In Praise of *Exo*

Exoneration examines the Rosenberg research, and comes to conclusions which are provocative and per... important than questions of guilt or innocence are the challenges this book makes to the justice system in our country. There are many studies of this historic case, but the Almans bring fresh insights and raise troubling questions.

Howard Zinn, author of *A People's History of the United States: 1492 – Present*

From historians to novelists, writers for decades have sought to capture U.S. political life at the chilling, anti-democratic moment epitomized by the Rosenberg-Sobell atomic conspiracy case. Some focused on the madness of the time; others on the human drama. With its meticulous rendering of both the back story of the era and its painstaking attention to the details of the trial, *Exoneration* is sure to become the bible of this cautionary chapter in U.S. history. As a revival of McCarthy-era smear tactics gains traction at this perilous moment in our fragile democracy, this book belongs on the shelves of every citizen who wants the truth behind the headlines.

Rob Okun, editor and exhibit organizer, *The Rosenbergs: Collected Visions of Artists and Writers*; *Unknown Secrets: Art and the Rosenberg Era*

Emily and David Alman have written a moving and cogent tribute to the work of the Committee to Secure Justice in the Rosenberg Case. These courageous men and women, including my father, Joe Brainin, fought (despite severe personal costs) to win clemency and defend our country's human and Constitutional values when others stood silent or joined the hysteria. The authors' perspective after more than a half-century is a valuable contribution to the history of our time.

David N. Brainin, son of Joseph Brainin, original member of the Committee

Excerpt from Robert Meeropol, son of Julius and Ethel Rosenberg, and board member of the National Committee to Reopen the Rosenberg Case (NCRRC), taken from his blog (http://www.rfc.org/blog/article/471), answering the question, **"How can you exonerate people who are guilty?"**

While many people equate the word "exoneration" with "innocence," the two words are not synonymous. I have been trying to explain this distinction for decades. I am very sympathetic to those who don't get it because it took me years to figure it out.

...There was, and remains to this day, no credible evidence that either of my parents helped steal what the prosecutors called "the secret of the atomic bomb."

...Even if my father and others conspired to commit espionage, they did not "steal the secret of the Atomic Bomb," and they did not commit treason, and the U.S Government was aware of this distinction all along. Yet the FBI, prosecutors, Judge, and even the President, intentionally propagated the "atomic espionage" and "treason" façade in my parents' case, and knowingly used these embellished and inflammatory allegations to justify killing them. My parents should be exonerated because their prosecution and execution were a result of a government orchestrated conspiracy to falsely enhance the charges against them.

Some say that this distinction is too subtle for people to comprehend. I don't think that's the case. I've found that most people grasp this concept readily when I've taken the time to explain it.

...Similarly, just as my brother and I can admit our earlier mistake in proclaiming our parents' total innocence, it is past time for the Executive Branch of the Federal Government to acknowledge that it was wrong to execute two people for a the crime they did not commit, and remove from their names all stigma that is associated with their commission of that act.

Exoneration

The Trial of Julius and Ethel Rosenberg
and Morton Sobell —
Prosecutorial deceptions, suborned perjuries,
anti-Semitism, and precedent for
today's unconstitutional trials

Emily Arnow Alman and David Alman

Memoir by Michael Meeropol

Foreword by Blanche Wiesen Cook and Gerald Markowitz

SAN 850-556X
Green Elms Press
PO Box 15186
Seattle, WA 98115
info@greenelmspress.com

Printed in the United States of America
ISBN 13: 978-0-9779058-3-6
ISBN 10: 0-9779058-3-7

Alman, Emily Arnow.

Exoneration : The Trial of Julius and Ethel Rosenberg and Morton Sobell — Prosecutorial deceptions, suborned perjuries, anti-Semitism, and precedent for today's unconstitutional trials / Emily Arnow Alman and David Alman. -- Seattle, WA : Green Elms Press, c2010.

p. ; cm.
ISBN: 978-0-9779058-3-6
Includes bibliographical references and index.

1. Rosenberg, Julius, 1918-1953--Trials, litigation, etc. 2. Rosenberg, Ethel, 1915-1953--Trials, litigation, etc. 3. Sobell, Morton--Trials, litigation, etc. 4. Trials (Espionage)--New York (State)--New York. 5. Trials (Conspiracy)--New York (State)--New York. 6. Antisemitism--United States--History--20th century. 7. Cold War. 8. United States--Social conditions--20th century. I. Alman, David, 1919- II. Title. III. Title: The Trial of Julius and Ethel Rosenberg and Morton Sobell — Prosecutorial deceptions, suborned perjuries, anti-Semitism, and precedent for today's unconstitutional trials.

KF224.R6 A46 2010   2009932788
345.73/0231--dc22   1003

Disclaimer:
The authors have striven for 100% accuracy in facts and figures. If inadvertent mistakes are found, the authors may amend these facts and figures in subsequent printings.

Acknowledgements

Some years have passed since Emily and I began writing this book, and in that time we sometimes lost track of good people who provided us with important documents that have helped illuminate the history we recounted. We thank them all.

I owe a very special gratitude to my daughter Jennifer whose patience and concern since Emily's death have helped sustain me.

In preparation of the final draft of the book, the very best criticism we received came from Michael and Robert Meeropol, the sons of the Rosenbergs, to whom an early draft of the book was shown about a year after Emily died. Assisting me was an uphill job for them. I was a difficult writer to deal with, and I blocked off lines of thought they brought to their reading of the book, and I was stubborn in what I believed were facts beyond challenge. Emily would have come to appreciate much sooner than I did how right they were in their outlook and in their courage and determination to speak the truth. I thank them for their remarkable patience and friendship.

The book might not have seen the light of day if not for an accidental "meeting" that put me in touch with Miryam Gordon, the publisher of Green Elms Press. I have never met her, but I have spoken to her many times on the phone and we have exchanged hundreds of emails. She has poured hundreds of hours into editing, designing, obtaining distinguished authorities to provide forewords, and all the other tasks that are usually performed by teams of experts in publishing. All without certainty of any compensation through book sales. I thank her for her commitment and her faith in the book.

Dedications

To our daughters Michelle and Jennifer, to their daughters CiCi, Heather, and Abigail, and to all those in the vast community of earnest men and women who labor so hard throughout their lifetimes to keep our Constitution supreme in the design of American justice.

Author's Note:

On March 18, 2004, Emily Hope Arnow Alman left us. I spent 68 years with her. I look everywhere I can, sometimes to God, sometimes to the mathematics of infinite possibilities, sometimes to the unknown complexities of chaos and matter, to allow me to meet and court her again.

Table of Contents

Photographs:

Special acknowledgment is made to Michael and Robert Meeropol for their permission to use the photo of Julius and Ethel Rosenberg in the park on the cover and also on page xlii.

Special acknowledgment is made to the Rosenberg Fund for Children (www.rfc.org) for permission to use the photos on pages 160 and 256.

From left, Abel and Anne Meeropol, adoptive parents of Michael and Robert Rosenberg, Gloria Agrin (standing), attorney, and grandmother Sophie Rosenberg, all part of the "community of support" that surrounded the Rosenberg children.

Memoir

by Michael Meeropol, son of Julius and Ethel Rosenberg

A community of support...

My brother and I have both described our memories of the three years and four months between the arrest of our mother in August of 1950 and the day (December 24, 1953) we met Anne and Abel Meeropol.[1] It was a bewildering set of experiences involving the arrests of our parents, living for a time with our maternal Grandmother, Tessie Greenglass, and her sister Chutcha, living for about a year with our grandma Sophie Rosenberg, living in a children's shelter, and for me, adjusting to two new schools, and more. In the summer of 1952, my brother and I moved from our grandmother Sophie's apartment in the Washington Heights section of Manhattan to a small detached one-story house in southern New Jersey. We lived with Ben and Sonia Bach, friends of our parents, until six months after our parents' executions in June 1953.

Those years also marked a period during which I learned that my parents had been accused of stealing the secret of the Atom Bomb (whatever that meant) and that they had lost the trial and been sentenced to death. I learned there were people who wanted clemency for them (I learned what the word "clemency" meant). I also learned that there were people out there, like the mother of a friend in my grandmother's neighborhood, who thought my parents were horrible – I heard the word "communist" in anger for the first time in her apartment.

It was during this intensely disruptive period in my brother's and my lives – a period that shaped us both in ways, I am sure, that we are still grappling with even 56 years later – that we met and in some ways bonded with Emily and Dave Alman. There was something quite special about them. The fact that they had two daughters, Shelley and Jenny who were Rob's and my age was significant.[2] However, I think it just had something to do with them as people – we connected with them in a special way. There were other new people who entered our lives during this period as well – Manny Bloch, of course (our parents' attorney), and Frances and Ben Minor who lived in my grandmother's neighborhood and offered friendship with their son, Michael, who was my age. When we lived in New Jersey, Ben and Sonia introduced us to neighbors and friends who

---

1 For my version, see *We Are Your Sons*, pp. 5-255. For Robert's version, see *An Execution In The Family*, pp. 1-17

2 See *We Are Your Sons*, pp. 146, 222, 238, for specific references to Shelley Alman.

supported clemency for our parents and we formed friendships with kids our age.[3]

However, Emily and Dave became such an important part of our lives during that year that when we began to live with Anne and Abel Meeropol and stopped seeing the Almans (the Meeropols were advised that one of the ways we could "get past" the intense trauma of losing our parents was to have a "normal" life that involved not "dwelling" on the past) I missed them. Five years later when we began to have family visits, it was a pleasure to re-connect with the Alman family. We visited them on their farm in New Jersey, and in New York. Rob actually went to Jenny's eighth grade prom. From time to time, I've corresponded with and visited with Michelle. Mainly, I've had correspondence and visits over the years with Emily and Dave – and since Emily's passing, with Dave alone.

After Manny Bloch and Gloria Agrin (Bloch's legal assistant), Dave and Emily personified the struggle to save my parents' lives. Manny had been this incredible father figure during the years between the trial and the last visit we had with him in January of 1954, shortly before his untimely death. Gloria, who had been engaged to marry Manny, later married Barney Josephson, the man who owned the nightclub where our father (Abel's) song "*Strange Fruit*" was first performed by Billie Holiday. Abel and Anne had been friendly with Barney before he married Gloria, and so we got together with them regularly. In fact, after they got married, it became a yearly ritual for Abel, Anne, Robby and me to have our Christmas Eve (the night we met the Meeropols) "anniversary dinner" at Barney's restaurant.

I remember spending many hours visiting with Gloria and Barney throughout my high school years, furthering the political and cultural education that I got from Anne and Abel and even learning a little bit about the case because of Gloria's personal involvement. One year, when Abel was dodging a subpoena from the House Un-American Activities Committee, I actually lived with Barney and Gloria during the last few weeks of my school year.

---

3 For meeting with Ben and Frances and becoming friends with their older son Michael, see *We Are Your Sons*, p. 111. I had the pleasure of re-connecting with Michael during college and interviewing both Ben and Frances for the writing of *WAYS*. It was this community of individuals who rallied around Rob and me both before and after we began to live with Anne and Abel which helped us make the transition from the trauma of the years 1950-53 to normal childhoods. We have always been incredibly grateful to all who helped. Some we remained friends with and others we lost track of, but we appreciate them all. It was just such help that inspired Rob to form The Rosenberg Fund for Children in 1990. He wanted to create an institution that would be there for children in similar circumstances to ours. (www.rfc.org).

As an adult in my twenties, and especially in my thirties when I began to seriously research the case, I started to learn both about the details of the government frame-up and about the struggle to save my parents' lives. In doing so, I integrated memories of books I had read earlier as well as conversations with Shelley Alman about her parents' activities on the behalf of the Committee – conversations from when I was a teenager. It was during those visits with the Almans that I learned that, though Manny had played the key legal role – and the equally important role of chief morale building for my parents as their only link to the outside world aside from family members, the National Committee to Secure Justice in the Rosenberg Case, the organization that almost succeeded in saving their lives, had had an entirely independent existence from Manny. In my thirties, as I researched for my sections of our book, We Are Your Sons, I had further discussions with Emily and Dave and Shelley, learning for the first time that Committee members sometimes found themselves in conflict with Manny about strategy.

With the benefit of history, I now realize that it was the work of the Committee that was most crucial in raising doubts in ordinary people's minds, and that led thousands to send telegrams to President Eisenhower in June of 1953, urging that he commute the sentences. They used the trial record itself to show the incredible miscarriage of justice that occurred in Judge Irving Kaufman's Court and they got a tremendous response. Emily once told me that a member of Congress said, "You don't know how close you actually came [to saving my parents]."

I am very happy and Emily and Dave were able to finish so much work on this book before we lost Emily. I have enormous respect and grateful affection for both of them. I am not an objective reader when it comes to their descriptions of their own actions and motivations. I am positive, however, that every word written in this book is either a heartfelt scrupulously honest recollection of what Dave and Emily were thinking at the time or their best retrospective conclusions about the issues in my parents' case which have benefited from decades of thought and research.

There is an enormous archive of materials from the National Committee to Secure Justice in the Rosenberg Case as well as their own personal papers from those years. This has allowed the Almans to consult contemporaneously created records to keep their memories accurate. There also is a vast archive of US government documents, wrung from the government as a result of a partially successful Freedom of Information Act lawsuit that my brother and I initiated in 1975. Close to 180,000 pages of previously secret US government documents are now available for perusal, and Emily and Dave make good use of them. The various archives provide a record for independent scholars to consult. (Just check out the endnotes in this book!)

Though it was William A. Reuben who wrote the series of articles in the *National Guardian* that raised the first doubts about the fairness of my parents' trial and the case in general, and though the Committee was formed in his apartment, the key to the formation, activities and successes of the Committee was the energy and persistence and leadership provided by Emily and Dave Alman. Thus, Emily and Dave provide a unique perspective and understanding of the case within this book. This perspective derives from who they are as people. They were (and are) independent thinkers with incredibly strong personalities who refused to succumb to pressure either from organizations of the left or institutions of authority within the government.

It is not surprising that Emily never joined the Communist Party, but was once expelled from a local branch because of some anti-authoritarian statements she had previously made. Emily actually defended herself at the meeting called to determine her expulsion. (She wasn't even a member!) Though Dave had been a member, he left in 1939 when he denounced the Hitler-Stalin Pact.

It is also not surprising that the fact that though Julius and Ethel were Communists who might have approved of Emily's expulsion, this did not deter either Emily or Dave from attempting to save their lives and win them a new trial. In fact, until they were convinced by both the 1995 release of materials from the US government's Venona Project and the statement by my parents' codefendant Morton Sobell in September of 2008, Dave and Emily had believed my parents were innocent not just of the charges of treason and atomic espionage that were the basis of the death sentences, but of all espionage charges. They vigorously defended my parents in their writings and personal activities from 1953 on.[4] (Emily was the catalyst for the creation of the National Committee to Reopen the Rosenberg Case in 1974, an organization whose initial event at Carnegie Hall that year was keynoted by Emily. It was she who persuaded my brother and me to become actively involved.)

In forming the Committee in late 1951, and vigorously fighting hard to save our parents for the next 18 months, Emily and Dave (and the others whose names they rescue from historical obscurity – some of whom I have met, some of whom I never, unfortunately, had a chance to meet and thank) took on the United States government, the established media and the organized Jewish establishment in the United States, with potentially serious personal consequences. When my daughter Ivy interviewed Emily and Dave in her film Heir To An Execution, Emily told her that she and Dave assumed they would be arrested after the executions.

---

4   For an example, see the review by Emily Alman of Louis Nizer's awful book, *The Implosion Conspiracy*, in *Jewish Currents* magazine in 1973.

In addition, for the first year of the Committee's existence, they also resisted the official left, the Communist Party, which had made the decision to distance themselves from our parents and, in fact, had ordered people not to get involved in defense efforts. One official tried to persuade Dave and Emily to disband the Committee arguing that "in every battle, 'we must accept some casualties.'" Later, I personally met a friend of my mother's who told my wife Ann (the woman was too ashamed to tell me directly) that she had been ordered by her Communist Party superiors to have nothing to do with helping defend my mother and father when they had initially been arrested. The Communist Party got involved at the end of 1952, and there is no question that their international contacts helped create a groundswell of public support for clemency, particularly in Western Europe. However, had Emily and Dave not formed the Committee against all odds, the Communist Party members would have found no movement to support.

What was it about Emily and Dave, which led them to make these personal decisions? I think Dave summarizes it well in the first chapter, but a careful reading of the entire book reveals how truly special they are. They both possess strong analytical minds and have incredible intellectual and personal courage. Imagine what it took for Dave to tell his Communist Party comrades that Stalin's decision to sign the pact with Hitler (a decision that some historians, not all of them pro-Communists and fellow travelers, were still justifying 60 years later) was a great betrayal of socialist internationalist principles. Imagine what it took for Emily and Dave and the handful of people who formed the Committee to recognize, as Dave and Emily so ruefully but proudly assert in this book, that they all were "God's second choice to save the Rosenbergs' lives... that God's first choice was anyone but us. [but] ... all there was, was us." Finally, they were stubborn as Hell.

I know Dave and Emily wrote this book because they wanted to make the case for the exoneration of Ethel and Julius Rosenberg and Morton Sobell. Today as I write this, Dave is the president of a new incarnation of the National Committee to Reopen the Rosenberg Case. Dave hopes that if this book receives wide distribution, it will spark a new national conversation about the case, especially now that the question of my father's involvement in passing classified information to the Soviet Union during World War II has been settled (at least to my and my brother's satisfaction).

Whereas virtually all published discussions of the case since 1953 have focused on the issue of total guilt or innocence, this book presents a novel interpretation. Dave and Emily argue that, as early as 1948, the US government had detailed information about an individual who was code-named Liberal. This person, Dave and Emily surmise, could have easily been identified as Julius Rosenberg long before 1950, yet the government chose to ignore the information. The government chose to resurrect and redefine the case against the spy code-named Liberal only after the Soviet Union had exploded its atom bomb in 1949, after the memories of the wartime alliance had been dimmed by years of postwar conflict over Eastern Europe (including the blockade of Berlin and the subsequent airlift in 1948), after the New Deal coalition that had included Communists and fellow travelers was destroyed in the Presidential election of 1948 – the liberals rallying to anti-communism and helping marginalize and soundly defeat Henry Wallace's third party campaign. This time the charge in public and in court (though not in the indictment) would be treason – giving aid and comfort to an enemy.

Dave and Emily also wrote this book because they believe that there was serious anti-Semitism involved in the decision to prosecute Jews for espionage both in the United States and in the Soviet bloc.

The Almans deserve a wide and respectful hearing from experts in law, history and politics as well as the general citizenry. Read this book for the incredible story of courage and action. Read it for the surprises. (Did you know Senator Joseph McCarthy was in favor of clemency for the Rosenbergs and that the Committee had indirect contact with him to explore whether he should make a public statement?) Read it for the drama of those last incredible months before June 19, 1953. Read it to discover some truly unsung American heroes – not just Dave and Emily though you get to know them best through this book, but also Joseph Brainin, Aaron Schneider, Peggy Strauss, Yuri Suhl, Norma Aronson, Bill Wolf, Louis Harap, Don Rothenberg and the thousands of ordinary Americans who wrote letters to Presidents Eisenhower and Truman, gave money to the Committee, marched in picket lines and later, gave money to a fund so that Robby and I were guaranteed an education and a good start in life.

Read this book, too, because, in recalling the story of how a handful of people stood up to the US government (and at the same time ignored the fears of the remnants of the organized left) and were able to touch the consciences of millions of people around the world and thousands within the United States, we can be reminded of the very best in our American culture – a culture that for all its conformism, materialism, fear, willful ignorance, bigotry and racism also embodies the striving of human beings to be better, to create a sense of community and empathy for those less fortunate, to hold a abiding belief in justice for all, and above all else, to have the courage to stand up for what one believes in. When you read this story, I hope you will feel, as I did, a certain pride that American culture, even in the 1950s, gave us Emily and Dave Alman and all those others, named and un-named, who joined together, fought the good fight, and almost saved my parents' lives.

I also hope you will feel pride that thousands of Americans ignored the lies of the Justice Department that accused the Committee of being a Communist Front organization. They thought for themselves about the trial, and decided that there was sufficient doubt about its fairness and the appropriateness of the sentence to raise their voices in protest, even at the height of the Cold War in the midst of a hot war in Korea. The fact that the government went ahead with the executions despite the outpouring of protest and world wide condemnation should not blind us to the significance of the work of those thousands of Americans and their "agitators," the Committee members, including of course Emily and Dave Alman.

Foreword

by Blanche Wiesen Cook, Distinguished Professor of History, John Jay College and Graduate Center, CUNY
and Gerald Markowitz, Distinguished Professor of History, John Jay College and Graduate Center, CUNY

The Rosenbergs And The Crimes Of A Century...

When all the ashes of the 20th Century settle and all the lies are laid to rest, the assassination of Julius and Ethel Rosenberg will continue to loom enormous. The sacrifice of the Rosenbergs will forever be a monument to a century of violence, holocaust, and hatred; a ceremonial slaughter in a vastly wicked time. Seen in full light, and from a distance, the contest seems bizarre: The Rosenbergs and the Bomb – Two proud Jews confronted by a bloated, brutal, twisted state. "The Crime of the Century" sketched on a jello box; or exploded upon Hiroshima, Nagasaki, Nevada, the Pacific Islands ....

To contemplate the Rosenberg case demands that we pause to reconsider our own lives, our own dedication to truth, hope, justice. Who were we then? Who are we now? What kind of world can we imagine? How can we participate? Who were Julius and Ethel Rosenberg? What did they read? What did they sing? What did they believe? What was their crime? Two ordinary, Jewish, New Yorkers who believed in a non-fascist future; who believed a new day might dawn – without pogroms, without racism, poverty, or war. Communists believed those things during the depression and after the great anti-fascist war.

Just as World War I was followed by Red Scare and the deportation of countless resident "aliens," mostly Jewish and deemed un-American, so, too, World War II was followed by Red Scare and the deportation of hundreds of un-American resident "aliens." Citizen Reds were hounded and harassed; across the country, teachers were silenced and fired. Hollywood was politically deboned. By February 1951, any attorney who was or had been a member of the Communist Party was "relieved of membership" of the American Bar Association. That month, Dr W.E.B. DuBois and other leaders of the Peace Information Center were indicted for failure to register as agents of a "foreign principal" for circulating the Stockholm Peace Appeal against nuclear weapons.

The Cold War froze all reality, froze information, froze our hearts and minds. It began immediately after the Allied victory of 1945; or it never really ended after 1917 – which was how Nazis gained so much ground during the l930s – so widely perceived as the acceptable alternative to Communists. Hitler's initial targets were "Jewish Communist Traitors;" they would be silenced, disappeared. Nazis were dangerous, but Communists were demons; they had no souls; no love in their hearts. But then Nazis over-reached, and the Cold War was suspended. Peace and a new path that led to human rights might have followed the Allied victory, but the Cold War hardened the future. Atomic victory forecast an American Century, and Communism would be rendered dust.

To combat the "Red Menace," Congress voted for the permanent militarization of America, and introduced a military-fueled economy. The unemployment rate fell to a postwar low of 1.8% in October 1953. Fueling this great growth was consumer spending and the rapid expansion of the military-industrial complex. In fact, the Cold War made it all possible: The endless array of cars, washing machines, dryers, refrigerators, television sets, and record players would have been inconceivable without the massive military spending that infused billions of dollars into the economy. Hindsight gives us the facts: in 1949, Congress appropriated $14 billion for the military. In 1953, Congress appropriated $50 billion for the military. Between 1953 and 1959, 50% of Congress' budget went for defense spending.

The globalization of American influence and power which occurred during the 1950s was unprecedented. Some called it neo-imperialism, some post-colonialism. Whatever it was called, the rhetoric of freedom, liberation, and global democracy camouflaged the modern era of dirty tricks from disinformation to counterinsurgency. Eisenhower's demeanor as a bumbling, do-nothing president covered up the fact that he was, in part, a covert president who routinely resorted to national security/CIA operations that toppled democratically elected governments considered unfriendly to U.S. interests. In 1953, the United States overthrew Iran's popular, elected, nationalist government of Mohammed Mossadegh. The CIA chief in Iran, Kermit Roosevelt, dismissed Mossadegh as weak and irrelevant, and claimed his support was limited to some "bearded religious mullahs" and communist students. In 1954, the United States overthrew Guatemala's popular, elected, nationalist government of Jacobo Arbenz Guzman, because he was inimical to the interests of the United Fruit Company. These activities ended democratic processes for decades, and defined the course of U.S. relations far into the future.

In March 1954, the U.S. National Security Council legitimized these activities with a new policy: NSC 5412 determined that "in the interests of world peace and U.S. national security, the overt foreign activities of the U.S. government should be supplemented by covert operations." The Central Intelligence Agency's mandate to conduct "espionage and counter-espionage operations abroad" was now expanded. All covert operations were planned and executed so that "U.S. Government responsibility for them is not evident ... and if uncovered the U.S. Government can plausibly disclaim any responsibility for them." The details of these policies remained secret, classified and unknown to most Americans, who nevertheless supported the mandates of the Red Scare – whatever its excesses.

The Red Scare was increasingly propped up by a strident, bipartisan anti-liberalism that manifested itself as McCarthyism. New Deal and Fair Deal Democrats, many of whom ran fast to board the Red Scare train, were called "commiecrats" and "phony egg-sucking liberals" by Senator Joseph McCarthy whose name came to dominate the decade. Actually the anti-communist crusade began long before, and during the New Deal was dominated by Martin Dies' House Committee on Un-American Activities (HUAC), begun in 1938. HUAC achieved a new level of significance in 1948, when young Congressman Richard Nixon decided that his career would most benefit from the kind of personal crusade against communists and Jews that helped him win a particularly ugly California election over New Dealer Helen Gahagan Douglas.

President Harry S. Truman, himself the target of anti-liberal attacks, was among the first anti-communist crusaders. In 1947, Truman's Executive Order 9835 introduced loyalty oaths and a monumental purge of federal government workers. Quickly copied by state and local governments, political orthodoxy was now required for educators, entertainers, journalists, diplomats, and all public officials. Thousands of teachers were fired and such politically radical music groups as The Weavers were banned from the airwaves. Even their most popular nonpolitical song, "Goodnight Irene," at the top of the hit parade, was permanently removed from radio broadcast throughout America. Truman's loyalty program instituted an intellectual means test for American leadership or even civic participation. To ferret out the "disloyal," esteemed Americans were routinely asked:

> "Have you ever read Karl Marx?"

> "What do you think of Henry Wallace's third-party effort?"

> "Have you ever had Negroes in your home?"

> "There is a suspicion that you are in sympathy with the underprivileged. Is this true?" "Did you ever write a letter to the Red Cross about segregation of blood?"

> "Have you ever read Thomas Paine? Upton Sinclair?"

> "When you were in X's home, did X's wife dress conventionally when she received her guests?"

Unionists and labor activists were particularly targeted. Shortly after World War II, several large strikes paralyzed major industrial centers. In 1946, the number of strikes and the number of workers involved surpassed all previous records. Communists and radicals had been elected to leadership positions of several major unions, including the United Electrical Workers, Mike Quill's Transport Workers Union, the National Maritime Workers, Harry Bridges' International Longshoremen's Association, the Mine Mill and Smelters Workers Union, and seemed generally to dominate the CIO (Congress of Industrial Organizations). By 1950, radicals had been systematically removed from all leadership positions within the CIO. Those unions which refused to purge radicals were expelled from the CIO.

After World War II, labor and radical parties won elections in Italy, Great Britain, France, Greece and Austria. Opposed to poverty and to a renewed anti-Russian crusade, the left and old New Deal coalition in the United States represented a threat to the emerging Cold War consensus. The new military-industrial coalition, was dedicated to the American Century – the dominance of U.S. industry and ideology worldwide. Radical political groups, such as Henry Wallace's 1948 Progressive Party, endorsed Soviet-American friendship, and the emergence of an anti-Cold War peace movement. It was deemed an "un-American" road-block against the American Century.

To destroy all such challenges, a massive "anti-Communist" crusade targeted all left-liberal nonconformist thought. To maintain the pressure against radicalism, the HUAC and the Senate Internal Security Subcommittee went "into the field." From Milwaukee to Detroit to Pittsburgh to Baltimore to Hillsboro, North Carolina, to Los Angeles, special investigators sniffed out and purged everyone from red to mauve. McCarthy's associate Roy Cohn described "the way to get results: Hold our hearings, get these people in public session, have them claim the Fifth Amendment, have the witnesses name them as Communists, have them fired."

Although these activities did not destroy unionism absolutely, they permanently altered the relationship between labor and management. Labor militancy, familiar to the 1930s, virtually disappeared. "Sweetheart contracts" to protect immediate bread-and-butter interests were negotiated, but at the expense of independent power for the union movement – economically and politically.

Privatization and political orthodoxy were reinforced by several major political show trials. From the Smith Act indictments of 28 July 1948, which resulted in the longest criminal trial in U.S. history, to the indictment of career diplomat Alger Hiss in December 1948, to the execution of Ethel and Julius Rosenberg on 19 June 1953, to the harassment and degradation of Owen Lattimore and other Asian diplomats who "lost" China, and atomic scientist J. Robert Oppenheimer, declared a security risk in June 1954, the 1950s bore witness to the politics of Red Scare, silence and control.

On July 28, 1948, a federal grand jury in New York indicted twelve members of the national board of the U.S. Communist Party. They were charged with violating the Alien Registration, or Smith Act of 1940 – the first peacetime sedition law in U.S. history since 1798. The law made it illegal to "knowingly or willfully advocate, abet, advise, or teach the duty, necessity, desirability, or propriety of overthrowing or destroying any government in the United States by force or violence." It also prohibited participation in the writing or circulation of materials advocating such ideas, and made membership in any group advocating such ideas illegal. The defendants were found guilty, and each received the maximum sentence of five years' imprisonment. Dozens of other Smith Act convictions followed.

In the summer of 1948, Alger Hiss, who had resigned from government service to become president of the Carnegie Endowment for International Peace, was named a Communist who passed secret documents by a self-confessed Communist spy, Whittaker Chambers, during HUAC's investigation of government espionage to expose the Democrats' "twenty years of treason." After Hiss denied the charges and sued Chambers for libel, Chambers led freshman Representative Richard Nixon and other members of HUAC to a pumpkin patch where the microfilmed documents were allegedly buried. With film cameras and radio crews at the ready, the pumpkin patch brigade unearthed the "evidence." The statute of limitation on espionage having expired, Hiss could only be indicted for perjury. One trial ended in a hung jury; the second convicted him. Hiss was sentenced to five years in prison; and Richard Nixon who, as a member of HUAC, had led in questioning him, was catapulted into prominence. Nixon, among other committee members, repeatedly attacked the New Deal and members of the liberal Democratic establishment as "bleeding heart pinkies," dupes of the Soviet Union, actually spies.

When Russia exploded its first atomic bomb in 1949, the FBI launched an extensive hunt to find who had "stolen" the U.S. atomic secret. Unlike Alger Hiss, the Rosenbergs were not prominent, affluent, or important. They were hardworking people who owned a small business in New York's Lower East Side. The Rosenbergs and their co-defendant, Morton Sobell, were rank-and-file Jewish communists, idealists inspired by the united front visions of the New Deal era. Ethel Rosenberg's brother, David Greenglass, accused of stealing atomic secrets while a machinist at Los Alamos, New Mexico, where the first atomic bomb was assembled, confessed his own involvement and accused the Rosenbergs of espionage. When the Rosenbergs denied their guilt and refused to consider any of the many deals offered to them while in prison, the government escalated its case and accused them of "the crime of the century:" They personally gave the secret of the atom bomb to the Russians. As Judge Irving R. Kaufman sentenced the Rosenbergs to death in April 1951, he announced that they were responsible for every death and casualty in Korea. Eisenhower ignored all appeals for clemency from world leaders, including Pope Pius XII, and they were executed on 19 June 1953.

Their execution served as a demonstration and a warning: unrepentant communists were traitors and spies, and would be executed.

J. Robert Oppenheimer, director of the Los Alamos atomic project and widely hailed as the "father of the atomic bomb," fell victim to the McCarthy fervor in 1954. Never accused of mishandling documents or sharing secrets, he was nevertheless demeaned and publicly humiliated for having communist sympathies and communist relatives. Actually, Oppenheimer's "crime" was his opposition to the development of thermonuclear weapons (the H-Bomb). His former colleagues, Edward Teller and Lewis Strauss, dedicated to the repeated testing of the "hydrogen" bombs despite serious health questions about radioactive "fallout," initiated his removal from government service. On 29 June 1954, the Atomic Energy Commission declared Oppenheimer a "security risk," removed him from government influence and blocked his access to government "secrets," including his own reports and papers.

In the midst of these show trials Congress passed several laws that were among the most repressive in U.S. history. The Internal Security Act of 1950, passed over Truman's veto, established the Subversive Activities Control Board and prohibited any person to "combine, conspire or agree with any other persons which would substantially contribute to the establishment within the United States of a totalitarian dictatorship." "Communist-action" organizations were to register with the Attorney General and to report names of officers, sources of funds, and membership lists. The law contained the most controversial "concentration camp" provision: In the event of war or insurrection, the President might declare "an internal security emergency" and the Attorney General could then detain all persons for whom there were "reasonable grounds" to believe they "probably will engage in, or probably will conspire with others to engage in, acts of espionage or sabotage."

At its peak, in 1955, the FBI's security index of people to be arrested under this provision included 26,000 individuals – including union organizers, journalists, lawyers, physicians, scientists, and teachers. Congress subsequently appropriated funds for the Department of Justice to establish six detention camps in Arizona, Florida, Pennsylvania, Oklahoma, and California. In 1952, Congress also passed the Immigration and Naturalization Act (the McCarran-Walter Act) which instituted second class citizenship for the millions of naturalized Americans, who could now be, and were, deported by the score.

In addition to these infringements on freedom of speech, press, and assembly, the United States specifically limited its celebrated right to travel freely. In 1952, Truman's Secretary of State, Dean Acheson, declared that he would withhold passports from anyone there was "reason to believe" was in the Communist Party, or who might be "going abroad to engage in activities which will advance the communist movement," or whose "conduct abroad is likely to be contrary to the best interest of the United States." As a result, passports were routinely with-held from those who wrote or spoke critically of U.S. policies, whether or not they were communist. Between May 1951 and May 1952, 300 Americans were denied the right to travel internationally. Ruth Shipley, then head of the passport office, reportedly boasted, "Nobody critical of U.S. foreign policy would leave the country." Succeeded by Frances Knight, whose policies were even more vigorous, passports were withheld from numerous citizens for the greatest variety of rea-sons, including Supreme Court Justice William O. Douglas (to go to China); Ring Lardner, Jr., a blacklisted Hollywood writer; Arthur Miller (prevented from trav-eling to Brussels to see a production of his anti-McCarthy play, "The Crucible"); Otto Nathan, a German-Jewish refugee who was Einstein's best friend and advi-sor; and Paul Robeson, then the most famous black activist and performer, who was denied the right to travel between 1950 and 1958.

Perhaps the most insidious effort to limit and erase dissent and to achieve a one-note culture was to be found in the annals of the Hollywood blacklist, which remained in place for over a generation. HUAC invaded Hollywood twice, in 1947 and again in 1951. Never satisfied, HUAC returned to the subject of Hollywood subversion – in 1953, 1955, 1956, and 1958.

Dedicated to the elimination of all pro-New Deal producers, directors, screen-writers and stars, HUAC intended – by its weapons of publicity and expo-sure – to destroy their reputations, credibility, and very presence in American cultural life. Above all, HUAC was dedicated to ending Hollywood's love-affair with the US-USSR Grand Alliance of World War II. A controlled, de-radicalized Hollywood taught America to love the Germans and hate the Russians almost as soon as World War II ended. Such films as Mission to Moscow (1943), Song of Russia (1943), and Days of Glory (1944) seemed to HUAC particularly un-American in their celebration of the wartime alliance, and the heroic Russian people – whose wartime casualty record of twenty million dead was now trivial-ized as Soviet propaganda. Everybody associated with such films became suspect. Innocence could only be proven by denouncing communism, communists, and everybody "soft" on the communist menace.

From 1947 on, Hollywood was divided between those who named names with enthusiasm, and those who refused to testify for reasons of self-protection or principle. Wrapped in rigid legalese, HUAC eliminated all choices: one could take the Fifth Amendment and be condemned as an enemy of the state; or one could be a friendly witness, name names, and be given a hero's handshake, which guar-anteed continued access to work. Seventy-two friendly witnesses named over 300 film people who they considered past or present "communists" or "communist sympathizers." Screen Actors Guild President Ronald Reagan, George Murphy, Robert Montgomery, Robert Taylor, and Gary Cooper were among HUAC's most enthusiastic and "friendly" witnesses. They did more than denounce the communist influence on Hollywood. They invented a town honeycombed with stinging red bees. Gary Cooper, for example, testified that he had "turned down" many scripts "because I thought they were tinged with communist ideas." But he could not remember any of them.

Those who refused to name names were held in contempt of Congress, imprisoned, and blacklisted. Lives were destroyed. Many creative artists were never again employed; others moved to Europe or Mexico. Some changed their names. A small number were luckier and began working again during the 1960s. Alvah Bessie, Howard Da Silva, Dashiell Hammett, Lillian Hellman, Zero Mostel, Dorothy Parker, Anne Revere, Gale Sondergaard, and Dalton Trumbo (who called the era "the Time of the Toad") were among many whose lives and work were permanently affected. For a time, some Hollywood notables organized to resist the outrages and established a Committee for the First Amendment, including John Huston, Lauren Bacall, Frank Sinatra, Groucho Marx, Humphrey Bogart, Judy Garland, and others. They, too, were condemned for their efforts. Katharine Hepburn was told by Louis B. Mayer that there was so much opposition to her principled stand that he could not employ her again until she "became publicly acceptable." Humphrey Bogart was so harassed he quickly apologized for his "ill-advised" actions on behalf of the committee. John Huston explained, "Bogart owns a 54-foot yawl. When you own a 54-foot yawl, you've got to provide for her upkeep."

McCarthy's crusade against communists in government resulted in thousands of early retirements and hundreds of fired diplomats. But his activities backfired. After McCarthy aides Roy Cohn and David Schein toured U.S. diplomatic posts in 1953, the Mayor of Berlin told Adlai Stevenson that "McCarthy had done more to hurt America abroad in eight months than Soviet propaganda did in eight years." In all European cities, the morale of the U.S. diplomatic corps was depressed, destroyed. Committed to the removal of all "queers," "drunks," "perverts," and political activists who had kept the State Department both "soft on communism" and "limp-wristed," McCarthy and his crowd aimed fast and wild. On 8 April 1954, A.A. Berle noted in his diary, "Jane and Andrew Carey back from Ethiopia because, may God forgive us, the Security Service ... decided that Andy was a security risk because he had married Jane. The real reason was that they had invited Adlai Stevenson to dinner... These are two conservative Republicans, who had behaved approximately like human beings. It makes you a bit sick."

McCarthy's final play was his attack on the Army as a hotbed of subversion. He had finally gone too far. Eisenhower had long resisted pressure to condemn McCarthy. To the dismay of many of his friends, Eisenhower had refused "to get into the gutter with that guy." Now, he took a stand. He refused to hand over military papers for the Army-McCarthy hearings. It was all over. Twenty million

Americans bore witness to McCarthy's gratuitous announcement that Frederick Fisher, the legal assistant to the army's chief counsel, Joseph Welch, had once been a member of the National Lawyers' Guild, an organization of militant left-leaning lawyers, which had defended communists. Finally, McCarthy outdid himself. Hammering on and on, he lost the support of his own audience. No one would ever forget the mood of that moment when Welch said, "Let us not assassinate this lad further, Senator. You have done enough. Have you no sense of decency, sir, at long last? Have you left no sense of decency?"

On 11 November 1954 the Senate voted 67 to 22 to condemn McCarthy for his abusive behavior. He had sullied the honor of the Senate and "acted contrary to Senatorial traditions."

McCarthy's crusade had been acceptable until it was done unto them. It had been a bipartisan massacre. When Eisenhower boasted that his administration had fired 1,456 federal workers within his first four months in office, and 2,200 shortly thereafter, the Democrats boasted that they had done even better when in office – and they had.

For all the damage done, the American Century was short-lived and fraught with horror, violence, war. Actually, from our 21st Century perspective, we see it now as the century of total war – that has led nowhere in particular. Communism is dismantled; the USSR is dead. War rages everywhere and hatreds abound. So we must again ask: What was it all about? Was it worth the price? Who were the victims? What was the victory? Where do we go from here?

In the end, we have several facts. The Rosenbergs refused to bow or grovel; they never went supine. Eisenhower said, "see, they love their ideology more than their children." In the face of power unbridled, arrogant, obscene, they rejected a deal, a cynical and crass propaganda deal that would have set them free, made them rich, transformed their future.

Because of the Freedom of Information Act, the CIA released an astounding 22 January 1953 memo, detailing a modest proposal. If the Rosenbergs would agree to "appeal to Jews in all countries to get out of the communist movement and seek to destroy it," their sentences could be commuted. The "advantages" of this scheme could "scarcely be overstated from a psychological warfare standpoint."

"The couple is ideally situated to serve as leading instruments of a psychological warfare campaign designed to split world communism on the Jewish issue, to create disaffected groups within the membership of the Parties, to utilize these groups for further infiltration and for intelligence work...."

The Rosenbergs should be handled tactfully: People of their sort "can be swayed by duty [not by] self-interest. They should not be asked to trade their principles for their lives – for one thing, such an appeal to cowardice would almost certainly fail." They should be instead "offered two things psychologically:

(1) an opportunity to recant while preserving their self-respect and honor; (2) a new purpose in life."

The psychological strategists of the CIA thought the "ideal emissaries" to introduce this proposal "would be highly intelligent rabbis, representing reformed Judaism, with a radical background or sympathetic understanding of radicalism, and with psychiatric knowledge .... Should the operation succeed, generous commutation appears indicated -- both to encourage others to defect and to utilize the Rosenbergs as figures in an effective international psychological warfare campaign against communism primarily on the Jewish question."

This political warfare deal coincided with qualms expressed by members of the State Department who were concerned that the Rosenbergs execution would harm America's interests throughout Europe, seething with protests and almost unanimous opposition. From France (where posters of smiling Ike featured a mouth full of his perfectly white teeth, each one an electric chair), U.S. ambassador C. Douglas Dillon urged Eisenhower to stay the execution. It would be a public relations disaster. The "great majority of French people of all political leanings feel that the death sentence is completely unjustified," and due entirely to the "political climate peculiar to the United States." Even those who considered the Rosenbergs guilty of something, believed the death sentence absurd when compared with the 14 year prison term meted to British atomic scientist/spy Klaus Fuchs (the German-born son of a Lutheran minister). In addition, there were all the doubts about David Greenglass' reliability, his undenied perjury, his wife's awareness that her husband was "an hysteric," and a liar. This is a story about love and hate. A morality play, the unnecessary passion killing of the Cold War is an epic that will never die.

For all the CIA's psychological enthusiasm, did nobody pause to consider this family's dance of death? Who was David Greenglass, Ethel's baby brother? His mother loved him best. What had he stolen? A tool? Was it irradiated? Was his mind fried? His heart dried? His soul emptied? What was his deal? With whom did he make it? Where did he hide? Where do they hide when they kill their sisters?

Then there were the children, and the world's reaction to ten year old Michael's letter, a plea to Eisenhower on behalf of himself and his six year old brother Robert, "Please let mommy and daddy go and not let anything happen to them ...."

Eisenhower was unmoved. He refused to appear "weak and fearful" in the face of subversion. "The action of these people has exposed to greater danger of death literally millions of our citizens." Ike concluded, "they have even stooped to dragging in young and innocent children in order to serve their own purposes."

Liberal Eisenhower, who wanted World War II to be "the last civil war to tear humanity apart," and even Eleanor Roosevelt saw virtue in the sacrifice of

Ethel and Julius Rosenberg. ER was silent about the Rosenberg case as it unfolded, but she endorsed their death – for Cold War reasons. Although she abhorred Joseph McCarthy's "gestapo" excesses, and opposed the death penalty in general, on 11 December 1952, she detailed her views in her *My Day* column.

> I am getting a considerable number of letters, all Communist-inspired so far as I can see, from people urging me to do something to prevent the execution of Julius and Ethel Rosenberg, who... were found guilty of being members of an atom-bomb espionage ring.
>
> This Communist-inspired campaign is certainly going to do the Rosenbergs more harm than good. Some of the writers try to make it appear that this sentence was imposed on the Rosenbergs because they are Jews and is intended to start anti-Jewish activities in this country. That is utter nonsense.
>
> The question of civil liberties in this case has been carefully watched. It is odd that the Soviets should harp on this when they themselves have come out openly in an anti-Semitic campaign.
>
> I do not believe in capital punishment, but we do have capital punishment in our country. I do not know if putting the Rosenbergs to death will do us more good than if they were under a sentence of life imprisonment, but this country operates under law and as long as we have laws we must live up to them.
>
> Without question, the authorities in our country have given careful consideration as to whether the security of the United States would be benefitted by death or life imprisonment. Punishment of this kind is used as a deterrent for others who might be tempted to do likewise and that also must have been given careful consideration.

The crime of the century. The Rosenbergs did it. What had they done? The Almans conclude that Julius transmitted classified information to our wartime ally, during the war. But he and Ethel were both executed for treason. Who else was executed for giving secrets to a wartime ally? Indeed, who among the known and named Nazi collaborators, American business leaders and bankers were executed, imprisoned, even indicted, for trading with the enemy throughout the war?

The Rosenbergs were the exemplars who paid with their lives – two Jews from Seward Park High School and City College, betrayed by their families, sacrificed by the state, abandoned by the Communist Party – which fled into silence and fear; supported nonetheless by radical individuals who remained independent and determined. Journalists and activists around the original National Guardian – Jim Aronson, Cedric Belfrage, Bill Reuben; later joined by Virginia Gardner, Helen Sobell, Carl Marzani, Emily and David Alman. They wrote and organized and would not let the story settle.

Ethel Rosenberg would be almost 90 now. On 24 January 1953, she wrote a poem to her sons,

IF WE DIE

You shall know, my sons ....

Why we leave the song unsung,

the book unread, the work undone.....

Work and build my sons, and build

a monument to love and joy,

to human worth, to faith we kept

for you, my sons.....

All over the world there are and will always be children of the Rosenbergs – individuals with courage, eager to carry on, to resist tyranny, to challenge authority, to make it better, to contemplate the possibilities of creating a caring society with security and justice for all.

Here, Emily and David Alman have given us a book of hope with which to journey again along roads that go beyond "borderless, mythological ethnic prejudices." After 60 years of courageous, often lonely, activism during America's meanest moment when hysteria was elevated to a political platform and Constitutional precepts were undermined, the story of their determination to build a mass movement for justice and law is critical and encouraging. Their daily efforts to mobilize a mass movement for sanity during a time of brutal bitter madness, roused millions of people who petitioned and demonstrated – despite the refusal of every major newspaper and radio station to accept their news releases and ads. Their ability not to give up, not to give in, not to be censored or self-censored in that vicious climate in which two people were accused of one crime and executed for another, fortifies us as we assess new facts and ongoing debates, and continue to struggle for the triumph of legal precepts, democratic legislation, and human rights. In the 21st Century, already stained by torture, terror, and new levels of tyranny, the Almans' commitment to return to "a Constitutional system of justice" remains our most vital, important, urgent goal.

Chronology

1950

Early spring. Emily Alman is introduced to Ethel Rosenberg in a mothers/children park near Knickerbocker Village on the Lower East Side, New York City.

June 15. Ethel Rosenberg's brother, David Greenglass, a machinist, is arrested on a charge of conspiring to commit espionage on behalf of the Soviet Union.

July 17. Ethel Rosenberg's husband, Julius, an engineer, is arrested and charged with being a member of the conspiracy for which David Greenglass was arrested.

August 11. Ethel Rosenberg is arrested and charged with being a member of the conspiracy.

August 18. Morton Sobell, an engineer and college classmate of Julius Rosenberg, is arrested and charged with being a member of the conspiracy.

1951

March 6-29. The defendants are tried in the federal courthouse at Foley Square, New York City, on a charge of having conspired to pass classified information in 1944-1945 to our then military ally, the Soviet Union. Presiding over the trial is Judge Irving R. Kaufman; the chief prosecutors were U.S. Attorney Irving Saypol and Assistant U.S. Attorney Roy Cohn.

April 5. The defendants are found guilty. Ethel and Julius Rosenberg are sentenced to death; Morton Sobell is sentenced to 30 years imprisonment; David Greenglass receives a 15-year prison sentence.

September-October. Emily Alman and William A. Reuben, the author of a series of articles in the National Guardian in which he brands the key elements of the prosecution's case as "hoaxes," initiate the Committee to

Secure Justice in the Rosenberg Case. The Committee asks for a new trial and, if that fails, for a reduction of the sentences and for clemency for the Rosenberg couple.

1952

All defense petitions for hearings on appeals are rejected.

All petitions for the Supreme Court to review the case are denied.

Trials, similar to the Rosenberg trial in 1951, are held in Moscow and Prague. The charge is espionage and treason on behalf of the United States Almost all the defendants are Jewish. Twenty-seven defendants are executed.

December. Eighteen months after the Rosenberg trial, two FBI agents acknowledged in affidavits that, at the instruction of the prosecution, they enabled a key government witness to perjure himself at the trial.[1,2]

1953

All further petitions for hearings on appeals are rejected.

All further petitions for a Supreme Court review of the trial are denied.

January 20. President Harry S. Truman leaves office; a petition for clemency for the Rosenbergs passes to incoming President Dwight D. Eisenhower.

February 11. President Eisenhower denies clemency.

February 13. The Vatican reveals that Pope Pius XII had appealed for clemency for the Rosenbergs while President Truman was in office. The Pope's appeal was concealed by the U.S. Attorney General and was never made known to either President. Also concealed were appeals by 3000 Protestant ministers and leading rabbis. Others joining appeals for clemency were Albert Einstein, Harold Urey and other leading scientists who had worked on the atom bomb, and the heads of European countries allied with the United States.

March. Discovery of new evidence of perjuries by the Greenglasses.

June 8. Judge Kaufman refuses to grant a hearing on new evidence.

June 16. Supreme Court Justice William O. Douglas grants stay of execution to give defendants time to petition for a hearing on a new appeal stating that the defendants were prosecuted and sentenced under the wrong law.

June 19. Supreme Court justices called back from their vacations for an unprecedented session at which they vacate the stay of execution. Three justices dissent.

June 19. Julius and Ethel Rosenberg are executed.

1955

In Moscow, the post-Stalin Communist government exonerates the executed defendants tried in 1952 for espionage and treason on behalf of the United States.

1963

April. In Prague, the executed defendants in the Slansky trial are exonerated (In May 1968, there is another exoneration in which the executed were fully "restored" to their previous status as loyal citizens).

1973

Five of the trial jurors in the Rosenberg trial reveal they had been persuaded by the prosecution's arguments that the defendants were being tried for spying for an enemy nation during the Cold War, that is, for treason.[3]

1973-1983

Lawsuits by Michael and Robert Meeropol, sons of the Rosenbergs, to compel the Department of Justice to comply with the Freedom of Information Act resulted in scores of thousands of relevant government documents being made available to the public. These documents shed light on suborned perjuries and other misconduct by the prosecution at the trial; and of a pre-determination of guilt by the judge. Many of those documents comprise the documentation for this book.

1976

May 13. Irving Saypol, the former chief prosecutor at the Rosenberg trial, is indicted by a special prosecutor for perjury and bribery during his tenure as a New York State judge.

1986

June 23. Roy Cohn, the former assistant prosecutor at the Rosenberg trial is disbarred for stealing client funds, perjury and other unethical conduct.

1993

August 16. A mock trial of the Rosenbergs at the American Bar Association annual meeting returns Not Guilty verdicts.

1995

The famous Venona/FBI decoded messages are made public. A number of these confirm that there had been contact between Julius Rosenberg and Soviet espionage personnel in the United States during World War II. None of the decoded messages support the prosecution's charge that the crime was committed during the Cold War or that technical information on the atom bomb had been passed.

2001

December. In a book by a New York Times reporter, Sam Roberts, and on television and on CBS' 60 Minutes, David Greenglass confesses that, at the instruction of the prosecution, he had given perjured testimony against his sister, Ethel Rosenberg.[4]

2008

September. Nearly all the 1950 grand jury minutes that resulted in the indictment of the defendants were released. The minutes disclose that, although Ruth Greenglass, David Greenglass' wife, had testified at the trial that Ethel Rosenberg had typed up David Greenglass' espionage notes for Julius Rosenberg, the only notes she mentions at the grand jury hearings were notes she alone prepared.[5]

Morton Sobell publicly acknowledges that in the 1940s, he and Julius Rosenberg had passed non-atomic classified information to the Soviet Union.

Ethel and Julius, 1942

Chapter 1 | The bonding of strangers

The city of life...

New York City was our city, Emily's and mine. We were born in it, went to school in it, grew up in its poverty, absorbed its street-smarts, breathed in its clamorous energy. I carried Emily's schoolbooks, mentally assassinated every tall hulk of a boy who talked to her, wrote poems to her, eloped with her, turned a lathe in a shipyard repairing troop ships, scribbled would-be novels. One bright summer day in 1942, Emily and I walked down Fifth Avenue, pregnant with our first daughter, looking into the windows of great stores, feeling the pulse of the time, amused by snobby window mannequins pretending not to notice us, warmed by the sun and the sleepy young soldiers and their clinging girls, got caught up in the surging crowds crossing the streets as though we were members of a multitudinous biblical crossing to somewhere sublime. There is a great happiness in carrying a full womb in New York City, the City of *life*.

The city of death...

In our New York City, media headlines four years after the war described the peace. The *New York Daily Mirror* told us the authorities were taking great precautions: "ORDER RED VESSELS HALTED IN BAY TO UNDERGO SEARCH FOR EXPLOSIVES." On February 12, 1950, the *New York Journal-American* told us that "PORT'S SECURITY IS NON-EXISTENT."[6] By September 1950, the New York Times was preparing us to expect heavy casualties from Soviet atom bomb attacks: "BOMB TOLL IN CITY OF 160,000 IS SEEN," but one month later it cited a warning from a U.S. Senator: "TYDINGS SAYS BOMB CAN KILL A MILLION."[7] The *New York Daily Mirror* had already trumped this figure in February with an estimate of nationwide casualties: "WARNS H-BLITZ COULD KILL 15,000,000."[8] Six months later the same newspaper quoted a general as saying

> Within 10 seconds after it is dropped on N.Y. or any other city an atom bomb would kill almost every living thing within a half mile radius of the blast and spread horrible destruction for miles more.[9]

Some newspapers claimed an exodus from New York City was already underway. "CITY FOLKS FEAR OF BOMBS AIDS BOOM IN RURAL REALTY;" "DOOM OF 27 U.S. CITIES BY H-BOMBS ENVISIONED;" "WAR PERILS START WAVE OF ANXIETIES;" "WHEN RUSSIANS STRIKE IT WILL BE WITH PLENTY OF A-BOMBS ON NEW YORK AND WASHINGTON, D.C.;" "RUSSIA CAN A-BOMB US NOW."[10] One newspaper assured us its headline was a "grim estimate reached in the highest echelons of the Pentagon." The *New*

York Journal-American warned us no one would come out alive if we were atom-bombed: "WARN H BOMB BLITZ COULD DESTROY ALL NY."[11]

We were told the Russians were trying to smuggle atom bombs into the city to be detonated in our neighborhoods, targeting the Holland Tunnel at rush hour, targeting Central Park on Sunday where the worshippers at St. Patrick's Cathedral went afterward to receive the blessings of the sun, targeting the midtown garment center with its heavy-breathing cutters huddled over massive tables, its stitchers squinting into their sewing machines, its barrel-chested hat blockers marooned in steam, and legions of foremen, snappers, designers, managers, vice presidents, presidents, bosses' sons, daughters, nephews, nieces, aunts and indescribables rushing in and out of elevators, barking orders, curses, insults and prayers. Elsewhere, the public schools' masses of children were huddled under snow-white sheets per atom bomb drill instructions from City Hall. One drill instruction told the teachers to warn the children against peeking outside the sheets because the blinding light of a nearby atomic explosion might injure their eyes.

Everyone prayed in those days that a new Hiroshima would not unfold at the next tick of a second.

Over the summer months of 1950, we began to learn the names of those who, we were told, had enabled the Russians to threaten to turn Fifth Avenue, the garment center, Brooklyn Bridge, the Empire State Building, our tenements and our mansions and Emily and David and little Michelle and Jennifer into radioactive ash.

Why we wrote this book...

Emily and I began to write *Exoneration* in 1995, and I have had to complete it without Emily, since her death in 2004. Our subject is an unfinished chapter in American history, and an important unfinished business of our lives known as the Rosenberg-Sobell case.

Despite a number of excellent factual studies of the trial over the past five decades, the true dimensions of the human, ethnic, and Constitutional tragedies embodied in the case had never been fully explored. The appropriate focus of previous studies had been on whether the trial, the verdicts, and the sentences were shaped by the evidence or by political expediency. But the Rosenberg-Sobell case is not simply an espionage case. It is an event precipitated by monumental forces competing for world dominion, and was shaped in part by borderless, mythological ethnic prejudices.

There was barely a mention in previous studies, for example, that the 1951 trial, with its all-Jewish cast of defendants, had its counterparts in trials in 1952, in Moscow and Prague, in which the defendants were also all-Jewish or nearly all-Jewish, and in which the defendants were charged with espionage and treason.

We believe that many principles of American justice were eroded by precedents injected into the Rosenberg-Sobell trial. The Founders of our Constitution wanted our system of justice to rest on democratically enacted laws, not on fickle or ambitious or vain or self-serving men and women. Every law would prescribe a punishment for its violation. No man or woman who violated one law would be punished by reference to another law that was not violated. By conducting "bait and switch" prosecutions, in which formal indictments for one crime were superseded in the courtroom by oral prosecutions for another crime, the Constitution was dealt a severe blow, one that resonates to this very day. Every blow to the Constitution takes its toll in human tragedy.

We wrote this book in the hope that it will increase public awareness of the necessity for returning to a Constitutional system of justice.

Case summary...

The official description of the Rosenberg-Sobell case is that in the 1940s, after the start of World War II, Julius Rosenberg, an engineer, and his wife, Ethel, and Morton Sobell, an engineer and classmate of Julius Rosenberg, and David Greenglass, Ethel Rosenberg's brother, conspired to obtain atomic bomb information for transmittal to the Soviet Union, our then ally. Greenglass was assigned by the army to Los Alamos, NM, as a machinist in a workshop attached to the research laboratory that produced the atom bomb. He became the prosecution's chief witness.

The defendants' ascribed motive for the crime was their belief in Communism and their desire to enable the Soviet Union to destroy the United States. They were tried before a jury in New York City in March 1951, and were found guilty. Julius and Ethel Rosenberg were sentenced to death; the other defendants received long prison sentences.

The Supreme Court declined to review the case nine times.

Basing ourselves on newspaper accounts of the trial, we initially accepted the official version. A case of idealism, we thought, misused for espionage and treason. Our only quarrel was with the death sentences. We were opposed to capital punishment for any crime whatsoever.

During the months that followed the trial, however, a different version of the case emerged. It began with a series of articles by William Reuben, a former American Civil Liberties Union (ACLU) public relations director, appearing in the *National Guardian*, a left-wing weekly newspaper. Reuben claimed the charge relating to the atom bomb, and the imputed intent of the defendants to help the Soviet Union destroy the United States, had been prosecution hoaxes for which no evidence had been presented.

That began our decades-long exploration of the Rosenberg-Sobell case which, to this day, eludes closure.

In September 2008, Morton Sobell, who had served eighteen years of his thirty-year prison sentence, confessed that, during the 1940s, he and Julius Rosenberg had passed non-atomic classified information to the Soviet Union.

The confession would not have surprised Emily, nor did it surprise me. After reading Sobell's confession in the *New York Times*, I did what Emily would have done. I telephoned Morton Sobell to tell him he had done the right thing by his admission. Emily and I had very long ago assumed the possibility of what Sobell confirmed.

Two presidents troubled by the prosecution...

Two presidents, twenty years apart, signaled uncertainty about the prosecutions' conduct. President Lyndon B. Johnson, a Democrat, made inquiries into the case as far back as March 1953, and later, in his last week in office in January 1969, undoubtedly had a hand in Morton Sobell's early release from prison. President Richard Nixon, a Republican, had been present when President Dwight D. Eisenhower was advised by his Attorney General to deny clemency to the Rosenbergs. Nixon said in respect to one defendant, Ethel Rosenberg,

> If I had known – if we had known that at the time –
> if President Eisenhower had known it, he might have
> taken a different view with regard to her. In other words,
> tainted evidence, even though a person is totally guilty,
> is a reason to get him off.[12]

Nixon attributed the "tainted evidence" to "overzealous prosecutors, and those that are assisting prosecutors, like J. Edgar Hoover..."

Haunting questions...

A great many questions were spawned by the Rosenberg-Sobell trial, some focusing narrowly on the conduct of the trial, others dealing broadly with the historical conflicts and schisms mirrored by the trial. Was communism the inspiration for the crime? Was justice the inspiration for the prosecution? Why did the Supreme Court refuse to review the case? Why did the post-German-occupation leaders of France and other European nations intervene on the side of the Rosenbergs? Why did Pope Pius XII do so?

The most profound question of all, the question that has haunted students of the case for more than half a century is this: why did Julius and Ethel Rosenberg, a couple in their thirties, the parents of two very young sons, choose to be executed rather than confess? A glib answer was given long ago: they wanted to be martyrs for Communism. But they did not defend Communism at their trial; they did not declare it superior to capitalism; they did not claim the Soviet system was better than ours. They simply said they were innocent. In her last letter to President Eisenhower, delivered to him a few hours before her execution, Ethel Rosenberg admitted "a certain innate shyness, an embarrassment almost, comparable to that which the ordinary person feels in the presence of the great and the famous" had restrained her from communicating with him to ask that her and her husband's lives be spared.

We, too, were haunted by the question, and especially so for a personal reason we will shortly describe. Among the tasks we set ourselves in this book was to try to find an answer that was more credible than the glib and unsupportable one.

There were other important questions spawned by the case. The 1951 New York City trial had its counterparts in trials in 1952 in Moscow and Prague, in which the defendants were also all-Jewish or nearly all-Jewish, and in which the defendants were charged with espionage and treason, and in which more than 20 death sentences were imposed. The three trials raised a troubling question: why did the law enforcement agencies of the United States, Moscow and Prague seem unable to find non-Jewish Soviet spies and traitors in their respective populations?

Nine months after the New York trial, federal law enforcement officials issued a statement with which the law enforcement agencies of Moscow and Prague were undoubtedly in full agreement. Disloyal persons, our law enforcement officials told the media, would rarely be found among persons of "pure Anglo-Saxon stock."[13]

There were troubling precedents arising out of the prosecutorial and judicial conduct at the Rosenberg-Sobell trial, creating models for other trials. A new court system was created out of those precedents in later years, one in which the Constitution has no place, and the courts are accountable only to the transient occupants of the White House.

Shortly after the death sentences were imposed, George F. Kennan, a high ranking State Department official who had designed the "containment" policy against the Soviet Union and against communism in other countries, became concerned with the direction which the nation was being led. In an essay in the New York Times, he asked whether the United States was beginning to resemble the

> very power we are trying to combat: intolerant, secretive, suspicious, cruel, and terrified of internal dissension because we have lost our own belief in ourselves and in the power of our ideals.[14]

Who we were – 1...

At the time of the Rosenberg-Sobell trial, in March 1951, we lived in New York City with our two young daughters in a small three-room apartment in a rent-controlled multi-building complex known as Knickerbocker Village, not far from the Jewish ghetto in which I had been raised.

Emily, then 29, was a Hunter College graduate and was employed as a New York City Probation officer and, on a part-time basis, as a social worker for elderly people at the 92nd Street YMCA. She would go on to get a doctorate in sociology, would later chair the Sociology Department of Douglas College at Rutgers University and, afterward, begin another career as a practicing attorney. I was 32, had been a machinist during World War II, and then became a New York State Parole Officer, from which I resigned to become a full-time writer after having had several novels published. I later became a businessman and an activist.

A civics textbook of the streets...

Emily and I were far from being versed in law in 1950 and in the immediate subsequent years. But we had been Probation and Parole officers for about a year, occupations to which we had brought a special knowledge we – and especially I – had obtained on the streets, as well as in our homes, at school, with the police and with friends who were storefront lawyers on the Lower East Side. We knew there were two kinds of trials, those conducted by honest officials and those that weren't. We knew about plea bargaining, bribed judges, bribed prosecutors, bribed or blackmailed witnesses. We knew corruption was not all of one kind. An official who would disdain a financial bribe might nevertheless perpetrate illegalities against defendants whose color or religion or politics or sex he or she abhorred.

When we became involved in law enforcement, we obtained new knowledge that reinforced what we already knew. Emily learned why some probationers were routinely treated more kindly than others. I learned why certain felons who repeatedly violated parole received reprimands from judges, while the same judges sent other parole violators back to prison to complete their sentences. We also learned why, administratively, certain probationers and parolees never found themselves in court for violations they had committed, while others consumed courtroom calendars for the pettiest of infractions.

I was not surprised by what I learned because my own dealings with police at a very early age had prepared me well. When I was thirteen years old I decided I wanted to join my father in peddling ice cream and inflated toys in the traffic at the corners of Canal Street and Broadway, not far from the Holland Tunnel. My father told me the traffic cop would expect a daily bribe, although my father believed it would be twenty-five cents a day rather than the dollar he and the other adult peddlers paid. I asked my father why the cop had to be paid. "Because it's his traffic," my father said.

Sure enough, after I had gone into the traffic a few times, the traffic cop, whom the peddlers called Mad Dog behind his back and 'Sir' to his face, motioned me to join him in a little hallway on the street. Mad Dog asked me, "You know you got to pay rent?"

"Yes, sir," I said.

He put out his hand. I put a dime in his palm. "You sonofabitch," he said. "You're only, what, twelve? And you already know how to Jew us down."

"Yes, sir," I said.

On our way home that evening, my father surprised me. "Don't be too mad at Mad Dog," he said. "He's got a son crippled with polio, about your age. If it happened to you, I'd be a mad dog, too."

I didn't have to worry about polio because my mother made me wear anti-polio camphor balls wrapped in a handkerchief around my neck.

Our street civics lessons did not make Emily or me cynical. Maybe sad at times, maybe a little judgmental. But hardly even skeptical, until the Rosenberg-Sobell case.

Neighborhood news...

On an afternoon on April 5, 1951, a neighbor knocked at our door and told us that two other neighbors, whom we didn't know, had just been sentenced to death.

Our condemned neighbors lived in another of the Knickerbocker Village buildings. We had been reading about their trial in the newspapers. They had passed secret information about the atom bomb to the Soviet Union during World War II and afterward, when the Cold War had begun and the Soviet Union had become our designated enemy. So far as we could tell from the news stories, the trial had been tolerably fair. The tangible and circumstantial evidence (though never actually described in the newspaper stories) must have been good enough to justify the guilty verdicts, although the death sentences troubled us.

Our interest in the case was heightened by a past occurrence. One spring day in 1950, Emily had taken our daughters, Michelle, then eight, and Jennifer, two, to a nearby park with another neighbor and her child. Our neighbor saw a woman she knew, and she introduced her to Emily. "This is Ethel Rosenberg," she said. Emily and Ethel Rosenberg talked for a little while. Ethel had her two small sons with her, close in age to our daughters. It was a pleasant conversation, as Emily remembered it. And then Ethel got up and left with her sons, and she and Emily never saw each other again.

Emily's brief conversation with Ethel Rosenberg, which might have dimmed in memory over time, now became, instead, a persistently relived occurrence.

The woman who had simply been another young mother on a park bench with whom Emily had spoken was now a young mother who had been sentenced to death.

Their execution was set for the following month. We knew, however, that executions were usually held up while legal appeals were pending.

There were similarities in our lives that gave the Rosenbergs' a claim to our attention. They had graduated from Seward Park High School, as we had; they had two very young children, as did we; like us, they were Jewish, and had been born into similar poverty. It was impossible to look at their photographs and not share with them another resonance. They had bonded with each other at an early age, as had we. They had expressed idealistic visions of a more benign society, as had we, although they trusted Communism to realize their visions, while our trust was not in any single philosophy or political theory. We had drawn the conclusion from history that humankind moves slowly, painfully and sometimes chaotically, toward a better life. Or so we hoped.

Our opposition to their death sentences was, of course, shaped by our views on capital punishment. But these views soon became the least of our reasons for questioning the sentences.

We had been greatly surprised by Reuben's claims, for nothing in the newspaper reports of the trial had indicated any reason for doubting the essential elements of the prosecution's claims. Some claims may have been exaggerated, some may have been oratorical flourishes. There may have been some fevered oratory by the prosecution in which the defendants were blamed for our casualties in the Korean War and in future wars, but that kind of oratory was common, and was expected to be sensibly discounted by jurors.

The same, we thought, might be said of Reuben's claims. His description of some of the prosecution's claims as "hoaxes" may have been an author's oratorical flourishes. We intended to find out for ourselves.

Who we were – 2...

We were what are often called "children of the Great Depression." We had experienced that unstable and tumultuous time at first through our parents, and then directly, when we gradually entered the wider world beyond our homes. In our mid-teens our expectations for the future were bare. The advantages of education and the rewards of hard work and entrepreneurship promised us in our classrooms had become irrelevant. Formerly self-reliant and well educated men and women sat on the same government-issue metal folding chairs as did many of our parents, waiting for their names to be called by investigators for Home Relief assistance, the name given in those years to what we now call "welfare." A question we asked ourselves was whether we must follow our parents into those chairs, and for how long?

Unbeknownst to us, our country was on the cusp of change. The widespread hunger and hopelessness that had overcome many millions of Americans under President Herbert Hoover had begun to slowly give way to new perceptions and new beliefs under President Franklin D. Roosevelt: an era of a government's monumental indifference to its suffering population was being replaced by a government that created millions of jobs, a system of pensions and health services for the aged, and unemployment insurance. Unionization and the formation of cooperatives were encouraged as protective measures in confrontation with corporate power. In teenagers and young adults, the resurrective spirit behind what became known as the New Deal began to create expectations of ordered, stable and creative lives in the foreseeable future. Our moods were lifted by President Roosevelt's advice: *We have nothing to fear but fear itself!*

Emily and her mother...

Emily was deeply influenced by her mother, a Lower East Side social worker who chose to work among the poor at a poverty-level wage, rather than rise into administrative levels of charity where the poor were rarely seen. Emily's father, a sometime businessman and composer, had died when Emily was twelve.

At an early age, Emily felt drawn to the troubled and lost. In a time when street corner orators were hailing Socialism or Communism or Fascism as paths to national salvation, Emily chose triage as her philosophy: respect for the hurt and the hungry, the dispossessed, the abandoned, the inconsolable and the crazy. She declined the orators' solutions: she regarded fascism as a moribund panacea marked by slavery and death, and socialism and communism as ideals-still-in-the-making, still fully susceptible to deceit, demagoguery and corruption.

A story about Emily...

One evening, after she had been a Probation Officer for a few months, Emily warned me she might be fired for something she was about to do at work. The next day, she asked the sitting judge in the court to which she was assigned whether she could speak privately to him when court was over.

"What about?" he asked.

"If I start explaining it to you now, I don't think I'll get far. I just want ten minutes, Your Honor."

After a moment he said, "Ten minutes. I'll have one of the assistant DAs join us in chambers, if you don't mind. You'll both be off the clock."

When they were seated in chambers, Emily said, "Each of my probationers' cases takes about four or five minutes to process in court. An assistant DA rattles off the charge in about thirty seconds or less. Your Honor asks them did they do what they're charged with, hooking or petty theft or getting into a brawl. They try to explain, but Your Honor says, 'Yes or no?' Sometimes Your Honor says, 'Spare me the violins, just say 'Yes or No...''"

"I see where this is going," the judge interrupted her. "Here's what I say to you, Emily. Spare me the violins. I know my job. Anything else?"

The prosecutor said, "If you do what I suspect she wants, we'd have to have twenty-four hour court sessions."

"Your Honor, I've only used up four minutes of my ten," Emily said. "A lot of the women complain they don't get their day in court. All they're allowed to say is 'Yes' or 'No.' I can't tell you how many of them tell me they're disappointed, that there's no difference between a court that tells them to shut up except 'Yes' or 'No' and a John or father or brother or boyfriend or pimp who smacks them around until they get the answer they want."

"Whhhooooaaa," the prosecutor said. "Stop right there, Emily. Comparing His Honor to a pimp? Are you crazy?"

"I still have five minutes," Emily said. "What I'm suggesting, Your Honor, is that you let one or two of them every day have her day in court, tell you about her life. They need somebody important to hear what they have to say. Maybe it'll give them some hope. Maybe some dignity and respect instead of being made to feel like what their boyfriends or pimps call them."

"The pimp stuff again!" the prosecutor cried out. "I don't believe what I'm hearing."

"Time's up, Emily," the judge said.

"I just want to assure you, Your Honor," the prosecutor said, "that I think this is the stupidest thing I ever heard. I'm praying that you don't lock Emily up just to teach her a lesson in respect for Your Honor."

The judge looked at Emily in silence for a moment. "This is so outrageous, Emily, that I don't want to respond to you in my present state of mind. What I think I should do is tell you we can meet again tomorrow after court. I want you to think very carefully about what you want to say to me then. I hope what you say to me tomorrow will make me forget what you said to me today." He turned to the prosecutor. "You be there, too. Off the clock."

The next day, Emily began the meeting by saying, "I'm not a lawyer, but I imagine that there was a time when Mr. Prosecutor here was quizzed by a committee of some kind to explain why he wanted to be a prosecutor. I imagine there was a day when Your Honor appeared before a committee to explain why you wanted to be a judge. All I'm asking is that the women whose conduct I supervise be allowed to express in more than a single syllable an explanation of their lives and what they hope for. The men in their lives demand of them only a positive single syllable response to whatever it is the men want. The court allows my probationers to choose between two one-syllable words, which is not a huge improvement. These women should be given the right to describe their lives to an official tribune of the state, an authority that has power, the same authority that arrested them for their conduct, incarcerated them at times, put them on probation at times, but never gave them an opportunity to describe their lives."

"That's hokum," the prosecutor said. "Every one of these women has a case file, every one of them has been interviewed at great length by intake officers, and some of them have been interviewed more than once and they tell a different story each time."

"No," Emily said. "They tell their story to laundry-list clerks. Name, address, how old were you, where did you meet, did you seek medical attention, for how long, when did he leave, who does the baby live with, how long did you live there, where did you get the knife, did you sign a foster parent agreement. This tells these women how unimportant their lives are to us. These women should be given a chance to describe their lives in a place that considers their lives important. They should be allowed to describe themselves to someone with authority, in a courtroom with a judge and his gavel up on a bench, an American flag in the corner, and a Bible to swear on and a stenographer and a bailiff and reporters and some spectators."

"Emily," the judge said. "Do you honestly think that would make any difference in their behavior? That the hookers and knifers would reform and become nurses and Big Sisters?"

"What we do for them now isn't turning them into Florence Nightingales, either," Emily said. "No, I don't know what the impact of having their day in court would be. Except that as humans who've been arrested, they have a right to it. Maybe they won't go on nursing the grudge that they never had their day in court, that they were treated as insignificant trash. Maybe some of them will take it as a vote of confidence. I don't know."

There was silence for a few moments. The judge said, "I'm relieved, Emily, for your sake, that you didn't make any comparisons to pimps this time."

The prosecutor said, "She didn't do so directly, Your Honor. But it was there, indirectly, when she talked about the syllables. You remember, certain men only want one-syllable answers..."

"For the record," Emily broke in, "I haven't made the connections in my mind that the prosecutor has in his. I didn't ask to meet with any pimps about this problem."

"Well," the judge said, "You don't sound as outrageous as you did yesterday. But as impractical as hell. How could it be done? You're not an attorney. I can't allow you to act as one and conduct an examination."

"You can appoint a lawyer," Emily said.

"I don't have a budget for assigned counsel in misdemeanors."

"You can ask a law student to do it."

"Is there anything you don't have an answer for?"

"Try me," Emily said.

In the end, the judge agreed that he would permit Emily to select one probationer, once a week, to describe her life, in fifteen minutes or less. None of the other judges followed the judge's example.

Years later, when she became a lawyer, Emily saw to it that her clients, many of whom she represented pro bono, had their day in court, had a chance to utter what was relevant to them in their lives, however irrelevant their lives might be to a judge or prosecutor.

David...

I was at first less skeptical about the usefulness of programmatic ideals than was Emily. I believed that if ideals were used corruptly, the corrupters could be easily replaced. I became a Communist for a number of years. I agreed that all natural resources should be publicly owned and managed for the good of society, that the profit motive was the problem and not the salvation of the United States. But I argued with my comrades that death sentences in the Soviet Union were as much a product of imperfect leaders as they were in the United States. I argued against the Communists' notion that men and women condemned to death for vile crimes were less worthy of help than men and women condemned to death because they were militant unionists or civil rights activists. I argued that the American Communist leaders were trying in vain to impose the history of Communist Russia on the United States. When, in 1939, the Stalin and Hitler regimes made a compact, I argued that the Soviet Union had betrayed the prayers of hundreds of millions of human beings. That ended my Communist affiliation.

But neither Emily nor I would distance ourselves from actions on behalf of the poor, the condemned or the discriminated against, regardless of who sponsored the actions. We had learned from reading Mahatma Gandhi that if you want to sincerely stand with the wronged, you must be willing to do so with people who stand for them for other reasons than yours. In those years, neither the Democratic nor the Republican Party would march for any cause that favored economic, racial, ethnic or gender equality. They left it to the Socialists, the Communists, the unionists, the anti-lynching groups, the anti-anti-Semites and the equality-for-women groups to move the nation, march by march and arrest by arrest, toward the equalities that have now been partially achieved.

A story about David...

In 1950, seven Virginia black men were marked for execution, having been convicted of raping a white woman. Because their attorneys were all local white men who had advised their clients to confess and had reluctantly and poorly defended those who refused to confess, it was impossible to know whether all seven men, or some of them, or none of them, were guilty. A man I knew, an

African-American lawyer, decided to let other lawyers make the cold rounds of the appellate courts to save the condemned men, while he would make the rounds of churches, unions, newspapers, and liberal organizations to rouse public opinion against their executions. I had just had a novel accepted for publication and felt a freedom that was new to me, and I asked him whether I could help in some way.

We explained to white preachers and priests why there were grounds for believing that the defendants had not been fairly tried. Afterward, back in his car, we debated whether we had swayed, offended, or bored the church leaders.

There came a February day when it was clear that scores of legal motions and tens of thousands of prayers for compassion had made no mark on the stone faced judges in Virginia and Washington, D.C., nor on the Virginia Governor.

"You may as well go on home," my friend said. "I'll go sit with one of the families."

"I want to do that, too," I said.

He drove us to a town called Martinsville, and he stopped on a street corner in the Jim Crow section of town. He told me to wait for him. He left the car and walked over to a taxi and spoke to the driver. Then he came back. "He'll take you to one of the families," he said.

The driver took us deep into farm country, past shacks and huts and tin patched structures, and he stopped outside a dilapidated old shack where half a dozen black men, some young, some old, all of them armed with rifles of one kind or another, stood and eyed me as I got out of the taxi. There were half a dozen old cars parked under some nearby trees. "Bill Patterson wanted me to be here tonight," I told the nearest of them. They stepped away from the door.

It was cold inside, made only a little warmer by a small pot-belly stove. There were two rooms, a small, back one, in which a ten-year old girl sat on a cot, a baby in her arms, her thumb in the baby's mouth, a blanket over her shoulders. She looked at me without any expression. The outer, larger room had a bed, a table, some chairs and the pot-belly stove. A woman lay on the bed, covered with several blankets that did not hide her trembling and her sometimes whole-body spasms. She made crying, broken sounds, she moaned and sometimes struck her head with her fist. Two women sat on the bed on either side of her, sometimes reaching out to touch her cheek or lips or wrist.

I sat on a chair facing the bed, not knowing what to do, thinking, "Maybe I'm doing something just by being here."

From time to time, one or two of the armed men came in and talked briefly with the women and went out again.

The sun went down and two oil lamps were lit. The little girl in the other room, her blanket still over her shoulders, the baby still in her arms, came in and climbed up on the bed and began saying out loud, "It's going to be alright, Mama. It's going to be alright, Mama..."

The whispering of the men outside waxed and waned and, when it waned, the quiet became unbearable.

About an hour or so later, I heard a car drive down the dirt road and stop near the door. The women and the little girl and the woman shivering in the bed became very still. We heard a car door open. We heard the men outside speaking to whoever had been in the car. And then there was silence. And then an old man opened the door briefly, his lips tightly shut. He nodded at the two women on the bed and shut the door. And then the silence was broken by the woman striking herself in the head and the little girl crying, "It's going to be alright, Mama..."

That was one month before the Rosenberg-Sobell trial began.

Emily's initiative...

An evening in fall 1951. Emily and I had put our daughters to bed and spent a quarter of an hour or so listening to the news on the radio. Emily said she didn't want to listen to the radio, she wanted to talk. I shut off the radio. We both stood at a window looking out at an old red brick Roman Catholic church that served as a school for the children of second generation Italian families.

"Ever since the April death sentences against the Rosenbergs, I can't get Ethel out of my mind," Emily said. "She is a woman I talked with. I still hear the sound and the rhythm of her voice. I see her eyes. Michelle and Jenny were with me in the park that day and they heard and saw her, they saw her sons. My mind is filled with her."

I thought I knew what was coming.

"What I have trouble with is understanding the silence," Emily said. "When two neighbors are about to be killed, how can neighbors be silent? I can't accept that. We have to do something."

I thought, "Emily doesn't know how immovable officials become after they order executions."

"Emily, I have to tell you something," I said.

"Yes?" The impatience of patience in her voice was clear to me.

I said, "It's one thing to pit yourself against a bunch of Tammany Hall judges who tell you they don't want to hear violins. It's another thing to take on J. Edgar Hoover, the FBI, the Department of Justice and the federal judges. They are the government of the United States of America. They can hurt us badly, our daughters and you and me."

I was not a total stranger to threatening situations. But facing down policemen who told me and a black man in a small Virginia city that we were disorderly because we were walking down a street together was nowhere near as threatening as being marked for punishment by the United States government.

All she did was look at me with a mixture of sadness and regret, and I knew in that moment that I could lose her, that my life would never be the same again if I said another cautionary word. So I didn't.

Meeting the defense attorney...

Emily's first step was to locate Emanuel Bloch, the Rosenbergs' attorney. We met with him at his very modest office, within walking distance of the federal courthouse. He had a small waiting room and a lone secretary.

Emily told him we had two concerns: were the Reuben articles accurate in their accusations of misconduct by the prosecutors and the judge? Was there any way in which we might help the Rosenbergs' sons?

Bloch was in his late forties, a seasoned civil rights attorney, but nothing had prepared him to defend people indicted for conspiring to commit espionage. He was a sole practitioner, and he needed help in trying the case, but almost every attorney he approached, he told us, had declined to become involved. Bloch's father, Alexander, was also an attorney and well on in years. For the record, he became Ethel Rosenberg's attorney. A young woman attorney, Gloria Agrin, volunteered to assist Bloch in technical matters and law research, but the weight of the case was on Bloch's shoulders alone. Among his problems was that he had no investigative facilities and hardly any funds. We learned later that the Communist Party, which we mistakenly assumed would assist him financially in the Rosenbergs' defense, did not do so.

Consequently, Bloch stood virtually alone for his clients in the courtroom and took the full brunt of responsibility for the verdict and the sentences. Morton Sobell, we later learned, had been represented by two attorneys, neither of them with a significant background in criminal law, who were of little assistance to either Bloch or to their client.

On the day we first spoke with him, Bloch was in a state of extreme tension and exhaustion. From the moment the trial ended on March 29, 1951, and before the sentences had been pronounced, he had single-handedly begun the laborious task of analyzing the 2600-page trial record for judicial errors and prosecutorial misconduct on which his appeals would be based. It was just as well, he told us, that because of his representation of the Rosenbergs, many of his other clients had left him. He had also learned that an attempt was being made to prosecute him under the "white slavery" Mann Act for traveling from New York City to Washington D.C. and sharing a hotel room with his fiancée.

Bloch told us Reuben's analysis of the trial was essentially correct. Emily said we wanted to read the trial record for ourselves and asked that he lend us a copy. He seemed reluctant to do so. The few copies he had, he told us, were being passed around among attorneys whose help he was seeking. He also told us he doubted that non-lawyers would understand the nuances and courtroom rituals of the Federal judicial system. He was, correctly, unimpressed by Emily's previous employment as a New York City probation officer and mine as a New York State parole officer.

Bloch, we later learned, had one more reason for not wishing to let us read the trial record: he was concerned that we would regard as errors certain decisions he had made during the trial in respect to cross examination of witnesses, certain advice he had given his clients, and his acceptance without challenge of certain testimony by prosecution witnesses and several prosecution exhibits.

In the end, Bloch reluctantly accepted our assurances that if there were matters we did not understand in the trial record, we would discuss them with him, which we did, although not always to his or our satisfaction. As for the Rosenbergs' sons, Bloch told us, their paternal grandmother and other close relatives were presently taking care of them. He was concerned, however, that new difficulties might arise when the older of the two, Michael, returned to school in September. "I promised my clients that I'd protect the boys as if they were my own," he told us. "And that's what I intend doing."

During our conversation he raised, with a touch of bitterness, one other matter. "Do you think," he asked us, "that it was pure coincidence that all the defendants were Jewish and that the chief prosecutors and the judge were also Jewish?"

I thought to myself: the defendants were New Yorkers and the prosecutors and the judge were New Yorkers, and it would hardly be remarkable that they were all Jewish.

Emily and I remained politely silent.

Bloch must have understood our silence. He said, "Did you know that the trial was originally set for New Mexico, where the alleged crime occurred and that the first indictment was written by the U.S. Attorney in Albuquerque?"

"Is that routine?" I asked. "To move trials from where defendants were first indicted to where they live?"

He asked, "Is it routine in New York City, where about a third of the population is Jewish, to empanel a jury without a single Jewish juror?"

His questions made us uncomfortable and our responses did the same for him. We left Bloch with the trial transcript in our hands and with uncertainty about his implication that there had been an anti-Semitic factor at the trial. Our discomfort had arisen not because what he was implying was unbelievable, but because we did not want to confront the possibility that it *was* believable.

In our minds, if our reading of the trial record supported Reuben's claims of deceitful misconduct by the prosecutors, Bloch would have strong grounds on which to appeal for reversing the verdicts, and there might even be a basis for an appeal to public opinion if the prosecutorial misconduct had been deliberate.

The ethnic implications of Bloch's questions, even if to some degree true, would muddy the picture with unprovable and inflammatory claims.

Months later, we found that Bloch's questions were being asked throughout Jewish communities everywhere, and not only among Jews, and not only in the United States.

We were not yet aware that the following year would be marked by espionage/treason trials of Jews in Moscow and Prague.

We made inquiries among our lawyer friends about the three Jewish officials who had represented the government at the trial. Federal Judge Irving Kaufman, who had presided at the trial, had been appointed to his post less than two years before the trial. The chief prosecutor, U.S. Attorney Irving Saypol, had begun his career as a Tammany Hall official. His chief assistant prosecutor, a relative, had been Roy Cohn, a very bright young lawyer. The judge and the two prosecutors owed their appointments to Tammany Hall, the oldest political machine in the state. Inevitably, as was true for many Tammany beneficiaries, Saypol and Cohn later found themselves facing the judgment of reform-minded prosecutors and colleagues.[15, 16]

There were also two other assistant prosecutors – Myles Lane and James Kilsheimer II, neither of them Jewish – who played minor roles at the trial.

Justice officials' next move...

Less than a week after being sentenced, Ethel Rosenberg was transferred to the death house at Sing Sing, drastically reducing the family's and Bloch's visits to her, thereby creating arbitrary hardships for visitation and the preparation of appeals. One month later, Julius Rosenberg was transferred to the death house.

If Emily had any reservations about the course she was set on, the transfers erased them. She regarded the hasty pre-appeal transfers to the death house to be a deliberate cruelty, intended to isolate the Rosenbergs from their family and sons, and to arouse in them a sense of abandonment that would discourage any faith they might have in obtaining relief of their situation.

The trial record...

On studying the voluminous trial record, we came to a troubling conclusion: the defendants had not actually been prosecuted for conspiring to pass information to a wartime ally in 1944-1945. Their formal indictment described the conspiracy as lasting from 1944-1950, but the last alleged espionage act listed in the indictment was in 1945. The chronological facts were ignored and the formal indictment was replaced by an oral indictment in the courtroom in which the crime was described as having been committed during the Cold War years, at a time when fear of a Soviet atom bomb attack was widespread.

The chief prosecutor declared at the trial that the defendants had joined

> in a deliberate, carefully planned conspiracy to deliver
> to the Soviet Union, the information and the weapons
> which the Soviet Union could use to destroy us...[17]

The prosecution declared, on 18 occasions at the trial, that the defendants had committed treason.

The judge, in his instructions to the jury, legitimated the accusation of treason, telling the jurors that "irrational sympathies must not shield proven traitors."[18]

Article III of the Constitution forbids prosecutors and judges from labeling as treason acts that do not fit its precise Constitutional description: *Treason against the United States, shall consist only in levying War against them, or in adhering to their Enemies, giving them Aid and Comfort.*

The prosecution did not point to any criminal acts committed by the defendants after the Allied victory in 1945. It simply repeatedly described the acts as having been committed on behalf of an enemy nation. The jurors, as the reader will discover, believed the defendants were being tried for committing treasonable acts on behalf of an enemy, and found them guilty of treason.

Reuben's claim that the prosecution had perpetrated two major hoaxes on the jurors was justified. The prosecution had presented neither tangible nor circumstantial evidence to support the accusation that the defendants had passed atomic information to the Soviet Union. Another hoax – that the atom bomb had been enveloped in such secrecy that the Soviet Union could not have developed its own bomb by 1949 without having been helped by defendants – was debatable. Later, in our examination of thousands of government documents in the 1970s relating to the case and the atom bomb, we discovered that General Leslie Groves, who headed the atom bomb project, had informed the Secretary of War, in 1946, that the Soviet Union either already had its own atom bomb or would have it shortly.

Among the discoveries made by the authors in their examination of another set of government documents in 1995, was that the espionage committed in 1944-1945 had been discovered in 1948, not in 1950, as Justice officials and the FBI claimed. In those intervening years, the Soviet Union detonated its first atom bomb. Had the defendants been tried before the Soviet's acquired their atom bomb, the applicable laws and the public's residual admiration for our ally's immense sacrifices of life (20 million casualties), would have resulted in sentences that would have, with good behavior, reunited the defendants with their families in three or four years.

By trying the defendants under an oral indictment in the courtroom, for committing treason on behalf of an enemy, Julius and Ethel Rosenberg were executed, Morton Sobell was sentenced to 30 years imprisonment, and the government's chief witness, David Greenglass, was sentenced to fifteen years.

The Committee to Secure Justice in the Rosenberg Case...

With the help of William Reuben, Emily formed a committee to organize public support for legal motions to obtain a new trial or a reduction of the sentences or, if those motions were rejected, to obtain clemency for the Rosenbergs from President Harry S. Truman or his successor, Dwight D. Eisenhower.

The formation of the Committee was undoubtedly a surprise to Justice officials. In mid-20th century United States, there was the most widespread hostility, even to the point of violence, toward dissenters of any kind. This hostility would seem to logically preclude any public efforts to challenge the mandated fate of persons who were regarded as Communist traitors.

Although Justice officials had to know, from FBI reports, that the initiative for creating the Committee had not come from Communists, and that the Communist Party was utterly opposed to its formation, they very quickly told the media that the Committee was a "Communist-led" group. Justice officials also had to have known that emissaries from the Communist Party knocked on our door, and on the doors of other Committee members, asking us in the most urgent terms to dissolve the Committee. We will describe these efforts in greater detail later. The fact is that Justice officials and the Communist Party saw eye to eye on the Committee during most of its of existence.

A Committee of Unimportant Persons...

The make-up of the Committee to Secure Justice in the Rosenberg-Sobell Case was hardly daunting to Justice officials. Reuben, a highly decorated World War II veteran, had found only a left-wing limited-circulation weekly, the *National Guardian*, willing to air his views of the trial. Emily had never helped form a committee of any kind in the past, and was not known as an activist outside her immediate circle of friends. I had had several novels published, none of which became best-sellers. The other members of the Committee emerged from our joint lists of people we knew who might lead us to people we didn't know.

Two newly-minted lawyer neighbors with young children said they wished us well when we asked them to join the Committee. They would support the Committee's activities, they said, but would not join it, and were unhappy that we were not as cautious as they were.

"We wish we didn't feel we have to do this," Emily told them. "What we're afraid of is waking up one day and wishing, for the sake of our kids, we had tried to save the America we grew up in."

Many other friends and neighbors expressed similar cautions. Some predicted that in the prevailing political climate, the Committee would have a very short and unsatisfactory life.

Cautious or not, our lawyer-neighbors, put us in touch with a typesetter named Norma Aronson, who knew many local politicians, including several Borough Presidents. She was bright and independent and had come to the same conclusions as we had about the case, and became our first new member. Among her first accomplishments was finding a sympathetic printer who agreed to publish, at cost, 10,000 copies of the trial record. Norma recommended that we speak with Aaron Schneider, a veteran union organizer who at that time had become disenchanted with what he regarded his union leaders' weakness for gaining the approval of government officials and employers. Aaron and Emily and I met for lunch at a cafeteria on East Broadway. We became instant friends, having much in common in our opinions of the political left and the right. Aaron had many contacts in the State assembly and senate, and in the New York City Council. Among Aaron's accomplishments for the Committee was to create a channel in 1953 to Senator Joseph McCarthy, enabling us to discuss with the Senator a possible role by him in encouraging President Eisenhower to grant clemency to the Rosenbergs.

One of my acquaintances, Yuri Suhl, a poet and novelist whom I had met at a writers' meeting, was impressively sensible, upbeat and witty. Suhl knew a fellow by the name of Joseph Brainin, a publicist for a number of well established, well-funded Jewish organizations with large support staffs. Reuben and Emily and I met with Brainin, a man with a skeptic's wit. He told us drily that if he joined the Committee he would never again be retained by the leaders of well-funded Jewish organizations. Fortunately for us and for him, there were exceptions to his prediction. He was also innovative and daring. During a past fund-raising drive for a major Jewish charity, he announced that he would be a passenger in a plane that would fly upside down, trailing a banner, the length of Manhattan, a stunt that was considered impressive in the 1940s. He also had a great many friends in the city's cultural and intellectual sphere. Best of all, he had come to the same conclusions we had simply by reading the same newspapers we did.

Brainin became the Chairman of the Committee and its chief timekeeper. He set a limit to our debates. When he looked at his watch for the second time during a discussion, we knew it was time to come to a decision. If we ignored his signal, he would give us a baleful look and say, "We are talking, talking, talking and the Rosenbergs' clock is ticking, ticking, ticking and we have to act before the ticking stops."

Emily and I both knew Milton Ost, a writer and publicist, whose free-lance assignments left him little spare time, but who nevertheless prepared our early press releases and other materials and continued to share his thinking and advice all through the campaign for clemency. One day a young film/drama critic, sports writer and reporter for the Jewish Telegraphic Agency, William Wolf, came to see us to offer his help. We had him meet Ost and they worked in tandem for a while until we were able, six or seven months after the Committee was formed, to pay Wolf a very bare salary so that he might give the clemency campaign all his time. To preserve his occasional free-lance assignments, he chose to work under the name Ted Jacobs. He was ten years younger than we were, and was sometimes very obviously hesitant to quarrel with decisions made by the older Committee members. He quickly learned that being the youngest among us did not make him less wise than the oldest.

Yuri Suhl brought Louis Harap, a Harvard educated editor of *Jewish Life*, a left-wing political-cultural magazine, to our attention, telling us that Harap, like many leftists, was searching for a way out of the sectarianism of left-wing politics. Harap was a thoughtful person and a devoted student of Jewish history. He was also a good listener and a source of historical anecdotes to support his approval or disapproval of projected actions.

Suhl also suggested that we talk to Peggy Strauss, at that time the vice president for sales at a leading clothing firm. She was the only person on the Committee with a steady well-paying job. She was quiet and unassuming, although her contacts in the intellectual and cultural life in the city were very wide. She was not a debater, and she would speak only once or twice during discussions, always with concern for how the public would interpret our statements and actions. She was also an expert at what were then called *kaffee klatches*, an ornamental name for small breakfasts, lunches or dinners at which there would be discussions and fund raising.

At some time in the second month of assembling a Committee, Aaron Schneider introduced us to Don Rothenberg, an Ohio war veteran who had headed a local veteran's organization in Cleveland and had then moved into Democratic Party politics with an eye, he told us, to running for Congress in 1954 or 1956. He was bright, well read, cheerful and optimistic. When we suggested to him that being a Committee member might end his chances of ever being nominated to run for Congress, he took a position very much like Emily's.

He said, "First things first. In 1951, my platform is triage for the Rosenbergs."

Among his accomplishments in the new trial/clemency campaign was to win the support of Senator William Langer of North Dakota, a member of the Senate Judiciary Committee.

Helen Sobell, the wife of Morton Sobell, became the last of the members of the Committee. She was a very persuasive speaker and many doors opened to her that might otherwise have remained shut. She was understandably driven harder than the rest of us and, possibly because of that, would always vote "Yes" on any action anyone proposed, which often left her in the minority. This was not a failing, for she had a quick mind and could instantly grasp the good that might come out of any suggested action, and was articulate in explaining her vote.

Although the Committee adopted a formal structure after most of its members were assembled, it remained a flexible entity that repeatedly sought consultation and advice from sympathetic lawyers, scientists, and the clergy, one of whom, Father Clarence Duffy, predicted that Pope Pius XII would support a clemency appeal.

We were not a Committee of Very Important Persons. We were unquestionably insular. All of us were Jewish, with bonds of common experience and history. Every one of us had lost grandparents, aunts, uncles, cousins, to the Holocaust that had begun when most of us were adolescents and had ended only after we were bringing our own children into the world. In the main we had few networking friends among non-Jews. The lifestyles of the Committee members were very low middle-class or working class.

"We are God's second choice," Brainin said.

We all, except Emily, realized we were a committee of Very Unimportant Persons. Emily agreed we were Unimportant but, she said, we were *Exceptionally* Unimportant, which made a difference.

Drawings of Ethel and Julius Rosenberg by Picasso in 1952;
Morton Sobell post-incarceration and during the trial period (undated).

Chapter 2 | The people of the trial

Defendants Julius and Ethel Rosenberg…

Both Rosenbergs were raised in New York City's poor lower East Side families. Julius' father had owned a dry-cleaning store in Harlem for a year, but when the store failed, the family moved back to the East Side, to a fifth floor cold-water flat. Ethel Rosenberg's (nee Greenglass) father earned a livelihood by repairing the sewing machines of the poor. Both Rosenbergs attended public school and Hebrew schools, and both graduated from Seward Park High School.

For want of funds, Julius' photograph — like those of many other students in 1933 — is absent from his graduation yearbook. Julius was a serious college-bound student, although his religious feelings had led his father to hope that Julius would become a rabbi, and for a time it is likely that Julius may have thought so, too. He was an active and observant Jew who took prizes in religious exposition and sold candy at street corners to raise money for his synagogue's activities.

At City College of New York (CCNY), Rosenberg appears to have been caught up by student enthusiasm for the New Deal, and in protests against the anti-Semitic agenda of Nazi Germany. The Brown Shirts, a Nazi off-campus organization, may have done more to make him a Communist than the young Communists at the college. One afternoon, a group of Brown Shirts stopped Rosenberg on campus and asked him what the letters CCNY stood for, and then told him they stood for 'Christian College, Now Yiddish.' They subjected other students they thought were Jewish to beatings and other indignities. The college administration refused to intervene.

In 1934, twenty-one students were expelled from CCNY for disrupting an administration-sponsored celebration of Mussolini's fascist regime in Italy; Julius was not among the expelled, but he was among the many hundreds of students who expressed opposition to the expulsions, for which they were labeled "guttersnipes" by the president of the college.[19]

The FBI opened files on both Rosenbergs in the late 1930s, when the nation was still wrestling with poverty and when the fear of war focused on Nazi Germany. Both the Rosenbergs, according to FBI informants, were unionists, affiliated with the American Labor Party, supporters of the Loyalist government in Spain which was defending itself against a Nazi-financed rebellion led by General Francisco Franco.

The Rosenbergs advocated an end to a Congressional ban against selling arms to the Spanish Loyalist government. After Franco's victory, they became contributors to a Canadian-led movement seeking to raise funds for orphanages in France, England, the Soviet Union, and Mexico, for the children of parents killed in the Spanish Civil War. The Rosenbergs were also reported by FBI informants to have been present at left-wing public rallies, and were said to have regularly read the Communist newspaper, the *Daily Worker* and other radical literature.

Although Julius gradually evolved into a Communist or near-Communist, he seems to have been intellectually attracted to Communism rather than driven to it by his experiences. He does not appear to have felt especially deprived by poverty, probably because he had a nourishing, affectionate life within his family and, at a fairly early age, with Ethel. He had a practical turn of mind, and his radical leanings didn't leave him with a distaste for business. He also had an orderly sense, to which his preference for socialism over capitalism may have been related; as a young man in the Depression years, he saw capitalism as chaotic and anarchistic, driven by uncontrollable individualistic forces, while socialism appeared to hold out the promise of a rationally planned economic order.

Ethel Greenglass, a few years older than Julius, was a clerical worker who hoped to become a singer. She was active in neighborhood dramatic groups and in other neighborhood activities. She was the first secretary of the East Side Defense Council, during World War II. Ethel was more the dreamer than was Julius but, aspiring to a profession that could be advanced only partly by learning, she was never quite sure of herself, never quite certain she had the driving energy that leads to the realization of creative dreams. She was a constant self-improver, taking lessons in parenting, for example, a virtually unheard of step for Lower East Side mothers. Another unusual step among these women was Ethel's attempt to cope with her uncertainties by seeking professional counseling for herself.

Ethel and Julius had met at a fund raising affair at a seaman's union in a small rented hall on Delancey Street, a main thoroughfare on the Lower East Side, where Ethel was a featured singer, and they seem to have been immediately attracted to each other. Their shared political activities included support of petitions and other actions to persuade President Roosevelt to lift the arms embargo against the democratically elected government of Spain. At the trial, their pro-Loyalist sympathies were introduced as proof of their hostility to the United States.

The Rosenbergs were married in June 1939, in an old synagogue nestled among ancient tenements on New York's lower East Side at Sheriff and Rivington Streets, not far from the East River, close to the tenements in which Emily lived with her mother and sister, and I with my parents.

In early 1950, Ethel and Julius were raising two sons and living their lives according to beliefs they had gradually acquired since their teens, and that had been encouraged during the twelve year presidency of Franklin Roosevelt: that working people should be aided in their efforts to improve their lives through union organization; that minorities and women should be supported in their efforts to obtain equality of opportunity; that free speech and free assembly were as much the right of leftists as of rightists. Beyond that, they shared the illusions of many others that the Soviet Union was a work in progress toward the realization of a society free of competition for power, space, and the daily necessities of life.

Whether they were card-carrying Communists is another question. It is very possible that, like most people who believed in one or another form of socialism, they may have never been members of the Communist Party, although they may have shared the views of the Communist Party on many issues.

A major break in the informal alliance of Communists and non-Communists came in August 1939, when the American Communist Party, by its support of the Stalin-Hitler Pact, lost whatever good will it had earned among non-Communists in the past. It also lost many members. For at least the next two years, few people broke bread with the Communists, and many people never broke bread with them again, even after the Communist Party leaders declared their support for the war against the Axis Powers, a change which was reasonably interpretable as being in conformance with the Soviet Union's interests after it was attacked by Nazi Germany in June 1941. The Rosenbergs' reaction to the Stalin-Hitler Pact is not known. It is probable that they accepted it without protest. Their faith in the Soviet Union was unquestioning, and they undoubtedly discounted reports of Stalin's brutality and anti-Semitism as "capitalist propaganda."

In their daily lives, the Rosenbergs at no time appeared to devote a great deal of time to what the FBI labeled as "Communist activities," but were content, for the most part, to contribute small sums of money to various causes, reading radical and Communist literature, attending public meetings called to promote equality or to protest perceived injustices, and signing and gathering nominating petitions for, in some cases, successful Communist candidates for elective New York City posts, although only Ethel appears to have been involved in contributing to these petitions. One of these election petitions was introduced at the trial, by the prosecution, to prove the "unAmericanism" of the Rosenbergs: the petition was on behalf of a Communist African-American attorney seeking a seat on the New York City Council..

Julius Rosenberg had been a junior engineer for the Army Signal Corps, during the war. In 1941, he was questioned about an unidentified informant's statement that he had been a member of the Communist Party while at CCNY. He denied the accusation and the matter was dropped. But in 1945, the Communist charge was revived. In the previous year, he and Morton Sobell had begun passing classified information to the Soviet Union, but there was nothing in the 1945 charge to indicate this was known to the FBI.

There is no reliable version of how the two men came to undertake passing information to the Soviet Union. In some versions, Julius Rosenberg offered to do so to a Communist official, who then put him in touch with a Soviet espionage controller in the United States. In other versions, he was recruited by a Soviet agent.

His motives were clear. As a Communist, he believed the Soviet Union was the forerunner of a new egalitarian, exploitation-free society. The Kansas-born leader of the Communist Party, Earl Browder, had coined a slogan for the time: *Communism is 20th Century Americanism.* This undoubtedly encouraged a belief among many Communists that the United States and the Soviet Union were moving toward similar destinies. (Browder was expelled from the Communist Party in 1946 by a wing of the Party that, with the help of Stalin's aides, renounced Browder's slogan, which they believed was making Communists "soft" on capitalism.)

The "similar destinies" concept was encouraged by the American public's palpable appreciation of the fact that the Soviet Union bore the brunt of the war in the European theater of operations, an attitude that would have been interpreted by Julius Rosenberg as assuring him of some degree of sympathy if his service to the Soviet Union was discovered. In a 2001 memoir by Alexander Feklisov, Rosenberg's Soviet espionage controller,[20] Rosenberg is depicted as a highly idealistic individual who believed that in World War II "the human race was fighting an enemy attempting to erase thousands of years of civilization...The issue that most troubled him was the extermination of the Jews..."[21]

There still remains some uncertainty that either of the Rosenbergs were members of the Communist Party. According to one historian, the FBI had in its possession two photostats of Julius' Communist Party membership cards, one for December 1939, and the other for 1944.[22] The alleged membership cards were not shown to Rosenberg in 1941 or 1945, nor were they introduced as evidence at the trial in 1951, possibly because that would have given the defense the right to examine them for authenticity.

Also uncertain is when Julius Rosenberg learned the United States was attempting to develop an atomic weapon in World War II. Unsupported testimony by Greenglass asserted that Rosenberg knew of it in 1944. However, the credibility of this testimony is diminished by additional testimony from Greenglass that, in spite of having been employed since July 1944, in a machine shop attached to an atomic development operation,[23] where there were frequent warnings about exposure to radiation, and articles on the atom bomb in the local media, he first learned about the atom bomb from Julius Rosenberg in December 1944, or January 1945.

News that an atom bomb was being developed began appearing in the media by late 1943 and early 1944, in spite of efforts by the War Department and other government agencies to suppress it.

In a memorandum dated January 3, 1944, War Department officials took note of a news story dated December 6, 1943, in which the *Nashville Tennessean* informed its readers that the United States was developing a "new and secret explosive."[24] Three other Tennessee newspapers carried the same story. By late summer 1944, the news stories had found a name for the secret explosive, and the War Department began sending officers to news reporters to discover their sources of information about what the reporters were describing as a race between Nazi Germany and the United States to develop an atomic bomb. One reporter, Betty Lersch, who had sent such a story over the Trans Radio Press Service, told a War Department officer that the story was "all over Washington."[25] While the major media largely complied with the War Department's request for secrecy, the news was breaking through in the local media, especially in areas that were active in research and development of the atom bomb.

When Julius Rosenberg was arrested on July 17, 1950, the Rosenbergs' apartment was searched by a team of seven FBI agents[26] and an inventory was made of their findings.[27] The FBI agents found none of the paraphernalia customarily used by professional spies, such as secret inks, mini-cameras, mini-films, short wave radio devices, false passports or other false or blank documents, air or ship or railroad tickets, passport photographs, code books, hollow pens or pencils or coins, articles of furniture adapted for photography or copying, articles of disguise, and so on. Nor were any classified government documents of any kind found. The only article taken by the FBI from the apartment for introduction at the trial by the prosecution was a collection can for the orphans of Spanish soldiers killed during the Spanish civil war in 1936, which became prosecution's Exhibit 27.[28]

A series of decoded cables between Soviet espionage agents in the United States and the Soviet espionage center in Moscow, known as the *Venona/ FBI* messages (detailed later), made no reference to the Rosenbergs, Sobell, or the Greenglasses after 1945. None of the messages indicated the nature of the information that was being passed on, and none were introduced at the trial in 1951, although most of the decoded messages had been available to the Justice Department in 1948.

Defendant Morton Sobell...

The FBI file on Morton Sobell had been begun at least ten years before the FBI placed his file on a Justice official's desk in 1950. On December 15, 1941, FBI Director Hoover notified the Director of Naval Intelligence that Sobell, who was working for the Navy at the time

> appears on the active indices of the American Peace Mobilization and the American Youth Congress. These organizations are believed to conduct subversive activities.[29]

Morton Sobell was born in 1917, to parents who had been raised in a small Russian village. Their families left for the United States at the turn of the century, and lived on the lower East Side. Rose Pasternak, later Morton's mother, dropped out of high school to work as a sewing machine operator; Louis, his father-to-be, worked as a cigar maker and attended Cooper Union, from which he graduated as a civil engineer in 1915, and then married Rose. Louis' engineering degree notwithstanding, the couple lived in a one-and-a-half room cold water tenement flat with Rose's mother and their baby. Engineering as a profession was all but closed to Jews in the first twenty five years of the 20th century.

In 1921, Louis, who had been apprenticed to an apothecary as a boy, entered Columbia College of Pharmacy, and in 1927, he borrowed funds from a relative to purchase a drug store in the Bronx, New York. He was the store's sole employee, and kept it open seven days a week from 8 A.M. to 11 P.M. His son recalled bringing meals to his father at the store, taunted by children calling out "kike" and "Christ killer."[30]

Reading, discussion and debate were important activities in the Sobell home. Rose's brothers were radicals, and one of them became a labor organizer. Rose became a Communist, and it appears that Louis was close to being one. Consequently, discussions on American history, national and international affairs, unionism, and socialism had provided the intellectual atmosphere in which Sobell, who had a special interest in science, grew up. He took gold medals in physics and mathematics. At CCNY, he opted for the engineering school, his father's unhappy experience notwithstanding. Sobell was active politically (he relates an outcry over a Reserve Officers Training Corps (ROTC) pamphlet containing the statement "democracy leads to mobocracy"), and he joined the Young Communist League branch at the college. After graduation, he relates that he

> looked around, read the want ads in the *Times*, and made the rounds of the employment agencies where I was told, without any apology, that no Jews were wanted.[31]

With the help of an aide to the Borough President of Manhattan, Sobell obtained employment, in 1939, at the Bureau of Ordnance in the Navy Department in Washington, D.C. He shared an apartment with a friend, Max Elitcher, who also worked at the Ordnance Bureau, and both became Communist Party members.

Shortly after, Sobell began having qualms about the Communist Party's political positions, particularly after the Soviet-Nazi Pact.

> In the 1940s, the question of Communist Party membership was considered a personal matter, at least in the circles in which I traveled. I can't recall ever asking anyone if he was a member of the Party, or anyone ever asking me. My own ambivalence toward some of the positions taken by the Party made me especially

reluctant to recruit anyone. I did not feel I could defend
every shift in the Party line.[32]

It was about this time that he and Julius Rosenberg, according to Sobell's
confession in 2008, began to pass classified non-atomic technical information to
the Soviet Union.

In 1945, he and Helen Levitov, who had a daughter from a previous mar-
riage, were married. Two years later, he went to work for Reeves Instrument Co.,
a firm started by one of Sobell's coworkers at General Electric. Sobell was asked
to sign an affidavit stating that he was not then, and had never been, a member of the Communist Party, which he did. He had not been a member of the
Communist Party since leaving Washington, and apparently gave no thought to
the past membership aspect of the affidavit. In any case, he did not equate his past
membership in the Communist Party with disloyalty to the United States.

Sobell faced two problems. He was or had been a Communist, and shared
with other dissenters the fears that they were targeted for reprisals and punishment. The fear was especially great when there were children involved. It was one
thing to "stand firm," holding to one's faith in the eventual abatement of political
repression, it was another to accept for one's family whatever suffering was in
store. Faith provided no timetable for the realization of normalcy, and one could
wait in vain and lose not only livelihood, but freedom as well. But he was also
different from other dissenters because he had passed classified information to
the Soviet Union. Sobell denied, in his confession, that what he had done was
espionage, except in a very narrow technical sense. His sole aim, he said, had
been to aid an ally, not to harm the United States. In a letter to the *New York
Times* on September 18, 2008, one week after having made his admission to a
Times reporter, Sobell wrote, "I helped an ally (admittedly illegally) during World
War II. I chose not to cooperate with the government in 1950. The issues are now
with the historians."[33]

In the immediate post-World War II world, the outline of a nightmare had
begun to take shape in the minds of many liberals, dissenters, Communists and
independent thinkers. Failure to adhere to the prevailing models of political cor-
rectness was becoming synonymous with, at best, indifference to American values, or, at worst, with treason.

In the summer of 1950, Sobell's fear that his having passed information to
the Soviet Union during World War II might become known was aggravated by
the arrest of David Greenglass on June 15. He became more certain that the FBI
would call on him when he learned that, on the day following Greenglass' arrest,
Julius Rosenberg had been questioned by the FBI.

The Sobells discussed leaving the country but, Sobell wrote

> ...it seemed an enormous step. Mexico seemed most
> practicable. We had talked of going there on vacation. It
> was close and living there was inexpensive. If we went,
> perhaps it would be merely a long summer vacation.
> We could go with an open mind, look around, and then
> decide our course of action.[34]

The Sobells came to a decision, within a week of David Greenglass' arrest. Under their own names, they and their two children flew to Mexico. In the authors' interviews with Morton Sobell, and in an affidavit by him to the U.S. Court of Appeals on September 23, 1953,[35] Sobell pointed out that he had made no secret of his destination when he took the family to Mexico, had bought round-trip tickets,[36] and registered his camera with U.S. custom officials at Dallas Airport, so that he would not have to pay duty on the camera on his return,[37] did not put up their home for sale, and rented an apartment in Mexico City under his own name.

While in Mexico, however, Sobell purchased a new set of glasses under the name 'M. Sand;'[38] registered at a hotel in Vera Cruz as 'Morton Sand;'[39] registered at a Tampico hotel as 'Marvin Solt;'[40] and purchased a flight from Vera Cruz to Tampico as 'M. Sand,' and a flight from Tampico to Mexico City as 'Morton Salt.'[41] He also sent letters to a friend and relative with variations on his name in the return address.

On August 8, three weeks after Julius Rosenberg's arrest, the Sobell family took vaccination shots to return to the United States.[42] The FBI knew that the Sobell family was in Mexico, but the prosecution made no attempt to have Sobell extradited. Instead, the prosecution arranged with Mexican police to apprehend Sobell on suspicion of "bank robbery," after which the police drove Sobell, his wife and two children overnight to Laredo, Texas, where they were turned over to waiting Justice officials. The next day, a New York Times headline read "Engineer is Seized at Laredo as Spy for Russian Ring." Without identifying its source, the Times reported

> it is believed that [the Sobells] were awaiting Russian
> visas for a Scandinavian country from which they would
> proceed to the Soviet Union or a satellite.[43]

Other newspapers reported "seizure" of Sobell in a similar vein. At the trial, however, the prosecutors proffered no witnesses to support the "Russian visas" story that Justice officials had aired in the media in August 1950.

Defendant David Greenglass...

David and Ethel Greenglass had spent their childhoods in poverty on the Lower East Side of Manhattan. They were raised, like the Rosenbergs and Sobells, in a cultural mix of American values as portrayed by their school teachers, tabloids and Hollywood, and Jewish values derived from tradition and religion. The latter provided two rationales with which to understand personal destiny: first, poverty could be overcome by heroic effort; second, one must accept poverty, as well as sickness and other unhappy conditions, as God's will. These two rationales were reconcilable. If one escaped poverty, that, too, was God's will.

Their parents appear to have been focused on a single goal: survival; all else was an unattainable frill. Their father was immersed for all his waking hours in mending the broken sewing machines of the poor; their mother was a disappointed, bitter, angry, possibly physically abusive parent.

Ethel Greenglass, who would become Ethel Rosenberg, was six years older than brother David. David and Ethel, in whose charge he was often placed, had a common bond of restlessness. By coincidence, Greenglass and his mother, Tessie, were known to Cecilia G. Arnow, the mother of one of the authors, Emily. Cecilia was a legendary social worker at the Grand Street Settlement House, not far from the East River, where Tessie belonged to the Cecilia G. Arnow Mother's Club, and where David Greenglass spent time at social activities. Cecilia described him to us as a "fumbler," an erratic and unstable boy.

As a young adult, David Greenglass appears to have been volatile, impressionable, intellectually dependent on persons he professed to admire, and envious of individuals he believed had attained "status." At the same time, he harbored feelings of contempt for "status" people, and he appears to have opportunistically played back to them what he believed they wanted to hear.

He expressed idealistic hopes of socialism, and had joined the Young Communist League. His army letters to his wife, Ruth, contain expressions of yearning for a better world, and he wrote of attempts he had made to share his ideals with other soldiers.

It is possible, however, that Greenglass was writing what he thought Ruth wanted to read and show to the Rosenbergs, for none of his former army comrades interviewed by the FBI were called to testify that he had tried to recruit them to Communism or, more to the point, to an espionage ring.[44]

The pair were married when they were barely out of their teens. They had known each other since childhood. From Ruth's documented comments, it is clear that she knew early on that David would need constant comforting, solace and reassurance, and these needs apparently corresponded to her need to be a caring person. Greenglass appears to have been dreamy, moody, easily distracted and, as later events showed, belligerent and violent.

He was drafted into the army, where his last assignment, in 1944, was as a machinist at the then-secret atomic bomb research and development center in Los Alamos, New Mexico. Unhappy at their separation, Ruth moved to Albuquerque, New Mexico, where they rented an apartment.

According to the testimony of the Greenglasses, Julius Rosenberg invited David Greenglass to obtain information on the atom bomb for him, which he would pass on to a Soviet agent. Greenglass testified that this did not involve stealing any documents, sketches, photographs or data in any other format. Instead, he would depend for his information on conversations with other persons in the machine shop, and with a junior scientist for whom he made lens molds, and by eavesdropping on conversations in which he was not involved.

After his return to New York and his discharge from the Army in February 1946, Greenglass joined a small business started by his brother Bernard with Julius Rosenberg and a non-family partner, which afterward became the G. and R. Engineering Company and then Pitt Machine Products, Inc.

The source of Greenglass' investment in the company — $1100 — was never explained by him, but there is documentation that points to Greenglass' involvement while at Los Alamos in thefts of material, including uranium.[45]

The relations between Greenglass and Rosenberg at their small company were hostile. Rosenberg, the head of the company, complained that Greenglass' technical and supervisory skills were unsatisfactory; Greenglass complained that Rosenberg, who acted as the salesman for the company, brought in insufficient business. The company went into debt, which aggravated the relations between the two men and raised new issues between them, such as their respective share of the liabilities of the company. When the business became so unprofitable that none of the partners were drawing salaries, confrontations between Rosenberg and Greenglass became more acrimonious. One argument became so violent that the two men had to be separated by Greenglass' brother Bernard, an incident that Rosenberg and Greenglass both testified to at the trial.[46]

In August 1949, Greenglass withdrew from the business and asked that his investment be returned to him. When Rosenberg responded that the business lacked funds with which to buy out his share, Greenglass demanded a personal note from Rosenberg to cover the return, which Rosenberg refused to give him.[47] The dispute remained alive even after both men had been arrested, when Greenglass instructed O. John Rogge, his attorney, to sue Rosenberg for return of the investment.[48]

Ruth Greenglass shared her husband's hostility to Julius, and may have had an hostility of her own to Ethel. Just as there were marked differences in the educational and occupational backgrounds of her husband and Julius, there were obvious differences between the cultural and matrimonial attainments of the two women. Both were strong women, but Ethel was a singer and actress, even if still on an amateur level, and had married an engineer, which in their families and social circles, elevated her status.

There was also a decided contrast in their residences: Ruth lived in a walk-up cold water flat with primitive in-the-hall shared toilet facilities, while Ethel lived in a controlled-rent building with an elevator, laundry room and other amenities. Ethel's children would be raised amidst a modest sufficiency while her — Ruth's — children might always lack for something.

In February 1950, FBI agents came to Greenglass' apartment. Neither Greenglass nor the FBI ever disclosed the reason for the interview. Asked at the trial about the interview, Greenglass replied, "I don't recall exactly what the whole conversation was about."[49]

Information that came to light after the trial indicated several possible reasons for the FBI's visit. The Greenglasses' bank records in New Mexico showed deposits that were significantly greater than the combined income of Greenglass and his wife Ruth; and there was suspicion that he had been involved in black market activities in New Mexico. An investigation conducted by Walter and Miriam Schneir, authors of *Invitation to an Inquest,* disclosed that in New Mexico, the Greenglasses repeatedly deposited sums of money that could not possibly have come from their salaries alone.[50] Greenglass would testify to having received a single payment of $500 from Harry Gold,[51] a spy not associated with the Rosenberg-Sobell-Greenglass group, but the New Mexico deposits were numerous, totaling thousands of dollars. At no time did the Greenglasses claim that they had received any compensation for spying beyond the $500. Their bank deposits in New Mexico were known to the prosecution, but not to the defense until long after the trial.

There were also FBI files that showed Greenglass to have been a member of the Young Communist League before he was drafted. The files also noted that his sister, Ethel, was married to Julius Rosenberg, an engineer, and that, in 1945, Rosenberg had been dismissed from his wartime job at the Signal Corps on the grounds that he was a Communist.

Other misfortunes beset the Greenglasses. Shortly after the February visit by the FBI, Ruth, six months pregnant with their second child, was almost burned to death when the gas stove they used for heating their apartment ignited her nightgown, and she had to be hospitalized for two months. Soon after giving birth, Ruth came down with an infection caused by her burns, and was hospitalized again, leaving her husband with a child and a baby to care for. Greenglass took a leave of absence from his job, apparently reducing their income to zero, although later events indicated that he had a sum of money — possibly between five and ten thousand dollars — that he kept in a place other than a bank.

The Greenglasses believed that they had been under surveillance for months before David Greenglass' arrest in mid-June 1950, and became certain of it in May, when the surveillance appears to have been deliberately made obvious to them, serving as an additional intensification of the state of apprehension in which they lived. According to Ruth Greenglass, as reported by Robert H. Goldman, an attorney with the O. John Rogge law firm representing the Greenglasses

> They had been under surveillance by the FBI for several weeks. In particular, they had noticed a car of the Acme Construction Company, 1400 First Avenue in Manhattan. She [Ruth Greenglass] ascertained there was no such Company.[52]

Although Greenglass' first statement to the FBI when he was arrested in June 1950, was never made available, he appears to have acknowledged the existence of an espionage operation. When Greenglass learned that his statement had the potential for resulting in a death sentence, he elaborated on it by naming his wife as having had a hand in recruiting him at the behest of Julius Rosenberg. The testimony he subsequently gave against his sister and brother-in-law, which, long after his release from prison, he admitted publicly (2001) was perjured, he blamed on instructions given him by the prosecutors.

There is no indication Ruth Greenglass felt astonished or betrayed when she learned David had implicated her in the conspiracy. She quickly made it clear to the prosecutors the cooperation of her husband depended on her not being indicted. This is borne out in a Justice Department memorandum by Warren Olney III, then an assistant attorney general:

Query

> Why wasn't Ruth Greenglass prosecuted for her part in this conspiracy?

Comment

> Obviously, naming her as a defendant would not only in all likelihood have destroyed her valuable cooperation but would undoubtedly have had an adverse effect on the key Government witness, David Greenglass.[53]

With David Greenglass' arrest, Ruth was confronted with imminent tragedy. Her children faced the loss of their father, possibly for a very long time, possibly forever, and she faced the loss of the boy-man to whom she had devoted herself. Whatever it was he had done at Los Alamos was foolish, but no worse than what other men had done.

There was a striking similarity in Ruth's attitude to David's incrimination of her to that of Tessie, David's mother, in respect to his incrimination of his sister

Ethel. Perhaps in Tessie's eyes, David's offering of his sister to the prosecutors required that Ethel make a similar offering of her husband who, in turn, would confess and offer up others.

Such an attitude must be understood in the context of Tessie's life. Formerly of Austria, Tessie knew the nuances of danger and understood her son and daughter and son-in-law were being threatened with death, and she believed they had to understand very clearly what they must do to save themselves. America was not the damnable inferno of anti-Semitism that Russia and Poland had been, but the fact was only Jews would be sitting at the defense table at the trial in the federal courthouse. The fact the chief prosecutor and his chief assistant were both Jewish was not at all reassuring and, later, when it was announced that a Jewish judge would preside at the trial, the situation became even more ominous: every ghetto in Europe had had small numbers of Jews who bought immunity from the Holocaust by sacrificing other Jews.

Justice officials, the prosecutors, the judge and Tammany Hall...

Most of the players on the government's side in the Rosenberg-Sobell case were protégés or clients of New York's then pre-eminent political machine, Tammany Hall, the oldest political machine in the nation. Upon the success of the American Revolution, a loose alliance of New York politicians, speculators and middlemen who had formerly expedited, through the King's appointed governors, the sale of judgeships, clerkships and a variety of business licenses to harbor masters, importers, exporters and overseers of the slave trade (in mid-18th Century New York, 10% of the population were slaves), seized the opportunity provided them by the infant democracy to enlarge their operations. The Hall created a shadow government that handled the exchange of money for the purchase of appointments to the bench and to other city offices, for licenses or permits to maintain roads, run ferries, practice law and other professions, without the necessity of meeting the educational or training or financial qualifications that unbefriended citizens had to meet. The public government legalized and enforced the arrangements made in the shadows. Tammany Hall, like all political machines, also developed client relationships with persons who needed votes to make their dreams come true.

One hundred and sixty years later, the Hall was still making certain that appointees and candidates for election were loyal to the arrangements the Hall made in the shadows with its unpublicized beneficiaries. Among others, the Hall enabled Irving Kaufman, who presided at the Rosenberg-Sobell trial, to become a Federal judge; Irving Saypol, who would be the chief prosecutor, to become the United States Attorney for the Southern District of New York; and Roy Cohn, Saypol's relative and chief assistant, and Myles Lane, another Saypol assistant, to become Assistant U.S. Attorneys.

Irving Saypol was a former chairman of Tammany Hall's Law Committee. Albert Cohn, the father of Roy Cohn, was a politically powerful New York State judge; Irving Kaufman obtained his Federal judgeship with the help of Tammany's Judge Albert Cohn. Myles Lane, who had been promised the United States Attorney title that went, instead, to Saypol, was impatiently waiting his turn.

At the time the Rosenberg-Sobell case began, Tammany Hall's power was beginning to be challenged by reform groups, but it would be years, long after Saypol, Cohn, Lane, and Kaufman had reaped the benefits of their association with the Hall, that reformers would succeed in ousting a number of the most criminally-inclined beneficiaries of the Hall's power.

In one nine year period, 1963-1972, after a reform movement had temporarily succeeded in establishing higher aptitude and character thresholds for prosecutorial and judicial posts, thirteen New York State judges were formally indicted for various crimes, including acceptance of bribes, bankruptcy fraud, selling and transporting stolen treasury bills, perjury, bail bond fraud, shoplifting, moral turpitude, liquor license fraud, fraudulent campaign fund schemes, and influence peddling. Two were found not guilty, four were convicted and sent to prison, and the remainder were censured, removed or permitted to resign.[54]

Had the review of judges accused of crimes been extended a few more years, it would have included Irving Saypol, who became a New York State judge shortly after the Rosenberg-Sobell case ended. In 1976, Justice Saypol was indicted for bribery and perjury.[55] *The State of New York v. Irving Saypol* is discussed later.

Roy Cohn, Saypol's assistant and, like him a beneficiary of Tammany Hall's power, was repeatedly during his professional career challenged for his fitness and character, but he was protected from formal judgment for many years by the patriotic media-image created for him and for Saypol by their roles in the Rosenberg-Sobell case. So certain was Cohn that his patriotic aura would protect him from judgment that he made a point of being openly contemptuous of indictments in which he and/or his friends were accused of felonious crimes.

Cohn's biographer, Nicholas von Hoffman, quotes a description by Joey Adams, a comedian and Cohn admirer, of a dinner at which Cohn was guest of honor, in which the guests included Stanley Friedman (Cohn's partner, convicted on a Federal racketeering charge and sentenced to prison), Donald Manes (a politician who committed suicide after his dishonesty was discovered), and Mario Biaggi (a Bronx congressman imprisoned after being convicted in Federal court on 15 counts of racketeering). Cohn is quoted as telling the dinner guests, "If you're indicted, you're invited."[56] Roy Cohn, however, did eventually face the judgment of his peers, and was disbarred.

Judge Kaufman, who had been a federal judge for eighteen months when the Rosenberg-Sobell case arose, took a step that precluded the possibility that a more seasoned judge might be given the assignment to preside over the trial. According to Roy Cohn, Judge Kaufman aggressively enlisted his help in pressuring the clerk in charge of the criminal court calendar to give him the assignment. Cohn gave this graphic account of Kaufman's pressure

> He wanted the Rosenberg case as much as he wanted the judgeship — and when Irving wants something he doesn't stop, he doesn't leave you alone until you do what he wants.

> We were vacationing in Florida during the Christmas season of 1950. Irving and his wife were in Boca Raton, I was in Palm Beach. We might as well have been in the same room. I think he called me fifty times a day. 'Call Dave Sweeney [the calendar clerk]. Call Dave Sweeney. If you don't call him some other judge is liable to put pressure on him. Everybody wants the case, you got to get to it, Roy. Call Dave Sweeney.'[57]

Some believe Kaufman wanted the assignment because he saw the trial as step toward nomination to the U.S. Supreme Court. Others believe he wanted to make it clear that "establishment" Jews loathed Communist Jews, a belief that is supported by a diary entry by Gordon Dean, Chairman of the Atomic Energy Commission, in which he wrote that Kaufman had told the prosecution on February 7, 1951, one month before the trial, that he intended to sentence Julius Rosenberg to death.[58] On March 16, 1951, ten days after the start of the trial, FBI Director J. Edgar Hoover was informed that Ray Whearty, a Department of Justice official, had reason to believe that "if he doesn't change his mind," Kaufman would sentence Julius Rosenberg to death.[59]

Whatever Kaufman's motives, his desire to preside over the case was undoubtedly welcomed by Justice officials who were seeking a "balance solution" to counter suspicions of an anti-Semitic factor in the case because of the all-Jewish cast of defendants.

An all-Jewish cast...

We must, before entering the courtroom, take account of the ethnicity shared by the defendants and two of the prosecutors and the judge. They brought to the trial definitive aspects of their upbringing, and they shared, through the extermination of their closest kin in Europe, the single most significant experience in the lives of all Jews of the 20th Century.

Anti-Semitism in the United States always had, with some exceptional moments, the quality of a moderate, low-grade chronic fever. Rarely did the prejudice reach the level of violent behavior exhibited against African-American slaves and their descendants, American Indians, Asians and, for a time, against

Catholics, and never did the bias ignite the ferocious pogroms that swept Russia and Poland from time to time. But as the 19ᵗʰ Century entered its last decades, and the 20ᵗʰ began its first, the great increase in immigration of Russians, Poles, Germans, Italians and other national groups to the United States, coupled with a number of recession-depression cycles (every twenty or thirty years since the early 1700s), led to pseudo-scientific, physical and legal attacks on the newly landed foreigners. The attacks were rarely against immigrants from northwestern Europe; the most frequent targets were those who arrived from eastern, central and southern Europe.

It was in the densely packed firetraps in the slums of New York, Chicago, Pittsburgh, San Francisco and other industrial cities and towns, that the newcomers, in their millions — Christians of Old World Christianities, Jews, Muslims, deists, atheists, indifferentists — were confronted with prejudice against some Gods, but not others, with ridiculed ancestries, histories, colors, languages, ceremonies and troublesome customs. The immigrants viewed the derisions of their Gods and customs as echoes from a receding past, against which they deafened themselves. Their lives not being at stake, few chose to openly confront remnant rumblings of another place and time.

What these immigrants regarded as prejudice and derision was, in the eyes of law enforcement bureaucracies and prestigious academics, venerable historical truths that needed no further examination. In respect to Jews, the teachings were unquestionably venerable. They had been nineteen centuries in the making. Neither intelligence, nor power, nor class status nor religion, nor color prevented anti-Jewish prejudice or, for that matter, prejudice of any kind, from taking root among significant sections of the public, from the very poor to the very rich, from the disenfranchised to those at the highest levels of government.

The unquestioned venerable "truths" that underlay prejudice passed effortlessly through the curricula of esteemed American universities and across thousands of pulpits and made the rounds of numberless high and low private clubs and secret societies. Illiteracy was no bar to these teachings: they were as well known to the besotted or bewildered followers of the Grand Wizards of the Ku Klux Klan as they were to the sons and daughters of the educated merchants and pundits of New England and the offspring of the post-bellum cotton princes of the South.

What the literate and illiterate learned of antiquity was that Jews and other satanic creatures were engaged in a conspiracy to bring down the Christian world by amassing and hoarding fortunes in gold and silver, by spreading plagues and causing other disasters. In the 14ᵗʰ Century, according to the anecdotal-reliant historians of the time, the Jews let loose the bubonic plague in Europe, an offense for which thousands of Jews were massacred, after which the plague faded away.

The educated circles in the United States took on the task of restricting Jewish immigration in the first decade of the 20th Century, with a great boost from Harvard's president, A. Lawrence Lowell, an active member of the Immigration Restriction League, who wrote that he had distinct misgivings about the Jews' "peculiar traits."[60]

Two events, in 1915, reveal the extremes to which anti-Jewish prejudice affected Americans at the time. In August 1915, Leo M. Frank, a Texas-born Jewish factory manager in Atlanta, Georgia, was found guilty of raping and strangling a 14-year-old girl, and was sentenced to death. The prosecutor, the media, and the local churches identified the crime as a Jewish ritual to obtain the blood of a Christian child. A black man had confessed to the crime before Frank's trial, but later testified that he had confessed in return for a bribe by Frank. Because persistent doubts of Frank's guilt were widespread, the governor commuted Frank' sentence to life. Overnight, a lynch mob that included Christian clergy, two former judges and a former sheriff dragged Frank from his prison cell and hung him.[61] (In 1982, the confession by the black man was validated by an eyewitness, also black, who had seen the original confessor dragging the girl's body. In 1986, Frank was granted a posthumous pardon by the Georgia Pardons and Parole Board.[62])

Six months after Leo Frank was lynched, President Woodrow Wilson nominated Louis Brandeis for a seat on the Supreme Court. Brandeis was the first Jew to be so nominated. Former President William Taft described the nomination as "a fearful shock...one of the deepest wounds that I have ever had as an American..."[63] Senator Henry Cabot Lodge, Massachusetts, declared that "Converting the United States into a Government by foreign groups is to me the most fatal thing that can happen to our Government..." Six former presidents of the American Bar Association denounced Brandeis as unfit. The *New York Tribune* labeled the nomination "A ghastly joke." The *New York Sun* wrote that Brandeis was "utterly and even ridiculously unfit."[64] Four months of debate and poorly disguised ethnic insults passed before the Senate, to its credit, ratified the nomination.

Earlier, President Wilson had wanted to nominate Brandeis as his Attorney General, but political and corporate opposition to having a Jew in that post was even greater than to having Brandeis on the Supreme Court. It would take another 59 years for the "establishment" to agree that a Jew, an eminent legal practitioner and scholar, Edward Hirsch Levi, could be trusted to function as the nation's chief law enforcement officer.

Several years after the Frank and Brandeis affairs, the Russian Revolution set off a new spate of anti-Semitic sentiment in high places in the United States and Great Britain. At the onset of the Communist-led Revolution in 1918, David R.

Francis, Secretary of the Interior, who later became the American ambassador to Russia, wrote

> The Bolshevik leaders here, most of whom are Jews and 90 percent of whom are returned exiles, care little for Russia or any other country but are internationalists and they are trying to start a worldwide social revolution.[65]

Winston Churchill, then head of the British war ministry, shared the ambassador's outlook, writing in 1920

> There is no need to exaggerate the part played in the creation of Bolshevism and in the actual bringing about of the Russian Revolution by these international and for the most part atheistical Jews…Moreover, the principal inspiration and driving power comes from the Jewish leaders…And the prominent, if not indeed the principal, part in the system of terrorism applied by the Extraordinary Commissions for Combating Counter-Revolution has been taken by Jews, and in some notable cases by Jewesses.[66]

At about this time, a document, *The Protocols of the Elders of Zion*,[67] forged at the turn of the 19th Century by an anti-Semitic group associated with Tsar Nicholas II's police, began to be widely distributed in civil and government circles. The *Protocols* described a conspiracy by Jews to disrupt the political and economic systems of major nations, replacing these with Communism, which would permit the Jews to rule the world. Non-Jews would become servants and subjects of the Jews, and the religion and culture of Christianity would be destroyed. Among those who found the *Protocols* persuasive was auto pioneer Henry Ford, who praised, published, and distributed the forged document to millions of Americans in the 1920s.

The *Protocols* also became reading matter at the Department of Justice. Young J. Edgar Hoover found the *Protocols* interesting enough to share with his colleagues. According to a recent Hoover biographer, in 1920, Hoover, then chief of the General Intelligence Division of the Department of Justice, sent for twelve copies of the *Protocols*, after which he asked "the State Department to check on whether six particular Bolshevist leaders were Jewish."[68] He also ordered an investigation of Eamon de Valera, president of Ireland, to discover whether he was Jewish.[69]

The views of Hoover and like-thinking associates in respect to immigrants from Eastern Europe, and to Jews in particular, were encouraged by academics, eugenicists and opportunistic politicians on the streets, and in the Oval

Office. The immigration restriction movement succeeded, in 1924, in reducing immigration by 80%, and specifically restricting immigration from eastern and southern Europe to a maximum of 10% of the remaining 20%.[70] The two most adversely affected groups were Jewish and Italian immigrants. President Calvin Coolidge approved the Act, declaring that "America must remain American."

Those immigrants already in the United States were also under attack for their purported "subversive" beliefs, for harboring in their midst militant unionists led by American-born labor leaders, and for their assumed "pro-Soviet," "seditious" and" insurrectionist" behavior. Among J. Edgar Hoover's earliest accomplishments at the Department of Justice was to expedite the deportation of 1,119 foreign born "radicals" in 1920, none of them charged with indictable offenses, almost all of whom were Jewish.[71] He followed that up with other similarly ethnically skewed deportations.

Jews remained "persons of interest" for Hoover throughout his life, in part because he was surrounded by like-thinking officials throughout his career who reinforced his bias, and in part because his anti-Semitism was embedded in an outlook that regarded all non-Anglo-Saxons as potential enemies of American society. Even after substantial sections of the population, including many Anglo-Saxon conservatives, were abandoning such prejudices, Hoover remained adamant against changes that would in any way signal to non-Anglo-Saxon population groups that they were regarded as equals.

J. Edgar Hoover's obsession with the Jews...

In 1958, 38 years after reading and distributing copies of the *Protocols*, and five years after the execution of the Rosenbergs, Hoover, at that time in his 34th year as Director of the FBI, felt moved to appeal to Jews to abandon what he perceived to be their attraction to Communism. In *Masters of Deceit*, subtitled *The Story of Communism in America and How to Fight It*,[72] he included a special chapter on American Jews. Aware that his views might be attacked as anti-Semitic, Hoover adroitly labeled the chapter as **The Communist Attack on Judaism**, and worded his complaint against the Jews as applicable only to those Jews who were Communists.

> It is a matter of record that numerous Communist Party leaders call themselves Jews and claim a Jewish origin. This does not, however, make them Jews, any more than William Z. Foster's Catholic background and Earl Browder's Protestant background give them any standing in present-day Catholic and Protestant communities in the United States.[73]

Hoover never felt the need to single out Catholics and Protestants in respect to Communism, or to complain that Catholic Foster's and Protestant Browder's names were, during the Great Depression, widely known and held in high esteem among the Christian poor and by many Christian intellectuals. Hoover went on, for 19 pages, of reasons for Jews to turn their backs on Communism, after which he issued a warning.

> Where communist infiltration tactics have succeeded in Jewish organizations, it has been because of a failure on the part of leaders and members alike to be vigilant and thwart the communist tactic of infiltration into the Jewish community just as it has sought to infiltrate every other organization.[74]

What Hoover did not do is cite events that led him to his perception of the Jews' weakness for "Communism." At the very time Hoover was condemning Jews for their failures to combat Communism, Dr. J. B. Matthews, HUAC's expert on religion, was arguing

> "The largest single group supporting the Communist apparatus in the United States today is composed of Protestant clergymen."[75]

(Probably the best known lay Catholic in the nation, Dorothy Day, founder of the Catholic Worker movement, famously complained that when she helped the poor she was called a saint, but when she asked why there were poor she was called a Communist.) In New York City, home to the largest number of Jews in the United States, the only Communists elected to the New York City Council in mid-20th Century were an Italian American, nominally Catholic, and an African American, nominally Protestant.

Hoover's warning to and about Jews was not the result of his experience in law enforcement, but the consequence of a lifelong prejudice that was in direct conflict with his own data. Communist membership, to use Hoover's figures, had fallen to 22,600 in 1955, when he was preparing his warning, and "by the summer of 1957 membership had further declined."[76] The adult population of Jews in 1957 was approximately 3.5 million. If every member of the Communist Party at that time had been Jewish, the percent of the Jewish population who were Communists would have been .00645%, meaning that 99.99% of Jews were non-Communists, if not actually anti-Communists.

Unlike some other law enforcement officials, Hoover would never identify the *Protocols* as a fraudulent document, neither in speech nor print. By contrast, Richard Helms, who would later become Director of the CIA, told a subcommittee of the Senate Judiciary Committee investigating internal security laws in 1961

that more than 60 years ago, the czarist intelligence service concocted and ped-
dled a confection called the *"Protocols of the Elders of Zion."*[77] The *Protocols* are
still being used, along with the Rosenberg-Sobell case, by domestic and foreign
anti-Semitic organizations.

Hoover's suspicion of Jews was not only a justification for making them
the "usual suspects" in espionage cases, but was also expressed by Hoover in his
administrative leadership of the FBI. He ordered that Jews were to be hired only
in very low token numbers. William Sullivan, Hoover's aide for 30 years, once
virtually pleaded with the Director to relinquish his anti-Jewish bias.

> In over 8000 agents, how many are Jewish? Very few,
> a relatively handful...You have always had one Jewish
> official up front for people to see.[78]

Frank Donner, a former American Civil Liberties Union attorney, went
even further, writing

> Hoover's racism...is now too well established to require
> elaboration. Not only were Jews shunned as agent mate-
> rial, but anti-Semitism flourished, especially in the core
> of functionaries surrounding Hoover.[79]

Hoover also saw to it that women would not be hired as agents, and blacks
were hired only to do menial jobs as chauffeurs and porters. On numerous occasions, complaints arose that Hoover's hiring and other administrative policies violated Civil Service codes and laws, to which he replied that the security of the
United States required the isolation of the FBI from routine regulations that might
affect its performance. On one occasion, when a Justice official attempted to assert
the Department's authority over the FBI, Hoover contemptuously referred to the
official as a "Lebanese Jew,"[80] and continued his autonomous directorship of the
agency.

Turning the Jews into a suspect population...

From 1928 onward, and especially after 1933, when the Nazis seized power
in Germany, American Jews were among a large number of Americans of diverse
religious beliefs who conducted protests against Nazi Germany's anti-Jewish
crusade, and against its remilitarization program. Many were also critical of the
adamant refusal of the U.S. State Department to limit trade between American
businesses, including major banks, and Germany. A further reason for these protests was that the Nazi government was using the profits from trade with the
United States to build up its armed forces. The quarrel with the State Department
was further exacerbated by its refusal to admit all but a few of the scores of thousands of Jews fleeing Germany. By 1940, the number of American Jewish persons

among those who had openly protested the ongoing German massacres by picketing Germany's consular offices and conducting large public protest meetings,
was a frequent subject of FBI surveillance and of a great many FBI files.

A buzz phrase was later used by the FBI and Congressional "loyalty"
committees to justify the labeling of tens of thousands of protesting anti-Nazi
Americans, Jewish and non-Jewish, as 'Communists,' on the grounds that they
had been *"premature anti-fascists,"* that is, anti-fascists before Pearl Harbor.
Among these were Americans who had passed on to the FBI information on
Nazi operatives in the United States.[81]

As a result of Hoover's exceedingly broad definition of "enemies" of the
American way of life, millions of Americans ended up in FBI "disloyalty" files,
and a significant number of them were Jewish. The Jewish presence in those files
ultimately left its mark on the conduct and the outcome of the Rosenberg-Sobell
case.

Unfair and damaging as the ethnic-slanted Hoover files were to Jews, they
were equally unfair to the nation at large, because they shielded from discovery an
untold number of American spies-for-pay for the Soviet Union, Nazi Germany,
Imperial Japan and undoubtedly other countries as well. So committed were the
FBI and other law enforcement agencies to Hoover's dictum that the search for
spies must focus on dissenters and non-Anglo Saxons that it was not until almost
two decades after Hoover's death, in 1972, that discoveries were made of Soviet
spies-for-pay in the FBI itself, as well as in the CIA and the military.

The complexities of a shared ethnicity...

The ethnicity shared by the chief prosecutors, the judge and the defendants
in the Rosenberg-Sobell case was not an inconsequential factor in the drama that
unfolded at the trial.

It would have been impossible, in the 1950s, for anyone of Jewish descent
to be untouched by the Holocaust, 20th Century's phenomenon of ultimate anti-
Semitism. For twelve years, the methodical extinction of kin evoked nightmar-
ish dreams and anxieties in American Jews who had witnessed or heard reports
from childhood onward of unthinkable brutalities at the hands of an inexplicable
humanity chanting "Death to the Jews!"

For many Jews, the label "genocidal" appended to Germany was a
euphemism for a borderless global hostility to the Jewish people. They and
many non-Jews were deeply troubled during the twelve years of slaughter
by the silence of the world's Christian churches, whose Savior was a Jew. The
churches' silence was taken by many to be a sign of indifference or worse.
Hardly reassuring to American Jews immediately after victory in 1945 was a
massive welcome by the government to the thousands of very recent German
participants in the Holocaust, a phenomenon we will shortly describe.

Verbal graffiti of the time...

Although by 1950, the "Communist-traitor" phrase had become a staple in the utterances of moderate, as well as extremist members of Congress, their usual discreet avoidance of the fuller phrase used by the German Nazis — *Jew-Communist-traitor* — was nevertheless readable on many of their lips. The unspoken word — 'Jew' — in anti-Communist political and social tirades had become a vocal form of anti-Semitic graffiti.

Judge Kaufman and prosecutors Saypol and Cohn, like the defendants, could not have been unaware of the ethnically truncated phrases describing "Communist traitors." At odd moments, troubling shadows must have fallen across their perceptions of themselves, a dim awareness that they were already behaving as though their own survival was literally at stake, that within their life-times they and their families might find themselves in an unimaginable America.

Such fleeting self-disturbing thoughts would have been nourished by what they learned in their adult years. As young adults, Judge Kaufman and prose-cutors Saypol and Cohn would have experienced, at the very least, "moderate" anti-Semitic acts and attitudes. They came into adulthood during a time of quota systems for the admission of Jews to major universities and in industry and pro-fessions. There were residential areas closed to Jews, even in New York City, by "gentlemen's agreements" among real estate owners and agents. There were hotels and resorts that would not accept, or would actively discourage Jewish guests.

The judge and prosecutors may have learned from table-talk in their childhoods that these discriminations sometimes received encouragement at the highest levels of government. One president — Calvin Coolidge — believed Jews lacked acceptable bloodlines for integration or assimilation, and had favored immigration laws that drastically reduced the number of Jewish immi-grants, while increasing the number of non-Jews permitted to enter the United States.[82]

From table-talk or first-hand, they would have learned that State Department officials were rigidly opposed to any form of assistance to Jews who were trying to escape the Nazi death camps. In May 1943, the Swedish govern-ment proposed that the German government be requested to release 20,000 Jewish children, which Sweden offered to shelter for the remainder of the war. The State Department took five months to respond, and rejected the proposal because it might antagonize the Nazi government with which we were at war.[83] By then, of course, more than another 20,000 Jewish children had been mur-dered. In response to another proposal for saving the Jews, the State Department redefined European Jews as "enemy aliens," and protested "granting to a special group of enemy aliens relief measures which we have in the past denied to Allied peoples."[84]

It is very likely Judge Kaufman might have heard from his father, who was a successful businessman, that objections to proposals for saving endangered Jews had been made by the Secretary of State because the proposals might require the use of funds allocated for the war effort. The truth was otherwise. Jewish businessmen in the United States and abroad had offered to raise the funds needed to enact life-saving proposals, and many non-Jewish businessmen were already expending funds and risking their lives to save Jews and were offering to defer being repaid until after the war.

Many American Jews of that time felt that they lived within a Christian nation that was tolerant of Jews, but the durability of tolerance was unknown. Tolerance breeds politeness, not enlightenment or equality. A popular joke of the time went as follows: What is a kike? A kike is a Jewish gentleman who has just left the room.

Coping with ethnicity: the prosecutors, the judge...

Prosecutor Irving Saypol appears to have coped with being Jewish by creating in himself a separate persona who was capable of anti-Semitic acts his non-prosecutorial persona would have denounced. For example, in his first attempt to obtain a perjury conviction against William Remington, a government employee who had been labeled a Communist espionage agent by Elizabeth Bentley, a self-confessed but never-indicted spy, Saypol had badgered a witness he was cross-examining in order to make it clear to the jury the witness was Jewish, although this wasn't evident from the witness' name, nor was it relevant to the prosecution. Remington was convicted, but the U.S. Circuit Court of Appeals reversed the verdict, taking pains to admonish Saypol because

> On cross-examination the prosecutor continued his inquiry of this matter long after it became clear that the change of name had no relevancy to any issue at the trial, and could only serve to arouse possible racial prejudice on the part of the jury.[85]

Remington's attorney also subsequently discovered that the foreman of the grand jury that had indicted Remington was John Brunini, the literary collaborator of Elizabeth Bentley, who had a financial stake in the sale of her book on Communism, a fact known to Saypol, but only after the trial by Remington's lawyer.[86]

Like Judge Kaufman, Irving Saypol actively sought his role in the Rosenberg-Sobell case. On September 11, 1950, he wrote to the Assistant Attorney General to press for eliminating a possibility that the trial would be conducted by the U.S. Attorney for New Mexico, only to be informed, on September 19, that venue might still "lie in the District of New Mexico."[87]

Roy Cohn, the youngest of the prosecutors, had been six years old when Hitler came to power, and was twenty three years old at the start of the Rosenberg-Sobell case, in 1950. His growing awareness of the Holocaust during his formative years must have been deeply traumatic; he appears to have coped with being Jewish by adopting the language of anti-Semites as his own. One Cohn biographer cites Cohn as frequently using the word "kike" to describe Jews, and to take pleasure in being called "kike" by his lovers and others. He called a well known publisher of the time "Jewhouse," and would characterize statements by Jews as "typical kike remarks."[88]

Judge Kaufman coped with being Jewish in his college years at Fordham University, a Catholic institution, by excelling in Christian studies (his classmates nicknamed him 'Pope Kaufman').[89]

We earlier described his efforts to obtain, with the help of Roy Cohn, the assignment to preside at the Rosenberg-Sobell trial. After obtaining the assignment, he signaled to Justice officials, before the trial began, that he believed the defendants were guilty, and he intended imposing death sentences on them. Kaufman may have been impelled by a need to demonstrate to the officials he was one of them, in spite of being Jewish.

He may have been particularly affected by the outcome of a political trial that took place one year preceding the Rosenberg-Sobell trial, which involved another federal judge, Samuel Kaufman, older than Irving Kaufman, and unrelated to him.

Judge Samuel Kaufman had presided over the first trial of Alger Hiss, who had occupied key positions in the New Deal administration, and who had been accused by Whittaker Chambers, a former Communist, of being a Russian agent. Hiss was being tried for perjury for denying he had known Chambers. Hiss' attorney requested that Judge Samuel Kaufman compare the testimony given by Chambers at his grand jury appearance with his testimony at the trial. The judge did so and found

> 19 very substantial discrepancies between the testimony
> he [Chambers] has given before the Grand Jury on his
> first appearance and the testimony he has given at this
> trial.[90]

When the jury announced its inability to reach a verdict, Judge Samuel Kaufman was threatened with impeachment by members of Congress, and Representative Richard Nixon of California asked that the House Un-American Activities Committee subpoena the jurors to find out whether any of them were Communists.[91]

The attacks on Judge Samuel Kaufman must have given the younger Kaufman clear reason to fear Communists, for it was plain to him that the application of Constitutionally-mandated rights to Communist defendants could lead to his denunciation, as it had to many other public officials who, blindly or knowingly, had ignored the new philosophy that had affected every government office. It is possible the attacks on the older Kaufman led the younger Kaufman to make a public display of his political distance from the Rosenberg-Sobell defendants by obtaining the assignment to preside at their trial, where he could make his position unmistakably clear to his non-Jewish colleagues.

That the older Kaufman went one way and the younger another sheds light on the different ways that judges and other officials reacted under the political and social stresses affecting the country in mid-20th century America, when the preservation of personal integrity, professional identity and reputation were at stake for both sides in trials involving alleged subversives and traitors.

Such actions — the assumption by Saypol of an anti-Semitic persona, the requests by Cohn to be addressed in abusive anti-Semitic phrases, the pretrial assurances by Kaufman to chief officials in the Department of Justice that he would sentence Julius Rosenberg to death — are clear indications by the trio that they were aware of the life-long suspicions of Jews shared by FBI Director J. Edgar Hoover and his like-minded associates in government and Congress. Their actions were deliberate demonstrations of a deeply felt need to deny they harbored the disloyal traits many government officials attributed to Jews. They understood that Hoover's own reputation and fame as a spy catcher rested on the outcome of the case he had passed on to them, and that if he suffered disappointment, their careers and good names would be in jeopardy.

They also knew the prosecution of an all-Jewish cast of defendants would be heard by some sections of the public, American and elsewhere in the world, as an ominous echo, however faint, of the human pathology that created the Holocaust. That likelihood was increased by the absence of tangible evidence of the crime. They could not have been unaware that the ethnicity of the people they were describing in their inflammatory speech would inevitably arouse the same nuanced anti-Semitism the Appellate Court had described in Saypol's conduct in the Remington case. The presence of the unarticulated ethnic adjective accompanying the "Communist traitor" accusations would be palpable.

The times of the people of the trial..

The final weeks of 1945 were a puzzling time. On the one hand, we were celebrating the peace that followed the loss of 60 million human beings who paid the price of a would-be German Century. But deaths in such numbers become abstractions beyond our understanding, so the conversations in our homes and on the streets dealt with what was comprehensible. In local cafeterias, the talk was of how quickly the defense factories could be converted to turning out cars, bicycles, skates, radios, tables and furniture. The older diners, depending on their political outlooks, were either lauding the Four Freedoms promised by the late four-term President Franklin Roosevelt or debating whether his successor, Harry Truman, shared Roosevelt's compassion. At the Grand Street Settlement House, where Emily's mother was the sole social worker, the little dance floor shook to the jitterbugging couples, some reunited for the first time in several years, moving to the beat of a '78' needle phonograph. The drums of war were already dimming in memory. "Not for long," some said. "We're gonna have to show the Russkies who won the war."

From what we read in the newspapers, the British, the Russians and the French and other liberated nations were also in the grip of expectancy, although their circumstances were not quite like ours. Their German occupiers had executed tens of thousands of the citizens of the occupied countries, laid waste to their industry and agriculture, and imposed anarchy and brutality in their governments.

But that was yesterday. From 1945 to 1949, expectations were high for the victors and the liberated. The momentum of anticipated relief for hundreds of millions of human beings seemed unstoppable, and was so universal and logical that the power of its passion and vast numbers would surely precipitate into something real, something you could carry with you, something you could say you had.

By 1949, those expectation also became yesterday.

What became clear to thoughtful people was that the atomic bomb – the "big stick" – had become paramount in American relations with the rest of the world and we would not hesitate to use it.

The Soviet Union had its own "big stick:" an enormous population and a land mass to match; a firm grip on the governments of the nations on its borders; and a potential ally, China, with an even greater population and comparable land mass in which a Communist revolution would soon be victorious.

Later, sometimes years later, we discovered what had transpired in the power rooms in Washington and Moscow, and we learned how American and Russian statesmen had shredded the peace we had so innocently celebrated. Grandiose visions were in vogue at the American and Russian seats of power, each expressed in simple expressions: *American Century, Soviet Century.* Readjustment, reconstruction and rehabilitation were Out. Dominance of the world was In.

The Century visionaries were not new. Twenty-five years earlier, hyperoptimistic visions of dominance sprang up among the successful new Communist leaders in Moscow, who believed that the irresistible superiority of a collectively owned and operated society would soon sweep away capitalism throughout the world. A corresponding vision, born of fright, led to the landing of American

troops on Soviet soil in 1919, in an attempt to destroy the Communist government before it could put its philosophy into practice. The attempt failed.

In 1941, apparently believing the Soviet Union would be badly weakened
in the coming conflict with Germany, the icon of the visionaries of an "American
Century," Henry Luce, the head of the Time-Life publishing empire, proposed
that upon the conclusion of World War II, the United States

> should exert upon the world the full impact of our influ-
> ence, for such purposes as we see fit and by such means
> as we see fit.[92]

The American and Soviet Century agendas were tactically removed from
public display from 1941 to 1945, when the United States, the Soviet Union, and
Great Britain became allied against the Axis Powers. The goal of the Axis was the
destruction of the Soviet Union and the weakening of the United States as a world
power. Having warded off, at an enormous cost, the threat to the existence of one
ally and to the global power of the other, the former allies ungagged their visionaries and split into two sides: the Free World, led by the United States, and the
Socialist World, led by the Soviet Union. True to form, the Free and the Socialist
visionaries cloaked their battle cries in a defensive vocabulary. Each was preparing for war to defend itself from the other.

In the Soviet Union, where much of the nation's productive resources were
in ruins, and in which the population was still mourning the loss of 20 million
men and women, an expanding militarization placed severe limitations on the
materials and facilities for producing what families needed: shelter, food, clothing, furniture, schools, hospitals and services. The survivors had anticipated a
renewal of what they had been told was the nation's epic journey to Socialism
with, perhaps, more freedom on the near horizon. Instead, the Stalin government
declared that its wartime ally, the United States, had almost overnight become
its designated enemy. *Pravda*, the official organ of the Soviet Communist Party,
warned its readers that the United States was

> feverishly preparing for a new world war, they are send-
> ing more and more of their spies to the U.S.S.R. and
> the people's democracies, trying to succeed where the
> Hitlerites failed – trying to create a subversive terrorist
> "fifth column" in the U.S.S.R.[93]

In the United States, a corresponding demonization of the Soviet Union was
underway, succinctly expressed by a leading Democratic Senator from Nevada, who
would describe the Soviet Union as "the most serious danger to the continuance of a
free America that this Nation has faced since the days of our war for independence."[94]

The American Century bloc asserted that its agenda was America's destiny: a vast expansion of American military, economic and political power throughout the world, giving the United States an unchallenged dominance over all other nations. The bloc had supporters on every level of government and Congress, and in mega-corporate boardrooms and the media. It frequently had the ear of almost every president after President Roosevelt's death.

Both American and Soviet leaders knew their world-dominating aspirations required non-dissenting, lockstep populations for their ambitions to be realized. The Stalin-led commissars quickly "cleansed" the government of officials, scientists and writers who were critical of the Soviet Century agenda, labeling them "peaceniks" and traitors.

American Century proponents likewise began to tag dissenters as traitors. Thousands of Americans were paraded in the media as "treacherous Communists," after these labels were attached to them at Congressional and state legislative committee hearings. The media parades were modeled on similar events that had enabled the destruction of democracy in Germany prior to Hitler's seizure of power.

Among the first of the American skeptics to fall was Secretary of War Henry Stimson, a conservative Republican who had served five presidents in one capacity or another, beginning with Theodore Roosevelt in 1906. Stimson believed the Soviet Union would soon have its own atomic bomb and it was in our interests to agree to share information on the bomb so that the two nations, through the United Nations, might together prevent its proliferation across the planet.

On September 11, 1945, Stimson wrote to President Harry S. Truman that he recognized "the ultimate importance of a change in Russian attitude toward individual liberty" but he believed the change

> will come slowly and gradually and I am satisfied that we should not delay our approach to Russia in the matter of the atomic bomb until that process has been completed....I believe that this long process of change in Russia is more likely to be expedited by the closer relationship in the matter of the atomic bomb...[95]

Ten days later Stimson resigned, possibly because of age and because his beliefs were anathema to what future President Dwight D. Eisenhower would call the "military-industrial complex." Eisenhower would warn the nation that the "complex" had "the potential for the disastrous rise of misplaced power," and

> We must never let the weight of this combination endanger our liberties or democratic processes."[96]

"Blow them off the face of the earth"...

Thirty years later, we learned from government documents what happened immediately after Stimson resigned. Robert Patterson, appointed to succeed him, promptly requested that General Leslie Groves, who had overseen the huge program for development of the atom bomb, submit a "first strike" nuclear war plan against the Soviet Union. Groves submitted the plan on February 12, 1946. It read, in part

> 1. This report is submitted in compliance with instructions received in your TOP SECRET memorandum of 29 January 1946 on the same subject. 2. The atomic bomb which will be available to the armed forces of the United States in January 1948, 1949 and 1950 will be of the same general type as the bombs dropped on Japan in August of 1945...[97]

Groves' report contained a warning:

> It is to be expected that any enemy will attempt with all his resources to destroy the carrying plane. It is essential that we make realistic estimates of losses en route to a target area in order that the final delivery of a sufficient number of bombs may be insured. *The failure to deliver a few atomic bombs during the initial attack may permit a determined enemy to organize a counter attack with atomic bombs and deal us a severe blow.*

The italicized portion was included in a draft of Groves' report, but was deleted from the copy sent to the War Department. The draft's most important deleted clause, "may permit a determined enemy to organize a counter attack with atom bombs," was an acknowledgment by Groves, in 1946, that the Soviet Union was expected to have atomic bombs within two years.

President Truman agreed that the Soviet Union had to be restrained, but he regarded the extremist steps being weighed by the new Secretary of War and the American Century proponents as posing a great risk for the United States. He vetoed the first-strike plan and demanded the Secretary of War disown it, publicly. David McCullough, in his biography of Truman, wrote in the fall of 1946,

> At the Pentagon, at Truman's request, Secretaries Patterson and Forrestal [James V. Forrestal, Secretary of the Navy] issued a joint statement denying they knew of any responsible Army or Navy officer who had ever advocated or even suggested a policy or a plan of attacking Russia.[98]

From that moment on, the American Century proponents labeled the president "soft on communism;" in some quarters he was labeled a "traitor."

In the 1948 presidential election, the Republican Party leaders, who supported the American Century agenda, made a broadside attack on the loyalty of the 20 million-plus Democratic voters, publicly labeling them "Commiecrats."[99]

The "Commiecrats" sent Truman back to the White House, after which his disappointed rival, New York Governor Thomas E. Dewey, described for the *New York Times* what the United States should now expect: Soviet planes would "bomb the great production centers and cities of the continental United States, with the Red pilots bailing out to become prisoners of war." The Russians, Dewey said, could use Chinese satellite troops to overrun Alaska, and the "enemy would then have air and land bases for the hordes of Asia on the North American continent."[100]

The Governor called for a volunteer force from every nation to fight Communism and "specifically recommended that the youth of Germany and Japan should be eligible" to join this force. The past experience of the German soldiers in fighting the Red Army was expected to be an invaluable asset in a war against totalitarian Communism.

When, in 1949, the Soviet Union detonated its first atom bomb, some members of Congress and a number of newspapers went public with calls for an immediate first-strike atom bomb attack on the designated enemy. Senator Brien McMahon, Chairman of the Joint Committee on Atomic Energy, argued that the United States must

> blow them [Soviet Union] off the face of the earth, quick, before they do the same to us – we haven't much time.[101]

The *Manchester Morning Union* declared, in February 1950, that a first-strike atom bomb attack on the Soviet Union would be the single most significant step

> for peace in the world today. As well as our only salvation from impending destruction. We cannot delay longer.[102]

Atomics, a periodical dealing with atomic energy, noted the news that the Soviets had detonated an atom bomb was

> being screamed from banner headlines in every newspaper from Los Angeles to Portland, Maine, and radio commentators have worked themselves into a minor panic, many of them have the country practically at war with Russia.[103]

A new commonly accepted myth arose. The United States alone had possessed the "secret" of the atom bomb; the Soviets had lacked the "secret" until American Communist spies stole and passed it on to the Kremlin. The FBI, the public was given to understand, had undertaken a massive hunt to discover the spies.

The impact of these events and the fevered oratory that accompanied them sent a depressing message to the populations of the two powers that had designated each other as enemies. What a significant portion of the human race had thought was an unstoppable universal wave of hope was stoppable, after all.

Disappointment began to enter into our conversations. The jitterbugging in the dance halls went on, but many of us with spouses and children danced halfheartedly. A popular song, *We'll Meet Again*, began to lose the promise of its lyrics and became remote and nostalgic and sadly unbelievable.

"The less...hampered by idealistic slogans, the better..."

From 1949 onward, Congress and much of the media began to describe the United States as a besieged nation, virtually ringed by Red atomic missile carriers and overrun by treacherous American Communists eagerly awaiting a Soviet invasion. The White House adopted a "containment" policy that would supply arms, funds and advisors to any nation confronted by the threat of Soviet domination or of a revolution from within.

George F. Kennan, a State Department official who had authored President Truman's policy of military containment of the Soviet Union, argued that the nation's survival was being undermined by the public's preference for an attempt to negotiate a detente with the Soviet Union, a preference he laid to traditional American idealism. Americans, he wrote, must

> cease to talk about vague and unreal objectives such as human rights, the raising of living standards and democratization. The day is not far off when we are going to have to deal in straight power concepts. The less we are then hampered by idealistic slogans the better.[104]

An even franker and sterner statement of what was demanded of Americans was made by Air Force General James H. Doolittle, a highly decorated war hero.

> Hitherto acceptable norms of human conduct do not apply. If the United States is to survive, long-standing concepts of 'fair play' must be reconsidered...It may be necessary that the American people be made acquainted with, understand and support this fundamental *repugnant philosophy*.[105]   (italics added)

Although their prescriptions for America's survival were essentially the same, Kennan and Doolittle were concerned with two different America's. Doolittle would place no limits on the alterations in American life and outlook that stemmed from the "repugnant philosophy." Kennan's concern was for the survival of the "old" traditional America, and he soon repudiated that part of his advice that he believed endangered the America he wanted to save. By coincidence or by design, one month after the Rosenbergs were sentenced to death, Kennan wrote, in the *New York Times*, that the new philosophy being pressed on the public created

> a danger that something may occur in our own minds and souls which will make us no longer like the persons by whose efforts this republic was founded and held together, but rather like the representatives of that very power we are trying to combat: intolerant, secretive, suspicious, cruel, and terrified of internal dissension because we have lost our own belief in ourselves and in the power of our ideals.[106]

Thereafter, Kennan, once celebrated for his firm anti-Communist, anti-Soviet prescriptions, had his loyalty challenged by a Senate Communist-hunting committee.[107]

The displacement of adherence to the Constitution was encouraged by two rationales: *Better safe than sorry!* and *The Constitution is not a suicide pact!*

A Hiroshimic fear...

The rigidly controlled newspapers and radio commentators in the Soviet Union and the corresponding free media in the United States were, in respect to the drive for world supremacy, indistinguishable. Both represented their governments' feverish programs for mutual atomic destruction as being entirely defensive. In the name of patriotism, pundits in English and Russian asked their populations to sacrifice their longings for peace and dignified lives so that great portions of the wealth of each nation could be diverted into creating more powerful atom bombs, greater armies, and a storm of atomic bomb tests that poisoned the world's atmosphere.

The pleas aroused a Hiroshimic fear among American and Soviet populations that they might at any time be transformed into ash by incendiary ICBM's from the Kremlin or the Pentagon.

Cleansing America...

We do not know whether correspondingly fearsome headlines in *Pravda* and *Izvestia* accompanied espionage-treason trials in Moscow and elsewhere in

1952; it is likely they did. It would have hardly mattered if they did not. There simply were no visible critics and nay sayers to which the Soviet government was answerable. Those who had once spoken out were in prison or dead.

The inconvenient American Constitution did not permit the institution of a Soviet-style monolithic-minded society. The best our own totalitarian-inclined extremists could do was to conduct serial Congressional and local investigations of dissenters, accompanied by expressions of rage by high officials and the media against Americans who, disagreeing with the government's foreign policy, found themselves described as siding with the enemy. In tune with the "repugnant policy," our prosecutors protested against "technicalities" of law that allowed "worshippers" of our enemy to thwart justice and to move about freely through neighborhoods that might soon become cauldrons of fire and death.

Volunteers were being asked to come forward for civilian defense duties in New York. Atom bomb shelter areas were set aside to which children and adults could flee when the bombings of the city began. All New York school children were dog-tagged to make them more easily identifiable during and after the bombings. Air-raid drills were conducted for the first time in New York's history.

Two presidents speak: "Hang a few traitors": "I would kill the S.O.B.s"...

The malevolence toward dissenters of any kind was not fully satisfied by arrests and indictments. There arose a sentiment in Congress, the White House and the media for "vigilante justice" against "liberals, pinkos, socialists and communists." Westbrook Pegler, a widely syndicated columnist for a major New York newspaper, wrote

> The only sensible and courageous way to deal with Communists in our midst is to make membership in Communist organizations or covert subsidies a capital offense and shoot or otherwise put to death all persons convicted of such.[108]

Senator Karl Mundt of South Dakota argued at an American Legion meeting for "vigilante action to combat Communism" by organizing anticommunist posses "in every American town."[109]

President Truman, faced with the decision of labor unions to resist erosion of the value of their members' wages because of steeply rising prices for food and other necessities, a decision he interpreted as due to 'Communist influence,' drafted a speech in which he declared

> Let's give the country back to the people. Let's put transportation and production back to work, hang a few

traitors, and make our own country safe for democracy.
Come on, boys, let's do the job![110]

He was persuaded by his advisors to leave out the call for hanging unionists.

Truman's successor, Dwight D. Eisenhower, was not immune to the vigilante sentiments expressed by his colleagues. In an exchange between Supreme Court Chief Justice Earl Warren and President Eisenhower, after he had completed his second term, Eisenhower complained about Supreme Court opinions that upheld Constitutional rights for dissenters, including Communists. Justice Warren wrote

> I tried to explain that in the judging process we were obliged to judge Communists by the same rules that we applied to all others. He [Eisenhower] refused to accept this statement, and I asked him: 'What would you do with Communists in America? 'I would kill the S.O.B.s', he said.[111]

Congress outlaws "rats", "vermin", "tarantulas"...

In October 1950, six months before the Rosenberg-Sobell trial, Congress debated and passed the Internal Security Act, declaring that there was a "world communist movement," the purpose of which was "by treachery, deceit, infiltration into other groups (governmental and otherwise), espionage, sabotage, terrorism, and any other means," to establish Communist dictatorships everywhere in the world "through the medium of a world-wide Communist organization."[112] It found that there were legions of treacherous Americans "numbering thousands of adherents, rigidly and ruthlessly disciplined," waiting for the right moment to paralyze our defenses against an invasion from the Soviet Union.[113]

The Act created a giant funnel through which all persons who failed to satisfy a government agency or a Congressional investigating committee that they were not dissenters or potential or actual spies and traitors, could be sent to detention camps without having been tried or sentenced for any crimes. The Act declared the worldwide communist conspiracy was so vast that "adequate surveillance to prevent espionage and sabotage" was impossible, thus invoking a rationale for incarcerating persons against whom the government did not have any evidence of having ever contemplated or committed a crime.[114] The Act permitted the Executive to bypass the courts in order to detain for indefinite terms "persons who there is reasonable ground to believe probably will commit or conspire with others to commit espionage or sabotage,"[115] and automatically transferred the citizenship of native-born and naturalized Americans to Soviet citizenship if they "participate in the world Communist movement."[116] The Act created one formal imprisonment procedure: an individual failing to register with the Department of Justice as an actual or potential traitor to the United States could be punished by a $10,000 fine and "imprisonment for not more than five years, or by both such fine and imprisonment."[117]

Congressional supporters of the Act likened its opponents in Congress and among the public to "political parties [that] are infiltrated with these agents of Moscow,"[118] "infected rats on ships touching American ports,"[119] "vermin,"[120] "tarantulas,"[121] and so on.

One of the members of Congress who voted nay on the Act was Representative Usher Burdick of North Dakota.

> I do not stand aside in patriotism to this government, because my folks have been in it since 1634, in every war we have ever had...But on this occasion I think we are voting because we think the people want us [to] strangle men who think, even though they think wrong. I would not stop man from thinking, if he was thinking wrong. Let him think...[122]

Another Representative, Vito Marcantonio, said

> We are carrying our country back to the period of the alien and sedition laws. We are carrying the Nation back to the period of the fugitive slave laws, and the period of the Dred Scott decision...You are killing the America of the American Revolution.[123]

The vote for the Act was overwhelming in the House and the Senate. President Harry Truman vetoed it; his veto was overridden.

The Act proved unenforceable, for almost every clause violated the Constitution. But its purpose – arousing fear of debating government decisions relating to foreign policy and national security – achieved considerable success. Among other things, the public faced the reality that six camps had actually been set up for the detention of "disloyal" Americans: in Oklahoma, California, Arizona (2), Pennsylvania, and Florida.

In a look at these detention camps in a 1955 report, the *New York Times* found that the camps had amenities, such as showers and laundries, which had been absent from the camps into which the German Nazis had shuttled millions of its citizens, and concluded

> There is nothing at any of the camps to suggest the 'concentration camps' that horrified the free world in World War II.[124]

The *Times'* reporter was in error. The Nazi concentration camps did have showers, although they delivered Zyklon B gas, rather than water.

Bringing home new civics lessons...

State and local law enforcement agencies were encouraged to develop their own loyalty checks. In Michigan, "writing or speaking subversive words," was made punishable by life imprisonment. In Tennessee, Communist Party membership was made punishable by death; in Virginia, anyone found "lurking with intent to spy" was subject to the death penalty.[125] Los Angeles required any "subversive" passing through the city to register at the Sheriff's Office. Jacksonville, Florida, set up an agency at which citizens had to register if they had ever corresponded with present or former communists. In Birmingham, Alabama, and in Macon, Georgia, "communists" were required to leave town in 48 hours or face six months in prison.[126]

Within and from the White House and Congress and the state capitols, down to local precincts, wards and parishes, the torrent of accusations of disloyalty spread through the nation. The "repugnant philosophy" was declared the new Americanism. To discuss and debate was treason. To be fearful and silent was the mark of patriotism.

The Great Turnabout: altering the nation's memory...

There was one more signal with ethnic overtones which the Jewish judge and prosecutors could not have missed. For lack of a proper pejorative adjective, we call it The Turnabout.

At the same time as noJustice officials were preparing the case against the defendants, they were deeply involved in a project called "Paperclip," an operation aimed at modifying the public's perceptions of the Nazi Germans as practitioners of shocking crimes and cruelties before and during the war.[127] The burden of condemnation had to be lifted from the Germans, especially from its military and industrial leaders with whom our megacorporate CEO's had always had good relations in wartime as well as in peace.[128]

The Turnabout began with an announcement by the War Department in October 1945, one month after Secretary of War Stimson's resignation, that a number of "carefully selected" German scientists and technologists were being brought to the United States who would, however, be unavailable for interviews or photographs.[129] The War Department issued a peculiarly worded press release stating

> The Secretary of War has approved a project whereby certain understanding German scientists and technicians are being brought to this country to ensure that

we take full advantage of those significant developments
which are deemed vital to our national security.[130]

The War Department press release did not describe what was the "certain
understanding" Germans understood.

The newly imported former enemies were experts in military strategy and
armaments, concentration camp administration, disinformation techniques,
human experimentation, and other skills the American Century proponents
apparently believed would be useful to our government in the foreseeable near
future.

Although the 10,000-plus "carefully selected" Germans brought into
our military installations and laboratories, aircraft industries, biological insti-
tutes, university political science faculties, and other areas of life were initially
described by the War Department as "temporary" visitors, they were permitted
to bring their spouses and children,[131] and their applications for American citizenship were expedited.

The entry into the United States of Germans who had been active enemies
was illegal under immigration laws and past Executive Orders, but President
Truman had been persuaded to allow the German experts to enter the United
States, although he had stipulated that entry would be denied to Germans who
were wanted for war crimes or who had been Nazi activists. The task of overlooking the violation of immigration laws and President Truman's stipulation barring
active German Nazis and war criminals from entering the United States fell to
the Department of Justice. To overcome the stipulation, a "legal" solution was
hatched: the president would empower the Attorney General and the Secretary
of State to jointly waive the prohibitions if "extraordinary circumstances" arose.
"Extraordinary circumstances" quickly became the everyday norm.

The havens chosen in the United States for the thousands of former enemy
Germans were often prestigious and well-paying. The faculty of Georgetown
University, to name only one of the educational havens, had to learn to deal with
a new colleague, Constantine Boldyreff, whom the Army knew to have overseen
Russian slave labor for the Nazis during the war. Boldyreff appeared as a teacher
of psychological warfare at the university's Foreign Service Institute.[132]

The engineering staff at Bell Aircraft, one of the aircraft companies that
became a haven for the incoming Germans, was one day introduced to a new
colleague, Walter Dornberger, a Nazi general who had overseen the production
schedules at Nordhausen, one of the sites at which German V1 and V2 rockets
were constructed for the bombardment of London, which had resulted in 80,000
casualties, 30,000 of them fatal. The rockets had required the labor of 20,000 prisoners from a nearby concentration camp named Dora; before Germany's defeat,
most of Dora's inmates had died of "starvation, disease, or by execution."[133]

Army and Justice officials found it impossible to keep the illegal importation of these "carefully selected" German experts secret for long. Federal and state officials had to give orientation lectures to puzzled university department heads, industrial plant managers, laboratory chiefs, and other administrators who would host the new arrivals. Not all the selected hosts were certain of the "Americanism" of the Turnabout. Many of them were aware, if they declined to collaborate, they might be risking their careers and livelihoods.

Their dilemma was shared by secretaries, clerks, and supervisory staffs, especially in the Justice Department, which conducted the preparation and processing of the paperwork expediting the entry into the United States of so many former active enemies and fugitives from west and east European war crimes tribunals. A number of Justice personnel were overtaken by doubts and disquiet, particularly among those who had lost family members to the Nazi armed forces. For many personnel, to simply obey orders, in the face of very troubling moral questions, would have violated an essential component of their self-image as Americans. Thus, much of the "leakage" of the secret program of infusion of Nazi Germans into American life was driven by conscience.

There is documentation of resistance to executing the secret program within the Justice Department, centered on the very criminality of the Nazi Germans the Turnabout managers wanted the public to forget. In a letter of October 20, 1950, from Attorney General J. Howard McGrath to Secretary of State Dean Acheson, evidently in response to a complaint that Justice was dragging its feet in expediting the entry of the Nazi experts into the United States, McGrath wrote that steps were being taken to overcome obstacles that prohibited entry to certain categories of Germans. To

> alleviate undue hardship, the Attorney General has exercised his discretionary authority...to grant temporary admission to aliens in category 2 where the only ground of exclusion is the alien's nominal membership, whether present or past, in either the Nazi, Fascist, Falangist or other totalitarian party or organization.[134]

The exclusion would also be lifted for Germans (and officials appointed by the Nazis in occupied countries) who said they had not "voluntarily taken part in any atrocities committed by such totalitarian party or organization."

State Department officials found McGrath's response unsatisfactory, and wrote him, on November 28, that there should be no need for obtaining his discretionary authority for the admission of Germans who had belonged to any Nazi organizations, because not all Nazi organizations could be held to be truly Nazi. For example, the Nazi armed forces and their various supporting organizations were military, not political entities. None of these military forces, he was told, "were a 'section, subsidiary, branch, affiliate, or subdivision' of the parent Nazi or Fascist parties."[135]

But a week later, even the distinction between the Nazi/Fascist political and military organizations was deemed to create an undue hardship for Nazi experts awaiting entry. On December 5, 1950, the Under Secretary of State wrote to McGrath to say if the exclusion for entry into the United States could be lifted for persons who had not "voluntarily taken part in any atrocities," it should also be lifted for persons who said they had not voluntarily joined Nazi or Fascist parties.[136]

Attorney General McGrath complied. He was a leading member of the Democratic Party, and among his tasks was the obvious one of refuting, in deeds, the "Commiecrat" and disloyal labels pinned on his party by Republicans and extremists. One step in that direction had been his authorizing the indictments in the Rosenberg-Sobell case under an inapplicable law – the Espionage Act of 1917 – rather than Atomic Energy Act of 1946. Another was his facilitating illegal entry of "ex-" Nazis and war criminals into the United States. To have refused to do so would have been taken as proof of McGrath's personal "softness", if not sympathy, toward Communism, and would have lent credibility to the slanders against his party. Accordingly, McGrath waved the Nazis in.

The national commander of the war veterans' largest organization, the American Legion, made no protest to the entry into the United States of the ranking Nazi officers who had led the Nazi troops in the shooting of his comrades. Instead, he declared that our country was being "infiltrated by a 'secret battalion' of 75,000 'trained Communists' and an 'auxiliary corps' of up to one million dupes, camp followers, secret sympathizers, and casual supporters."[137]

Eventually, a great many of the "rehabilitated" Nazis became citizens and some came to occupy positions of great prestige and authority. Wernher von Braun, a German rocket scientist who had utilized slave labor at the German Mittelwerk V-2 rocket plant to produce the lethal missiles that rained death over London, and who had been a major in the Nazi SS, the elite corps that acted as Hitler's bodyguard,[138] became the first Director of NASA's George C. Marshall Space Flight Center.[139] Another former member of the elite SS, Kurt Debus, eventually became the first Director of the Kennedy Space Center.[140]

The Turnabout managers evidently felt it necessary to denigrate World War II and to withhold recognition of its nearly one million American casualties. So strong was their grip on Congress that it was not until 1993, 48 years after the end of World War II, and after the demise of the Soviet government, that a bill could be enacted in Congress to create a National World War II Memorial in Washington, D.C. to honor the uniformed men and women who had fought in World War II. Memorials in the national capital honoring those who fought in the "right" wars – the wars in Korea and Vietnam, respectively – were approved thirteen and seven years before the memorial for those who had served in World War II.

The Great Turnabout: Europe...

The Turnabout was imposed in Europe as well as in the United States. Tens of thousands of Nazi leaders and war criminals were recruited in Europe to lend us their expertise in our military, security and foreign policy operations.[141] This required that we virtually halt all war criminal trials, with the result that more than 90% of the accused war criminals went unpunished. Of 106,000 individuals accused of war crimes, only 6,500 (6%) were convicted. As of 1997, 52 years after the end of the war, German prosecutors were still "investigating" charges against unindicted Nazi war criminals.[142]

The denazification process in Europe was halted on the pretext that the Nazi label had been falsely pinned on Germans by Communists and by "Jewish interests." When criticism was raised against the halting of denazification and the infusion of the de-prefixed Germans into American life, it was identified as Jewish prejudice. Major Lyman White, a special investigations officer for the Army, noted the criticism and wrote

> While critical comment must be evaluated in the light of the natural Jewish bias against anything Nazi, it is, however a matter to be watched, and, if possible, counteracted lest it lead to official restrictive action...[143]

Major White, who, like his superiors, apparently did not share the bias of most Americans against anything Nazi, assigned a public relations officer to see to it that "human interest stories" be used to "take the focus away from controversial topics."

The halting of the denazification process and most of the war criminal trials created an anti-American mood among many Europeans, who had a few years earlier experienced Nazi atrocities first-hand, and now witnessed the criminals going free and resuming their lives or boarding planes and ships bound for the United States.

The Soviets do half a Turnabout...

Captured Nazis with special knowledge and skills that would be useful in a war with the United States were being shipped into the Soviet Union and shepherded into engineering and weapons development centers. A former American Air Vice-Marshal estimated that 300,000 German aerospace engineers and technicians were relocated to the Soviet Union immediately after the war.[144]

This number seems high, but the Air Vice-Marshal pointed out that Allied bombing constantly pushed the German airplane factories eastward, so that by

the end of the war there was a great concentration of German aerospace expertise relatively close to the Soviet border. More important, however, the Soviets
acquired several high-level nuclear physicists, including Gustave Hertz, a Nobel
prize winner, who were able to make important contributions to the Soviet atom
bomb development program.[145]

It does not appear, however, that the Soviet commissars attempted to
describe the relocated Germans as benign, an attempt that would have been
instantly doomed by the many Russians who had survived the war but whose 20
million closest relatives had not. The relocated Germans were repatriated within
a decade.

Nevertheless, by coincidence or design, before the Germans were repatriated, there were events in Moscow that were probably applauded by many of
them. To foster support for the premise the Soviet Union was being targeted for
atom bomb attacks by the United States, Stalin initiated a vigorous anti-Semitic
campaign, and it was during the period of the Germans' stay in the Soviet Union
that the previously mentioned arrests and trials of large numbers of Jews on
charges of espionage and treason took place.[146]

The 'everywhere' of the Turnabout...

The Turnabout popped up in cartoons and skits as well as in the streams
of memoranda and documents generated by government officials. On television,
Nazi's were portrayed as bumbling dimwits instead of inciters and participants
in the deaths, worldwide, of 60 million human beings. The familiar Nazi enemy
was now bifurcated in the media and popular culture: there was, on one side, a
miniature little mustached devil, a misbegotten loner and psychopath; and on the
adjacent side there was the German nation, its SS troops, its Gestapo, its legions
of exterminators, its known and unknown fugitives from war crimes tribunals,
all of them suddenly decent, forgivable folk, suffering understandably from loss
of memory of any bad behavior. What the German folk did recall – and it was
their most important credential of friendship with us – was that they had killed
twenty million Russians. A discreet silence was maintained over the nearly one
million casualties they and their Japanese allies had inflicted on Americans.

7000 American military casualties of the Turnabout...

The phenomenon of our country becoming a haven for Nazi war criminals
left its mark for many decades on our landscape. It made itself felt in school systems throughout the country, in which for many years the Holocaust and other
Nazi atrocities, including those against American soldiers, were largely absent
from history textbooks and classrooms. In 1988, 43 years after the end of the
war, a nationwide history program on the Holocaust was denied federal funding
because, said one opponent of the program, the "Nazi point of view, however

unpopular, is still a point of view and is not presented, nor is that of the Ku Klux Klan."[147]

The Turnabout injected Nazi procedures into our defense research, causing thousands of American soldiers and civilians to be victimized by experimental programs brought to us by imported Nazi scientists who were infused into our universities and defense establishments.

One of these procedures was revealed 40 years after the fact, when U.S. Army Sergeant James Stanley brought suit for the devastating disorder and damage inflicted on his life by experiments conducted in association with Nazi scientists employed in 1953 at the Edgewood Arsenal, Maryland.

A leading expert in this and similar experiments, which eventually involved 7000 American soldiers, was Hans Trurnit, a Nazi Party doctor who, before being welcomed to the United States, participated in a study at Dachau concentration camp at which inmates were experimentally frozen to death.

The experiments at Edgewood Arsenal began with a Nazi protocol based on experiments performed on slave laborers in Europe. In the Edgewood Arsenal experiments, the American soldiers were not told what effect the experiments would have on them. They were told only that the experiments were for the purpose of devising greater protection for the troops, and it was for those purposes the soldiers gave their consent.

Among the experimental treatments given to Sergeant Stanley and the other subjects were high doses of heroin, lysergic acid diethylamide (LSD), amphetamines, and other drugs; they were subjected to experimental hypnosis, lobotomies, electroshock, sensory deprivation and other procedures developed by interrogators in the Nazi concentration camps. The experiments altered the characters of Sergeant Stanley and the other soldiers. They experienced hallucinations, sleeplessness, irrational and suicidal ideation; they committed uncharacteristic acts of violence against themselves and others and, in many cases, as a result of these effects, became estranged from their spouses and children.[148]

In answer to Sergeant Stanley's suit, the majority of the justices of the U.S. Supreme Court, in an opinion written by Justice Antonin Scalia, refused to permit Sergeant Stanley to bring suit against the government for these experiments to which the victims had never given consent. Associate Justice Scalia wrote that the military operates under

> the need for special regulations in relation to military discipline, and the consequent need and justification for a special and exclusive system of military justice is too obvious to require extensive discussion; no military organization can function without strict discipline and regulation that would be unacceptable in a civilian setting.[149]

In effect, the Scalia ruling held that Constitutional protections against indiscriminate harm do not apply to members of the armed forces if they volunteer for experiments which have been falsely described to them. Rights they had before volunteering are lost to them at the moment of volunteering, and the usual obligations of officers to the men under their command to be truthful to them and to respect their humanity, no longer applied.

Supreme Court Justice William J. Brennan dissented from the majority opinion, writing

> the Government of the United States treated thousands of its citizens as though they were laboratory animals, dosing them with this dangerous drug without their consent. * * * The medical trials at Nuremberg in 1947 deeply impressed on the world that experimenting with unknowing human subjects is morally and legally unacceptable. The United States Military Tribunal established the Nuremberg Code as a standard against which to judge German scientists who experimented with human subjects. Its first principle was: *1. The voluntary consent of the human subject is absolutely essential.*[150]

The Scalia ruling legitimized the use in the United States military the procedural protocols and immorality of experiments practiced by the Nazi scientists and overseers of the Nazi slave camps. Our officials had condemned these protocols and their inhumanity before and during World War II.

Forgiving the massacre of 71 American prisoners of war...

During the World War II Battle of the Ardennes, also called the Battle of the Bulge (December 16, 1944–January 16, 1945), 71 American prisoners of war were massacred. The total American battle deaths at Ardennes were 19,000. An American war-crimes court subsequently conducted a trial of the German officers and soldiers involved in the massacre; 74 of them were convicted, of which 43 were sentenced to be hanged. During the Turnabout, however, the Office of the Judge Advocate found there had been prosecutorial misconduct at the trial of the German defendants, and recommended the death sentences be commuted to life imprisonment. None of the condemned was hanged and, by 1956, every one of the convicted Germans had been freed.[151]

In 1985, 40 years after the Turnabout began, President Ronald Reagan, predicting an Armageddon at which the Soviet "evil empire" would be destroyed, was still courting the German nation to stand with the United States. Absent from his statements regarding Germany was even the subtlest acknowledgment that there had ever been a Nazi German assault on the United States and its allies or on humanity in general.

The Great Turnabout: altering America/Americanism...

The solicitation to Nazi Germans to share in the shaping of post-war America, and the adoption by our political leadership and the media of the "repugnant philosophy" championed by extremist visionaries of an American Century, were abrasive to the viscerally understood meaning of the word Americanism. Just as the Nazi-Soviet Pact had dealt a blow to those who saw the Soviet Union as a beacon against the threat to humanity by German Nazism, the Turnabout was a blow to Americans who internalized the certainty their country was a fortress against the cruelty and immorality of Nazi practices.

In the Turnabout, the "repugnant philosophy" had undeniably found a home in three powerful agencies of government. The violation of immigration laws and Presidential Orders by Justice officials had enabled State and War Department officials to recruit the century's most expert mass murderers and genocidal practitioners to prepare us for our future role in history.

At the very time Justice officials were enabling the illegal importation of these experts, they were also being called on by Congress and large sections of the media to set aside Constitutional "technicalities" in order to destroy the "Communist" conspiracy threatening our survival. The first order of business, Congress signaled, was to discover the American Communist spies who had stolen the secret of the atom bomb and delivered it to the Soviet Union.

Hope ran high that outright evidence of David Greenglass' perjury would be
enough to win the Rosenbergs a reprieve from execution.
Article printed May 4, 1953 in the New York Times.

ROSENBERG RALLY HEARS NEW STORY

It Is About Greenglass Paper
Said to Belie Testimony He
Gave at Atom Spy Trial

A memorandum supposedly written by David Greenglass, confessed atomic spy, was featured yesterday as new "evidence" at a rally on behalf of Julius and Ethel Rosenberg, convicted and under death sentence as his fellow conspirators. Last night it was reported the Federal Bureau of Investigation was looking into the wanderings of such a document.

O. John Rogge, Greenglass' attorney, confirmed that there had been a handwritten memorandum by Greenglass, apparently similar to a document printed in the French press several times since April 18. Mr. Rogge said the original memorandum appeared to have been "filched" from his files, and had been missing when the F. B. I. first inquired about it last Wednesday—only to turn up in the files the next day.

One version of the memorandum by Greenglass, a former atomic bomb worker at Los Alamos, N. M., who had testified that he gave Rosenberg his brother-in-law, a long description of the secret bomb in September, 1945, was announced by Joseph Brainin, chairman of the Committee to Secure Justice in the Rosenberg Case.

At a rally attended by 10,000 persons at Triborough Stadium, Randall's Island, Mr. Brainin said that this copy had been authenticated by Elizabeth McCarthy, Boston handwriting expert. In it, he said, Greenglass related in June, 1950, his "approximate statements to the F. B. I."

This showed, Mr. Brainin said, that Greenglass did not remember one point the F. B. I. raised, but wrote "I allowed it in the statement." The document, Mr. Brainin said, contained other points that were "the absolute opposite of what Greenglass' testified to in court," and left out all mention of having passed any atomic secrets to Julius Rosenberg and any reference to Ethel Rosenberg.

Asked for comment, Mr. Rogge said that Greenglass at first "told part of his story to the F. B. I.," and then later gave the rest. Greenglass is serving a fifteen-year sentence as a confessed spy. The Rosenbergs, who insist they are innocent, have been in the death house at Sing Sing Prison since April, 1951, and are awaiting the outcome of their third appeal to the Supreme Court.

Chapter 3 | The prosecution's dilemma

A matter of evidence...

The official history of the Rosenberg-Sobell case has the FBI giving Justice officials dossiers on David Greenglass, Julius Rosenberg and Morton Sobell, all suspected espionage agents in the spring of 1950. In June 1950, David Greenglass, who had been a machinist at the Los Alamos atomic bomb development center, was arrested on an espionage charge, following which he confessed and implicated his wife, Ruth, and his brother-in-law, Julius Rosenberg, who was arrested one month later. A month after that, Greenglass expanded his confession to include his sister, Ethel Rosenberg, and she was arrested on the same charge in August.

David Greenglass' confession presented a problem to Justice officials. There was insufficient tangible or credible circumstantial evidence to support his confession, or his implication of Ruth Greenglass or Julius Rosenberg or Morton Sobell in espionage. A Justice Department official advised Everett Grantham, the U.S. Attorney in New Mexico, who was presenting the case to a grand jury in Albuquerque, that there was insufficient evidence beyond David's statement to satisfy his grand jury's investigation in respect to Ruth Greenglass. A testy exchange of letters and memoranda then passed between top Justice Department officials and FBI Director J. Edgar Hoover, regarding the lack of evidence. William E. Foley, Chief of the Internal Security Section, Department of Justice, told Grantham that he had been informed by an FBI official

> that the Department has been furnished with all information
> which the Bureau has in the matter.[152]

J. Edgar Hoover followed up two weeks later with a letter to Attorney General J. Howard McGrath, nominally his superior, to complain that Justice officials constantly delayed prosecution of spies, whose names he had passed on to them, because the officials wanted to go to court with an "absolutely air-tight case."

McGrath replied to Hoover on August 2, 1950, reminding him

> If we do not have sufficient evidence, admissible in court,
> to convict them the prosecutions will fail. Obviously a
> series of cases which result in acquittals, or which have
> to be abandoned by the government, would create a very
> bad impression upon the public in general and would be
> most advantageous to the subversive elements.[153]

McGrath added, possibly with some sarcasm, he

> would like to suggest that you furnish the result of your
> investigations in these cases to the Department at an
> earlier stage in the proceedings.

Justice officials past history of dead-end leads and Not Guilty verdicts...

In June 1945, at the insistence of FBI Director J. Edgar Hoover, Justice officials had convened a grand jury to approve the indictment of six editors and
scholars associated with *Amerasia*, a journal largely devoted to events in the Far
East. Hoover believed the six were Communist espionage agents for the Soviet
Union, although James McInerney, an official in the Criminal Division of the
Justice Department, described the evidence presented by Hoover as "a little above
the level of teacup gossip."[154] Justice officials were faced with two bad choices: to
conduct the trial with insufficient evidence, risking Not Guilty verdicts, or declining to proceed, and face denunciation by Hoover and his friends in Congress
and the media for being overly concerned with Constitutional "technicalities"
in respect to the legal rights of spies and traitors. Justice officials then compromised by indicting the six for unlawful possession of classified government documents, a non-capital offense. The grand jury approved the indictments for only
three defendants. Two of those three subsequently plea-bargained and their cases
ended with the imposition of modest fines. All charges against the third were
dropped.

Hoover was indignant, complaining in a memorandum that "it is hard to
tell whether govmt is representing the govmt or the defendants."[155]

By contrast, in early 1946, Canadian law enforcement officials, basing
themselves on information from Igor Gouzenko, a defecting cipher clerk in the
Soviet embassy in Ottawa, tried 21 people on various espionage charges relating
to the atomic bomb, of which nine were convicted. One of the nine was Allen
Nunn May, a British physicist, who was sentenced to 10 years in prison. May
denied he was a Communist and said his conscience had led him to share knowledge of atomic energy with the Soviet Union. His attorney compared what May
had done with the actions of a physician who believes that all humankind should
benefit from his knowledge of a new treatment for a disease. May was released
from prison after six years and eight months.

Five days after Gouzenko's defection, FBI Director Hoover sent two
agents to Ottawa for a briefing by the Canadian authorities, and to interview the
defecting cipher clerk. Since Hoover had a well known contempt for foreign law
enforcement agencies, a month passed before the Canadians permitted the FBI
agents to question Gouzenko.

Gouzenko told the two agents that in May 1945, he had learned that an assistant to Edward R. Stettinius, the U.S. Secretary of State, was a Soviet agent. When this was reported back to Hoover, he at once assumed the agent was Alger Hiss, the subject of one of the FBI's million-plus "Red files," although Hiss had never been an assistant to Stettinius.[156] Hiss had come to Hoover's attention six years earlier, when a former Communist, Whittaker Chambers, had told a State Department official that Hiss, then an employee in the State Department, was a Communist.[157]

Hoover placed Hiss and his wife under surveillance, and put a wiretap on their phones, but after twenty-one months he was unable to find any evidence that Hiss was a Communist or a Soviet agent.[158]

Another unsatisfactory investigation and prosecution involved Nicolai G. Redin, a young Russian naval officer. On March 26, 1946, based on information placed on their desks by the FBI, Justice officials ordered the arrest of Redin and charged him with trying to acquire atomic and other classified information. At Redin's trial in Portland, Oregon, in June 1946, the key prosecution witness testified he had sold Redin classified information. U.S. Attorney Victor Anderson told the jury if Redin had not been caught, his "success would have been greater than that of the Russian hordes that swept to the palaces of Berlin."[159] He also warned the jury if they did not find Redin guilty, they would be branding the FBI agents as "perjurers."

It turned out, however, the data found in Redin's possession was information available at any public library. After ten hours of deliberation, a jury of seven men and five women, found Redin not guilty.

Two years later, in August 1948, Justice officials indicted Alger Hiss for perjury for denying that he knew Whittaker Chambers, who had confessed to spying for the Soviet Union in the 1930s, and who had named Hiss as an accomplice. The jury was unable to agree on Hiss' guilt.

Justice officials under duress...

After the 1949 test of the Soviet atomic bomb, Congress and the media put great pressure on Justice officials for a genuine Communist spy prosecution victory. To Justice officials' complaints of inadequate evidence, J. Edgar Hoover advised them to prosecute without regard to Constitutional "technicalities." Justice officials had to quickly confront their previously described dilemma: what to do with David Greenglass' confession of espionage for which there was no supporting evidence?

Justice officials' solution...

Department of Justice documents made available in the 1970s make it clear that, in the absence of evidence, Justice officials and the prosecutors decided to apply maximum pressure on the two defendants who were withholding confessions. To make certain Greenglass would stand by his confession in the courtroom, the prosecution came to an agreement with him that his wife would not be prosecuted.

When the anticipated confessions were not immediately forthcoming from Julius Rosenberg or Morton Sobell, J. Edgar Hoover persuaded Justice officials and the prosecutors to indict Ethel Rosenberg on the same capital charge as her husband. Her indictment, Hoover said, "might serve as a lever in this matter" with which to pry a confession from her husband.[160] According to one of Hoover's biographers, however, "Hoover and Ladd [D.M. Ladd, another high ranking FBI official] tacitly admitted there was no real case against Ethel."[161]

It fell to the chief assistant prosecutor, Roy Cohn, to enable Ethel Rosenberg's indictment. He promptly conferred with O. John Rogge, Greenglass' attorney, after which, Cohn wrote, he went to David Greenglass and told him

> that we knew he was protecting Ethel, and that unless he told us what *he* knew about her activities we could not guarantee that Ruth, his wife, would be safe from prosecution...Such was my message to him, and he responded with alacrity.[162]

Both Greenglasses agreed to testify that Ethel had typed up espionage information from David Greenglass to Julius Rosenberg, making her an accomplice in the conspiracy. The problem was, however, there was no credible evidence such information had ever been in David Greenglass' possession, or had ever been typed by Ethel Rosenberg. There was no evidence there had ever been originals of the "copies" or likenesses prepared for the trial by David Greenglass. Under cross-examination, he admitted he had made the copies in his cell, based entirely on his memory.

The evidence problem in respect to Ethel Rosenberg did not improve over time. An acknowledgment of this came one month before the trial, at a meeting of Justice officials with a Congressional Committee, where Myles Lane, an assistant prosecutor, told the meeting that

> The case is not too strong against Mrs. Rosenberg. But for the purpose of acting as a deterrent, I think it is very important that she be convicted, too, and given a stiff sentence.[163]

When, finally, it became clear to Justice officials that there would be no confession other than David Greenglass' and that they would have to go to trial, they apparently decided on the "two indictment" solution, described earlier. A formal indictment would charge the defendants with conspiring to commit espionage for the Soviet Union from1944–1950, with the last espionage act occurring in 1945; the extension to 1950 included a purported attempt in that year to flee the country. In the courtroom, however, an oral, inflammatory, indictment would charge the defendants with passing classified information relating to the atom bomb to the Soviet Union to enable it to launch an atom bomb attack on the United States during the Cold War. It was the prosecution's hope that the enormity of the oral indictment, with its evocative threat of pain and death confronting the jurors' families as a result of the defendants' treason, would mask the lack of actual evidence of the charges.

The likenesses of evidence...

Sobell's confession in 2008 made it clear that he, Julius Rosenberg, and David Greenglass did pass non-atomic classified information to the Soviet Union in the 1940s. One would think, then, his confession validated the evidence brought to court by the prosecution, at least to the extent that it applied to the formal indictment. But this was not the case.

The 32 Exhibits of evidence submitted to the court by the prosecution were, in respect to acts of espionage, likenesses of evidence the prosecution would have wanted to have, but didn't.

Exhibit 1. A copy of the security regulations at Los Alamos, New Mexico.

Exhibit 2. A copy of a sketch of a high-explosive lens mold drawn for the trial in 1951 by David Greenglass that he said was a duplicate of one he had drawn in 1945, six years earlier, which he testified he had given to Julius Rosenberg.

Exhibit 3. Photographs of Ann Sidorovich, a friend of the Rosenbergs, and her husband Michael. Ann Sidorovich's name would be mentioned by David Greenglass during his testimony. The Sidoroviches were on the prosecutors' witness list, but were not called to testify.

Exhibit 4. A box of Jell-O purchased by the prosecutors in 1951 for use at the trial, introduced as similar to a box of Jell-O the Greenglasses testified was in the Rosenbergs' apartment in January 1945.

Exhibits 4a & 4b. In the presence of the jurors, David Greenglass cut a Jell-O box side into two irregular halves, which he testified were similar to a Jell-O box panel cut in halves in the Rosenbergs' apartment in January 1945, one half given to the Greenglasses by Julius Rosenberg, that would match a portion of a Jell-O box panel half that Harry Gold would show to David Greenglass in Albuquerque, New Mexico.

Exhibit 5. A portrait photograph of Harry Gold from FBI files.

Exhibits 6 & 7. Two lens mold sketches drawn for use at the trial in 1951 by David Greenglass, both of them similar to two sketches he testified he had given to Harry Gold on June 3, 1945.

Exhibit 8. A sketch[164] and description[165] of the atom bomb David Greenglass prepared for the trial in 1951 that he testified were similar to a sketch and description he had made for Julius Rosenberg in 1945.

Exhibits 9a & 9b. David and Ruth Greenglass' photographs, described as "passport photographs." David Greenglass testified he had them taken at Julius Rosenberg's request and had given them to him, although they were never found to have been in the possession of the Rosenbergs or anyone directly or indirectly connected with them. Ten years after the trial, the authors of *Invitation to an Inquest*, a 1983 account of the trial, took copies of Exhibits 9a & 9b to the photography shop at which the photographs had been taken, and asked that the owner authenticate them. The owner said the Exhibit photos did not meet the dimension requirements to be passport photos; a subsequent effort by him to obtain the originals from the FBI failed because, he was told by the FBI, the Department of Justice had destroyed the originals.[166]

Exhibit 10. A brown manila paper wrapper said to have contained $4000 David Greenglass said he received from Julius Rosenberg. The FBI sent the paper wrapper to its identification laboratory, which reported it had found no fingerprints or other identifying clues on or in the wrapper.[167] The report was never made known to the defense or the jury.

Exhibit 11. A photograph of Anatoli Yakovlev from FBI files. Yakovlev was a Soviet consular official, to whom Harry Gold testified he passed classified information. Yakovlev left the United States in December 1946.

Exhibit 12. A photograph of Klaus Fuchs from FBI files.

Exhibit 13. A family photograph of David and Ruth Greenglass.

Exhibits 14a & 14b. Two halves of a sheet of paper Harry Gold testified were similar to two halves he had once been given by Yakovlev to be used to identify himself to other spies. The prosecutors made no claim that the Rosenbergs or Sobell or any one known to them were recipients of either of the halves or had ever met with anyone who had either of the halves.

Exhibit 15. A visa document from FBI files for Yakovlev, issued by the Immigration and Nationalization Service (INS).

Exhibit 16. A copy of a Hilton Hotel registration card for Harry Gold for June 2 or 3, 1945, the original of which the FBI claimed to have returned to the Hilton Hotel at its request. The original was therefore not available for comparison with the copy.

Exhibit 17. A copy of Ruth Greenglass' Albuquerque, New Mexico, bank account.

Exhibits 18a to Exhibit 18k. Morton Sobell's Selective Service file. The prosecutors did not claim there were any false or misleading statements by Sobell in the file.

Exhibits 19 & 20. Copies of directives from Los Alamos officials relating to the presence of physicist Neils Bohr and other prominent personnel at Los Alamos.

Exhibit 21. A card filled out at a Vera Cruz optical store where Morton Sobell had purchased a new set of glasses under the name 'M. Sand.'

Exhibits 22a & 22b. Morton Sobell's hotel registration in Vera Cruz, Mexico, in which he used the name 'Morton Sand.'

Exhibits 23a & 23b. Morton Sobell's hotel registration in Tampico, Mexico, in which he used the name 'Marvin Solt.'

Exhibits 24a & 24b. Mexican airlines registration cards for Morton Sobell, one for 'M. Sand' in a flight from Vera Cruz to Tampico, another for 'Morton Salt' in a flight from Tampico to Mexico City.

Exhibit 25. Copy of an Immigration and Naturalization Service (INS) official's entry card for Morton Sobell reading, in part, "circumstances of the departure of Sobell from Mexico to the United States."

Exhibits 26a to 26j. Relating to Yakovlev's sailing from the United States in December 1946, with details about his stateroom and family.

Exhibit 27. A collection can found in the Rosenbergs' apartment for raising funds for children orphaned during the Spanish Civil War of 1936-1939.

Exhibit 28. Photographs of several console tables the prosecutors claimed were "likenesses" of a console table Greenglasses testified had been adapted by Julius Rosenberg for espionage purposes. The console table itself was not introduced as evidence by the prosecution, although it had been available to the FBI.

Exhibit 29. A sketch of the Rosenbergs' apartment made by the prosecution and shown to Julius Rosenberg with a request that he point to where the console table had stood.

Exhibits 30a to 30d. Photographs of four wristwatches David Greenglass testified he believed the Rosenbergs had received from the Soviet Union by way of reward, and that had been taken by the FBI when they searched the Rosenbergs' apartment. None of the watches were entered as evidence.

Exhibit 31. A photostat of a 1939 petition for a place on the ballot for Peter Cacchione, a successful Communist candidate for New York City Council, signed by Ethel Rosenberg.

Exhibit 32. A photograph of a photography store a street away from the Foley Square courthouse, at which the prosecutors claimed, through the testimony of the owner, that the Rosenbergs had had passport photos taken in May or June 1950. Neither the passport photos nor negatives of them were introduced as exhibits.

Why likenesses instead of the real thing...?

The prosecution claimed it had to rely on likenesses of evidence of atomic espionage passed to the Soviet Union because the originals were in Moscow. In that case, there was only the word of the prosecution's chief witnesses, the Greenglasses, that there had ever been originals and that the originals had been given to Julius Rosenberg.

Let us assume the validity of the prosecution's claim. There were three means by which the originals would have found their way to Moscow. They could have been cabled in code to Moscow; they could have been sent to Moscow through a clandestine radio; they could have been brought to Moscow in person through the use of a privileged diplomatic pouch or by a clever personal courier.

The choice made by Moscow for information on the atom bomb is indisputably via encoded cable. The spy universally credited with having given the Soviet Union the most definitive and scientifically useful information about the development of the American atom bomb was Klaus Fuchs, an eminent German-born British physicist who worked at Harwell, the British atom bomb development center, and who also spent time working at the Los Alamos, NM atom bomb center. Fuchs fell under suspicion some time after June 1944, when a paper he had written on a phase of atomic bomb research, *Fluctuations and the Efficiency of a Diffusion Plant*, appeared nine days later in a cable to Moscow from New York, which had been decoded by the Venona/FBI Project.[168]

The Soviet Union's choice of cable for transmitting urgent and top priority information from espionage sources was dictated by the wartime situation. Neither ships nor planes could be depended on to reach their destinations. Transmission by clandestine radio was subject to a variety of problems, including natural or intentional interference. Finally, the Soviet espionage agencies used a two-tiered encryption system they believed was invulnerable.

Some 3000 cabled messages between the United States and the Soviet Union were decoded/translated by the Venona/FBI operation. Twenty of those messages alluded directly or indirectly to the Rosenbergs and Greenglasses, but none of these dealt with atomic espionage or any other specific areas of espionage. Julius Rosenberg and Morton Sobell were passing classified information to the Soviet Union, but the information was certainly not as described by Justice officials. It was neither so urgent nor important enough to warrant encoding and cabling, and was apparently conveyed by less than quick and reliable routes. Unlike the decoded cables involving Klaus Fuchs, those concerning the American defendants relate only to their educational attainments, their health, their political reliability, and their recommendations of other persons as possible sources of information.

If, as Justice officials told the public, the information passed by Rosenberg-Sobell was history-making and treasonable in magnitude, it would have been news to Soviet espionage officials. They did not did not think highly enough of the Rosenberg-Sobell operation to take great pains to conceal Julius Rosenberg's identity in their encoded cables to the Moscow espionage center. As the reader will find later, while other spies, like Fuchs, were never mentioned by their true names in the encoded cables, Ruth Greenglass' name and address appeared un-encoded in the otherwise encoded cables, as did Ethel Rosenberg's first name, her relation to David Greenglass, and the true names of several of Julius Rosenberg's associates. In short, by using real names of persons within the Rosenberg family and circle of friends in otherwise encoded messages, the Soviet espionage operation did not appear overly concerned that Julius Rosenberg's identity would be discovered.

If, as Justice officials claimed, the originals of the atom bomb sketches David Greenglass prepared for the trial were in Moscow, they would have been found among the 3000 decoded messages that contained the spectacularly authentic atom bomb information from Fuchs. The absence of cabled atomic-related infor-mation from Julius Rosenberg in any of the 3000 decoded cables makes it highly unlikely that he passed such information to the Soviet Union.

If we assume, nevertheless, there were originals bearing atomic informa-tion that could not be brought to court because they were in Moscow, how do we account for the prosecution's preference for bringing "likenesses" of other evidence to court when the originals were in their hands or were at an address known to them? Two examples: Exhibits 30a to 30d were photographs of watches David Greenglass testified were gifts to Julius Rosenberg from the Soviet Union. The prosecution had the original watches and could have produced them in court, which would have allowed the jurors to examine them. They brought pho-tographs of the watches, instead, which did not permit examination.

Likewise, Exhibit 28, a series of photographs of various console tables "like" a Rosenberg console table the Greenglasses' testified had been adapted for 35 mm photography of classified materials. The console table had been in the Rosenbergs' apartment on the two separate days Julius and Ethel Rosenberg were arrested, but was never confiscated by the FBI agents who searched the apart-ment. The clear explanation for the failure of the FBI agents to confiscate the console table they saw in the Rosenbergs' apartment was that it did not have the adaptations to it described by the Greenglasses. Nor did the photographic "like-nesses" of other console tables brought to court by the prosecution have such adaptations. The prosecution placed on the jurors the burden of imagining the claimed adaptations in the photographs shown them.

The only Exhibits of original items introduced by the prosecution were circumstantial evidence of an intent by Morton Sobell, when he was in Mexico with his family, to conceal his whereabouts. More on this later.

An evaluation of FBI Director J. Edgar Hoover's skill as a spy hunter by his close colleague and former assistant, William C. Sullivan, from Page 183 of his book, *The Bureau: My Thirty Years in Hoover's FBI.*

Espionage   183

the best examples of this inefficiency occurred early in World War II. One of our agents in the New York office got a phone call from a man who claimed to be a member of a Nazi sabotage squad. He said a group of them had landed off the coast of Long Island on the previous day from a German U-boat and he wanted to turn himself and the others in to the FBI. The agent laughed. "Yesterday Napoleon called," he told the desperate German and slammed down the phone. Somehow the German gathered up what was left of his courage and called back the next day. Luckily another agent answered the phone. When the newspapers wrote it up, the headlines read "FBI CAPTURES GERMAN SABOTEURS" and the story praised the bureau for its "brilliant investigative work."

When it came to the realities of espionage, J. Edgar Hoover was as much a head-in-the-clouds amateur as our legal attaché in Paris. He didn't believe that an agent of the FBI would ever defect or sell information to the enemy. I knew that the men in the FBI were human, though, and I always worried that their personal or financial problems could leave them vulnerable to our enemies. Hoover also put Capitol Hill off-limits for FBI surveillance. If an FBI agent had a Soviet or Czech or Rumanian agent under observation, he could follow his subject to the bottom of Capitol Hill but no further. Of course, once the Soviets and other eastern bloc agents caught on to Hoover's policy, Capitol Hill became their favorite place to meet. It was fortunate that Hoover never realized his ambition, which was to direct worldwide intelligence.

Washington and Moscow. The messages had been gathered by a United States Military Intelligence officer who kept them all through the war without telling anyone what he was doing. When the war ended, he told the FBI what he had. As soon as Hoover saw how many communications were involved, he realized that there was so much valuable material that he had to share some of it. He kept most

Chapter 4 | Spies in America

A clue to an American spy from a British spy...

The first credible proof of Soviet espionage at the United States atomic research and development centers came in January 1950, when Klaus Fuchs confessed to Britain's Scotland Yard that he had passed classified atomic weapons information to the Soviet Union in both Britain and the United States, and that he had been aided in the United States by an American courier whose identity Fuchs said he didn't know. He had given his British interrogators two clues to the courier: a physical description and a set of dates on which he had met with the courier in Boston, New York and Santa Fe, NM.

Fuchs had been an outspoken anti-Nazi and a Communist when Hitler came to power. There had been nightmares in young Fuchs' life, undoubtedly related to devastating emotional and psychological stresses caused by the danger to the family from the triumphant Nazis. His father, a prominent Protestant theologian, was imprisoned, his mother and a sister committed suicide.

Fuchs' father had been deeply troubled that many of his fellow-clergy were making their peace with the Nazi dictatorship. In a pamphlet, *Christ in Catastrophe*, Fuchs' father described a nightmare in which he saw his children murdered, and heard a voice that asked, *"What do you want? Shall they keep their lives by losing their conscience?"*[169]

After the Nazi consolidation of power, Fuchs fled Germany and made his way to Great Britain, where he began a career as a scientist. With the start of the war with Germany, he was rounded up as an enemy alien, and sent to a detention camp in Canada, where he was segregated for a time with detainees described as incorrigible Nazis. Intervention by his English friends and colleagues resulted in his return to Great Britain, where he was very shortly assigned to the Tube Alloys project, the code name for the British atomic bomb research establishment. Fuchs eventually became a British citizen.

In the Tube Alloys project Fuchs established himself as a first-rate scientist and a prolific author of scientific papers relating to important areas of work on the atom bomb. He traveled between Great Britain and the United States and was a member of the British mission involved with U.S. Atomic Energy Commission officials in discussions on the declassification of atomic information.

A bachelor, Fuchs was considered warm and genial, with none of the behavioral traits people sometimes retrospectively associate with unexpected criminal activity or pathology.

There are conflicting and controversial versions of why suspicion fell on Fuchs in 1949, or earlier. In one version, in 1949, the FBI had notified the British security forces that American code breakers had decrypted the classified scientific paper referred to in the previous section, after which suspicion fell on Fuchs as one of a number of suspects who might have passed the paper to the Soviets.

In another version, Fuchs had become concerned that his father, who had been offered a prestigious teaching post in Soviet-dominated East Germany in 1949, might be held hostage by the German Communists in an attempt to pry atomic information from Fuchs. Fuchs relayed his concern to the chief security officer at the British atomic energy research center, saying that he was considering resigning his post to discourage the East Germans from using his father as a hostage. That had alerted the British to the possibility that Fuchs had passed information to the Soviets in the past.

A third version was that about a year after Igor Gouzenko defected to the Canadians, the police found Fuchs' name and pre-war address in the home of Maurice Halperin, an American mathematician whose FBI dossier described him as a Communist and probable spy, but who was never tried for espionage or any other offense.

So far as is known, Fuchs was almost at once informed of the suspicion he was under in late 1949, but he was not formally arrested until February 2, 1950. He made his first confession on January 27, 1950, and a second one on January 30, 1950. Presumably the reason for the delay in arresting him was to permit British security forces to keep him under surveillance to determine whether he would contact other spies in the time he remained free. There were no indictments of other persons for espionage that followed from his surveillance.

For a number of months prior to his first confession, Fuchs met irregularly with William Skardon, a middle-aged veteran British security officer, who told Fuchs he knew he had been involved with the Soviets, and invited Fuchs to unburden himself of that part of his life.

A day came in January 1950, when Fuchs agreed he wanted to talk about his past actions and the dilemma in which he said he found himself. He admired the people of his adopted country, he found in their moderate ways an example he wanted to follow, and he wished to spend the rest of his life among them as a respected scientist. But he had given classified information to another country, to a recent ally that was now seen in some quarters as an enemy.

The names of the Rosenbergs or Sobell or the Greenglasses do not appear in any of Fuchs' statements.

Although Fuchs' espionage continued into the Cold War, he was not regarded by the British as a traitor. In March 1950, he was sentenced to 14 years imprisonment, and was released after serving nine years and four months, and subsequently became Deputy Director of the Institute for Nuclear Research near Dresden, East Germany.

That the FBI had had a dossier on Fuchs since at least 1944, but had not placed him under surveillance during his trips to the United States, was an embarrassment to FBI Director J. Edgar Hoover, with which he dealt by denying any knowledge of Fuchs when the matter was explored at an executive session of the Congressional Joint Atomic Energy Commission.[170] His denial was challenged by General Groves, whose security section had sent Fuchs' name to the FBI in 1943.[171] That the FBI was kept informed of Fuchs' movements is demonstrated in a July 2, 1946, letter to Hoover by Lt. Col. Charles H. Banks, a member of Groves' security section, advising Hoover that

> I wish to inform you that Dr. K. Fuchs returned to the United Kingdom on 28 June 1946 by bomber from Montreal.[172]

The FBI also seems to have been totally unaware of the American courier who regularly obtained classified information from Fuchs to be passed on to the Soviet Union.

Hoover requested that the British permit the FBI to interview Fuchs, but British security authorities refused until four months had passed. The FBI Director's reputation for contempt of foreign security agencies was being repaid.

Upon Fuchs' arrest and confession, Hoover ordered his agents to make an immediate search of the FBI's files for dissenters and Communists who would fit the description of the courier provided by Fuchs and who could have been in the cities on the dates Fuchs said he met with him.

According to Robert Lamphere, an FBI agent whose specialty was espionage, Fuchs' sister, who was a patient in a Massachusetts mental hospital, and her husband, had seen Fuchs' American courier in 1945 or 1946. They gave FBI agents a physical description of the man: "white male, age 40 to 45, five feet eight inches tall, dark-brown hair, broad build, round face."[173] Lamphere wrote that this description was checked against "that given by Fuchs himself, and it was a match."

On May 26, 1950, during one of the permitted interviews with Fuchs, his FBI interviewers learned that Fuchs had called the courier 'Raymond,' although this may not have been his true name, and they cabled the information to Hoover.[174]

In a *Reader's Digest* article by Hoover titled "Crime of the Century," written in 1950, before the Rosenberg-Sobell trial, but published in May 1951, two months after the trial, Hoover wrote that the FBI had conducted a diligent investigation of more than 1200 suspects who might have fit the physical description of "Raymond."[175]

Hoover's first candidate for "Raymond," according to his account, was James Davidson, who had the age and physical and professional attributes described for "Raymond." Hoover sent "photographs of many different individuals" and of Davidson to the British in March 1950, to show to Fuchs, who reportedly "rejected all except one - a picture of the man we call James Davidson."[176] But Hoover decided, in spite of Fuchs' identification of Davidson, that he was not "Raymond," possibly because Davidson could have proved he was elsewhere at the times he was supposed to have been meeting Fuchs.

The FBI continued to rake through its "Red" files, and eventually, Hoover wrote,

> one suspect was beginning to stand out. He was around 40, brown-haired and stocky, and while not a first-generation American he had come to the United States as a small child and might easily be mistaken for a native... His name was Harry Gold.[177]

However, Harry Gold had not been "from 40 to 45 years of age" when he was Fuchs courier and when his sister and brother-in-law had seen him. Gold, born in 1910, had been about 34 when Fuchs first met "Raymond" and about 36 when he saw him for the last time.

Gold was not "five feet eight inches tall, broad build, round face," as FBI agent Lamphere said he had learned from Fuchs' sister. Gold, according to his description in Hoover's *Reader's Digest* article, was a "little, five-foot six-inch" man."[178] The differences in the descriptions may have been due to inaccuracies in Fuchs' sister's perceptions, but Hoover was silent on this matter. It is possible that Fuchs had lied when he identified "Davidson" as "Raymond," but it was equally possible that Fuchs was lying when he subsequently identified Gold as "Raymond." Or that he had lied in both identifications. Since Gold eventually confessed to being "Raymond," that should have closed the matter, but Gold may have had other motives for confessing to being "Raymond" than actually being "Raymond."

"I am the man to whom Klaus Fuchs gave his information"...

Gold had been known to the FBI from at least 1947, when he and Abraham Brothman, a chemical engineer who was then Gold's employer, were summoned to testify before a grand jury by U.S. Attorney Irving Saypol on accusations made by Elizabeth Bentley, a former Communist who had named scores of persons as Communist spies, although none were ever convicted of espionage. To Saypol's disappointment, the grand jury declined to indict either Brothman or Gold.

According to Hoover's *Reader's Digest* account, beginning on May 15, 1950, Gold, who at that time was working as a chemist at a Philadelphia hospital, was interviewed several times by FBI agents on suspicion that he had been Fuchs' courier. He was able to identify Fuchs from newspaper photographs, but denied having ever met him.[179] Photographs and films were secretly made of Gold, and these were sent to the two FBI agents who, by that time, had been permitted to interview Fuchs.

On May 19, Gold was asked whether he would permit FBI agents to search his home, and he agreed. Inexplicably, however, the search was not made until May 22, giving Gold several days to destroy any evidence that would tie him to espionage or, alternatively, something had been found in an illegal search that required "laundering" by finding it again during a legal search or, alternatively, nothing had been found during an illegal search and something had been placed in his apartment by the FBI agents who would "discover" it when they made a legal search. These alternative explanations for the failure of the FBI agents to make a prompt search of Gold's home may also point to poor training in the handling of espionage suspects, a strong possibility based on a description of Hoover's "expertise" as a spy hunter by a long term colleague, William Sullivan, the FBI's Assistant Director for Intelligence, who wrote

> when it came to the realities of espionage, J. Edgar Hoover was…a head-in-the-clouds amateur.[180]

Hoover's amateurishness in espionage was not due entirely to his technical incompetence, but was an inevitable consequence of his intractable belief that spies for the Soviet Union would be found only among the ranks of liberals, dissenters, Communists, homosexuals, and other "deviants."

On May 22, the day the belated search was conducted, FBI agents said they found a map of Santa Fe in Gold's home, which appeared to contradict a statement Gold had made to the FBI to the effect that he had never been west of the Mississippi River. When the map was shown to Gold, Hoover wrote, "his mouth fell open." A few moments later, "Gold blurted out, 'I...I am the man to whom Klaus Fuchs gave his information.'"[181] Gold then agreed to permit photographic stills and motion picture films made of him, which were sent to the two FBI agents in London.

Less than an hour later, according to Hoover, "quite by coincidence"

> a cable from London was received at FBI headquarters in Washington, saying that Dr. Fuchs, after seeing the secretly taken movies, had identified Harry Gold as his American partner. Two days later, after viewing the movies made with Gold's cooperation, Fuchs was positive this was the man.[182]

On May 24, 1950, according to Robert Lamphere, who had shown photographs and motion pictures of Gold – and of no one else – to Fuchs, the latter had finally said, "Yes, that is my American contact." This was the same reply he had given when he had been shown photographs of James Davidson.

Harry Gold, persona 1...

Harry Gold lived, it might be said, in the shadow of his younger brother, Joseph. Joseph was tall, athletic, bright, and outgoing, while Harry was short, sickly, bright, and a loner, and an easy target of anti-Semitic bullies. Their father was a carpenter, and the family lived in one of the poorer sections of Philadelphia.

Harry Gold was an erratic student. He attended the University of Pennsylvania for a while, but left in mid-term 1932. Some time later, he was accepted by the Drexel School of Technology for evening study, and two years later was studying at Xavier, a Catholic university in Cincinnati, Ohio, from which he received a Bachelor of Science degree in June 1940.[183] By then, he was thirty years of age. His working life had begun in 1929, when he was nineteen, with the Pennsylvania Sugar Company, which he left 17 years later to work at a laboratory run by Abe Brothman. In 1942, Gold was classified 4F, unsuitable for military service by his draft board; by contrast, his brother Joseph was accepted into the armed forces, and earned three bronze stars while on duty in the South Pacific.

What the FBI knew of Gold in 1947 was that he was a bachelor who lived at home. He did not date, party or go to dances. He had one friend, Tom Black, a chemist who had once tried to recruit him into the Communist Party, but Gold had declined, saying that he didn't like Communists and "thought they were a lot of wacked-up bohemians."[184]

Gold related that in the fall of 1936, while working for the Pennsylvania Sugar Company, a man calling himself Paul Smith had suggested that "I might be interested in aiding the procurement of industrial information for the Soviet Union." Over a two-year period, Gold furnished Smith with "data concerning processes that were being worked on in the laboratory of the Pennsylvania Sugar Company and subsidiaries." Gold's engagement in industrial espionage, according to what he told the FBI, was not for financial or ideological reasons. He said, "Here, I would like to make the following statement: All of the expenses involved in any work that I did were paid for by me entirely out of my own funds."[185]

Gold appears to have been attracted to the secrecy and intrigue of spying. He also admitted to having stolen $600.00 worth of materials, over a two year period, from the sugar-refining firm.

Gold related that in July 1940, he was contacted by Jacob Golos, who managed Amtorg, the Soviet trading company in the United States. Gold agreed to provide Golos with information, but "it was pretty sporadic."

The Golos relationship did not last long. "I knew Golos for a very brief time, and he was followed very shortly by a man called Sam, about the end of 1940."

Gold was overstating the length of time he had known Golos, the truth being, as he subsequently told the FBI, he had never met Golos, according to a July 11, 1950, Justice Department memorandum

On May 22, 1950, following his arrest for espionage, Gold admitted that he had never known Golos, as he had previously testified before the grand jury.[186]

The man called 'Sam' told Gold "that there was not much purpose to continuing this work in general, and that the best thing I could do would be to forget about it." But after Germany attacked the Soviet Union in 1941, Gold said, Sam requested he resume his previous role as a spy. In early 1944, Sam told Gold that he was to embark on a project "of so critical a nature that I was to think twice and three times before I ever spoke a word concerning it to anyone or before I made a move."

Harry Gold, persona 2...

There was another Harry Gold persona, stranger than the one originally described in the FBI's files.

Gold had told Brothman, his employer, that about a dozen years earlier he had met and fallen in love with a woman named Helen, who had "one brown eye and one blue eye." He lost Helen to Frank, a wealthy man whose uncle owned a peanut-chew factory. Through Helen he had met Sarah, a "comely, good looking" model at Gimbels' Department store in Philadelphia. He had a rival for Sarah's affections, a pimp who wanted to turn her into a prostitute. To save Sarah from the pimp, Gold married her. Sarah gave birth to twins, Essie and David. Gold bought a house for the family. David developed polio, but recovered. In 1945, Brothman offered Gold a job in New York, but Gold declined it because Sarah did not want to leave Abington, the Philadelphia suburb in which they lived. Because Gold had to travel a great deal, he and Sarah grew apart, and Sarah began an affair with "an elderly, rich real estate broker." The family broke up and Gold moved out of the house. Gold would go to Abington to secretly watch Essie and David play in the park, because it was too painful for him to visit them in their home. He was also deeply affected by the wartime death of his brother, Joseph, during a parachute jump in New Guinea. To replace Joseph, Gold's parents took in a cousin whose name was also Joseph.[187]

The FBI checked these hitherto unknown events in Harry Gold's history, and established beyond any doubt that there had been no Helens or Sarahs or pimps or Essies or Davids in Gold's life. He never had a spousal home. There was no elderly real estate broker alienating the affections of a non-existent Sarah, His brother Joseph was alive and well.

Gold was very proud of the imaginative and elaborate fantasies he created for himself. (Once, under cross-examination at his trial in November 1950, he said, "It is a wonder that steam didn't come out of my ears at times."[188])

Just as he had fabricated a romantic and parental life, he fabricated, sometimes absurdly, elements of his life as a spy, and continued to do so even during his prison years. In 1965, in his fifteenth year of imprisonment, he wrote an 89-page letter to a member of his attorney's law firm about *Invitation to an Inquest*, a book on the Rosenberg-Sobell case.[189] In his letter, he describes an event involving an exchange of purses by two spies (to which he never testified in court), which he describes as

> an old, old dodge; I may even have invented it.[190]

He complained that *Invitation to an Inquest* contained an

> overwhelming mass of factual and circumstantial items to demonstrate that I am a weirdly twisted creature, one who could most easily confuse self-created fantasy with reality - or could be led that way.[191]

Gold tells his attorney not to challenge any accusations made against him...

After the FBI obtained Gold's self-identification as "Raymond," he was arrested on the capital charge of conspiring to commit espionage for the Soviet Union. The indictment for conspiring, rather than for committing espionage, was a tacit acknowledgment that neither the FBI, nor Gold in his confessions, had provided any tangible evidence of espionage.

At his appearance in court, Gold told the judge he had no attorney and wanted one appointed for him who had no radical connections. On the following day, June 1, 1950, the court provided him with attorney John D.M. Hamilton, a former chairman of the National Committee of the Republican Party.

We know from a Justice memorandum of June 19, 1950, that attorney Hamilton had told Gold he didn't think the prosecution could make a *prima facie* case against him "based solely on an uncorroborated confession" but, to Hamilton's surprise, Gold instructed him not to challenge the charges made against him by the prosecution, thus freeing the prosecution from the obligation of producing proof of any act attributed to him.[192]

There was now a *quid pro quo* agreement between Gold and the prosecution. Gold would confess to crimes for which Justice lacked evidence, implicating others in a conspiracy to commit espionage for which the prosecutors also lacked evidence. In return, the prosecution would not ask for the death penalty for Gold.

In court, on Gold's instructions, Hamilton said

> I would be perfectly willing on behalf of the defendant to accept any statement of the crime that he [the prosecutor] might make, without supporting evidence.[193]

The spy who knew no spies...

Gold seemed eager to erase any doubts the prosecution might have of his willingness to cooperate, essentially because he did not want to die, and possibly because something totally unexpected and irresistible was waiting for him: the prospect of historic immortality. The names of Fuchs and Gold would be eternally and inseparably interwoven in the written histories of events that had affected the future of nations. He had been a minor spy for well over a decade, mainly for the excitement of it, even paying his own expenses, and here he was, suddenly thrust on the international stage as a world-class spy, partnered with a world-class scientist. This was real life, more exciting than any of his daydreams and fantasies.

As for corroboration of Gold's confession that he was "Raymond," Fuchs would be his silent corroborator. Fuchs had, in his confession, given the approximate dates on which he had met "Raymond" in New York, Boston and Santa Fe. As mentioned, Gold had ordered his attorney to accept as true any acts the prosecution would attribute to Gold, which would have included Gold being present in the cities on the dates Fuchs had said he met his courier.

More was wanted of Gold than his agreement that he was "Raymond." Having been part of the Soviet Union's spy apparatus in the United States for fourteen years, the names of other American spies for whom he had been a courier were expected from him. Press releases from the Justice Department promised sensational exposures and trials based on what Gold would reveal. But the name of only one indictable suspect crossed his lips, and this suspect could not be indicted for espionage because neither Gold nor the FBI provided any evidence to support such a charge. Instead, the suspect was indicted for perjury for denying he knew Gold was a spy. The trial jury acquitted him.[194]

Justice officials were not pleased.

Gold's stubborn refusal to identify himself as a Communist or a 'leftist' of any kind was another disappointment. Instead, Gold described himself as an *anti*-Communist. This was unsatisfactory to Hoover and other Justice officials. The Congressional investigating committees and the media wanted the prefix 'Communist' to accompany 'spy.' Without that pejorative label, there was no political capital to make of Gold's confession. A spy who was simply a spy was, in the political climate of the time, unproductive. A spy who could be called a *Communist* spy was proof that there were legions of American traitors in the service of the Soviet Union. A *Communist* spy was also a resource to be mined for the names and activities of other Communist spies, each of which could become a new source for the exposure of new spies. There seemed no logical reason why a man who confessed to a capital crime on behalf of the Soviet Union would not confess to being a Communist.

Hoover solved the problem by confessing on Gold's behalf what Gold would not confess himself. Hoover declared Gold to have been a Communist, writing of Gold in the *Reader's Digest*

> Although too late he had come at last to see that Communism had robbed him of the conscience of a free American, completely paralyzing his power of moral resistance. No spiritual force was left within him to stay his deeds of treason.[195]

One cannot rule out Gold as "Raymond," nor can one rule out that the role of "Raymond" was given to him by Hoover, who may have shared with other officials an assumption that it did not matter whether a specific allegation fit a specific "Communist" because such people, like habitual criminals, were capable of any crimes with which they were charged.

From Harry Gold to David Greenglass...

On June 2, 1950, according to FBI accounts, Gold provided the agency with a connective thread that would lead to David Greenglass. On that day Gold recounted a May 1945, conversation he said he'd had with his Russian controller, 'John,' about an appointment with Klaus Fuchs in Santa Fe in June 1945. During their conversation, 'John'

> supplied me with a name and address of a man in Albuquerque, New Mexico, and instructed me to contact this man while I was there. I believe JOHN told me to contact the man's wife in case the man was not there. JOHN told me that I would receive information from this man, which I was to deliver to JOHN. JOHN gave me an envelope containing about $500. I was instructed to give this money to the man in Albuquerque in payment for the information.[196]

According to the FBI's account, Gold went on to say he had met the man, an army machinist, in June 1945, but could not recall the man's name.

A date-deleted FBI memorandum indicates that on June 15, 1950 (the day of David Greenglass' arrest), photographs were shown "to HARRY GOLD in Philadelphia and that HARRY GOLD identified the photograph of DAVID GREENGLASS and RUTH GREENGLASS standing in front of a porch of a house in Albuquerque, New Mexico" and that Gold wrote on the back of the photograph that this was the man he contacted in Albuquerque "on instructions from his Soviet espionage superior 'JOHN.'"[197]

Gold's identification of David Greenglass, in June 1950, was not, however, when Greenglass first came to the attention of the FBI. Four months earlier, in February 1950, FBI agents interviewed Greenglass in his apartment in New York City, either on suspicion of espionage, or of black market dealings when he had worked at Los Alamos. Neither Greenglass nor the FBI ever disclosed the reason for the interview.[198]

SECRET   6

We feel that because—and it is my personal conviction, and
this morning I checked with the Department, and they agreed—
that the only thing that will break this man Rosenberg is the
prospect of a death penalty or getting the chair, plus that if
we can convict his wife, too, and give her a stiff sentence of
25 or 30 years, that combination may serve to make this fellow
disgorge and give us the information on these other individuals.
I can't guarantee that.

   The Chairman. He is pretty tough, isn't he?

   Mr. Lane. It is about the only thing you can use as a lever
on those people.

   The Chairman. In other words, what you are saying is that

   The Chairman. In other words, what you are saying is that
you think what you want to do is have Greenglass divulge some
now secret information on the chance that the death penalty would
then result to Rosenberg.

   Mr. Lane. Yes.

   The Chairman. Now, the question is—which Mr. Dean has
spoken to—the material we are going to give is not in your
opinion and in the opinion of the Military Liaison Committee,
prejudicial.

   Mr. Dean. We are convinced the Russians have it. It is
generally not the dimensions but the rough shape of the HE,
the number of detonators, that there is an initiator and it has
beryllium in it. We don't know—with very clever cross examina-

From Page 6 of the secret minutes of a February 8, 1950 meeting of Department of Justice officials, members of the Congressional
Joint Committee on Atomic Energy, and officials of the Atomic Energy
Commission. Justice officials in this meeting sought tacit Congressional
approval to coach David Greenglass by giving him "now secret" information, which he would claim in his testimony to have given Julius Rosenberg,
although he could not have had this information in 1944-45. Approval was
given, thus enabling and encouraging him to give perjured testimony.

Chapter 5 | On the eve of trial

Two logical questions...

In view of Sobell's 2008 confession, isn't the matter of evidence moot?

It would be moot if the issue was simply the guilt or innocence of the defendants. As we have shown, however, there were two indictments – a written, official indictment charging conspiracy to commit espionage without any allusion to an intent to injure the United States, and an oral one charging the defendants with intending the greatest harm imaginable: treason. Sobell's 2008 statements support the major portion of the official indictment, but the guilty verdicts, in the words of the prosecution, the judge and the jurors, were based on the charge of treason.

For which of these indictments was evidence presented? If evidence was introduced supporting the official indictment in which no intent to injure the United States was charged, how do we account for the prosecution's oft-repeated charge of treason in the courtroom? If evidence was introduced to support the treason charge, it is nowhere in the trial record. Under these circumstances, Sobell's 2008 confession hardly makes the absence of evidence moot.

Among those in Congress who knew the evidence the prosecution would bring to the trial, its quality was considered unremarkable, and remained so even after Congress gave the prosecution an opportunity to enhance it.

In the eight months that had passed since the first arrests in the Rosenberg-Sobell case, the history of Soviet atomic espionage had begun to take on a recognizable order. There were important dates on which, from an analysis of the activities of several major scientists and others involved in espionage, the Soviet Union had received classified information on gaseous diffusion, plutonium production piles, implosion techniques and other vital processes for creating atomic weapons. A hierarchy of spies was beginning to emerge, based on their contributions to the Soviet atomic weapons program.

The Congressional Joint Committee on Atomic Energy (JCAE) was preparing to issue a 222-page appraisal of Soviet espionage, in which it would rate the importance to the Soviet Union of a number of individual spies. In April 1951, shortly after the Rosenberg-Sobell trial ended, the report was finalized and printed. Klaus Fuchs led the list, followed by Bruno Pontecorvo, an Italian physicist, Allan Nunn May, and David Greenglass. The latter three, according to the appraisal, "all rank well below Fuchs in importance."[199] The appraisal stated that, "Fuchs alone has influenced the safety of more people, and accomplished greater damage than any other spy, not only in the history of the United States, but in the history of nations."

The combined espionage of the four spies, the appraisal went on, enabled the Soviet Union to achieve its atomic goal "at least 18 months" sooner than if it had not had their assistance. This was reasonably close to estimates by many scientists. It was far less, however, than the politically-driven estimates of many in government. In July 1945, for example, Gen. Leslie Grove, then head of the atom bomb project, attempted to insert a prediction into a speech by President Truman that it would take "10 to 25 years" for any other nation to develop an atom bomb.[200] The President declined the prediction. (The reader will recall that in his first-strike scenario for the War Department in 1946, Groves assumed the Soviets would have their own atom bomb not in "10 to 25 years" but in two years.)

Since they would have been consulted by those who wrote the JCAE appraisal, Justice officials and the prosecutors would have, at the least, suspected that the JCAE regarded David Greenglass, the Rosenbergs, and Morton Sobell as low in importance among Soviet spies. In a direct reference to the Rosenbergs, the appraisal observed that among their espionage activities, "none relate directly to atomic energy, except as they focus through Greenglass, who is Ethel Rosenberg's brother."[201] Unlike Fuchs, Pontecorvo, May, Greenglass, and Gold, the Rosenbergs and Sobell were not even listed in the appraisal's Table of Contents.

An objective pre-trial view of the Rosenberg-Sobell case would not have encouraged its elevation to the world stage.

The Greenglass dilemma...

Very early on, Justice officials knew Greenglass would be a troublesome witness. Shortly after his arrest, but before Julius Rosenberg's arrest, an undated, handwritten Justice Department memorandum signed by "G.F.K." commented that Greenglass' statements did not warrant Rosenberg's arrest:

> There is presently not sufficient evidence on which to arrest Rosenberg and Mrs. Greenglass. As to Rosenberg, we have only Greenglass' statement which he probably will repudiate. As I recall, Gold didn't implicate Greenglass.[202]

The source of G.F.K.'s concern that Greenglass might retract his implication of Julius Rosenberg was an FBI memorandum, date deleted, with the information that "Greenglass stated that under no circumstances would he testify against Rosenberg."[203]

Even more troublesome was the prospect of David Greenglass' anticipated testimony regarding the atom bomb. He told the FBI and the prosecution that the only classified information he had obtained was data given to him by a junior scientist for whom he had machined a lens mold. He had not stolen any diagrams, blueprints, photographs, reports or other classified documents. He had not obtained access to secret rooms, cabinets or files. He had not attended any scientific or engineering conferences or seminars or discussions at the Los Alamos atomic energy center. Instead, he told the prosecutors, he eavesdropped on conversations in the machine shop and locked them in his memory. To access what he had heard, he delved "into the recesses of my mind and brought it forth and put it down on paper."[204] He did not explain how he acquired the knowledge to assemble the bits of information he obtained through eavesdropping into sketches of a completed, working atom bomb.

It was clear to the prosecutors that Greenglass' *modus operandi* was not likely to allow him access to high level classified information about the atom bomb. Less, in fact, than what had been published under government auspices in August 1945, within days of the Hiroshima-Nagasaki bombings. *Atomic Energy for Military Purposes,* written by H. D. Smyth, a scientist involved in the research and development of the atom bomb, made clear that all the scientific information needed for developing an atom bomb was known to the international scientific community as far back as 1940. Smyth wrote

> Looking backward on the year 1940, we see that all the prerequisites to a serious attack on the problem of producing atomic bombs and controlling atomic power were at hand.[205]

The prosecutors were concerned that Greenglass' description of his espionage techniques might not impress the jurors, especially when they learned the result of his attempt to improve his skills at a technical school. On cross-examination, he would certainly be asked what grades he had gotten in his upgrade courses, and Greenglass would have to testify he failed them all.[206]

And, finally, Greenglass told the prosecution he had never been present when Rosenberg had passed information on to someone else. He testified that on one occasion Rosenberg introduced him to a Russian man, who queried him about the lens molds during a car ride in Manhattan

> Greenglass: He wanted to know the formula of the curve on the lens; he wanted to know the H.E. [high explosive] used, and means of detonation; and I drove around —
>
> The Court: And what, means of detonation?
>
> The Witness: That's right; and I drove around, and being very busy with my driving, I didn't pay too much attention to what he was saying, but the things he wanted to

know, I had no direct knowledge of and I couldn't give a
positive answer.[207]

Greenglass testified that at some point the man got out of the car and went
off with Julius Rosenberg. Greenglass was unable to give a description of the man.

The prosecution looks for another candidate for confession...

As matters stood after the arrest of Julius Rosenberg, who had been
expected to corroborate Greenglass' confession, the prosecution lacked any other
witness to corroborate the latter's anticipated confession.

To find such a witness, FBI searched their "disloyal" files for Julius
Rosenberg's engineering school classmates. They found two Rosenberg class-
mates who had been Communists. One of them, Max Elitcher, had been mentioned by his true name in a Venona message, the text of which indicated that
Julius Rosenberg had visited Elitcher in Washington, D.C. in July 1944. According
to FBI memoranda, Elitcher told the FBI he had been approached by Rosenberg
several times to join a spy ring, but he had never agreed to do so. He also told the
FBI Rosenberg told him Sobell was also involved in espionage.

Elitcher agreed to testify for the prosecution and was never indicted,
although he confessed, to the FBI, and at the trial, that he had falsely stated in a
Loyalty Oath he had never been a Communist. His testimony, although useful,
was a step removed from what was needed — confession from another member
of the conspiracy.

The other classmate was Morton Sobell, who was arrested shortly after
Ethel Rosenberg was indicted. Sobell declared his innocence.

Justice officials now had three defendants who would not confess — the
Rosenbergs and Sobell — and were compelled to repeatedly file requests to the
court for adjournment of trial dates. August, September, October, November,
December 1950 and January and February 1951, passed before the officials
accepted the reality of the situation: the anticipated confessions would not be
forthcoming.

"Sanitizing" the spectacle...

When Justice officials realized they had no choice but to go to trial, they
had to confront the troublesome spectacle of an all-Jewish cast of defendants.

The instant reaction by the largest Jewish daily newspaper in the country, the *Forward*, to the arrest of David Greenglass, must have come as a
surprise to Justice officials. The *Forward*, one of the most vocal anti-Communist and anti-Soviet newspapers in the nation, offered him legal assistance. The only explanation for the *Forward*'s offer of support to Greenglass
was that its editors perceived anti-Semitism lurking in the shadows.

To make matters worse, Justice officials must have known from their sources in the Soviet Union that preparations had been underway in Moscow and some of its satellite states, since 1948, for espionage-treason trials in which all or most of the defendants would be Jewish. The wisdom of staging a similar ethnic spectacle in the United States was questionable.

Another problem was that, in mid-20th Century, the Holocaust was very fresh in memory, and everyone knew a key German justification for the Holocaust had been that Jews, by their nature, conducted themselves as spies and traitors in whatever country they resided.

It does not appear from the available documentation that any of the Justice officials directly involved in selecting the prosecutors in the Rosenberg-Sobell case were Jewish, although a few years after the executions, when articles critical of the trial began to appear in non-Communist periodicals and in books by mainstream publishers, a Justice official who was Jewish was assigned to reply to the critics.[208]

Since it was apparent to Justice officials that other sections of the public, Jewish and non-Jewish, might react as the *Forward* had, the supervising Justice officials undertook to "sanitize" the situation by choosing to try the case in New York, where they could put together a team of four prosecutors, two of whom, including the chief prosecutor, would be Jewish. This decision was finalized in late September 1950, or afterward, according to a letter to U.S. Attorney Saypol from the Assistant Attorney General.[209] The judge at the trial would be Federal Judge Irving Kaufman, who was Jewish, and who had actively sought the assignment.

But there were imponderables, one of which was a small possibility that placing the trial in the federal courthouse in New York City's Foley Square, not far from the Lower East Side's Jewish ghetto, where 300,000 Jews lived within a square mile of tenements and near-tenements, might result in street protests. Most of the ghetto inhabitants were immigrants; they had come to America to get away from anti-Semitism. There was nothing meek about them. And there was also the possibility that among the 1.7 million Jews in the city who lived outside the Ghetto, there would be a fair number who might also erroneously equate a cast of all-Jewish defendants with ethnic prejudice. And there was the problem that one or more Jews on the jury might wonder whether there might be a flaw in FBI espionage-treason investigations that turned up only Jewish suspects.

On the other hand, the leaders of major Jewish organization were making no protest about the arrests, and it was likely that ethnic loyalty would not extend to Communist Jews.

There would have also been imponderables if Albuquerque, NM, the jurisdictional venue for federal crimes committed at Los Alamos, had been chosen for the trial. Actually, the first indictment in the case had been issued in Albuquerque. But a jury of New Mexico citizens might be even less readable than a jury of New

Yorkers. Twenty years earlier, New Mexico voters had elected a Jewish governor. So had New York voters, but that was hardly a surprise.

A promise to Greenglass, quickly broken...

David Greenglass was also moody, resistant, unpredictable, and intractable at times, and frequently demanded the right to consult with his wife before finalizing his agreements and statements. As a result, the prosecution's treatment of him varied from harsh to considerate, going so far at one point that he was led to believe he would not be named a defendant at the trial or, if this could not be arranged, that he would be given a suspended sentence for his role in the conspiracy.

The defense attorneys became indirectly aware of the prosecution's problem with Greenglass because of superseding indictments Saypol had drawn up. Ordinarily, superseding indictments reflect new information and new defendants, but in this case they also reflected stages in the negotiations between the prosecution and David and Ruth Greenglass, as well as with Harry Gold and Max Elitcher.

Until August 17, 1950, David Greenglass had been named a defendant in every indictment drawn up by the U.S. Attorney in Albuquerque, NM, and by Saypol in New York. An indictment on that date altered Greenglass' status to "co-conspirator," which meant that, unlike his status in previous indictments as a defendant, he would not be on trial alongside the Rosenbergs and Sobell, and would not be subject to a jury verdict or sentencing. His wife would not be tried at all.

The defense attorneys regarded this sudden leniency toward the Greenglasses in the August indictment as a sign of the prosecution's uncertain control of the couple, as well as of the Greenglasses' distrust of the prosecution. As David Greenglass later confessed, the prosecutors had compelled him to give perjured testimony against the Rosenbergs.[210] It undoubtedly occurred to Greenglass that if the prosecutors wanted to seal his lips afterward, they might recommend he be given a death sentence. The August 17 indictment would have been written to allay his fears by removing him as a defendant. The truth was, of course, the prosecution could have tried Greenglass and his wife separately at a later trial.

Emanuel Bloch, the attorney for the Rosenbergs, at once informed Federal Judge T. Hoyt Davis that David Greenglass' new status as a co-conspirator instead of defendant, was proof that Greenglass' confession was suspect because it had been obtained by a deal that spared his life by putting the Rosenbergs' lives at risk. Bloch wanted a formal hearing on the matter.

Saypol may not have foreseen how transparent his alteration of Greenglass' status would be, and he promptly instructed assistant prosecutor Myles Lane to do something to ward off Bloch's threat to litigate the removal of Greenglass as a defendant.

Lane quickly arranged for a meeting on August 23, 1950, with two partners of O. John Rogge, the Greenglasses' attorney. One of the partners described in a memo what then transpired.

> [Lane] told us that Bloch had earlier in the day argued to the judge at the arraignment of his clients that they were absolutely innocent and that from the fact that Greenglass was not indicted but merely named as a co-conspirator in the New York indictment, it looked to Bloch as if the government had made a deal with you as Greenglass' attorney. Lane felt that we would now have to consider the question of whether it was OK that Greenglass be indicted here in a superseding indictment and not merely named as a co-conspirator. He would then be a defendant and be tried here in New York but would testify against the others. HJF [Herbert J. Fabricant, a Rogge partner] told Lane...that it would seem that such an arrangement would probably be approved by OJR [Rogge].[211]

The new situation, created by Bloch's threat to pursue the Saypol-Greenglass arrangement in the courts, compelled Saypol to renege on his agreement not to try Greenglass on the capital charge of conspiracy. In short, the one-time defendant, now only a co-conspirator, would have to become a defendant again, a drastic change of status.

Shortly after the meeting referred to above, one of the Rogge firm lawyers gave Ruth Greenglass the bad news, and reported to Rogge her disappointment

> that Dave may not get a suspended sentence and is worried about the kind of treatment he will get.[212]

It is clear, from the phrase "Dave may not get a suspended sentence," that Greenglass had been told by the prosecution, prior to Bloch's threat to pursue the August 17 "deal" indictment, that an attempt would be made to reduce his penalty to a suspended sentence, a promise Saypol later made clear he had never intended to keep. At David Greenglass' sentencing, he told the court

> Mr. Saypol: I recommend that the defendant be imprisoned for a term of 15 years.[213]

Although Bloch could not have known that Saypol had held out hope of a suspended sentence to David Greenglass at the time, he was determined to thwart any deal in any way possible.

Greenglass' attorney under indictment...

Surprisingly, the Greenglasses' attorney, O. John Rogge, did not challenge the change of David Greenglass' status from co-conspirator to codefendant, a failure that may have reflected a unique situation — a major conflict of interest — confronting Rogge, a former U.S. Attorney.

Justice officials with whom Rogge negotiated on behalf of the Greenglasses were, in that same year, preparing to bring Rogge and other individuals to trial on the grounds that, as officials of a peace organization, they had failed to register as "subversives."

Four years earlier, Rogge, then a Special Assistant to the U.S. Attorney General, had publicly revealed the close wartime association of a number of prominent American oil businessmen and a Montana senator with the recently defeated Nazi government, following which the Attorney General fired Rogge for making an unauthorized disclosure of illegal wartime trading with the enemy.[214] Subsequently, Rogge, a firm anti-Communist, became identified with former Vice President Henry Wallace's advocacy of an extension of the wartime alliance of the allied powers, including the Soviet Union, and of adherence to the Constitution in legislation related to national security. Rogge also began to represent African-Americans and other people not in the mainstream of American life, and even at one time had been co-counsel with Emanuel Bloch in defending six African-American men in Trenton, New Jersey, who had been charged in 1949 with murder. In March of 1950, Rogge also became an attorney for the anti-Stalinist Tito government, and had registered as an attorney for that country.

The 1950 indictment against Rogge involved the violation of a statute requiring the officers of organizations listed by the Attorney General as subversive to register with the Department of Justice. Rogge was an officer of the World Peace Council, a listed organization. Rogge's codefendant would be W.E.B. DuBois, also an officer of the Council, a world-famous African-American scholar and historian in his eighties, a founder of the NAACP, known internationally also as a sociologist and philosopher. DuBois had support in his defense from educators, intellectuals, writers and other groups in the United States and abroad.

If found guilty, Rogge and DuBois faced imprisonment of up to five years and a fine of $10,000. Rogge also faced disbarment, and the loss of his status and identity in the legal and political milieu in which he was a recognized force.

Rogge's role on the World Peace Council was not clear. He was not in complete agreement with its views, which he felt were often partial to the Soviet Union, and he was expressing his differences with the Soviet Union publicly.

At some point before the trial of Rogge and DuBois, which took place in November 1951, after the Rosenberg-Sobell trial, Rogge agreed to become the prosecution's chief witness against Dubois.

It was undoubtedly foreseeable to Rogge that his status as a defendant in the registration case might be said to influence his representation of his clients in the Rosenberg-Sobell case.

Support for such an inference could be drawn from his decision not to resist the new indictment by Saypol that would change David Greenglass' status from co-conspirator to codefendant in a capital case.

Rogge may have signaled his intent to be agreeable to Justice officials as early as ten days after becoming the Greenglasses' attorney, according to a June 28, 1950, memorandum from Assistant Attorney General James M. McInerney, in which he recounted a discussion on June 26, 1950, with Rogge, after the latter had held a meeting with an FBI official. McInerney wrote

> Mr. Rogge stated, "I have had occasion to criticize my country several times in the past five years but I believe that my country is entitled to protection against the commission of espionage and I am going to see that it receives that protection insofar as it is consistent with my representation of my client in this case." He repeated the first part of this quotation on two or three occasions during the interview and seemed to derive some pleasure from its patriotic sound.[215]

McInerney's comment on Rogge's patriotism may have been triggered, not by Rogge's remarks, but by Rogge having blown the whistle on corporations that were illegally, if not actually treasonably, trading with World War II enemies of the United States, which many Justice officials were aware of, but about which they had chosen to remain silent.

Justice officials could take no satisfaction from Rogge's testimony against Dubois, at their trial in November 1951, at which Gloria Agrin, who had assisted Bloch in his defense of the Rosenbergs, was chief defense counsel. At a memorable moment, Rogge was asked by the prosecution to identify DuBois in the courtroom. He hesitated for a few moments, at which point DuBois stood up and said, "Here I am."[216]

Federal Judge James McGuire subsequently told the prosecution it had made a poor case and he directed the jurors to acquit the defendants.

Attorney Rogge will reappear later in an action that may have been intended to aid the defense in its appeals.

A Congressional committee gives the green light to suborn perjury...

Since he had not stolen any secret documents or other materials to pass on to Julius Rosenberg and Harry Gold, Greenglass would have to demonstrate that his eavesdropping enabled him to comprehend the design and functions of the components of the atom bomb, however roughly, and to render them in sketches and explanatory text. He would not have to be accurate in the sketches and explanations he would testify he prepared, since the indictment was for conspiracy to pass the information, rather than for doing so accurately. But, if the information was shown on cross-examination to be grossly inaccurate, or if a lingering doubt remained regarding his capacity to understand the structure and function of the bomb, one or more jurors might question his credibility. A single juror who doubted Greenglass' credibility would be enough to produce a hung jury.

Justice officials asked Atomic Energy Commission (AEC) experts to evaluate Greenglass' comprehension of the information he said he had overheard. The experts spent six hours with Greenglass, and on February 6, 1951, the AEC Director of Classification wrote, "We do not believe that Greenglass is very well informed", and that his technical information was limited.[217]

Justice officials promptly took a step that, in the past, has been interpreted as simply a means of ensuring that if Greenglass inadvertently revealed any atomic information at the trial presumably not already known to the Soviet Union, Justice officials and the prosecution would not be faulted as lax in respect to national security.

Two days after receiving the experts' report, Justice officials and Atomic Energy Commission officials met with members of the Congressional Joint Committee on Atomic Energy (JCAE) to seek their protection, in the event it was needed. The members of the JCAE agreed that the trial was of the greatest importance and that no effort should be spared to obtain guilty verdicts and death sentences against the Rosenbergs so that they would confess and reveal the entire scope and personnel of the spy ring. After hearing from Justice and AEC officials what David Greenglass' testimony was likely to include, the JCAE agreed that the risk of transmitting new information to the Soviet Union was minimal and worth taking, and that the JCAE would support Justice and AEC officials if any criticism of them arose in respect to safeguarding national security.[218]

There is another explanation for the meeting with the JCAE, but of a less benign character. The AEC experts' report cited above made it unlikely that Greenglass' unsatisfactory grasp of the workings and construction of the atom bomb would lead him to disclose anything new or useful to the Soviet Union in his testimony. A careful reading of the minutes of the February 8 meeting, held one month before the start of the trial, supports the less benign view of its purpose: it was to gain the assent of the JCAE for AEC experts to enable Greenglass' testimony to convey to the jurors the impression that his atom bomb sketches had been a virtual blueprint for making an atom bomb. To accomplish this, Greenglass would have to be coached — that is, enabled to claim he had passed on to Julius Rosenberg more information than he had had in 1944-1945.

Since Greenglass was certain to be asked on cross-examination whether he had been coached, he would have to perjure himself with a denial. It was also possible that AEC officials might be subpoenaed and would likewise have to deny any knowledge of coaching.

The purpose of the February 8 meeting with the JCAE, then, was to obtain a promise of protection if the suborned perjuries were discovered. The request would have to be worded very carefully, and the word 'coaching' would never be uttered.

Among those present at the February 8 meeting were Myles Lane for Justice, Gordon Dean for the AEC, and Senators and Representatives in the leadership of the JCAE.

Lane and Dean began by telling the JCAE leaders that it was of the utmost importance that Julius Rosenberg receive a death sentence at the trial. Dean said

> In order to convict Rosenberg, and particularly to get
> the death penalty imposed… Greenglass will have to
> from the stand reveal certain information that he passed
> on to Rosenberg.[219]

Rosenberg was described as "the keystone to a lot of other potential espionage agents,"[220] the "key to the whole picture. He is the cornerstone,"[221] and,

> Rosenberg is the king pin of a very large ring, and if
> there is any way of breaking him by having the shadow
> of a death penalty over him, we want to do it.[222]

The importance of Julius Rosenberg as an espionage agent was, in the minds of JCAE members, nowhere near as high as Lane and Dean described it and they considered Fuchs, a highly regarded physicist, to have been in a class by himself in respect to the importance of the information he had passed on to the Soviet Union. Dean was aware of this and, very early on, told the JCAE members that the information Greenglass might disclose "will not give the Russians any more than they already knew through Fuchs."[223]

This statement told the JCAE that the machinist's witness testimony of what he had passed on to Julius Rosenberg would be elevated closer to, but would not be more than, the information passed on by Fuchs.

Lane told the meeting there were certain risks in having Greenglass disclose in the courtroom the full extent of the information he had passed on to Rosenberg. There was an uncertainty, he said, that the Soviet Union had ever received the information.

> Yakovlev [a Soviet espionage controller for Harry Gold]
> certainly got this information, and with a period of five

years lapsing since that happened, I am sure — I am fairly
sure — he must have turned it over to his superiors.[224]

Lane did not explain why he was only "fairly sure," six years after the information had been passed to the Soviet espionage controller, that Yakovlev had
delivered such vital information about the atom bomb to his government. If
Yakovlev had not sent the information on in an encoded cable or in a diplomatic
pouch in 1945, he certainly would have delivered it in person when he returned to
the Soviet Union, in 1946. We will see why Lane mentioned this highly improbable possibility.

Another risk, according to Gordon Dean, arose from Greenglass' uncertainty that he remembered the information he had passed on, and that he may
have passed on information of which he had no recollection. Dean said

> The only danger there seems to be in the situation is if
> a very clever man with a scientific background is doing
> the cross-examination of Greenglass and refreshed his
> [Greenglass'] recollection on something he hasn't told
> us.[225]

The Chairman of the JCAE, Senator Brien McMahon of Connecticut,
seems to have immediately understood what Lane and Dean wanted. He asked
Lane

> In other words, what you are saying is that you think
> what you want to do is have Greenglass divulge now
> secret information on the chance that the death penalty
> would then result to Rosenberg.

> Mr. Lane: Yes.[226]

"Now secret information," in 1951, could only mean information Greenglass
did not have, and could not have passed on to Rosenberg in 1945. The Lane-Dean
references to "uncertainties" were intended to make it appear that the "now secret
information" would not really be "new to Greenglass" but simply the product of
Greenglass' "refreshed" memory.

Senator Bourke B. Hickenlooper of Iowa also understood what Justice officials wanted. He asked "what would we be giving up or what would we be disclosing" that would not have been passed on to the Soviet Union in 1945? Addressing
Lane, he said

> As I understand it, you are raising the question that
> there may have been something that he [Greenglass] has
> forgotten that he didn't turn over that may come out in
> cross-examination. Is that the point?

Mr. Lane: That is one of the points we considered, and that is why we have these men from the Atomic Energy Commission, Friday, to give him a trial run along the lines of the cross-examination he might receive at the trial, in the hope of being able in so doing to elicit from him any information he might have which he hasn't given to us lawyers.[227]

Hickenlooper observed

If they [the Soviet Union] know anything, then the only people who don't know it is the American public and some other people, but if the people who can use it already have it, I am questioning whether there would be any material harm in using it in a trial.[228]

Rep. Sterling Cole of New York may have been even more insightful than the two Senators. What he believed he had heard from Lane and Dean was that, eight months after the defendants' arrests, Justice officials were concerned that there wasn't enough evidence to be certain of a conviction. Cole pointedly asked Lane why the prosecutors needed more evidence to justify death sentences than they needed to simply obtain convictions. Lane did not challenge Cole's conclusion.

Mr. Lane: Mr. Congressman, I think you know that it is not too difficulty [sic] to get a conviction in some conspiracy cases. You have to prove the [indecipherable] agreement plus an overt act. But to get a death penalty, I seriously doubt from my own experience, that any judge would impose a death penalty merely because a man testified there was an agreement and they passed out information respecting the number of people that were working there [Los Alamos] or the names of scientists who were working there.[229]

Lane also told the meeting

The case is not too strong against Mrs. Rosenberg. But for the purpose of acting as a deterrent, I think it is very important that she be convicted, too, and given a stiff sentence.[230]

Toward the end of the meeting, Senator Hickenlooper gave Lane and Dean his support for coaching Greenglass:

> …my own personal opinion has been for some time and
> is now that there are very powerful arguments for the
> most vigorous prosecution of these people… to intro-
> duce fully sufficient evidence to hook this fellow [Julius
> Rosenberg] with the most severe penalty you can give.[231]

Senator John W. Bricker of Ohio made clear he understood that Justice and AEC officials wanted protection against the consequences that might follow if the coaching became known. He told Lane and Dean they had friends in Congress on their side.

> As I understand it, all this is to see that there is no criti-
> cism of the Department of Justice or the Atomic Energy
> Commission after the trial is over if something comes
> up that we don't anticipate.[232]

Those present at the February 8 meeting apparently regarded as justifi-able a decision to coach Greenglass, to allow him to display to the jurors, by his sketches and explanations, the enormity of what had been taken from the United States and put into the hands of the enemy. Coaching Greenglass would make it virtually certain the jurors would vote Guilty and that the judge would have justification for inflicting death sentences, and would increase the likelihood that confessions would follow.

Justice and AEC officials may have regarded the possibility of Greenglass' coaching and perjury becoming known as very unlikely. The AEC coaching experts, although probably reluctant to become involved, could be depended on to keep silent. Greenglass, knowing his life — and possibly his wife's — was at stake, was sure to follow a carefully laid out testimonial script and, if asked whether he had been coached, to reply in the negative.

The thinking of those attending the February 8 meeting appears to have been that coaching Greenglass was an action to enable justice to be done. If the action was discovered, who would not forgive everyone on the government's side for having taken a patriot's risk?

Ruth Greenglass Grand Jury testimony, 1950, regarding her handwritten notes on the atom bomb for Julius Rosenberg:

> Q And what did Rosenberg say? A. Well, he was pleased at receiving the information.
>
> Q Didn't you write that down on a piece of paper?
>
> A Yes, I wrote that down on a piece of paper and he took it with him.
>
> Q In longhand? A Yes.
>
> Q And did you write it down in his presence?
>
> A I believe so.

David Greenglass trial testimony (1951) from the Trial Record (page 723):

> 2sh   Greenglass-direct   723
>
> Q   Then what?   A And they set that up and each sentence was read over and typed down in correct grammatical fashion.
>
> Q   Who did the typing, Mr. Greenglass? A Ethel did the typing and Ruth and Julius and Ethel did the correction of the grammar.

Ruth Greenglass trial testimony (1951) from the Trial Record (pages 1010-11):

> Q   All right. Now what occurred after the typewriter was placed on the bridge table?   A   Well, Ethel was typing the notes and David was helping her when she couldn't
>
>   1011
>
> make out his handwriting and explained the technical terms and spelled them out for her, and Julius and I helped her with the phraseology when it got a little too lengthy, wordy.

Chapter 6 | The trial

The courtroom as world stage...

Irving Saypol was a practiced hand at converting courtroom trials into theater. Some months before being assigned to the Rosenberg-Sobell case he had persuaded a jury, without citing a single act of violence, that books on history and philosophy could be truly incendiary, which resulted in prison sentences for ten Communist leaders.

His success lay in his ability to divert jurors from their roles as triers of fact and to recruit them as patriotic defenders of national security and domestic and foreign policy. At the March 1951, trial, he adeptly confronted the jurors with the Cold War, the atom bomb as foreign policy, the fear of an atom bomb attack on New York City, and other issues roiling them and the public.

The juror-candidates learn what is wanted of them...

Unlike many other cities in which the electorate had moved to the political right as a result of the Cold War, New York City voters favored New Deal and liberal candidates for public office and, in the immediate post-war years, had elected two Communists to the City Council.

Rather than risk putting the verdicts in the hands of unpredictable New Yorkers, the prosecution chose to eliminate as much of the "mix" of the city as was possible. A wry wisdom among New York City lawyers in mid-20th Century was that the Tammany Hall appointees in charge of compiling jury-candidate lists could produce a jury of any desirable bias. The mechanics of jury selection had for a long time been managed in such a way that random selection had been superseded by "selective randomization." Jury pools could be largely city-wide but "spiced" with a helping of candidate-jurors from areas of the city that were known for specific political, social or ethnic biases. Candidate-jurors were also drawn from at least a dozen small towns north of the city when, in Tammany Hall's cynical parlance, there were "not enough" candidate-jurors among New York City's nearly 8,000,000 residents. As a result, jury panels could be drawn that had only a passing resemblance to the overall demographics of the city.

Five of the jurors at the Rosenberg-Sobell trial were not from New York City at all, but from White Plains, Mamaroneck, Scarsdale, Dobbs Ferry, and Mt. Vernon.

A second step in diluting the New York City "mix" was Judge Kaufman's decision to pass the jury candidates through a political "filter" test, at the request of the prosecution, which would eliminate any candidates who admitted to reading newspapers or journals, or having been members of organizations that had been declared subversive by the U.S. Attorney General, who was, of course, an adversarial party in the case. The defense attorneys did not object to the "filter" test *per se*, but did object to the Court using the descriptive word "subversive" which was in the title of the Attorney General's list.[233] The judge agreed not to articulate the universally known unarticulated word.

Judge Kaufman then enlarged the "filter" to include 300 publications and organizations, many of them of a purely liberal persuasion, The list included religious publications, such as *The Protestant*, and minority-defense organizations such as American Committee for the Protection of the Foreign Born, American Jewish Labor Council, American Student Union, Commonwealth College, Civil Rights Congress, Independent Socialist League, Jewish Peoples Committee, National Negro Congress, Peoples Institute of Applied Religion, School of Jewish Studies, Southern Negro Youth Congress, etc.[234] They were also asked whether they or family members had ever been associated with the Abraham Lincoln Brigade (consisting of American volunteers who fought alongside the Spanish Loyalist army against a fascist army funded and armed by Nazi Germany).

Surprisingly, for a panel of New Yorkers, only one candidate-juror admitted that he did not always obey the Attorney General's proscribed reading list, saying that he occasionally read *In Fact*, a liberal monthly newsletter. Judge Kaufman excused him from serving.[235, 236]

Prospective jurors were asked whether any of them "oppose the use of atomic weapons in time of war,"[237] a matter wholly extraneous to jurors as triers of fact. The jurors were also asked whether any of them "favor the platform urged by Russia [at] the United Nations regarding the use and development and supervision of atomic energy,"[238] which was likewise a diversion from their roles, or whether "any juror or member of the juror's family attended the College of the City of New York known as C.C.N.Y."[239] a similar diversion with a distinct ethnic undertone.

The judge went on to ask whether any of the prospective jurors or relatives or close friends had "ever been the subject of any investigation or accusation by any Committee of Congress" or whether any prospective juror had "such prejudice or bias against the House Committee on Un-American Activities" or other committees or agencies "that it would so influence your judgment that you would be unable to arrive at a just and honest verdict?"[240] Such questions were certain to remind the juror-candidates of the Congressional assault on the Hiss trial jurors who had brought an unsatisfactory verdict one year earlier at the first Hiss trial.

The prospective jurors were asked whether "any juror or member of his family or close personal friend" has "signed an election petition nominating Benjamin J. Davis" [an African-American Communist candidate for the New York City Council].[241] The judge also asked the prospective jurors whether they would be influenced by anti-Communist or pro-Communist materials, which were not identified, and they all answered in the negative.

There was no disqualification of potential jurors who admitted they read or subscribed to anti-Communist periodicals, and whose backgrounds or family, friendship or social circles might bias them against Communists. The judge allowed such jurors to be seated if they said that despite their anti-Communist bias, they felt they could dispassionately decide the guilt or innocence of the defendants.

Whether Judge Kaufman's comprehensive inquiry into the mindsets of the jurors always produced honest answers is uncertain. One of the obvious problems that would have confronted at least some of the prospective jurors was that honest answers to many of the highly charged questions might cost some of them their jobs, friends, and amity within the family. It is likely that some prospective jurors chose to be silent rather than make troubling admissions. But, having been silent, they faced the possibility that if they were seated as members of a jury that could not reach a verdict or that found for the defendants, there would be swift and certain repercussions.

The occupations of the jurors were only marginally close to the New York City "mix": a Macy's store manager, a restaurant owner, a company auditor, an estimator for a publishing firm, two accountants, an official of a municipal agency, a bank examiner, a bookkeeper, a switch-board operator, a waiter at a tennis club, and an employee of the Consolidated Edison Company.[242]

Approximately 70% of New Yorkers at the time were Protestants and Catholics; Jews would account for most of the remaining 30%. A panel of 95 candidates had been drawn from the 300 candidate-jurors, of which 18 (19%) were Jewish. One candidate was challenged by the defense, ten by the prosecution, and seven were eliminated for consideration by the judge because they admitted to being biased against capital punishment, leaving no Jews on the jury. (The Supreme Court ruled in a later case that candidate jurors in capital cases could not be eliminated simply because they were opposed to capital punishment. They had to be asked by the presiding judge whether, in spite of their bias against capital punishment, they could deliberate the question of guilt objectively.)

Saypol had achieved his first purpose as soon as the curtain went up at the trial. The jurors knew what was expected of them.

The prosecution's witness list and its Nobel-level scientists...

The prosecution's witness list was read to the prospective jurors, resulting in worldwide headlines because of the prominence and reputations of many of the witnesses. Among the 102 listed witnesses was Harold Urey, a Nobel laureate in chemistry, who had been on the team of scientists that had produced the atom bomb; Dr. J. Robert Oppenheimer, former scientific head of the Los

Alamos atomic bomb project; Dr. George B. Kistiakowski, an eminent physicist; and General Leslie R. Groves, former head of the atomic research and development project.[243]

One prospective juror requested he be excused because his daughter had worked for Dr. Urey, and he was afraid he would be biased. Judge Kaufman excused him,[244] but did not inquire of the other juror-candidates whether the appearance of the eminent scientists' names on the prosecution's witness list might prejudice them in any way.

The prosecutors' witness list also included the names of friends of the Rosenbergs and members of Morton Sobell's family. The appearance of these names on the witness list astonished and dismayed the defendants and their attorneys, for their names sent a message to the jurors that the defendants' families and friends might testify against them.

By the end of the trial, however, not one of the three eminent scientists or General Groves had been called by the prosecutors. A junior scientist and an engineer who testified did not mention or allude to the Rosenbergs or Sobell nor did they testify to any knowledge of espionage at Los Alamos. Nor had any of the Rosenbergs' friends or any member of Sobell's family been called to testify by the prosecutors.

Of the 102 witnesses on the prosecution's list, 23 were called. Three (David Greenglass and his wife, and Max Elitcher) gave testimony against the Rosenbergs and Sobell relating to espionage. One witness, Harry Gold, testified against the Greenglasses. The remaining witnesses testified to the Sobell family being brought across the border to Laredo, Texas, where Morton Sobell had been placed under arrest by FBI agents, and to collateral matters relating to the operations and security at Los Alamos, New Mexico in 1945; two witnesses testified to personal correspondence with Morton Sobell unrelated to espionage; another, to phone calls that a witness thought, but could not be sure, came from Julius Rosenberg. Several witnesses testified to the use of aliases by Sobell while he was in Mexico. There were three rebuttal witnesses brought by the prosecutors, but none of them testified to any knowledge of espionage activities by the defendants.

The jurors now "knew" that the accusations against the defendants would come from impeccable, world-renowned witnesses. Later, one of the defendants' appeals mentioned the prosecution's failure to call any of these impeccable witnesses. Justice officials replied that it had been unnecessary to call them.

The opening statements...

After the indictment was read to the jurors, both sides made their opening statements. Irving Saypol immediately set the stage for transposing the crime from the time of its actual commission to the Cold War era. The inspiration for the defendants' treasonous behavior, he told the jurors, was an alien ideology to which they were fanatically devoted.

> The evidence will show that the loyalty and the allegiance of the Rosenbergs and Sobell were not to our country, but that it was to Communism, Communism in this country and Communism throughout the world.[245]

The defendants' aim, he told the jurors, was destruction of the United States.

> [B]y their rank disloyalty to this country these defendants joined with their co-conspirators in a deliberate, carefully planned conspiracy to deliver to the Soviet Union, the information and the weapons which the Soviet Union could use to destroy us...[246]

In their opening statements, the defense attorneys pressed the jurors "to use your mind and your reason" rather than be swayed by the prosecution's oratory. They were aware the spoken words of prosecutors leave a more lasting impression on jurors than the language of written indictments, and for that reason they objected to Saypol's references to the defendants' desire to destroy the United States, since the formal indictment nowhere charged that the defendants intended any harm to the United States, although the statute under which they were indicted would have permitted such a phrase to be used. The phrase was omitted because it would have raised the level of proof that would have been needed to secure guilty verdicts and to avert a reversal by the appellate court if the verdict was appealed.

The testimony...

There are, today, three certainties about the testimony that were not present in 1951. The first certainty, which emerged only recently, was that Julius Rosenberg and Morton Sobell had engaged in espionage for the Soviet Union in the 1940s. Sobell has specifically denied, however, that atomic espionage was involved.

The second certainty is, in effect, a confession by David Greenglass before the trial that he would testify to acts of which he had no knowledge, except as they were described to him by the FBI. In a memorandum to his attorney shortly after his arrest, he described several events he related to the FBI during his first interviews[247] (the memorandum came to light in spring 1953). At one point, his interrogators interrupted him and suggested he alter his description of the event by adding something of which he had no knowledge. In the memorandum, Greenglass notes, "I didn't remember this, but I allowed it in the statement."

A similar expression of his willingness to describe events related to him by the FBI, but of which he had no personal knowledge, appeared during his testimony. Asked during cross-examination about his early statements to the FBI, Greenglass replied:

> The Witness:
> I - I had told them about this - what they put in the statement, what they wanted me to put into the statement, what they wanted me to put into the statement in the first thing, they told me was just to make a general statement, that is all.[248]

The third certainty is owed to Michael and Robert Meeropol, sons of the Rosenbergs, who sued to compel Justice officials to comply with the Freedom of Action Act in the 1970s. As a result, the public learned that the oral charge of atomic espionage by Julius Rosenberg rested on perjured testimony by David Greenglass. Greenglass testified that, without coaching, and based solely on eavesdropping, he was able to comprehend and prepare sketches and explanations of the working of an atom bomb. He passed the information to Julius Rosenberg, who then purportedly passed it on to the Soviet Union. No other act of espionage was charged to Julius Rosenberg.

The 1970s also produced documentary evidence of perjury and deceit in respect to five other oral claims made by the prosecution:

> the claim that Ethel Rosenberg typed up Greenglass' handwritten notes and thereby became a member of the conspiracy;

> the claim, in a headline-producing announcement by the prosecution, that the Greenglasses' testimony would be corroborated by William Perl, a former CCNY classmate of Julius Rosenberg;

> the claim that the console table had been adapted for espionage photography and that it had been a gift from the Soviet Union to Julius Rosenberg;

> the claim that Julius Rosenberg had sent Harry Gold to Albuquerque, in 1945, to obtain classified information from David Greenglass;

> the claim that the Rosenbergs had passport photographs taken in May or June 1950 or at any other time.

The authenticity of five of these claims is undermined by documentary evidence of perjury; the sixth claim — the media-headlined prosecution claim of future corroboration by William Perl of some aspects of David Greenglass' testimony — is undermined by documentary evidence of collusion between the prosecution and the judge to enable the claim to be made, and in the fact that Perl was never called to the witness stand by the prosecution.

These six claims were fundamental to the prosecution's case, and the most important of them was the first, that David Greenglass had passed atom bomb information to Julius Rosenberg, who then passed it on to a Soviet agent. There were other claims that were extensions and elaborations of the six important claims, for which not even "likenesses" of evidence were introduced.

A cautionary note on the testimony...

In the testimonial/evidentiary records of trials there are always oddities, seemingly mutually exclusive declarations by a witness, patent absurdities, and rulings from the bench that are illogical, illegal, or biased. None of these events, taken singly or together, are indications of the probability of a defendant's innocence or guilt. In the overwhelming number of trials, these oddities and contradictions are simply indications of carelessness, impatience, irritability, or other human failings. In our account of the trial, we have avoided any reference to such occurrences.

Greenglass' coached atom bomb testimony...

David Greenglass testified that in September 1945, he gave Julius Rosenberg a sketch of the atom bomb and a multi-page explanation of its parts and their functions. To support Greenglass' testimony, the prosecution introduced Exhibit 8, a sketch of the atom bomb, accompanied by written explanations.[249]

Greenglass testified that he had prepared a copy of the sketch and the explanation on the previous day. The explanatory material Greenglass had prepared read as follows:

> I have 'a', which points to two detonators, each mold. Each high explosive lens, there were 36 of them, that I have pointed to as 'b' had two detonators on them; that is, two detonators connected to capacitors which were charged by suitable apparatus and was set to go off by a switch that would throw all 72 condensers at once. There were two detonators on each lens so in case of failure of one, the other would go off. And beneath the high explosive lens there was 'c', I have marked, a beryllium plastic sphere, which is a shield for the h.e., the high explosive. Then I have 'e,' which is the plutonium

itself, which is fissionable material. That is also a sphere. Inside that sphere is a 'd', is beryllium. Inside the beryllium there are conical shaped holes 'f', marked 'f'.

Now, the beryllium shield protects the high explosive from the radiation of the plutonium. This is to prevent the h.e. from deteriorating and not go off until it is set off. At the time of the discharge of the condensers the high explosive lens implode, giving a concentric implosion to the plutonium sphere on the inside. This in turn does the same to the beryllium, and the beryllium is the neutron source which ejects neutrons into the plutonium, which is now at a super or hypercritical stage because of the high pressure heat, and nuclear fission takes place...The switch that set it off was set off by a barometric pressure device, and the bomb itself was on a parachute.[250]

An unexpected motion by the defense...

After introducing Exhibit 8, the proceedings took an unexpected turn. The Rosenbergs' attorney, Emanuel Bloch, without consulting the two attorneys for Sobell, made a motion to impound Exhibit 8 and the testimony relating to it, saying that his motive was to make certain "even at this late date, this information may not be used to the advantage of a foreign power."[251]

Saypol, caught by surprise, said, "That is a rather strange request coming from the defendants."

Judge Kaufman, also surprised, said he welcomed the suggestion and asked Bloch whether he also wanted the courtroom cleared of all spectators, to which Bloch agreed. But Saypol foresaw a new possibility, that the prosecution might enable Greenglass to make an impressive presentation of the atom bomb to the jury and, at the same time, avoid any cross-examination of the witness by getting a stipulation from the defense that Exhibit 8 was authentic and that Greenglass had been capable of creating it without being coached.

In support of Bloch's motion, Saypol told the court that there had been a meeting on February 8 with AEC officials and JCAE leaders that was concerned particularly with the danger that secret atomic information might be disclosed at the trial.[252]

Judge Kaufman understood at once what Saypol was after.

The Court: ...Perhaps we can even avoid this matter of clearing the courtroom if counsel stipulate right now

> that the matters that were described, as he [Greenglass] is
> about to describe, were of a secret and confidential nature.

Bloch agreed, but one of Sobell's attorneys did not, saying

> I do not feel that an attorney for a defendant in a crimi-
> nal case should make concessions which will serve the
> People from the necessity of proving things which in the
> course of proof we may be able to refute.[253]

Judge Kaufman argued, unsuccessfully, with Sobell's attorneys, that the stipulation Saypol sought would not injure their client, but they continued to decline. At one point the judge addressed himself to Bloch, saying, "I under-stand that you are willing to concede the testimony concerning that particular phase of it, is that correct?" Bloch avoided a direct response, possibly because he was alarmed at how quickly his motion to impound was being altered by Judge Kaufman into a motion that would relieve the prosecution of the need to prove the authenticity of Exhibit 8. He was also concerned that the judge would inter-pret such a stipulation to mean the defense would not be permitted to challenge Greenglass' ability to have prepared the sketch and the explanations without hav-ing been coached. Bloch replied simply that the testimony should be given after the court was cleared.

The court was then cleared of spectators, though not of the press, which was admonished by the judge to use "your good taste and good judgment on the matter of publishing portions of this testimony."[254] He ordered Exhibit 8 impounded after the jury had seen and heard testimony on it.

After the spectators had been readmitted to the courtroom, Bloch cross-examined Greenglass on Greenglass' ability to have created, from overheard con-versations, the sketches and descriptions of the atom bomb he testified to passing on to Rosenberg, and to reproduce these six years later from memory. He asked Greenglass about his training as a machinist and whether he had ever taken advanced courses to improve his skills. Greenglass replied that he had taken an advanced course at Brooklyn Polytech.

> Bloch: How long did you go to Brooklyn Polytech?
>
> A. Six months.
>
> Q. And how many courses did you take during those six
> months?
>
> A. About eight different courses.
>
> Q. And did you fail —

Mr. Cohn: Oh, I object to that, your Honor. What difference does it make?[255]

After some discussion, Judge Kaufman permitted Bloch to ask the question.

Q. How many of the eight courses that you took did you
fail?

A. I failed them all.[256]

Judge Kaufman broke in to say he didn't know why Greenglass was being
questioned about his educational attainments. He told the jurors, in effect, that
Greenglass' sketches and descriptions of the atom bomb were beyond challenge, since their accuracy was irrelevant and could not be used to cast doubt on
Greenglass' ability to have created them in 1945.[257] The defendants were being
charged, Judge Kaufman told the jurors, with conspiring to pass classified information to the Soviet Union, but the accuracy of that information was irrelevant
to the crime.

The judge was correct in his legal description of the crime, but he was
imputing an intent to Bloch's cross-examination that obscured its purpose. Bloch
was attempting to show, not that Exhibit 8 was an inaccurate description of an
atom bomb, but that Greenglass was lying when he claimed to have produced
Exhibit 8 unaided.[258] At one point Judge Kaufman himself put the question to
Greenglass.

The Court:… Those sketches that are in evidence, are
they the product of your own mind? By that I mean,
were you helped by anybody on the outside in drawing
those sketches?

The Witness: Nobody else, just myself.[259]

If the jurors understood that Bloch was not challenging the accuracy of Exhibit 8, but was challenging Greenglass' truthfulness in denying that he had been coached, they might have reason to doubt his
credibility as a whole, and reasonable doubt could mean the difference
between life and death for the defendants. By making it appear to the jurors
that Bloch was arguing an irrelevant point — the accuracy of Exhibit 8 —
Judge Kaufman obscured the issue that Bloch tried to put before the jurors.

The prosecution did not call on any of the scientists on its witness list to
authenticate Exhibit 8. Instead, it called John A. Derry, an engineer with no post-
graduate training, who had been assigned to Los Alamos by the Army, and who
had not worked on the atom bomb, to authenticate Exhibit 8. He testified that
Exhibit 8 "substantially gives the principle involved" in the operation of an atom
bomb. Bloch asked him whether a machinist without engineering or scientific

training "would be able to describe accurately the functions of the atom bomb and its component parts."[260]

Judge Kaufman declared (*sua sponte*) that he objected to the question and was sustaining his objection, and Derry was not permitted to answer the question.

Earlier, to bolster Greenglass' skills and credibility, the prosecutors had him testify that he had been promoted to foreman of the machine shop and was given the rank of T/4 sergeant.[261] In 1961, in answer to an inquiry from the authors of *Invitation to an_Inquest*, the Army public relations office wrote them that Greenglass had been a "T/5 corporal" throughout his army service at Los Alamos, and Army records did not indicate that Greenglass had ever been promoted to "assistant foreman or foreman of the 'E' shop."[262]

Justice officials succeeded in keeping Exhibit 8 impounded for the next fifteen years, over the objections of defense lawyers who wanted to submit it to scientists who had themselves worked on the atom bomb.

After Exhibit 8 was unimpounded, in 1966, it quickly found its way into the mainstream media, which solicited opinions from scientists on the accuracy and importance of what Greenglass testified he had turned over to Julius Rosenberg and Harry Gold, and on Greenglass' ability — given his limited education — to have drawn the atom bomb sketches in Exhibit 8 without assistance.

Philip Morrison, a physicist involved in the development of the atom bomb, expressed surprise that during his testimony, Derry had failed to "correct or disassociate himself and his own testimony from the errors in the Greenglass testimony," and

> If, in truth, Major Derry had occasion to see the actual atomic bomb under development at Los Alamos "many times," as he stated, he ought to have added "and it did not look like that..."[263]

Henry Linschitz, a chemist who had headed up an explosives section at Los Alamos, described Exhibit 8 as a "childlike caricature."[264] In the end, even with coaching, Greenglass had been unable, in the opinions of scientists who had worked on the atom bomb, to give a credible description of the weapon.

The Greenglasses testify against Ethel Rosenberg...

Greenglass testified he and his wife, Ruth, brought his Exhibit 8 sketch and explanatory notes to the Rosenberg apartment. His wife had remarked

> that the handwriting would be bad and would need interpretation, and Julius said there was nothing to worry about as Ethel would type it up, retype the information.[265]

He testified that the Rosenbergs brought a bridge table into their living room to facilitate Ethel Rosenberg's typing.

> Mr. Cohn. Who did the typing, Mr. Greenglass?
>
> A. Ethel did the typing and Ruth and Julius and Ethel did the correction of the grammar.[266]

Ruth Greenglass corroborated her husband's testimony.

> A. Ethel got out a typewriter and sat down to work on the notes.
>
> Q. On what type of typewriter was it? I mean, was it a standard model or a portable model or what?
>
> A. It was a portable — I believe it was a Remington.
>
> Q. And where was the typewriter placed?
>
> A. On the bridge table.[267]

In his summation to the jury, prosecutor Saypol described the typing scene.

> Just so had she on countless other occasions sat at that typewriter and struck the keys, blow by blow, against her own country in the interests of the Soviets.[268]

In the fall of 2008, Ruth Greenglass' testimony at the August 30, 1950 grand jury hearing became available. There is no mention in it of Ethel Rosenberg's typing any of David Greenglass' notes. Instead, it is Ruth Greenglass who writes — not types — information prepared by her husband, which she personally passes on to Julius Rosenberg.

After testifying to the jury that she passed information to her brother-in-law, Myles Lane asked her:

> Q. And what did Rosenberg say?
>
> A. Well, he was pleased at receiving the information.
>
> Q. Didn't you write that down on a piece of paper?
>
> A. Yes, I wrote that down on a piece of paper and he took it with him.
>
> Q. In longhand?
>
> A. Yes.
>
> Q. And did you write it down in his presence?
>
> A. I believe so.[269]

The earliest reference by the FBI to any typing by Ethel Rosenberg was in an FBI memorandum dated late February 1951, eight months after Greenglass' arrest, and one month before the trial.[270] That was the month in which Myles Lane told the JCAE and the AEC officials that "The case is not too strong against Mrs. Rosenberg."[271]

Twenty eight years later, in a 1979 an interview with the authors of *The Rosenberg File* at the office of her attorney, Ruth Greenglass

> conceded that she never had the details of the September 1945 typing scene fixed in her mind. She just assumed "that we probably went over there and did it at that time, frankly, because that would have been the way it would have been done."[272]

Fifty years after the trial, David Greenglass, in a CBS *60 Minutes* television program in December 2001, and in *The Brother*, published in 2001, based on interviews with Sam Roberts, a *New York Times* reporter, admitted that the typing may have been done by his wife. Roberts asked David Greenglass whether he stood by his testimony about his sister typing his notes, he replied

> Yeah, I don't remember that at all. I frankly think my wife did the typing, but I don't remember.[273]

In December 2001, on CBS' *60 Minutes* television show, Greenglass repeated his admission that he had lied in his testimony against his sister.[274]

There was, of course, a purpose to the prosecution's subornation of perjury against Ethel Rosenberg. The prosecution felt it needed a specific act by Ethel Rosenberg, in furtherance of the conspiracy, in order to justify her indictment. Otherwise, some jurors might be inclined to regard her role as wifely and passive and, if they could not agree on a verdict for her, or found her not guilty, her life would no longer be a bargaining chip in the prosecution's attempt to secure her husband's confession.

The corroboration witness who didn't...

Toward the end of the Greenglasses' testimony on March 15, 1951, the *New York Times* and other newspapers front-paged a prosecution press release announcing the arrest of William Perl, a former classmate of Julius Rosenberg and Morton Sobell, who, the press release said, would corroborate some portions of the Greenglasses' testimony against the Rosenbergs.

The *New York Times* headline read, "COLUMBIA TEACHER ARRESTED, LINKED TO 2 ON TRIAL AS SPIES."[275] The announcement also informed the media that Perl's true name was Mutterperl and that his father "was a native of

Russia."[276] Since the jurors were not sequestered, it was very likely that some, if not all, the jurors would have read the story.

The defense attorneys promptly complained to Judge Kaufman that Saypol's headlined press release might have been read by the jurors,[277] but Judge Kaufman did not ask the jurors whether they had done so. Instead, he accepted Saypol's assurance that the arrest and press announcement had been a routine matter and had not been intended to influence the jurors. Perl, however, was never called to the witness stand, despite the headlined press release.

Subsequent events produced the startling information that Judge Kaufman had a direct hand in facilitating Saypol's use of the Perl indictment to make the false announcement. Perl's indictment had been sealed, and Saypol wanted it unsealed on March 14, 1951, for the purpose of his announcement to the press.[278] Unsealing Perl's indictment required a hearing and an order by a judge. Saypol made his request for unsealing the indictment after business hours at the courthouse, when it was unlikely that a federal judge would still be available. As it happened, however, on that day Judge Kaufman stayed late and was available to conduct the hearing. Since Saypol was about to link Perl, the subject of the indictment, to the Rosenberg-Sobell case, the presence of defense attorneys at the hearing was legally required. Nevertheless, the hearing was conducted with the prosecution alone, and Judge Kaufman granted Saypol's motion ex parte, allowing him to make his announcement to the media. The media headlines could not have come as a surprise to Judge Kaufman, nor would he have been surprised, if he had chosen to ask, to learn that the jurors had read the media headlines he had enabled.

Perl declined to become a corroborating witness for Saypol and, in May 1953, was tried on four counts of perjury. The jury acquitted him on two counts and found him guilty of perjury on the counts of falsely denying that he knew Julius Rosenberg and Morton Sobell. Perl was sentenced to two concurrent five-year prison terms.

The false-corroboration prosecution announcement was eventually placed before the U.S. Court of Appeals, which termed the announcement "reprehensible,"[279] but chose not to act on it.

The Greenglasses testify to seeing a console table...

The Greenglasses testified that the Soviets had shown their appreciation to the Rosenbergs by rewarding them with a console table, several watches and a special citation. Ruth Greenglass testified that Julius Rosenberg had shown her a console table he said he had received as a gift from "a friend," and that he had turned the table on its side to show her a unique feature.

> Mr. Kilsheimer: And what did he show you when he turned the table on its side?

A. There was a portion of the table that was hollowed out for a lamp to fit underneath it so that the table could be used for photograph purposes, and he said when he used the table he darkened the room so that there would be no other light and he wouldn't be obvious to anyone looking in.

Q. And did Julius tell you what he photographed using the table?

A. Yes. He took pictures on microfilm of the typewritten notes.[280]

Earlier, David Greenglass had testified that he believed "they had told me they received a console table from the Russians."[281] The prosecutors did not enter the purported console table into evidence.

Julius Rosenberg was asked by Bloch how he had obtained the console table. He replied that he had purchased it from the R.H. Macy department store in New York City and had paid for it by check.

E.H. Bloch: And how much did you pay for that console table?

A. It was somewhere about $21.[282]

Later, Saypol, in the presence of the jury, said, "Do you know, Mr. Rosenberg, that we have asked Macy's to find that check and they can't find it?" And then he added, "Don't you know, Mr. Rosenberg, that you couldn't buy a console table in Macy's, if they had it, in 1944 and 1945, for less than $85?" Ordinarily, the opposing attorney would object to such remarks because they constituted uncorroborated and uncross-examinable testimony by an unsworn witness, a prosecutor, in the presence of the jurors. Inexplicably, neither the defense attorneys nor the judge objected,[283] and the jurors were left to accept as fact that Macy's had no record of such a console table and that, if they had one, its price would have been at least four times as much as Julius Rosenberg claimed.

At the time the FBI searched the Rosenberg apartment in July 1950, the FBI agents had seen a console table, but it had not been adapted for photography or for any other special use and it was not taken away by them for laboratory inspection or for use as an exhibit by the prosecution, and it was never brought into court by the prosecution. The FBI's inventory of the contents of the Rosenberg's apartment mentions a "table," without further description.[284] No strips or frames or bits of microfilm were offered into evidence, nor micro-film cameras or other micro-filming equipment.

The prosecution evidently had a need for an "espionage-adapted" console table to fit a pre-conceived espionage scenario: Greenglass would bring stolen documents to Rosenberg to film, after which Greenglass would return the documents to where they belonged. But Greenglass denied having stolen or copied or even peeked at any classified documents. Possibly, the prosecution may have believed that other spies brought Rosenberg such documents to film, but no evidence was brought into court to support this possibility. Nevertheless, the prosecution could not let go of the non-existent "espionage-adapted" console table and used the Greenglass testimony about it to provide the jurors with a graphic image of a spy at work.

The actual console table was found in spring, 1953, by Leon Summit, an investigative reporter for the *National Guardian*, who located it through interviews with Rosenberg family members Summit brought the table to a Macy's official who, in an affidavit, identified it as a table sold by Macy's in 1944-1945 for $19 plus tax.[285]

The discovery of the console table created an embarrassing question for the prosecution and the FBI: If David Greenglass had mentioned the console table during his many hours of interrogation after his arrest, why had the FBI not taken the console table as evidence when they searched the Rosenbergs' apartment on July 17, 1950, the day they arrested Julius Rosenberg, or on August 11, 1950, when they arrested Ethel Rosenberg?

Justice officials put the question to the Director of the FBI. On March 30, 1953, FBI Director Hoover replied to Warren Olney III, Assistant Attorney General,

> For your information, at the time of the arrest of Julius Rosenberg, on July 17, 1950, Bureau agents searched his apartment and were unable to locate the console table described by Greenglass among Rosenberg's furnishings.[286]

Hoover's information to Olney may have been accurate because, if the FBI agents searching the Rosenbergs' apartment were looking for "the console table described by Greenglass," they would have been searching for a console table with a hollowed out portion for use in microfilming. The console table they found in the apartment lacked the adaptations described by Greenglass.

A Justice Department memorandum dated April 20, 1953, attempted to pass responsibility for the disparity between Greenglass' testimony regarding an "espionage-adapted" table and the true table, on to Greenglass' shoulders alone. The Justice memorandum read, in part

> On 3-25-53, Bureau agent exhibited photographs of this table to David Greenglass who advised table appeared to be same type as one he saw in Rosenberg home, but he

could not be definite. Department has been advised of
the foregoing information.[287]

The memorandum then set the stage for relieving the FBI of responsibility in the matter by casting doubt on whether Greenglass "told all" on his arrest;
specifically whether he told the FBI about the console table before Julius
Rosenberg's arrest.

> Attached is a letter to NYO requesting search of its files
> and interviews of agents who handled Rosenberg case
> in an effort to fix time of Greenglass' story concerning
> console table and determine if specific search was made
> for such table at time of Rosenberg's arrest.

Thus, three weeks after FBI Director Hoover assured his superior that the
console table had not been in the Rosenbergs' apartment when it was searched,
the likelihood was raised that the table had been there, but that the FBI agents
had not made a specific search for it, because Greenglass had not mentioned it
in any of his statements in June, July or August, contrary to his testimony that
he told the FBI about the table at the time of his arrest, on June 15. In short, FBI
agents had probably seen the table on July 17, 1950, and again on August 11,
and found it ordinary, that is, not adapted for micro-filming. This probability is
supported by the authors' copy of the inventory list made by the FBI of what was
found in the Rosenbergs' apartment, although our copy may not be complete.[288]
A table, not further described, and a bookshelf are the only items of furniture
mentioned. Further, according to FBI agent Robert J. Lamphere, who had been
involved in preparing the case against the Rosenbergs, "The Rosenberg apartment
in Knickerbocker Village was thoroughly searched, but no important evidence
was found."[289]

Two weeks after the April 20 memorandum cited earlier, an FBI memorandum stated

> Rosenberg attorney now claims to have found table and
> states it was in Rosenberg apartment at time of arrest,
> proving that Greenglass withheld this information from
> FBI, otherwise FBI would have seized the table at the
> time of Rosenberg arrest... Reflet requested investiga-
> tion by NYO to determine when Greenglass told us
> about console table and if at time of search of apart-
> ment, agents knew about it and made specific search for
> such table. Bufiles were checked for this negatively.[290]

In other words, the FBI position was that it could not determine from its
records when David Greenglass first mentioned the console table.

As he had done in respect to his perjurious testimony regarding his sister's typing up his espionage notes, David Greenglass eventually confessed, in *The Brother*, published in 2001, that he had "never even seen the table,"[291] and had lied when he testified otherwise at the trial.[292]

None of the watches, or a certificate of recognition, which the Greenglasses described as gifts to the Rosenbergs from the Soviet government were entered into evidence.

The Greenglasses-Gold meeting June 3, 1945...

On June 2, 1950, according to FBI accounts, Gold provided the agency with a connective thread that would lead to David Greenglass. On that day Gold recounted a May 1945, conversation he said he'd had with his Russian controller, 'John,' about an appointment with Klaus Fuchs in Santa Fe in June 1945. During their conversation, 'John'

> supplied me with a name and address of a man in Albuquerque, New Mexico, and instructed me to contact this man while I was there. I believe JOHN told me to contact the man's wife in case the man was not there. JOHN told me that I would receive information from this man, which I was to deliver to JOHN. JOHN gave me an envelope containing about $500. I was instructed to give this money to the man in Albuquerque in payment for the information.[293]

Gold testified he traveled to Santa Fe, NM, to pick up classified atom bomb information from Klaus Fuchs on June 2, 1945.[294] He then took a bus in the evening to Albuquerque, went to an address at which 'John' had told him he would find the Greenglasses, but the Greenglasses were not in.

Prosecutor Lane asked him what he did at that point, and Gold replied

> A. I stayed that night — I finally managed to obtain a room in a hallway of a rooming house and then on Sunday morning I registered at the Hotel Hilton.
>
> Mr. Lane: Now, did you register under your own name?
>
> A. Yes, I did.
>
> Q. What name did you use?
>
> A. Harry Gold.
>
> Q. Now, what did you do on Sunday? That is, June 3, 1945?

A. On Sunday about 8:30 I went again to the High Street address. I was admitted, and I recall going up a very steep flight of steps. It was open [sic] by a young man of about 23 with dark hair. He was smiling. I said, Mr. Greenglass?" He answered in the affirmative. I said, "I came from Julius," and I showed him the piece of cardboard in my hand…[295]

David Greenglass testified similarly to Gold's salutation.[296]

With *I came from Julius,"* Gold, who had never met Julius Rosenberg, presented himself to the jurors as a close and trusted accomplice of 'Julius' in the espionage conspiracy, and effectively enlarged the conspiracy to include Fuchs and himself. His four-word salutation ascribed to Julius Rosenberg a specific act in the conspiracy: Julius Rosenberg had sent Gold to the Greenglasses to pick up classified information about the atom bomb for transmittal to the Soviet Union. The "piece of cardboard" mentioned by Gold was presumably a copy of one of the two halves of a Jell-O box side panel that had been described by the Greenglasses as having been cut by Julius Rosenberg.

Gold went on to testify that David Greenglass told him he would have to come back later because the material he intended giving him was not ready. Gold returned at approximately 3:00 p.m., obtained the material, and at about 3:15 p.m.

A. The three of us, Mr. Greenglass, Mrs. Greenglass and myself, left the Greenglasses' apartment and we walked along a slanting back street in Albuquerque and there in front of a small building, I left the Greenglasses.[297]

At 8 p.m., Gold boarded a train for Chicago.

Was there a June 3, 1945 meeting of Harry Gold and the Greenglasses?

The first doubts about the veracity of the testimony relating to the June 3 meeting arose from Greenglass' 1950 handwritten memorandum, that came to light in spring 1953, referred to earlier. The memorandum read, in part

I stated that I met Gold in N.M. at 209 High St. my place. They [the FBI] told me that I had told him to come back later because I didn't have it ready. I didn't remember this but I allowed it in the statement. *** But this I'll tell you I can honestly say the information I gave Gold may be not at all what I said in the statement.[298]

The Greenglass-Gold testimony regarding their June 3, 1945, meeting in Albuquerque was examined at some length in John Wexley's *The Judgment of*

Julius and Ethel Rosenberg,[299] and in Walter and Miriam Schneir's, *Invitation to an Inquest*.[300] In both studies, the authors raised the possibility that the June 3 meeting never occurred or, if it did, it was for another purpose than the one described in the testimony. Subsequently obtained Justice Department and FBI documents support their suspicions.

Where "I come from Julius" came from...

On August 1, 1950, Gold had told prosecutor Myles Lane he had been instructed to tell the Greenglasses at their Albuquerque meeting "that I brought records from the person whose name I recall as Ben in Brooklyn."[301] At some point between August 1950, and the March 1951 trial, the purpose of the Albuquerque meeting was altered: instead of Gold bringing records from 'Ben' to David Greenglass, its purpose was changed to Gold obtaining information from Greenglass, with the salutation altered from "I bring records from Ben" to "I came from Julius."

An FBI memorandum relates that on December 28, 1950, Greenglass and Gold were brought together in The Tombs, a New York City jail to "determine what transpired at their first meeting in Albuquerque." The phrase "at their first meeting" indicates that there may have been a second meeting, although no mention of this second meeting appeared in the testimony or in any other available government documents. The FBI memorandum read, in part,

> Concerning the reported salutation "Greetings from BEN." GREENGLASS says he had no recollection of such a statement made by GOLD, pointing out further that the name BEN would mean nothing to him. GREENGLASS proposed that possibly GOLD had said "greetings from Julius" which would of course make sense to GREENGLASS. GOLD'S spontaneous comment to this was that possibly GREENGLASS was right that he had mentioned the name of JULIUS rather than Ben. GOLD, however is not at all clear on this point.[302]

Thus, the salutation, *"I came from Julius,"* was suggested to Gold by David Greenglass seven months after Gold's arrest, and after Gold told the FBI that a different salutation, with a different name, had been used and that there had been a different purpose for the meeting.

During his testimony concerning his trip to Albuquerque, Gold referred to 'Julius' twice more

> A. Mrs. Greenglass told me that just before she had left New York City to come to Albuquerque she had spoken with Julius.[303]

And

> A. He [David Greenglass] told me that if I wished to get in touch with him then I could do so by calling his brother-in-law Julius, and he gave me the telephone number of Julius in New York City.[304]

But in a June 2, 1950, statement Gold had made to the FBI, he described Greenglass' advice differently.

> I was to call this man's father-in-law in the Bronx, New York. The father-in-law's first name was, or may have been Philip. This meeting never occurred, on the orders of John, who seemed to have lost interest when I mentioned the matter to him in the late Fall of 1945.[305]

In June, according to Gold, a central figure in the conspiracy had been 'Philip;' in August, he had been 'Ben;' in December, at David Greenglass' suggestion, 'Ben' became 'Julius;' in the courtroom in March 1951, an unspoken surname — 'Rosenberg' — was added to Gold's salutation by Gold's testimony that 'Julius' was twice mentioned to him by the Greenglasses who, if they had meant a Julius unrelated to them, would have added a surname — 'Julius Brown,' for example. Assuming, that is, they were using real names instead of cover-names. Gold, in fact, did not introduce himself as Harry to the Greenglasses, but as "Dave from Pittsburgh."[306]

Gold's presentation of his "piece of cardboard" would have been sufficient to identify him as the courier the Greenglasses had expected. The salutation mentioning 'Julius' violated the cautions Gold testified he used in his interactions with other spies.

The use of the improbable and unnecessary salutation and the two additional references by Gold to 'Julius' indicate that the essential purpose of the Gold-Greenglasses testimony about June 3 was to make it appear to the jurors that proof of Julius Rosenberg's involvement in atomic espionage came not only from the Greenglasses, but also from another spy — Harry Gold. In short, the prosecution was trying to compensate for the lack of corroboration of the Greenglasses' testimony against the Rosenbergs by using Gold's false salutation.

Wandering dangerously in a spy-conscious city...

In his study of the case, John Wexley pointed out Gold testified he had taken the Hilton hotel room *before* he learned that there would be a delay in obtaining the material from David Greenglass. If the delay had not occurred, Gold would have been able to leave the Greenglasses' apartment with the new material by 10:00 or 10:30 a.m.,[307] after which he could have taken the 12:55 p.m.

Superchief express train out of Albuquerque.[308] There had been no reason for him to register at the Hilton Hotel. Why did he do so?

If Gold had registered at the hotel as he testified, he would have felt compelled to use it because the delay in obtaining Greenglass' materials left him with a serious problem: he had on his person the classified atomic bomb information he had picked up from Fuchs on the previous day, and he had luggage (his trip to Santa Fe and Albuquerque spanned five-plus days, and he would have needed, at the least, a change of clothing, a shaving kit and other personal things). He testified that, because of the delay, he spent from approximately 9:30 a.m. to 3:00 p.m. on the streets of Albuquerque with his luggage and Fuchs' material. He carried these with him on his return to the Greenglass' apartment. After obtaining David Greenglasses' material, he carried his luggage and two sets of classified materials on a walk with the Greenglasses. Then he spent from approximately 3:30 p.m. to 7:30 p.m., an additional four hours, on Albuquerque's streets, with his luggage and classified materials. Possibly, he may have spent part of those four hours at the train station, but he made no such claim. Had he actually taken the room at the Hilton, he would not have had to spend nine-plus hours on the streets of a secrecy-conscious city filled with security agents because of its proximity to Los Alamos. Even if he had sat in the railroad station for some of that time, he would not have been safe from scrutiny.

In an 89 page letter Gold had written to his lawyer while in prison, he wrote that he took the Hilton Hotel room

> because it was a part of the Standard Operating Procedure, viz., with all that material from Fuchs on me, wandering an entire day around a relatively small town such as Albuquerque was a risk to be avoided.[309]

That is exactly the risk Gold testified he took. Although he mentions "wandering an entire day" with the material from Fuchs, in the letter Gold makes no mention of carrying any material from David Greenglass.

Gold testified he was so aware of the risks that he had argued with 'John' against going to Albuquerque. They were sitting at a cafe in New York and having a drink when 'John' told him where he would have to go

> Gold: I protested — [there was an interruption here on an objection by Bloch, and then Gold continued] I told Yakovlev that I did not wish to take on this additional task... I told Yakovlev that it was highly inadvisable to endanger the very important trip to see Dr. Fuchs with this additional task.[310]

Gold wanted nothing to delay his return to 'John' with Fuchs' information. On August 1, 1950, Myles Lane had asked Gold whether he and David Greenglass had discussed the atom bomb in Albuquerque. Gold replied

> I would like to emphasize that my principal desire after having obtained the information from Klaus Fuchs on the day previous was to get out of Albuquerque as fast as I could — I did not wish to prolong the discussion at all.[311]

At the trial he testified

> If I was going to actually get information, very usually a brief meeting was scheduled, the idea being to minimize the time of detection when information would be passed from the American to me.[312]

But Gold's behavior on June 3 — if that was the date and if there was a pickup from Greenglass — did not conform to his own rules of caution. As soon as the material was passed to him in the Greenglass apartment, he testified, the three spies, one of them carrying luggage and two sets of classified information "walked along a slanting back street in Albuquerque and there in front of a small building, I left the Greenglasses."[313]

Although his behavior in Albuquerque did not conform to his expressed fear that he might endanger Fuchs and himself, he preferred to say he had roamed the streets of Albuquerque rather than say he had ever set foot in the Hilton Hotel room he had taken on the morning of June 3. He wrote to his lawyer he could "recall absolutely nothing" about using the room.[314]

Elsewhere in his letter he wrote that he took the hotel room to "have some sort of address at which I could be called should space be available on a particular flight."[315] Since he did not return to the hotel after he registered,[316] this explanation also lacks credibility. Arguably, he may have intended to phone the hotel to determine whether there was an airline message for him, but he did not claim to have done so or to have telephoned the airline directly. In any case, he left by train.

Forging corroboration for the Hilton Hotel registration...

The prosecutors had prepared photostats of two Hilton registration cards signed by Gold, one for June 3, 1945, the other for September 19 of that year.[317] Walter and Miriam Schneir went on to prove that the June registration card was a forgery.

After ascertaining that Hilton registration cards were handled identically at all Hilton Hotels, the Schneirs asked a qualified handwriting expert to analyze the two photostats of Hilton registration cards for Harry Gold, the first for Albuquerque on June 3, 1945 (Exhibit 16), the second for Albuquerque for September 19, 1945, which was not an Exhibit. Both cards carried samples of the handwriting of Hilton personnel.

The handwriting expert found there was a high probability that samples of Gold's handwriting on both cards were his; it was doubtful the handwriting samples of a clerk whose initials were on both cards were from the same person; there were also indications the two cards "were not produced from the same printing form or plate."[318]

In his 89-page letter to his lawyer, Gold tried to explain away the handwriting expert's findings. The failure of the hotel clerk's handwriting on the registration card to match her handwriting on another card, Gold wrote, may have been due to a "crush at the registration desk"[319] during which the clerk might have been jostled by someone.

The Schneirs also discovered a serious error on the forger's part. Hilton uniform registration procedures placed the date of registration on both sides of the card; on the front side, the date is handwritten, and on the reverse side the date is stamped. The September 19, 1945 card has the correct date and format on both sides; the June 3, 1945 card carried the correct date on the front, but the stamped side carried the date of June 4, 1945, the day following the date on which Gold said he registered at the hotel. In both cards, the time of registration was carried only on the reverse side; the June 3, 1945 reverse side gives the time of registration as "12:36 p.m.," although Gold testified he had registered at the Hilton before 8:30 a.m. on that day. The '12:36 p.m.' time would not have made sense, even if Gold had registered at the hotel only after learning there would be a delay in obtaining Greenglass' materials. He knew by 9:30 a.m. there would be a delay. Why would he wander the streets with his luggage and Fuchs' material until 12:30 p.m. before going to the Hilton Hotel, and then not use the room?

In a pre-trial undated Department of Justice communication to the Atomic Energy Commission, listing the names of various FBI, AEC and other personnel who were available to testify at the Rosenberg-Sobell trial, an unnamed witness was said to be available to testify to

> A registration card of the Hilton Hotel, Albuquerque, New Mexico for "HARRY GOLD, <u>6923</u> Kindred Street, Philadelphia 24, Pennsylvania" reflecting GOLD represented the firm of "Terry and Seibert" and disclosing that the room was occupied by the registrant from 12:36 p.m. to 8:00 a.m., June 3, 1945.[320]

This registration card has Gold checking out of the hotel on June 3 at 8:00 a.m., having checked in at 12:36 p.m. on June 2, although he testified he was still in Santa Fe until very late afternoon of June 2, 1945.[321] Even if read another way, that Gold had checked in at 12:36 p.m. on June 3 and checked out at 8:00a.m. on June 4, it would have conflicted with his testimony that he took an evening train out of Albuquerque on June 3.

These discrepancies may reflect an uncertainty by the prosecutors about the day on which they believed, or wanted, the Gold-Greenglass meeting to have taken place. There are testimonial and documented variations on the date of Gold's presence in Albuquerque. At one point, David Greenglass testified that the visit occurred on "the third Sunday in June 1945."[322] On another occasion Greenglass said the visit took place in May 1945. In his confession, Fuchs had put his meeting with his courier in Santa Fe in late June 1945.[323]

As we have seen, the prosecution felt it necessary to prove Gold's presence in Albuquerque on June 3 by introducing a forged Hilton Hotel registration card. Wexley has argued that the June 3 date may have been chosen because, on June 4, Ruth Greenglass opened a bank account into which she deposited $400, which would seem to corroborate a June 3 payment of $500 to her husband by Gold. Wexley suggested, however, the $400 deposit on June 4 might have come from a black market operation in which the Greenglasses were involved.[324]

The Schneirs shared this suspicion. They reviewed the Greenglasses' various bank accounts and a safety deposit box,[325] but there were no bank records for 1944. The records for 1945-1946 showed that the Greenglasses' known incomes from the Army and Ruth Greenglass' clerical job did not fully account for their total deposits, to say nothing of funds they may have kept as cash in a safety deposit box or elsewhere. The Schneirs found

> over a ten month period [1945-1946] the Greenglasses
> deposited about $2200 in the First National Bank and
> $470 in the Albuquerque National Bank and that much
> or all of this money probably came from some source
> other than the regular salaries and Army allotment that
> they were receiving at the time.[326]

Justice officials were embarrassed by the exposure of the apparent forgery, and declared the Schneirs had unjustly imbued clerical errors with criminal intent. The officials ordered an investigation of the two cards, during which they were told that the original of the June 3 card had been returned to the Hilton Hotel at its request and that the hotel had destroyed the card. The September 19 card, which the Hilton Hotel did not request be returned, was destroyed by the FBI.

In a Justice Department memorandum of August 26, 1966, from Benjamin F. Pollack to Walter J. Yeagley, Pollack wrote

It must be conceded that the New York office of the FBI had no authority to destroy that card, since it is a rule of the FBI that no agent can destroy a court exhibit without authorization from Washington, which authorization was never given in this case.[327]

Pollack was wrong on the facts. The September 19, 1945 registration card destroyed by the FBI had not been an exhibit at the trial. It is likely the originals of both the June 3 and the September 19 registration cards were destroyed *after* the Schneirs determined that the June 3 card was a forgery.

Pollack left it to others who did not have the resources of the Justice Department to dig more deeply into what had happened. Pollack had once endangered his career in carrying out an assignment related to the Rosenberg-Sobell case, and he was not about to do so again. More about this later.

Scholars and journalists familiar with the operations of the FBI in the 1950s would have had no difficulty in believing it engaged in forgeries, and in identifying the FBI's Crime Record Division as having performed the forgery. According to M. Wesley Swearingen, an FBI agent who retired in 1977 after twenty five years with the Bureau, the Crime Record Division specialized in forgeries, anonymous threats and other "dirty tricks." Swearingen recounted a forgery by the Division in the Rosenberg-Sobell case of which he had personal knowledge, involving the author of a Broadway drama titled "The United States v. Julius and Ethel Rosenberg," described later.[328]

Another incongruity in the purported June 3 visit to the Greenglasses was Gold's appearance at the Greenglasses' apartment. After a thorough review by the authors of all espionage contacts associated with the Rosenberg-Sobell case, Gold's was the only "house call" made by an American spy to another American spy who was a stranger to him.

A questionable decision by the defense...

The defense chose not to cross-examine either Gold or Greenglass about the June 3 meeting, on the theory that Gold and Greenglass were each confirming that the other was a spy. However, neither, at that point in the trial, were testifying against the Rosenbergs or Sobell. The theory was totally inapplicable to the situation. When the jurors heard "I came from Julius," they "heard" the surname "Rosenberg." The jurors understood that Harry Gold was testifying against Julius Rosenberg.

A passport photographer's perjury confirmed by the FBI...

David Greenglass testified that Julius Rosenberg had told him, in late spring 1950, they would have to flee the country after Gold was arrested. Flight would involve a number of steps: Greenglass would go to Mexico City, where he would meet someone in a park at a statue of Columbus; they would exchange passwords; and the person would provide him with passports and funds that would take him, via Vera Cruz, "to Sweden or Switzerland, one or the other."[329]

Julius Rosenberg denied having had such discussions with Greenglass and, on cross-examination, denied he had had passport photographs taken in May or June 1950.

> Mr. Saypol: Did you in the month of June 1950, or in
> the month of May 1950, have any passport photographs
> taken of yourself?
>
> A: No, I did not.[330]

After the defense had ended its case, Saypol called Ben Schneider, owner of a small photography store near the federal courthouse, as a surprise rebuttal witness. Saypol claimed to have discovered the witness only on the previous day, the last day Rosenberg had been on the witness stand.

The defense requested the right to a *voir dire* examination of the surprise witness to learn something about his background, but Judge Kaufman ruled that the witness would testify without background questions by the defense.[331] The judge would permit the defense only to ask the photographer his place of business, and when he had first known he would be a witness, which the witness gave as the previous day.

This was a critical and unusual ruling. Lawyers for either side at trials are permitted to ask questions about the backgrounds, possible criminal records and current indictments, and other questions relating to the character and reputation of witnesses, and whether they had previously given testimony for the prosecution in other cases. Obtaining such information is inherent in the Constitutional right, under the Sixth Amendment, to confront one's witnesses.

The defense attorneys doubted Schneider was a "surprise" to Saypol, and believed his name had been deliberately kept off the witness list so that there would be no time for the defense to investigate him before his appearance in court. Schneider's testimony would be the last to be heard by the jurors.

An unprecedented procedure then occurred. Both Saypol and Judge Kaufman apparently became concerned that a refusal to permit *voir dire* questioning of the witness might be useful to the defense as an issue on appeal. Saypol offered to conduct the *voir dire* that was refused to Bloch, to which Judge Kaufman assented. Saypol then asked a few perfunctory questions of his intended witness, none of them relating to his background, character or previous appearances in court on behalf of prosecutors. When he was done, Saypol said he hoped the *voir dire* "has now been disposed of to his [Bloch's] satisfaction." Bloch replied, "No, it is not to my satisfaction." Judge Kaufman then said, "It is to my satisfaction."[332]

Saypol put into evidence prosecution Exhibit 32, a photograph of Schneider's store. The witness testified that, on a Saturday in May or June 1950, the Rosenbergs and their two sons came to his studio to have passport photographs taken. He remembered it was a Saturday, he testified, because he didn't usually keep the studio open on that day. Another reason Schneider remembered the Rosenbergs, he testified, was they ordered three dozen photographs.[333] As the Rosenbergs left the studio, the witness said, they told him they were going to France to take care of some property. He also remembered them, he said, because the boys were unruly.[334]

> Q. Now, when the [FBI] agents came to visit you yesterday, did they show you photographs?
>
> A. They did.
>
> Q. Was it from those photographs that you picked him [Julius Rosenberg] out?
>
> A. That's right.
>
> Q. And is it seeing him here now with his wife that recalls it to your memory that they were the persons who came in?
>
> A. That's right; that's right.[335]

Saypol's phrase "Was it from those photographs..." led to a reply that implied the witness had been shown photographs of a number of persons, from which he selected Julius Rosenberg. But according to a December 1, 1952 affidavit from FBI agent Walter C. Roettling the only photographs shown to the witness were those of Julius Rosenberg. Roettling affirmed in his affidavit, "I exhibited photographs of Julius Rosenberg and asked Mr. Schneider whether he had ever seen this man."[336]

On cross examination, Emanuel Bloch asked the witness whether he had negatives of the passport photographs he testified he took of the Rosenbergs.

> A. We don't keep the negatives.
>
> Q. You don't keep any negatives in your place?
>
> A. No.
>
> Q. Not one?
>
> A. We don't, no.
>
> Q. Not for a day?
>
> A. For a day, but after that —

Q. For two days?

Judge Kaufman interrupted Bloch and admonished him to "take it easy."
When Bloch resumed cross-examination, he repeated his last question

E. Bloch: For two days?

A. No, we don't.

Q. Never?

A. No.[337]

**

Q. Do you keep books?

A. Books?

Q. Do you keep books in your business?

A. No.

Q. Have you a record here to show that [sic] you sold to
the Rosenbergs?

A. No.[338]

Bloch elicited from Schneider that he had seen a photograph of the
Rosenbergs in a newspaper several weeks earlier, but didn't recognize Rosenberg
until FBI agents showed him photographs of Julius Rosenberg on the previous
day.

Earlier, Saypol had asked the witness

Q. And is that the last time you saw him [Rosenberg]
before today?

A. That's right.

One year later, the defense lawyers learned that the witness had, with
the FBI's and Saypol's knowledge, committed perjury in his reply. He had been
brought into the courtroom by two FBI agents on the day before he testified, at a
time when Julius Rosenberg was on the stand.

Ironically, the perjury became known through Oliver Pilat, a *New York Post*
reporter who was often called "Saypol's mouth" during the trial, because of Pilat's
custom of clearing his stories with the prosecutor.[339] In *The Atom Spies*, which
appeared after the trial and while the appeals were pending, Pilat acknowledged
Saypol's "consultative" assistance,[340] but inadvertently created problems for him
by writing

> While Julius [Rosenberg] was still on the stand, an FBI agent brought into the courtroom a photographer from a shop hardly a block away who recalled somebody resembling the description of Rosenberg, with two wild kids, coming in for passport photos. He [Schneider] wanted a look at Rosenberg to be sure, and when he took the look, he nodded.[341]

It was clear the prosecution had deliberately elicited the witness' perjury. Schneider's perjury became one of the issues on appeal, and was supported by an affidavit by an FBI agent in which the agent revealed that prosecutor Saypol

> directed that the photographer be brought to the United States Courthouse to confirm the identity of Rosenberg previously made.
>
> ***
>
> I brought Mr. Schneider into Courtroom 110, to the fore part of the courtroom inside the railing where there were two vacant seats. I instructed Mr. Schneider to look round the court room and see if he saw anybody he recognized. I did not point out any specific person to Mr. Schneider. Mr. Schneider looked around and, when he saw Julius Rosenberg, he stated to me that was the man whose picture he had taken.[342]

Even the FBI agent's affidavit was essentially deceptive, since Saypol had directed the FBI to bring Schneider into court on a day that Julius Rosenberg was on the stand, and was being addressed by name.

The contributions of the perjuries and deceits to the prosecution's case...

The six major perjuries and deceits described above were, in effect, the prosecution's full case.

The first suborned perjury was David Greenglass' denial that he had been coached to display to the jurors information about the atom bomb he did not have in 1944-1945. This enabled the prosecution to give the jurors the impression that Greenglass, through Julius Rosenberg, had given the Soviet Union a virtual blueprint for making their atom bomb.

The second suborned perjury was the testimony of both Greenglasses that Ethel Rosenberg had typed up David Greenglass' notes on the atom bomb, thus justifying her indictment on a capital charge. The officials knew from Ruth Greenglass' testimony at the grand jury hearings, on August 8, 1950, that her only reference to preparing notes for Julius Rosenberg were notes in her own handwriting.

The third was the prosecution's deceitful headline-making announcement, enabled by Judge Kaufman, that a new witness would corroborate the Greenglasses' testimony about Julius Rosenbergs' involvement in atom bomb espionage.

The fourth false claim was the "espionage-adapted" console table, which created for the jurors a dramatically graphic picture of Julius Rosenberg seated at the console table, the shades in his room drawn, reducing highly classified documents to postage-size dimensions for transmission to the Soviet Union.

The fifth false claim was the suborned perjury in Harry Gold's "I come from Julius" salutation at the purported June 3, 1945 meeting. The impact of the salutation on the jurors was to place Julius Rosenberg in the atom bomb espionage operation involving Greenglass and Gold.

The sixth suborned perjury was the passport photographer's unsupported testimony that he had taken Rosenberg family passport photos. His testimony was clearly intended to corroborate the Greenglasses' testimony that the Rosenbergs were planning to flee.

The Rosenbergs' defense…

The problem for the Rosenbergs' defense was that the charge in the formal indictment relating to obtaining non-atomic classified information for the Soviet Union during World War II was largely, but not entirely, true. But the accusations made in the oral indictment in the presence of the jurors — that the defendants were guilty of passing the secrets of the atom bomb to the Soviet Union, and that they were motivated by hatred of the United States — were false. The oral charges had dominated the prosecution's case and it was predictable that they would dominate the Rosenbergs' cross-examination.

A statement made later in the trial, by Judge Kaufman, illustrated the prosecution's deft transposition of the time of the crime from the years of amity and military alliance in World War II to the years of feverish hostility during the Cold War. The judge said,

> It is so difficult to make people realize that this country is engaged in a life and death struggle with a completely different system…I believe that never at any time in our history were we ever confronted to the same degree that we are today with such a challenge to our very existence.[343]

This was hardly an accurate description of the public's view of the Soviet Union during World War II, when the crime had been committed, nor could it have been a true reflection of Julius Rosenberg's and Morton Sobell's intent. Bloch and the other defense attorneys understood quite well that the testimony given by the Rosenbergs would be heard by the jurors in the context of fears aroused by the New York media headlines of anticipated human casualties during Soviet atom bomb attacks on the city. Simple denials by the defendants of specific acts described by the Greenglasses would hardly go far to overcome the widely held maxim of the time: *Better safe than sorry.* Assertions of loyalty and patriotism by defendants labeled as Communists would have little credibility.

The Rosenbergs and their defense attorneys took what they considered the least harmful approach: 1) they would deny the truth of all the acts the Greenglasses had attributed to them; 2) they would assert their loyalty and patriotism; 3) if they were asked questions relating to membership in the Communist Party, they would cite the Fifth Amendment. They were certainly aware that citing the Fifth Amendment could be taken as an evasive affirmative answer to the Communist question. But a 'No' answer to the Communist question, even if it was the truth, would most likely not be believed by the jurors, since such a response would be expected of Communists. A 'Yes' answer would be heard as 'Yes' not only to being a Communist, but also 'Yes' to being a traitor. A 'Yes' answer would also result in instant demands by the prosecutors that the Rosenbergs name their accomplices, a demand that had been upheld in other courts and hearings, on the grounds that once a defendant did not avail him or herself of the Fifth Amendment, there was no limit to the questions they had to answer. The requirement to name others — relatives, neighbors, colleagues, strangers — as "traitors" would certainly been a factor in their citing the Fifth Amendment.

The defense also faced very practical problems. In his direct examination of the Rosenbergs, Bloch had intended to show, among other things, that the Greenglasses' testimony had not been corroborated by any other witness. But the Perl announcement had an unsettling effect on Bloch and on the other defense attorneys. Just as Nobelist Harold Urey, J. Robert Oppenheimer and General Leslie Groves had been placed on the prosecution's witness list to deter the defense from challenging Greenglass' atom bomb testimony, so Perl had been announced as a witness to deter the defense from challenging the Greenglasses' testimony when the case for the defense was under way. The defense could not have foreseen that neither Urey, Oppenheimer, Groves, nor Perl would be called to testify, although the prosecution could still call any of them as rebuttal witnesses after the defense rested.

Bloch was also aware that simple denials by his clients would hardly be as dramatic for the jurors as the Greenglasses' testimony had been. The defense had nothing to rival Exhibit 8 or the torn Jell-O box panels or the tale of a late evening ride with an unknown Russian, with which to win the jurors' attention.

Julius Rosenberg's testimony...

Bloch took Julius Rosenberg through the testimony of the Greenglasses, listing each of their accusations and asking Rosenberg to comment on them. Did Rosenberg ever ask Ruth Greenglass to invite David Greenglass to join an espionage conspiracy. "I did not."

Had Rosenberg known in November 1944, there was a project called the Los Alamos Project? "I did not."

Rosenberg gave the same reply to whether he had ever asked for or received information bearing on the atom bomb from David or Ruth Greenglass.[344,345] Likewise, to whether he had ever told Greenglass there was an atom bomb project at Los Alamos or that Greenglass had described such a project to him,[346] and whether he arranged to have David Greenglass meet an unknown Russian one night in mid-Manhattan.[347]

When Bloch asked whether Rosenberg recalled that a friend, Ann Sidorovich, had been at the Rosenberg apartment one evening,[348] Judge Kaufman broke in to ask

> The Court: Did you ever discuss with Ann Sidorovich the respective preferences of economic systems between Russia and the United States?

Rosenberg replied

> A. ...in my normal social intercourse with my friends we discussed matters like that. And I believe there are merits in both systems, I mean from what I have been able to read and ascertain.

> The Court: I am not talking about your belief today. I am talking about your belief at that time, in January 1945.

> A. Well, that is what I am talking about...

> Mr. Bloch: Do you owe allegiance to any other country?

> A. No, I do not.[349]

Bloch asked whether Rosenberg would fight for the United States against any enemy, to which Rosenberg replied in the affirmative. Judge Kaufman turned the proceedings back to the issue of Communism

> The Court: Did you approve the communistic system of Russia over the capitalistic system in this country?

> A. I am not an expert on these things, your Honor, and I did not make any such direct statement.

> Mr. Bloch: Did you ever make any comparisons in the
> sense that the Court has asked you, about whether you
> preferred one system over another?
>
> A. No, I did not. I would like to state that my personal
> opinions are that the people of every country should
> decide by themselves what kind of government they
> want...
>
> Mr. Bloch: Do you believe in the overthrow of govern-
> ment by force and violence?
>
> A. I do not.
>
> Mr. Bloch: Do you believe — do you believe in anybody
> committing acts of espionage against his own country?
>
> A. I do not believe that.[350]

Judge Kaufman persisted in asking Julius Rosenberg about his views on Communism

> The Court: Well, did you ever belong to any group that
> discussed the system of Russia?
>
> A. Well, your Honor, if you are referring to political
> groups — is that what you are referring to?
>
> The Court: Any group.
>
> A. Well, your Honor, I feel at this time that I refuse to
> answer a question that might tend to incriminate me.[351]

Had Rosenberg told the Greenglasses, one evening, that Ethel was tired because she had been typing material for the Russians, and had she or he ever typed such material? He replied "I did not say anything of the sort" and "She did not," and "I did not."[352]

On cross-examination, Saypol asked whether Rosenberg and his class-mates at CCNY pursued any activities in common. Rosenberg replied

> A. ...if Mr. Saypol is referring to the Young Communist
> League or the Communist Party, I will not answer any
> question on it.[353]

There then followed a series of questions by Saypol that touched on whether during World War II Rosenberg had advocated opening a second front prior to the American June 6, 1945, landing in France and whether he felt the United States was not treating the Soviet Union as an equal ally. As to the second front,

Rosenberg replied affirmatively;[354] matters regarding equality among the allies, Rosenberg testified, "were up to the Governments, the British, American and the Russian Government."[355]

Saypol then asked Rosenberg whether he had expressed these opinions "in any Communist unit that you might have belonged to?" Rosenberg again invoked the Fifth Amendment protection against self-incrimination.

Saypol introduced into evidence Exhibit 27, a collection can for orphans of the 1936-1939 Spanish Civil War, which had been found in the Rosenberg's apartment by the FBI. Saypol asked whether Rosenberg had ever solicited funds or contributed funds to the Joint Anti-Fascist Refugee Committee, which sponsored the collection can. Rosenberg replied he had contributed but not solicited funds for the Committee.[356] Saypol described a public insurance and burial society — the International Workers Order (IWO) — as a Communist organization in which Rosenberg held a $5,000 life insurance policy and asked Rosenberg whether "Is it not a fact that it is a communist organization exclusively?" Rosenberg replied, "I don't believe it is a communist organization."[357]

Saypol then asked Rosenberg for the name of the person who had invited him to join the IWO, to which Rosenberg replied that he did not remember.

Saypol asked Rosenberg whether he had been a member of the Communist Party in 1945, when he was dismissed from his Army Signal Corps employment. Rosenberg invoked the Fifth Amendment. Saypol quoted from Rosenberg's denial, in 1948, that he was a Communist

> Saypol: And then you go on to say: "I am not now and never have been a communist member...Either the charge is based on a mistaken identity or a complete falsehood. In any event, it certainly has not the slightest basis in fact."[358]

Rosenberg acknowledged he had so replied. Saypol then asked whether the denial of Communist membership had been truthful, and Rosenberg responded by invoking the Fifth Amendment. Saypol pressed for an answer, and Judge Kaufman said he might overrule Rosenberg's reliance on the Fifth Amendment,[359] which meant Rosenberg would have to give a Yes or No answer to Saypol's question. Bloch argued Judge Kaufman could not deny a Constitutional protection to a defendant, and if Judge Kaufman did so, his ruling would become an issue on appeal if there was a guilty verdict.[360] Judge Kaufman, possibly thinking out loud, said he wanted to be careful not to

> The Court:
> ..jeopardize a case as important as this with a ruling that might prove to be error.[361]

At this point the trial was adjourned for the weekend. When the trial resumed on Monday, Saypol withdrew the question that had led to Judge Kaufman's threatened nullification of Rosenberg's right to invoke the Fifth Amendment.

Saypol continued his cross-examination of Julius Rosenberg by reciting the names of a number of various persons and asking Rosenberg whether he knew them, to which Rosenberg responded affirmatively for some, negatively for others. When his response was affirmative, Saypol then demanded to know when and where he had met the person, how often he saw the person and, in some instances, whether they exchanged Christmas cards and whether he had met the person at Communist meetings.[362] All the defense attorneys rose to protest that Saypol was asking Rosenberg about matters on which no testimony had been taken or proofs submitted. In effect, they were objecting that Saypol was being permitted to testify in the presence of the jury to unproven matters: for example, "Isn't it the fact that you gave her [a woman named Vivian Glassman] $2,000 to take out to somebody in Cleveland?" "Don't you know that he [a man named Alfred Sarant] is in Mexico?" "Don't you know, Mr. Rosenberg, that the Sidoroviches didn't move to Cleveland until December 1944?" "Didn't you know that Sobell was working for General Electric at that time in Ithaca, New York?" "Mr. Rosenberg, did you know that Mrs. Greenglass perhaps had telephoned to her husband in Albuquerque in November 1944?"[363]

These "questions" constituted uncorroborated testimony by Saypol, and by no other witness, and their effect on the jurors, as he surely knew, would be to make it appear to them that the events described by Saypol in his questions actually occurred and that the witness was being repeatedly evasive. In spite of vigorous objections and motions for mistrials by the defense, Kaufman did not disallow the prosecutor's charge-laden statements in the guise of questions.

Ethel Rosenberg's testimony...

Bloch's examination of Ethel Rosenberg elicited the same responses as her husband had given.

In his cross-examination, Saypol attacked Ethel Rosenberg's credibility on the grounds that at the grand jury hearings in the previous year she had declined to answer a number of questions by citing the privilege against self-incrimination, while at the trial she chose to answer some of these questions directly. Bloch objected, but Judge Kaufman upheld Saypol, telling the jurors that Ethel Rosenberg's decision to answer Saypol's questions directly rather than decline to answer them as she had the previous year at the grand jury hearing should be weighed by the jurors in evaluating her credibility.

Bloch, as it turned out, was right in his objection. Six years after the trial, the Supreme Court, in *Grunewald* v. *United States,* ruled that it violated the Constitutional rights of defendants for prosecutors to use a defendant's access to Fifth Amendment protections at grand jury hearings to attack the defendant's credibility at a jury trial.[364] To allow such a prosecutorial tactic, the Court ruled, would be tantamount to nullifying the protective purpose of the Fifth Amendment.

Sobell's attorneys decline to have him testify...

Sobell's attorneys did not have him take the stand. Their reasoning was that other than Elitcher's testimony about a late-night drive to Knickerbocker Village, where the Rosenbergs lived, for which there had been no corroborating testimony, the prosecution had not made a case against Sobell.

Summations: for the defendants...

Bloch appealed to the jurors to consider only those facts relating to the crime charged in the formal indictment, which was that the defendants conspired to pass classified information to the Soviet Union during World War II.[365] The defendants, he told the jurors, were not being tried for being Communists.

Bloch pointed out that the statute under which the defendants were tried made it a crime to transmit classified information "where there is intent or reason to believe that it would be to the injury of the United States," but that no claim was made in the indictment that the defendants had intended to injure the United States by their purported crime.

Bloch then took up the matter of tangible and circumstantial evidence. He examined the prosecution's exhibits for the jurors, pointing out that none of the exhibits corroborated a criminal act or intent to commit such an act by the defendants, and that few exhibits had any relation at all to the Rosenbergs.

Bloch argued that the Greenglasses had implicated the Rosenbergs in their crime because

> Bloch: Greenglass figured that if he could put the finger on somebody, he would lessen his own punishment; and he had to put the finger on somebody who was here in the United States, and he had to put the finger on somebody who was a clay-pigeon; and that man sitting there (indicating defendant Julius Rosenberg) is a clay-pigeon because he was fired from the Government service, because it was alleged that he was a member of the Communist Party; and he was a guy who was very open and expressed his views about the United States and the Soviet Union, which may have been all right when the Soviet Union and the United States were Allies, but today it is anathema ...[366]

In summary, Bloch emphasized the total absence of any tangible corroboration of the testimonies of the witnesses, and the threat of death sentences as motivating the Greenglasses' testimony and the threat of a perjury indictment motivating Elitcher's testimony.

Edward Kuntz, one of Sobell's two attorneys, told the jurors that Emanuel Bloch had been overly charitable toward the prosecution and its witnesses, and to Max Elitcher in particular. Elitcher had testified he had perjured himself in the past by denying he had been a Communist, and that he had been invited several times by Julius Rosenberg to become a spy, but had always given non-committal answers.

> Mr. Kuntz: I am not going to be charitable like Manny Bloch. I have tried cases a little longer than he has. I am through being charitable when the life of a man depends on my actions and my words. ... Why should I be charitable? When I cross-examined him [Elitcher], I asked him, "Elitcher, aren't you a liar?" and he said, "Yes." "Aren't you a perjurer?" He said, "Yes." How could I be charitable with... a man who will involve, who will kill another man to save his own miserable skin?"[367]

He went on to hold Saypol responsible for what he described as Elitcher's deceptive testimony, and argued it was impossible to adequately defend Sobell, because no one could point to any evidence of a crime; there was nothing in the prosecution's case against Sobell to challenge because Sobell had not been accused of any acts that were definable and capable of being analyzed and rebutted

> Mr. Kuntz: Somehow I do feel inadequate. I feel inadequate in this case for this reason. When somebody charges you in an indictment with doing certain things, you go out and you prepare to oppose them. I am telling you if you hunt from top to bottom of this indictment you won't find in there a word about Morton Sobell outside of the title in this case and in the parts that I read to you and look at how many pages it is with overt acts and everything; not a word about Morton Sobell.[368]

That ended Kuntz' summation, but a few moments later Saypol would bring him to his feet again.

Summation: for the prosecution...

Saypol began by comparing the American system of justice with that of the Soviet Union.[369] He quickly moved on to a personal issue, however, complaining that defense counsel — in particular, Edward Kuntz — had sought to confuse the jurors.

To understand what happened next, we must provide a little background. When Saypol had been chairman of Tammany Hall's Law Committee, he had arranged to void American Labor Party petitions that would have enabled Edward Kuntz to run for a judgeship. Now, for his summation in the Rosenberg-Sobell case, Saypol armed himself with an old copy of the *New York Law Journal*, in which a reporter had described Kuntz as a Communist, and which Saypol had informed Cohn he intended to read to the jurors. Cohn, afraid that if Saypol did so, there would be strong grounds for an appeal for reversal if the jurors brought in guilty verdicts, had notified Judge Kaufman of Saypol's intentions. Judge Kaufman shared Cohn's opinion that Saypol must be prevented from reading the material on Kuntz to the jurors.[370]

Saypol, mentioning Kuntz by name, told the jurors

> Mr. Saypol: I was a little puzzled by the vitriol in the latter attack, and as I sat and reflected I sent for another law book and I find that in 1936 a lawyer by the name of Edward Kuntz was a candidate for election to the Court of General Sessions.
>
> Mr. Kuntz: Wait a second. What has this got to do with this case?[371]
>
> The Court: No, let us not go into that.[372]

Saypol persisted, but Judge Kaufman cut him short, and Saypol had to continue his summation without pursuing his attack on Kuntz as a Communist.

On the subject of Kuntz' client, Saypol told the jurors

> Mr. Saypol: The association of Rosenberg and Sobell began at City College, and it continues until today. They have been held together by one common bond: Their mutual devotion to Communism and the Soviet Union, and their membership in this conspiracy to commit espionage for that Soviet Union.[373]

Saypol had raised the "intent to injure the United States" treason argument, which was absent from the indictment, in his opening statement in which he had said that in their

> rank disloyalty to this country these defendants joined with their co-conspirators in a deliberate, carefully planned conspiracy to deliver to the Soviet Union, the

information and the weapons which the Soviet Union could use to destroy us…[374]

Toward the end of his summation, Saypol may have become concerned about his repeated references to Communism, which would surely become the bases of appeals to the higher courts if guilty verdicts were returned. Saypol told the jurors that he didn't want them to "convict them [the defendants] merely because of their communist activity."[375]

Nevertheless,

> Communism, as the testimony has demonstrated, has a very definite place in this case because it is the communist ideology which teaches worship and devotion to the Soviet Union over our own government. It has provided the motive and inspiration for these people to do the terrible things which have been proven against them.[376]

Judge Kaufman's instructions to the jurors…

In making his charge to the jury, Judge Kaufman had to deal with the same problem the prosecution and the defense faced at the trial: he would be unable to lay out each side's tangible and circumstantial evidence, and their opposite interpretations of the testimony. He would, instead, as the prosecution had done, rely on history-as-evidence, express the crime as a Cold War event, describe the times as a clash of ideologies and nations, and accept the prosecution's descriptions of the defendants' motivations.

He called attention to the world situation and the hostility among nations, and in this way blurred for the jurors their legally stated role as finders of fact by giving them another role — guardians of national security. Because "of the development of highly destructive weapons," he told the jurors, the nation must

> guard against spying on the secrets of our defense, whether such spying is carried on through agents of foreign powers or through our own nationals who prefer to help a foreign power.[377]

The judge pointed out that the mere allegation of the defendants' guilt by the prosecution was not to be taken as proof of guilt. And then he legitimated the treason charge, saying,

> The Court: This does not mean that the mere allegation or use of the word "espionage" should justify convicting innocent persons; however, irrational sympathies must not shield proven traitors.[378]

The judge altered the meaning of the Constitution's definition of treason as giving aid to an enemy, by declaring,

> The Court: I charge you that whether the Union of Soviet Socialist Republics was an ally or friendly nation during the period of the alleged conspiracy is immaterial, and you are not to consider that at all in your deliberations.[379]

On the issue of Communism, Judge Kaufman said

> The Court: I wish to caution you most strenuously that proof of Communist Party membership or activity does not prove the offense charged in this indictment, but may be considered by you solely on the question of intent which is one element of the crime charged here. It will be up to you to determine whether you believe that testimony and, if so, the weight you will give it on the question of intention.[380]

He laid out the obligations of the jurors to deliberate without bias, and to take into a account the self-interest a witness might have in giving his or her testimony, the credibility of accomplice testimony, the necessity of avoiding inferences of guilt in respect to Sobell for not taking the stand, likewise for defendants who invoked the Fifth Amendment privilege against self-incrimination; and, finally, that a juror

> The Court: ...cannot allow a consideration of the punishment which may be inflicted upon the defendants to influence your verdict in any way; the desire to avoid the performance of an unpleasant task cannot influence your verdict.[381]

The verdicts...

About four hours into their deliberations the jurors sent a note to the judge stating

> One of the jurors has some doubt in his mind as to whether he can recommend leniency for one of the defendants. He is interested in knowing your mind on the matter.[382]

Judge Kaufman re-read to the jurors that portion of his charge that had dealt with punishment, and explained that "the question of possible punishment of the defendants in the event of conviction is no concern of the jury and should not in any sense enter into or influence your deliberations." He added the jurors could make a recommendation, if they chose to, but "it is my prerogative to follow or disregard any recommendation that you may make on the matter of punishment. Is that clear?"[383]

At about 20 minutes after midnight the jurors informed the court they wished to retire for the night "due to still existent dissident vote amongst us." Judge Kaufman said he would first ask the jurors "whether they have arrived upon a verdict as to any defendant," and to give him the verdict on that one defendant.

The elder Bloch, Alexander, objected, saying, "That is cruelty to us."

> The Court: Why prolong the agony? If they have it, they have it.
>
> Mr. Kuntz: Judge Kaufman, I have a sort of feeling that if you do that, that juror — now, I don't know who it is and I don't know for whom it is — might feel that this is a suggestion — [384]

Judge Kaufman insisted on obtaining a verdict that night on one or more defendants, if the jurors had one. Kuntz objected again that if Judge Kaufman made his request, it would place pressure on any dissident juror or jurors to yield to the majority. Judge Kaufman overruled the objection, but said he would leave it to the jurors to decide whether, if they had reached a verdict on any of the defendants, they wished to tell the court what that verdict was.

The jurors replied

> We have reached our verdict on two of the defendants and we prefer to reserve rendering our verdict on all these defendants until we have complete unanimity.[385]

The following morning, March 29, 1951, at 10 a.m., the jurors announced they had found all three defendants guilty as charged.

Judge Kaufman thanked the jurors, saying he agreed with their verdict.

> The Court: *** The thought that citizens of our country would lend themselves to the destruction of their own country by the most destructive weapon known to man is so shocking that I can't find words to describe this loathsome offense.[386]

In dismissing a jury it is customary, especially in trials that have attracted national and international media interest, for the presiding judge to advise the jurors that they are not obliged to discuss their verdicts with media reporters, friends or family. Judge Kaufman, however, went further:

> The Court: I just want to give you one last admonition
> before I send you off, and that is, please don't discuss this
> case, don't discuss your deliberations, don't discuss your
> verdict with members of the press or with anybody.[387]

Whether the jurors took Judge Kaufman's admonition as meaning that they would be breaking the law if they discussed their deliberations and verdict with the media or other inquirers (there is no such law), is not known, but it is a fact that twenty years were to pass before any of the jurors would speak to the media about the trial.

The sentences...

At the sentencing hearing Irving Saypol repeated the treason charge and urged Judge Kaufman to show no leniency

> Mr. Saypol: It would be delusion indeed to believe
> that the war in Korea is anything but a war inspired by
> Russia. It is not an ad hominem appeal to suggest that
> it is inferable that young American lives are being daily
> sacrificed in Korea in defense of our way of life. These
> defendants gave their allegiance to forces which now are
> proven is allied to the real enemy in that fight ... How
> could the life of a single individual engaged in such trea-
> sonable activities be weighed against the life of a single
> American soldier fighting in a distant land?[388]

The defense attorneys called Judge Kaufman's attention to the absence of tangible evidence of the commission of a crime, and argued, in effect, that the absence of such evidence was a rational reason for sentences far removed from the irreparable penalties at the judge's disposal.

Emanuel Bloch took on the judge's historical exposition to the jurors,

> Mr. E. H. Bloch: Now, your Honor, I would like the
> Court to ask itself this question — and I have to pres-
> ent a hypothetical state of facts: Assuming that the
> United States Government had found out in 1945 what
> they found out years later and which impelled them to
> bring these charges; one, would these defendants find
> themselves in a criminal court? And if, two, they found
> themselves as defendants, would there be the hullaba-
> loo and hysteria which has accompanied the progress of
> this criminal procedure?

The Court: You overlooked one very salient feature, and
that is that their activities didn't cease in 1945, but that
there was evidence in the case of continued activity in
espionage right on down, even during a period when it
was then apparent to everybody that we were now dealing with a hostile nation.[389]

Bloch pointed out that the overwhelming bulk of the testimony concerned
itself with the alleged theft of classified information relating to the atom bomb in
1945, and that the testimony relating to the later years was related to allegations
involving flight. He then said

Mr. E. H. Bloch: I am not saying that when a man com-
mits a criminal act he is to be condoned or his actions
are to be condoned or he is to be excused because he
lacks prescience and foresight of what the turns of history might bring about. I am not saying that at all. But I
do say that it would be unduly harsh and unduly severe
and unduly rigorous if an ideological approach, inspired
by motives and feelings that were prevalent amongst
great sections of the American population in 1944 and
1945, were translated, transmuted and transformed into
something as heinous as Mr. Saypol has just stated and
represented to the Court.[390]

In imposing his sentences on the defendants, Judge Kaufman may have
been especially concerned that the media might call attention to the difference
between the historical context he had proposed to the jurors and the one being
proposed by Emanuel Bloch. Consequently, he began by leading at once into the
treason theme to justify the sentences he would shortly announce

The Court: Citizens of this country who betray their
fellow countrymen can be under none of the delusions
about the benignity of Soviet power that they might
have had prior to World War II. The nature of Russian
terrorism is now self-evident. Idealism as a rationale
dissolves.[391]

He repeated the deceptive time transposition made during the trial, saying

the power which set the conspiracy in motion and prof-
ited from it was…openly hostile to the United States at
the time of the conspiracy.[392]

He then invoked the specter of Armageddon, with the defendants enrolled in a battle against God. The defendants, Kaufman declared

> made a choice of devoting themselves to the Russian ideology of denial of God, denial of the sanctity of the individual and aggression against free men everywhere instead of serving the cause of liberty and freedom. I consider your crime worse than murder. Plain deliberate contemplated murder is dwarfed in magnitude by comparison with the crime you have committed ... I believe your conduct in putting into the hands of the Russians the A-bomb years before our best scientists predicted Russia would perfect the bomb has already caused, in my opinion, the Communist aggression in Korea, with the resultant casualties exceeding 50,000 and who knows but that millions more of innocent people may pay the price of your treason. ...I feel that I must pass such sentence upon the principles in this diabolical conspiracy to destroy a God-fearing nation, which will demonstrate with finality that this nation's security must remain inviolate....It is not in my power, Julius and Ethel Rosenberg, to forgive you. Only the Lord can find mercy for what you have done. The sentence of the Court upon Julius and Ethel Rosenberg is, for the crime for which you have been convicted, you are hereby sentenced to the punishment of death, and it is ordered upon some day within the week beginning with Monday, May 21st, you shall be executed according to law.[393]

If the judge had prayed to God before sentencing the defendants, as the media later cited him saying, he may have been praying that, for just an instant, God would look away.

The jurors speak: they deliberated on the oral accusation of treason...

For twenty years, the jurors seem to have regarded Judge Kaufman's admonition not to discuss their verdict with anyone as binding. But in 1973, the National Public Affairs Center for Television (NPACT), a news programming group, succeeded in interviewing five jurors who had been on the Rosenberg-Sobell jury. The jurors' statements must be evaluated in the light of the more than twenty years that had passed since they voted their verdicts.

Among the interesting facts that came to light was that in his search for the jurors, the NPACT reporter discovered that one juror, Richard Booth, juror number 2, was not known to the employer he had said he worked for in 1951. In court at the time of the *voir dire*, Booth said he was employed as a caterer at the Seminole Club, a Long Island tennis club,[394] and this was repeated two years later in a February 6, 1953 memorandum to the Assistant Attorney General by Myles Lane.[395] But the NPACT reporter who had tried to locate Booth found that no one at the Seminole Club

> has ever heard of him, including Juan the bartender who worked there at the time of the trial. I have called all of the union locals to which he might have belonged in some aspect of catering or waiting work, with no success.[396]

There can be little doubt that every juror on the panel of jury-candidates was given a background check by the FBI, and probably a more comprehensive check was made of those who were actually seated. How did a juror unknown at his place of employment survive an FBI check? The first thought that springs to mind is that the NPACT reporter may have erred, but the record discloses that he successfully tracked down all the other living jurors. A second thought springs to mind: that Booth may have been a prosecution plant who would simply vanish. Earlier, we mentioned that, as a result of the Freedom of Information Act, students of the case learned that chief prosecutor Irving Saypol had installed John Brunini, the literary collaborator of Elizabeth Bentley, as foreman of the grand jury in the William Remington case.

In his interview, Vincent J. Lebonitte, the foreman of the Rosenberg-Sobell jury, related that he had persuaded a holdout juror to change his vote, not on the basis of the evidence, but by citing Judge Kaufman's instructions to the jury on the dangers the United States faced from the Soviet Union

> Q. How did you persuade the juror to vote with the rest of you?
>
> A. ...I do distinctly recall mentioning that possibly Ethel Rosenberg's actions some day might be responsible for your death, the death of your children, your family, and even her children for that matter.[397]

Lebonitte was advising the holdout juror, as Judge Kaufman had previously inferred to the jurors, that his duty as a trier of fact must be sublimated to a duty to take as true the dangers to the nation as described to him by public officials. Thus, although the world situation was not evidence of the defendants' purported hostility to the United States, it became, for Lebonitte, as it had for Judge Kaufman, an argument for their guilt.

The trial, Lebonitte told the interviewer, "had a very profound effect on me...something that affected my life very greatly."

> I had come to realize that this was not just a national situation but it had international ramifications which certainly had its corresponding effects on me.[398]

Lebonitte's interest in what he apparently regarded as the larger issues at the trial included concern that critics of the trial might find an anti-Semitic aspect in the case

> There was one observation I made after the trial which I think satisfied me as being the number one juror of the entire case and that was the fact that the defendants, both defendants Ethel and Julius, the prosecutor Irving Saypol and the Judge that presided during the trial [,] Irving Kaufman all happened to be of the same faith and this gave me a certain feeling of satisfaction knowing that the idea of prejudice did not creep in not just on one occasion but on no occasion whatsoever during the entire proceeding and this made me feel gosh, everything was right at least from that particular standpoint.[399]

James A. Gibbons, the holdout juror whose mind had been changed by Lebonitte, was a bookkeeper who lived in the Bronx, New York. His change of mind still seemed to trouble him, for he told a reporter in 1975

> I felt like Pontius Pilate washing his hands. If you know your Bible, you'll understand.[400]

Lebonitte and Gibbons were not the only jurors who had been led by Judge Kaufman's exposition into accepting the dangers posed by the world situation as an argument for the defendants' guilt. The NPACT interviewer asked juror Charles W. Christie, an auditor for an oil company, whether it had been difficult for him to come to a decision. Christie replied

> They committed treason, they were guilty, then, and as far as I'm concerned, they would still be guilty.[401]...At times, as I said before, I wavered, but as I recall it now, I waited until the end to make my final conclusions. But the wavering I had in the meantime was thinking of the fact that I had a family; I had two girls, and how they [the defendants] could expose their two children to such a fate.[402]

Juror Christie denied that the political beliefs of the defendants had played any role in his vote on the verdict.

> A. Let's talk about treason first and espionage. It was wrong then and it's wrong today in the same degree, as far as I'm concerned....The trial was not in any sense of the word, related to the communist party abroad or in this country. As far as I was concerned, it was a pure case of espionage on the part of these defendants. ... They [the defendants] were also American citizens. And this is the basis on which they were evaluated — not as Communists ... They were evaluated on the basis of American citizens committing a traitorous act.[403]

The interviewer asked what Christie felt should be understood about the trial, and he replied that the same trial, in the atmosphere prevailing in the 1970s, might have led to a different verdict because there was greater

> permissiveness on the part of the courts. I don't think the outcome would be the same, particularly the fact that the death penalty is practically outlawed, but aside from that, I have reservations that you'd even get the same verdict today.[404]

Another juror, Charles J. Duda, a bookkeeper who lived in Dobbs Ferry, New York, was asked whether there had been any debate in arriving at a verdict

> Oh, I don't think there was any real changing of minds. It was more hesitation. I think at the outset...I think it was just mainly the, well, do you want to use the word, Christian Attitude of a couple of the jurors towards the children.[405]

Asked about the Soviet Union as a factor at the trial, the juror replied

> Well, it was right after W.W. II, relatively a short time after, the Korean War was going on and Communism, it was a bad thing. After all we helped them in World War II, bailed them out and here they are coming back at us any way they could; taking over all these European nations and making slave states out of them so I think the feeling against Communism was much more prevalent than it is today.[406]

Asked about the factor of Communism at the trial, the juror said

> Well, maybe it [mattered] to people, the fact that they were Communists but, as I said before we were thoroughly briefed that this was not to enter into our deliberation...we didn't take that into consideration, in fact it was never brought up in our deliberation the word Communism because it was not part of the evidence.[407]

Another juror, Howard G. Becker, a Wall Street bank examiner who resided in Mamaroneck, New York, expressed surprise at the death penalty.

> I was surprised about the death penalty because up to that time the verdict had never been meted out to anyone in peace time. The most they ever got previous to that was life imprisonment and none of the jurors I'm sure thought that the death penalty would ever be meted out at the end of that trial.
>
> Q. Did it [communism] play a part in the trial?
>
> A. Well, as I recall it was brought quite often during the trial but as I recall the judge promptly overruled any mention of it during the trial.[408]

The interviewer asked the juror whether he had formed an impression of the Rosenbergs during the trial.

> A. Well, they gave the appearance of a very subdued couple and while they maintained that appearance during the whole trial as the evidence was presented they appeared more and more that they were duped into this probably by some Russian agents, probably to better their position in life and make some money and they thought this was the best way to do it and this was the impression I got.[409]

None of the jurors made mention of any tangible or circumstantial evidence that had entered into their deliberations and verdicts.

A senator endorses torture for Julius Rosenberg...

Shortly after trial ended, the Congressional Joint Committee on Atomic Energy (JCAE) issued its 222-page report on Soviet espionage. The JCAE members saw no reason to revise their pre-trial evaluations of Soviet spies. Fuchs remained most important by a wide margin; Bruno Pontecorvo was next, followed by Allen Nunn May, and Greenglass. The sensational Rosenberg-Sobell trial had done well in the media, but for those responsible for national security in government, the trial's outcome had the potential for embarrassment. Confessions were more distant than ever. There was no telling how the judges of the Court of Appeals or the Supreme Court would react to appeals. There were no sequel trials, and it became clear that the Justice Department's pre-trial announcement that it had 21,105 new espionage cases[410] had simply been a ploy by which to extract more funds from Congress. The chief prosecutor, Irving Saypol, promptly resigned from the Justice Department after the trial to become an obscure New York State judge. Roy Cohn, his chief assistant, stayed on for another year and then became chief counsel to Senator Joseph McCarthy's political investigating committee.

There may have been some animus among the JCAE members toward Justice officials and Saypol for needlessly involving them in coaching David Greenglass. The prosecution should have foreseen, if not actually known, that the Rosenbergs' lawyer would move to impound Greenglass' Exhibit 8 sketches and explanatory notes. Hadn't the purpose of the prosecution's scientist-heavy witness list been to discourage the lawyer from cross-examining Greenglass about Exhibit 8? Now, everyone would have to wait for two or more years while the defendants' appeals went on, during which there was always the possibility that some weak or spiteful person who knew about the coaching would blow the whistle, and the JCAE's role would come to light.

The partial minutes of a JCAE meeting, held after the Rosenbergs had been found guilty and sentenced to death, disclose how concerned its members were due to the failure to obtain confessions. According to the minutes, Senator Hickenlooper was prepared to encourage Justice officials to torture Julius Rosenberg to extract his confession. He told the meeting,

> There are ways of securing that information from this man. We don't have to beat him with a ball bat to do that[.] There are ways of securing that information. I think when this country is in peril, that those ways, which can be used, we should take the means necessary to get the information from his mind. I am perfectly aware of the Bill of Rights and a lot of other things, but this is a question of where this country is at stake in some degree at any rate. I would never criticize the use of particular methods I am thinking about.[411]

The JCAE members' concern about their role becoming known was premature by some twenty years. In the 1970s, the minutes of the February 8, 1951 meeting were discovered as a result of the enforcement of the Freedom of Information Act.

Committee Chairman Joseph Brainin addressing a rally
at Randall's Island, New York,
May 3, 1953.

Chapter 7 | Breaking the silence

The Committee to Secure Justice...

The authors were passive spectators in the account we have given so far of the Rosenberg-Sobell trial. Earlier, we wrote we had assumed from what we read in our newspapers in spring 1951, that the trial had been a reasonably fair one. Our first active interest in the case was solely due to the death sentences, and was driven, in part, by the fact that Emily had once had a brief conversation on a park bench with Ethel Rosenberg.

Subsequently, on reading a series of articles critical of the prosecutors and the judge by William A. Reuben, and our reading of the trial record, we became persuaded that the prosecution had resorted to a chronological deceit, as well as other deceits, to obtain guilty verdicts from the jurors. At Emily's initiative, and with the help of William Reuben, a Committee was formed to secure a new trial for the defendants or, if that failed, to obtain clemency for the Rosenbergs and a reduction in Morton Sobell's 30-year sentence. The Committee took no position on the innocence or guilt of the Rosenbergs or Sobell, but only on the conduct of the trial.

To give a formal structure to the Committee, which we described in detail in Chapter 1, we elected Joseph Brainin as Chairman, Louis Harap as President, and Emily as treasurer.

The Committee began with many handicaps, chief of which was that none of its members — with one exception — had any experience in organizing large numbers of people for any cause whatsoever. Joseph Brainin, the exception, had experience in organizing large major public events for Jewish organizations but, as he pointed out to us, he had done so with the help of substantial budgets, trained staffs and office support, to say nothing of target audiences already favorably disposed to support what was asked of them. A few other members had some limited experience in organizing anti-capital punishment actions, union locals, community-based actions and literary groups.

By way of material assets, the Committee had about a hundred dollars, acquired by passing the hat around, an ancient mimeograph machine on loan from a small print shop, a supportive weekly publication — the *National Guardian* — which had a very limited circulation, and one well worn copy of the 2600-page trial record, which all of us had read. We had no office or telephone, and no certainty that our audience — the general public — would respond sympathetically.

God's second choice...

All the members of the Committee were Jewish and, with one exception, poor or nearly poor. The one exception had reached middle-class status. Those who had children did not have savings accounts. What we had was what the Irish and Italian and Polish lower economic classes had: endless commentaries about America, Americanism and the impossible dream that Franklin Roosevelt, who had died in April 1945, would come back to save us once again.

We agreed, as Brainin put it, that we were God's second choice to save the Rosenbergs' lives. We agreed that God's first choice was anyone but us. On the other hand, all there was, was us.

Just as she would do many times in her life for others in other circumstances, Emily persuaded us we were chosen by God or History to do extraordinary things, that we had talents unknown to us, that we had courage beyond belief, that we were, she said, "mule-stubborn Americans," and that we would rouse an America we did not yet know existed.

Searching for a voice...

The Committee members' viewpoints on the direction the campaign should take were hardly unanimous, as they discovered at the first working meetings in Reuben's and the authors' apartments. Some members argued for a campaign based on two issues: prosecutorial and judicial misconduct, and on the horrors of capital punishment.

Brainin, the oldest among us, a veteran skeptic, but not a cynic, said, "People have become so used to horror, they no longer think that horror is so horrible. A lot of people will think we're using the 'horror' argument because we don't believe in our prosecutorial misconduct arguments."

Members argued that the misconduct issue should be used in the context of the repressive atmosphere created by right-wing extremists. But then, others argued, we would be alienating people who didn't believe a repressive atmosphere existed in the country or who felt that a repressive atmosphere was necessary. (Actually, we found there were people who believed the times called for limitations on freedom, and who supported clemency for the Rosenbergs because they believed that unfair trials went beyond the limitations acceptable to them.)

We spent days drafting statements, debating them, culling them, rereading them, and discovering that we were separating into two camps, one that railed against the courtroom injustice to the Rosenbergs and Sobell, the other that railed against worldwide injustice to the human race.

"One side," Emily said, "Is trying to do triage, to save a couple of lives by getting the public to care about courtroom deceits, perjuries, misconduct and illegal death sentences. The other side wants to show the public that extreme right wing politics, anti-Semitism and imperialism is at the heart of the case. One side is going to have to widen its angle of vision, the other side is going to have to narrow it."

She went on to say that, at some future time, historians and other writers would figure out the context in which the case had to be understood, but that was not our mission. "In fact," Emily said, "Our mission is to convince even right wingers and imperialists and even anti-Semites to save the Rosenbergs." Prophetic words, as it turned out.

Tabling some truths for another day...

One issue, more than any other, led to the most serious disagreements within the Committee in its effort to create a statement that would explain what had happened at the trial. Every member of the Committee agreed that the cast of all-Jewish defendants at the trial had been an historic anti-Semitic spectacle. Paradoxically, a majority of Committee members were strongly opposed to mentioning the spectacle directly or indirectly in the informational materials by which we hoped to gather public support for a new trial or clemency.

Brainin reflected the thinking of the majority, arguing that for many decades succeeding generations of Jewish leaders in the United States had followed a policy that rarely identified high public officials as anti-Semitic, regardless of evidence to the contrary. Experience had taught them that identifying an official as an anti-Semite would bring to the surface anti-Semitic sentiments in other officials who would rally in defense of their accused colleague. There was concern that compelling highly placed officials to defend themselves against accusations of anti-Semitism was bound to fracture the existing state of "tolerance" with which Jews were regarded in daily life. An existing invisible divide between "us" and "them" would then become very visible and, inevitably, punishing.

If we called attention to the anti-Semitic spectacle at the trial, Brainin said, we would be identifying J. Edgar Hoover and other Justice officials as anti-Semites and, in the ensuing recriminations, we would have created a distraction from the proofs we had of the prosecution's resort to deceptive "likenesses" of tangible and circumstantial evidence it wished it had, and the transposition of the time of the crime to the Cold War, and the improper references by the prosecution and the presiding judge to the crime as constituting treason, and other acts of misconduct throughout the trial. (We had no thought, then, that within the next two years we would have in our hands the proofs of suborned perjury and other deceptions.)

A minority argued that although anti-Semitic prejudices appeared to be dwindling in the general public,[412] they appeared to be increasing in Congress and the Executive. The forgiveness implicit in welcoming thousands of German Nazis to America whose anti-Semitism had risen to murderous heights not very long ago, was itself an act of anti-Semitism. Congress was actively giving cover to anti-Semites through its so-called "Communist" investigation committees that publicly paraded lists of "disloyal" citizens, in which the names of Jews always far outnumbered those of any other ethnic group.

Those who disagreed with Brainin pointed out that Congress was at this very time enacting legislation reducing Jewish immigration. The State Department had begun insisting that would-be immigrants be compelled to meet the requirements of Section 7(c) of the Immigration Act of 1924, in which they had to obtain certificates of good conduct from the law enforcement agencies of Germany, Poland, and other German-occupied countries in which Jews had been hiding and deemed "fugitives" by police agencies that had previously been rounding them up for the extermination camps.[413]

Thus, the argument went, there existed, within the government, an anti-Semitic spirit that had made the spectacle in the courtroom possible. The death sentences required us to call things by their right names. How would the public recognize the reality of where America was being led if we withheld the truth?

A digression into future knowledge...

Behind our debates lay a visceral knowledge reinforced by the past and our expectations that the future would reliably repeat it. Our visceral knowledge told us the all-Jewish cast of defendants had not been an accident, no more so than the ethnically-weighted lists of names of "disloyal" Americans were objective portraits of the American political landscape. Our examination of the conduct of the Rosenberg-Sobell case had raised disturbing questions in our minds.

Had there actually been a true effort by the FBI and other security agencies to find atomic spies? Had there been only a politically circumscribed spy hunt nuanced by ethnic prejudice? Over the next four decades a stream of government documents and a series of well-documented studies on espionage, sabotage, and treason gave credibility and substance to our questions.

Had the hunt for Soviet spies been ethnically and politically biased...?

As we pointed out earlier, J. Edgar Hoover's chief target was the ideologically-motivated [ethnic adjective omitted] Communist spy. The first twenty years of his professional life had been spent identifying, chasing, harassing and, through the Justice Department, deporting and imprisoning dissenters, protesters, mavericks, liberals, socialists, communists, and others, the most prominent among them being Jews, all of whom he suspected were varieties of Communists bent on destroying the United States. Because of the extraordinary breadth of Hoover's definition of 'Communism', he could provide Justice officials with "data" that led them to make the startling and extravagant claim that more than 20,000 Americans were indictable as Soviet spies.[414] This, despite Hoover's failure, in his 48 years as FBI Director, to provide Justice officials with no more than a handful of indictable Soviet-related spy suspects.

Hoover's ready condemnation of all dissenters was nuanced by his lifelong ethnic prejudice. As we have shown in the citations from his chapter on the Jews in *Masters of Deceit*, Hoover believed that Jews were especially receptive to hostile critics and enemies of the United States and, for that reason, would be found among the dissenting and seditious population in far greater numbers than any other ethnic group. In his view, an all-Jewish cast of defendants at an espionage-treason trial was a graphic image of truth.

The results of a later, unbiased search for spies...

In less than two decades after Hoover's death in 1972, when the search for spies was freed of his focus on dissenters and Jews, more than a dozen Americans were indicted for spying for the Soviet Union during the Cold War, none of them Jews and none of them in the FBI's "disloyal" files or motivated by any purpose other than financial rewards that rose in some instances to millions of dollars.

The spies-for-pay discovered after Hoover's death included several well placed agents in the FBI (Earl Pitts[415] and Robert Hannsen[416]); highly placed personnel in the CIA (Aldrich Ames,[417] Harold J. Nicholson[418]); in the armed forces (Army Lt. Colonel William H. Whalen,[419] Air Force Sgt. Herbert W. Boeckhaupt,[420] Army Intelligence officer Richard Craig Smith,[421] Chief Warrant Officer John Anthony Walker,[422] his son, Yeoman 3rd Class Michael Walker, his brother, Navy Lt. Commander Arthur Walker, and a friend Senior Chief Radioman Jerry Whitworth; Sgt. David S. Boone;[423] Marine Sgt. Clayton Lonetree[424]).

In 1988, three Americans, none of them with an eastern European heritage — Kurt Stand, his wife, Theresa Squillicote and a friend, James M. Clark — were tried for conspiring to commit espionage and attempted espionage, by passing classified information to East Germany, the Soviet Union and the Republic of South Africa, between 1974 and 1990. Theresa Squillicote had been an attorney at the Pentagon. Stand, her husband, had been active in the labor movement and was a member of the Democratic Socialists of America. Clark was a former U.S. Army civilian employee. All three were characterized by the prosecution as Communists. Financial awards also seem to have been involved. Clark confessed and testified against the other two, who were then found guilty. Although the United States was not at war with the recipients of their espionage, the sentences were harsh: Squillicote was sentenced to 22 years, her husband to 19 years. They had two young children at the time, 12 and 14 years of age.[425, 426] Clark was sentenced to twelve years imprisonment.

The Soviet Union paid its spies in the United States huge sums for much smaller stakes than atomic weapons. Aldrich Ames was paid $2.7 million for passing on to the Soviets the names of American spies in the Soviet Union, resulting in the executions of the agents he had betrayed;[427] Hanssen received $1,400,000 for his services;[428] Nicholson received at least $120,000.[429]

None of these spies were sentenced to death, although their crimes were committed during the Cold War and, in some cases, knowingly caused the deaths of other Americans.

The absence (?) of German and Japanese atom bomb spies in U.S...

Hoover and the other national security chiefs in World War II appear to have made a deliberate disconnect between German espionage in American defense industries and German espionage at U.S. atomic development centers. If a search was made at such centers for German or Japanese spies, the results remain concealed to this day. One may hunt through the relevant espionage libraries and browse through the Internet for hours at a time, seeking information on German or Japanese espionage directed at United States atomic facilities in World War II, to no avail. In 1962, the AEC issued the first volume of the definitive history of the development of the atom bomb, *The New World,* and in 1969 the second volume, *Atomic Shield,* appeared.[430] In their combined 1,484 pages, the only reference to atomic espionage is in the context of the Rosenberg-Sobell case. There is also a reference to withholding certain atomic information from Canada because the information might be passed on to the British.[431]

There are published works on German espionage in our defense industries and the military during World War II, in which German spies were caught, tried and sentenced. Other German spies are described as being cooperative, leading their interrogators to other spies, although never to atomic spies. A monumental study of German espionage during World War II, by David Kahn, an expert in cryptography and espionage, makes no mention of German atomic espionage.[432] Nor is there any mention of German espionage in the definitive history of the development of the atom bomb, *The Making of the Atomic Bomb,* by Richard Rhodes. He did find it strange that there was an absence of any American effort to discover the progress made by Nazi Germany in the development of its own atom bomb.

He wrote

> One of the mysteries of the Second World War was the lack of an early and dedicated American intelligence effort to discover the extent of German progress toward atomic bomb development. If, as the record repeatedly emphasizes, the United States was seriously worried that Germany might reverse the course of the war with such a surprise secret weapon, why did its intelligence organizations, or the Manhattan Project, not mount a major effort of espionage?[433]

In 1943, under the leadership of Gen. Leslie Groves, the leader of the atomic weapons development project, a group given the name 'ALSOS' was formed to gather and analyze information on German atomic weapons research acquired in Europe as the Germans began their long retreat to Berlin. Among the first things it learned was that Werner Heisenberg, who had won the Nobel prize in physics in 1932, and Otto Hahn, who would win a Nobel prize in 1944, were involved in the development of an atomic weapon in Nazi Germany. Information was also obtained on the importation of uranium and heavy water by Germany, both of which were necessary for the development of an atomic weapon.[434] If 'ALSOS' also discovered that the German government had sent or recruited spies to discover our own atomic development program, no word of it appeared. Nor did any appear after the German and Japanese surrender, when the Axis espionage files came into the hands of American military and civil authorities.

Concealing the extent of wartime German espionage and sabotage in the U.S....

In 1942, the first full year of World War II, German espionage enabled German submarines to sink 12 million tons of American shipping.[435] Not only were 1200 ships sunk in that year, some were sent down by German submarines in American waters, within sight of land. The German submarines could not have accomplished this staggering amount of damage without an enormous amount of information from espionage agents: the departure time of specific ships from specific American ports, the war personnel and materiel the ships carried, their destinations, the routes they would take, and interim information on where the ships might be at any given time.

German espionage was also evident in acts of sabotage against U.S. military installations and harbors, and began even before the declaration of war in 1941. In September 1940, a powerful explosion occurred at Hercules Powder, a munitions plant in New Jersey; on November 12, 1940, major explosions occurred at two munitions plants in New Jersey and one in Pennsylvania; in 1941 there were fires set in Navy Department offices in Washington, D.C. and at the Norfolk Navy Base; fires were set at the Franklin Arsenal in Philadelphia and at Indian Head, Maryland. In New Jersey, the Jersey City waterfront was destroyed by fire. On February 9, 1942, the *Normandie*, capable of carrying 10,000 troops, was set on fire, leading to it capsize in New York Harbor.[436]

In all, there were nearly 20,000 reported acts of sabotage. The FBI summed up the situation

> Between January 1940 and May 1945, the Bureau investigated 19,299 alleged cases of sabotage. Sabotage in some form was found in 2,282 incidences, primarily acts of spite, carelessness, malicious mischief, and the

like. *During World War II, not a single act of enemy-directed sabotage was discovered in the United States.*[437] (italics added)

To claim that not even one of over 19,000 "incidents" that destroyed and damaged troop ships, ports, arsenals and military offices, was "enemy-directed," would have, in another context, drawn accusations of being "soft" on an enemy.

Clues to non-ideologic, non-ethnic atomic spies...

As we mentioned earlier, Hoover's focus on ideologically-driven spies for the Soviet Union shielded, among others, atomic spies-for-pay for the Soviet Union. There had been clues to such spies in the Venona/FBI messages, made public in 1995. Venona/FBI message, No. 961, dated June 21, 1943, uses the code name 'Kvant' in describing a meeting in Washington, D.C. between 'Kvant' and a deputy for the Soviet ambassador, in which

> Kvant declared that he is convinced of the value of the materials and therefore expects from us a similar recompense for his labor — in the form of a financial reward.[438]

In the identification section of the message, 'Kvant' is described as "unidentified," but is declared interchangeable with another cover name, 'Quantum,' also unidentified, which means that more than one such message had been decoded and translated. The FBI was unable to find in its ethnically-skewed suspect population files a true name for 'Kvant' or 'Quantum.'

In a memoir by a Soviet espionage controller in the United States, Alexander Feklisov, who described himself as Julius Rosenberg's controller,[439] he confirmed the existence of 'Kvant' or 'Khvat' as a non-political spy-for-pay. 'Khvat' is quoted as telling his Soviet controller

> As far as I'm concerned, the Republicans, the Democrats, the Communists or the Fascists all belong in the same bag. If I'm dealing with you it's because I need money![440]

There were precise clues to the areas in atomic research in which spies-for-pay were operating. In his confession, Klaus Fuchs said he learned the Soviets had obtained information on an "electromagnetic method as an alternative means of separating the uranium isotopes,[441] and that the Soviets were interested in a "tritium bomb,"[442] information that no known or alleged Communist spy had passed on to the Soviets. Obviously, the Soviet Union had sources of information beyond the FBI's "usual suspects."

A clue to why spies-for-pay for the Soviet Union or Germany or any other country were not identified may be found in an interview by a television news group with Robert Lamphere, the FBI liaison with the Venona Project. Lamphere was thoroughly persuaded that in searching for Americans who were spying for the Soviet Union, the place to find them would be in the skewed "suspect population" files. When he was asked how the FBI had searched for the man said to be Klaus Fuchs' courier in the United States, he replied

> Immediately after we received the initial information; the description of the man — we began sending photographs, hundreds of photographs...of anyone who remotely met the description, anyone who had ever been involved with anybody — no matter how remotely that we suspected of Communist activities — or Soviet Intelligence activities.[443]

Asked whether he believed that "leftists" in general "must be put under surveillance," Lamphere answered in the affirmative.

For spies-for-pay, the warning flags would not have been dissent or ancestry, but bank deposits, safety boxes, life styles, requests for access to more secret locations and operations, frequent use of corporate channels not required in the course of their ordinary responsibilities, and personal secretiveness. The flags were ignored, not only by Hoover but also by other law enforcement agency heads.

The spy-immune corporate sector...

As post World War II history unfolded, it became plain that Hoover and other law enforcement heads had treated the corporate sector as immune to the temptations that had corrupted the loyalty of agents and officials of the FBI, the CIA and the armed forces.

A spate of well-documented books appeared that presented an entirely different view of loyalty and corporate behavior, among them were *Trading with the Enemy*, by Charles Higham, and *The Splendid Blond Beast*, by Christopher Simpson. They revealed many hundreds of high-level wartime contacts and transactions during World War II, between the German government and American industrial corporations, banks and communications firms, all of them involving informational channels to Berlin. Not a few of these American corporate entities played essential roles in the nation's atomic weapons program. Obvious as the corporate milieu would be as a "spyground," it was given a clean bill of health from the start of the work on the atom bomb by General Groves, who declared that, in respect to security at the atom bomb facilities, "we relied on the discretion and patriotism of American industry."[444]

We cite three examples of the close-knit relations during World War II between American corporations, some of them involved in the research and

development of the atomic bomb, and Nazi Germany. The wartime transactions with the enemy were enabled with the help of policy-making officials who later became Secretaries of State, Secretaries of Defense and who
occupied other posts in the cabinets of Presidents Truman and Eisenhower.

The services provided by our corporations to Nazi Germany included
wartime manufacture and repair of Axis military equipment in Germany and
elsewhere in Europe; shipment of military equipment from facilities in the
United States to known "blinds," companies outside the United States that trans-
shipped exports from the United States to the Axis powers; withholding from the
American war effort various patents and compounds needed by our armed forces,
while allowing these patents and compounds to be used by the Axis powers; participation by American corporations in profit-taking from the slave camps in
Germany, Poland and elsewhere in Europe, and from the looting of the treasuries
and assets of Nazi-occupied countries; and participation by American corporations in profit-taking from the murder of millions of Jews and the expropriation
of their properties and sale of the profitable parts of their remains.

Corporate "discretion and patriotism:" Du Pont...

The Du Pont company, a major participant in the building of the atom
bomb, placed a significant portion of its manufacturing facilities at the disposal
of the Nazi war effort through its subsidiary, General Motors, whose president,
William S. Knudsen, told reporters in 1933 that Germany was "the miracle of the
twentieth century."[445] From the outbreak of the war between the United States
and Nazi Germany, GM developed a production strategy with its German subsidiary, so that both sides might benefit from GM's expertise. Alfred P. Sloan,
chairman of GM, directed the operations of GM-USA at the same time that he
was a director of the operations of the German GM subsidiary, GM-Opel. The
GM-Opel plant at Russelsheim, Germany, manufactured military planes for the
Nazis throughout the war, producing 50% of the Junkers propulsion systems.[446]
In 1943, GM-USA was manufacturing equipment for the U.S. Air Force, while
GM-Opel was turning out Messerschmitt jet fighters for the Nazis — which could
fly faster than U.S. planes. In 1943, the gigantic GM-Opel plant was being run
with slave labor provided by the Buchenwald concentration camp. Meanwhile,
GM in Switzerland was repairing damaged Nazi trucks and converting them
from gasoline to wood-gasoline fuel.[447] In 1943, when it was discovered that GM
dealers in Axis areas were doing business in the Balkans, GM-USA ordered the
reports — but not the trade — to be suppressed.

GM-friendly policy makers at the State Department and in other govern-
ment agencies allowed the GM-Nazi collaboration to proceed without hindrance.
They did even more: *they rewarded GM's manufacturing efforts on behalf of Nazi
Germany.* In 1967, GM's friends in the United States government granted GM

a $33 million tax exemption for "the troubles and destruction occasioned to its airplane and motorized vehicle factories in Germany and Austria in World War II." Those factories had been producing equipment with which to kill American soldiers, sailors and airmen.[448]

Corporate "discretion and patriotism:" Ford...

The Ford Motor Company founder, Henry Ford, had an affectionate business relationship with Nazi Germany before and during the war. In 1936, the German subsidiary of Ford caught the aryanization fever (the forced sale of Jewish-owned factories, banks, and other businesses to non-Jewish Germans) and began buying up forced-sale Jewish properties.[449] Although Hitler was clearly preparing for war and considered the United States a future enemy, the German Ford subsidiary in that same year became deeply involved in German weapons production, including the building of trucks for the Nazi occupation troops in France.[450] In midst of the war, in April 1943, a U.S. Treasury Department report on Ford's subsidiaries in France concluded that the Ford subsidiaries' production "is solely for the benefit of Germany and the countries under its occupation" and that "the increased activity of the French Ford subsidiaries on behalf of Germans receives the commendation of the Ford family in America."[451] Like GM, Ford — at its truck manufacturing plant in Cologne — was supplied with slave labor from the Buchenwald concentration camp. In addition, the Nazis placed Russian prisoners of war at the disposal of Ford manufacturing plants in Germany.[452] Ford's service to the Nazi war effort wasn't confined to its subsidiaries. On May 29, 1942, for example, Ford shipped six cargoes of cars from its New Jersey plant to a company in Chile that had been placed on a list of enemy companies trading with the Axis powers. In October of that year, the United States Ambassador to London alerted Dean Acheson at the State Department that 2000 German Army trucks were going to be repaired by the Ford plant in Berne.[453] Dean Acheson chose not to act on the report.

Corporate "discretion and patriotism:" Standard Oil...

Standard Oil of New Jersey, the biggest oil company in the world in 1941, was owned by the Rockefeller family. Its bank was the Chase National Bank, also owned by the Rockefeller family. Its chairman was Walter C. Teagle, who was director of the I.G. Chemical Corporation, a subsidiary of I.G. Farben, a major German corporation. Edsel Ford, head of the Ford Motor Company, was a member of the I.G. Chemical board.[454] On March 5, 1941, Herman Göring, Hitler's second-in-command, paid Standard Oil an option of $11 million for use of oil resources controlled by Standard Oil even if the United States and Germany should go to war against each other.[455] Senate hearings on Standard Oil's war-time dealings with the Nazis were begun on May 1, 1942. Testimony and evidence revealed that Standard Oil had deliberately retarded production of a vital war material — acetic acid — in favor of the Nazi war machine; that due to a deal with I.G. Farben, Standard Oil was blocking American use of technology for producing another vital war material — synthetic ammonia, used in making explosives; that Standard Oil was restricting America's ability to produce hydrogen from natural gas and from obtaining paraflow, a product used for airplane lubrication at high altitudes; and that Standard Oil was blocking American efforts to produce synthetic rubber. Two years later, Standard Oil of New Jersey arrogantly sued the United States government to regain the synthetic rubber patents Standard Oil had tried to withhold from the wartime defense industries. A Federal judge subsequently ruled

> Standard Oil can be considered an enemy national in view of its relationship with I. G. Farben after the United States and Germany had become active enemies.[456]

Corporate "discretion and patriotism:" poetry sums it up...

It is clear, from these three examples, that the labyrinthine corporate channels required for doing business with Nazi Germany during the war, and the atmosphere of good-will that prevailed among the beneficiaries of those business transactions, would encourage and facilitate espionage, atomic and otherwise. Scores of American corporations were part of these mutual business relations with the enemy, but if the dogs of counterintelligence picked up scents of espionage and treason, neither the FBI nor any other law enforcement agency in civilian or military service responded.

Perhaps there is an explanation:

> Treason doth never prosper: what's the reason?
> For if it prosper, none dare call it treason.[457]

Politically and ethnically "clean" suspects at Los Alamos, NM...

In October 1950, five months before the Rosenberg-Sobell trial began, seven men were arrested, each of them found with very tangible evidence of theft of classified documents and materials from Los Alamos, NM, including photographs of stages in the assembly of the atom bomb, and other hard evidence of theft of classified information.[458] None of the suspects were Jewish.

In each instance the suspect was at Los Alamos during the period that the prosecution claimed, at the Rosenberg-Sobell trial, that classified information had been passed to the Soviet Union.

Alexander Von Der Luft, an enlisted man serving at Los Alamos from 1944 to 1946, was charged with removing "highly classified documents which contained certain production data." He pleaded guilty on August 21, 1947, and was sentenced to "a probationary period of 4 years," meaning that he served no time at all.[459]

Ernest Dineen Wallis, an enlisted man at Los Alamos at the same time as Von Der Luft, was charged with removing "certain classified negatives and photographs." He was indicted by a grand jury at Albuquerque on July 24, 1947, pleaded guilty, and was sentenced to a year and a day, and placed on probation, so that he, too, served no time at all.[460]

George Wellington Thompson served as an enlisted man at Los Alamos from August 1943 to September 1945, after which he became a civilian employee at Los Alamos until March 17, 1947. During the FBI investigation of Wallis (see above) the FBI found that "Thompson had in his possession a number of highly classified negatives and photographs which he had removed from Los Alamos." On March 11, 1948, he was sentenced for "theft of government property" and fined $125, but was not required to serve any time.[461]

Arnold F. Kivi, another enlisted man at Los Alamos, was found to have "removed certain highly classified photographs." He pleaded guilty to theft of government property and on October 16, 1947, was sentenced to serve 18 months in a Federal prison.[462]

Fred Girard Michaels was assigned to the Los Alamos project from December 1943 to January 1946. He was arrested by the FBI "for having highly classified photographs," was indicted at Albuquerque on February 12, 1948, but six weeks later, on April 1, 1948, the U.S. Attorney at Albuquerque had the charges against Michaels dismissed, closing the case.[463]

Ernest Lawrence Paporello was an enlisted man at Los Alamos from April 1944 to March 1946, and "removed certain highly classified photographs which depicted various phases of the assembly of a mock-up bomb." On March 4, 1948, he was convicted of "theft of government property" and was sentenced to 6 months imprisonment and fined $250.[464]

Sanford Lawrence Simons was at Los Alamos, as a soldier and civilian from August 1944 to July 3, 1946. The FBI found that Simons "took a piece of normal uranium and 1.032 grams of plutonium alloy" from Los Alamos. On September 13, 1950, he entered a plea of not guilty, but it was understood "that he will change this to a guilty plea in the near future."[465]

It is possible, although not certain, that if these seven men, or any one of them, had been vocal liberals, or socialists, or communists or communist-associated, or had been born into an ethnically suspect population, the FBI would have charged them with conspiring to steal atomic information for the Soviet Union. *Time Magazine* reported that two of the men, Von Der Luft and Wallis, had been cleared of espionage by the FBI because "they had had no foreign or subversive connections."[466] John Wexley, in *The Judgment of Julius and Ethel Rosenberg*, cites a statement by the FBI that Simons had "no known link with Communist or subversive organizations."[467]

We do not suggest that any of these men were spies. We do suggest the failure of our security agencies to find so much as one non-Jewish atomic spy was the result of a shared understanding, in mid-20th Century America, that finding just *any* atomic spy, to say nothing of finding a *German* atomic spy, would have been an impediment rather than a boon to the goals dictated by the American Century agenda.

The Pollard case...

Finally, there was one more event — another trial — thirty-two years after the Rosenbergs' sentences were carried out, that revealed the persistence of discriminatory justice against Jews, even after Hoover's death in 1972.

On November 20, 1985, Jay Pollard, a civilian Naval Intelligence analyst, was arrested and charged with spying for Israel; two days later his wife, Anne, a public relations manager, was also arrested. Both were Jewish. The materials Pollard had passed on to Israeli agents were mostly classified descriptions of military preparations by Arab countries and Palestinian groups against Israel, which had not been shared with Israel by the United States. Pollard was not charged with intent to harm the United States, and a plea bargain was agreed upon, with the understanding that Pollard would be sentenced to ten to fifteen years, which would enable him to be paroled after serving one-third of his sentence. His wife would be sentenced to five years. Prior to imposing the sentences, the presiding judge received a memorandum from Defense Secretary Caspar Weinberger urging that Pollard be shown no leniency, on the grounds that Pollard's espionage had provided Israel with secret information which, in turn, lessened Israel's motivation to share secrets with the United States. Weinberger's memorandum was briefly shown to Pollard and his lawyer, but they were not permitted to study it to make a detailed denial of its allegations.

At the urging of the prosecution, the judge ignored the terms of the plea bargain to which the prosecutors had formerly agreed, and sentenced Pollard to life imprisonment. The courts have since refused to permit Pollard's second lawyer to read the Weinberger document for purposes of an appeal, and it remains sealed to this day, twenty four years after it was given to the judge but not to the defendant or his then-lawyer. Anne Pollard was released after three years and four months. Pollard became eligible for parole after ten years but parole has been denied, and he is now in his twenty-fourth year of incarceration.

A review of cases involving espionage reveals that the Department of Justice asks for harsher sentences against spies who, for idealistic reasons, pass information to an ally, with no intent to harm the United States, than they recommend for spies-for-pay who pass information to an enemy, in which proven harm has been done. Call it random accident or the result of reflexive ethnic prejudice by the authorities, but the fact remains that, in national security cases, Jewish defendants are punished more severely than others. (There is, of course, a long history of similarly biased sentences against other minorities. In non-security criminal cases, there is a two-hundred year history of imposing more severe sentences against African-Americans, indigenous Americans, Hispanics, and Asians than against others for the commission of the same crimes.)

In all, approximately seventy Americans spied for other countries during and after the Cold War, on behalf of the Soviet Union, Poland, Saudi Arabia, China, Great Britain, South Africa, the Philippines, Egypt, South Korea, Greece, Iran, Cuba, East Germany, North Vietnam, Hungary, Czechoslovakia, a number of Latin American nations and others during and after the Cold War. Two were executed (the Rosenbergs), four were given life sentences, one of which was reduced to four years. Pollard was one of the remaining three whose life sentences was not reduced.[468]

3 trials for espionage-treason in three worldly cities...

Even as the Committee wrestled with the troublesome issue of whether to raise anti-Semitism as a factor in the trial, a new development arose. The 1951 Rosenberg-Sobell trial in New York City was to become one of three trials on espionage-treason indictments spawned by the Cold War. In each trial, casts of all-Jewish or nearly all-Jewish defendants would be sitting in the dock. The other two trials were conducted in 1952 in Moscow and Prague. The major difference between the Moscow-Prague trials and the New York City trial was in the description of the beneficiary of the crime: in Moscow-Prague it was a "capitalist imperialist power." In New York City it was a "godless Communist tyranny." With slight alterations, the fevered courtroom oratory of the prosecutors in the three cities was identical, as were the pre-trial determinations of guilt by the judges.

There was a troublesome irony in the situation: the Soviet Ministry for State Security of a nation with a long history of officially-sanctioned violent pogroms against its ancient Jewish population, and the Department of Justice of the United States, one of the freest nations on earth, both found it almost impossible to find spies and traitors except among their Jewish citizens.

As though to drive the irony home, nine months after the New York trial, federal law enforcement officials gave the public a rare insight into their view of the relationship of ethnicity to loyalty. The officials advised the media that disloyal persons would rarely be found among persons of "pure Anglo-Saxon stock."[469]

Other portentous similarities marked the three trials. The verdicts and sentences in all three cases were identical: guilty, followed by death sentences and long prison terms.

The three trials resulted in the execution of 28 men and women, 27 of whom were Jewish.

End of digression: decisions in the context of known and unknown history...

While much of what has been described above was not fully known to us in the fall of 1951, what we learned came as no surprise. In the end, the majority view in the Committee prevailed: what we presented to the public on behalf of the defendants would be based only on what we had in hand. We avoided any mention of anti-Semitism as an issue in the Committee's informational material. We took a position based on what we knew we could support by a recitation of the facts, which was that the defendants had not been fairly tried and sentenced.

But the anti-Semitism issue troubled us for all of the Committee's existence. If we had had foreknowledge of what we learned over time, would it have altered the majority decision? We cannot know. Would it have saved the Rosenbergs' lives? We cannot know that either.

We return now to the emergence of the Committee.

The Committee's advisors...

From the start of the Committee, we had been haunted by our lack of worldly experience. We were not equipped to be name-droppers, our personal phone books were empty of important people, we lunched in cafeterias and most of our information about important events and doings in the city, nation and world came, not from friends in high or low places, but from reading the *New York Times* which, we soon learned, was unfriendly to our cause.

We knew we had to quickly achieve diversity, if not within the Committee, then diversity of advice and guidance from persons whose life experiences were different from ours, who were associated with outlooks affected by other beliefs. We found our way over a period of several months as the result of a discovery that followed our first announcement of the formation of the Committee in the *National Guardian* (no mainstream newspaper would run our announcement).

We received responses from many individuals who said they had been trying to form similar committees in their cities and that they had reached out and received supportive responses from Protestant and Jewish clergy, local attorneys, scientists in academia, and others. They also surprised us with their generosity. Our first ledger book reveals that from mid-October to the end of December 1951, the Committee received approximately $9600 from 1200 contributors scattered across the country, for an average contribution of $8 per correspondent.[470] Many contributions during the Thanksgiving and Christmas months were in odd amounts (for example: $38, $46, $12, etc.), indicating to us that these were pooled contributions by more than one person. An interesting facet of the responses and contributions was that most of them came from women. It was possible, we thought, that more women than men were responding because one of the condemned was a woman and mother. Men, it seemed, may have had less compassion for the fate of their gender brothers.

Taking our cue from these donor-correspondents, we became bold enough to make contact, either directly or through some of our correspondents, with several prominent Protestant and Jewish clergy in the mid-west and with a Catholic priest in New York, Father Clarence Duffy, and they became the core of an informal group of advisors and consultants to our Committee. They also, at various times, played public roles as writers and speakers for a new trial or clemency and, in one instance, met as a committee with President Eisenhower to plead for clemency. It was with their guidance that, in less than twelve months, the campaign for clemency became a movement that evoked compassionate, intellectual, religious and legal support throughout the world.

The best known of our advisors were Bernard M. Loomer, Dean of the Divinity School of the University of Chicago, one of whose writings at the time, "The Size of God"[471] (in which he argued that God is the totality of the entire world of our experience rather than separate and apart from it), was being widely discussed and debated among theologians; Rabbi Abraham Cronbach of Cincinnati, Professor of Social Studies at Hebrew Union College, a leading pacifist; and Stephen Love, a prominent Chicago Catholic lawyer who was a member of the Fitness Committee of the Illinois Supreme Court, and whose clients included Chicago's surface-railway operators. We had made copies of the trial record available to them before they became advisors to the Committee. They were far more conservative than any of the Committee members and, for that reason, could challenge our thinking from the perspective of the wider audience that would be needed to turn the clemency campaign into a clemency movement.

Rabbi Cronbach was among the most conservative of the Committee's advisors, arguing against any criticism of Judge Kaufman on the grounds that "We advance our cause by winning friends, not by making enemies,"[472] and that although he had doubts of the Rosenbergs' guilt, he was inclined to waive his doubts in favor of moderation in pressing for clemency.[473] He believed that emphasis on the atmosphere of fright in which the trial was conducted and the harshness of the sentences would move the public more easily than a more confrontational approach. In a pamphlet, titled *Mercy for the Rosenbergs,* which the Committee published and distributed, he commented that

> Regrettably the Rosenberg case has become implicated
> with that deadly word [Communism]. Were the case to
> be judged on its merits, a great swell of protest would
> arise against the sentence of death. Public opinion would

> encourage and support the President in commuting the
> sentence. The issue has unhappily gotten entangled in
> clichés which cause Americans to forget that Americans
> are merciful.[474]

Although he maintained this position throughout the clemency campaign, he did alter an initial preference for a very low-key thrust by the Committee. As time went on, he encouraged the Committee's more vigorous advancement of its views and large public demonstrations of support for clemency.

Father Clarence Duffy of New York, who had advice for us from time to time, repeatedly told us he was certain that the head of his Church would intervene for saving the Rosenbergs' lives. His certainty was rewarded in the fourteenth month of the Committee's existence.

In addition to Loomer, Cronbach, Love and Duffy, many attorneys and scientists, including Harold Urey, the scientist-Nobelist who had been listed as a witness for the prosecution, and several judges, including James H. Wolfe, former Chief Justice of the Supreme Court of Utah, also made known their support for clemency. As a result, they came under attack from within and outside their professions. They must have been dismayed by public and private allegations that they had cast their lot with Communists and traitors, but there was about them a grim determination to hold fast to their views. As they saw themselves, they had cast their lot with the Constitution. Emily described them as "mule-stubborn Americans."

Committees spring up everywhere...

It was clear to us from the initial response to the Committee that there was, among independent-minded people and mavericks, a troubled reaction to the trial and its outcome. Although they had not read the trial transcript and relied solely on descriptions of the trial in the media, almost all of them expressed an awareness that a crime committed during the years of the wartime alliance had been prosecuted as a Cold War crime on behalf of an enemy. They were particularly disturbed at the death sentences. Very few correspondents alluded to anti-Semitism. Their reports on discussions with their local clergy revealed that the latter were also aware of the prosecution's relocation of the crime to the Cold War era, and were likewise disturbed at the death sentences.

By early 1952, the Committee realized that our correspondents wanted more than encouraging letters from us. They were asking us to provide information in distributable form, knowledgeable speakers, assistance in organizing public meetings, and were urging us to give the movement a national character. Almost all the Committee members, however, had full-time jobs, so that visits to other committees had to meet three requirements: the committees had to be, at most, a day's travel from New York City, their members had to agree to meet with our speakers on weekends, and the local committees had to pay the bus or train fares. Newark, Philadelphia, Washington, D.C., and Boston were the only cities close enough for one-day visits, but there were at least a dozen other cities, all more distant, in which committees had arisen, and we were receiving mail from persons in many small cities who were asking for assistance in publicizing the case. It soon became impossible to put off the requests of committees even in the most distant cities. And so in early spring 1952, a few members of the Committee began rearranging their lives so that they could take a week or so to travel to the Midwest and as far as California.

The Committee outgrows apartments and a tin cash box...

The contributions we received confronted us with the realization that we needed a bank. We were initially turned down by several banks, but one was eventually found that would accept our deposits, possibly, although not known by us for certain, with the help of the FBI, which undoubtedly wanted to keep an eye on our income and expenses. To make certain our finances would always be in order, we hired a secretary who could also function as a bookkeeper, and an accountant who oversaw our financial activities.

In the space of two months, the Committee had outgrown the limitations of apartments and needed an office and a full-time secretary to handle correspondence and routine chores. An office was not easy to obtain because any office rental agency that would put its facilities at the Committee's disposal assumed that it would invite a visit from the FBI or, worse, from the IRS.

Rental agents routinely told the Committee they were "full up" when we sought office space, but Emily found space in a three-story building, one floor of which was partitioned into small cubicles that could hold a desk and a single filing cabinet. Emily told the owner we believed the Rosenberg-Sobell trial had resulted in a miscarriage of justice; the owner said he was sympathetic to our cause because his father had been the victim of a frame-up in Washington D.C. by the Communists who, he told Emily, controlled the courts.

A printer is found for the Trial Record...

Because we had all become converts after reading the trial record, we agreed it would be the chief source of all our informational materials. We hoped to find a sympathetic printer who would publish the verbatim record at a very low cost to us, in quantities that would permit us to make copies available to the media, influential attorneys, judges, scientists, the leaders of the American Civil Liberties Union and other civil liberties organizations, members of Congress, and religious leaders and organizations.

Our typesetter member, Norma Aronson, had contacts in publishing and printing and she found a printer who agreed with us on the harshness of the death sentences, but it would be four or five months before the trial record would be available to us, partly because even in a small font size it would run over 1700 pages, and presented other formatting, printing and binding problems, to say nothing of financial problems. The printer, while agreeing to bill us without profit to his firm, reasonably asked the Committee to pay the cost of typesetting, paper, printing and binding, which we said we could do if he would permit us to pay these costs over a period of several months. We came to an agreement some time in March 1952, and the project got underway.

There were objections from attorneys, including Bloch, to publishing the trial record. They argued that lay people, however intelligent they might be, would not understand what they read in the record. For example, there was the argument that lay persons might assume that allegations by the prosecution or unsupported testimony by prosecution witnesses were facts, which could only seem to lend credibility to the prosecution's claims. One attorney suggested that if we insisted on publishing the trial record, we ought to inject explanations and clarifications at certain points, to keep readers from being led astray. If we did that, we replied, we would not be giving the reader a pristine trial record, and we therefore declined to add to, or subtract from, the record. We asked the doubters to have faith in the intelligence of the readers.

We were soon to discover that Justice officials took another view of the trial record, treating it as an apocryphal document, placing barriers to its access by other agencies of government, including the State Department. The trial record would not be made available to our own ambassadors who requested it, who were facing inquiries from European anti-Communist editors, lawyers and political leaders to whom the Committee had sent copies of the record when they became available.

The Committee does *not* get on the Attorney General's 'Subversive List,' but gets on the Communist Party's "unapproved" list...

It was obvious to us that the Committee and the campaign might be labeled "Communist controlled" by the U.S. Attorney General, since we were charging misconduct by the officials and prosecutors of the Department of Justice. It was also likely, we knew, that Justice officials would place FBI agents and informers among the volunteers who would be helping us and, in 1953, we learned from the *New York Times* and other newspapers that they had done so.[475] We had agreed early on, however, that we had nothing to hide and would never attach suspicion to anyone volunteering to lick stamps, make phone calls, run errands to and from printers, or perform any of the other daily chores the campaign required.

Predictably, Justice Department officials declared that the Committee had been created by the Communist Party, although they knew from their FBI agents and informants inside the Communist Party that the Communist leaders did everything they could to prevent the formation of the Committee.

Shortly after the *National Guardian* carried news of the Committee's formation, emissaries from the Communist Party called on Committee members to urge that they disband, arguing that the Attorney General would label the Committee a Communist organization and that its challenge to the fairness of the trial would create the impression that the "Communist" Committee was defending spies and traitors. This, in turn, would reflect badly on the Communist Party.

One of the emissaries came to the authors' apartment to make his argument. He was a civil rights leader whom David knew to be a courageous and honorable man. He told us that the Committee's efforts would adversely affect the possibility of favorable rulings in the appeals against the verdicts and sentences by a group of Communist leaders who had, in the previous year, been found guilty of "advocating the overthrow of the United States government." Most of the defendants had been given ten year prison terms, except for one, a much decorated war veteran, who was sentenced to seven years. The Communist leaders believed that a campaign for a new trial or clemency by the Committee would burden the convicted Communists with the stigma of "espionage" and "treason," which might prejudice the appellate judges against them.

The authors pointed out that none of the Communist leaders faced execution or 30 years of imprisonment and that if the Rosenbergs and Sobell were Communists, as the prosecution claimed, how could the Communist leaders abandon their comrades to execution and long imprisonment? Emily, who had always been very critical of the Communist Party, said she found it troubling that Communist leaders and the officials of the Justice Department shared the same aims in respect to the Committee, that is, to shut it down, and that these shared aims should also trouble the civil rights leader.

Our visitor argued that in every battle "we must accept some casualties." David replied that it would be more appropriate and compassionate to apply this observation to the relatively-lightly sentenced Communist leaders than to the Rosenbergs and Sobell.

Five months later, Gus Hall, a Communist Party leader, who was at that time in the Federal House of Detention with Morton Sobell, attempted to persuade Sobell to renounce the Committee's efforts, and was especially critical of Sobell's wife for speaking at public meetings about the case. According to an FBI memorandum, on April 17, 1952,

> Hall stated emphatically that this was the wrong thing for Helen Sobell to do and that he did not believe the Party was in favor of making appearances under the circumstances. Hall stated that he did not think these meetings called by the National Committee to Secure

Justice in the Rosenberg Case would do either Sobell
or the Rosenbergs any good, but on the contrary would
probably prove harmful. [476]

Later, when the Communist Party leaders saw the magnitude of support for
the clemency movement, they activated groups associated with the Communist
Party on behalf of clemency, but their activities were often provocative rather
than unifying, and sometimes were senseless. The Committee members frequently wondered out loud whether the FBI, through its infiltration and provocation program, was responsible for those groups' actions, which clearly supported
the Justice officials' caricatures of how dissidents behaved.

In spite of the "Red label" pinned on the Committee by Justice officials, it
was not placed on the Attorney General's list of "subversive" organizations. There
was good reason for this, since the Committee was not subversive, although this
was true of other organizations on the Attorney General's list. It was more likely
that Justice officials assumed that the Committee, emboldened by the growing
number of supporters for its aims, would go to court to challenge its placement
on the list. Ordinarily, this would not be seen as a problem to Justice officials. In
respect to the Committee, however, Justice officials would have assumed that the
Committee would make the Rosenberg-Sobell case the cornerstone of an appeal
against being on the Subversive List, and the very last thing in the world Justice
officials wanted was an airing of the case. Hence, the Committee would be labeled
"Communist" in communications by Justice officials to the media, but would not
be placed on the Attorney General's list.

A traditionally feisty media goes silent...

We had no exaggerated notion of the degree to which we could affect public opinion. What we hoped was that over the coming months the doubts we
shared about the fairness of the trial would light a spark in a mainstream news-
room in New York or Boston or Philadelphia or Los Angeles or wherever, that a
crusading reporter for a major newspaper or radio or television channel would
bring what we knew to audiences we could never reach by ourselves, and thereby
cause a new and fair trial to be held.

A mainstream media expose of the case was not to be. Among the first
difficulties encountered by the Committee was the refusal by every major newspaper and radio news program in New York to accept news of our existence or,
later, when funds were available, paid announcements of the Committee's existence and aims.

Advertising managers in the mainstream media uniformly informed
the Committee that they would not disseminate "Communist propaganda," by
accepting advertising from us. One advertising manager of a major New York
City newspaper told us that he would accept paid ads only if we agreed to a

header that read: *Warning: the following advertisement has been submitted by a group deemed by the Attorney General to be Subversive.* When we pointed out the Committee was not on the Attorney General's Subversive List, the editor offered to rewrite the warning: *The Following Advertisement Has Been Paid For By the Communist Party.* The major media ban on news of the clemency campaign and, later, on the discovery of new evidence, was only occasionally broken. But it was not the government that silenced the media, it was the media that silenced the media, driven by the same fears of denunciation that, in those years, faced every group, government official, and individual in American life.

The Committee calls its first public meeting...

By February of 1952, Committee members believed we had sufficient support to call a public meeting in New York City for the purpose of gaining new supporters and to undertake a publicly-supported *amicus brief* to the Supreme Court on behalf of a review of the case.

The owners of the first meeting hall we rented which could seat 1000 persons backed out of the contract ten days before the meeting, on the grounds they had not known we were a "Communist" organization. Aaron Schneider, who was owed a favor by leaders of the Knights of Columbus, a Catholic men's humanitarian-oriented organization, quickly obtained agreement by the Knights to rent us Pythian Hall, and we posted the change of place through mailings and the *National Guardian*. We were aware, of course, that rental of Pythian Hall to us must have had the approval of at least some authoritative level of the local Catholic hierarchy.

On the evening of March 12, 1952, almost 2000 persons showed up at the meeting (from a population half the size of what it is now); those who could not be seated were accommodated in a smaller room that could be addressed from the larger room by a loudspeaker. Among the speakers were William Reuben; Rabbi Louis D. Gross, editor of the *Jewish Examiner*; our chairman, Joseph Brainin; Mary Van Kleek, former Director of the Russell Sage Foundation, who described the sentences as a "breakdown in the hard-won safeguards of the American system of justice"; and Helen Sobell, wife of Morton Sobell. All the speakers respected the Committee's request that no issue other than a new trial or clemency be raised.

Through Emanuel Bloch, the Rosenbergs sent a message to the meeting, declaring

> We are an ordinary man and wife, and it is inevitable that ordinary people would be grievously persecuted by the history of the past few years...there are forces today which hope to silence by death those who speak for peace and democracy.[477]

The New York City public event had been successful in spite of the refusal of the major media to accept paid announcements of the meeting. There had been reporters from several major newspapers and wire services at the meeting, but whatever the reporters may have written did not see the light of day.

Harold Urey and Albert Einstein...

Through an acquaintance of Harold Urey, the most eminent name on the prosecutors' witness list, we had contacted the scientist and, in the course of a discussion, asked him whether he would comment on the appearance of his name on the witness list in view of the fact that he was never called to testify. Dr. Urey replied we were either misinformed or misrepresenting the witness list, that he had never been interviewed by the FBI or by any prosecutor for the purpose of testifying at the Rosenberg-Sobell trial.

A carbon copy of the trial record was given to Dr. Urey, and he found that he had, indeed, been listed by the prosecutors as one of their witnesses,[478] and that the court had been specifically assured by Prosecutor Roy Cohn he would testify.[479] Dr. Urey found that other experts on the atom bomb — Gen. Leslie R. Groves, Dr. George B. Kistiakowski, and Dr. J. Robert Oppenheimer — had also been listed as witnesses, but had also not testified. His reading of the trial record persuaded him that his name, like the other scientists' names on the prosecutors' witness list, had been a deception, and he found other deceptions as well in respect to the "scientific" testimony by David Greenglass. Nevertheless, he hesitated to make his conclusions known. He showed the trial record to an attorney he respected, and the attorney agreed with Urey that he had become associated with the Rosenberg-Sobell case by the prosecutors without ever having been consulted on the matter, and that his name on the witness list left the implication he had knowledge of a connection between the defendants and the theft of classified atomic bomb information at Los Alamos.

Later that year, on December 16, 1952, Urey wrote to Judge Kaufman

> I have read the testimony given at the trial, and though I have no legal experience in matters of this kind my competence is comparable to that of the jurors and the great public who are concerned about this matter.
>
> ...The government's case rests on the testimony of David and Ruth Greenglass, and this was flatly contradicted by Ethel and Julius Rosenberg. I found the testimony of the Rosenbergs more believable than that of the Greenglasses.[480]

The Committee pressed Urey to make a public statement on the case, but he preferred to see what the outcome of the various appeals would be, hoping, as did we, that the outcome would be a new trial. Another reason for his hesitation, we believe, was that he had consulted with Albert Einstein, and had learned Einstein did not want to comment on the case because he had been told that the Communist Party was behind the clemency campaign.

Shortly after our initial discussion with Dr. Urey, William Reuben succeeded in obtaining an appointment with Albert Einstein, and he and I drove to Einstein's home in Princeton, New Jersey. Since the appointment had been made for Reuben alone, he went in to see Einstein to ask whether he would permit me to participate in the discussion. Reuben then came out and told me that the FBI had pre-emptively sent a warning to Einstein that the "Communist-inspired" Committee would try to recruit him, that Emily and I were notorious Communists, along with Reuben and Bloch, and asserted that the Committee intended to make martyrs of the Rosenbergs rather than save their lives.

Einstein said he would see Reuben alone.

Meanwhile, I sat in the car and mused about the life of Emily and David, of our unexpected involvement in a national and international affair, of the seemingly absurd connections life made among people — what was I doing sitting in a car outside the home of Einstein, the most celebrated scientist of the time? What was Emily doing talking to Harold Urey, another great scientist? Emily and I had been door-knockers, and had suddenly become self-appointed "world knockers." Hardly a day or evening passed without us asking how, why, wherefrom? Emily always gave an answer that wasn't an answer except that there was no other answer: We and the other Committee members were doing what we did because no one else had appointed themselves to do what we had appointed ourselves to do. Emily revised Brainin's comment that we were God's second choice. She said, "God had to work with what was available down here. Maybe God had no other choice."

Reuben came back to the car with a message from Einstein: the scientist would review Greenglass' scientific exhibit and testimony (Exhibit 8), if Bloch succeeded in getting it unimpounded. We conveyed the message to Bloch, who replied that, given the nature of the time and the case, it would be legally impossible to unimpound the material, especially since it was he who had made the motion to impound it. He had done so to show that the Rosenbergs were as concerned as the prosecution had been about the possibility that the Soviets might still benefit from the information disclosed by Greenglass during his testimony.

Einstein's response to Bloch's reply was paraphrased to us by an intermediary: Einstein said he believed the Committee, the Almans, and Emanuel Bloch wanted to make certain the Rosenbergs were executed so that the Communists would have two martyrs for their cause. Otherwise, Bloch would not now be refusing to move to unimpound the impounded portion of Greenglass' testimony.

Einstein's position was hurtful. Our skins were not thick enough to ignore Einstein's acceptance of the FBI's accusation against us. Nor were the authors alone in that regard. Every member of the Committee was similarly affected.

Many months were to pass before Einstein realized, even if the goals imputed to us by Justice officials were true, we were not the issue. The issues were the baseless oral indictment, its cynical charge of treason, and the lives of two defendants and the freedom of a third.

The Trial Record arrives and is sent out...

The trial record was published in May 1952, in an initial printing of 5000 copies in two soft-cover volumes, each volume consisting of four sections; it was set in 9 point type that was easily readable by persons with average vision. Without charge to us, the printer boxed each set of eight volumes. We immediately sent out copies of the trial record to committees across the country and to journalists, lawyers, civil libertarians, scientists and clergy, select members of Congress, leaders of Jewish organizations, libraries in major cities, and to similar persons and groups in Canada, Great Britain, Ireland, France, and Italy, to the Chief Rabbi of Israel, the Archbishop of the Church of England, the Vatican, and to prominent theologians. We initially sent out 3000 copies, and sold the remainder to committees and individuals for $6.00 a set. Some months later the demand for copies caused us to order another printing of 5000 copies, most of which were sent to influential persons recommended to us by previous recipients and local committees. We raised the price of a boxed set to $10, which enabled us to pay the printer on time.

We informed local committees of the mailing of the trial record to influential persons in their cities, and suggested they let some weeks go by before contacting them. We learned that most of the recipients reacted positively to the trial record and were especially appreciative that the Committee had published it verbatim and without editorial comment. Few of them would join local committees but many agreed to act as advisors and to circulate their copies of the trial record to other persons who they thought would be helpful to the clemency campaign.

The leaders of major Jewish organizations ask their members to look away; major Jewish newspapers ask their readers to understand what they saw...

The leaders of the major Jewish organizations believed that, to minimize any repercussions against Jews in the politically heated atmosphere of the time, Jews must ignore the spectacle that had been staged in the courtroom in Manhattan's Foley Square. They must take on faith the descriptions by Justice officials of the defendants as traitors. For a Jew to express suspicion that the Rosenberg-Sobell case was a miscarriage of justice, either in respect to the verdicts or the sentences, was, the Jewish leaders believed, to make all Jews vulnerable to denunciation and penalization. Hence, the leaders were adamant in their insistence that the memberships of their organizations refrain from any acts that J. Edgar Hoover or other government officials might characterize as critical of the trial and its outcome.

The Jewish leaders' concern for their co-religionists was genuine. For more than a thousand years, responsible Jewish leaders have had to confront a dilemma: whether to look on in silence at assaults against a small number of Jews in order to preserve tolerance and life for a large number of Jews, or speak out in protest. A majority of the Committee members, including the authors, had themselves voted not to charge that anti-Semitism had been a factor at the trial, not because it had not been, but because we believed such a charge would distract from the factual case for a new trial or clemency.

The situation in mid-20th Century America was novel. The Rosenbergs and Sobell had not been targeted because they were Jews, but because they were Communists who had conspired to spy on behalf of the Soviet Union. But the searching spotlight by which our law enforcement agencies discovered "Communists" and spies was not directed equally at all segments of the population; the least attention was paid to that large segment of the population — Anglo-Saxons — from which officials anticipated finding very few Communists and spies, while the greatest attention was paid to a smaller segment — the foreign born and first-generation Americans — whose names dominated the lists of "Communists" and "Red spies" and "traitors" routinely made public by legislative and private "Communist"-hunting committees. The spectacle in the federal courthouse had not been anti-Semitic because the defendants were Jewish, but because there were no defendants who were not Jewish.

In this novel situation, a non-Jew who found fault with the Rosenberg-Sobell trial put only him or herself in harm's way. But a Jew who faulted the trial confirmed the bias among many American government officials that Jews were deservedly considered a suspect-population. This was the situation as interpreted by leaders of the major Jewish organizations.

There was some Old World truth in this interpretation, but not enough to remain undisturbed. The truth was that anti-Semitism in the United States had been frequently and publicly challenged at times, and in many ways. Old World passivity and resignation were not the norm in New World America.

I can best illustrate this point with an event that occurred in my early teens. On the eve of Yom Kippur, the holiest of days for Jews, a frightening rumor spread through the Lower East Side ghetto. Father Charles E. Coughlin, a Catholic priest with a large radio following, who had formed the Christian Front, a paramilitary organization, had, some people said, obtained the addresses of every synagogue in

the ghetto, and had instructed his Christian Front soldiers to set fire to the synagogues when they were filled with worshippers. The newspapers had carried stories
about Christian Fronters in the New York City Police Department, and it was estimated that 5000 policemen belonged to the Front.

I was concerned, not because I was a pious young Jew, but because of tales
my parents had told me of attacks on synagogues in Russia and Poland during their
childhood. When rumors of such impending assaults arose in the old country, the
rabbis and sextons would empty the synagogues of the Torah and of other holy
objects, and hide them everywhere they could except in their homes, where the
pogrommists would surely come to look for them. Then the ghetto streets would
empty.

In the evening the lamps were not lit. When the pogrommists came, they
would sack the synagogues, break the walls, defecate on the few books deliberately
left behind to appease them, destroy the benches, cupboards, shelves, the Ark of
the Torah. Then, depending on their mood, they would set fire to what remained of
the synagogue or they would fan out on the streets and break in the doors of a few
homes. Hours later, the streets would still be empty, the sky would slowly lose its
stars and, with the first gray of dawn, there would be heard the weeping and wailing
and tearing of clothes for the raped maidens and murdered brothers and fathers.

But this was the new country, where new traditions would be woven into life.
There were heated discussions on the tenement stairs, in the apartments, up on the
roof.

"We must demand police protection for our synagogues!"

"Are you crazy? You want the Christian Fronters to protect the synagogues?"

"What we need is to tell our own Jewish gangsters to show that they're Jews,
after all, and stand guard at the doors to the synagogues!"

"What? A dozen gangsters against thousands of Fronters?"

"This is what comes of having some Communists in our midst. I say, let's
promise to drive out every Communist if the Fronters will let us alone!"

"And Socialists too! And atheists too!"

"What are you saying? They're not Jews? Their children are not Jews?"

"Here's what to do: the Communists and Socialists don't believe in God. Let's
tell the Fronters they can do whatever they want to every man they find not in the
synagogue on Yom Kippur!"

"Since when do we Jews turn over other Jews to pogrommists?"

"To save our children's lives, everything is permissible!"

"Let's not go into the synagogues, but stand outside them, surround them so
that nobody can get to them to burn them down!"

"And not pray?"

"We will pray in the streets outside the synagogue. It's permissible, to save
lives!"

"I can see you don't understand Hebrew law!"

"Does the Torah tell us to go into a burning synagogue to pray? Of course not!"

Of course not, I thought. The Torah surely tells us to go down to the East River and gather stones, bricks, metal, nails and whatever else we can find. The same thought occurred to other teenagers and to many men.

On Yom Kippur, I stood outside the little Attorney Street synagogue with some other boys and adult men. I had been *bar mitzvah*ed in that synagogue and no longer had to sit in the balcony with my mother and other women. But I had no taste for religion.

In Hebrew class, I had told my rabbi, "Rabbi, I don't believe in God." The rabbi smiled at me. The rest of the class, all of them boys, fell silent. "You don't believe in God?" the rabbi asked, still smiling. I liked him. "No, rabbi, I don't believe in God." The rabbi began laughing and looked at the class. Then he stopped and addressed the class. "All right, all right, sly ones. Put your noses back in your books. The joke is over." He was still smiling. He sighed." All right," he said to me. "You, too, your nose back in your book." I put my nose back in my book. My rabbi went on smiling. He and I knew a really pious Jew does not have to believe in God.

The synagogue was bursting with praying men. Many fathers, including mine, had told their young sons to stay out of the synagogue. And so we did, but not far from our praying fathers and mothers. I wandered the nearby streets with other boys, ready to cry the alarm if the Christian Fronters showed up. The excitement of fear and the tension of fasting from sunup to sundown sharpened our alertness. Whenever we saw a patrolman come down the street, spinning his billy club and looking bored, we looked past him for signs that hundreds of Fronters might be close behind.

I prayed that Mad Dog, the traffic cop at Broadway and Canal whose son had been crippled by polio, was not a Fronter.

The hours wore on, the sun began to sink, the synagogue doors opened and the men in their dark suits and hats emerged and looked about them, and they were followed by the women and children who had chosen to be with them that day. The sexton came out, jangling his keys. He turned the top lock, the middle lock, the lower lock. He looked up and down the street. Then he went home.

We remained, walking the streets, the synagogue ever in our sights. Our mothers brought us roasted chicken thighs and soup and bread and fruit. The stars came out. Our mothers came to coax us home. "It's late," the mothers said. "The Fronters aren't coming. Come home."

My rabbi came by, smiling. He winked at me and went on. The sky became bare of stars. When the sun began to rise, we went home.

One day, some weeks later, my rabbi said to me, "I understand you, David. You don't believe in God, but you believe in synagogues. That's fine with God."

The leaders of the major Jewish organizations could not fully suppress their memberships' concern that something was amiss in the Rosenberg-Sobell case. Many of their members had already been exposed to questions about the trial and sentences, not by the Committee, but by major Jewish newspapers. With one small exception, every Jewish newspaper in the country was strongly anti-Communist, and the questions they raised about the case could hardly have been influenced by Communists.

Even before the trial had begun, these Jewish newspapers had sounded alarms about the possibility of anti-Semitism in the case. As early as June 19, 1950, nine months before the trial began, a member of the law firm representing the Greenglasses wrote a memorandum, based on an interview with Ruth Greenglass, in which he noted

> The *Jewish Daily Forward*, which is certainly not a leftist newspaper, is very excited about the anti-Semitic issue and has offered a lawyer.[481]

A week after the death sentences were pronounced, the anti-Communist *Jewish Day* editorialized

> One cannot overlook the Jewish element in this unfortunate Rosenberg trial...If the Rosenbergs are, as Judge Kaufman has said, guilty of the death of 50,000 American soldiers in Korea, one can easily hold the Rosenbergs and their like responsible for the atom war against America.[482]

A few days later, an editorial in *Jewish Day* asked

> What led the judge to give the extreme penalty...? Is it not perhaps the fact that the judge is a Jew and the defendants are Jews?...He [was] afraid that perhaps, if he were not to give them the death penalty, he would be suspected of not having done so because he is a Jew... Precisely because the judge should have been free from every Jewish complex — he should under no circumstances have issued the death sentence...[483]

On February 7, 1952, the anti-Communist English-Jewish weekly, *The Sentinel*, a Chicago publication, carried an editorial by a prominent rabbi.

> When Julius and Ethel Rosenberg were condemned to death...I condemned the verdict and accused the presiding judge, who happened to be a Jew, of leaning over backwards in his desire to show that Jews condemn treason...[484]

Three weeks later the editor of another anti-Communist Jewish publication, the *California Jewish Voice,* wrote

> My only concern was why a Jewish judge had to...decide a death penalty for peace-time espionage...To prove that he was unbiased, he acquiesced to legal murder in the time of national hysteria.[485]

In March 1952, the editor of the *Jewish Examiner* asked

> Did [Judge Kaufman] think that the death sentence against the Rosenbergs was necessary to counteract the anti-Semitic charge of communism against Jews in general? Apparently the jurist has not learned that anti-Semitism has nothing to do with the truth.[486]

These editorial reactions must be understood not only as they relate to the Rosenberg-Sobell case, but in the broader context of the known prejudicial mindsets of many public officials. We mentioned earlier the well-publicized claim in December 1951, by law enforcement officials, that the absence of Communists among the thousands of employees at the Oak Ridge atom bomb facility was due to "a predominance of pure Anglo-Saxon stock."[487] In that same period, eight New York City teachers, all of them Jewish, were fired from the public schools for "Communism." These events were followed by an outbreak of anti-Semitic vandalism, including the desecration of Jewish cemeteries and synagogues.

The editorials in the Jewish press and the general atmosphere of tension in respect to Jewish life at the time made it difficult for leaders of Jewish organizations to keep their memberships from thinking about and expressing themselves on the Rosenberg-Sobell case. The leaders were undoubtedly hearing from critical Justice officials on their inability to keep their memberships from supporting the new trial/clemency movement. There had been, for a considerable time, an informal working relationship between the Jewish leaders and FBI officials, in spite of the FBI's known anti-Semitic hiring policy and its suspect population files. This relationship was used by Jewish leaders in this period to demonstrate their sincerity in attempting to silence their memberships in respect to the Rosenberg-Sobell case.

Their efforts were acknowledged in a March 1952, communication from J. Edgar Hoover to Assistant Attorney General James M. McGranery, in which Hoover conveyed his satisfaction with the anti-clemency stance of a major Jewish anti-bias organization.

> There is being transmitted herewith for your information a Photostat of a memorandum which was sent out on February 28, 1952, to all Anti-Defamation League offices

by Mr. Arnold Forster of the New York Headquarters of that organization in connection with the Rosenberg matter. You will note that this memorandum by the Anti-Defamation League is for the purpose of alerting all Jewish groups against supporting any meetings or attempts to develop pro-Rosenberg sympathy among Jewish groups in their respective areas.[488]

On April 2, 1952, Benjamin R. Epstein, the National Director of the Anti-Defamation League wrote to Lou Nichols, a top FBI official

It was nice talking to you on the phone yesterday afternoon...I am enclosing for your information a copy of our current monthly ADL Bulletin, which will be in the mails within the next few days, and call your attention especially to the lead article, "Anti-Semitism and the atom spy trial...". We have been very pleased with the excellent relationship which exists between our various staff directors and representatives of the Bureau who frequently have sought our cooperation, which is always forthcoming.[489]

On May 18, 1952, the National Community Relations Advisory Council (NCRAC), a leadership group representing approximately fifty Jewish organizations, issued an anti-clemency press release to "Anglo-Jewish weeklies," which was "joined in by the American Jewish Committee, the American Jewish Congress, Anti-Defamation League of B'nai Brith, Jewish Labor Committee, Jewish War Veterans of the U.S., the Union of American Hebrew Congregations." The press release began with an acknowledgment that any "group of American citizens has a right to express its views as to the severity of the sentence in any criminal case." It went on

Attempts are being made, however, by a Communist inspired group called the National Committee to Secure Justice in the Rosenberg Case, to inject the false issue of anti-Semitism into the Rosenberg case. We condemn these efforts to mislead the people of this country by unsupported charges that the religious ancestry of the defendants was a factor in the case.[490]

The press release was a declaration without any supporting evidence for its claim that the Committee had injected the issue of anti-Semitism, and did not quote any statement made by the Committee in respect to anti-Semitism or, for that matter, to any other subject. Such declarations were repeatedly made by various anti-clemency groups during the campaign for clemency, but were never documented, because the Committee had determined that it would rely solely on the misconduct of the prosecutors and the judge to make its case to the public. The false claim that the Committee was charging anti-Semitism in the case was a claim that mirrored the Jewish leaders' knowledge that anti-Semitism had been, indeed, a significant factor in the case.

On June 5, 1952, several weeks after we had begun sending out copies of the trial record, a number of which went to the American Jewish Committee and other major Jewish organizations, Rabbi S. Andhil Fineberg, Director of Community Service for the AJC, released a seven page statement about the "troublesome controversy" that had arisen in Jewish communities because of the Rosenberg-Sobell case, with permission to reprint his statement restricted to "Jewish periodicals and within Jewish circles."[491]

Rabbi Fineberg's statement asserted

> The Committee for the Rosenbergs claims that anti-Semitism was rampant in the case because the jury included no Jews. But it also insists that anti-Semitism was present just because the judge and the prosecutor were Jews. This is the type of "proof" the Committee uses.[492]

His statement was devoid of any quotation from the Committee's press releases or publications or statements by speakers at public meetings. He went on to say

> readers and audiences of the Rosenberg Committee are being told...that Fascists have already gotten control of the United States and that every anti-Semitic act, whether in Miami, Philadelphia, Boston or Cicero, no matter whether it is the work of a few hoodlums or of a street gang, is the result of machinations of powerful unnamed plutocrats who will doom every Jew to death unless the "progressive" forces are strengthened.[493]

Rabbi Fineberg warned the Jewish community against sentimentality, writing that compassion for the children "subtly cloaks the guilty parents."[494] The rabbi's descriptions of statements by the Committee created problems for the American Jewish Committee, for many of their members had already seen the fact sheets and other materials distributed by the Committee, and some had seen or knew that the Committee was distributing the trial record, and did not find in the Committee's informational materials the allegations about anti-Semitism and "Fascist" control of the country to which Rabbi Fineberg alluded. He received praise and encouragement, however, from Justice officials and from

Judge Kaufman. On June 23, 1952, after the Committee had begun sending out copies of the trial record, Judge Kaufman wrote to Rabbi Fineberg

> Thank you for your letter of June 20th enclosing your statement on the Rosenberg case.
>
> I have been disturbed by the completely irresponsible and baseless propaganda put out by the Committee to Secure Justice for the Rosenbergs. Naturally, by reason of my position, I must remain mute even though the false line that is being followed by those responsible for this propaganda gives me great concern as an American and a Jew.
>
> It is of course gratifying to see that organizations such as yours and the Anti-Defamation League recognize the propaganda for what it is and are alerting those at whom it is aimed, lest they become dupes.
>
> I thought your statement was an excellent one and I was much encouraged by it.[495]

In our discussions with members of the AJC and other major Jewish organization, we found that what disturbed them most of all was Judge Kaufman's putting the blame for 50,000 American casualties in Korea on the defendants, although the crime they were said to have committed occurred half a decade before the Korean war. Judge Kaufman's words, they feared, would feed, rather than allay, anti-Semitism.

It soon became plain that many Jewish newspaper editors and the leaders of the major Jewish organizations, to which many of the editors belonged, found themselves on opposite sides of the Rosenberg-Sobell sentences, the editors condemning the sentences and questioning Kaufman's motives, the Jewish organization leaders finding the sentences acceptable and, in fact, strongly disapproving of any criticism of them.

The ACLU approves the verdicts and the sentences...

On May 2, 1952, the ACLU released a memorandum through Herbert Monte Levy, its staff counsel, in which it stated, incorrectly, that the Rosenbergs "were convicted by a jury of the crime of atomic espionage" (the charge had been conspiracy to commit espionage) and found no civil liberties violation in the prosecution's oral addition of the treason charge in the courtroom.[496] This was an unprecedented statement by an organization that had never before publicly taken sides in a case it did not take to court.

The memorandum stated that the Rosenbergs' appeal from the verdict and sentences had been

> examined by both Osmond K. Fraenkel, Esq., Chairman of the ACLU's Due Process Committee and a leading Constitutional authority, and by me. Both Mr. Fraenkel and I reached the conclusion that no valid civil liberties points had been raised, and that the case, was not one in which the ACLU should intervene.[497]

But it did intervene, by publicly justifying the conduct of the trial, by accepting, for the first time since its inception, the legitimacy of using ideology and history as evidence of the commission of a crime, and by justifying the death sentences.

> This was a conviction for espionage, which we believe to be the proper way to deal with communist totalitarianism.
>
> ***
>
> It might possibly be contended that there is a violation of the due process of law, in that the penalty is utterly unreasonable for the offense charged. However, it is our opinion that this argument would be totally without merit. Though there actually has never been an execution for espionage in peace time, persons have been sentenced to death for this in the past, although such sentences were never carried out.[498]

The ACLU memorandum took note of the oral addition of the treason charge at the trial.

> The crime of atomic espionage was a different crime from that of treason and there is no reason why the legislature could not have created such a crime and made it punishable by death...a prosecution under such a law is not improper, so long as the prosecution does not attempt to accuse the defendants of treason during the trial and thus turn the prosecution into one essentially for treason.[499]

As the ACLU officers knew from the trial record, but which they decided to ignore, the lead prosecutor, at his opening statement and throughout the trial, did describe the defendants as "traitors," described their activities as "traitorous" and "treasonable," claimed he would show the jury overwhelming "evidence of these traitorous acts," and referred repeatedly to their "betrayal" of the United States.[500] In his summation, Saypol had told the jurors that the defendants were driven to "serve the interests of a foreign power which today seeks to wipe us off the face of the earth."[501] Likewise, Judge Kaufman, in charging the jurors, had told them that "irrational sympathies must not shield proven traitors" and made other references to the defendants' "treachery" and "betrayal of their fellow countrymen."[502]

Not all ACLU chapters were of the same mind. In December 1952, the ACLU leaders felt compelled to disavow an appeal for clemency by its New Haven affiliate.

> The New Haven Civil Liberties Council, an affiliate of the Union, released to the press on November 24, 1952, a copy of a letter its executive committee had written to the President requesting commutation. This action was taken without prior consultation with, or the authority of, the National ACLU. It has been misconstrued by some organizations and individuals, and possibly by the public, as representing the position of the National ACLU.[503]

The accompanying press release explained that it should "not be interpreted to mean that the National ACLU approves or disapproves the death sentences." But the ACLU added

> the sentence is not so disproportionate to the severity of the crime as to amount to a denial of due process.[504]

As a rationale for the appropriateness of the death sentences, the ACLU leaders relied on Judge Kaufman's commentary on the world situation.

> It is argued that, since the Rosenbergs might have been given a lighter sentence had they been tried at the time of their commission of the crime, when the United States and Russia were allies, civil liberties would be violated were the sentence carried out now. But the conspiracy was found to have continued during at least the beginning of the cold war, and the trial judge also had a reasonable basis for consideration of present world circumstances, in evaluating the seriousness of the results of the crime committed several years earlier.[505]

A quarter of a century later, the ACLU leadership acknowledged that the FBI had had a direct hand in determining the ACLU's position in the Rosenberg-Sobell case. More later.

Letters from an organizer...

Some time in February or early March 1952, Emily suggested that I give up a part-time job and devote my time to the Committee. The Committee would try to pay a small weekly salary. We had a modest royalty from a paperback edition of my third novel and occasional checks for freelance writing chores, plus monetary assistance from our mothers. I was given a title — Executive Director — a euphemism for a combination jack-of-all-trades; I would be the designated liaison between the Committee and the various clemency groups that had sprung up around the country, and would visit them if they provided fares and lodging.

We were aware that while some committees would welcome the visitor they requested, others would fear a visit from the FBI or local police after a visit by the Committee. Such a fear emerged on March 27, 1952, in Pittsburgh, the first city I visited at a group's request. The correspondent for the group had written me to phone him when my bus arrived. I wrote to Emily

> Am in Pittsburgh about an hour now, still trying to get hold of one of my two friends. Mr. W. doesn't answer the phone, and the other has no listed phone.[506]

Late that evening, I gave up trying to reach my correspondent. The people in the Pittsburgh group obviously wanted to help the clemency movement but had become frightened by their own courage in asking for assistance from the Committee. So be it. The Pittsburgh group would find its way in its own fashion. Since I was due in Cincinnati the next evening, I took the next bus out. On March 29, 1952, I wrote to Emily that there had been

> a very good committee meeting last night in Cincinnati at the Hotel Olmstead. About a dozen people, 3 from the university, the others unaffiliated, several strangers unknown to anybody, but obviously decent people and would meet next week to plan a big public meeting, amicus circulation, and fund raising. They kept asking, 'Why wasn't something done before?' They had absolutely no knowledge of what had happened elsewhere...[507]

On the following day, I

> spent two hours with the gen'l counsel for the Cleveland ACLU, a middle of the road political figure, and obviously quite courageous... He will support a public meeting. But he also made it clear that the Cleveland ACLU was not going to openly buck the [national]

ACLU unless they have a chance to study the full trial record...They agreed to hold a public meeting to shoot for at least $2500 contribution to us, etc. A very good meeting, attended by people with extremely close connections with Council of Jewish Women, B'nai Brith, ACLU, Pioneer Women, Quakers, etc...

Emily had phoned me with the news that New York City's Madison Square Garden, which could seat 25,000 people, had agreed to rent the Garden for a public meeting. (But three weeks later, the owners of the Garden reneged on the contract, no reason given.)[508]

On March 31st, I wrote from Detroit

I had a long talk with the editor of the *Jewish Weekly News*. He was belligerently opposed, but after reading our news-fact sheet and talking, he agreed to consider a sort of exploratory editorial, and possibly even involvement in a public meeting.[509]

Later that day, on the way to Chicago, I wrote that the Rosenberg children seemed always to be in my consciousness, and "I talk about them at meetings, half afraid to because...some begin to wonder whether I talk about the kids to elicit sympathy for the case."

From Chicago, I reported that a group of scientists were forming a committee, and that a lay committee was "now in formation" with the support of a local rabbi.[510]

I wrote optimistically of my meetings with committees in St. Louis, where a rabbi invited me to return to address his congregation;[511] and in Los Angeles;[512] San Francisco;[513] and after my return to St. Louis.[514]

That spring Emily traveled too, taking our daughters with her, to Washington and to Baltimore, where she met with Rabbi Uri Miller, Chairman of the Social Justice Committee of the National Council of Rabbis. He was sympathetic, and said he would use his influence privately for clemency as well as signing an amicus brief to the Supreme Court and asking other rabbis to do likewise. In discussing the case with him, Emily spoke of her concern about the detention camps set up under the 1950 Internal Security Act, and the rabbi then told her that her concern was valid. He said he had protested the setting up of the "detention" camps to government officials he would not identify, and related they had replied as follows: the rabbi would have had more grounds for protest if the detention camps had been set up without facilities for prayer and kosher food.

The new trial/clemency movement grows...

I had been away for six weeks, and some important events had transpired in my absence. For one thing, the office had been moved. The Committee now occupied an entire floor in another small office building. We were receiving a great deal of mail and contributions from all over the country, mostly from individuals and small groups of people who had also written to the White House and to their elected representatives in Washington, D.C., and who wanted to know what else they could do. Interspersed among these favorable letters were "hate mail" letters and opposition letters of a more rational kind that disagreed with the Committee.

The writers of the more rational anti-clemency letters accepted the claims of Justice officials as true, and requested we state some basis for siding with "traitors" against our own country. We made certain to reply to these letters, and suggested that if the pamphlet of Reuben's articles in the *National Guardian* was not persuasive, we would inform them when the full trial record became available in a public library in their cities.

Another event — or series of events — of a very hopeful nature was the receipt of promised contributions from committees and individuals in the cities I had visited, as well as orders for large numbers of the Reuben pamphlets, fact sheets, and other printed information, and requests that we assist the committees in planning for public meetings by finding prominent persons as speakers.

A third welcome development was a positive response from many prominent persons to whom we had sent informational materials, who agreed to have their names as sponsors on the letterhead of the Committee's stationary, among them being well known writers, Protestant and Jewish clergy, scientists, physicians, a former governor of the U.S.-controlled Virgin Islands, educators, union officials, and a retired banker.[515] Not surprisingly, some of the sponsors were or had been actively involved in peace movements. Most of them were labeled "Communists" by HUAC and Justice officials, but none of them resigned as sponsors, and some agreed to speak at public meetings arranged by the committees around the country.

Every week brought us news that the promised public meetings in other cities were being held, with attendances of between several hundred and a thousand persons. Some were held at large churches (San Francisco), commercial meeting halls (Washington, D.C., Cleveland), major hotel auditoriums (Los Angeles, Philadelphia, Newark, Chicago, Detroit).

Unlike the New York City newspaper and radio media, the non-New York media were willing in many of the cities that had active committees to accept paid announcements for meetings and appeals for support, and to run news stories after the meetings, although, not surprisingly, these media dutifully ran the

Justice officials' warnings to the public that such meetings and their speakers were "Communist inspired."

Morton Sobell transferred to Alcatraz...

Justice Department documents obtained in the 1970s reveal that, because of reports by inmate-informants in 1952, Justice officials believed Sobell was on the verge of confessing, and therefore kept him in New York where FBI agents could take his statements.

We learned from an FBI memo dated March 15, 1954, that in 1952, the New York office of the FBI believed that "all legal proceedings" on behalf of Sobell had been terminated and this had encouraged them to make "a determined effort to seek the cooperation of Sobell."[516]

In late April or early May 1952, an inmate-informant at the Federal House of Detention told the FBI he had informed Sobell that if a new trial was won, there was a possibility Julius Rosenberg might testify against him. The inmate-informant reported that Sobell replied, "and to think that I could change this whole thing with a dime;" the informant said that Sobell told him he meant by this that he "could completely alter his position."[517]

On June 12, 1952 a Justice Department memorandum, based on the inmate-informant reports, concluded that

> Sobell is in an agitated frame of mind and that he was considering cooperating with the Government [but] wanted answers to the following questions:
>
> 1. If we would give him an assurance that if he talked this would not appear in the columns of two syndicated columnists;
>
> 2. Whether we would promise not to tell his wife or his lawyers of his cooperation;
>
> 3. Whether we would promise him to listen to him without asking any questions and if he desired not to cooperate to go out of the room;
>
> 4. What would be the Government's attitude if Sobell cooperated fully and then the Supreme Court granted his appeal and sent his case back for a new trial?[518]

Over the next months, the FBI agents decided that Sobell was not behaving in a manner that would support the inmate-informant's reports. A decision was then made to send Sobell to Alcatraz, three thousand miles from his family and attorney, in spite of the fact that he in no way fit any of the customary indicia by which prisoners were sent to Alcatraz. He had no history of violence, or a criminal background requiring imprisonment in a distant and high security facility.

On Thanksgiving Day 1952, Sobell was taken to Alcatraz. The inmate-informant reported he had suggested to Sobell "that the time had come to help himself," and that Sobell had replied, "I have a lawyer in San Francisco and there is an FBI office out there, too."[519]

Another FBI memorandum of that week had the inmate-informant reporting that before being taken to Alcatraz, Sobell had told him, "I have a story to tell and I know the FBI wants my story" and that he also said

> There is only one rope (that is, a means of escape) for the Rosenbergs and myself. Since the Rosenbergs stand the chance of losing their lives I will give them the chance of grabbing the rope.[520]

The inmate-informant expressed the opinion that Sobell would have confessed except that his wife would not permit him to, an opinion with which the FBI agreed.[521]

Another FBI memorandum of that week reported that the inmate-informant had "detected a letter on the subject's [Sobell's] person" addressed to Judge Kaufman, which read

> My innocense [sic] — the essential unfairness of the trial — these aspects of the case, there is no point to my now raising. However, when one compares the thirty years which I received with sentences in similar convictions of the past, it becomes evident that there must have been considerations beyond which the trial record reveals that entered into the final judgment. The sentence, it would seem, is predicated on some unstated element of the charge — something, perhaps, that the prosecution did not wish to reveal in open court. How else to explain the harsh severity of the sentence — and now — Alcatraz? I ask your Honor to reconsider the basic injustice of such procedure."[522]

The inmate-informant told the FBI the letter had not been mailed but that Sobell "requested it be sent with his personal belongings to Alcatraz."

After Sobell was transferred to Alcatraz, the FBI sought to find an Alcatraz inmate-informant to keep them abreast of the possibility that Sobell would be receptive to offers of reduction in his sentence in exchange for a confession. We will given an account of this later.

The media acknowledge the magnitude of support for clemency...

In December 1952, on the threshold of the New Year, a *New York World Telegram* columnist, Frederick Woltman, wrote a lengthy column that, in its own bent way, provided its readers — and the Committee — with an approximately accurate reprise of some of the Committee's accomplishments. The column carried the usual warning that the Committee's

> daily press releases, circulars and pamphlets could properly be tagged "Manufactured in Moscow."[523]

Woltman described the campaign at that point, as being "without parallel in the long, fruity history of Red propaganda ventures." He described clemency supporters as "suckers," and expressed indignation that the Committee's "literature has been circulated at churches of all denominations...throughout the nation." The Committee, he reported, was circulating "hundreds of thousands" of printed cards addressed to President Truman, as well as petitions and other materials. In November, the report went on, the Committee had launched a "Million Message" campaign for clemency, and had

> handed up [to the Supreme Court] a brief for a new trial bearing no less than 50,000 signatures. These, according to the Committee, were rounded up by 2000 sympathizers who rang doorbells for six months. Four fifths of the names came from outside New York City.

Woltman called attention to what he felt was a deplorable development

> After he imposed the death penalty April 5, 1951, Federal Judge Irving R. Kaufman received about 10,000 pieces of mail. About 99% were favorable. Then there was a lull until the Rosenberg committee started functioning last January.

> The inpouring mail since has overwhelmingly favored a lighter sentence. The Red campaign was working.

Woltman also repeated the falsehood that the Committee claimed the Rosenberg-Sobell case had been "a plot against Jews," and attacked Dr. Harry F. Ward, former chairman of the American Civil Liberties Union, who supported clemency, as having a "record of Communist associations," and went on to disparage Father Clarence E. Duffy, the Catholic priest who had characterized the death sentences as contrary to Christian beliefs. Woltman noted that Father Duffy had been forbidden by his superiors to celebrate mass publicly.

Another anti-clemency columnist, Howard Rushmore, who wrote for the *New York Journal-American*, sought to make news as well as report it. Early in

1952, a supporter had come to the Committee headquarters with Rabbi Meyer Sharff, a man in his sixties who, by his bearing and clothes, was unmistakably Orthodox. He headed a Brooklyn synagogue of working and middle class congregants. Some months earlier, he had been given informational material on the case by a member of his congregation, and had come to offer what help he could. He began by telling us he believed the United States to be the freest country in the world, and that he abhorred Communism and Stalin.

Turning to the Rosenberg-Sobell case, Rabbi Sharff said under Orthodox law an accused person could not be found guilty of a crime simply on the word of a witness, unless there was true corroborative evidence. This was especially so if the witness gained something substantial from his or her testimony. He was not saying, he told us, that American law was deficient in any way. He was addressing, he said, the duty of "true Jews" toward Jews who were tried and found guilty on the word of a witness who was rewarded for his testimony, and for whose testimony there was no corroborative evidence.

We asked whether he would make a public statement of his views, which he did, saying

> I have studied and pondered long over the facts in the Rosenberg Case, which concern not only one human being, but four living souls, a father, a mother, and two small sons. The saving of one soul, as the saying goes, is the saving of the souls of future generations...
>
> I consider it my profound duty to address myself to friends and foes, to all, be they Jews or non-Jews, irrespective of institutional affiliation, or political persuasion, to participate in the work of securing justice for the Rosenbergs and Sobell.[524]

The rabbi was indefatigable, speaking at large and small meetings in New York and across the country, and constantly challenging the ingenuity of the Committee's small staff, because he would not travel between sundown on Friday and sundown on Saturday, nor on Jewish holidays, nor would he speak publicly on the Sabbath or other holy days, and arrangements had to be made in the cities he was bound for to have his food certified as kosher by an Orthodox rabbi and, wherever possible, arrangements were made for him to have lodging with Orthodox families. This also meant that his host families might be subject to criticism because of his mission, but this did not deter them.

In June 1952, Howard Rushmore, in his column in the *New York Journal-American*, reported Rabbi Sharff had broken with the Committee because he had learned that it had been organized by Communists. A Committee member went to see the rabbi about Rushmore's column, and reported back to us that although the rabbi would not give him the details, he had met with Rushmore and several other persons who sought to persuade him to abandon his activities for clemency, and he had probably responded by saying that he would think about what they had told him. We believed it was likely some members of his congregation had been critical of his clemency activities, and we would have understood if he had ended his cooperation with us. Our hope was, if he withdrew from the campaign, he would not echo Rushmore's false charge that the Committee and the clemency campaign were Communist-led.

On the following day Rabbi Sharff sent word that Rushmore had been mistaken, and that he intended to keep his speaking engagements, which he did. Nor did he seek to play a less visible role, for in April of the following year, he gave the invocation at a clemency meeting of 10,000 persons at the TriBoro Stadium in Randall's Island, New York.[525, 526]

Rabbi Sharff's attitude reflected a sentiment we had found among other Orthodox Jews and their rabbis. They expressed a more indignant and angry reaction to the death sentences than many Reform, Conservative and unaffiliated Jews permitted themselves to show. This may have been due to the overall attitude of Orthodox Jews, who considered themselves to be the "true" Jews, Jews who took the Talmud, the book of Jewish law, as binding for the personal conduct of Jews everywhere in the world. The Talmud, in the main, required personal conduct to be uncompromisingly compassionate toward people who faced unbearable circumstances, and allowed for no exceptions that would permit a Jew to look away from the suffering of others.

Clemency in President Truman's hands...

The original execution date for the week of May 21, 1951, had been repeatedly postponed to meet the legal requirement for the filing and processing of appeals in Judge Kaufman's court, the U.S. Court of Appeals and the Supreme Court, which refused to accept the case for review each time an appeal reached its in-box. Every appeal filed in 1951 and 1952 had been denied, at which point Judge Kaufman ordered the executions to take place during the week of January 12, 1953.

In early December 1952, faced with an execution ordered for the following month, clemency was the Rosenbergs' only hope of staying alive. President Truman had an application from the Rosenbergs for clemency, and he had three options: he could grant clemency, or he could deny clemency, or he could pass the appeal on to Dwight Eisenhower, the president-elect, who would take office on January 20, 1953.

Committee members were mixed in their evaluation of the possibility Truman might grant clemency. A few believed he might do so during the Christmas season, but most of us did not. We felt Truman was a man with good basic instincts in situations that did not require profound self-examination, he was too insecure to act decisively according to his conscience, and acted instead on the advice or pressure of others. It is probable, some of us thought, he had had qualms about atom-bombing Hiroshima and Nagasaki, but he had yielded to the strident demands of General Groves and the extremists that the bomb had to be used to spare American lives, to justify its cost, and to demonstrate its power to the Soviet Union.[527]

Those on the Committee who thought Truman might grant clemency reasoned that he suspected the case against the Rosenbergs and Sobell had not been sound because he was aware of the pressures that had been brought on Justice officials to find Communists to prosecute for espionage. He had himself battled the extremists' pressure to impose loyalty oaths on the public (although he finally yielded to the pressure), and had resisted the extremists' attacks on civil liberties, as exemplified in the 1950 Internal Security Act, which he vetoed (his veto was overridden). Most of us believed the best we could hope for was that Truman would not deny clemency, leaving the decision to President-elect Eisenhower.

(Forty years later, we learned from a letter to the *New York Times* from Harvey M. Spear, a Justice Department official, that David K. Niles, an assistant to Truman, had consulted with him about a telephone call Judge Kaufman had made to Truman "urging him to commute to life imprisonment the death sentences Judge Kaufman had imposed on the Rosenbergs." The President answered that "if Judge Kaufman felt strongly enough to urge the President to commute the death sentences, then Judge Kaufman should commute the sentences himself."[528])

On the assumption that Truman would pass the clemency appeal to his successor, we combed the media and histories of World War II for clues to Eisenhower's character and outlook. We were struck by the fact that Eisenhower, like other life-long professional soldiers, had lived his life apart from the uncertainties and, sometimes, calamities, that face the overwhelming majority of Americans. Committee Chairman Brainin half-joked that Eisenhower had lived under socialism for the better part of his life, having had all his essential needs met. But he had, of course, also faced the grim dangers that professional soldiers face, if not the grim fears of loss of jobs or of costly illnesses or of impoverished old age.

While Eisenhower was generally portrayed as a wise and genial but firm father figure, there were times in his life when his actions had gone beyond paternal firmness. A Committee member called our attention to the fact that, in 1932, Eisenhower, then a major, had been among the officers led by General Douglas MacArthur in carrying out an attack with cavalry, guns, tanks and tear gas on 25,000 poverty-stricken American veterans of World War I and their families who had come to Washington to ask for assistance and jobs. Several veterans and two babies were killed, many others were wounded.[529] Another member called attention to Eisenhower's approval, in 1945, of the execution of Private Eddie Slovik, the first execution for desertion since the Civil War.[530] Slovik had told his commanding officer he was unable to face the fury and danger of battle, and that he would desert rather than do so, which he did. A great many prospective soldiers had been rejected for military service for essentially the same reasons given by Slovik. Eisenhower's decision to allow the execution to be carried out appeared to signal the absence of compassion for the life of a human being under his command who had been mistakenly allowed into the armed forces by an incompetent examiner who was also under the general's command.

We did not know at the time the later revelation by Chief Justice Earl Warren that Eisenhower was opposed to due process in trials involving persons labeled "Communists," and, asked how he believed their cases should be handled, had replied, "I would kill the S.O.Bs."[531]

The question we asked ourselves was: where within himself would Eisenhower find the compassion with which to grant clemency to the Rosenbergs?

A Clemency Vigil at the White House...?

We began discussing the possibility of conducting a Clemency Vigil at the White House. This led us inevitably to explore the impression the public had of the Committee's actions so far. Our public meetings had been peaceful, our language in our printed materials had been moderate and respectful, always hewing closely to the course we had set, sparing in our use of adjectives, careful to express the intensity of our emotions in words that emphasized fact rather than feeling. Now, with the imminence of executions, we had to elevate our efforts to a level that would inevitably reveal something of the emotions that drove us and yet, at the same time, we knew our words must remain within the boundary of peaceful and rational advocacy. The result, so far, based on what the many clemency committees had reported to us, was that, at the very least, half a million clemency communications had gone to the White House.

We found that other committees had also begun to discuss a national clemency vigil at the White House. In some cities, brief vigils had been held at Justice Department offices.

If a White House vigil attracted thousands of supporters, it would bring to the attention of the President and the public the broad spectrum of support the clemency movement had obtained. If the press releases and other materials associated with the Vigil made it clear that it was being held in support of a decision for clemency, and if its numbers and duration could be sustained, it might break through the anti-clemency stance of the mainstream media, and it might balance to some degree the anti-clemency sentiments being conveyed by Justice officials and others who had direct access to the President.

But if it attracted only a few hundred supporters, it would send an abysmally different kind of message.

We brought the suggestion for a White House Vigil to Dean Loomer, Rabbi Cronbach, Stephen Love, Father Duffy and to other consultants among the clergy, lawyers and scientists. They were supportive, with reservations. Some were afraid that a Vigil might be "too militant" if it numbered in the thousands, that such numbers, assuming they were realized, would spark violence. At the same time, they recognized that lesser numbers would most likely be interpreted, at best, as public indifference or, at worst, as support for executions. A few consultants, who had contacts in government, argued that a vigil would virtually shut the door on face-to-face efforts being made for clemency by acquaintances or friends of the President. But most of our supporters who had such contacts did not discourage the idea of a White House Vigil.

One probable boon from a vigil, its supporters argued, would be a decided increase in the activities of committees throughout the country. They would be energized to bring news of the Vigil to their communities, to raise funds with which to send participants to the Vigil, and to organize public meetings in its support.

So we were faced with a perplexing problem. Would either Truman or Eisenhower have the capacity to penetrate the fog of anti-Communism in respect to the misconduct, deceits and illegalities that had marked the trial? Did either have the strength to oppose the demand by Justice officials that the Rosenbergs be executed if they did not confess?

We had no answers. But we had begun to feel that however essential petitions and letters and telegrams were, they were largely invisible to the public, and that what we needed, within the bounds of orderliness and civility, was an action that through the numbers and visibility of its participants, conveyed their commitment to saving the Rosenbergs. This would hopefully encourage others to support clemency even if they did so only by lending their names to petitions.

Yes, yes, yes, that is so, we told one another, but we were never sure.

We were aware the media would echo the anticipated Justice officials' press releases labeling the Vigil another Communist operation, intended to embarrass the President and the United States. We were also quite certain that there would be a counter-vigil by opponents carrying placards, calling on the President to execute the Rosenbergs, and it would be photographs of their placards for execution rather than ours for clemency that would accompany the news stories.

The members of the Committee had to acknowledge a circumstance that would affect how each of us voted on the matter of a vigil. Most members of the Committee had acquired, early on in their lives, a prejudice against collaborating, by silence, in the arrogance and indifference of many government officials to the lives of ordinary people. We had lived through the officials' abandonment of millions of suffering Americans in the 1930s, through diversions of public moneys to favored interests and to ill-concealed contempt for Americans without wealth or power. Not until Franklin Roosevelt came on the scene did hunger and other problems of ordinary Americans become a proper subject for government officials to discuss over lunch. Had President Roosevelt been alive, we believed, there would have been no need for a clemency Vigil at the White House.

We did not quite trust soft-spoken appeals to government officials on issues of life, equality or freedom. We had all of us spent part of our childhood or adulthood amidst discussion and debate about what could be done to save our relatives in Europe from their fate at the hands of the Nazis. Some of us had wanted to bring the pressure of demonstrations and picket lines against our State Department to cease its affectionate relationship with Adolph Hitler and his government. We were told not to be impatient, rash, reckless, irresponsible. Others counseled us to bring what they believed to be the persuasive balm of reason and deference to the State Department so that it would coax the better side of Nazism to come to the fore. In the end, the "balm of reason" prevailed. And so we said *kaddish*, the prayer for the dead, for six million Jews.

The burdens of our prejudices and the discovery of the irrelevance of either counsels of militancy or of good manners to the fate of the six million who were murdered, made us cautious. And our timekeeper, Joseph Brainin, knew this (how could he not, having himself lost family to the Holocaust, and been through the discussions and debates?), and he saw the frowns on every face, and he let us talk and disagree, and talk again, and then he would say, "Friends, the clock is ticking..."

Our daily need to debate the wisdom of proposed actions and conduct, either among ourselves as a Committee, or with supporters who held conservative or, opposing, what we called "adventurous" views, created tensions within ourselves. The clock was, indeed, ticking and we were, indeed, talking. The nuances that differentiated one member's definition of "militancy" from another's became acute. Each of us experienced the constant fear that our personal advocacy of — or opposition to — a specific action or nuance was utterly wrong and would forever haunt us if the Rosenbergs were executed. A residual tremor of that fear remains in us to this day.

Our debates and discussions and soul searching about the Vigil were often on the run than around a table. Committee members were now constantly traveling to meet with committees in other cities. Distant cities, like Los Angeles, had to provide us with air fares, since six-day round-trip train travel wasted too much time. In addition, we had a Congressional-contact group in the Washington D.C. area to seek support from lawmakers; we were speaking at public meetings organized by other groups; we were kept busy answering mail from lawyers, clergy, journalists and others; we were constantly engaged in fund raising because our cash on hand was never enough to pay rent, legal fees, printers' bills, stationary, postage, travel expenses, and the meager salaries that were rarely paid on time.

Nevertheless, the sentiment in the Committee and among the consultants was to embark on a vigil. A final decision on such a step, we felt, could not be taken without consulting the Rosenbergs. Since we were not permitted to have any contact with them, we asked their attorney, Emanuel Bloch, to lay before them the pros and cons of a vigil, which he did, and shortly afterward told us that they approved of it.

A diversionary action by the Communist Party...

An occurrence shortly before starting the Vigil reinforced our concern for how the public perceived the clemency movement. From the very first public actions by the Committee it became clear that many rank-and-file Communists were disregarding their leaders' hostility to the clemency campaign and were accepting the Committee's guidelines for their personal participation in the campaign.

In late fall 1952, when this became clear to the Communist leaders, they began to plan, through the Civil Rights Congress, to develop independent actions on behalf of clemency. Those of us familiar with the past history of the Civil Rights Congress knew that it had a very honorable record of campaigning on behalf of wrongfully imprisoned dissenters and, in particular, on behalf of African-Americans who had been sentenced to death after guilty verdicts rendered by white-only juries for crimes they may not have committed. In many instances, no white defendants had ever been sentenced to death for similar crimes. We could not forget, however, that in the fall of 1951, one of the Civil Rights Congress' leaders had urged Committee members to abandon their efforts for a new trial and clemency, a wish identical to that of officials of the Justice Department.

The Civil Rights Congress announced in December 1952, that it would hold a public protest meeting on Christmas Eve at Sing Sing, at which Howard Fast, a noted writer and activist, would speak. Bloch conferred with the Rosenbergs about the announcement, and they replied in a telegram on December 19, 1952, in which they described the intended action as

> ILL ADVISED STOP DIRECT CONTINUING CAMPAIGN TO FEDERAL GOVERNMENT FOR RELIEF STOP SING SING AUTHORITIES NO LEGAL POWER TO INTERVENE IN OUR CASE STOP...[532]

In spite of the Rosenbergs' wishes, the demonstration at Sing Sing was held. Afterward, at a meeting at our request in which Joseph Brainin, Aaron Schneider, Emily, I and a representative of the Civil Rights

Congress participated, Emily pointed out that actions directed at non-policy making government agencies could not in any way help the Rosenbergs, no matter how dramatic the sponsors thought the actions were. All actions, she argued, had to be directed at persuading people to provide tangible support for a new trial and clemency in the form of respectful letters, telegrams and petitions to the White House.

Emily also had a more serious criticism to make. To attract participants to the Christmas Eve event at Sing Sing, the CRC had tossed leaflets announcing the action from windows and rooftops in New York City. Emily described such acts as burdening clemency supporters with the appearance of secrecy and deviousness. People advocating clemency for the Rosenbergs were not participating in an underground action, she told the CRC representative.

> The United States is not a fascist country and there is no reason for people who want to organize an action to be faceless. But you not only organized a useless action, you did it surreptitiously. If the FBI wanted to initiate an action that would give clemency supporters a bad name, it would do exactly what the CRC did.

Emily's reference to the FBI was not lost on the CRC representative, but he chose to pretend, by smiling when Emily made the remark, that she knew this was not the case. He said he had come to listen, and to correct any factual misunderstandings by the Committee, and that he would pass our opinions on to the Congress' Board of Directors. The Civil Rights Congress subsequently took few actions directly on behalf of the Rosenbergs, although it did add their names to actions the Congress took on behalf of other men and women in prison.

The Committee and the Moscow and Prague trials...

It had become a principle for the Committee that it would not stray from the Rosenberg-Sobell case to take up other public issues. But in November 1952, the Committee was compelled to rethink its position. On November 20, 1952, the Communist-led government of Czechoslovakia began a "purge" trial of Rudolph Slansky, who was Jewish, as were ten other of fourteen defendants who were former members of the Czechoslovakia Communist Party. The charges included sabotage, murder and treason and, in respect to eleven of the defendants, a belief in Zionism as the motive for the crimes. All the defendants, including Slansky, confessed and, like the other defendants, he was found guilty. On December 3, 1952, eleven of the accused, Slansky among them, were executed.

The Committee debated whether to issue a statement condemning the Slansky trial and the executions that followed as having been motivated by anti-Semitism (eleven of the fourteen defendants — nearly 80% — were Jewish, although the overwhelming number of Czechoslovakia Communist Party and its leaders were not Jewish). While, with one exception, the Committee members were agreed that the Slansky trial had been a travesty that deserved condemnation (the one member who disagreed believed that the unanimous confessions pointed to the guilt of the defendants), most of the Committee members had serious reservations about the wisdom of a condemnatory statement by the Committee. We had taken great pains to set a course for the clemency campaign we hoped other clemency committees would follow: to adhere to a single concern — a new trial or clemency and sentence reductions in the Rosenberg-Sobell case, based solely on proofs of prosecutorial and judicial misconduct. Our concern was that if we opened the Committee to other public issues, it could become a divisive forum for political and social agendas far wide of the Rosenberg-Sobell case, to the detriment of the clemency campaign. We had done everything we could to avoid giving a platform to other agendas and had even rejected an anti-capital punishment position, although a majority of Committee members were opposed to death sentences.

But we were not certain of our position in this instance. Brainin pointed out to the Committee that its silence on the Slansky trial could also become a divisive factor, since silence by us would be played to the public by Justice officials as "proof" that the Committee was controlled by Communists.

Our problem was aggravated by the position on the Slansky trial taken by the *National Guardian*, which had broken the press silence on the Rosenberg-Sobell case and had supported the Committee's actions, and which now accepted the Kremlin's version of the Slansky trial, as did the American Communist Party.

Before the Committee resolved the issue, the Soviet Union announced on January 13, 1953, that it had arrested nine doctors, all of them Jewish, and charged them with murder and with conspiracy to murder leading officials in Stalin's government. Joseph Brainin proposed that he issue a public statement, identifying himself as Chairman of the Committee, condemning what was apparently a new wave of Soviet anti-Semitism. Brainin had been secretary of a reception committee, a few years earlier, for a visit to the United States by Solomon Mikhoels, a Jewish actor in the Soviet Union who had died in 1948 in a car accident Brainin and many other persons suspected had been staged by the Stalin government, a suspicion that was heightened by Moscow's claim in the Jewish doctors' case that Mikhoels had once been a link between the Jewish doctors and American intelligence agencies. Brainin's proposal was quickly approved by a majority of the Committee, including the authors, although a minority argued that Brainin's statement would open the door to the injection of other issues into the campaign for clemency.

On January 28, 1953, the *New York Post* carried a headline reading: HEAD OF ROSENBERG COMMITTEE BLASTS MOSCOW PURGE OF JEWISH DOCTORS.

Brainin branded the charges against the Soviet defendants "illogical" and "fantastic." Asked about attributions to the Committee of charges that the Rosenberg-Sobell case was the result of anti-Semitism, Brainin told the *New York Post* the Committee had

> "never injected the issue of anti-Semitism." There were some people, he said, who felt that the sentencing judge — Federal Judge Irving R. Kaufman — had been super-sensitive because he was a Jew and therefore unduly harsh, "but at no time did I believe there was an anti-Semitic element to the trial or that it was conducted against the Rosenbergs as Jews."[533]

Fortunately for the defendant doctors, after Stalin's death on March 5, 1953, the successor government dropped the charges and exonerated the defendants.

What was not known at the time was that, in August 1952, the Soviet Union had secretly conducted a trial of the members of the Jewish Anti-fascist Committee and executed fifteen defendants.

Justice officials and a number of Jewish leaders continued to utilize the Prague executions and the aborted trial of the Jewish doctor defendants in Moscow to discourage the growing support for clemency and a new trial, not only in the United States, but in Europe and the rest of the world as well. The clemency campaign, its detractors argued, was not being pursued on behalf of the Rosenbergs and Sobell, but was intended to deflect attention from Soviet anti-Semitic trials and executions. There is no doubt that when the various Communist Parties saw the very large numbers of Americans and Europeans who were supporting the clemency movement, they felt encouraged to try to use the clemency movement to dull the public's accurate perceptions of anti-Semitism in Stalin's long reign. It is also certain that our Justice officials and many media commentators attempted to use the Stalinist anti-Semitic trials to dull the public's perceptions of the prosecutorial and judicial deceptions that led to the guilty verdicts and draconian sentences in the Rosenberg-Sobell case.

Top photo: Rabbi Abraham Cronbach, Sophie Rosenberg, Robby Rosenberg
(seated between adults) and Michael Rosenberg, outside the White House
Bottom photo: Emily Alman, Sophie Rosenberg, Robby Rosenberg (left) and
Michael Rosenberg, walking with Vigil participants

Chapter 8 | Pope Pius XII, 3000 American Protestant ministers and rabbis

A winter Vigil at the White House...

In mid-December 1952, we called the committee leaders in the various cities to tell them that we hoped to begin a Vigil at the White House as early as Sunday, December 28. Our intention was to maintain the Vigil until January 17 or 18, 1953, at which time, on the urging of several of our advisors, we would suspend the Vigil for a short time so that when the new president and his family went to the White House for the first time after his inauguration, they would not face what they might interpret to be a hostile picket line.

At the start of the White House Vigil, before the presidency changed hands, the participants initially numbered between five hundred people during daylight hours and early evening, when the temperatures were in the thirties, and two hundred people during the long hours from midnight to dawn, when the cold seemed colder in the darkness and was made colder still by the empty streets and the usually empty park opposite the White House.

Very visible by day and night were the Washington D. C. police and FBI agents, their presence especially welcome at night when occasional small pro-execution groups, usually accompanied by news photographers, came out of the darkness intent on provoking fights with Vigil participants. We had anticipated this and had cautioned the Vigil participants to ignore all provocations, even physical provocation, because we believed Justice officials would advise the police to deter provocative actions that might call attention to the Vigil. The police allowed small groups carrying pro-execution placards to join the Vigil, but almost as soon as news photographers had gotten the pictures they sought, the groups left.

We quickly discovered the Vigil would require us to add another person to the staff, which now numbered four persons. Emily was the logical choice. She had been an organizing inspiration for the Committee, and the first to have faith that the public silence could be overcome. To add oversight of the Vigil to her responsibilities, she would have to give up her employment at the 92nd Street YMCA.

Emily went to see an officer of the Board of Directors of the Y at which she was employed. He was a prominent Catholic layman, an attorney and an official of a Loyalty Board appointed by President Truman to screen civil service employees for Communist sympathies. Emily told him she was deeply disturbed at the death sentences given to the Rosenbergs, and had also become convinced from reading the trial record that the Rosenbergs and Sobell had not been fairly tried. She was part of the Committee trying to obtain a new trial or clemency for the defendants.

The official said he appreciated her frankness and regretted that the Y would lose her services, but he did not see how her employment could continue at the Y, since he was sworn to root out Communism, which he assumed she embraced as a philosophy. She told him that she was not an ideologue for any party, and that her actions were not dictated by dogma but by feelings that transcended partisanship of any kind, except a reverence for life and for what she called the American scripture, the Constitution. He acknowledged that such feelings were possible, and they discussed the appearance of human feelings in public life for a little while, a subject that seemed to interest him, because he prolonged the discussion several times when Emily thought it had come to an end. Before she left, he said, "If I'm ever in deep trouble, Emily, I hope someone like you comes along to help me." To which Emily replied, "Our country is in very deep trouble right now, and I hope you come along to get us out of it."

Emily had left him a copy of the trial record, but she never heard from him again. She said her discussion with him left her with the impression he was a good person who did not know that people could extricate themselves from the milieus in which their thoughts and feelings were not always their own. He *wanted* to help, Emily said, but was afraid that some part of him would become unrecognizable to everyone around him — his family, his church, the leaders of his party, his friends and, for a while, even to himself.

Walking the Vigil...

The clemency Vigil participants were warmly and well dressed (Emily had sent word to the supporting committees that participants in the Vigil were expected to wear their "Sunday best" every day). They formed two lines of marchers on the sidewalk along the White House fence, each line moving two abreast.

At some point in the early morning the participants would stop while a clergyman gave a brief invocation, followed by the singing of the Star Spangled Banner, after which the marching would resume. Most of the placards read CLEMENCY FOR THE ROSENBERGS; some asked for clemency on humanitarian grounds, or because the acknowledged perjuries by the passport photographer had laid a shadow of doubt on the verdicts; some placards read THE ELECTRIC CHAIR CANNOT KILL THE DOUBTS IN THE ROSENBERG CASE.

The police objected to the participants chanting clemency slogans, which the police described as "shouting," but now and then a chant would begin and last for several minutes before it faded away. There was singing, mostly spirituals, although the police objected to singing, too, but rarely enforced their objections, and never did so during the midnight-to-dawn hours.

Most of the early participants at the Vigil came from New York City, New Jersey, Philadelphia, Baltimore and Washington, D.C. About one in every fifteen was African-American. We had expected to see many more women than men on the vigil, but to our surprise their numbers were almost equal.

The participation of large numbers of blacks in the Vigil, and public expressions of support for clemency by many black ministers, was due in part, we believe, to the post-World War II (1946-1951) spate of fatalities inflicted on African-Americans, by the authorities and white racists. The fatalities were not at all confined to the south, but occurred in northern states as well. In that five year period, 170 African-American men, women and children were known to have been killed: 90 by police and prison guards; 40 by white men (only two of whom served prison time, but most of the remainder were never tried); 21 men were lynched; 17 were executed after trials of doubtful validity; two of the executed were children, aged 14 and 15.[534] Jewish participation in protests against the lynchings had been prominent, and persisted during the movement for equality during the next three decades that followed.

The time spent at the Vigil varied among the participants. Some spent an hour or two, and left. Some local people joined the Vigil during their lunch hour or for half an hour after work, and others came after dinner. But since the buses and trains continued to bring new participants, the numbers remained relatively stable, and most participants followed a two-hours-on and two-hours-off schedule. Many of the participants were housewives, mothers, grandmothers, active or retired teachers, clerks, seamen from nearby Baltimore, workingmen, storekeepers, salesmen and sales women, college students and occasional faculty members from universities in New York, Philadelphia, Princeton and Baltimore. There were almost always a number of the clergy at the Vigil, as well as a few lawyers and, occasionally, physicians and scientists.

There were frequent brief exchanges between passersby and the participants. Most of the passersby were politely curious, some of them were encouraging, and some were hostile.

Committee member Aaron Schneider, who had experience in dealing amicably with the police during his years as a union organizer, was able to obtain police permission for the Vigil leaders to bring coffee and doughnuts to the participants several times a day. The simple fact of recognizing the authority of the police by negotiating the arrangement with them softened to some degree a recognizable tension between them and the participants.

Tessie Greenglass visits her daughter at Sing Sing...

At the time of the Vigil, two mothers, Sophie Rosenberg, Julius Rosenberg's mother, and Tessie Greenglass, Ethel Rosenberg's mother, tried, each in her own way, to save the lives of their children. Sophie Rosenberg asked the Committee to arrange for her to participate as a speaker at public meetings, to walk at the Vigil and to be present at interviews with prominent people whose support we sought, and she also made efforts, which were unsuccessful, to see the President.

Tessie Greenglass' effort was directed at persuading her daughter and son-in-law to confess. She told O. John Rogge, her son's attorney, she wished to visit Julius Rosenberg at Sing Sing (although she had yet to visit her daughter, who had been at Sing Sing since the spring of 1951). Rogge informed the FBI of Tessie Greenglass' wish; the FBI replied it would neither oppose nor support her petition to visit her son-in-law.[535] Her petition was denied, whereupon she visited her daughter at Sing Sing.

Very likely, Tessie was certain her son-in-law, Julius Rosenberg, was guilty, and that her daughter was probably guilty as well. She may have even understood that their refusal to confess was based on the prosecution's transformation of the time of the crime and its description as treason. "This is to let you know my mother was here on Monday," Ethel wrote to Bloch.

> Now brace yourself for a shock; fact is, I am still in a state of stupefaction...I pointed out to her that... if I, while awaiting electrocution, was not afraid to continue to assert my innocence and give the lie to his [David Greenglass'] story, why couldn't he, in a far more advantageous position, be man enough to own up, at long last, to this lie, and help to save my life, instead of letting it be forfeited to save his face?...Said she, "So what would have been so terrible if you had backed up his story?" — I guess my mouth kind of fell open. "What," I replied, "and take the blame for a crime I never committed...?" She shrugged her shoulders indifferently and maintained doggedly, "You wouldn't be here."[536]

Tessie never visited her daughter again.

Urey and Einstein speak out...

During the first weeks of 1953, the number of Vigil participants was increased by a special 11-car train that brought 1100 new participants from New York,[537] and by nearly another 1000 who arrived by trains, buses and cars from other cities. An ecumenical religious organization made its facility, Inspiration House, available as a meeting place where participants from around the country could meet one another, and where they could spend time when they were away from the Vigil. The Inspiration House people also helped find homes to accommodate Vigil participants for several days at a time, and directed us to boarding houses that would accommodate participants at far lower charges than hotels would.

With the influx of more participants, now well over a thousand during the daylight and early evening hours, Aaron Schneider negotiated with the police for permission for the participants to march three abreast, which the police agreed to after consulting with, as one police official told him, "other interested parties."

Within a few days, new developments brought a great boost to the morale of the participants. On January 5, 1953 — the fourteenth month of the Committee's efforts — the *New York Times* printed the first pro-new trial/clemency appeal to appear in that newspaper. It was a letter to the newspaper by Dr. Harold C. Urey.[538]

After expressing his doubts about the credibility of the prosecutors' chief witnesses, Urey wrote

> We are engaged in a cold war with the tyranni-
> cal Government of the U.S.S.R. We wish to win the
> approval and loyalty of the good people of the world.
> Would it not be embarrassing if, after the execution
> of the Rosenbergs, it could be shown that the United
> States had executed two innocent people and let a guilty
> one go completely free? [Urey is referring here to Ruth
> Greenglass, who was not tried, although she confessed]

One week later, the *New York Times* published a letter in support of Urey's position from Albert Einstein, in which the scientist wrote

> My conscience compels me to urge you to commute the
> death sentence of Julius and Ethel Rosenberg.
>
> This appeal to you is prompted by the same reasons
> which were set forth so convincingly by my distin-
> guished colleague, Harold C. Urey, in his letter of Jan.
> 5, 1953.[539]

New signs sprouted up on the Vigil line, accompanied by new leaflets, quoting from Urey's and Einstein's statements.

Other prominent Americans were announcing their support, among them writers: W.E.B. DuBois, Nelson Algren, I.F. Stone, Waldo Frank, Dashiell Hammet; actors and singers: Ossie Davis, Paul Robeson, Ruby Dee, Gale Sondergaard, Howard DaSilva; scientists: Harlow Shapley, E.U. Condon, Philip Morrison, Gene Weltfish; Linus Pauling; artists: Rockwell Kent, Robert Gwathmey, Pablo Picasso. They were quickly labeled Communists or "Communist dupes" by HUAC.[540]

During weekdays, some participants in the Vigil left the line to keep pre-arranged appointments with members of Congress to solicit support for clemency.

This was an uphill mission, considering that over two-thirds of the members of Congress had voted to override President Truman's veto of the Internal Security Act of 1950.

Nevertheless, a few members of Congress endorsed clemency. Rep. Robert J. Crosser, of Ohio, did so because he was opposed to capital punishment. Another was Senator William Langer of North Dakota, a supporter of the Internal Security Act, who later spoke at public meetings for clemency.

Committee member Don Rothenberg kept a log of his, Emily's and other callers' contacts with members of Congress in the winter and spring of 1953; excerpts from the callers' notes reflect the fear by elected lawmakers to act on their beliefs.

> Against capital punishment but feels inadequate to intervene (NY); Has been seen by several delegations from his district, but will take no action. (NY); Says Rosenberg are guilty — but death sentence is too harsh. (NY); For clemency — but will not issue public statement. (NY); Undecided — cites 'separation of powers' — will do nothing. (NY); Is for clemency but will not intervene — was misinterpreted once and is shy of open statements. (OH); She was definitely for clemency...Is frightened — but still potentially helpful. (OH);...[she] will not intervene with Justice Department (through fear of sticking neck out). (PA); Friendly and sympathetic, concerned about the death penalty (WA); Thinks penalty too severe — but doubts possibility of congressional action. (WA); For clemency — but won't take initiative alone. (WI)[541]

The Committee members agreed that every one of us must spend some time at the White House Vigil, to walk alongside the many thousands, of men and women our actions had brought to Washington from the near and most distant cities of the country.

The White House by day, by night...

The Vigil and the lights of the Truman White House after midnight... A room was suddenly lit or another suddenly darkened. Was the outgoing President restless? Was he searching for another defining act of his personal history? Had the Rosenbergs crossed his mind? Or was he fast asleep, and was the suddenly lit room a place in which an aide had remembered an unfinished chore?

By day, the White House seemed a more prosaic place. Moving vans were carrying the stuff of the Trumans' lives out; other vans were carrying the stuff of the Eisenhowers' lives in.

Grandstands had been erected on Pennsylvania Avenue to seat the spectators who would come to cheer Dwight D. Eisenhower on the most remarkable day of his life.

My hopes were higher at night, for I imagined the outgoing President, alone except for Bess, asking himself whether he wanted to end his presidency with a tinge of regret for something undone.

My hopes were lower by day, for I imagined the incoming President surrounded by urgent voices demanding his attention, none of them advising him to begin his presidency with an act of humanity.

A new application for clemency to two presidents...

On January 9, in a new application for clemency, the Rosenbergs wrote, in part

> No sentences of death are merited here. Our alleged crime was not treason. There was no charge of traffick with an enemy...[542]

> ...We are husband and wife. We are firmly united by the ties of marriage, the love we bear our two fine sons and one another. We have never known the ease of riches or even comfort. At times we have felt the pangs of want. We come from a humble background and we are humble people. Were it not for the criminal accusations against us, we would have lived out our lives simply, like most people, unknown to the world, except for those few whose lives crossed ours...[543]

> If we are innocent, as we proclaim, we shall have the opportunity to vindicate ourselves. If we have erred, as others say, then it is in the interests of the United States not to depart from its heritage of openheartedness and its ideals of equality before the law by stooping to a vengeful and savage deed.[544]

Some of us wondered if the Rosenbergs' affidavit had been too stiff-necked.

If President Truman was going to reject or grant clemency, he had only a short time to do so. All of us in the Committee prayed for the grant, but not all of us placed hope in the man who had let himself be persuaded to hurl atomic bombs at hundreds of thousands of civilians, adults and children. It was not hard for us to believe he could easily be persuaded to take two more lives to appease his opponents.

The imminence of the executions if neither president granted clemency, created an underlying somber mood in us, mixed with stubbornness aroused by the Rosenbergs' tone in their appeal for clemency. Many hundreds of thousands of us were speaking to our government in our petitions and letters and in our miles of marching at the Vigil and elsewhere. In truth, we were not standing hat in hand to ask for mercy but, as the country's Founders had done, asking not for charity, but for justice.

The Vigil pauses, the new president announces his decision...

The Vigil now numbered over 2000 marchers during the day, and about a third of that number through the night. More participants were on their way, and we began to anticipate that within a few days the Vigil would number 3000 or more marchers at any one time, and we would have to again ask the police to expand the limits they had placed on the length of the Vigil or permit the participants to march four or five abreast.

A two-day national clemency and prayer meeting was arranged to start on January 4, at the Washington National Guard Armory, but the ubiquitous "other interested parties" persuaded the Armory officials to cancel the permit.[545]

In major cities, local committees conducted actions of their own. On January 8, 1953, a day of rain, 2000 persons held a Vigil at New York City's Strauss Square on the Lower East Side, addressed by a former state attorney and the Radio City Synagogue rabbi and W.E.B. Dubois.[546] On the same day, 300 persons at Los Angeles' City Hall, among them Helen Sobell, marched for clemency, led by ministers of the Long Beach Christian Church and the Bethal Baptist Church, and in Philadelphia, 45 Protestant ministers sent off a letter to President Truman, writing, "We beg you to commute this sentence from motives of justice and mercy and for the sake of America's good name throughout the world." In Newark, N.J., a 43-car motorcade drove through the city, bearing streamers that read "Clemency for the Rosenbergs." In Asbury Park, N.J., the radio silence imposed on the campaign was broken by a half hour dramatization of the campaign for clemency over WJLK, and a quarter page ad for clemency appeared in the Asbury Park Press. Objective news stories of the campaign also appeared in the Trenton, N.J. press.[547, 548, 549]

Over the next weeks, as we had anticipated, the Vigil numbers grew. The police permitted the participants to march four and five abreast, and the sheer pressure of numbers forced the marchers to exceed the limits set by the police.

When the Vigil had begun on December 27, 1952, a number of marchers had carried placards that read "This Is the Vigil's 1st Day," and each day's number had been changed at midnight, a reminder to us, and to spectators, that the 18th day — January 12, 1953, had been set by Judge Kaufman as the next date for executing the Rosenbergs. Before that date, on January 10, the Rosenbergs were granted a mandatory stay of execution to permit them to file an appeal for clemency with the new president. The date on the placards continued to be changed until January 18, 1953, the 24th day of the first Vigil, when the Vigil was suspended in observance of the inauguration and the Eisenhower family's entry into the White House.

While we had originally planned to suspend the Vigil on January 18, 1953, as an act of courtesy and civility, another important reason began to emerge. Small groups of pro-execution marchers were being permitted by the police to behave more provocatively than in the past. We didn't think the "other interested parties" would have been distressed if violence flared up at the Vigil on inauguration day, giving them an opportunity to portray clemency supporters as spoilers of a hallmark day for the country — the peaceful change of one set of political leaders for another.

Although there were never more than five or six pro-execution people on the Vigil line, they were now permitted to shout insults, obscenities and threats at the pro-clemency marchers. The pro-clemency marchers observed the rule we had laid down: they were not to respond to anything the pro-execution marchers said or did, because that would divert attention from our purpose. Aaron Schneider called the attention of the police chief in charge of the Vigil detail to the increasing number of provocations, but it was plain that the chief's hands were tied. Schneider, using his union contacts, saw to it that a number of very tall and muscular unionists, mostly carpenters and furriers, came up from New York and Philadelphia, to join the Vigil. They were to abide by the same rules set for everyone, so that their only contribution to inhibiting provocation was their physically intimidating presence. Their essential role was to escort Vigil participants away from the Vigil who were unable to resist responding to provocations.

At the same time, we repeatedly made very public our intention to suspend the Vigil on inauguration day, and our reasons for doing so.

January 19 passed in silence from President Truman.

The new president took the oath of office. The former president and his family left the White House. The new president's family moved into the White House.

Three weeks later, on February 11, 1953, the new president denied the Rosenbergs' application for clemency.

The Vigil resumes...

Within hours of the announcement of the President's denial of clemency, the Committee began receiving phone calls and telegrams from committees and individuals throughout the country. The mood of most of these communications was dismay, filled with foreboding, ringing with disbelief, and sometimes tearful. Some callers expressed anger at the Committee, for having halted the first Vigil in order not to antagonize the new president and his family when they moved into the White House. "What you showed him," one committee chairman said, "Was that you felt you owed him the kind of deference that would let him get away with murder." No one was calling to urge us to fold our tent.

While there had been reservations among a number of conservative and religious personalities about the wisdom of the first Vigil at the White House, there were no reservations to resuming the Vigil after the President's action. In a few days, the eastern seaboard committees had provided 2000 men and women with which to begin the first day of the renewed winter Vigil for clemency. As it happened, that day's rain was so heavy the number of participants fluctuated wildly, a few times falling to no more than twenty persons, and at other times, when the rain eased up, rising to 2000 again.

The rising number of Vigil participants did little to raise the Committee's mood. Although the President's decision had not come as a surprise, it was nevertheless a great disappointment. We had hoped the very newness of his position would make him want to present himself as a moderate statesman who abjured irreversible steps and notions of infallibility. To make matters worse, on the day following the announcement of his decision, several mainstream newspapers carried a public statement strongly opposing clemency, signed by clergy and other professionals and businessmen. The six signers described themselves as

> representatives of the three major religious groups of the United States — Charles E. Wilson, industrialist and former president of General Electric Company; Samuel I. Rosenman, former Supreme Court Justice, New York State, and former counsel to President Roosevelt and President Truman; Clarence E. Manion, professor of law and former Dean of the College of Law of Notre Dame University; Rev. Daniel A. Poling, editor of "The Christian Herald"; Father Joseph N. Moody of Cathedral College, New York; and Rabbi William F. Rosenblum of Temple Israel, New York.[550]

These were men who were not generally regarded as spokespersons for their religious affiliations. Wilson was a very wealthy businessman, with no known deep interest in religion; Rosenman was a former judge and friend and advisor to a past president; Manion was an academician, with an expertise in law; Poling, the editor of the "Christian Herald," held himself out to be an expert on Communism; Moody was an academician; and the sixth, Rosenblum, had a congregation that undoubtedly included a fair number of clemency supporters.

Their statement read

> Those who join in organized campaigns for clemency in this case have knowingly or unknowingly given assistance to Communist propaganda.
>
> Appeals in regard to clemency should be directed to the Rosenbergs themselves. They have revealed no regret for the harm which they have done our nation nor any desire to assist the Department of Justice. They have failed to take steps that might warrant clemency.[551]

This was the first public statement we had seen in which any of the clergy opposed clemency. Coming so quickly after President Eisenhower's decision, it was disheartening. But one of our clergy advisors told us to take heart from the statement because, he said, whoever had initiated it had undoubtedly first called on American bishops or cardinals of the Catholic Church, and on well known Protestant ministers and rabbis, and all had apparently declined to sign the statement.

We were somewhat relieved by his assurances, but we were not cheered. If some in the clergy began publicly opposing clemency, we could expect defections from among the 3000 Protestant clergy who had already given clemency their support. And defections by the clergy would undoubtedly lead to defections by lay professionals. This would inevitably have a negative effect on support from the general public.

We were due for an uplifting surprise.

Pope Pius XII intervenes for clemency...

On February 14, a few days after the statement of the six appeared, the *New York Times* carried a Page 1 headline reading POPE MADE APPEAL TO AID ROSENBERGS, PLEA ONE OF MERCY.[552] Other newspapers also headlined the story. The *New York World Telegram* headline ran the whole length of the first page, and read POPE URGED MERCY FOR A-SPIES.[553] The news programs on radio and television reported similarly. The Pope's intervention was front-paged throughout the world.

The *Times* report quoted the Vatican newspaper *L'Osservatore Romano* as writing "that when it was a matter of saving human lives, the Pope never refused to intervene." The report laid the Pope's action to pressure from the Italian Communist press, but then went on to say, "Actual intervention, however, was made as a result of appeals to the Pope from Catholics in several countries."

The report also revealed that, in December 1952, the Apostolic Delegation, "at the request of the Holy See," had notified the United States Attorney General, James P. McGranery, that the Pope had received "numerous and urgent" appeals for intervention. McGranery did not reveal the notification to the Truman White House, nor State Department, nor to others in the Justice Department, nor did he pass the information on to anyone in the incoming Eisenhower administration.

The *Washington Post* asked, "Who at the Justice Department received the notice of the Pope's action, and what did he do with it?"[554]

On the previous day, February 13, on the bottom of a Rome embassy cable to the Secretary of State, a handwritten comment informed State that, in December 1952, the Papal Representative in Washington had "brought to the attention of the Democratic Attorney General" that the Vatican was receiving requests for intervention on behalf of the Rosenbergs. The preceding portion of the cable informed the Secretary that on February 14, *L'Osservatore Romano*, the Vatican newspaper, would release a statement announcing

> Now it should be known that His Holiness without being able to enter into the merits of the case never refuses his interest whenever it is requested in order to save human lives because of the high motives of charity innate to his apostolic ministry. As he has compassionately done in several other similar cases, also in this case he has not failed to intervene....[555]

We later learned that another clemency plea arrived at the Justice Department after the Papal Nuncio had communicated with McGranery, this time from the Chief Rabbinate of France, which represented the French Orthodox, Conservative, and Reform rabbis. This plea was also withheld from the Truman and Eisenhower administrations by McGranery.

We suddenly saw the January statement by the six "religious" leaders in a new light. McGranery had known that the December notification had been intended to alert him that the Pope would soon intervene for clemency, and that the Papal message to him could not be kept secret for long. He or someone acting at his instructions had attempted to preempt an appeal by the Pope by arranging for an endorsement of the executions by the clergy. But, as our clergy advisor had told us, whoever had initiated the statement had been unable to get so much as a one prominent and authoritative religious figure — Catholic, Protestant or Jewish — to sign the statement. Now, with the news of the Pope's intervention, we were cheered.

The next day, February 15, the New York Times ran another Page 1 headline, POPE MADE NO PLEA TO AID ROSENBERGS. Ignoring the very clear phrase in the Vatican's statement — *As he [the Pope] has compassionately done in several other similar cases, also in this case he has not failed to intervene...—* the *Times* wrote

> James P. McGranery, former United States Attorney General, made clear yesterday that Pope Pius XII had not made a personal plea for clemency for Julius and Ethel Rosenberg, atomic spies condemned to death, but only had transmitted the information that the Vatican had received "numerous and urgent appeals on their behalf."[556]

McGranery, who had been made a knight by the Pope, admitted that in December 1952, he had received notification from the Papal Nuncio which he had not shared with other officials, including President Truman, that the Pope had received many appeals for intervention.

The *Times* ended its story with a complaint that, because of the White House Vigil, "forests of placards blocked the White House view for camera-carrying tourists, and interfered with pedestrian use of the sidewalks."

Mainstream media editors were confronted with a dilemma: they could trust their reading of the Vatican's statement that the Pope "has not failed to intervene," and charitably ignore McGranery denial, or they could, as the *New York Times* had done, fall in step with Justice officials and pretend they had not read what they read, or they could stop running any stories on what the Pope had done.

In the main, they accepted the *Times'* approach by suspending their comprehension of the Vatican's statement. Others chose a less humiliating course by dropping the story.

We and our advisors were astonished, not so much by McGranery's irrational actions, as by the willingness of media editors to pretend they could not comprehend what they read, rather than stray from the government's line.

McGranery's concealment of the Pope's and the French Rabbinate's appeals shed light on the severe pressures under which he and other government officials were working. Officials never knew when acts of commission or omission might create vulnerabilities for them.

McGranery may have felt embarrassed by the Pope's politically incorrect humanity. Perhaps he was afraid the Pope's intervention would reflect badly on him and other Catholics. He may have been concerned that his colleagues and others in government would think he harbored sympathy for the Pope's plea.

He would have been especially concerned with the fevered Congressional inquisitors who were constantly seeking men and women in government who could be said to be linked to Communism and treason.

In what had become an unending storm of political denunciations, McGranery, like his colleagues throughout government, was perpetually running for cover.

McGranery's concealment of the Pope's clear intention to intervene was not passively accepted by the clergy. Rev. Jesse William Stitt, a Presbyterian minister, immediately called attention to the fact that Truman and Eisenhower had not learned of the clemency pleas by thousands of American Protestant ministers. In a letter to G. Bromley Oxnam, a bishop of the Methodist church with highly placed contacts in government, Rev. Stitt requested that a petition he had enclosed, signed by 2258 Protestant ministers, be brought personally to the attention of Secretary of State John Foster Dulles, in the hope that Dulles would "use his personal influence with the President to reconsider his refusal to commute the death sentence."

Rev Stitt wrote

> The puzzling and shocking fact that, according to the press, the Pope's appeal did not reach either President Truman's or President Eisenhower's desk has led us to fear that the various communications we have sent to both men have been withheld and pigeon-holed, and we are therefore extremely anxious to...bring this Protestant appeal in person to Mr. Dulles.[557]

Bishop Oxnam forwarded the letter and the petition to Dulles, commenting that although he was not aligning himself with efforts on behalf of the Rosenbergs, he felt Dulles should be made aware of the sentiments expressed in the petition.

At the same time, Bernard Loomer, Dean of the Divinity School at Chicago University, one of the Committee's principal advisors, wrote to President Eisenhower as spokesman for 2300 Protestant ministers, asking for an appointment.[558]

On March 10,1953, the hitherto concealed French rabbis' appeal became known when Rev. Harold S. Williamson, pastor of New York's Church of the Rugged Cross, made it public. The appeal to the President read

> The Rabbinate of France, profoundly moved by the death sentence pronounced on Ethel and Julius Rosenberg, but wishing to avoid any exploitation of this plea for political purposes, respectfully appeal directly to you, to implore you to use your prerogative of clemency in their behalf...The French Rabbinate joins with all the European persons — sincere friends of American democracy — in asking this measure of clemency in the

very name of our common ideal of justice and of generosity which we derive from the Bible.[559]

The following month, on April 16, 1953, *L'Osservatore Romano*, the Vatican
newspaper, published a lengthy elaboration of the Pope's plea, the first part of
which dealt with the background of the Pope's appeal; the second part, titled "The
Significance of an Intervention," is excerpted below.

> Not all the petitions addressed to his paternal heart were
> from Communists. The death penalty is an extreme rem-
> edy which no matter what the crime it aims to punish,
> arouses in certain people a lively repugnance...Further,
> the case of the young couple sentenced to die together
> is so pitiful as to arouse sincere commiseration even in
> those not animated by any ignoble partisan interest in
> wanting to save their lives...
>
> The Communists, who bear the full responsibility for
> this pitiful drama, wanted to use it as an expedient of
> their propaganda against the United States, claim-
> ing reasons of justice and humanity and rejecting the
> results of the trial. But this is no reason why the sad fate
> of the couple and their children should remain without
> an echo in the hearts of many and all the less so in the
> heart of the Holy Father....[560]

The Committee made an 8-page booklet of the Vatican's statement and distributed 10,000 copies among the clergy, members of Congress, lawyers, editors
of the New York Times and other mainstream media and lay people. The first
copy off the press went to Father Clarence Duffy, whom we began calling "the
Prophet."

A new execution date, and a stay of execution...

On February 16, five days after the president rejected the Rosenbergs' petition for clemency, Judge Kaufman set the week of March 9 for the executions to
take place.

On the following day the U.S. Court of Appeals stayed the new execution
date to permit a second appeal to the Supreme Court. Previously, the appellate
court had denied a motion for a new trial on the grounds that the Rosenbergs'
lawyer could have moved for a mistrial at one point during the trial, but failed
to do so. Justice officials argued that since the lawyer had erred at the trial, the
defendants should not be granted a stay to argue the point before the Supreme
Court. Judge Learned Hand, the senior judge of the Court of Appeals, disagreed.

> People don't dispose of lives, just because an attorney
> didn't make a point...You can't undo a death sentence.
> There are some Justices on the Supreme Court on whom
> the conduct of the Prosecuting Attorney might make an
> impression. Your duty, Mr. Prosecutor, is to seek justice,
> not to act as a timekeeper.[561]

The quickness with which the Court of Appeals had acted, and the criticism made of the prosecution, appeared to some to be a signal of hope for the defendants. For many months — since February 1952 — they had had a succession of doomsday rejections of appeals by the district courts, the appellate court and refusal by the Supreme Court to accept the case for review. Now, over the passing of a few days, we found ourselves nurturing optimistic expectations of a turn-around in the Rosenbergs' situation and we heard ourselves praising the clergy for speaking out and celebrating the power of righteous courts to correct wrongs. We had been arguing that a miscarriage of justice had occurred, not because our legal institutions were flawed, but because of human weakness and misconduct. Vindication for our argument, we began to hope, was just over the horizon.

A letter dated February 20, 1953, from the head of the Cincinnati clemency committee to Rabbi Cronbach described the emotional lift the Pope, the Protestant ministers, the rabbinate and the Court of Appeals decision had given us.

> In the short space of two weeks the whole complex of
> the case has changed. Where, a short time ago we were
> filled with despair, there is now a strong feeling of hope
> among people working to help the Rosenbergs.[562]

Letters and phone calls from committees around the country were spirited and supportive. For one thing, public clemency meetings had been planned before the stay was granted, and the local committees had decided not to cancel them, finding the stay had created so much hope and feelings of optimism that they began to think of the planned events as celebrations. Further, there was strong sentiment for maintaining the clemency Vigil at the White House, together with assurances that committees from as far away as Los Angeles and Seattle would provide participants and funds for food and lodging.

The Vigil grew in numbers. Prior to the president's denial of clemency, the Vigil had involved more than 5000 persons who had participated in it at one time or another. After February 13, the number doubled, meaning that there had been a great increase in clemency supporters and financial contributions in the cities and towns from which the participants came.

The White House Vigil had inspired an enormous number of letters, telegrams and multi-signature petitions to the White House, and had succeeded in overcoming, on a modest scale, the silence of the media and the stigmatization of the clemency movement as "seditious." In New York, Chicago, Los Angeles and Philadelphia, the media silence was broken, although the news stories continued to describe the campaign as Communist-led, and often gave more space to the very small numbers of pro-execution groups than to the thousands of pro-clemency marchers. Recognition was now widespread regarding doubt of the fairness of the trial and even greater doubt of the legality and morality of the death sentences.

Pro-execution letters to the White House...

There were supportive, as well as critical, communications to President Eisenhower following his denial of clemency. A letter pre-dating the President's action by two days from the Shoshone County Anti-Communist Association of Idaho stated

> ...should the President grant clemency, it will be another weakening of our national defenses, and would encourage others in positions of trust to betray our country without fear of consequences...the verdict was upheld by the highest court of our land...For what purposes was the Rosenberg trial held, at high cost to the government, if that verdict is cast aside due to the high pressure of subversive groups appealing for their type of "fairness"?[563]

A woman in New Hampshire wrote to an aide to the President several days after his decision

> If you have any influence with the President please don't let him be swayed by the Pope. Let's get rid of those traitors, the Rosenbergs. And let's for the love of God stop letting Britain dictate to us. Let's blockade the coast of China.[564]

A letter from a Jewish war veteran advised the President he "did exactly the correct thing and I wish to say that most of my friends agree that the punishment fits the crime."[565]

Another letter, addressed to the Attorney General from the president of the Philadelphia Zionist Council, who identified himself as a Republican, wrote

> practically 100% of the Jewish community in Philadelphia feels that the action taken by the President was one based solely on the merits of the case and had nothing whatsoever to do with the religion of the defendants.

> The very small group here who have expressed opinions
> to the contrary are typical of a certain type you have in
> the American Labor Party in New York.[566]

But it was clear that the palpable history of the moment was the great proliferation of pro-clemency letters and telegrams and petitions to the White House, and the unchanging small number of pro-execution communications and advocates.

The Vigil had moved the clemency movement forward: it had brought nationwide attention to the undeserved and illegal death sentences, the perjuries, the deceptive witness list and the misconduct of the prosecutors. It had inspired an enormous upsurge of clemency communications to the White House. We estimated that, from the start of the Vigil at the end of December, to the end of February, approximately half a million new telegrams and pro-clemency petitions with multiple names had arrived at the White House. In the third week of February, a CBS commentator reported that mail to the White House had risen from the usual 25,000 daily to 35,000, and nearly half of the increased mail favored clemency.[567]

When clemency supporters spoke at public meetings and knocked at doors and sent out mailings, very few among the audiences and respondents echoed the invectives flowing from Justice officials. Some disagreed with the door-knockers and sent them away empty-handed, but they only rarely warned them not to return. We were, when all was said and done, still living among the civil Americans described in our school textbooks.

At a private meeting with several dozen rank-and-file members of Hadassah, a Zionist Jewish women's organization, one of them asked Emily whether the Committee was not creating difficulties for American Jews by challenging the trial and sentences. Emily replied that the American people were not hostile to attempts to secure justice.

"The hostility doesn't come from the American people. It is only the movers and shakers in Congress and the White House who have lost the civility and humanity our school teachers told us was the American Way. You requested this private meeting, not because you are afraid of some vigilantes breaking down your door, or because of what Hadassah officials will say about you, but because you're afraid of what the FBI and Senator Joseph McCarthy will say, which is what your Hadassah leaders are afraid of, too. I'm prepared not to say another word about the Rosenbergs this evening. Let's talk instead about how we can save American civility and humanity and who we must save it from."

Later, Emily told the Committee, "They were ahead of me. They turned down the suggestion to talk about civility instead of the Rosenbergs. Most of them had already made up their minds to get information from us to allow them to sign a petition or make a cash contribution or spread the word to someone else."

The media in the smaller cities repeated the 'Communist-led' descriptives but were generally fairer in their reportage on the Vigil, in acknowledging the existence of local clemency committees. This was also true of local radio newscasts, some of which interviewed pro-clemency marchers as well as their opponents.

A mainstream newspaper breaks ranks...

In late January, the *Chicago Daily News* astonished other mainstream newspapers throughout the country by printing an editorial advocating clemency, on the grounds that clemency would preserve the possibility that the Rosenbergs would one day confess.[568] Although it was the only newspaper of its stature to do so, a number of other mainstream newspapers softened, to some degree, their previously unalterable pro-execution stance. Also later that month, *Newsweek* became the first of the major weeklies to acknowledge that the pro-clemency campaign was drawing significant support from persons who believed the Rosenbergs had been properly found guilty.[569]

The Turnabout shows up at the White House Vigil...

The new optimism felt by Committee members was accompanied by an impression that fresh perceptions were emerging among the public creating greater receptivity to the clemency movement. Troublesome aspects of the "repugnant philosophy" manifested by the Turnabout, were becoming apparent, one of which related directly to clemency. Among the acts of forgiveness and rewards being shown to Nazi war criminals was the commutation of the death sentences of 43 Nazi army officers and enlisted men who had been found guilty of participating in the massacre of 71 American prisoners of war at the Battle of the Bulge in 1944-1945. Following the imposition of the death sentences against the German soldiers and officers in 1946, an outcry arose in Congress, led by Senator Joseph McCarthy, that the trial of the German defendants had been unfair and that their confessions had been obtained by torture.[570] Over a period of two years, clemency was granted to every one of the condemned men and, by 1956, all had been freed.

Plainly, the matter of dispensing justice through clemency had become politicized by the government, being made available for crimes committed against Americans by former enemy nationals, but withheld for crimes by Americans who held unapproved political beliefs. But there was more: on the same news pages that carried stories of a new (for Americans) philosophy of justice, there were also stories of officially-sanctioned book-burnings (including works by Mark Twain) at the instigation of Roy Cohn, the former chief assistant prosecutor at the Rosenberg-Sobell trial, and carried out by American agencies abroad.[571]

Later that year, there would be book-burnings in the United States with the approval of President Eisenhower. Americans were being asked to endorse politicized justice, book burnings, and denunciations of non-conformists as conduct consistent with traditional concepts of Americanism.

George Kennan's unexpected public declaration, in May 1951, that it was impossible for Americanism to co-exist with the repressive measures advocated by extremists in Congress and the Executive, was a reflection of substantial public sentiment by conservative as well as liberal Americans.

New issues become relevant to clemency...

The Vigil had succeeded as a powerful symbol in support of justice, and in making the simple slogans of the campaign familiar to the public. The clemency campaign now had to move on from symbols and slogans and purely factual information to a substantive dialogue for a traditional non-politicized philosophy of justice. The Committee believed the time had come to place the new trial/clemency movement alongside the rise of public concern for the path down which the "repugnant philosophy" was taking the country, to acknowledge that the issue of clemency was not isolated from other debated issues.

This new outlook was a reversal of the Committee's past position, which was to ignore all issues except the trial-based prosecutorial misconduct in the Rosenberg-Sobell case. We had been concerned that pleading the case in the context of any other issue would be divisive and would harm the clemency effort. The most vigorous supporters of this outlook had been our conservative advisors among the clergy and laity. Now these same advisors were advocating that the clemency movement make its case in the broader context of the political currents that had shaped the case, and that were now, many believed, affecting the decisions of the appellate court and the Supreme Court.

The Committee members came to the conclusion that the dedicated participants at the Vigil would now be more effective by participating in dialogues in their home cities and towns than by marching at the White House. Even before that decision was made, a number of committee leaders in the larger cities had raised the matter. There was a new receptivity to the clemency movement in their cities, but many of the most articulate advocates for clemency were marching in Washington, D.C. instead of knocking at doors in Shaker Heights, Cleveland. If a need to re-establish the Vigil arose, we were confident we would have the numbers.

The political atmosphere seemed conducive to such a move. In a good number of cities there was now a willingness by the press and radio stations to take advertisements for clemency activities, although the media continued to attach the Communist label to the committees. This had become a tolerable burden because experience was teaching many people that the label 'Communist' was being used to describe criticism and dissent of any kind and, frequently, was drawing resentment, especially among Democratic voters whose party was still being referred to by Republican leaders as the "Commiecrat" Party.

The Committee also saw signs of support for a new trial and clemency from many persons who were acting independently of the clemency committees. All committees had made the White House the sole intended recipient of communications for clemency, but we heard from many sources that letters and petitions in great numbers were also being directed to Justice officials and to the judiciary.

At a court hearing immediately following the President's denial of clemency, at which Judge Kaufman would set a new execution date, Myles Lane, who had argued for key members of the House and Senate to enable David Greenglass to testify perjuriously about Exhibit 8, urged the judge to set an early execution date because, he said, the Communists were "attempting to vilify and harass everyone who has been associated with the trial and conviction of the Rosenbergs."

Judge Kaufman agreed

> The harassment has stepped up both in temper and tempo since the ruling of President Eisenhower. It is the most amazing thing, the way telegrams and telephone calls come into my chambers.[572]

The judge, addressing Emanuel Bloch, went on to say that the Committee was spreading misstatements and circulating "half truths about the case," to which Bloch replied that he was not an agent of the Committee and was no more responsible for the Committee's activities than he was for "the Pope's interest and intervention in this case." Judge Kaufman replied that he had "no knowledge of the Pope's intercession..."

A conservative publisher finds 47% of housewives favor clemency...

However much Justice officials and others pretended there was overwhelming support for the death sentences, they had reason to believe otherwise. A White House memorandum dated April 21, 1953, referring to a survey by McFadden Publications, a conservative publisher, stated the survey

> indicates that 52.5% of 200 housewives approve of the death sentence; 24% recommend life; 16.9% favor deportation; and 14.7% suggest some punishment other than death because of the children.[573]

Much as Justice officials wished to do so, it was impossible to pretend that the movement for clemency was too insignificant to be acknowledged other than by making statements condemning it. The acknowledgment was made without enthusiasm. Daniel L. Lyons, the U.S. Pardon Attorney agreed to meet with a pro-clemency union group in the last week of February. In a memorandum to J. Edgar Hoover, Assistant Attorney General Warren Olney III reported the union group's spokesperson

> expressed the view during the interview that the Department of Justice should offer no opposition to any motion for a stay of execution which was to be made on behalf of Julius and Ethel Rosenberg.[574]

Justice officials rejected the views expressed at the interview, and Olney sent the names of the unionists to the FBI "for your information." The fact remained, however, that before the Vigil and the Pope's intervention, no Justice official would have deigned to meet with anyone associated with the clemency movement.

Until the President's denial of clemency in February, no member of Congress had, to our knowledge, so much as asked any officials for information on the case or had indicated that any of his or her constituents favored clemency. In March, Senator Lyndon B. Johnson of Texas, at that time a member of the Senate Armed Services Committee, addressed himself to the Secretary of State because a constituent had raised a question concerning a foreign entity, the Vatican, and requested information about Pope Pius XII's intervention for clemency.[575]

The Assistant Secretary wrote two letters in reply, although the first one was not sent for reasons which become obvious upon reading. The first reply contained the following observation

> There is nothing in the record of the Rosenberg case to indicate that Julius and Ethel Rosenberg are Catholics, and their active implication in the conspiracy of which they were found guilty would be inconsistent with their being devout followers of any religion. It is consequently not likely that the religious persuasion of the Rosenbergs had anything to do with the interest of the Vatican in the Rosenberg case.[576]

The second reply omitted the above in its entirety, saying instead that the Pope had not made a plea for clemency, but had only reported to "the appropriate American officials" that he had received petitions on behalf of the Rosenbergs.[577]

Documents and events of later years (1965 and 1969), when Johnson was President, indicate his continuing interest in the case, and a probable intervention by him on Morton Sobell's behalf.

American Protestant ministers press for clemency...

After the Pope's intervention became public, there came a noticeable increase in the dialogue between lay clemency supporters and the clergy. There was a widespread assumption, among the Protestant and Jewish clergy, that the Pope, known as a fierce enemy of Communism, had defied the most conservative forces in the Vatican in making his plea for clemency, and had knowingly placed himself in the way of political criticism from American officials. Many of the clergy, even those hostile to the Catholic Church, felt that the Pope had set an example for them to follow.

An indication of the effect of the Pope's intervention on the American Protestant clergy came from the traditionally anti-Catholic south. In the spring of 1953, more than thirty Virginia Protestant ministers agreed to sign a nationally circulated letter to the President, asking for commutation of the Rosenbergs' death sentences, and an unknown number of others did so independently. Their congregations were in Richmond, Portsmouth, Hampton, Lexington, Suffolk, Norfolk, Cumberland, Craigsville, Danville, Smithfield, Philmont, Lurey, Petersburg, Alexandria, Franklin, among other Virginia towns. The clemency movement was reaching into what has often been called the "heartland of America."

A quarter of a century later, through the Freedom of Information Act, we obtained a partial list of over 2000 American pro-clemency clergy that had been sent in April 1954, to various government departments, including the State Department, for the information of their officials and for whatever uses they might make of the list.[578]

These clergy were among a much larger number, some 3000 Protestant ministers nationally, most of them co-signers of a clemency letter to the president, and a large number who wrote to the White House independently, at the end of December 1952, and throughout the first half of 1953.

The strong response from the Protestant ministers was, for the Committee, validation of our belief that the Rosenberg-Sobell case and the death sentences were opposed by large sections of the public. The Committee also felt validated for its distribution of the verbatim trial record to many of the clergy and, in particular, to those who held high positions in their denominations. We assumed, correctly, as we found out, that the clergy would take the trial record to attorneys for their denominations and churches, and we believed, also correctly, that many of these attorneys would tell the clergy they were on firm ground in their appeals for clemency, and possibly for a new trial as well. This gave us an insight into the outlook of both lawyers and clergy of a traditionally conservative section of the public.

The authors analyzed the government's list of 2000 clergy and found more than 500 (25%) of the clergy came from small towns of less than 10,000 persons, in 1953. We learned the names of these towns from a partial sampling of clergy whose surnames began with A or B. Their congregations were in **West Virginia**: Clay; **Arkansas**: New Underwood, Batesville; **Colorado**: La Junta, Elizabeth; **Iowa**: Madrid, Osage, Riceville, Shelby, Osceola, Mitchville; **N. Carolina**: Carthage, Warsaw, Graham; **Montana**: Fort Shorn, Ekalaka; **South Carolina**: Bamberg, St. George; **Oklahoma**: Medford, Carrier; **Louisiana**: Boothville; **South Dakota**: Beresford, Mobridge; **Nebraska** (the U.S. Attorney General's home state): Avoca, Red Cloud, Minatare, Laurel.[579]

We asked ourselves how the clergy and laity in those small towns learned about the questions arising from the Rosenberg-Sobell trial and the existence of a new trial/clemency movement.

In 1952-1953 there were no local newspapers or radio stations in those towns that would have accepted announcements of any kind from the Committee. Television was absent from most homes in 1953, and that medium, too, was closed to the Committee. Few, if any, of these towns had any lay organizations other than the American Legion or local business and school groups.

Some of these towns may have had their local mavericks or radicals, and some of these may have corresponded with mavericks in the larger cities. What the small towns definitely had were churches and church organizations and these communicated with, and received information from, regional and national offices. It was through these communications, the authors believe, that the clemency effort percolated into small towns and cities alike. An indication that this was so can be found in the status of the clergy on the government's list: at least ten of the supporters identified themselves as officers of national and regional church organizations.

Justice officials undoubtedly analyzed the list as we did, and found what we found. Predictably, Dr. J. B. Matthews, HUAC's expert on religion, issued a statement declaring, "The largest single group supporting the Communist apparatus in the United States today is composed of Protestant clergymen."[580]

Neither the records nor our memory of those days indicate that any of the clergy abandoned their efforts for clemency as a result of Dr. Matthews' statement, or because of criticism of them by government officials or private persons.

The Vigil participants go home to speak to their neighbors...

The mood of the spectators, during the weeks before the new pause in the Vigil, was far more civil and inquisitive than it had been prior to the denial of clemency. The Justice officials' concealment of the Pope's plea had been so astonishing that the public could no longer reflexively believe claims that the information circulated by new trial/clemency supporters was false.

Pressure grew for the President to meet with a representative committee of the clergy, headed by Bernard Loomer, who was publicly known to be an advisor to the Committee. On March 6, a group of 104 clergymen issued an open letter to the President, urging him to give a positive response to the request for a meeting by Loomer, and emphasizing their concern that the President's advisors were concealing religious support for clemency from him.

> It is indeed regrettable that the Pope's message was not communicated to you until after you had announced your decision. That circumstance suggests the possibility that you may wish to order an examination of all appeals for mercy with a view to re-evaluating their importance.[581]

Among the sponsors of the open letter were the Bishops of the Protestant Episcopal Diocese of Georgia and the Diocese of Kansas, and the head of the Central Pennsylvania Synod of the United Lutheran Church.

Clemency meetings, in cities across the country, were drawing larger audiences than they had in the past. In Los Angeles, an overflow public meeting at the Embassy Auditorium drew more than 3600 persons, where they heard Rev. Stephen Fritchman describe the voices for clemency as the "voices of the...vehemently anti-Communist," concerned "with the name and honor of the United States of America — with our record of justice as a people."[582] Other public meetings in the larger cities, such as New York and Chicago drew similarly large audiences.

A cautious optimism...

A cautious optimism began to fill us and, at the same time, we dreaded the worst. Our optimism put faith in public opinion; our apprehensions led us to look for a miracle. We asked ourselves unsettling questions. Could a factor in President Eisenhower's denial of clemency have been an assumption — possibly a correct one — that if he granted clemency the Committee would want to continue to seek a new trial for the Rosenbergs and Sobell? Would this factor remain if the Committee, assuming that it had the Rosenbergs' and Sobell's approval, gave its word to the Justice Department that it would fold its tent if clemency was granted?

Joseph Brainin said, "The Justice Department will say we're not offering them anything. We can fold our tent, but some other concerned people may put up a new one." Another Committee member said, "It won't give Justice officials what they're looking for, confessions to vindicate their conduct."

We tried to cling to our optimism, by believing that the Court of Appeals would look favorably on a petition for a hearing on one of the many issues placed before it, although so far the defendants had had an unbroken series of denials of hearings, even in instances where the judges found misconduct by the prosecutors. And, if the Court of Appeals denied every petition for a hearing, we desperately wanted to believe the Supreme Court would finally accept the case for review.

As we saw the situation, the President was being asked to choose between political expediency and the preservation of America's reputation for moderation and humanity. We did not know whether it would be possible to raise the movement for clemency to a level that would make it more expedient to grant clemency than to accept the Justice officials' recommendations against it.

One criminal attorney told us Justice officials and the judge had to be aware that, if neither confessions nor clemency intervened, they might be committing "felony murder," a murder committed during the commission of another crime — in this case, conducting a deliberately flawed trial — in which murder had not been contemplated. Would this deter them? "I've heard murderers say," the lawyer told us, "their victims brought the murders on themselves by resisting being robbed or raped." Then he added, "If I was on the prosecution team, what I'd be telling myself right now is that the Rosenbergs are calling the shots, forcing us to turn the screw, and it's the Rosenbergs, not us, responsible if anything happens that wasn't planned by us."

We were dismayed by the prophecy inherent in the lawyer's description of the officials' rationalization. At one of our dismay meetings, Emily suddenly said, "New slogan: BDTD. Better denial than dismay."

A $25-per-plate Clemency Dinner for 1000 guests...

The Committee became emboldened to schedule a major clemency event at a large public hotel in New York City. We had in mind a thousand-person $25-per-plate dinner ($25 was significant money in 1953), dietary-laws-observed (we did not wish to see news stories attacking the Committee for serving non-kosher food to the Jews among the guests). Several large and prestigious hotels either refused to contract for the dinner or asked for rental fees far beyond our means. One large hotel did sign a contract, but notified the Committee a week later that the waiters' union shop chairman said his members would not serve dinner to "commies." A week later a contract was signed with another large hotel, the Capitol, whose management and personnel assured us our guests would be treated as would any other guests at the hotel. We invited a British member of Parliament, Sydney Silverman, to be one of the featured speakers. Silverman was an executive board member of the World Jewish Congress, a decidedly anti-Communist organization; another speaker was Prof. Stephen Love, a key advisor; a third was Mary Church Terrel, a 90 year old African-American educator.

The dinner went almost as planned, with 1100 guests from almost every state in the Union. But British M.P. Silverman was refused a visa by the State Department, and a tape recording of his speech, rushed by airplane from London several days after his visa was denied, never arrived at the Committee office or at the dinner.

As we had anticipated, a substantial number of lawyers were among the guests, and Stephen Love addressed them specifically, commenting on the absence of evidence and the non-credible elements in David Greenglass' testimony. He challenged the impression held by many lawyers that the U.S. Court of Appeals had upheld the reliability of the prosecution's evidence. He pointed out that none of the appellants' petitions for hearings, on any points of appeal, had been granted, that without the grant of a hearing the appellants could not subpoena witnesses and documents with which to present their appeals. The appellate judges had shown that they were not entirely satisfied with some aspects of the trial, but had not agreed to hold a hearing on that which troubled them.

Mary Church Terrel, who had been born in 1863, the year in which President Lincoln had issued the Emancipation Proclamation, had been an educator and a founder of the NAACP. She told the guests the Rosenberg-Sobell case was not an aberration, that our history was studded with tragic miscarriages of justice and with great movements by ordinary people to undo the injustices.

Later that month, a clemency meeting with 2000 participants was held at Carnegie Hall by the National Council of the Arts, Sciences, and Professions, at which the speakers included William Harrison, the associate editor of the *Boston Chronicle*, Prof. Louise Pettibone Smith, who taught Biblical history at Wellesley, Rev. Kenneth R. Forbes, the executive chairman of the Episcopal League for Social Action, and Dr. Bernard Loomer.[583]

Support for clemency in the shadows of a city's government...

The success of the March dinner at the Capitol and the Carnegie Hall meeting led us to an even more ambitious undertaking, to hold a public meeting at New York's Triboro Stadium at Randall's Island, which could seat 10,000 persons (not the Committee's first choice, which was Madison Square Garden, seating 20,000, but whose manager told us with absolute finality that no clemency meeting would ever take place under the Garden's roof). We did not know, at this point, that at the Randall Island meeting the Committee would be able to make two sensational items of new evidence public that pointed directly to perjury by the Greenglasses.

The very act of conducting a public meeting at Randall's Island signified another barrier had been overcome. The Stadium was New York City property, overseen by the Parks Department. Controversial rentals would have to have the approval of the Mayor and all the Borough Presidents, to say nothing of influential business, political and religious leaders. ('Religious leaders' in this context was a buzz phrase for the Catholic hierarchy, which was headed in New York City at the time by Francis Cardinal Spellman, a friend of Roy Cohn, the former assistant prosecutor at the Rosenberg-Sobell trial. The Protestant and rabbinical powers in the community would not be expected to oppose rental of the Stadium to the Committee, not because they all supported clemency but because they were not friends of Roy Cohn). The Mayor at that time was Vincent R. Impellitteri, a man with the traditional Tammany Hall credentials for his position; in November, he would be defeated for re-election by the then Borough President of Manhattan, Robert F. Wagner, Jr. Our fear was that neither candidate would dare make a decision, in April, that might cost him votes in November, and that this might foreclose the possibility of approval of our request for renting the Stadium.

Committee member Norma Aronson, who had successfully obtained a publisher for the trial record, had also seen to it that whatever mailings and press releases we issued were also sent to all major New York City officials and political and religious leaders, thus keeping them more informed about the case and the clemency campaign than they would have been from reading or listening to the media.

In the second week of April, the Committee was assured by an authority in whom we had confidence that the stadium was ours.

As it turned out, we had to face the hurdle of obtaining approval to have our meeting at the Stadium twice: the weather forecast on April 25, for April 26, was very heavy rains. We debated whether to go ahead with the meeting, even though the stadium was not enclosed. To ask for a new date would encourage the opposition — and our good authority assured us the opposition within the city administration and the religious community had not yet given up the goal of canceling our contract. But having come this far, we were willing to take the risk, and we asked for a new contract for the Stadium for May 3. In two days, we were notified the new date had been approved. Someone — or, more likely, more than a few someones in the city administration and the religious community — felt very strongly about free speech for everyone and, possibly, for clemency for the Rosenbergs.

New evidence emerges...

Before the Stadium meeting took place, two articles of new evidence came our way, one in document form, the other, the actual console table the Greenglasses had testified had been adapted for espionage. Both articles of evidence supported defense contentions that the Greenglasses had committed perjury.

In March 1953, a "To whom it may concern" manila envelope was left in the Committee's office, on a desk routinely used for sorting the daily mail. When the Committee secretary began clearing the desk she looked at the contents of the envelope, understood their importance and brought the envelope to Joseph Brainin, the only Committee member in the office at that time. He saw, instantly, the contents had come from the files of O. John Rogge, the attorney for the Greenglasses.

There were photostats of two documents in the envelope: one was a copy of a handwritten memorandum from David Greenglass to O. John Rogge, written shortly after Greenglass had made his first statements to the FBI, in which he wrote that he had agreed to attest to actions the FBI said he had participated in, but of which he had no personal knowledge.

The second photostat was a memorandum to Rogge, from an associate, in which he described an interview with Ruth Greenglass in June 1950, where she told him her husband lied easily, had a 'tendency to hysteria' and to delirium, and

> She had known him since she was ten years old. She said
> that he would say things were so even if they were not.
> He talked of suicide as if he were a character in the mov-
> ies, but she didn't think he would do it.[584]

That evening, Brainin disclosed the contents of the envelope to Emily and me and to Aaron Schneider. He pointed out the documents might be forgeries created to entrap the Committee and to undermine the clemency campaign. He suggested that for the immediate future, knowledge of the documents go no further than the four of us. If Justice officials intended to entrap Committee members in a criminal prosecution of some sort, we would want at least six or seven Committee members to be able to honestly say they had no knowledge of the documents.

We debated bringing the documents to Emanuel Bloch's attention, since he was an even more important target for Justice officials than were Committee members. We were aware that if the documents were authentic, their possession by anyone other than Greenglass' attorney could create serious legal problems that could be used to distract attention from what the documents revealed. On the other hand, if the documents were authentic, they would surely save the Rosenbergs' lives.

We decided to bring the documents to Bloch. On reading them, he became visibly upset, and told us if the documents had been stolen from Rogge's office, he could not use them without risking the probability their importance would be obscured in the court by a hue and cry by the prosecutors that the thieves must be found and prosecuted, and he would be among those suspected of theft, and would be investigated for both criminal and ethical misconduct, and possibly barred from continuing to represent the Rosenbergs. He also pointed out the members of the Committee, if they used the documents in any way, could be accused of using stolen documents, and might also be prosecuted for theft. The effect on the clemency campaign could be disastrous.

Bloch, exhausted, sleepless, still terribly understaffed, but doggedly researching and writing appeals for the Rosenbergs, told us bluntly, "The only protection my clients have in the courts is me, and I can't risk them losing me. There's nothing I'll stop at to continue giving them that protection. You people are wonderful, but I'll denounce you publicly, if you do anything that endangers my representation of Julie and Ethel."

Brainin argued we had shed sufficient light on the case to inhibit Justice officials from using our possession of the documents as a diversion to interfere with Bloch's right to go on with his appeals, although Justice officials might undoubtedly try to do so. "The world is watching, and this may protect us. But time's not on our side," Brainin said.

Time was definitely not on our side. Judge Kaufman had set a new date — June 15 — for the executions. We had little more than 60 days, to authenticate the documents and to persuade Bloch to use them. Under the federal court rules, Bloch had to first bring a motion to the District Court, that is to, Judge Kaufman; and to bring a motion to the Court of Appeals if Kaufman rejected it; if that court rejected it, he would have to appeal anew to the Supreme Court to review the case.

We decided to submit the handwritten memorandum from David Greenglass to Elizabeth McCarthy, an eminent handwriting analyst, who told us she would need samples of his handwriting and that her examination of the documents would take about a month. We scoured records of the business partnerships in which David Greenglass had been involved with Julius Rosenberg and others after the war, and family correspondence and brief notes, which we turned over to the handwriting expert.

Ms. McCarthy's estimate that it would take her a month or more, possibly as late as May, meant we had far fewer than 60 days to use the documents effectively.

We came to a decision: we had to make the documents public before their authentication. The risk to each of us personally was far less than the risk to the Rosenbergs, if we withheld evidence of David Greenglass' perjury. There was still the possibility that the documents were forgeries intended to reflect badly on the clemency movement. But two lives were at stake and, it seemed to us, the documents had the ring of truth. Making the handwritten documents public would, of course, force Bloch to commit himself to going into court with them if they were authenticated. If, as a result, the court would find a pretext to bar Bloch from continuing to represent the Rosenbergs, there was not an attorney in sight who could take his place. A court-appointed attorney was certainly unlikely to have the Rosenbergs' confidence or trust. But, as Brainin had said, the world was watching, which would help the Rosenbergs, and the clock was ticking.

It was now an undeniable fact the Rosenberg-Sobell case was no longer working itself out in deep shadow, as had been largely true until early 1953. Whatever Justice officials did now had to be done in some degree of daylight. Public reaction to penalizing Bloch and the Rosenbergs for bringing a perjury-revealing authenticated Greenglass document to court could aggravate the problems that already faced Justice officials in their pursuit of the Rosenbergs and Sobell's confessions. Or so we told ourselves and one another. We also agreed, for Bloch's protection, to refrain from any further discussion of the Greenglass memorandum with him, until we obtained authentication.

We had several sets of photostats made, one of which Joseph Brainin took to editors at the *New York Times*, the *New York Post*, and several other newspapers. Every editor declined to accept the photostats, although one suggested that if a legitimate European newspaper published the documents, he would then consider running them as a story. We felt we had no time to lose and, because Brainin had contacts with several French journalists, we urged him to go to France with the documents as quickly as possible, which he did.

The Greenglass' memorandum appeared on April 18, 1953, in *Le Combat*, a non-Communist French newspaper, and it was quickly taken up by other newspapers in France and other European countries.

The memo was not reported on immediately in the United States, except by the *National Guardian* and the small-circulation left-wing press.

State Department officials notified American diplomatic and consular officials at once that the documents cited by *Le Combat* were probably forgeries, and that a statement on the matter would shortly be made by Justice Department officials.

On May 1, Elizabeth McCarthy notified us that after comparing samples of Greenglass' handwriting with the handwriting of the author of the memorandum, "I can come to no other conclusion than that they were written by one and the same person."[585] We immediately made the authentication available to the media. Three days later, on May 4, the documents were also authenticated by David Greenglass' attorney, O.J. Rogge.[586]

On that same day, six weeks after Brainin had offered the *New York Times* the Greenglass memorandum story, the newspaper covered it in the context of reporting on the May 3 meeting at the Triboro Stadium in New York City, to which 10,000 persons had come, and at which Joseph Brainin described the David Greenglass memorandum and its significance. The *New York Times* reported Brainin's account, and added that the Greenglass memorandum had been authenticated by Greenglass' attorney. The *Times* wrote

> Mr. Rogge said the original memorandum appeared to
> have been 'filched' from his files, and had been missing
> when the F.B.I. first inquired about it last Wednesday —
> only to turn up in the files the next day.[587]

The *New York Post* also covered the Stadium meeting, but made no mention of the Greenglass memorandum. It devoted three paragraphs, instead, to objections by spectators to having their pictures taken by *Post* photographers.[588]

On the day on which the *New York Times* had made public the Greenglass memorandum, a meeting was held at Rogge's office, at which Bloch and Herbert J. Fabricant, a Rogge partner, were present.[589]

Rogge told Bloch and Fabricant that, on the previous Wednesday, his staff had discovered that the Greenglass memorandum was missing from the case file, but was found in the file the next morning, and he had then turned the memorandum over to the FBI.

Bloch said he had received a cable from France, some two weeks earlier, from a French attorney stating the memorandum had been published in a French newspaper and that he would request the newspaper to send Bloch "complete photostatic documents." Several days later, Bloch received the photostats from the lawyer, who wrote he was sending another set to the Committee.

On April 24, Bloch wrote to the French attorney, acknowledging he had received the photostats, writing that he could not "vouch for the authenticity of the documents which you sent me."

"My first reaction to these documents," Bloch told Rogge and Fabricant, "was that they were spurious."

> Then the Committee tried to buttonhole me. Unless these documents are absolutely genuine they are of absolutely no earthly use to me and if they are genuine, then it is for me as a lawyer to analyze and set [sic] whether they could aid at all legally to help my clients.[590]

Bloch turned to Rogge and asked him whether the documents were genuine or spurious.

Rogge avoided giving a direct response, saying he recalled

> seeing in the file on Thursday morning a memorandum of 3 pages (numbered in three pages) in David's writing which I have turned over to the FBI at their request to see if they could find out how this document appeared in the file on Thursday when it had been — when it had not been in the file in the preceding afternoon.
>
> ✳✳✳
>
> It seems to me that the FBI will be able to compare through a handwriting expert and if they say it is a replica then it would appear that it is genuine and if they say it is not his handwriting, then it would be a spurious document.[591]

Two days after this meeting, on May 6, Rogge wrote to Bloch, mistakenly saying that at the May 4 meeting he had advised Bloch the documents were authentic, and had been stolen from the files by persons unknown. He said Bloch was obligated to return whatever copies he had and "refrain from disclosing or using the contents thereof in any manner or fashion."[592] On the other hand, Rogge's letter went on, Bloch was free to use whatever legal processes were available to him to obtain permission to use the documents.

Rogge was being legally correct. The documents had become publicly known, having been read aloud at the Triboro Stadium and cited in Committee press releases, and had received a very modest amount of mainstream press coverage, but Rogge could not assent to their use by Bloch. Whether Bloch was free to make the documents the basis of a motion in court, however, was another matter. Bloch wrote to the Bar Ethics Committee for guidance,[593] and, after receiving its reply, proceeded to prepare a motion for a hearing on the Greenglass memorandum, the console table, and several other points.

The French press took the occasion to chide the American media for allowing *Le Combat* to scoop the American media on a uniquely American story relating to a sensational American trial, all because, the French said, our media was afraid of being denounced by government officials for printing a fact.

The prevailing assumption by many persons has been that the documents were stolen from Rogge's files. One writer has said that David Brown, an FBI-informant who had chaired the Los Angeles Clemency Committee, had told the FBI the Committee had paid a professional thief $25,000 to steal them.[594] Aside from the unreliability of FBI-informants, the tale does not explain how the Committee could have known what was in the files to be worth the risks involved, to say nothing of finding the funds to pay the thief.

Rogge's statement that the memorandum had been 'filched' from his files by an unauthorized person was not credible. If an unauthorized person had done so, why would he or she make copies and then run the risk of returning the originals to the files? Only a member of the Rogge firm would have dared put the memoranda back in the files after the FBI had been told that they had been stolen. And, we believe, only someone who had a deeply ingrained professional and proprietary sense of the importance of retaining originals of documents would have put them back where they belonged.

If someone in the Rogge firm had wanted the Committee — and Bloch — to know of the existence of the documents, it is likely that a person so motivated would have simply made copies and found a way to put them in the Committee's hands. This is what we believe happened. As for who that person was, our belief is that O. John Rogge himself arranged for us to have the documents. He was a good human being who had been ground down by Justice officials for whom he had once worked, and he had the decency to try, in his own way, to prevent the execution of the Rosenbergs. It is significant that, although he knew he would have had the full support of Justice officials if he attempted to prevent Bloch from going to court with the documents, he chose not to impede Bloch's wish to do so.

New evidence: the console table is found...

The Greenglasses had testified at the trial they had seen a console table in the Rosenbergs' apartment that had been hollowed out and adapted for microphotography for espionage purposes. David Greenglass had testified that Julius Rosenberg had told him that the console table had been a gift from the Russians.

Julius Rosenberg had testified on direct that the table had not been adapted in any way for microfilming, and that he had purchased the table for approximately $21.00 at R.H. Macy's in New York City, in 1944 or 1945.[595]

The console table had not been brought into court as an exhibit by the prosecutors; instead, they had brought photographs of what they said were "similar" tables. At no time had the prosecutors indicated they had been unable to locate the table itself.

We earlier recounted the discovery of the console table and the Macy's Department store affidavit of its authenticity.

The new evidence was believed by Bloch and other attorneys to be such stark proof of perjury and prosecutorial misconduct at the trial that the U.S. Court of Appeals would have no choice but to grant a hearing at which the defense would have an opportunity to bring tangible evidence — the console table and the Greenglass memorandum — before the judges.

A German Turnabout guest debates clemency...

Brainin had been right. Enough light now shone on the case to inhibit attempts by Justice officials to prevent Bloch and the Committee from using the new evidence in the courts of law and public opinion.

The new evidence increased public receptivity to the Committee's materials and arguments. In some parts of the country the response by lawyers and judges was particularly encouraging and, in the case of a judge in Michigan, was surprising because of his boldness. Committee member Aaron Schneider described to us an organizing trip he had taken, during which he stopped in Lansing, Michigan, where he met the judge.

> Aside from some sonofabitch who tried to get me to meet some people in the Lansing woods, I was doing fine. At one point I go to see one of the local ACLU lawyers. This guy tells me with a straight face that he's hardly ever heard of the case...Anyway, this ACLU choir boy

suggests I see a local judge to see whether the judge will sign a petition.

Off I go to see the judge. I go to his court and ask the security officer to mention to the judge that I'm a stranger in town and I'd like to see him for a couple of minutes. I must have made it seem pretty urgent because in a couple of minutes the judge was out in the corridor, asking me what I wanted. I started telling him about the Rosenbergs, and after about a minute he interrupted me and said, "I was in the middle of a case when I came out to see you. Let me go back and finish it. Then I want you to come into the courtroom and address me on the case for ten minutes. I'll see to it that there are some reporters on hand. When you finish, I'll give you a kind of verdict, for whatever it's worth."

I went into the courtroom when his case was finished, and I talked about the case, and handed him a copy of the court transcript. When I was done, the judge said, "I still don't know the facts, but in this country we don't execute people if there's the slightest doubt of their guilt. I'm going to write to the President and ask for clemency, and I urge everyone in this courtroom to do likewise."

That local judge in Lansing put his career on the line for the Rosenbergs. To me he exemplified a part of America I hadn't seen before.[596]

Two important debates on clemency took place in April. The first was sponsored by an uncommitted liberal group, and was to have been between a pro-clemency attorney and Paul Windels, a prominent New York attorney. The pro-clemency attorney fell ill on the day before the debate, no other attorney could be found to replace him, and Mr. Windels graciously agreed to accept me, a non-attorney, as his opponent.

What was most significant about that debate was Windels, who was familiar with the trial record, and who said he was troubled by many aspects of the trial, acknowledged that his belief in the guilt of the defendants and the justness of their sentences, was based, not on the record, but on the fact the verdicts and sentences had withstood all defense appeals. He said the refusal of the Supreme Court to review the case was itself an argument for the guilt of the defendants. He said it was inconceivable to him that the judicial process could result in so egregious a miscarriage of justice as critics claimed had occurred.[597]

Consequently, the audience's questions after the debate were centered on factual aspects of the trial and testimony, and Windels and I were not very far apart in the answers we gave.

A far stranger debate occurred later that month, when I debated the Rosenbergs' death sentences with a *Reader's Digest* associate, a German national who had entered the United States through one of the Turnabout programs that welcomed loosely-defined non-Nazi German experts on Communism. The debate was held before a largely Jewish middle-class audience, members of a major Jewish organization whose leaders had somewhat softened their original hostility to debates on the issue of clemency.

I spoke first and received, when I was done, a smattering of polite applause. Then the non-Nazi German spoke, and from that moment on fear and dismay began to shade every face in the audience. His prelude to discussing the Rosenbergs' death sentences was an impassioned speech on the dangers of the lure of Communism to people who believed that they were in some way victimized by history. He seemed utterly unaware that when he demanded the execution of the Rosenbergs, his audience would hear him demanding the blood of two more Jews. His condemnations evoked tortuous memories, grief, and anger. When he fervently exhorted his listeners — who had lost entire generations of families to the gas chambers of the Master Race — to extirpate from their midst all Jews who had succumbed to the temptations and taints of Communism, there was utter silence in the hall.

The pro-execution debater let something loose in that hall that emptied it of any curiosity or emotion except, perhaps, despair.

When he was done, there were a few faint sobs and mutterings. The scheduled Question-and-Answer period was not mentioned, because the members of the audience were elsewhere, in a dark place we reserve for experiencing what we can neither express nor forget. The subject was no longer the imminent executions of the Rosenbergs, but the execution of six million and two Jews. No one's voice broke the silence. The only sounds were those the audience made as it shuffled up the aisles and through the doors.

The media forgets whose flag flies overhead...

With the discovery of the Greenglass memorandum and the console table, we had hoped the media would, as it almost always did when prosecutorial misconduct in high profile cases becomes evident, begin to explore the new evidence, if not the conduct of the trial itself. Ordinarily, the mainstream media, having gotten the scent of misdeeds by important officials, would have begun a dedicated search for the truth, and a Pulitzer journalism prize for public service. The Rosenberg-Sobell case, as J. Edgar Hoover had written, was "The Crime of the Century," and the executions were scheduled to take place in a very short time.

But a media search for facts was not to be. Other than the *New York Times,* none of the mainstream newspapers gave more than a superficial prosecution-press release account of the new evidence.[598] This was one of the occasions that caused great puzzlement to the media abroad. The submissive deference of our media — the traditional *feisty* American media — to the press handouts of Justice officials was inexplicable to the journalists of the democracies that had found a thousand ways to resist their German iron-fisted occupiers and executioners. To the media abroad, the unquestioning acceptance of government press-releases as gospel truth was inconsistent with democracy and, in particular, with an American democracy that prided itself on having an aggressive truth-seeking press.

Even after the Greenglass memorandum had been authenticated, and photographs of the console table (top, bottom, sides and undersides) accompanied by the Macy's affidavit, had been brought to the media, silence followed, except when the media ran Justice Department press releases with tales about the "suspicious origins" of the new evidence and condemnation of its use as "propaganda."

The prosecution-friendly news stories on the Rosenberg-Sobell case in the mainstream media were never accompanied by so much as a stray question mark. It was not that freedom of the press had been taken away; it had been given away.

Ethnic and civil rights memberships vote with their feet...

In the weeks immediately following the Vigil, we had urged clemency supporters to augment the Committee's informational materials, by raising issues that were in one way or another relevant to the case: in particular the politicization of review procedures by government officials, which allowed them to expedite reversals of death sentences for scores of convicted Nazi murderers of American prisoners of war while, at the same time, rigidly denouncing the clemency campaign for the Rosenbergs. The results, in which the discovery of new evidence also played a role, were quickly evident.

Many people who had acknowledged in the past that the Rosenbergs and Sobell had not had a fair and impartial trial, had nevertheless declined to put their names to clemency petitions. As they sometimes put it, "By doing something you feel is right for some people, you could also be doing something wrong for the country." Many were now persuaded otherwise. Greater numbers of the Protestant and Jewish clergy were putting their names to petitions, and greater numbers of their congregations were doing so. We also now had the support of Dorothy Day, the leader of the Catholic Workers movement, as well as support from other members of the Catholic laity. The memberships of the major Jewish organization, some sections of which had been favorable to clemency in the past, were joined by many more.

Our personal contacts among the second tier leaders of Jewish organizations told us some of the top leaders were shifting away from their previous rigid opposition to the new trial/clemency movement.

Years later, we found documentary proof this was so. In a "Confidential Memorandum" on March 30, 1953, an American Jewish Committee (AJC) official in Florida was told that although "most of the organized committees for clemency for the Rosenbergs are activated and led by Communists," the AJC does not oppose clemency *per se*, but opposes only clemency appeals put forward "on the grounds that the Rosenbergs were denied fair judicial process because they were Jews." The memorandum went on

> We would therefore urge persons who are impelled by conscience to object on humanitarian grounds to the rigor of the sentence to make certain that their impulses are not exploited for these subversive purposes. We would never urge a person who feels the sentence is unjust not to express himself to the President in an upright and straightforward manner.[599]

The qualified acceptance of clemency support by major Jewish organizations had been an inevitable development. Jewish organization leaders could not continue to parrot the invective of FBI and Justice officials, who were known to practice anti-Semitism in their agencies, and who were implementing the "repugnant philosophy" by forgiving the Nazi participants in the Holocaust and in the Malmedy massacres of American prisoners of war. It is likely that at least some of these leaders were relieved to have found a supportive approach to clemency, not because they were compelled to find one, but because they wished to find one.

Likewise, the memberships of many ACLU chapters, although their national leaders remained rigid in support of the verdicts and sentences. Committees across the country were reporting the appearance of known ACLU members at public meetings and signing clemency petitions. One committee chairman, who was close to a number of ACLU activists in his city, told me, "The ACLU leadership up in New York know that a lot of people are involved who don't ordinarily support any kinds of causes, and they're sticking their necks out signing petitions or sending letters. Leadership knows if a vote was taken on clemency in the ACLU, a majority would support it. There's not going to be a vote, but the leaders can't sit back and do nothing while their members are out there signing petitions. They tell me maybe their national officers know something they don't know, but they read our stuff and sign petitions and kick in with a couple of bucks anyway. For a lot of them, to see the ACLU trailing the Pope, really hurts."

At a Committee meeting in late April 1953, based on reports from approximately forty committees in as many cities and towns, and in discussions with our advisors, we estimated that at least two million clemency communications, by way of multi-signature petitions and personal letters, had been sent to the White House.

A rally in Paris, June 1953, in support of clemency for the Rosenbergs

Chapter 9 | The clemency movement abroad (See Appendix)

For clemency: The Pope, heads of State, royalty, rightists, leftists, millions...

The Trial Record contributed greatly to the understanding of the case abroad. Even the very incomplete and biased reports from our media, which were widely read in Europe and elsewhere, played an unanticipated role in the emergence of foreign clemency movements. Events reported in the American media, like denials of the Pope's intervention, were astonishing to many abroad, causing resentment and support for a new trial or clemency.

Acknowledgment that a worldwide clemency movement was underway came in a December 20, 1952 Paris-to-State Department Information Bulletin that went to our missions in Germany, Italy, Spain, Portugal, Morocco, Tunisia, Sweden, Yugoslavia, the Netherlands, Belgium, South Vietnam, and Algiers. In most of these countries, "committees for clemency" had been formed by self-appointed non-Communist persons and groups, in the fall of 1951, in the same way that our Committee had begun.

At this point in the book, however, rather than interrupt our account of the post-sentencing developments and the emergence of the clemency movement in the United States, we refer the reader to the Appendix for a comprehensive account of the clemency movements in Europe, Canada, South America, and elsewhere in the world.

Rally for clemency, late spring 1953, Washington, D.C.

Chapter 10 | The legal appeals/The silence of the robed

Expectations...

The attorneys for the Rosenbergs and Sobell were joined in their appeals by John F. Finerty, a veteran attorney in capital cases, several of which had attracted worldwide interest: the case of Nicola Sacco and Bartolomeo Vanzetti, two Massachusetts unionists convicted for murder and executed in 1927, and exonerated fifty years later by order of the Governor of Massachusetts; another was Tom Mooney, a California unionist, and his wife Rena, who were tried, along with Warren K. Billings, another unionist, on a charge of bombing a California Preparedness Day Parade in 1916. Mooney and Billings were found guilty and sentenced to death, but their sentences were subsequently commuted to life imprisonment. Mooney was eventually pardoned by a California governor on the grounds that "Thomas J. Mooney is wholly innocent...his conviction was based wholly on perjured testimony presented by representatives of the State of California."[600]

Appeals in federal cases, and in most state cases as well, are two step procedures, the first of which is a petition to the appropriate court, to be granted a hearing at which an appeal may be supported by subpoenaed witnesses and documents. In this first step, appellants must prove to the court, by argument, that if they are granted a hearing, there is a reasonable chance that they may prevail. In the absence of a hearing, they do not have the right to subpoena witnesses and documents. If a hearing is denied, the appellant may appeal the denial all the way up to the Supreme Court, if that court decides to consider it. If the Supreme Court declines to review the lower court's denial of a hearing, that ends the matter. If the right to a hearing is granted, but fails to convince the appellate court of its merit, the court's decision may be appealed to the Supreme Court, which may or may not agree to consider the appeal.

The expectations of the Rosenbergs' and Sobell's attorneys in respect to the fate of their appeals were initially optimistic. A few years earlier, hearings had been granted to defendants convicted of espionage and treason on behalf of Nazi Germany, and in several instances the verdicts were set aside. The legal points on which the reversals had been made were in some of these cases very similar to those being made on behalf of the Rosenbergs and Sobell.

Attorneys not involved in the case told the Committee to keep its expectations low. For one thing, they said, the appellate system had Closure as its chief goal. Justice, they told us, ran a poor second. Closure as an appellate goal was inherited from the days when colonial courts were expected to expedite, not delay, execution of the king's purpose, whether it be the levying of a tax, a fine or a hanging. We were also told that judges, like everyone else in government at that time, must be expected to take great care not to become targets of denunciations from Congressional inquisitors.

The chief obstacle Bloch faced, the lawyers said, was that if so much as a single hearing on any point of appeal was granted, it might lead to an order for a new trial. A retrial would inevitably be conducted under heightened scrutiny by the media and the public, which would discourage the reappearance of previous prosecutorial misconduct; it was even probable that another judge would preside. A prosecutorial transposition of the time of the crime would be made more difficult, and the oral treason charge could not be repeated. For that reason, appeals for hearings would be resisted with all the power at the disposal of the Department of Justice.

There did come a moment in June, when it appeared that a hearing on a point on appeal might be granted. Justice officials declared such a hearing might be calamitous. The *New York Times* headlined the Justice officials' response on page Page 1, "CASE SEEN IN PERIL," and quoted Supreme Court Justice Robert Jackson as saying

> The probabilities are that if the Atomic Energy Act covers the case [as opposed to the 1917 Espionage Act], the whole case is out.[601]

The *Times* paraphrased Robert L. Stern, the Acting Solicitor General as saying that

> The Government did not think it could win a case on an indictment brought under the Atomic Energy Act.[602]

Nothing was more risky, the lawyers went on to say, than predicting the outcomes of petitions for hearings in a country in which "loose cannon" judges, stubbornly quoting the Constitution to the consternation of Congress and the Executive, appeared with surprising frequency.

We asked whether the attorneys believed that Bloch shared their outlook. "Every bit of it," we were assured, "and especially the 'loose cannon' part. Otherwise, he couldn't go on."

A missing element in the appeals...

As we have seen, the defendants were not tried for the actual crime, which was passing (or conspiring to pass) classified information to an allied nation in time of war. They were tried for a crime, invented by the prosecution with the cooperation of the judge, in which the defendants were orally charged throughout the trial with having passed atomic information to an enemy in time of war.

In retrospect, the defense attorneys did not display a persistent awareness that it was the oral indictment and its time transposition that were constantly placed before the jurors, while the formal indictment was read to the jurors at the start of the trial and rarely referred to after that. The appeals properly related to the formal indictment but mistakenly ignored the impact on the jurors of the reiterations by the prosecution and the judge that they were confronted with a Cold War crime. It was what the jurors heard from the representatives of the government, not the words of the formal indictment, that became embedded in the jurors' memories, as their later interviews revealed.

The "public climate" appeal...

The Rosenberg-Sobell attorneys undertook a review of public opinion polls that had been taken during and after World War II by professional polling organizations, to show that the prosecution had deliberately sought to create and exploit fears by the jurors of a Soviet atom bomb attack on their city. The defense demonstrated that, by the time of Winston Churchill's famous "Iron Curtain" speech on March 6, 1946 at Fulton, Missouri, a speech that was widely interpreted as a call for war against the Soviet Union,[603] the public had already begun to be persuaded that an armed attack on the United States by the Soviet Union was virtually certain.

In a public opinion poll taken in January 1950, six months before David Greenglass' arrest, this opinion was expressed by 70% of the respondents.[604]

A poll taken in October 1949, after the public learned that the Soviet Union had tested an atom bomb, revealed that 77% of the population believed that in the event of war, the United States would be atom-bombed.[605] In December 1950, three months before the start of the trial, a national cross-section of the public was asked whether they feared that their own communities might be atom-bombed: 16% of residents of small towns replied in the affirmative; for small cities the affirmatives were 25%; in cities with over 100,000 population, the affirmatives were 41%. In coastal areas, including New York City, 63 percent of those polled said they "had thought about this."[606]

In their appeal for a hearing, the defense attorneys also cited the pretrial headlines predicting casualties of a Soviet atom bomb attack on New York City that we cited in Chapter 1, and cited a favorable ruling by the U.S. Court of Appeals, in a case similar to the Rosenberg-Sobell case, in respect to pretrial publicity (*Delaney v. United States*).[607] The Appeals Court warned

> One cannot assume that the average juror is so endowed with a sense of detachment, so clear in his introspective perception of his own mental processes, that he may confidently exclude even the unconscious influence of

his preconceptions as to probable guilt, engendered by a pervasive pretrial publicity.[608]

The Appeals Court had also rejected the notion that defense attorneys, on *voir dire*, can always pinpoint and exclude jurors who have been influenced by pretrial publicity.

> Since he [Delaney] was obliged to stand trial in the hostile atmosphere engendered by the extra-courtroom publicity, he had little or no reason for assuming that one juror rather than another would be more likely to be influenced, consciously or unconsciously, by his preconceptions — all of them having affirmed, in answer to inquiry by the trial judge, that they were prepared to determine Delaney's guilt or innocence solely on the basis of evidence produced at the trial.[609]

In their response, Justice attorneys denied the indoctrination of fear had ever existed, there was no proof that any juror's objectivity had been affected by the news stories, the jurors had been warned by Judge Kaufman against being influenced by what they had read in the media, and argued that no hearing on the issue was required.[610]

The appellants also argued that Justice officials and the prosecution had fed false and inflammatory stories to the media, to which Justice attorneys replied that such statements had not been inflammatory, had been "few in number and, moreover, were simply a method of answering the legitimate questions of the press," and had had no "impact on petitioners' trial."[611] The appeal, according to Justice attorneys, was an attack on

> the freedom of the press in reporting the public details of the prosecution of war-time spies.[612]

In their ruling, the appellate judges wrote that if a defendant "believes that pretrial publicity has been such as to render impossible the selection of an impartial jury," he

> may move for a change of venue or for a continuance until the public clamor shall have subsided. The petitioners took neither of these courses.[613]

As for jurors being influenced by the media, the appellate judges said

> On the *voir dire* the prospective jurors were carefully questioned as to whether they had read or heard about the case and a jury was selected satisfactory to the defendants, who did not even use all the peremptory

> challenges permitted them. Nor do they allege that any
> trial juror was in fact prejudiced by the publicity now
> asserted to have made a fair trial impossible.[614]

The judges were technically correct that the defense attorneys could have moved for a change of venue or of a continuance, but drew the incorrect conclusion that defendants sentenced to death must pay the penalty for the failure of an attorney to make a timely motion. A very significant number of verdicts and sentences in capital cases have been reversed because defense attorneys, by oversight or bad judgment, failed to move to properly protect the rights of defendants to fair trials.

It may be that the defense attorneys had wrongly resigned themselves to an inescapable reality: there was no credible possibility that the "public clamor" could be avoided by moving the trial elsewhere in the United States, or by asking for a reasonable lapse of time to allow the clamor to subside. The "clamor" was part of the nation's daily fare for the next thirty-plus years, with President Ronald Reagan, in 1989, still invoking the specter of an atomic Armageddon.

The appellate judges chose not to confront this reality or to acknowledge that there was an actual solution to the problem: to hold a hearing and take the testimony of expert witnesses. If, as a result, the verdicts and sentences were set aside, a new trial could be held, beginning with a more thorough and objective examination of prospective jurors. This solution undoubtedly occurred to the appellate judges, but it entailed the certain risk of a Congressional and media assault on their reputations and careers, and on the judiciary as a whole.

Nor could, as occasionally happens, information on jurors' prejudices become known shortly after the verdicts. The jurors had been instructed by Judge Kaufman not to discuss their verdicts with the media or anyone else, an instruction with no basis in law that was adhered to by the jurors for 20 years. When the jurors began to speak out, the reasons they gave for voting Guilty were overladen with fear for the lives of their families, confirming the impact of the perceived imminence of New York City being atom bombed by the Soviet Union.

As we pointed out earlier, in 1973, jury foreman Vincent Lebonitte described how he had persuaded a holdout juror to change his vote, not on the basis of the evidence, but on a hypothetical scenario drawn from newspaper headlines and prosecutorial charges of treason, involving an atom bomb attack by the Soviet Union, on New York City and on other cities in the United States.[615] Another juror, Charles W. Christie, an auditor for an oil company, told his interviewer

> [I] was thinking of the fact that I had a family; I had two
> girls, and how they [the defendants] could expose their
> two children to such a fate.[616]

The appellate judges rejected the defendants' petition to hold a hearing on the issue of a prejudicial atmosphere.

The "console table" appeal...

On June 8, 1953, Emanuel Bloch and Malcolm Sharp, a professor of law at Chicago University, spoke for two hours in Judge Kaufman's court, arguing on a motion for a hearing on the console table and on several other issues, as well.

Bloch and Sharp presented to the court, along with the newly found table, a Macy's official's affidavit, stating that its model number identified it as one of a number of tables sold by the store in 1944-1945, for approximately $19.00 plus sales tax.[617]

The lawyers argued that Greenglass' credibility, in respect to the use of the table for spy purposes, was belied by the absence of any alterations to the table that would have adapted it for microfilming or other espionage purposes, and because Julius Rosenberg's testimony about its place of purchase and price was supported by the Macy's affidavit. A hearing was necessary, they argued, to bring the table to court as tangible evidence that it had never been altered for any purpose, and to determine the role of the prosecutors in obtaining testimony that transformed an ordinary console table into an "espionage-adapted" table that didn't exist. They offered to permit Judge Kaufman to inspect the table before he came to a decision on their petition; he declined to look at it.

Judge Kaufman ruled the motion for a hearing required the Rosenbergs first prove that the newly found console table was the one that had been in their apartment, proof of which they could not produce, Judge Kaufman said, because "one such table must look very much like another."[618] On the other hand, he said, the prosecutors were not required to prove the table described by Greenglass ever existed because the prosecutors never had it in their possession and had relied solely on the Greenglasses' testimony that there had been such a table.[619] Also, if Greenglass perjured himself in his testimony about the table, there was no proof that the prosecutors were aware of any perjury.[620] Further, Judge Kaufman said, the table had been discovered too late to be used in an appeal. Finally, the whole matter of the console table was being exaggerated, the judge said, because the console table testimony took up only an "infinitesimal amount of time at the trial."[621] The petition for a hearing on the console table was denied.

The passport photographer's perjury appeal...

The defense appeals argued that Ben Schneider, the "surprise witness" photographer who had testified to having made passport photos for the Rosenbergs, although he had not been able to produce either negatives or sales transaction records to substantiate his claims, had committed perjury, with the knowledge of the prosecutors. The photographer witness had testified he had not seen the

Rosenbergs between the time he had allegedly taken their photographs in the spring of 1950, and the day he testified in court in March 1951. The defense learned after the trial had ended that on Saypol's instructions Schneider had been brought into court by the FBI on the day before he testified, at a time when Julius Rosenberg was on the stand and had been easily identifiable because he was referred to by name when being questioned. Justice officials were compelled to admit that this was so, since reporters had witnessed the photographer's presence in the courtroom. An FBI agent's affidavit admitted that Schneider had been brought into the courtroom at Saypol's request, but denied that anyone had identified Rosenberg to Schneider.[622]

On appeal the judges upheld Judge Kaufman's ruling that Schneider's testimony, that he had not seen the Rosenbergs between spring of 1950 and the day he testified, had not been perjurious because when he was asked whether he had seen the Rosenbergs "before today," that is, the day he testified, he was "really" being asked "before the trial" (the verbatim trial record notwithstanding), making his answer honest because it was not "intentionally false."[623] The petition for a hearing on the photographer's perjury was denied.

The FBI-directed Greenglass perjury appeal...

The appellants' appeals argued the prosecution had knowingly used perjured testimony when David Greenglass stated on cross-examination that when he was arrested, he disclosed all the major incidents involving the Rosenbergs to which he subsequently testified in court.[624] The point of the appeal was that the Greenglasses' testimony was not based on events that actually occurred, but were inventions created during a protracted period of negotiations with Saypol. The appellants cited Saypol's serial indictments, the June 1950 handwritten David Greenglass memorandum to his attorney, in which he acknowledged permitting the FBI to insert incidents into his statements that were unknown to him,[625] and a statement by Saypol conceding Greenglass had denied his guilt for a period of time after his arrest.

In Saypol's statement at Greenglass' sentencing on April 6, 1951, Saypol admitted Greenglass had not "told all" when he was arrested, but had, instead, vehemently denied his guilt. Saypol told the court that it was only

> through Ruth Greenglass, his wife, came the subsequent recantation of those protestations, their repudiation and the disclosure of the facts by both of them.[626]

After a Justice Department attorney replied to the appellants' appeal, Judge Kaufman retired for fifteen minutes and returned with a written opinion which took thirty-two minutes to read.[627] He denied the motion in its entirety. It was obvious, from a logistical view, that the judge's decision had been written before arguments on the motion had been heard.

In respect to Greenglass' admission in his June 1950, memorandum to O. John Rogge, that he permitted the FBI to "remember" for him events he did not recall, Judge Kaufman found this too "feeble" to warrant action by the court, but even if this was proof of perjury, he wrote, it did not prove that the prosecution knew that Greenglass had given perjured testimony.

Judge Kaufman found there were insufficient grounds to warrant a hearing on Greenglass' admission of perjury, and added

> It is worthy of re-emphasis that no one Government witness has recanted after all these years...[628]

His phrase "all these years" referred to the 25 months which had passed since he had sentenced the Rosenbergs to death.

In the past, appeals in many capital cases had gone on for many years. For example, appeals by Nicola Sacco and Bartolomeo Vanzetti ran for six years before the appellants were executed, in 1927. Caryl Chessman, known as the "Red Light Bandit," was sentenced to death in 1948, but as of 1953, the execution was yet to be carried out. (Chessman was executed in 1960.)

The recantation Judge Kaufman had alluded to came forty-eight years later, from the chief witness, David Greenglass, too late for the Rosenbergs or Kaufman, but not too late for history.

The appellate judges upheld Judge Kaufman's denials of hearings on any issue brought before him.

The Greenglass "atom bomb perjury" appeal...

Greenglass' capacity to sketch and describe the atom bomb from overheard conversations in 1944-45, and to repeat the feat again, from memory in 1951, was challenged in a petition for a hearing supported by affidavits from four prominent scientists who had been involved in the development of the atom bomb at Los Alamos. In his testimony, Greenglass had denied he had received assistance from any source in creating the sketches and the description at the time of the trial.

Greenglass had been specifically asked, at the trial, whether he had relied solely on his memory when he had drawn the sketches in 1951, for the trial. "I did," Greenglass replied.[629]

> Mr. E.A. Bloch: Now, were you given any reference books or text books while you were in jail since your arrest, relating to any scientific matter?
>
> A. No. I didn't — nobody gave me any.

> Q. Did you read any scientific books while you have
> been in jail?
>
> A. Just science-fiction.[630]

Judge Kaufman joined the inquiry.

> The Court: ...let me ask you. These sketches that are in
> evidence, are they the products of your own mind? By
> that I mean, were you helped by anybody outside in
> drawing these sketches?
>
> A. Nobody else, just myself.
>
> The Court: Did anybody tell you to change any line here
> or change any line there?
>
> A. Nobody told me anything like that.[631]

Bloch did not know, of course, that on February 2, 1951, Justice officials had arranged for Greenglass to meet for six hours with a group of AEC scientists who would evaluate the claims Greenglass intended to make in his testimony.[632] They concluded that Greenglass was not competent "beyond his abilities as a machine shop man," that he could be "confused by competent technical cross examination," and lacked knowledge of many of the components of the atom bomb.

Bloch was also unaware that, six days after the AEC interviews, on February 8, 1951, AEC officials were pressured by Congressional leaders to permit AEC experts to coach Greenglass for his trial testimony.

Emanuel Bloch had obtained information that pointed very clearly to consultation and reading matter on the atom bomb being made available to Greenglass during his pre-trial incarceration, enabling him to prepare the atom bomb sketches and the explanatory material. The appellants' petition pointed out

> The suppression concerning the truth, that a hearing
> on this petition will more fully reveal, that these exhib-
> its were literally "manufactured" for trial, is a most
> profound imposition upon the court and a measure of
> the magnitude of the extent to which the evidence on
> which the petitioners were convicted was a result of
> fabrication.[633]

Justice attorneys, arguing against a hearing on this point, contended that Bloch had, on cross-examination, put Greenglass' lack of a scientific education before the jurors, and the jurors had found Greenglass' testimony credible, which should bring closure to the question of Greenglass' credibility.[634]

The affidavits of the four atomic scientists, who had been involved in the research and development of the atom bomb, stated they did not believe that Greenglass could have prepared the sketches and the written material unaided. Justice attorneys argued that none of these scientists

> was in a position to give an opinion about the quality of his abilities which, no matter what his education, may have been adequate for this purpose.[635]

The appellate judges dismissed the affidavits of the four scientists

> who express the opinion that Greenglass, with his limited education as shown at the trial, could not have made the sketches from memory. Since none of them knew Greenglass, none was in a position to give an opinion about the quality of his memory which, no matter what his education, may have been amply sufficient for this purpose.[636]

What the appellate judges wrote about the inability of the four scientists to have an "opinion about the quality of his [Greenglass'] memory" was, of course, equally true of the jurors, since the jurors did not know Greenglass, and were being asked to evaluate an exceptional, not an ordinary, event within their experience: the ability of an untrained person to render the complex graphics and documentation of what had taken massive numbers of scientists and engineers to devise over a four year period of intense research and development.

In any case, the appellate judges declared, the jurors found Greenglass' testimony credible, and therefore upheld the lower court's denial of a hearing. In making this decision, the appellate judges chose to ignore the essential point made in the petition: that if Greenglass appeared to be credible to the jurors, it was because he had been coached by being supplied with printed matter relevant to the testimony he would give involving Exhibit 8 and several similar exhibits. The petition for a hearing on the coaching of Greenglass was denied.

The prosecutions' false promise of "corroboration" appeal...

The appellants argued Saypol had misled the court and the jurors by his spurious announcement that William Perl would be called to corroborate portions of the Greenglasses' testimony against the Rosenbergs. Justice attorneys replied the defense attorneys had not asked for a mistrial when the media "carried a statement ascribed to the then United States Attorney," and it was too late to do so after the trial.[637]

The appellate judges noted that, in Saypol's statement to the media,

> Mr. Saypol said also that Perl had been listed as a witness in the current espionage trial. His special role on the stand, Mr. Saypol added, was to corroborate certain statements made by David Greenglass and the latter's wife, who are key Government witnesses at the trial.[638]

The judges examined the statement, and the fact that Saypol never did call Perl to the stand at the Rosenberg-Sobell trial, and added

> Such a statement to the press in the course of a trial we regard as wholly reprehensible.

The judges found, however, that the defendants — or their lawyers — were to blame in the situation.

> Nevertheless we are not prepared to hold that it vitiates the jury's verdict when there is no allegation or evidence that any juror read the newspaper story and the defendants deliberately elected not to ask for a mistrial.[639]

But the judges were not being asked to vitiate the verdict. They were being asked to hold a hearing at which witnesses could be called (including Saypol and jurors), and documents subpoenaed, to support the appellants' contentions that the prosecution's misconduct was deliberately contrived to mislead the jury. The appellate judges denied the hearing, apparently satisfying themselves they had equally admonished the prosecutor for misconduct and the defense attorneys for failing to make a motion, though sparing the judge any criticism for failing to poll the jurors on whether they had read the Perl headlines, or for his *ex parte* hearings on unsealing the Perl indictment, described earlier.

The false charge of "treason" appeal...

The appellants appealed against the prosecution's oral charge in the courtroom that the defendants conspired to commit treason on behalf of an enemy. The Constitution does not permit prosecution for treason except for *acts* of treason. An act of treason can only be committed on behalf of an enemy nation with which the United States is at war, or by an act of war against the United States. In *Cramer v. United States*, a treason case concerning an American citizen accused of sheltering a German saboteur during World War II, the Supreme Court set aside a guilty verdict on this point, finding that the framers of the Constitution

> wrote into the organic act of the new government a prohibition of legislative or judicial creation of new treasons.[640]

None of the acts described by the Greenglasses or Max Elitcher or Harry Gold were said by them to have occurred at a time when the Soviet Union was considered an enemy nation or, to put it more positively, all the acts were committed when the Soviet Union was our active ally.

The jurors, as their interviews show, accepted treason as the crime on which they deliberated.

A quarter of a century after the trial, we learned that the appellants' appeal on the treason issue had led to disagreement among Justice officials on how it should be answered. In a November 5, 1952, memorandum by Robert L. Stern, the Acting Solicitor General, Stern noted that the appellants had argued "that their convictions were unlawful because not in conformity with the treason clause in the Constitution."[641] There was strong opinion in the Department that no reply should be made at all on the treason point, according to the memorandum, because

> Although our arguments seem plausible on their face, deeper analysis of the problem raises difficulties. Our own internal discussions have indicated considerable disagreement. Conceivably the memorandum might provoke the [Supreme]Court into a more profound inquiry into the question.

In the end, Justice attorneys decided to respond with virtual silence to the appellant's complaint that the trial had been illegally conducted for the crime of treason, arguing that the prosecution had alluded to the defendants as traitors only 18 times.

The appellate judges, like the troubled Justice officials who decided that the less said the better in respect to the treason appeal, denied the appeal for a hearing on the treason point with seven words: "[W]e hold that it is without merit."[642]

Reduction of sentences appeal...

While at least one of the U.S. Appellate Court judges appeared sympathetic to an appeal for a hearing for a reduction of the death sentences and Sobell's 30 year prison sentence, he held that the Appellate and Supreme Court had "no power to modify sentences," and that such power lay exclusively with the sentencing judge.[643] While the appeal attacked the sentences for their harshness, it also argued that the sentences were outside the law, a point the Appellate Court chose to ignore. Later, when another appeal was pressed, this time arguing that defendants had been tried under the wrong law, and that the correct law prohibited death sentences unless recommended by the trial jury, it was met with silence by both the Appellate and the Supreme Court.

The Sobell kidnapping appeal...

Two aspects of Sobell's appeals were unique to him: first, since he had not been charged with conspiring to commit espionage relating to the atom bomb, his lawyer argued he should have been tried separately from the Rosenbergs, so whatever the jurors perceived to be the weight of evidence against the Rosenbergs should not have also weighed against Sobell.[644]

Justice attorneys responded that the indictment had covered "general" espionage, making the conspiracy a single one, and that it was therefore proper for Sobell to be held liable for the acts of the Rosenbergs.[645] They did not, however, identify specifically what Sobell conspired to steal that justified his inclusion in the "general" conspiracy. On the other hand, Justice attorneys argued, it would not be proper for Sobell to benefit from doubts cast on the credibility of the testimony of the Greenglasses and other witnesses against the Rosenbergs because, "The case against petitioner depended only slightly on the testimony of the Greenglasses."[646]

On February 25, 1952, by a vote of 2 to 1, the appellate judges upheld the Justice attorneys' position. The dissenter was Judge Jerome Frank, who held Sobell should have been tried separately.

In another petition, Sobell argued he and his family had been kidnapped in Mexico by Mexican police on behalf of the FBI *after* the FBI learned that he and his family had taken the requisite vaccinations for return to the United States.[647] Justice attorneys were unable to show, in their arguments opposing Sobell's appeal, that any country other than the United States required a vaccination certificate in 1950.

The purpose of the kidnapping, the appeal claimed, was to enable Justice officials to announce that they had apprehended a "Red spy" in flight. At no time did Sobell know he had been indicted, for his indictment had been sealed and was not made public until after his arrest.

Justice attorneys responded by a declaration that did not contradict the allegation

> Whether he was unceremoniously thrown out by the police with or without the help and direction of the F.B.I. or punctiliously ejected under the regular procedures of the Mexican immigration authorities makes no difference: in either event, he did not return voluntarily to stand trial.[648]

The judges of the Court of Appeals put their stamp of approval on the kidnapping.

> Sobell's forced return to the United States was certainly relevant to the government's theory that he had fled to Mexico to escape prosecution, for otherwise the jury

might have inferred that he had returned voluntarily to stand trial.[649]

The petition for a hearing on the kidnapping issue was denied.

There were no other appeals by the Rosenbergs or Sobell until a week before the final execution date.

From left to right, the defense team, Daniel Marshall, Fyke Farmer, Emanuel
Bloch and John Finerty.

Chapter 11 | The Justices ponder being unequal to the Executive and Congress

June 1953: conflicting prayers and expectations...

The month of June 1953 was vital to the expectations of Justice officials and Judge Kaufman. If confessions were not obtained from either of the Rosenbergs in that month, the executions would have to be carried through. The president had already denied clemency in February, giving the Rosenbergs almost five months in which to face up to the reality that whether they lived or died was in their hands alone. Every appeal had been exhausted. In mid-month June, the Supreme Court justices would be off on their vacations, after having declined for the seventh time to accept the case for review. Justice officials and J. Edgar Hoover had agreed that the confessions would most likely be made in either Julius' or Ethel Rosenberg's cell at Sing Sing, when it became clear to the Rosenbergs that they had only minutes to live. The FBI agents and stenographers who would take the confessions had been selected and given instructions on their comportment with the Rosenbergs. Meanwhile, the executioner would go on with his preparations.

What was most important, then, was to quickly dispose of any unanticipated last minute attempts to obtain a stay of execution from one of the Supreme Court justices before the Court adjourned for the summer. A stay would give the Rosenbergs at least five more months in which to continue to withhold their confessions, and five more months for pro-clemency petitions to be counted at the White House.

"It's September 1951 all, over again," Brainin said. "All there is, is us."

But it wasn't quite like September 1951. At that time, we knew, because of the appeals being prepared, that the Rosenbergs might have at least another year to live. Now, their lives might end before the month was over.

Our phones rang day and night with what should have been uplifting news. More churches, more lawyers, more scientists, more everyday people signing and speaking, more of everything we wanted to hear, but we sensed a new rigidity in statements flowing from Justice officials and a new curtness in the courts.

We met with our principal advisors among the Christian clergy and the rabbis, academics, scientists, historians, several union leaders, a smattering of writers and musicians, some of them mainstream Americans who had become mainstream mavericks by their outspokenness on the Rosenberg-Sobell case.

Our mood was somber. One historian told us, "I talked to a Congressman and he says we're just spinning our wheels. He says there are facts in the case that couldn't be brought out at the trial, or even afterward, for reasons of national security, and everybody who has heard these facts believes the Rosenbergs are as guilty as hell. The courts, the media and everybody in public life has gotten the word."

We responded that unless there was secret evidence of an intent by the defendants to enable the destruction of the United States by the Soviet Union, there was no basis for the treason verdicts or the sentences. (Actually, since the United States had never declared war against the Soviet Union, it was questionable, from a legal standpoint, whether the defendants could have been charged with treason even if they had spied during the Cold War.)

It was not the first time we had heard intimations of secret evidence in the hands of Justice officials. But what can one do with "secret evidence?" It can't be confirmed or refuted, since it can't be known and examined. How can one determine whether "secret evidence" is the genuine asset of a dedicated public servant or the counterfeit coin of an opportunistic prosecutor?

There were bizarre schemes brought to the Committee for saving the Rosenbergs' lives. One such scheme involved blowing up the power lines on which Sing Sing depended for its executions. Another involved the threat of self-immolation outside the White House. We did not know whether the schemers were FBI-provocateurs or honest people at their wits' end. Whatever they were, they were turned gently away.

A businessman told me that he had a plan for saving the Rosenbergs' lives and wanted to meet me in a public park at sundown. I declined the park locale, but agreed to meet over coffee in a local cafeteria, during daylight hours.

"You know it's over when all you've got left is a Supreme Court that's already turned you down half a dozen times," the businessman told me. He was a middle-aged man who had contributed modest amounts of money to the Committee through a woman friend he described as his secretary. She would bring the money, in cash, to the Committee office once every few months, never more than a hundred dollars or so, and ask for samples of our latest leaflets, pamphlets, public letters and so on.

"You're not going to save the Rosenbergs," he said. "Nothing's going to work now. Bloch did all he could but the courts aren't going to give him the right time. So what do you do when you run out of speeches and Popes and Protestants and rabbis and out of appeals and out of everything else? What do you do?"

The question was rhetorical. And, as Brainin would say, the clock was ticking. I waited for the man to go on.

"So, my friend, here is a new plan," the man said. "It's not mine alone, it's a plan by me and a half dozen other men with some money. I can't tell you whether one of them is a lawyer, but I have to tell you that a lawyer says the plan is feasible.

"Now, this is it. The Rosenbergs are federal prisoners, but they're being held in a New York State prison at Sing Sing, and that's where the execution is going to take place. Under New York law, there is no crime comparable to the federal law under which the Rosenbergs were indicted, and therefore, under New

York law a legal argument can be made that the Rosenbergs can't be lawfully executed in a New York prison. I know what you're thinking: the Rosenbergs can be transferred to another state for the executions. But hear me out — the same legal argument can be made in any state. The real problem is this — under the present hysteria, what New York judge would listen to a motion along these lines and find for the Rosenbergs? I don't have to answer this question for you, do I?"

"Go ahead," I said, hoping that the man had a really practical plan in mind.

"The fact is, a smart lawyer can tie up the executions for six months, at least. Okay? Now, the fact is that there are a few bottom-line judges in New York who would give us a friendly decision, provided that a decision that benefits the Rosenbergs also benefits the judge. You understand what I'm saying? Okay. The judge's decision would tie up the case in the courts for six months to a year, and by that time — who knows?"

I took a few moments to think the suggestion over and to make some guesses about the man sitting opposite me. "I can see why you wanted to meet when the sun went down," I said. "And I think I see where this is going. You're about to tell me that you've already sounded out a bagman, and he gave you a figure that would be attractive to a judge. You and the other money men have a nice sum to contribute, but you need still more, and you want to approach other sympathetic money men, and you want me to vouch for you in my capacity as a Committee member."

"You got it," the man said.

"I was a New York State parole officer for a little while," I told him, "and I got to know a number of guys who got involved in scams like this one. I think you ought to worry about whoever got you into this."

For all I knew, the man might have been truly naïve.

What the man didn't know was that such a scheme had come up six months earlier, involving another group of businessmen. In that case, I had been told the name of the bagman the group had contacted. He was a New York State senator, and, according to one of the Committee members who knew him, the bagman was honest in the sense that he did not take money for services he could not render. The bagman told the Committee member he had canvassed the appropriate judges on behalf of the group, and had been turned down by every judge.[650]

3 high ranking officials submit proposals for clemency...

In the early days of the Committee, in September 1951, Emily had argued that we must make no assumptions about who might be for or against clemency, and had specifically said she expected clemency to receive support from some "right-wingers" and even from some anti-Semites. Twenty years later, we learned how prophetic she had been. In 1953, three prominent individuals in government proposed clemency. One of them was a known anti-Semite.

One of the three was C. Douglas Dillon, a member of one of the wealthiest and most powerful families in the United States, and at that time the U.S. Ambassador to France, who would later become Secretary of the Treasury under President John F. Kennedy.

On May 15, Dillon cabled the Secretary of State that it was in American interests to grant clemency to the Rosenbergs, and that it was an illusion to think arguments for clemency were inspired principally by

> Communist propaganda or that people who take this position are unconscious dupes of Communists. Fact is that the great majority of French people of all political leanings feel that the death sentence is completely unjustified from moral standpoint and is due only to political climate peculiar to United States...[651]

On June 9, Dillon wrote the Secretary once again that he and his principal advisors "would be very pleased if it should be possible to commute death sentence."[652]

Another proposal for clemency was made by Allen Dulles, Director of the CIA, who was described by a leading historian as having "made no secret of his hatred for Jews or his contempt for the British, and he 'peppered his conversations with anti-Semitic and anglophobic remarks.'"[653] Dulles' brother, John Foster Dulles, was then Secretary of State.

The Dulles brothers had been law partners in an international legal firm among whose clients were pre- and post-World War II German cartels and corporations. Both appeared to share their German clients' view of Jews. In John Foster Dulles' State Department, as in that Department under previous Secretaries, it was "not unusual to find references to 'oily Jews' in official diplomatic reports of both the United States and Britain."[654]

Dulles wanted to introduce his proposal without claiming authorship. According to A.H. Belmont, one of J. Edgar Hoover's top FBI aides, early in 1953 he received an interoffice memorandum from Dulles prepared by an unidentified Central Intelligence Agency employee.[655] The CIA Director's modesty may have simply been the means by which he could deny authorship if the proposal became public and aroused criticism.

Dulles began his proposal, which he dated January 22, 1953, two days after Eisenhower's inauguration, with the following statement

> A concerted effort to convince Julius and Ethel Rosenberg, convicted atom spies now under sentence of death, that the Soviet regime they serve is persecuting

and ultimately bent on exterminating the Jews under its sovereignty. The action desired of the Rosenbergs is that they appeal to Jews in all countries to get out of the communist movement and seek to destroy it. In return, death sentences would be commuted.[656]

Dulles believed that this offer to the Rosenbergs would succeed because

> people of the sort of the Rosenbergs can be swayed by duty where they cannot be swayed by considerations of self-interest. They should not be asked to trade their principles for their lives — for one thing, such an appeal to cowardice would almost certainly fail. The argument should be rather that they are about to die for a system that has betrayed and is destroying their own people, that they have the moral obligation of influencing other Jews against communism. In short, they would be offered two things psychologically: (1) an opportunity to recant while preserving their self-respect and honor; (2) a new purpose in life.

Realization of the aims of the Dulles clemency proposal required the recruitment of very special people.

> Perhaps the ideal emissaries would be highly intelligent rabbis, representing reformed [sic] Judaism, with a radical background or sympathetic understanding of radicalism, and with psychiatric knowledge. Such men can be found.

There was, of course, the danger that the Rosenbergs might reject such emissaries at the start because "they may wish to die as martyrs," in which case "the execution should proceed and the emissaries should preserve total silence."[657]

In May 1953, the CIA Director apparently learned that U.S. Ambassador to France, C. Douglas Dillon, had recommended the President grant clemency, and it is likely that Dulles pressed his proposal as a better alternative because Dillon's recommendation required the government to "surrender" to the "Communist-led" clemency movement, whereas Dulles' clemency proposal imposed a *quid pro quo* condition on the Rosenbergs. They would denounce communism, and the Soviet Union, and, in return, would receive clemency.

Justice officials would have seen two major problems with Dulles' proposal. The first, which he probably would not have understood, was if the proposal became public, some people — and certainly Jewish leaders in the United States and abroad — would complain that it libeled Jews as being especially attracted to communism. Dulles would not have understood this concern because he shared J. Edgar Hoover's belief that Jews *were* prone to communist thinking, and this "fact" was at the heart of his proposal. He was offering the Jews redemption through the Rosenbergs who, having been communist sinners themselves, had the moral authority to become the saviors of their fellow Jews. Dulles' clemency proposal was intended to be to the Rosenbergs what the road to Damascus had been to Paul, a revelatory experience which would inspire the Rosenbergs to become anti-communist apostles to their communist-prone co-religionists.

The second problem for Justice officials was that the Rosenbergs' "conversion" to anti-communism would not be an actual confession of guilt accompanied by the names of accomplice spies and traitors. The Rosenbergs' "conversion" would leave in place all the accusations of misconduct against Justice officials, the prosecutors and the judge. At best, the officials' reputations would be left in a hazy limbo in which their vindication would never be clearly achieved.

For Justice officials, there was no other path to vindication of their conduct of the Rosenberg-Sobell trial except through confessions; the spur to confession lay in the imminence of executions.

A third proposal came from C. D. Jackson, an Eisenhower presidential aide, who was also the publisher of *Life*. Jackson was a member of the White House Psychological Strategy Board, a group that dealt with the manipulation of public opinion on the Rosenberg-Sobell case and other problematic issues. J. Edgar Hoover, in a memorandum to Attorney General Brownell, reported that Jackson had suggested using

> a prominent Jewish psychiatrist such as Dr. Karl Binger
> to insinuate himself into the confidence of Julius and
> Ethel Rosenberg.[658]

The objective appears to have been to secure from the Rosenbergs a statement that dealt mainly with regret and remorse, but was not quite a full confession.

Hoover expressed his opposition to Jackson's suggestion, telling Brownell that Dr. Binger had been used in Alger Hiss' defense and had appeared poorly during his cross-examination. Hoover went on to emphasize the need for full confessions, writing that Judge Kaufman had "indicated to the Rosenbergs' attorney and relatives that the Rosenbergs can save themselves by making full disclosures."

Justice officials' overtures and threats to the Rosenbergs...

Justice officials staged a public "overture" to the Rosenbergs on June 1, 1953, sending two U.S. Marshals to Sing Sing to serve execution papers on the couple, and to inform them that they were scheduled for execution at approximately 11:00 p.m. on June 18, the day of their fourteenth wedding anniversary.

The next day, James V. Bennett, Director of the Federal Prisons, appeared at Sing Sing with an offer to spare the Rosenbergs' lives if they confessed their guilt. Justice officials undoubtedly chose Bennett for this mission because it would have been undesirable to send someone who was familiar with the case, which would have encouraged the Rosenbergs to argue their innocence. What Justice officials wanted was to make clear to the Rosenbergs there was nothing to discuss except their confessions. If the Rosenbergs quickly realized it was pointless to argue their case with Bennett, all they would be left with was the fear of death.

Julius Rosenberg described the meeting with Bennett in a letter to his attorney. Bennett opened the conversation by saying that if Rosenberg wanted to cooperate with the government, he, Bennett, would make arrangements for Rosenberg to speak with the proper Justice officials. If the officials were convinced that Rosenberg had "fully cooperated with the government they will have a basis to recommend clemency."[659]

Rosenberg wrote his attorney that he told Bennett he was being told to "cooperate or die."

> It is a terrible thing to do to offer to barter life by "talking..". He [Bennett] said "Why do you know that I didn't sleep last night when I knew I had to see you and Ethel the next day and talk to you about this matter. Why, I was terribly worried." How do you think we feel sitting here waiting for death for over two years when we are innocent. My family has gone through great suffering...Then you talk to me about this.[660]

Bennett countered Rosenberg's assertions of innocence by what he believed were factual proofs of his guilt, Bennett said he had read in the newspapers. He told Rosenberg, for example, he had read that Elizabeth Bentley, a confessed spy who had never been indicted, had described espionage dealings with Rosenberg (Bentley made no mention of either of the Rosenbergs in her testimony); all the courts had upheld the conduct of the trial and the Pope had not intervened for clemency. It became clear to Julius Rosenberg that Bennett did not even understand the newspaper accounts of the case.

After spending a fruitless hour with Julius Rosenberg, Bennett went to Ethel Rosenberg's cell and told her the purpose of his visit. When Ethel Rosenberg asserted her and her husband's innocence, Bennett suggested she might help herself by simply acknowledging that she knew her husband to be guilty without acknowledging that she was equally guilty. Ethel Rosenberg quoted Bennett as saying

But now take a family, for example. One member might
not be actively engaged in certain activities, but still have
knowledge concerning another member's activities.[661]

Her reply, Ethel Rosenberg wrote, "was exceedingly polite" She reiterated
that she and her husband were innocent.

Bennett told Ethel Rosenberg

Well, the government claims to have in its possession,
documents and statements that would dispute that, so
if only you were willing to cooperate, there might be a
basis for a commutation —

Ethel Rosenberg replied

If you are persuading me to confess...on the basis of evidence with which I was never confronted in court, then
obviously the validity of this evidence must be strongly
questioned.

Ethel Rosenberg wrote that she had begun to feel "sorry for him; just
another cog in a wheel, doing a lousy, thankless job..."

One of her last statements to Bennett was

Camouflage it, glamorize it, whitewash it in any way you
choose, but this is coercion, this is pressure, this is torture. Let me say to you in all sobriety. You will come to
me at ten minutes of 11:00 p.m. on Thursday, June 18,
and the fact of my innocence will not have changed in
the slightest.[662]

On June 5, Bennett reported to Justice officials on his visit to the Rosenbergs
at Sing Sing, from which the following are excerpts.

...I questioned some of his [Rosenberg's] statements and
repeatedly told him that he ought somehow to be able
to disabuse those familiar with the case of the feeling
he had failed to make a full disclosure and had not been
cooperative. Each time he protested his innocence. He
also claims that he was convicted on the basis of perjured
testimony and trickery on the part of the prosecutor...

* * *

I next went to the women's cellblock, where I saw Mrs.
Rosenberg. I followed about the same approach in telling
her that the purpose of my visit was to see how she was

getting along and also to ascertain whether she by any chance desired me to put her in touch with the proper Government agents so that she could have an opportunity to make any statement or give any information about her case that would be helpful to the Government in solving some unanswered questions relating to the whole matter. She said that...she had no intention of putting her finger on somebody else or giving false or misleading information even though it might have the effect of staying her own execution...

Realizing that I wasn't getting anywhere, I asked the Warden to bring in Julius...Both Julius and Ethel again protested that they would have no messages and no information and that the only thing I could do for them would be to present to the Attorney General a recommendation that their sentence be commuted.[663]

With one remarkable exception, the mainstream media found nothing wrong with the Attorney General's "confess or die" position. But an editorial in a Texas newspaper, the *Laredo Times,* declared

This is a chapter in our history on the level of communist or fascist thinking. In our minds, under this type of thinking, it was impossible for the Rosenbergs to get a fair trial.[664]

Justice officials seemed unable to imagine the death threat would not succeed. They prepared to have at Sing Sing, on the morning of the day of the executions, two high-ranking FBI agents and Anthony Villano, a young stenographer, who could transcribe 170 words a minute. Villano would bring enough supplies for a month, so that if the confession process became prolonged there would be no narrative gaps due to material or mechanical problems. The two high-ranking FBI agents would be given thirteen pages of questions to put to either or both of the Rosenbergs. In addition, there was to be an open telephone line from Sing Sing to the White House.[665]

A careful clemency exchange with Senator Joseph McCarthy...

In April 1953, during a discussion between Committee member Aaron Schneider and a Milwaukee businessman who was a clemency supporter, the latter mentioned that he had access, through a friend, to Senator Joseph McCarthy, and that the Senator, surprisingly, had not been exploiting the Rosenberg-Sobell case in his attacks on Communists. He also called to Aaron Schneider's attention that in 1949, McCarthy had openly opposed the death sentences for the 43 German officers and soldiers who had been condemned for the murders of 71 American prisoners of war in what became known as the Malmedy Massacre, which we dealt with earlier. He proposed to sound out McCarthy on what his reaction would be if the President granted clemency. If the Senator said he would not be critical, would he consider communicating this informally to the White House?

The Committee's first concern with this suggestion was that such a request might result in a public statement by McCarthy opposing clemency, but after some discussion we agreed an anti-clemency statement by the Senator would come as no surprise to anyone.

The Senator's irresponsible tactics toward those he called "Communists" did not inspire trust. It was likely, most of us believed, his opposition to the death sentences for the German soldiers may have been due to the very large number of voters of German ancestry in Wisconsin, rather than to the immorality of capital punishment. On the other hand, we were trying to save two lives and the Senator had been uncharacteristically silent about the Rosenberg-Sobell case. It was possible our Milwaukee clemency supporter had a useful insight into the man and the situation. We encouraged the Milwaukee clemency supporter make an inquiry.

Some weeks later, Aaron Schneider received word the Senator had replied that he would not be critical if President Eisenhower granted clemency, but he did not believe that an informal assurance of this to the White House could be kept secret and, once it became public, it might adversely affect the possibility of clemency. To support his prediction, the Senator described a recent dispute he'd had with the White House. In early spring 1953, he had entered into direct negotiations with Greek ship owners for the purpose of obtaining their agreement to stop permitting their ships to be used for trade with Communist countries. The State Department and the White House became furious with him, since foreign relations were exclusively the province of the Executive. McCarthy believed if it became known he would not condemn a grant of clemency, the President might publicly interpret this assurance as a recommendation for clemency, and would reject it to show his independence of McCarthy. But, we were told, the Senator might rethink his position on letting the White House know his intentions if the Committee still thought he should do so.

The Committee was uncertain how to respond. Was the Senator being honest with us about his views? The newspapers confirmed the story of his negotiations with the Greek ship owners. The whole matter of McCarthy and clemency had suddenly acquired an air of unreality. Might the Rosenbergs be executed as an anti-McCarthy gesture? It would be one of the most cynical parodies of justice imaginable.

While we pondered McCarthy we also pondered Eisenhower. From our reading of Eisenhower's background, we found few signs of a compassionate nature in his official persona. We were aware of significant incidents in Eisenhower's life in which compassion had eluded him. The first, which we mentioned earlier, was Eisenhower's participation, when he was a major under General Douglas MacArthur, in the armed attack on 25,000 American World War I veterans and their families who had marched to Washington D.C. during the Great Depression, many of them homeless and all of them hungry.

At least one biographer has written that "Eisenhower had disapproved" of the action.[666] In 1932, Eisenhower had come to a moment in his adult life when he had a very hard choice to make, one that would surely obliterate all his dreams if he acted on his disapproval of carrying out a physical attack on his unarmed former fellow soldiers. (Ironically, thirteen years later, he led the Allied military forces to a victory in Europe, one consequence of which was that, for the first time, military attacks against unarmed civilians became defined as crimes against humanity).

Another incident mentioned earlier was the execution of Private Eddie Slovik. Later, we learned of a third incident, which the President recounted to a delegation of clergymen who were urging him to grant clemency to the Rosenbergs. After the Allied landing at Normandy, the President told the clergy, some American soldiers started raping, stealing, and pillaging. The mayor of one of the villages told Eisenhower that he was advising his people to arm themselves against the Americans. Eisenhower then decided to make an example of two American soldiers who had been convicted of criminal conduct, and had them publicly executed.[667]

One of the troubling aspects of these incidents was that they involved Eisenhower in carrying out assaults on the lives of American soldiers or war veterans, not as punishment for crimes, but for expedient purposes.

We also recognized that he was not allied with political extremists, although he would make, as Truman had done, "small" concessions to them in an attempt to exercise some control over their agenda. It was obvious from his speeches and those of officials close to him that, over the very strong objections of extremists, he was trying to end the Korean War through negotiations. General Douglas MacArthur, a very popular military hero at the time, declared that peace without victory in Korea would be a great victory for Communism. The President went on to make a negotiated peace.

Eisenhower had also made it plain he would send financial aid to France to pursue its war in Indochina but would not send troops to Vietnam. He had also, by extremist standards, failed to cleanse the government of "Communist" agents. Later, when he left office, he warned the nation against the "military-industrial complex," and its reach for total power.

Was he prepared to incur greater hostility from the extremists by an act of clemency for the Rosenbergs? We thought his decisions for life or death for people whose fate he would decide, could be affected by considerations unrelated to the deeds or misdeeds that had put condemned human beings in his hands. We did not think President Eisenhower would be deterred by compassion or historical factors from doing what McCarthy predicted he might do.

We suggested to the Milwaukee clemency supporter that the Senator be informed the Committee was unwilling to take the risk that he might be correct in his prediction of the President's response to learning McCarthy would be silent if clemency was extended to the Rosenbergs. The Committee asked the contact in Milwaukee to simply thank the Senator for giving us his views.

A new Vigil at the White House...

On June 13, 1953, the Committee re-established the Vigil at the White House. Very quickly, the Vigil participants numbered in the thousands.

Some of our legal advisors said they believed that somewhere in the judicial mangle spawned by the Rosenberg-Sobell case, a court would find a circumstance that would deflect Justice officials from their course. Others said they believed that the President would deliberately withhold a grant of clemency until the last minute in the hope that the Rosenbergs would, as the first of them entered the death chamber, blurt out a confession.

Others wondered out loud whether the Rosenbergs should make "compromise confessions," in which, even if their confessions were false, admit to conspiring to commit espionage, but refuse to name accomplices.

Still others wondered whether a grand gesture by the Committee was called for, an immediate withdrawal of all vigils, meetings, petitions and other clemency actions, announcing that by our silence we were putting all our faith in the President to do what he believed to be right and moral, so that he would not have to ask himself whether he was surrendering to the "Communists" if he chose to grant clemency to the Rosenbergs.

Most of the Committee members and its advisors juggled all these desperate and despairing thoughts at one and the same time. For some, the "big picture" became a form of rationalizing the irrational — we were struggling for the great principles of American justice, for truth, integrity, honesty, fairness. For others, the "small picture" infused their thoughts and feelings — a man and a woman trapped in our political storms — wondering each moment to whom and to what to commit their lives: to children, at the cost of what the man and woman considered to be truth and honor, or to truth and honor, at the cost of their sons and the cycles of days and years they had anticipated for themselves.

Our sense of despair was not only for the Rosenbergs. It was for human history and its unglorious repetitions, for the looming inevitability that the God-fearing man in the White House would permit the March 1951, spectacle in Foley Square to follow the same course as the spectacles mounted in Moscow and Prague and, before that, in Berlin.. But that could not be, we told ourselves. At the last moment, our President would relent.

Those of us who believed in God imagined scores of millions of prayers rising from everywhere on earth to protect the Rosenbergs; those of us who were not Believers or who did not know what to believe, prayed anyway. It was the least that some could do, it was the most that some could do. We wondered to ourselves what the Rosenbergs were praying for. *Punish us only for the crime we committed, and for no other,* perhaps.

The clergy had agreed the Committee should designate June 6 and 7 as special weekend days of prayers in churches and synagogues, and pressure should be increased for a positive response to the request by the group of ministers led by Rev. Loomer to speak directly to the President.

Meanwhile, the actions taken by clemency committees in the smaller cities had caught the attention of their local media, and the reports the Committee received from them indicated many thousands of communications for clemency were arriving at the White House, daily.

The various city and state committees in the big metropolitan centers — Boston, Chicago, Detroit, Cleveland, Los Angeles, New York, Philadelphia — were conducting clemency motorcades, floats, parades, street meetings, picket lines at Department of Justice offices, clemency rallies in squares and market-places, interfaith prayer meetings, house gatherings, petition distributions and sendoffs at train and bus stations for thousands of supporters headed for the clemency Vigil.

A maverick lawyer appears...

A Tennessee lawyer — Fyke Farmer — had read the trial record while traveling in Europe in 1952, and became convinced that the defendants had not been fairly tried. He had been persuaded to read the record after he had read *Freedom's Execution*, a pamphlet by Irwin Edelman, a Californian who can best be described as an anti-Stalin Communist.

Farmer believed the law under which the Rosenbergs and Sobell should have been tried was the Atomic Energy Act of 1946, rather than the one under which they had been indicted, the Espionage Act of 1917. The essential difference between the two Acts, in respect to the Rosenbergs, was under the 1946 Act, if they had been found guilty, the presiding judge could not have imposed death sentences without the approval of the jury, and then, only if the indictment stated that the crime had been committed with intent to injure the United States.

In May 1953, Farmer attempted to discuss the matter with Bloch, but had been rebuffed. Emily and I and the other Committee members were made aware of the rebuff when we first met Farmer. An arrangement was subsequently made for both lawyers to be present at a Committee member's apartment, but although Farmer had come to discuss the case with Bloch, Bloch refused and left after staying only a little while.

Bloch had been aware of the 1946 Act, and had cited it in the fall of 1952, in a petition for review by the Supreme Court, observing

> Congress in passing the Atomic Energy Act of 1946 (42 U.S.C.A. Sec. 1816) did not see fit to prescribe the death penalty for atomic espionage except where there exists an intent to injure the United States.[668]

Edelman, whose pamphlet had aroused Farmer's interest, was a clemency supporter but was also an outspoken critic of the Committee, which he believed was deliberately concealing legal errors made by Bloch.[669] Among Bloch's errors, Edelman argued, was Bloch's motion to impound Exhibit 8 during David Greenglass' testimony, and Bloch's failure to call atomic scientists to refute David Greenglass' testimony.

An FBI operation in the Los Angeles clemency committee...

Before publishing his views on Bloch's conduct of the defense of the Rosenbergs, Edelman had conferred with the leaders of the Los Angeles clemency committee, of which he was a member. The leaders rejected his views and then, unbelievably, expelled him from the committee.

While the national Committee had no control over what local committees did, we had always made it clear to them we believed very strongly that anyone who supported clemency, regardless of their views on other matters, had a place at the table. Neither Edelman nor the Los Angeles committee informed us of his expulsion when it occurred, and we learned about it only shortly before Fyke Farmer came into the case.

Our original assumption was Communists in the Los Angeles committee had orchestrated Edelman's expulsion. According to a clemency supporter from Los Angeles who was in New York when we learned of it, Edelman was offensive to Communists in the committee because he was a follower of Stalin's most vocal critic, Leon Trotsky, who had been murdered in 1940, apparently by an assassin acting under Stalin's orders.

We believed this was a likely explanation for Edelman's unwarranted expulsion, although the general conduct of the Los Angeles committee's activities did not seem to us to bear a "Stalinist" stamp. Two years later, in May 1955, however, we learned from the *New York Times* that the FBI may have been involved in the expulsion of Edelman as part of its disruption program within organizations that Justice officials deemed subversive. David Brown, who had been a leader in the Los Angeles Committee to Save the Rosenbergs, had been a paid FBI informant at the time of Edelman's expulsion.

The *New York Times* subhead on the story read, *Testifies He Got Pay as Head of Unit to Save Rosenbergs and as Counter-Spy.*

> A recanting Federal Bureau of Investigation informer testified yesterday that he had received $75 a week as head of a "Committee to Save the Rosenbergs" while drawing his regular pay as a counter-spy for the F.B.I.
>
> ***
>
> Brown, under cross-examination at a hearing of the Subversives Activities Control Board in the Federal Building, volunteered testimony that his oral reports to the F.B.I. were laced with falsehoods. He resorted to fabrications, he said, so he could continue to draw pay as an informer. He had testified previously that the pay ranged from $25 a week to $250 monthly.[670]

As had happened in the case of a number of other FBI agents and informers, Brown felt remorse for his actions, and now refused to identify as a Communist anyone he had worked with in the Los Angeles committee. He was not asked any questions relating to Edelman. (The *New York Times* did not explain why it labeled Brown a "counter-spy," which inferred that the clemency Committee was an espionage operation. Not even the Justice Department had used such language in its reference to the Committee.)

Later, we will show the FBI routinely used its agents, informants and other cooperative contacts in clemency, civil liberties and anti-bias groups to encourage dissension, suspicion and expulsions. Former FBI agent M. Wesley Swearingen, a twenty-five year veteran of the FBI, cited earlier, disclosed deliberate incitements of violence by an African-American group against a playwright who was a clemency supporter.[671]

We are unable to state with any certainty that FBI-informant Brown had initiated a move to expel Edelman. We do know his job description for the FBI would have encouraged him to do so.

Criticism of Bloch's representation of the Rosenbergs...

Edelman's criticism of Bloch's motion to impound Greenglass' testimony and sketches relating to the atom bomb had also been made by attorneys and knowledgeable laymen, as had been Bloch's failure to call on eminent scientists to refute David Greenglass' testimony. There was general agreement among the critics that the impounding motion had been a mistake; there was considerable disagreement among the critics in respect to Bloch's not having called on a scientist to attack the Exhibit 8 material, because it had been reasonable for Bloch to believe only a scientist of Harold Urey's stature could have helped the defense. Or so it appeared, because of the prosecution's deceptive witness list. It was not until the trial was over that the defense realized the prosecution had placed Urey's name on the witness list with no intention of calling him to the stand.

In the midst of attempts the Committee was making to persuade Bloch to find common ground with Fyke Farmer, Harold Urey sent a telegram, dated June 12, 1953, to President Eisenhower, in which he asked to see the President "to be allowed to present my understanding of the case to you, Mr. President." He had previously that week asked to see Attorney General Herbert Brownell, but an appointment was refused. In his telegram, Urey wrote

> New evidence makes it even more plain what was plain
> enough before, that the prosecution's case has no logic in
> it, and that it depends upon the blowing up of patently
> perjured testimony.[672]

The President declined to see him.

Some of Bloch's misjudgments and oversights may have been the consequence of his virtual abandonment by other attorneys because of their fear of being labeled "Communist," if they assisted him, and because his exhausting labors may have sometimes clouded his judgment. His theory of the case — that the Greenglasses and Gold were telling the truth in respect to their own criminal activity, but had falsely implicated the Rosenbergs — led him to pass up opportunities to challenge their testimonies, as he did in respect to the purported June 3, 1945, Gold visit to the Greenglasses in Albuquerque.

It must have been exceedingly painful to him in early June 1953, when criticism of him by some attorneys was used to diminish the paramount responsibility of the prosecutorial and judicial authorities for the tragedy in the making.

Our belief was whatever legal errors Bloch made in his defense of the Rosenbergs, he made no errors of the heart in his efforts to save their lives. And in his appeals, which no attorney has criticized, he was utterly correct; the appeals were denied, not because of errors by him, but because the appellate judges feared the extremists' wrath that would come their way if they granted a hearing on any issue on appeal.

We believe Bloch was utterly wrong in his resistance to Fyke Farmer's intervention (which he supported only at the last minute), but we did not agree with a proposal by Edelman to reorient the campaign for clemency, which would shift the primary focus away from the Justice Department and the White House to the Rosenbergs' lawyer and to the Committee and to the clemency movement for having "covered up" Bloch's errors. Edelman held that the public should be asked to urge the President to grant clemency because the defense had been bungled, and the public should be directed to write to Emanuel Bloch to urge him to enter a motion for a new trial, giving his own errors as grounds, "and showing, of course, the scandalous manner in which the judge took advantage" of his errors. If we did not adopt this reorientation, Edelman wrote, it was because we did not want to save the Rosenbergs' lives.

Edelman's premise was that if Bloch had not committed any errors, there would not have been Guilty verdicts. This was not a real-world supposition. The transposition of the time of the crime to the Cold War years, the deceptive witness list, the suborned perjuries, the transformation of the charge into treason, and the prosecutors' deliberate use of the fear by the jurors that they and their families faced imminent annihilation by Soviet atom bomb attacks on New York City, had been willful orchestrations by Justice officials and the prosecutors, and were properly challenged on appeal. Edelman's view implied that by putting the onus on Bloch, the government would have a face-saving way of granting clemency. He appeared unaware of the possibility that Justice officials were not seeking face-saving reasons to grant clemency, but were seeking confessions from the Rosenbergs to justify a deliberately designed miscarriage of justice.

Nevertheless, the Committee discussed Edelman's views within and outside the Committee. Blaming the defense for inadequate representation might conceivably give the courts or the White House a ground for clemency. But none of our advisors among the clergy or lawyers or scientists or educators, including the most conservative and the most "leftist" of them, believed it would result in clemency. An appeal for clemency on the grounds of inadequate legal representation would, in effect, ask Eisenhower to acknowledge that Bloch presumably did not adequately challenge prosecutorial and judicial misconduct. The "inadequate representation" argument, Brainin said, required that Eisenhower "confess that everything the Committee said about the trial was true."

Even the most critical attorneys derided the idea that any court would sustain an "inadequate representation" appeal, even if Bloch himself made it. He had performed extremely well, they said. He had dared to defend the Rosenbergs, when no one else would do so. He had made errors, but they did not even come close to constituting inadequate representation.

The Committee believed its obligation, at this point, was to give whatever help it could to Farmer and Bloch, and to do all it could to demonstrate Farmer's views were not in conflict with Bloch's appeals, and no developments on the legal front should obscure the fact that the reasons for seeking clemency were unchanged. Those reasons had won the world's attention and had overcome the isolation of the defendants. Fyke Farmer's "wrong law" issue reinforced the relevance and gravity of the previously raised issues.

New appeals for stays of executions and reversal of verdicts...

On Saturday, June 13, Bloch filed a petition in Washington D.C. for a stay of execution with Supreme Court Justice Robert H. Jackson. Jackson recommended the Court order oral argument on the petition when it met on Monday.

On the same day, Fyke Farmer filed a petition for a writ of *habeas corpus* with Federal Judge Edward Dimock in New York City. That evening, with Daniel Marshall, another attorney, he left a letter with Kaufman's law clerk asking permission to argue the petition before Kaufman the next morning.

The substance of Farmer's petition was that Justice officials had indicted the defendants under the wrong law, the Espionage Act of 1917, which Farmer said was inapplicable in cases involving atomic espionage, a crime for which Congress had explicitly written the Atomic Energy Act of 1946. Farmer argued that since the indictment had not charged "the defendants conspired with intent to injure the United States, they were not punishable by death," because the Congress in enacting the Atomic Energy Act ameliorated the penalty provisions for atomic espionage by "depriving the courts of any authority to impose the death sentence for any offenses of the type under consideration here except upon recommendation of the jury," and restricting the jury's power to recommend death to cases where the offense "was committed with intent to injure the United States."[673]

Part of Farmer's argument was not novel to the appeals on behalf of the Rosenbergs, and had first been raised in Bloch's summation at the trial, when he pointed out that no claim was made by the prosecution that the defendants had intended to injure the United States.[674]

Both Farmer and Bloch, in their separate appeals, had argued that Judge Kaufman's justification for the death sentences against the Rosenbergs was patently illegal, irrespective of which law prevailed. Before sentencing the defendants, Judge Kaufman had stated that the law provided if the espionage

> or the conspiracy to commit espionage is committed during the time of war, the punishment might be death or imprisonment for not more than thirty years. If the espionage or conspiracy to commit espionage is committed at any other time, the maximum punishment is imprisonment for not more than 20 years.

> In the case before me, the conspiracy as alleged and proven commenced on or about June 6, 1944, at which time the country was at war. Therefore, the maximum penalty is death or imprisonment for not more than 30 years.[675]

Bloch argued that Judge Kaufman's finding that the crime was committed while the United States was at war was a travesty of reality, since it was not the

United States and the Soviet Union that were at war with each other, but both of them at war against the Berlin-Tokyo Axis.

There was no obstacle to making the arguments of both lawyers. What there was, however, was an artificial obstacle created by Bloch, who opposed Farmer's entry into the case and sent a telegram to Kaufman disavowing any responsibility for, or reliance, on Farmer's petition.

The authors and other Committee members attempted to discuss with Bloch the possibility that the Farmer petition raised valid issues, but Bloch was adamant in his belief he had raised the right issues for the courts, his appeals were rooted in the trial record, while the arguments centering on the 1946 Act were based on abstract legal arguments unrelated to what had actually happened at the trial and, for that reason, even if valid, were easily dismissable.

In hindsight, we believe that Bloch had succumbed to an untenable premise: if he had been right in raising the issues central to all his appeals, then there could be no other significant issues that were also right and useful.

Later, in an extraordinary declaration in person to the Supreme Court, Bloch, weeping, acknowledged these errors and pleaded with the Court to deal with the substance and not the dissonance that had accompanied Farmer's petition.

24/7...

From late May 1953, onward, the Committee office had remained open twenty-fours a day. All Committee members, wherever they were, kept in touch with the office or by calling one another's home numbers, since the office line was constantly busy. One fear we had was that, in spite of the fact that the execution was set for Thursday, the 18th, Justice officials had the power to arbitrarily carry out the execution at any time before or after that date, unless a temporary stay was granted by a court.

Our fear of the execution being moved up was, in part, due to the large numbers of participants in the Vigil at the White House. The *New York Times* estimated that there were 7000 participants, 2000 of which had come from Philadelphia and New York;[676] the *Washington Post* put the number precisely at 6832, and quoted the Deputy Police Chief as saying that it was the "largest picket line he had ever seen at the White House."[677]

Aaron Schneider, who led the Vigil that week, later told us of his fears on that day: a Vigil so large might lead Justice officials to seek to deter the Vigil from becoming even larger by confronting the Rosenbergs with the choice of confessing or being executed within hours. While there were motions at the Supreme Court for reconsideration of past refusals to review the case, and Bloch's petition for a stay of execution filed with Justice Jackson, there was no actual stay of execution and there was no rule, in the absence of a stay, requiring Justice officials to await the outcome of appeals.

The nine Justices had met on Saturday, June 13, to dispose of the request by the defendants for a rehearing, but their decision would not be announced until Monday, June 15, the last day of the Supreme Court's term for 1953; the next day the justices would begin their summer vacations.

Shortly after noon on Monday, June 15, the day before the Supreme Court justices would begin their vacations, the court convened and Chief Justice Fred M. Vinson announced three decisions on the Rosenberg case: the Supreme Court would not hold a hearing on the request for a stay; it would not grant a stay; it would not reconsider its refusal to review the case.[678]

As soon as the Chief Justice finished his announcements, John F. Finerty, who had joined Bloch in the proceedings, arose and informed the justices that he wished to file a petition for a writ of habeas corpus on behalf of the Rosenbergs which, if granted

> would have called for what would have amounted to a review of whether the Rosenbergs were being legally held for execution.[679]

The Chief Justice told Finerty he would have to file his petition with the court clerk, which Finerty did within two hours, causing the court to reconvene. At about six o'clock, the Chief Justice announced that the Court was denying Finerty the right to file his petition. A dissent was recorded for Justice Hugo L. Black. Justice Felix Frankfurter issued a statement in which he said he did not agree with the court's denial of Finerty's right to file his petition, because there should have been a full hearing and oral argument on the matter.

Bloch announced he and two other attorneys would attempt to see Justice William O. Douglas to argue the case for a stay; Douglas saw Bloch later that day and listened to his arguments, but said nothing encouraging.

Shortly after the Supreme Court decisions became known, Kaufman, in New York, announced he had rejected Farmer's petition, calling Farmer an "interloper" and "intruder," and saying that Farmer's petition verged "on contemptuousness."[680] Farmer had anticipated Kaufman's response, and he and Marshall left for Washington, D.C., where they would try to meet with Justice Black.

On the next day, June 16, two sets of attorneys, one led by Bloch, the other by Farmer, were in the lawyers' lounge of the Supreme Court, both waiting to see Justice Douglas. Farmer had hoped to meet with Justice Black, but he had been unreachable. Bloch and Farmer did not speak to each other in the lounge.

A direct appeal for clemency went to the President that day from the Rosenbergs. It read, in part

We, Julius and Ethel Rosenberg, husband and wife, are now confined in the Death House in Sing Sing Prison, awaiting electrocution on June 18, our fourteenth wedding anniversary. We address this petition to you for the exercise of your supreme power to prevent — "a crime worse than murder" — our unjust deaths.

***

We told you the truth: we are innocent. The truth does not change. We now again solemnly declare our innocence.

***

...our accusers torture us, in the face of death, with the guarantee of life for the price of a confession of guilt. Close upon the execution date — as though to draw upon the last full measure of dread of death and love of life — their high negotiator came bearing this tainted proffer of life. We refuse this iniquitous bargain, even as perhaps the last few days of our young lives are slipping away. We cannot besmirch our names by bearing false witness to save ourselves. Do not dishonor America, Mr. President, by considering as a condition of our right to survive, the delivery of a confession of guilt of a crime we did not commit.[681]

The Chief Justice passes control of his Court to the Attorney General...

Shortly before noon, Farmer and Marshall met with Justice Douglas; also present were James Kilsheimer and several other Justice officials. Farmer made his "wrong law" argument. There is no record of the discussion that took place, but we can be certain that Kilsheimer and other Justice officials disputed Farmer's arguments.

Douglas spent the rest of the day and part of the evening studying Farmer's 61 page petition. Early in the evening the lawyers, who had spent the day waiting in the lounge, were told Douglas would not come to a decision that evening.[682]

At 11 p.m. that same evening, at his request, Attorney General Brownell met with Chief Justice Fred M. Vinson, without a defense attorney present. Their meeting constituted a hearing in violation of Judicial Canon 17, which, in 1953, expressly prohibited hearings "where interests to be affected thereby are not represented." The hearing came to light twenty years later, in an interoffice FBI memorandum in which Judge Kaufman was cited as saying he had learned from Kilsheimer

the Attorney General and Chief Justice Vinson met at
11:00 p.m. to determine whether to call the complete
Court into session to dispose of Fyke Farmer's motion.
Judge Kaufman advised that as of 7:30 p.m., Douglas
was disposed to grant the writ. However, after he came
back from dinner, he was wavering and undecided.
Judge Kaufman said that even if Douglas does throw out
the motion, Justice Frankfurter will hear it.[683]

An addendum to the memorandum said that at 11:15 a.m. on June 17,

Judge Kaufman had very confidentially advised that at
the meeting between the Attorney General and Chief
Justice Vinson last night, Justice Vinson said that if a
stay is granted he will call the full Court into session
Thursday morning to vacate it.[684]

Not only were the Attorney General and the Chief Justice engaged in a forbidden *ex parte* hearing on June 16, but the Chief Justice had never seen Farmer's
petition for a writ, and had not read Douglas' reasons for granting a stay of execution (which had not yet been written), but was nevertheless committing himself
to vacating a stay if it was granted. Legally, this is known as prejudgment, another
forbidden act.

The Committee's clergy advisors meet with President Eisenhower...

Another meeting also took place that day, June 16, when President
Eisenhower, his White House encircled by thousands of participants in the clemency Vigil, agreed to see Dr. Bernard Loomer, two other Protestant ministers,
and Rabbi Abraham Cronbach.[685]

Dr. Loomer's account of the meeting described the President's demeanor
as cheerful and warm. "After a brief exchange of pleasantries, dealing mostly with
golf and fishing," Loomer told the President why they had sought the meeting.

The President, rocking back and forth on his swivel
chair, listened with apparent intentness to my statement,
which probably took about seven minutes. I was not
interrupted at any point. I offered two considerations
in favor of clemency, based on the assumption that the
Rosenbergs were guilty as charged (a proposition about
which I had and still have grave doubts with respect to
the evidence presented at the trial).[686]

Loomer told the President that "the execution of the Rosenbergs would
result in their becoming martyrs for the cause of Communism," and that the

Communists "may actually have preferred to have the Rosenbergs executed." The case, Loomer went on, "was a symbolic occasion transcending in meaning and importance the Rosenbergs themselves." He told the president

> America's problem then was to choose that symbol which would best represent to Americans and to the peoples of other nations the kind of society Americans wanted to preserve. I suggested that the symbol of execution would not indicate America's strength but rather her weakness: our fears, anxieties, hysteria, and defensiveness...It would be the act of a politically and spiritually immature people.

The President replied he had a number of other factors to consider in respect to clemency, an important one being the deterrent effect of executions. He gave as an example the public execution he had ordered of two American soldiers, described earlier. Loomer suggested that executions might "not control committed Communists in the same way he could control soldiers under his command."

> Well, Doctor, replied the President, I don't for a minute define Communism as a religion or a faith as you do. I grant that it is a fanaticism, but not a faith. The only thing that Communists are interested in is the improvement of material conditions. Don't they call it a material dialectic or something like that? But they are not concerned about the immortal soul of the individual.

The subject turned to the Rosenbergs themselves.

> These people, said the President flatly, did what they did for money. They don't deserve our sympathy. The President linked their activities with the course of the Korean War. Who knows, he asked, how many hundreds and thousands of deaths and casualties they are responsible for?

The President went on to say the Rosenbergs' trial "has been reviewed several times by the Supreme Court. They would never have been given this kind of treatment in Russia."

As for clemency, the President said the clergy didn't realize that

> if I were to commute their sentence to one of life imprisonment, under federal law they would be eligible for parole in fifteen years.

Rev. Daniel Ridout of Baltimore said he would like to remind the President of Portia's speech on the quality of mercy in *The Merchant of Venice*, but the President interrupted him and

> leaned far forward on his desk and said that since he had come in contact with this case he had gotten out his Shakespeare and had been reading *The Merchant of Venice*. He said he was aware of the points we were urging on him. As a matter of fact, added the President, I don't mind telling you gentlemen that I resent being reminded of my Christian obligations.[687]

The discussion ended shortly after, with Rabbi Cronbach telling the President "the prayers of the people would support the President as he sought divine guidance in making his decision."

Justice Douglas grants a stay of executions...

The next morning, June 17, at about 11:00 a.m., Justice Douglas announced he had ordered a stay of execution of the Rosenbergs

> pending further proceedings in the United States District Court to determine the question of the applicability of the penal provisions of § 10 of the Atomic Energy Act, and pending a timely appeal to the Court of Appeals from the ruling of the District Court.[688]

His grounds, briefly, were that under the Atomic Energy Act of 1946, "the District Court is without power to impose the death penalty except 'upon recommendation of the jury' and 'where the offense was committed with an intent to injure the United States.'"[689]

Douglas wrote

> It is important that the country be protected against the nefarious plans of spies who would destroy us.
>
> It is also important that before we allow human lives to be snuffed out we be sure — emphatically sure — that we act within the law. If we are not sure, there will be lingering doubts to plague the conscience after the event.
>
> I have serious doubts whether this death sentence may be imposed for the offense except and unless a jury recommends it. The Rosenbergs should have an opportunity to litigate that issue.[690]

The authors were at the Committee office in New York that morning, and it took a little while for the meaning of the stay to sink in. Douglas was directing the District Court — that is, Judge Kaufman — to determine whether he had been bound by the sentencing restrictions of the 1946 Atomic Energy Act, in which case the death sentences — as well as Sobell's thirty year sentence — were unlawful. And if the 1946 Act was applicable to the sentences, the defense was certain to argue that it was applicable to the overall charge of conspiracy, in which case a new trial under the 1946 Act would be necessary. Should Kaufman, as was likely, very quickly decide that the 1946 Act was not applicable, Douglas' stay required that timely appeal be taken to the Court of Appeals.

The most immediate meaning of the stay of the Rosenbergs' executions was an indeterminate reprieve, certainly not less than five or six months, since whatever decision the Court of Appeals made would then be appealed to the next term of the Supreme Court by either Justice officials or the defendants' lawyers. But even the six-month figure appeared too conservative, and we began to believe the Rosenbergs had been reprieved for at least a year.

The surge in sentiment for clemency among the public would have an opportunity to become even greater and those members of Congress who we believed favored clemency but who had chosen to be "careful" might be persuaded to make their views public, as Senator William Langer of North Dakota did.

The office telephone was ringing with congratulatory messages, and there was jubilation among the participants at the White House Vigil and, within an hour most of them were streaming into bus terminals and Union Station or already homeward bound in crowded cars. The offices of the clemency committees in Philadelphia, New York, San Francisco, Los Angeles, Boston, Cleveland, Chicago and elsewhere were preparing celebrations.

At Sing Sing, we were told, the Rosenbergs wept when they heard the news on the radio. Bloch had never mentioned Fyke Farmer to them, but they were surely interested in learning who Farmer was. It was the best news they had received from any court since their arrests in July and August of 1950.

In the midst of celebration, a phone call...

In the Supreme Court lawyers' lounge Bloch went over to Farmer and threw his arms around him.[691] Bloch returned to his hotel with his colleagues and friends, where they rested and allowed the tensions of the immediate past days to lift from them. Although Farmer and Marshall had not joined the celebrants, Bloch made a point of denigrating his own abilities as a lawyer, and praising Farmer and Marshall for theirs.[692]

Shortly after six o'clock, there was a telephone call for Bloch, and he was told by a news service that the Supreme Court Justices had been called back from their vacations for a special session on the motion of the Attorney General. None of the defense attorneys had been notified of the motion or given an opportunity to oppose it.

Attorney General Brownell knew, as the June 17 FBI memorandum cited earlier shows, that if he had notified the defense attorneys of his motion, as the rules required, and if both sides had argued before Chief Justice Vinson, the outcome would not have been affected: Vinson was already committed to reconvening the Supreme Court and vacating Douglas' stay.

In short, Brownell had had nothing to lose by obeying the rules and the law. He appears to have chosen to send an in-your-face warning to Bloch and Farmer and every lawyer in the country that neither he nor other Justice officials considered themselves bound by *ex parte* prohibitions, or by court rules or by legalisms in respect to the Rosenbergs.

Brownell's open disregard for the court rules was likely impelled by the prospect that a disaster for the Justice Department might be in the making, one that might even lead the president to feel that he had been let down by his trusted Attorney General.

Brownell had every reason to feel nothing had gone right in the Rosenberg-Sobell case since the arrests of the defendants. Irving Saypol was no longer at the Justice Department, and Roy Cohn was demanding a very significant promotion at the Department, and neither could be openly criticized or made to answer for their carelessness in respect to evidence (the console table), or perjury (the photographer witness), or their bad judgment (the deceptive witness list), all of which had probably been unnecessary, but had become the subject of worldwide headlines. J. Edgar Hoover had permitted his agents to participate in the photographer's perjury, but it would be indiscreet to hold him accountable. O. John Rogge, himself a former Justice Department attorney, the lawyer for three prosecution witnesses, had somehow been unable to keep his files locked and had permitted a memorandum by David Greenglass, acknowledging that he was willing to say what the FBI told him to say, to fall into the hands of the Communist committee for clemency and then into the hands of reporters. And Judge Kaufman had succumbed at the end of the trial to the temptation to make historic-sounding speeches about world affairs and about his consultations with God, with the result that the defense had been mining Kaufman's speeches for issues to appeal, and the Pope and the Protestant and Jewish clergy were declaring that Kaufman hadn't been listening to God at all. Had Kaufman not specifically declared that he was sentencing the Rosenbergs to death because of their atomic espionage, this Fyke Farmer lawyer would not now be waving the 1946 Atomic Energy Act at the Supreme Court.

It was mystifying: Why had prior Attorney General McGrath and his people taken a very ordinary case of espionage and carelessly let it grow into a *cause célèbre*? The Communists had seized upon the Justice officials' carelessness and the judge's ego-driven behavior, and had been permitted to distort the issues almost beyond repair. There was no orderly exit from the befogged maze, in which sight of the national interest was being lost. What was needed now was a no-nonsense action, a door-slamming, after which there would be nothing more to be said.

That appears to have been the purpose of Brownell's misconduct, to bring everything in the Rosenberg-Sobell case to an abrupt close; the form that closure would take was entirely up to the defendants. The first step was to lock the defense lawyers out of the judicial process, and that started with the *ex parte* agreement between him and Chief Justice Vinson, to force the Supreme Court to declare the case closed. Twenty-five months had been dithered away by the District and Appeals courts and by a loose cannon Supreme Court justice, arousing vain hopes in the Rosenbergs. If they had been taken to the death chamber in May 1951, when they had been scheduled to be executed, Justice officials would have had instant closure by confessions or executions, and the case would have been history, and the Executive would not have been hamstrung by delays, stays, vigils, the clergy pushing its way into the White House to make demands on the president, to say nothing of interference by impertinent heads of foreign states who, if not for Marshall Plan dollars, would be bowing to Stalin. The dithering had to end.

Slamming the Supreme Court's door on the Rosenbergs would be a dooms-day message to them: you have a couple of hours to make up your minds. You can no longer use the Supreme Court or any other court to squeeze us for time. Confess, or the law will take its course.

And if there were any other Fyke Farmers on their way to Washington armed with the Constitution, Brownell wanted them to know that law was no longer a winning game in the nation's capital.

Our celebration had been premature.

In the afternoon of that day, President Eisenhower gave his approval to the burning of books that were politically incorrect, telling a press conference that "it was all right with him if the State Department burns books which openly appeal for the Communist way of life."

> He added that he believes no one in government should
> do anything which would contribute to destruction of
> the United States.[693]

The media noted that Eisenhower's approval of book burning was in con-flict with a statement he had made three days earlier, on June 14, when he had told an assembly of Dartmouth students

> Don't join the book burners. Don't think you are going
> to conceal faults by concealing evidence that they ever
> existed.[694]

On that same day, the Constitutional provision for the independence of the judiciary came under attack by a group of congressmen, headed by Representative W.M. Wheeler, of Georgia. Wheeler announced on the House floor that he would introduce a bill to impeach Justice Douglas for granting the stay of execution to the Rosenbergs. Cheers and applause greeted Representative Wheeler's statement that he could not "sit idly by without seeking to do something about it."[695]

June 18-19, 1953: The Supreme Court justices, vexed and perplexed...

At two o'clock on the afternoon of the next day, June 18, the nine Supreme Court justices convened to deal with Douglas' stay of execution for the Rosenbergs.

The justices knew they would be deliberating not simply the vacation of a stay of execution requested by the Attorney General, an action they had never taken before, or the possibility of error in the selection of the proper law under which an indictment should have been drawn. Whatever they decided would affect the agenda of the prevailing political powers in and out of government, and would affect the fraternity of colleagues and everyday acquaintances with whom they shared lifelong interests and beliefs.

The Rosenbergs and Sobell, although principals in the underlying litigation before them, would not have been the focus of the justices' deliberations. The defendants came from a distant stratum of life, one of continued poverty or near-poverty, of Old Testament Jewishness and its stiff-necked defiance of, and contempt for, the variety of coercive powers that had slashed at them for thousands of years. These were not the every-day acquaintances of the Supreme Court justices, not even of the one Justice who was Jewish.

A majority of the justices had, on seven previous occasions, refused to review the trial record in the Rosenberg-Sobell case. The two reasons most frequently given for the Court's failure to review the trial are 1) that the Supreme Court does not review contested facts, but only alleged errors by the court or purported violations of Constitutional rights, and that when such errors had been brought on appeal to the U.S. Court of Appeals in the Rosenberg-Sobell case, the trial judge's actions were upheld; 2) that the Supreme Court cannot review every appeal it receives.

As to the first "reason," the Supreme Court was expressly created as the tribunal of last resort, and the appellate court as an intermediary way-station whose decisions are final, only if not appealed, or if they are upheld by the Supreme Court. To believe that the Court did not accept the case for review because the lower appellate court had found no basis for a hearing on any issue of appeal, is to say the Court had abandoned its guardianship obligation to the Constitution.

As to the second "reason," it is true the Supreme Court cannot accept every appeal brought to it. The public assumes the Supreme Court accepts cases by evaluating the comparative importance to the nation of the issues submitted to it for review. The importance of the Rosenberg-Sobell case was laid down by Federal Judge Kaufman himself, who had declared the lives of American soldiers in Korea and "millions more of innocent people," as well as our relations with a rival world power, were elements of the case.

Was the Rosenberg-Sobell case important enough for the Supreme Court to have accepted it? The authors surveyed all Supreme Court cases on which decisions were rendered in the last half of 1953 and all of 1954, since Supreme Court cases were accepted for review approximately six months before the decisions were read. This was the period during which the Rosenberg-Sobell appeals to the Supreme Court were filed.

Of the 103 cases accepted by the Supreme Court for the time in question, 13 were tax cases (in one of which $500 was one of the factors in dispute); four were deportation cases; two involved disbarments; four related to interstate commerce, seven involved unfair labor practices; another seven were admiralty cases; three involved illegal entry and search; four dealt with jurisdictional matters; two dealt with bankruptcy; two dealt with school segregation (one of which was the historic *Brown v. Board of Education* case); four involved restraint of trade; two concerned airline schedules; another two related to statutes of limitations. The remaining 57 cases dealt with water rights, life insurance, copyright, medical malpractice and similar matters.

Every one of these 103 cases was important to the petitioners for review, and one of them — *Brown v. Board of Education* — was of great importance to the nation because of the Court's ultimate affirmance of the doctrine of identical access to education for all Americans.

By any realistic measure of the importance of the Rosenberg-Sobell case to the nation, the trial required review. The case was at least as important as all but one of those the Supreme Court agreed to review at that time. If the verdicts and sentences remained intact, a *de facto* alteration of the treason clause in the Constitution would be left in place to become a precedent at future trials; the prosecutorial practice of charging "conspiracy" in evidenceless trials would be greatly encouraged; a precedent would be set for overlooking the subornation of perjury by prosecutors if they chose not to examine and take custody of physical evidence — in this case, the console table; the prosecutorial selection of laws by their degree of punishment rather than by their applicability to the crimes charged would likewise be encouraged.

The Supreme Court had an historic as well as Constitutional obligation to review the Rosenberg-Sobell trial, because of the unprecedented and disquieting spectacle the trial had created for the nation and the world.

Chief Justice Vinson and Attorney General Brownell indisputably held the case to be of utmost importance, although for reasons other than those mentioned above. Justice Vinson recognized its importance by taking the unprecedented step of aborting the vacation plans of the other eight justices, so that they could convene to take another unprecedented step, by reversing a stay of execution granted by one of them.

An important truth must have been in the justices' minds that day, one that may have been in their thoughts for many months, and that had disposed a majority of them to vote against reviewing the conduct of the trial. They knew that, with the exception of the sole act of refusal to grant review, any actions by the Court in the Rosenberg-Sobell case could lead to explosive political and historical consequences, and could result in repercussions from the dominant Congressional bloc that could affect the workings and personnel of justice at its highest level. The Supreme Court had over the many years of its existence frequently been the target of powerful political groups unhappy with its decisions. The most recent attack on the Court had come less than twenty years earlier, when President Franklin Roosevelt had threatened to pack the Court with additional justices who would vote to uphold New Deal legislation. His threat was averted in part by the decision of several justices that it was wiser to find New Deal legislation Constitutional than to risk the transformation of the Court from a caucus of nine justices, most of them conservative, to an assembly of as many as fifteen (one additional justice for every justice over seventy years of age), in which liberals might constitute a majority.

The justices were aware that a decision leaving Justice Douglas' stay in place could also become the provocation for an assault on the jurisdiction of the Supreme Court. National security cases had already been taken from them, in part, by the 1950 Internal Security Act, which permitted the imprisonment of "loyalty risks," simply on the findings of presidential Loyalty Boards. Such a step could lead not only to a devaluation of the legal and moral authority of the Supreme Court, but would, in essence, signal the devaluation of the Constitution as the source of law and justice. (A second major devaluation of the Constitution began twenty five years later, when President Jimmy Carter signed the Foreign Intelligence Act, which led, by additional legislation and Presidential Orders over the next quarter of a century, to a second Court system under Executive rather than Constitutional control.)

Among the headlines that surely caught the justices' attention, on the morning of June 18, were those dealing with Representative Wheeler's bill for the impeachment of Justice Douglas, which had quickly been seconded by nine other members of the House. The justices surely knew the would-be impeachers would not hesitate to add new names to the impeachment list. The justices could have taken only small comfort from the knowledge that the threat to impeach Douglas was not the first in the history of the Supreme Court. There had been other justices threatened with impeachment, although only one — Samuel Chase — had actually been impeached by the House, but was acquitted by the Senate, in 1805.

Chase had been impeached because, among other things, as an ultra-conservative, he had challenged the Jefferson administration's view that laws prohibiting criticism of government officials were unConstitutional.

The justices knew a decision *not* to vacate Douglas' stay, while very ordinary and in keeping with the traditional deliberative character of the Supreme Court, would be declared by many public officials and large sections of the media to be an astonishing victory for Communism. The justices' reputations and characters and patriotism could be irrevocably stained and adversely treated, in the present, and in the histories to be written of the time.

The justices also knew a truth that was masked by the grandeur of their titles: they were essentially powerless. The Supreme Court did not have the authority to enforce its own decisions, but must depend on the Executive to do so on behalf of the Court, and on the Congress to respect decisions that reined in its power. A glaring historical example of the powerlessness of the Supreme Court had to be on the justices' minds at the very time they were considering the fate of the Rosenbergs. They had been discussing *Brown v. Board of Education*, an appeal against federally-supported segregated schools. If the appeal was upheld, it would supplant *Plessy v. Ferguson* (1896), in which the Court had ordered that separate-but-equal educational facilities would be given to whites and African-Americans in publicly-supported schools. The justices were aware that the "equal" requirement in the *Plessy* decision had been ignored for fifty eight years by every one of the twelve presidents and twenty three U.S. Attorneys General who followed the 1896 decision. The Supreme Court simply did not have the power to enforce its rulings if the Executive and Congress chose to ignore them.

(A year after the execution of the Rosenbergs, *Plessy* was replaced by *Brown v. Board of_Education*, under the leadership of Chief Justice Earl Warren, who was appointed by Eisenhower after Justice Vinson's death, in 1953, after which Warren was threatened with impeachment for thirteen of his sixteen years on the bench.[696])

The task, then, of each of the nine justices, on this afternoon, was to keep his balance in the political tempest through which he lived from day to day, to weigh the importance of the personal, class and professional ties that bound him to government officials who were involved in the Rosenberg-Sobell case, to weigh the written law, and to weigh the fact of powerlessness.

The justices knew Brownell had, to all intents and purposes, brushed aside considerations of law and precedent and, by recalling the Court, their Chief Justice had yielded to the Attorney General at the *ex parte* hearing. They could vote to let Douglas' stay of execution remain in force, and invite denunciation, but if the Executive branch was determined to execute the Rosenbergs that day, Brownell's abandonment of legalities signaled that there would be executions, leaving the justices denounced and humiliated, and the Rosenbergs dead. Failure to do the Attorney General's bidding would have branded the Supreme Court as being nothing more than a dispensable vestigial appendage of the Executive branch of government.

As experienced veterans and beneficiaries of political wars, they knew the Executive's purpose was not to execute the Rosenbergs, but to compel their confessions, and what the Executive wanted the judges to do was to signal to the Rosenbergs' that their lives were in their own hands.

The specter of a new trial...

There were no verbatim records made of the arguments before the Supreme Court on that day, and so there are only newspaper reports and law clerks' diaries on which to rely, but it is safe to assume that, after the Solicitor General made the remarks we cite below, the arguments for the lawyers on both sides hewed closely to the arguments previously detailed.

The Justice Department's Solicitor General, Robert Stern, argued to the justices that if the Rosenbergs and Sobell had been brought to trial under the Atomic Energy Act of 1946,

> the case would have been thrown out so quickly the Government would have been a laughing stock.[697]

Stern's warning was, in essence, correct. If the Supreme Court, by leaving Douglas' stay in place, allowed the Rosenbergs to proceed with an appeal on the wrong-law issue, and if they succeeded in obtaining a new trial under the 1946 Act, the outcome would very probably be different from the outcome at the first trial. Because of heightened public and professional scrutiny, the transposition of the time of the crime, the deceptive witness list, the perjuries, and the inflation of the crime to treason, could not be repeated. It is doubtful Congressional members of the JCAE would have, for the second time, agreed to facilitate David Greenglass' perjuries relating to the atom bomb. Without the transposition of the time of the crime, the prosecution's and the judge's use of Cold War history as evidence would have lacked relevancy. The probability of a Not Guilty verdict would be high. The probability of confessions would evaporate. The damage to the Department of Justice for its misconduct in the first trial would have been incalculable.

Even if the defendants were found guilty under the 1946 Act, the penalties would be relatively moderate. The maximum penalty would be ten years imprisonment and a $10,000 fine, since the prosecution would not have been able to show any intent to harm the United States. With time off for good behavior the defendants might be home in four years. As a fallout of such a drastic change in the outcome, the reputations of everyone on the government's side at the first trial would have suffered.

Thus, Stern's overstatement was not simply a lawyer's oratorical flourish. It reflected the deep concern by Brownell and other Justice officials, and by Judge Kaufman, that an extraordinary unraveling of the Rosenberg-Sobell case might occur if a majority of the nine justices did not agree to vacate Justice Douglas' stay of execution.

John Finerty, Bloch's associate, told the justices bluntly that if they did not vacate Justice Douglas' stay, and if a lower court or the Supreme Court should find that a retrial was necessary because the indictment had been based on the wrong law, the case against the defendants would be seen in a far less earth-shaking light than it had been presented. He faulted Justice officials and the prosecutors and the judge for what he said was disregard for the law, and told the justices "There never was a more crooked District Attorney in New York than the one who tried the Rosenbergs."[698]

Fyke Farmer's turn came next, and he made the "wrong law" arguments, and declared the death sentences against the Rosenbergs were illegal and should be vacated by the Court, and the verdicts and sentences should be set aside, and the defendants retried under the proper law.

Earlier, after Stern had completed his arguments, Bloch told the justices he had been wrong in rejecting the advice pressed on him by Farmer and Marshall. His statement was the confession of an exhausted man, a mystified man who, since the arrest of Julius Rosenberg in July 1950, had labored virtually alone, preparing the defense, researching and writing appeals with valid issues — perjury, prosecutorial misconduct, new evidence — who was suddenly, in a few days, surrounded by attorneys he did not know, pressing on him issues that did not grow out of the conduct of the trial, and then usurping his role, filing their own motions and — astonishingly — winning a stay of execution from a justice who had previously done little to help the Rosenbergs. When Bloch took his seat again, many saw him as a displaced man, suddenly irrelevant to a monumental case in which he had successfully protected the Rosenbergs from Judge Kaufman's repeated orders for execution.

When the arguments were over, Chief Justice Vinson said the Court would announce its decision the next morning.

Bloch searches for another courtroom in which to plead for the Rosenbergs...

Bloch could not let the hours go by without trying to open doors into courtrooms in which, however improbable, his clients might find safe haven.

Even as he had evaluated and confessed his errors, Bloch had also evaluated the significance of Brownell's *ex parte* dealings with the Chief Justice. He pondered the meaning of the deliberate and illegal exclusion of the defense from the hearing on Brownell's motion to have the Supreme Court reconvene for the purpose of vacating Douglas' stay. He understood its immediate aim had been to persuade his clients to abandon all hope of judicial salvation; to acknowledge that they alone could save themselves.

Farmer and Marshall had raised a valid issue, but the Brownell-Vinson collusion told Bloch the Farmer-Marshall argument would get short shrift. It was very unlikely, he believed, the justices would even be permitted to discuss the grounds of Douglas' stay. He believed the justices would be compelled to simply vote Yea or Nay on whether to vacate the stay. Brownell and Vinson could be certain a majority would vote Yea, based on their past votes against reviewing the case.

In his desperation to find another courtroom in which to plead, Bloch placed a phone call that evening to Arthur Kinoy, in New York. Kinoy was then a very young lawyer who later became a highly respected Constitutional attorney and teacher, who had offered in the past to help Bloch. Kinoy has described the call.

> When I picked up the phone, Emanuel Bloch, the chief counsel for Julius and Ethel Rosenberg, was on the line from Washington. I had never heard anyone quite so distraught and upset as Manny Bloch sounded. He stuttered, then blurted out, "They may vacate Douglas' stay. The execution may go ahead tomorrow night."[699]

Bloch pleaded with Kinoy to try to get the Court of Appeals to accept some legal issue for consideration, which would result in a stay of execution, however brief, until the issue was resolved or the higher court was called into session again to vacate it on another motion by Brownell. Bloch was desperate to prolong life, one day at a time, for the Rosenbergs, in the belief that every day they lived would bring more lawyers, more judges, more clemency supporters to their side.

Kinoy's account has given us a glimpse of the turmoil in the minds of both the lawyers and the judges who at one time or another were confronted with the Rosenberg-Sobell case.

Kinoy and his young colleagues, Frank Donner and Marshall Perlin, stayed up through the night and, by five o'clock in the morning, had developed a variation of Farmer's argument that Judge Kaufman had lacked the authority to sentence the Rosenbergs to death. On the assumption that the Supreme Court would vacate Douglas' stay that morning, Kinoy would seek out a Court of Appeals judge with whom to file a new motion for a review of the "right law" issue.

> The only way we could do so was by going back to the trial judge in the case, Irving Kaufman, and starting all over again. There was no hope of getting Kaufman to grant any relief, particularly if the Supreme Court

vacated Douglas' stay, for Kaufman's own reputation as a
judge depended upon a full vindication of the propriety
of the death penalty he himself had mandated.[700]

What the young lawyers needed was Kaufman's formal denial of their petition for a stay of execution, which they could then take on an emergency basis
to a Court of Appeals judge. They found two attorneys who were willing to take
the petition to Judge Kaufman that morning, and instructed them not to waste
time trying to persuade the unpersuadable judge, but to get his denial as quickly
as possible.

Meanwhile, Kinoy and Perlin drove to New Haven, Connecticut, where
they waited until they got word that Judge Kaufman's denial was in hand, after
which they went to the office of Chief Judge Thomas Swan, of the Court of
Appeals, where they were joined by a third lawyer, Samuel Gruber. They had
little hope of success, for Swan was among the most conservative of judges. While
waiting they received word that the Supreme Court had vacated Douglas' stay
and that the Rosenbergs were scheduled to be executed that evening.

After about an hour of discussion, Judge Swan told the lawyers the issue
they had raised made sense to him. Kinoy quotes Swan as saying

> I'll tell you what I'll do. I can't grant a stay by myself,
> after the High Court has vacated Douglas' stay. But what
> I can do is convene a panel of this court this afternoon,
> two judges of the court and myself to hear your applica-
> tion and I'll vote for the stay. I'll convene a panel if you
> can get one other member of our court to agree to sit on
> the panel and consider granting the stay.[701]

Swan suggested that they immediately call on Judge Jerome Frank, the
most liberal judge on the court. Frank had dissented from the decision of his
colleagues in respect to Sobell, who he felt should have been tried separately
from the Rosenbergs. It was now two o'clock in the afternoon. Judge Swan put
his car and chauffeur at the lawyers' disposal. Then he telephoned Judge Frank,
who met Kinoy and Perlin at his door, and told them Judge Swan had arranged
an open telephone line between New Haven and Sing Sing, so that
if a stay was issued by the panel, the authorities at Sing Sing could be notified
without delay.

The lawyers spent an hour laying out their case to Judge Frank and answering his questions. Then there was a moment of silence. Kinoy wrote

> Then he said something that I shall never forget. He said
> to us in soft, slow words, "If I were as young as you are,
> I would be sitting where you are now and saying and

arguing what you are arguing. You are right to do so. But when you are as old as I am, you will understand why I cannot do what you ask. I cannot do it."[702]

The attorneys were unable to find another judge who would consider sitting on a panel to decide whether to issue a stay of execution for the Rosenbergs after the Supreme Court had vacated Douglas' stay.

There is no doubt that if the panel had been convened, and if it had granted the stay, the Court of Appeals judges would have been pilloried and threatened with impeachment. The conservative Judge Swan had been willing to take the risk; the liberal Judge Frank chose to live to fight another day.

Six justices abandon co-equality with the Executive and Congress...

Shortly after noon on June 19, the justices took their seats. A motion to hear argument was voted down. By the votes of Chief Justice Vinson and Justices Harold H. Burton, Tom C. Clark, Robert H. Jackson, Sherman Minton and Stanley F. Reed, the stay of executions of the Rosenbergs was vacated. The dissenters were Justices Black, Douglas and Frankfurter.

The dissents revealed that Bloch had properly evaluated the significance of the illegal *ex parte* collusion between Brownell and Vinson. It had been intended to prevent the justices from deliberating on Douglas' grounds for issuing his stay of the Rosenbergs' executions. The collusive duo had obtained what they wanted of the justices: a repeat of the previous refusals by a majority of the justices to review any aspect of the case. The majority of justices had abdicated the deliberative function of their existence and their independence from the Executive, and had agreed, at Brownell-Vinson's bidding, to send a message to the Rosenbergs on Sing Sing's death row: abandon hope in us; if you want to save your lives, a stenographer is waiting.

In his dissent, Justice Black wrote

> Concededly, an individual Justice has power to grant stays where substantial questions are raised. He not merely has power to do so; there is a serious obligation upon him to grant a stay where new substantial questions are presented. Where the life or death of citizens is involved, that obligation is all the heavier. Surely the Court is not here establishing a precedent which will require it to call extra sessions during vacation every time a federal or state official asks it to hasten the electrocution of defendants without affording this Court adequate time or opportunity for exploration and study of serious legal questions.[703]

Justice Frankfurter wrote

> Arguments by counsel are an indispensable adjunct of
> the judicial process, and responsible arguments require
> adequate opportunity for preparation. They must be
> pressed with the force of partisanship. And because
> arguments are partisan, judgment further presupposes
> ample time and an unhurried mind for independent
> study and reflection by judges as a basis for discussion
> in conference...We have not had in this case carefully
> prepared argument. We have not had what cannot exist
> without that essential preliminary. We have not had
> the basis for reaching conclusions and for supporting
> them in opinions. Can it be said that there was time to
> go through the process by which cases are customarily
> decided here?[704]

Justice Douglas wrote

> A suggestion is made that the question comes too late
> — that since the Rosenbergs did not raise this question
> [the 1946 Atomic Energy Act] on appeal, they are barred
> from raising it now. But the question of an unlawful sen-
> tence is never barred. No man or woman should go to
> death under an unlawful sentence merely because his
> lawyer failed to raise the point. It is that function, among
> others, that the Great Writ [Habeas Corpus] serves. I
> adhere to the views stated by Chief Justice Hughes for
> a unanimous Court in Bowen v. Johnston: "It must
> never be forgotten that the writ of habeas corpus is the
> precious safeguard of personal liberty, and there is no
> higher duty than to maintain it unimpaired."[705]

William H. Rehnquist, who thirty three years later became Chief Justice of
the Supreme Court, and who on June 19, 1953, was clerk to Justice Jackson, wrote
to the justice, "It is too bad that drawing and quartering has been abolished," and
that the Rosenbergs were "fitting candidates" for execution.[706]

Philip Elman, at one time Frankfurter's law clerk, commented in an oral
history project by Columbia University

> The Rosenberg case is the most disgusting, saddest,
> despicable episode in the Court's history in my lifetime.
> This has nothing to do with whether the Rosenbergs
> were guilty or innocent, whether Irving Kaufman

should have been impeached for his conduct of the trial, any of those things. I'm thinking about the way the case was handled in the Supreme Court...We knew the Supreme Court was one institution that worked the way it was supposed to work, where people got a fair shake, where equal justice under law was more than a slogan. And here the whole thing was falling down and we were shattered. This was our court, the Supreme Court of the United States for which we had feelings of admiration and closeness.[707]

After the announcement that a majority of the justices had voted to vacate Douglas' stay, Bloch rose asked that the Court stay the executions, so that he would have time to make one more appeal to the President for clemency. Marshall also moved for a stay, to argue his point that Congress had nowhere given the Court the authority to override a stay by a justice of the Supreme Court. Vinson then declared the justices would reconvene later that afternoon to announce the Court's decisions on the two motions, and the justices withdrew.

Within minutes, however, the justices returned and Vinson announced that the motions by Bloch and Marshall had been denied. Black alone had dissented.

Brownell knew he had involved himself and the Chief Justice in a major violation of the judicial rules, and of the Rosenbergs' rights to due process; he may have been unaware that the FBI's and Judge Kaufman's communications had left a paper trail of what he and Justice Vinson had done, which became public in the 1970s. He created his own version of the events. In *Advising Ike,* published in 1993, Brownell omitted any reference to his participation in the meeting with Justice Vinson, and wrote it had taken place *after* Justice Douglas issued his stay.

When the date for execution approached, Justice William Douglas of the Supreme Court granted a stay of execution on a point of law not theretofore raised. He did this shortly after the Court had adjourned for the summer and without consulting the other justices. I thereupon instructed the Justice Department to petition Chief Justice Vinson to call an unprecedented special meeting of the Court to review the stay. He granted the petition, and the Court met and reversed Justice Douglas' action.[708]

What one of the Justices knew...

For one of the justices of the Supreme Court, who had had a liberal background before he became a justice — Felix Frankfurter, a defender of Sacco and

Vanzetti, the two Italian-born unionists who were executed in Massachusetts in 1927 — the demand on him and the other justices to decide the fate of the Rosenbergs without reviewing their trial and deliberating on the issues, had been made all the more difficult because Frankfurter had knowledge he had acquired about the atom bomb during the war. His knowledge had a direct bearing on the prosecution's claim to the scientific secrecy surrounding the atom bomb.

According to an April 26, 1945 memorandum prepared by Frankfurter, in 1939, the year in which he became a Supreme Court justice, he had met Niels Bohr, an eminent Danish physicist who had won the Nobel Prize for his work on atomic structure in 1922, and they became warm friends. When the Nazis invaded Denmark in 1940, Bohr and his family became "house prisoners" (Bohr's mother was Jewish). In 1943, they escaped, after which Bohr began working in England on the development of the atom bomb; toward the end of 1943, Bohr joined the scientists at Los Alamos, New Mexico to continue working on the bomb.

Frankfurter's memorandum stated that

> Some time before Professor Bohr's arrival in this country I had been approached by some distinguished American scientists, because of past academic associations, to advise them on a matter that seemed to them of the greatest importance to our national interest and presented to them difficulties with which they, as scientists, were unable to cope since they were problems not within their technical competence. I had thus become aware of X — aware, that is, that there was such a thing as X and of its significance, but I have never been told and do not at this moment know anything that could convey to anyone any valuable information about it. Knowing, however, the general range of Professor Bohr's work in the field of physics, I had reason for assuming that his gifts were being availed of for the common cause.[709]

Subsequently, at a lunch with Bohr, Frankfurter wrote

> I made a very oblique reference to X, so that if I was right in my assumption that Professor Bohr was sharing in it, he would know that I knew something about it, and, if not, I could easily turn my question into other channels...it soon became clear to both of us that two such persons, who had been so long and so deeply preoccupied with the menace of Hitlerism and who were so deeply engaged in the common cause, could talk about the implications of X without either making any

disclosure to the other...Professor Bohr then expressed to me his conviction that X might be one of the greatest boons to mankind or might become the greatest disaster...He was a man weighed down with a conscience and with an almost overwhelming solicitude for the dangers of our people.

Frankfurter thought it was his duty to personally relay to President Roosevelt the concerns expressed by Bohr and by American scientists as well. Using language almost identical to that used by Secretary of War Henry Stimson in 1945, Frankfurter wrote

> that it might be disastrous to the whole endeavor of achieving sound international relations with Russia, if Russia should learn on her own about X rather than that the existence of X should be utilized by this country and Great Britain as a means of exploring the possibility of effective international arrangements with Russia.

Frankfurter added

> Professor Bohr made me feel that it would not be too difficult, on the basis of the scientific situation antedating the war, for Russia to gain the necessary information, to say nothing of other factors that militate against assuring non-disclosure.[710]

President Roosevelt subsequently met directly with Bohr, and encouraged further communications from Frankfurter and Bohr on atomic weapons and international relations.

Frankfurter's April 26, 1945 memorandum was apparently addressed to General Leslie Groves' attention, and was probably written at Groves' request, since Groves kept a very close watch on atomic scientists and their friends.

The memorandum and possibly some related documents, were put into a sealed envelope, to which was appended a statement:

> The attached envelope is the property of Mr. Justice Felix Frankfurter and is to be returned to him, unopened, when military security permits. The envelope contains secret official papers pertaining to the MED [Manhattan Engineering Project, code-name for development of atomic weapons].

> This envelope should be opened by no one other than Mr. Justice Frankfurter in his lifetime. In the event of his

> death before it is returned to him, it should be turned
> over to the then Secretary of War with an explanation
> of what it contains. Such an explanation can be given by
> Major General L. R. Groves, Lt. Col. John Lansdale, Jr.,
> or Lt. Col. William A. Consodine.[711]

A handwritten note at the bottom of the statement reads, "Returned to Mr. Frankfurter 1/15/47."

The memorandum and the "sealed envelope" statement by Groves reveal that scientists in general, among them Niels Bohr, one of the most senior scientists involved in the development of the atom bomb, believed there were no scientific or engineering secrets impeding the Soviet Union's development of the atom bomb, contrary to the claim the prosecution had made at the Rosenberg-Sobell trial.

One of the persons named as qualified to explain the contents of the sealed envelope containing Frankfurter's memorandum, Lt. Col. John Lansdale, Jr., was a prosecution witness at the Rosenberg-Sobell trial, testifying on secrecy measures at the Los Alamos atom bomb facility, during which he testified Neils Bohr was code-named Nicholas Baker at Los Alamos, and Bohr

> was a Danish scientist whom I can best describe as being
> the pioneer and granddaddy, you might say, of nuclear
> physics.[712]

A question for Frankfurter, first posed in 1952, when the initial appeal for review was filed with the Supreme Court by Bloch, must have been whether he should have informed the prosecution and the defense that he had personal information bearing on the secrecy aspect of the prosecution's case, and when he should have made that disclosure. Conceivably, the disclosure might have been grounds for a request by Justice officials that he recuse himself, at least on any appeal involving the matter of secrecy. It is also possible Groves or Lansdale, knowing what Frankfurter knew, might have alerted Justice officials and the prosecution, who decided not to ask for recusal because that would have alerted the defense to explore the secrecy issue more deeply. In any case, a majority of justices voted not to review the case, making the recusal issue moot.

At this moment, when it was clear to Frankfurter that the Rosenbergs' lives were hours, not weeks or months away from being terminated, a disclosure by a fourteen-year veteran of the Court that he had first-hand knowledge that the opinions of the highest scientific authorities in the world were opposed to the opinions of the laymen who constituted the judge, the prosecutors and the jury, could conceivably have had a salutary effect on other justices of the Court, and on Appeals judges like Jerome Frank, who might have taken heart from Frankfurter's boldness.

Frankfurter was an honorable man. One may say that, in the Rosenberg case, Frankfurter stumbled by his silence, although we may want to recognize that he was, like many other Americans in the 1950s, pushed before he stumbled.

Justice Frankfurter had voted not to vacate Justice Douglas' stay, and would later write an expanded opinion on why he did so.

The Rosenbergs address the president and write a farewell to their sons...

Bloch had handed Solicitor General Stern another plea for clemency addressed to the President, and returned to his hotel. Not long afterward the President issued his reply

> When in their own solemn judgment the Tribunals of the United States have adjudged them guilty and their sentence just, I will not intervene in this matter. The executions of two human beings is a grave matter. But even graver is the thought of the millions of dead whose death may be directly attributable to what these spies have done. I deny the petition.[713]

Bloch was determined to try once more. He left his hotel and took a hand-written letter, dated June 15, from Ethel Rosenberg, addressed to the President, and hurried past a hastily reconstituted clemency Vigil to the White House gates and asked a guard to give the letter to the President.

Ethel Rosenberg's letter read, in part

> At various intervals during the two long and bitter years I have spent in the Death House at Sing Sing, I have had the impulse to address myself to the President of the United States. Always, in the end, a certain innate shyness, an embarrassment almost, comparable to that which the ordinary person feels in the presence of the great and the famous, prevailed upon me not to do so.
>
> * * *
>
> True, to date, you have not seen fit to spare our lives. Be that as it may, it is my humble belief that the burdens of your office and the exigencies of the times have allowed of no genuine opportunity, as yet, for your more personal consideration.
>
> It is chiefly the death sentence I would entreat you to ponder. I would entreat you to ask yourself whether that sentence does not serve the ends of "force and violence"

rather than an enlightened justice. Even granting the assumption that the convictions had been properly procured (and there now exists incontrovertible evidence to the contrary), the steadfast denial of guilt, extending over a protracted period of solitary confinement and enforced separation from our loved ones, makes of the death penalty an act of vengeance.

* * *

Take counsel with the mother of your only son; her heart which understands my grief so well and my longing to see my sons grown to manhood like her own, with loving husband at my side even as you are at hers...[714]

The President's quick reply to her letter, given through a White House public relations aide, was

The President states, in his conviction, it adds nothing to the issues covered in his statement this afternoon.[715]

Ethel Rosenberg, on behalf of her husband and herself, wrote to their sons that day.

Only this morning it looked like we might be together again after all. Now that this cannot be I want so much for you to know all that I have come to know. Unfortunately I may write only a few simple words; the rest your own lives must teach you, even as mine taught me.

* * *

Be comforted, then, that we were serene and understood with the deepest kind of understanding that civilization had not as yet progressed to the point where life did not have to be lost for the sake of life; and that we were comforted in the sure knowledge that others would carry on after us.

We wish we might have had the tremendous joy and gratification of living our lives out with you...Always remember that we were innocent and could not wrong our conscience.[716]

Emily Alman addressing a grieving crowd on 17th Street in New York City, as
they hear the news that the executions have taken place and their clemency
efforts have failed. June 19, 1953.

Chapter 12 | 6,000,027, counting Berlin, Moscow, and Prague

6,000,029, counting New York...

Bloch was no longer trying to salvage another day of life for his clients. He was trying to win *hours*. He appealed to Judge Kaufman not to execute the Rosenbergs that evening, which was the beginning of the Jewish Sabbath, but to wait until the Sabbath was over. Judge Kaufman did not make an immediate reply.

The executions had been set for the previous day at 11 p.m., and it was assumed by everyone the time for the executions on June 19 would be unchanged. But the momentum created by Attorney General Brownell for applying terminal pressure on the Rosenbergs to confess had been heightened by the high Court's compliant nullification of Douglas' stay of execution. A decision was made by Justice officials and the judge to notify the Rosenbergs that they would be executed three hours earlier than the schedule called for. The reason given them — and the public — for their early executions was that Justice officials and the judge wanted to show their respect for the Jewish Sabbath.

It became necessary to send out a search party to find and bring in the executioner, who had not expected to be on hand to make his preparations until 9 p.m.[717]

I was in Washington when the justices, undoubtedly not entirely at peace with themselves, but at least free of fear of the wrath of those they had silently acknowledged to be their masters in the Executive and the Congress, hung up their robes to leave the Capital. Emily had returned to New York, on the previous evening. On the telephone, she told me she was concerned with what might happen on New York's streets in a few hours. "I can't tell you what it's like," she said. "People can't find words to describe what they know will happen. Everyone is tight-lipped. I'm tight-lipped. The phones are tight-lipped. People call and ask if there's any hope and I tell them, 'Yesterday, there was Justice Douglas, and maybe an hour from now there may be Justice X or maybe clemency,' and they hang up." I said I would try to get a flight back to New York within the hour, but it was raining and there might be a delay. "I'm with Aaron, right now," I told Emily, "and we're talking to the Vigil marchers who didn't go home after Douglas' stay yesterday. They're leaving Inspiration House, and rounding up others at Union Station or Greyhound, to return to the Vigil at the White House. Aaron wants to stay with them."

I did not tell Emily what Aaron and I observed. There were more groups of recognizable anti-clemency groups in Lafayette park opposite the White House than we had ever seen before. They didn't carry signs. But they did carry baseball bats and lead pipes. They milled about the park, eyeing the Vigil participants. The police studiously ignored them.

A light rain was falling. I took a cab to the airport.

The authorities debate whom to execute first...

Justice officials had to decide the order in which to execute the Rosenbergs. The Warden favored executing Ethel Rosenberg first because he believed Julius Rosenberg would break down and deliver the sought-for confession. J. Edgar Hoover overruled him on a point of public relations.

> Nothing would embarrass the Bureau more than to have the wife, and mother of two children, die and the husband survive. It would, Lou Nichols [a high-ranking Hoover aide] agreed, be a public relations nightmare.[718]

Hoover had a special problem. He had urged Justice officials to indict Ethel Rosenberg, not for information she might have about an espionage conspiracy, but because her indictment for a capital offense, to use his words, "might serve as a lever" to compel her husband's confession.[719] His agency had been unable to provide any evidence of her complicity in the alleged conspiracy,[720] and he may have been concerned that his recommendation might become known one day. According to his aides, he was certain when Ethel Rosenberg realized the execution of her husband had actually been carried through, she would confess to save her life.

Shortly before the sun went down to signal the coming of the Sabbath, the Warden finished his check-list in the death chamber: the five required witnesses were in their seats; the Justice officials' signatures were on the forms for the rental of the electric chair from the State of New York; the voltage tests had been completed to the executioner's satisfaction; the line-of-sight arrangements had been completed between the Warden and the FBI agents who would be observing each of the condemned prisoner's behavior for signs of willingness that the death chamber become their confessional, upon which, by agreed-upon hand signals to the Warden, he would stay the executioner's hand. Or would not, as the case might be.

The Warden signaled his aides to ignite the stake that was called the electric chair.

At 8:02 p.m., Julius Rosenberg was declared dead.

At 8:08 p.m., Ethel Rosenberg was declared dead.

A Hoover biographer noted that Alan H. Belmont, a top Hoover aide, had to repeat to Hoover three times, that Ethel Rosenberg was dead before Hoover gave any sign of comprehension that the executions were over.[721]

Emily had searched for a place in New York where, on the early evening of June 19, the uncharacteristically tight-lipped citizens might stand together in prayer, in inextinguishable hope, in stubborn faith, that after sunset the couple in Sing Sing would still be alive. The City's leaders and "interested persons" who held the keys to Union Square, where bronze statues of George Washington and Abe Lincoln look down from time to time on gatherings of citizens seeking redress, granted a permit for the gathering.

As the first of thousands of clemency supporters entered Union Square, the police announced the permit would not be honored. A phalanx of officers pushed 10,000 tight-lipped and distraught citizens to 17th Street, just north of Union Square and then blocked off all entrances to the street. Joseph Brainin, Emily, I and others spoke to the gathering from a hastily erected platform, with a hastily erected public address system.

Volunteer messengers ran to the platform from a public telephone booth a street away, bringing news from a lawyer on the scene in Washington, and from radio reports. Emily told the gathering that not all was lost, that our lawyers were still knocking at judges' doors, that a Vigil was still on at the White House. At 8:03 p.m. Emily's voice faltered for a moment, and then she told the gathering there was still hope of saving Ethel Rosenberg, and at 8:08 p.m., the police shut down the public address system.

Aaron Schneider described to Emily what happened at the Vigil when the news of the executions came through.

> ...one of the FBI guys comes over and tells me that the Rosenbergs had just been executed. They started crying on the picket line. I looked around me. We had over five hundred people on the picket line, 500 people crying. Across the street the hoodlums were waiting for us. On other streets there were people watching us quietly. I could feel the sadism all around us. I looked at my 500 mourners. I knew I had to get them out of Washington. The Police Chief was standing a few feet away. "Take your people across to the Park," he told me. It would be one bloody night if I did. I took his arm, and when he tried to shake me off I held on tighter. "You and me are going to march these people to the buses that are waiting for them," I told him. I was counting on the cops protecting us in order to protect their chief. I knew that if he really wanted to, he could shake himself loose. He didn't. Maybe he had a thought about something pleasant. Maybe he figured, what the hell, just this one time. So we marched arm in arm, him and me, the 500 crying

people, and the cops. The buses pulled out and everybody went home, Emily.[722]

That evening Emily telephoned the Warden and identified herself, and said she wanted to claim the bodies of the Rosenbergs, that they were to be buried in a Jewish cemetery in accordance with Jewish ritual and rabbinical law. The Warden, she told us, seemed pleased.

The *New York Times* reconsidered its denial that the Pope had intervened for clemency. On June 21, 1953, a *Times* review of the case observed

> Pope Pius XII, while avoiding any discussion of the mer-
> its of the case, had expressed a hope that justice would
> be tempered by mercy.[723]

The *Daily News*[724] and the *Daily Mirror*, two of New York City's most vigor-ous anti-clemency newspapers, estimated that twelve thousand mourners filled the funeral hall and the adjoining streets, although the *Daily Mirror* acknowl-edged that the Committee claimed more than twice that number. It also reported

> Twenty five picked detectives of the Special Services
> Squad watched for Red Agitators.[725]

The local Fur Workers Union, at the request of the Committee, had pro-vided a 24-hour honor guard to watch over the caskets. The furrier-men came bearing flags and black armbands. Their presence — they were all very muscular and serious — helped keep order in the funeral home and at the cemetery.

During the service Emanuel Bloch, exhausted and enraged, used the word "murder" to describe what the officials and judges and the president had done to the Rosenbergs. We were now living, he told the mourners, under a fascist dictatorship in civilian garb, for what had happened to the Rosenbergs could not have occurred in a democratic America. (Seven months later, at age 52, Bloch died of a heart attack, making moot an action by several lawyers to have him disbarred for his criticisms of the Attorney General and President Eisenhower at the Rosenbergs' funeral.)

Rabbi Abraham Cronbach told the mourners that their most difficult task was to

> avoid hatred, rancor, and retaliation. Well worth heed-
> ing are those ancient Jewish words: "Thou shalt take no
> revenge. Thou shalt bear no grudge...Thou shalt not hate
> thy brother in thy heart." Though the judges and the
> executive rendered a verdict which broke our hearts, we
> must remember that they did the right as they under-
> stood the right. Still, we should not hate. We should not
> be vindictive. Hatred killed Julius and Ethel Rosenberg.

Vindictiveness destroyed this young man and woman. We who achieved a spiritual triumph when we struggled to avert this tragedy — let us not now succumb to spiritual defeat.[726]

There was a brief stirring of disapproval among the mourners, but the rabbi went on.

Let us give our detractors not a scintilla of an excuse for impugning the caliber of our citizenship. Let us make it unmistakably clear that we cannot possibly gain by anything through which America is injured. We gain if America gains. We lose if America loses. Our citizenship should stand beyond reproach.

These things we must do if we would bring about a brighter day for our America and a happier time for all humanity.

The rabbi was appealing to human stubbornness, to make a path where there was none, over stones, over blood, behind and before the weeping mothers, before and behind the falsely stoic fathers, before and behind the faces of bewildered children, before and behind our puzzled selves, seeking the way to an elusive humanhood…

The Committee members look inside themselves…

For a brief few weeks that followed the executions, the Committee members became incommunicative with one another. What was there to say? In the minds of each of us there appeared self-inflicted judgments of personal failure. We had adopted policies that had not won enough supporters to the Rosenbergs' and Sobell's cause. We had rejected policies that might have won those supporters. We had misread events, overstated our reach, been too timid about some issues, too aggressive about other issues, we became too broad, we had remained too parochial, we had put off going to meetings that might have made the difference, we had fallen asleep on buses and trains when we should have been awake and marvelously creative.

Mingling with these critical thoughts and moods there appeared to us another set of perceptions. We were seared with the mystery of the human spirit, its awesome surprises, its embrace of love unto death, its dangerous insistence that suffering would not be our crazy species' immutable fate. We found ourselves tempted or driven by despair to visions of an unreal time, saw our endless multitudes approaching a broad and golden infinite place, heard our species' exalted cries: At last! At last!

At last what?

It was easier to speak of matters farther from the depths and closer to our line of sight. We spoke of sorrow not only for the Rosenbergs but for the nation. We told ourselves the heirs of the Founders deserved better than a government of men who were fearful of obeying the laws and the Constitution, fearful of being Americans. We asked, 'How much farther down a dark and lawless road would they take us?'

Emily kept telling us not to be afraid of looking inward, outward, downward, upward, whateverward. "We are all one species," she said, "we and those we despise and those who despise us." She put into words the terrible knowledge we had acquired. Otherwise ordinary human beings who, at some long past time in their lives, would never have thought they would one day put two humans to the stake, did so to the applause of their kin, colleagues and mentors. They could not stop themselves, she said, because they were afraid to stop themselves. And what about us? she asked. Where will our own fears take us? She reminded us that Rabbi Cronbach told us hatred had killed the Rosenbergs and warned us against being guided by hatred ourselves.

We sat in our apartments with one another, those whose advice had often prevailed and those whose advice had often been tabled, without rancor. Emily asked, What have we learned? We were not certain. We said we learned how little the many ask of their leaders and how little they receive. Our leaders, we said, thrive in the altitudes of power and wealth and intrigue and wars, while the overwhelming numbers of us pray for lifetimes of warmth and intimacy for ourselves and our children. We learned, we said, that this is not the concern of our leaders.

In the midst of our irritability and sadness, Emily turned to Brainin and said, "Joe, do the thing you always do."

Brainin looked at his watch and said, "Friends, the clock is ticking for Sobell..."

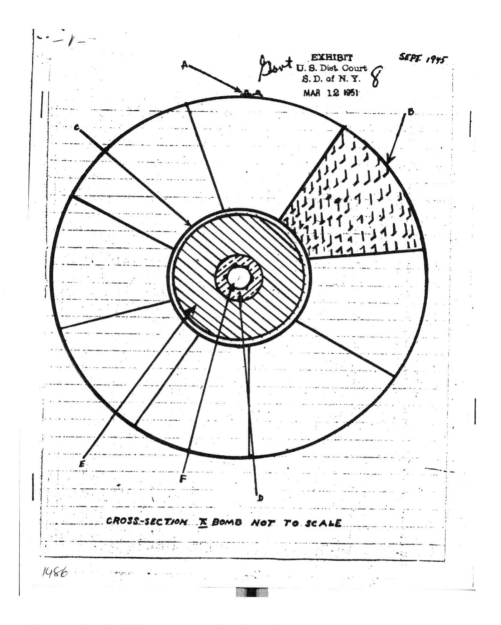

Prosecution Exhibit 8, purported to be a depiction of the atom bomb, hand-drawn by David Greenglass for trial in 1951, recreating from memory a similar drawing he testified that he had drawn and given to Julius Rosenberg in 1945. On seeing it in 1966, Henry Linschitz, a chemist who had headed up an explosives section at Los Alamos, described Exhibit 8 as a "childlike caricature."

Chapter 13 | The life of the cosmos goes on

Whispers of truth in the media...

With the departure of the executioner, an inescapable truth must have begun to haunt Justice officials and Judge Kaufman, and even Saypol and Cohn. Not even confessions by the defendants would have brought closure to the case. However patriotic or fearful the officials' motives had been, they had created an uneasy theatrical bedazzlement, a gnarl of tales told by terror-stricken witnesses, a tangled mis-shuffle of history, all of which held together for the few weeks it took to bring on the verdicts, after which the tales began to unravel. The officials had created so contrived a case that, in the end, even if the defendants had confessed, the confessions would have been judged by many to have also been contrived, that is, fiction inspired by a wish to live. The blessings of closure were more distant than ever.

Nine months after the executions, on March 17, 1954, the *New York Times* carried the remarks of Dr. James Beckerly, Director of the AEC Classification office, who had been directly involved in the preparation of David Greenglass' testimony at the trial in March 1951. According to the *New York Times*, Dr. Beckerly said

> it was time to stop 'kidding' ourselves about atomic 'secrets' and time to stop believing that Soviet scientists are incompetent.

> The atom bomb and the hydrogen bomb were not stolen from us by spies, Dr. Beckerly emphasized. Espionage played a minor role in the attainment of successful weapons by the Soviets, he said.[727]

One month later, the prestigious *Columbia Law Review*, while echoing the prosecution's complaint about the 25-month "protracted" duration of the Rosenberg appeals, nevertheless found the trial deeply flawed. On the matter of the inflammatory accusations in the courtroom that the defendants were Communists, the *Review* stated that such accusations would "induce the jury more readily to return a verdict of guilty."[728]

> Had the trial judge excluded such testimony he would thereby have forestalled any taint of prejudice, but he might also have precluded a verdict of guilty.[729]

On the vacating of Douglas' stay, the *Review* stated

> While members of the Supreme Court have consistently granted stays without question as to the source of their

power or the validity of their orders, the action of the
Supreme Court in vacating the stay is unprecedented.[730]

***

The inevitable conclusion is that in this last stage of an
extraordinarily protracted litigation, the rights of the
Rosenbergs did not receive the precise and extensive
consideration that must characterize the administration
of the criminal law.[731]

Two months later, there came about a most unlikely casualty of the
Rosenberg-Sobell case. General Leslie Groves, who had organized the atom-
bomb research and development effort, and who had reported back to his commander in August 1945, that he had fulfilled his mission, suffered a humiliating
fall from grace. At a hearing on May 10, 1954, on whether to deprive Dr. J. Robert
Oppenheimer, the chief scientist of the atom bomb project, of his security clear-
ance on suspicion of disloyalty, a discussion arose about the Rosenberg-Sobell
case. General Groves commented

No, I think the data that went out in the case of the
Rosenbergs was of minor value. I would never say that
in public. Again, that is something, while it is not secret,
I think should be kept very quiet because irrespective of
the value of that in the over-all picture, the Rosenbergs
deserved to hang and I would not like to say anything
that would make people say General Groves thinks they
didn't do much damage after all.[732]

An interoffice FBI memorandum of May 11, 1954, described the reaction
of AEC officials to General Groves' comments.

On May 10, 1954, Dave Teeple, Assistant to AEC
Chairman Strauss, advised that the AEC was delet-
ing portions of the testimony of General Groves from
the transcript of the Oppenheimer hearings, since it
was felt that the statement made by Groves was irrelevant and was unfortunate in that it could be used
by the Communists for propaganda in the event the
[Greenglass] testimony was ever released to the press.[733]

The writer of the memorandum concluded that if Groves' views became
known, the Communists would claim that "the Rosenbergs were executed for the
furnishing of information of minor value to the Russians."

In *Now It Can Be Told*, General Groves' account of the creation of the atom
bomb, there is no mention of the Rosenbergs or of the Oppenheimer hearing, but

he cites a letter of July 20, 1943, in which he informed an official that he wanted Oppenheimer on the atom bomb project "irrespective of the information which you have concerning Mr. Oppenheimer. He is absolutely essential to the project."[734] The pejorative information about the scientist whose exemplary leadership gave us the atom bomb was, of course, that Oppenheimer was a Communist.

Schoolmasters and Justice officials retaliate against the sons...

After the executions of the Rosenbergs, Michael Rosenberg, who was ten years old, and Robert, who was six, lived with friends of their parents, Sonia and Ben Bach, a chicken-feed salesman, in Toms River, New Jersey, who had two children of their own. In 1954, New Jersey school officials declared that the Rosenberg boys, who had been attending a Toms River school for a year and a half, were not New Jersey residents and would no longer be permitted to attend New Jersey's schools.

From among a number of offers of asylum, including one from a Protestant school in France, and another from a communal farm in Israel, and offers of adoption by the Bachs and by other friends and supporters of the Rosenbergs, a decision was made by the boys' paternal grandmother, Sophie Rosenberg, and by Emanuel Bloch, that the boys should be placed with Anne and Abel Meeropol in New York City, where public opinion would be more likely to shield the boys from politically compliant schoolmasters.

Anne Meeropol, a nursery school director, had lost two children at childbirth; Abel Meeropol, whose professional name was Lewis Allan, was a playwright and successful songwriter, his two best known songs being *Strange Fruit*, made famous by the blues singer Billie Holiday, and *The House I live In*, which he wrote with Earl Robinson, and which was sung by Frank Sinatra at a White House performance during President Richard Nixon's administration.

The Rosenberg boys, according to their account in *We Are Your Sons*,[735] were happy with the Meeropols, but they suffered another loss in1954, with the death of their closest friend and protector, Emanuel Bloch.

With Bloch's death, a semi-private and ostensibly non-political group, the New York Society for the Prevention of Cruelty to Children, filed a petition to remove the Rosenbergs' sons from the Meeropols, on the grounds that the children were being exploited and could therefore not develop "normal and healthy attitudes." The Society's petition gave no examples of the purported exploitation.

One evening, a Society officer and an official of the Jewish Board of Guardians and two policemen came to the Meeropols' home, claiming that the children had been ordered by New York Judge Jacob Panken of the Children's Court to appear before him that evening, and threatened to take the boys by force if the Meeropols tried to stop them. The Meeropols called several lawyers to seek help, and one of them reached the judge, who denied that he had ordered the children to be brought to court that evening.

The next day a hearing was held before Judge Panken, who ordered the children to be removed to a shelter in upstate New York. On the following day Bloch's father, Alexander, and two other attorneys: Gloria Algrin and Malcolm Sharp, obtained a writ of *habeas corpus* for the release of the children. At a hearing before Justice Robert McNally, the judge ordered the children brought to court the next morning.

On the following day, Justice McNally placed the children with their paternal grandmother. The surrogate court also appointed the grandmother and Kenneth D. Johnson, Dean of the New York School of Social Work, as co-guardians of the children.

Justice officials were apparently displeased that the attempt to separate the children from their grandmother and the Meeropols had failed. In a letter dated May 3, 1954, from Warren Olney III, Assistant Attorney General, Criminal Division, to a probation officer of the New York City Domestic Relations Court, who had written him for information about the Meeropols, Olney replied that he could not reveal information on the Meeropols contained in the FBI files, but he could pass on to her information "contained in public sources and [that] may be of interest you."

Olney informed the probation officer

> The records of the Board of Elections, Bronx, New York,
> reflect that Anne Meeropol registered to vote as an affili-
> ate of the American Labor Party for the years 1937-1944
> and for 1952.[736]

Olney wrote that the House Un-American Activities Committee and the California Committee on Un-American Activities had both found the American Labor Party to be under "Communist domination." On July 24, 1947, Olney wrote, the *Daily Worker* had praised a satire on investigating committees "by Lewis Allan and Elmer Bernstein." Also, a publication, *Jewish Life*, that had been described as a Communist publication by the California Committee on Un-American Activities, had featured poems by Lewis Allan in three of its issues, and that the *Daily People's World*, which the California Committee described as a Communist newspaper, had, on May 10, 1951, "carried a poem by Lewis Allen entitled 'Teacher, May I Leave the Room?'"

Olney also revealed

> Records of the Department of Health, New York City,
> reflect on Certificate 9200 that Abel Meeropolsky was
> born in Manhattan, New York, on July 14, 1903. His

> father was listed as Leo Meeropolsky, born in Russia, age
> 30, and his mother Sophie Blum, also born in Russia.

In all, Olney cited 25 items he believed constituted derogatory information about the Meeropols.

In 1957, Dean Johnson helped finalize the adoption of the boys by the Meeropols.

Michael Meeropol became a professor of economics; Robert Meeropol is a member of the Massachusetts State Bar and is head of the Rosenberg Fund for Children, which provides grants for educational and emotional needs of children whose parents have been imprisoned or otherwise sorely penalized for union or civil rights activities, and to young people who have themselves been penalized for such activities. The brothers have written two books on their respective journeys from childhood to maturity: *We are Your Sons*, published in 1975, written jointly, and *An Execution in the Family*, published in 2003, written by Robert Meeropol. Michael Meeropol also edited *The Rosenberg Letters*, published in 1994.

The FBI Director retaliates against the authors...

Among the FBI documents made available in the 1970s, a small number related to the authors. One set of documents revealed that FBI Director J. Edgar Hoover had determined we might be the neighbors to whom the Rosenbergs, according to a jailhouse informant, gave a Leica camera and $7000 for safekeeping. This would have made us accomplices of the defendants.

After the execution of the Rosenbergs, we became farmers in New Jersey for thirteen years, and it was in the third year of our farming that the FBI decided that the "lead" given them by the informant in 1951 was now "hot," and began an investigation to discover what we had done with the $7000 and the camera.[737] The FBI questioned our relatives, neighbors, grocer, pharmacist, grain supplier, mortgage holder and others, everyone except the authors. Our nearest farm neighbor agreed to permit the FBI to build a potato storage bin, at taxpayer expense, very close to, and with a direct view of our farmhouse. The potato bin was constantly occupied by immaculately dressed FBI agents with binoculars in hand.

On October 23, 1956, the Newark, N.J. FBI office notified Hoover that the surveillances revealed

> they are home most of the time...to perform the routine
> duties of feeding chickens and gathering eggs.[738]

The Newark FBI office said that it will plan "towards the development of a highly confidential source which may be of value in this case."

Four months later, on February 19, 1957, the Newark office reported that it was unable to determine whether Emily or David had "offered a Leica camera for sale or where they brought film for processing." But the Newark office had good news for the Director. The local pharmacist was willing to notify the Newark FBI office if we brought film to him for processing, and would

> make marks on any film returned to ALMAN and suggest to him that these marks indicate something is wrong with his camera and that he should bring it in for an examination.[739]

Our camera, however, was an inexpensive pawnshop-rescue Miranda, and our finances were unenviable. To save the farm from foreclosure, Emily had begun to drive a station wagon load of crated eggs to sell door-to-door in New York City twice weekly, except for one week when the station wagon was repossessed and we had to ask our mothers, with whose financial help we had made the down payment on the farm, to chip in to retrieve the wagon. The most valuable object retrieved with the wagon was Emily's doctoral thesis on the effects of hallucinogenic drugs on the self-perceptions of non-addicted people.

To discover whether we had $7000, the FBI agents recruited a local grocer to tell us he wanted to get out of the grocery business and would sell his store to us, but only for cash, so he would not have to report the transaction to the IRS. But we had become farmers in order to realize personal ambitions, Emily to earn a doctorate in sociology at the New School for Social Research, I to complete a novel. The flexibility of farm life suited us and our two daughters' needs. In any case, we were in enough debt to last us for quite a while, without incurring more to buy a grocery store we didn't want. We thanked the storekeeper, but declined his offer. It was not until we read the FBI account of the investigation that we realized who had led the grocer to make his offer.

On June 23, 1957, with no progress to report, the Newark FBI agents proposed to Hoover that they ask us directly whether we had ever been given $7000 and a Leica camera by Julius Rosenberg.[740]

Three weeks later, on July 18, 1957, Hoover replied to the Newark FBI office in a two page memorandum, on each page of which he warned the Newark FBI office not to attempt to speak directly to the Almans. He wrote

> an approach to the Almans at this time might be utilized as a basis for directing adverse criticism of the Bureau's investigative activities.[741]

We have never been able to understand exactly what Mr. Hoover's statement meant.

The "investigation" lingered for a while longer, but the FBI's potato bin was a poor shield against hot weather. The constant presence of ants, spiders, mosquitoes and snakes were troublesome to the FBI agents, and finally only the potatoes and the happy potato farmer occupied the bin, and when we woke in the mornings and looked out our windows, there were no peeping Edgars for us to wave at.

House Un-American Activities Committee retaliates against the Committee...

After two critical books on the Rosenberg-Sobell case, William A. Reuben's *The Atom Spy Hoax*[742] and John Wexley's *The Judgment of Julius and Ethel Rosenberg*[743] appeared, the House Un-American Activities Committee (HUAC) subpoenaed the authors, and many other people who had been active in the clemency campaign, to hearings in Washington, D.C.

We were living on our little chicken farm in New Jersey at the time. The HUAC hearings became a great source of comfort to us. Our farm was in a highly conservative rural community, and we were one of the few Jewish families in the area. We initially believed news of our involvement in the new trial/clemency campaign might arouse hostility and possible violence against us and our daughters.

Instead, our neighbors and the merchants we dealt with, with very few exceptions, chose to wait and see. Many of them had had their own unhappy experiences with government bureaucrats and office-holders. Indeed, a fellow New Jerseyan — a former chairman of HUAC, Representative J. Parnell Thomas — had recently been convicted and sentenced to three years imprisonment for padding his payroll with relatives. So our neighbors were hardly naive about the uses to which some public servants put their power.

The New Jersey newspapers ran front-page stories on our testimony at the HUAC hearings, but few of our neighbors or Emily's egg-route customers chose to withdraw their neighborliness or their patronage. Although our neighbors chose not to query us on what they had heard and read, we voluntarily enlightened them.

The authors testified at the HUAC hearings that the Committee had raised $300,000, from the late fall of 1951 to the end of June 1953.[744] HUAC accountants studied the Committee's well-kept financial records, which had been audited by a CPA of impeccable reputation. HUAC had access to bills, ticket stubs, and receipts from merchants, printers, buses, railroads, and airlines, records of funds sent to the Committee by other committees and so on. We kept from HUAC the names of the many thousands of men and women who sent us, on average, about $40 over a period of approximately 20 months. HUAC's accountants found that the funds had been spent on legal fees, on printing and distributing 10,000 copies of the trial record, numerous fact sheets, on advertising, on bus and train and plane fares, and on hotels at which HUAC's members would never be found.

The HUAC chairman declined to call any of the scientists who had spoken out for clemency or the clergy who had met with the president or any of the attorneys or judges who had expressed any doubts about the fairness of the trial and sentences. Instead, HUAC subpoenaed activists of clemency committees from a dozen states to ask them HUAC's standard inquisitorial question: Are you now, or have you ever been a member of the Communist Party?

Emily wanted to respond to the question in one of two ways. Her first choice was to honestly say that she was not and never had been a Communist, that she considered herself, in fact, an anti-Communist. She suggested I say I had once been a Communist but had not been one for at least fifteen years. Her second choice was that we reply that the Constitution protected Americans from having to answer to elected or appointed officials for their political beliefs or affiliations. In 1787, the Founders saw to it that the new government's Constitution would forbid officials to ask such questions.

The problem with Emily's second choice was that the courts had overruled the Founders' Constitution and made political beliefs subject to question. A witness must reply "Yes" or "No" to such questions, or invoke the protection of the Fifth Amendment. The problem with her first choice, to answer 'No' to the Communist question was that HUAC hearings were accompanied by professional false witnesses who were always prepared to swear that a witness who responded 'No' was committing perjury. Indictments and fines and imprisonment often followed.

I agreed in principle with Emily's choices, but believed, nonetheless, that we should answer the political-affiliation question by citing the Fifth Amendment protection against self-incrimination. It was pointless to needlessly subject oneself to punishment. There could be no shame in seeking the protection of the Fifth Amendment, which enabled a great many Americans to avoid the unearned punishment that HUAC and its clones had in mind for them. Protection of the citizenry had been the intent of the Founders when they put the Fifth Amendment into the Constitution. True, citing the Fifth Amendment was widely interpreted as an "admission" that one was a Communist. But it was the only defense against harsh penalties that HUAC, with the help of Justice officials, let loose at "recalcitrant" witnesses at their televised HUAC hearings.

In the end, I persuaded Emily that we should decline to answer the inquisitorial question on Fifth Amendment grounds, although we would also declare that the inquisitors had no right to ask the question.

I had been wrong. Emily had been right, of course. We should have given only a principled answer, one honoring Washington, Jefferson, Paine, Franklin and those other mule-stubborn Americans. They had not risked the royal hangman's noose so that a hundred and eighty years later, we would acknowledge that officials, high or low, had the right to ask us questions they were forbidden to ask by the Constitution.

The House of Representatives formally abolished HUAC in 1975.

The Greenglasses confront another broken promise...

David Greenglass would have been eligible for parole in 1955, in anticipation of which Ruth Greenglass wrote to Frederic de Hoffman, Vice President of General Dynamics Corporation, who had been involved in the 1951 AEC's assessment of her husband's anticipated testimony on the atom bomb. She received this reply.

> In your letter you state that your husband believes that I told him during the 1951 official hearings that he should get in touch with me if "I could be of any assistance" to him. I feel that I should inform you that I did not make any such statement, particularly inasmuch as my contact with your husband was purely in the nature of my assisting in an interview on behalf of the United States Government.
>
> With respect to your particular inquiry, there is no job opening within the General Dynamics Corporation which your husband, David Greenglass, could be asked to fill.[745]

David Greenglass was not to leave prison until 1960, except for a day of leave to attend his mother's — Tessie Greenglass' — funeral in 1958.

Ruth Greenglass died on April 7, 2008.

Harry Gold was released from prison in 1966, after serving half of his 30 year sentence, and became a hospital chemist. In August 1972, he died during a heart operation, but his death was not made public until February 1974. His family established the Harry Gold Award in Research or Teaching in Clinical Pharmacology.

Morton Sobell: Justice officials' last hope of vindication...

Sobell, imprisoned at Alcatraz, had become the last chance of vindication for Justice officials and the judge.

We earlier described attempts by the FBI, in 1952, through a prison informant, to find in Sobell's behavior in prison some signs of "softness" in his insistence on his innocence. Either on his own or at the suggestion of the FBI, the informant had told Sobell it was possible that if the Rosenbergs won a new trial,

Julius Rosenberg would testify against him, and Sobell had then made a veiled threat of retaliation against Rosenberg. The prison-informant also told the FBI that Sobell had indicated a willingness to cooperate if certain conditions were met.[746] Sobell, however, had not given prison officials any sign that lent credibility to the prison-informant's reports, and he was transferred to Alcatraz.

On August 21, 1953, a memorandum from FBI Director Hoover advised the San Francisco FBI office, "With the Rosenbergs now dead, our efforts should be concentrated in the case toward securing complete disclosure from Sobell," and

> In that connection, the San Francisco office is requested to discreetly consult with Alcatraz authorities concerning the feasibility of developing an inmate as a confidential source who might be in a position to win the confidence of Sobell and obtain information of value.[747]

On September 18, the San Francisco office replied the Alcatraz warden was opposed to cultivating a prison-informant to befriend Sobell, because too many other persons in the prison would have to be drawn into the arrangement. The San Francisco FBI office was prepared, however, to try to persuade the warden to drop his objections because it had found an inmate who it believed would be suitable to the task.

> Recently, while interviewing Erich Gimpel, German Saboteur, who is serving a life sentence at Alcatraz, on another matter, indicated to SA [Special Agent] Ralph Lindsey, that he had talked to the subject and had played chess with him. Gimpel stated that the subject was reluctant to discuss anything personal with him.[748]

Gimpel was not long available as an informant.

In 1944, he and an accomplice had been put ashore in Maine, from a German submarine. The accomplice gave himself up, and Gimpel was apprehended. Gimpel was tried for conspiring to commit wartime sabotage and espionage, found guilty and sentenced to death. President Truman commuted the death sentence and Gimpel was sent to Alcatraz.[749] Soon after the FBI recommended him as an inmate-informer against Sobell, he was pardoned by President Eisenhower. Gimpel, a grateful beneficiary of the Turnabout, went home to Germany.

On March 30, 1954, the New York FBI office sent a memorandum to Hoover in which, for reasons unknown, it made the assumption that "all [Sobell's] appeals and all actions in the US Courts have been terminated," and recommended that "positive action be taken to secure the cooperation of Sobell."

NY has taken into consideration the personal character and makeup of Sobell as obtained from comments made by officials in the Federal House of Detention and the NYC Prison (in which Sobell had been detained), and from the comments of Max Elitcher, potential informant [name deleted] and the experience of the agents who were assigned to the trial of Julius and Ethel Rosenberg and Sobell. The sum of these observations is that Sobell is arrogant, stubborn, proud, self-centered, and egotistical. It is the opinion of Max Elitcher, that Sobell, because of his pride, would never humble himself to seek out aid from the Bureau.[750]

The New York FBI office recommended against any attempt to gain Sobell's cooperation through his parents, his wife, or through efforts by the warden or the chaplain at Alcatraz. Even a direct appeal to him by an FBI agent would be unwise because the appeal

would be broadcast in every Communist newspaper in and outside the country. Since his cause is practically dead, NY does not care to run the risk of revitalizing it.[751]

Nevertheless, the memorandum went on, the former prison-informant's reports indicated that Sobell was aware there were options at his disposal, although his wife stood in the way of acting on them. The New York FBI office proposed that, on the pretext of disposing of certain items taken from Sobell when he was brought over the border from Mexico in 1950, a matter that would ordinarily be discussed with Sobell's attorney, an FBI agent would discuss the matter directly with Sobell at Alcatraz. This would ensure Sobell's "pride is satisfied" and might encourage him to indicate he was interested in cooperating. If that occurred

The agent should thereupon handle Sobell immediately in such a manner as to strengthen and enlarge upon any such cooperation.[752]

On April 2, the San Francisco office notified Hoover it agreed with the New York FBI's recommendation. It also suggested a way to remove Sobell's wife as an obstacle to the FBI's hopes for Sobell's cooperation. The San Francisco office wrote that Helen Sobell was

a dominating influence on him and strengthened him to "hold fast." If it should ever be learned by the subject that his wife is unfaithful to him, such information may be utilized as a wedge to break this influence.[753]

One problem, however, the memorandum went on, was

The San Francisco files do not contain sufficient information concerning the personal activities of subject's wife to know if she may be engaged in any extra marital relations or susceptible to such behavior.

If such information became available, it would

have to come to subject's attention in a most circumspect manner; however, it is felt that if such information is available, it may be of value in the future handling of this case.

Since Helen Sobell would soon travel from New York to visit her husband, the memorandum went on, information on her private life might be obtained by having "her activities covered during the trip from New York to San Francisco."

Two weeks later, on April 16, in a telegram to both the New York and San Francisco FBI offices, Director Hoover vetoed the suggested surveillance on Sobell's wife.

It is felt that in view of the possibility of unfavorable publicity to the Bureau coming from such activity, no attempt should be made to develop information on Mrs. Sobell's activities en route San Francisco.[754]

A note appended to the telegram explained the "possible embarrassment to the Bureau is extremely strong as the problem of informing Sobell would arise, as well as the possibility of having a surveillance detected."

On April 21, the New York FBI office informed Hoover that it agreed with his veto of the surveillance proposed by the San Francisco office.

For the information of the Bureau and San Francisco, on one occasion in 1952, Helen Sobell visited her husband at West Street Federal House of Detention. She was accompanied by an unidentified male negro [sic] who waited for her while she visited subject and who accompanied her from the prison. This fact was made known to all the inmates of the prison and many of them made remarks to Sobell to the effect that his wife was 'running around' with a negro [sic]. This had no effect on Sobell.[755]

The suggestion that an FBI agent visit Sobell, on the pretext of asking him how he wanted to dispose of personal items, was not carried through at the time, possibly because Sobell's imprisonment at Alcatraz had become a public issue. Shortly after the executions of the Rosenbergs, the Committee, with Sobell's approval, had begun a campaign to raise funds for his legal appeals for a new trial, and for his transfer from Alcatraz to a prison 3000 miles closer to his family.

The campaign was gaining strong support, including that of Senator William Langer, of North Dakota, chairman of the Senate Judiciary Committee, who had previously questioned the fairness of the Rosenberg-Sobell trial.

Justice officials viewed the campaign as a threat to their hopes for gaining Sobell's confession. The slightest success in the campaign — a transfer, for example — might encourage Sobell to believe that public pressure as well as his legal appeals might eventually result in his obtaining a new trial or early release. Any approach to him by the FBI while he was in a hopeful state of mind would result in rejection and, if the Bureau's effort became public, there might possibly be unfavorable publicity.

On December 10, 1953, Leland Boardman, the Bureau's third-ranking official, noted in an inter-office memorandum that the Communist *Daily Worker* had reported on December 9, that a brief was filed with the Senate Judiciary Committee

> requesting an investigation of the conduct of the US Attorney General's office in the Rosenberg and Sobell cases...The petition was presented to Sen. William Langer, Chairman of the Judiciary Committee, by Joseph Brainin and Daniel G. Marshall of Los Angeles.[756]

The Senator had authorized Brainin to tell the press that the Senator had said: 'I shall not allow it to gather dust.'

The following month, on January 19, 1954, the San Francisco FBI office notified Hoover that the *San Francisco News* had quoted Helen Sobell, on January 5, as saying the campaign on behalf of her husband had the backing of two Nobel Prize scientists, Harold Urey and Linus Pauling.[757]

On April 27, the New York FBI office reported that many requests to transfer Sobell out of Alcatraz were being directed at James V. Bennett, Director of Prisons, but that Sobell's transfer would "not be to the interest of this investigation" and "would just destroy any chance of getting his cooperation." Bennett, the report advised, should make his denial of a transfer public, so that Sobell would give up hope of leaving Alcatraz.[758] Meanwhile, the FBI continued to add to its disloyalty files the names of persons requesting Sobell's transfer.[759]

It was not until July 1954, that the FBI felt it advisable to pursue the pretext approach to Sobell. On July 15, Hoover informed the San Francisco FBI office

You are authorized to designate an older agent with a personality which will inspire confidence for the contact. He should make a thorough review of the Sobell case and be completely familiar with all its aspects...

Sobell's cooperation should not be directly solicited, but should be given every opportunity to talk if he so desires...

It is suggested that the contact be made neither directly after nor directly before a visit from his wife, and thought should be given to selection of the most propitious time.[760]

On August 27, Fred R. Elledge, a veteran FBI agent, made the pretext visit to Sobell at Alcatraz, spending approximately one and a half hours with him. The meeting began badly, because the Alcatraz officials had led Sobell to expect to see his attorney. When Sobell agreed to see Elledge, a fair amount of time was spent on going through the pretext of asking Sobell about the disposition of the items taken from him in 1950. Elledge laid the groundwork for returning by saying that there were other items still to come.[761]

At one point, according to Elledge's report, he warned Sobell that the campaign being conducted on his behalf was not in his best interests.

The actions and the activities of the Committee to Secure Justice for Morton Sobell and the Rosenberg case was broached to Sobell with the query if he actually thought the activities of this committee was accomplishing anything in his behalf. It was suggested to him that this committee was actually using his name as an excuse to conduct rallies, collect funds, and further exploit his case as a cause célèbre...and was also using his wife and exploiting her for this same purpose and that she was being exhibited throughout the country and they were preying upon her remorse and feelings in this matter to further their own purposes."[762]

Sobell asked why, if the FBI believed the Sobell Committee's efforts were fruitless, the Bureau was "so concerned over these activities." Elledge replied that apparently Sobell believed that "myriads of agents and perhaps others were aware of and behind the suggestion made by the interviewing agent," but that was not the case, and the agent's comments about the Committee and its exploitation of

Sobell and his wife "were the sole observations of the interviewing agent, given as the observations of a husband and father."

In his discussion with Sobell, Elledge made an allusion to rumors of Helen Sobell's infidelity and denied that "the FBI in New York or any other place had anything do with the accusations against his wife's morals."

Elledge wrote that he had been firm and critical with Sobell, and he had "sharply criticized" Sobell for saying that Elledge was using a "line," and "it was an insult to the intelligence of the interviewing agent to be accused of trying to use a 'line' toward him."

Elledge wrote he had been initially offended by Sobell.

> At this point it might be stated that at the outset of the interview, Sobell assumed a very superior air and had a smirk constantly upon his face.

But after Elledge's criticisms and rebukes, according to his report

> it was noted that the smirk had entirely disappeared and Sobell seemed to be deeply perturbed and concerned regarding the fact that his wife might possibly be being used by the committee.

Elledge reported that he had told Sobell that he, the agent, could do nothing for him.

> It was suggested that there was only one person who could do anything for him. At this point Sobell remarked, "No platitutes [sic] please." His remark was immediately challenged and it was pointed out to him that he should make a distinction between platitutes and actuality.[763]

Two days later, on August 29, Sobell wrote his attorney and apprised him of the FBI agent's visit. He described Elledge as a "very nice chap — he must have read Dale Carnegie, Advanced Course — you know — sincere."[764]

On September 1, Elledge made another visit to Sobell. He reported he had told Sobell to put any thoughts of martyrdom aside, and "consider solely what would be to the best interests of himself, his wife and family."[765]

Elledge pointed out to Sobell he had not taken the stand to deny his guilt, and this reminded him of Thomas Henry McMonigle, a rapist and murderer

> who was apprehended, tried and convicted, for the kidnapping and rape murder of a 17 year old high school girl. McMonigle never once professed his innocence or denied the charges against him. His sole statements were those damning the arresting officers, the officers of

the court, the prison officials and any others who had brought him to justice.[766]

Elledge concluded the visit by telling Sobell he should not be under the illusion

> that you can do nothing to help yourself. Don't sell yourself short. It is my opinion that you can do more to help yourself than all the attorneys, all the committees, or all your professional friends."

But the following month, on October 13, the San Francisco FBI office recommended to Hoover that Elledge's visits to Sobell be suspended for the immediate future. The suggestion was rejected by Hoover. The officials had learned that Sobell's attorney, wife, and parents had been informed about the visits, but they had no clue to the feelings Sobell had expressed about them.[767]

On November 11, Helen Sobell wrote to Hoover

> You must know that from the time that my husband, I, and my children were brutally and illegally kidnapped in August 1950, by your agents, my husband has been constantly pressured to confess to a crime which he has not committed. All of the various types of pressures which were used culminated in the choice of Alcatraz as the place of imprisonment for my husband, and in his being sent there on Thanksgiving Day of 1952. There is nothing in my husband's history, in prison or out, which could justify a decision to send him to Alcatraz. He does not belong in any prison; he certainly does not belong in Alcatraz.

> Recently, perhaps under the impression that a man who is beginning his fifth year in prison has lost some of his integrity, courage, or honesty, your agents have again begun their harassment of my husband. Perhaps, too, your office may be motivated by the fact that so many and such powerful forces are protesting against the use of Alcatraz as a third degree method in the case of my young scientist.[768]

Among the assertions made to her husband, she wrote, was that "confidential sources available to the F.B.I. had information that my husband was being deserted...I am convinced that the truth must come to light. When it is known, my husband will be free to return to his family who love him, in honor and with dignity."

Elledge went to see Sobell again, on November 24. After an opening discussion on the items that were the usual pretext for Elledge's visits, he reprimanded Sobell for the publicity given to his visits, and "that he expected to see his name in the paper again" because of his latest visit; and that the newspaper stories had not been truthful and had not been in accordance with the prior expressions made by Sobell.[769]

When Sobell pointed out he could not have been the author of the news articles, Elledge replied the news story "was an example of how he was being 'used' by certain people." Elledge reported that he had told Sobell "he had yet to say word one in explanation of his association with the Rosenbergs," he was not suggesting that Sobell perjure himself but to merely make a "statement of facts." He reminded Sobell, he reported, that Sobell had claimed he had not taken the stand at the trial on the advice of his attorneys, but Elledge, "was not aware of what he had used as an excuse for not having talked since then." Elledge told Sobell that he "had been scrupulously honest and truthful in his actions and statements toward Sobell," but he "was now doubtful as to Sobell's real attitude," and it "had been the last thought of the agent to harass Sobell in any way."

Elledge then told Sobell that "in view of the apparent misunderstanding and feeling on the part of Sobell that this would be the agent's concluding visit," unless Sobell specifically requested to see him. Elledge reported that his conduct of the visit "appeared to have a terrific impact on Sobell" and Sobell was in a state "of dejection and uncertainty." Elledge concluded his report with a statement that the real problem was that "Sobell might be willing, insofar as he is concerned, to tell everything he knows but is deterred from doing so for fear of alienating his wife's affections."

Four months later, on March 15, 1955, the San Francisco FBI office reported to Hoover, "There has been no indication that Sobell is desirous of contacting an Agent of the FBI...It is the recommendation of the San Francisco Office that no further attempts to interview Sobell be made at this time."[770]

In his book, *On Doing Time,* Sobell wrote that the FBI had succumbed to wishful thinking, mistaking his civility toward Elledge as a sign of interest in cooperation, unaware that the company of non-inmates and non-guards was rarely refused by prisoners at Alcatraz.

When Elledge had reprimanded him for being civil during the visits, and hostile afterward, Sobell wrote

> I made it clear to him that even if Hitler — I couldn't
> think of a more extreme example — had come to visit me
> on the Rock I would probably have sat down and talked
> with him, as I had in fact done with our G-man."[771]

In February 1958, Sobell's supporters succeeded in their efforts to have Sobell transferred from Alcatraz to the federal penitentiary at Atlanta, Georgia, 3000 miles closer to his family.

Justice officials: silence is the safest response to critical citizens...
John Wexley's *The Judgment of Julius and Ethel Rosenberg* and William Reuben's *The Atom Bomb Hoax* had received very favorable reviews. Wexley's analysis of the trial established so strong a case for doubting the integrity of the prosecutors and the impartiality of the judge, that Justice officials assigned a staff lawyer, Benjamin F. Pollack, to prepare a reply to Wexley.

Pollack's 112 page reply, in the form of a memorandum, was completed on November 7, 1957, but was not released for sixteen years, and then only because an enterprising reporter obtained a copy, which he made public. The Pollack memorandum simply reiterated all the past responses to criticism, but did not address the most-often voiced criticism that the crime had been committed at the height of the popularity of the alliance with the Soviet Union, and not, as the prosecution and judge persuaded the jurors, during the Cold War, that there had been no intent to harm the United States, and there had been no tangible evidence of the crime.

The Pollack memorandum also created a problem for Justice officials because it contained a statement by Pollack that was unacceptable to them.

> This is not to say that the writer of this memorandum concurs in the sentences imposed; he would have been inclined to be lenient with Morton Sobell, because he was not connected with the atomic bomb espionage, and with Ethel Rosenberg because she was the mother of two small boys.[772]

Because of their inability to provide a credible response to critics, Justice officials seem to have decided it was wiser to remain silent, than to attempt to defend the conduct of the trial. That would explain the suppression of the Pollack memorandum and, following that, the placing of rigid obstacles in the way of Jim Bishop, a conservative and best-selling author, who wished to write a book on the case. Bishop assured Justice officials and the judge the book would be entirely favorable to them. A previous book by Bishop, *The Day Christ Died*, had been widely acclaimed.

In the course of describing his book to Judge Kaufman, Bishop told him that he intended to interview Helen Sobell. According to a memorandum dated November 12, 1957, from FBI Director Hoover to two of his aides, Judge Kaufman had phoned to tell him Bishop's purpose in interviewing Helen Sobell was to "preclude the charge being made that the book was slanted."[773] Hoover wrote that he told Judge Kaufman such an interview

> would be unwise, because anything said could be used out of context unless Bishop had somebody sitting in on the interview who would know what had or had not been said. I further stated that nothing would be gained by such an interview since it would still be claimed that the book was slanted, and it would be much better to steer clear of something of this type.

Hoover directed one of his aides "to speak to Jim Bishop concerning this matter." The interview with Helen Sobell was cancelled.

Bishop asked to see the impounded Exhibit 8, and for the next seventeen months he was shuttled between Justice, AEC officials and Judge Kaufman, each of them denying that they had the authority to show him the impounded exhibit.[774] On February 4, Bishop wrote a letter to President Eisenhower, in which he described his intended book as the story of

> the problems and frustrations of the scientists who were trying to devise the first atom bomb while the servants of the Soviet Union were trying to steal it.[775]

On March 6, 1959, Benjamin H. Pollack, the author of the suppressed memorandum on the case, declared in a memorandum, that Hoover was opposed to Bishop's project, and

> had expressed a disinclination to such a publication. Mr. Hoover felt that the Government might be embarrassed by such publication at this time and that it would give the Communists ground for further propaganda.[776]

Three weeks later, Pollack notified the deputy chief of Justice's Criminal Division that, on March 24, 1959, Judge Kaufman

> told me he felt obliged to write Mr. Bishop and emphasize the fact that he, Judge Kaufman, had never requested Mr. Bishop to write the book he planned with respect to the Rosenberg case or any of the other spy cases.[777]

Judge Kaufman wanted to be sure, now, that Exhibit 8 would stay out of Bishop's reach. He told Pollack to appear before him to make a motion for a hearing on unimpounding Exhibit 8; an AEC official would be present to declare the impounded material to be secret and classified, following which Judge Kaufman would rule that Exhibit 8 would remain impounded.

There was an unspoken problem in the situation that every participant at the hearing had to be aware of: Morton Sobell, who was still actively seeking relief in the appellate courts in 1959, had an interest in unimpounding Exhibit 8 far greater than Bishop's, since he believed the impounded testimony would give him a strong basis for a motion for a new trial. Legally, Sobell should have been informed of the hearing, so that his attorney could appear to protect his interests, but Judge Kaufman chose once again to violate the prohibition against *ex parte* procedures. He also chose to conduct the hearing, not in open court, but in his robing room, which was not accessible to the public or the media.

Pollack provided the details of the *ex parte* hearing to the deputy chief of his Department.

> On the following day, Wednesday, March 25 at 2 p.m. we met in the robing room of Judge Kaufman in Court Room 9 with the following present: Judge Kaufman, his law clerk, his deputy marshal, Mr. Slavin (one of the court reporters at the trial of United States v. Rosenberg et al. in March 1951, and who transcribed the testimony with respect to the impounded exhibit), Mr. Lawrence the clerk of the court, Mr. Charles L. Marshall, Director, Division of Classification of Atomic Energy Commission, who happened to be one of the nuclear scientists who was connected with the Rosenberg case in 1951, and myself.[778]

Pollack dutifully made his motion, which Judge Kaufman granted. He ordered an envelope containing Exhibit 8 to be opened. Mr. Marshall examined the contents, Mr. Slavin read his short-hand notes, and the contents were returned to the envelope, which was then resealed. Then Marshall stated

> In my opinion as Director of Classification, Atomic Energy Commission, I still consider this exhibit classified information and I shall so inform my agency.

Marshall repeated his finding, in a letter to the Acting Assistant Attorney General, writing, "It will not be possible, therefore, to make this material available to Mr. Bishop."[779]

On January 27, 1960, the Assistant Attorney General wrote to the Chairman of the AEC, arguing for keeping Exhibit 8 classified, not for legal or security reasons but because

> As you are no doubt aware, the Rosenberg-Sobell case at the time it was prosecuted by this Department and

at all subsequent times has been seized upon by the
Communist Party, both locally and internationally as
excellent grist for their propaganda mills in an effort
to discredit the Judicial system of this government.
The committees organized for this purpose have, with
little respect for truth or law, twisted facts and words to
accomplish this end.

* * *

...I suggest for your consideration the probable adverse
effects of a *nunc pro tunc* declassification in such a highly
sensitive area.[780]

The Chairman of the AEC agreed. Silence was safer than refutation. Bishop
dropped the project. That year, another of his books was published, *The Day
Christ Was Born*.

Judge Kaufman "raises hell" with judges considering a Sobell appeal...

An FBI memorandum, dated December 21, 1962, related that Judge
Kaufman, who had by then been promoted to the U.S. Court of Appeals for New
York, Southern District, had called from New York, perturbed because the U.S.
Court of Appeals for the Connecticut District was considering an appeal by Sobell,
and that Kaufman said he had "raised hell" with one of the judges — Thurgood
Marshall — whom he characterized as naive and inexperienced.[781] (Marshall was
later appointed to the U.S. Supreme Court.) Kaufman was upset because Marshall
had asked the U.S. attorney representing the Justice Department whether, if
Sobell had been tried in recent years, "wouldn't it be necessary for the Court to
reverse the decision," because of the Supreme Court's decision in another case?
The U.S. Attorney had replied, "Probably." The memorandum reported that Judge
Kaufman had denounced the U.S. Attorney as "stupid" for making that reply, and

Judge Kaufman was of the opinion that this might very
well be the straw that breaks the camel's back and as a
result obtain Sobell's freedom.

But the Court of Appeals declined to apply the Supreme Court's ruling
to Sobell.

When a defendant who has been tried fairly in accordance with the law as it was understood at the time
seeks judicial relief because of new light on a point of
law affecting an aspect of his trial, his request must be
balanced against the rightful claims of organized society
as reflected in the penal laws.[782]

The Court did not explain how applying a Supreme Court ruling to Sobell would violate the "rightful claims of organized society."

On March 21, 1965, an article in the *New York Times* stated that, in reply to an appeal to First Lady Lady Bird Johnson by Helen Sobell that she intervene for humanitarian reasons with the President for the release of her husband, the Pardon Attorney had responded that if Sobell based his petition "on his belief that his sentence was excessive...we would be glad to give it consideration."

On March 24, 1965, an FBI interoffice memorandum advised that Judge Kaufman had read the story.

> Yesterday afternoon, Inspector Wick of your office received a telephone call from Judge Kaufman expressing concern about efforts to free Morton Sobell...Judge Kaufman commented to the effect that Sobell should serve his entire [thirty year] sentence.[783]

"...smothered and forced out of the public eye"...

On October 16, 1965, William C. Sullivan, a top FBI official, learned that television time was being sought by Walter and Miriam Schneir, whose book on the case, *Invitation to an Inquest*, had just been published. Sullivan's informant, whose name was not mentioned in the memorandum, indicated that he was in a position to influence the decision on whether the Schneirs would be given television time. Sullivan wrote

> I took the liberty of telling [name deleted] to instruct [name deleted] not to permit the Schneirs to go on his television program for no good would accrue from it. [name deleted] will handle this matter. It had to be expedited because [name deleted] wanted an answer right away.
>
> * * *
>
> As I see it, the first thing we should do in this matter is to take careful steps to secure the cooperation of friendly television stations and prevent this subversive effort from being successful. It should be kept off television programs and smothered and forced out of the public eye thereby.[784]

Sullivan went on to recommend the FBI "start preparing an exhaustive brief refuting this book to be held in readiness in the event that it is needed urgently." Sullivan was apparently unaware that a refutation of the Wexley book — the 112 page Pollack memorandum — had, by then, been under Justice Department lock and key for eight years, and would not be released — and then not voluntarily — for another eight years.

Sullivan also proposed an FBI letter go to all field offices, directing them to try to learn in advance of efforts to put the Schneirs on television programs and to take steps to prevent their appearance.[785]

The judge "felt that the Attorney General should be informed…"

On May 2, 1969, Sullivan was informed that a play — *The United States vs. Julius and Ethel Rosenberg* — was "currently showing in Cleveland, Ohio, which is critical of the Government's handling of that case."[786] (The play was subsequently moved to New York City.) A week earlier, on April 29, Judge Kaufman had telephoned FBI Director Hoover

> alarmed that the "New York Times" reviewed this play two weeks in a row, on April 20 and 27, 1969, which was highly unusual…The Judge added that he felt the Attorney General should be informed, and the Director advised that he would let the Attorney General know.

The FBI files were combed for Donald Martin Freed, the playwright, and Larry Tarrant, the director, as well as for the members of the cast, but there was no identifiable derogatory information on Tarrant or any of the performers in Cleveland, New York, or Bureau files.

There was, however, "derogatory information" on Freed: his FBI dossier revealed that he had been involved in activities in support of equal rights for African-Americans. Two months after Judge Kaufman's telephone call, action was taken against Freed, as part of an FBI program of disruption of relationships between white civil liberties advocates and African-Americans. M. Wesley Swearingen, a twenty five year veteran FBI agent we mentioned earlier, has described how the disruption was accomplished.

> Two months after Kaufman's call to Hoover, Hoover authorized the San Francisco FBI office on July 1, 1969, to pass out 200 copies of a leaflet, created and printed by the Crime Records Division, in the vicinity of a Black Panther Party-sponsored national conference in Oakland, California, alleging that "Donald Freed is a PIG" [slang for police-informer].

The FBI's leaflet read in part:

> We don't know what breed of a pig he is, but Freed is a LAPD [Los Angeles Police Department] PIG, an FBI PIG, a CIA PIG or maybe even a Sheriff PIG — but he is a pig,

an informer who deals with his fellow pigs and betrays us all.[787]

The FBI-created leaflet was signed *All Power to the People.*

Exhibit 8 is brought into the light...

On April 4, 1966, a hearing was held by U.S. District Court Judge Edmund L. Palmieri at which the U.S. attorney, for the first time, made no objection to a limited unimpoundment of Exhibit 8, so that Sobell's attorney could use it as a basis for a new appeal.[788]

On April 11, 1966, several days after Exhibit 8 was released to Sobell's attorney by the court, a memo to FBI Director Hoover, from which the sender's name was deleted, informed the Director

> On 4/6/66 Judge Irving Kaufman, U.S. Court of Appeals, called me from his home, in regard to an article which appeared in the New York Times 4/6/66, indicating that "U.S. Releases A-Bomb Sketch to Sobell for Use in an Appeal."
>
> Judge Kaufman was very much concerned about the fact that this information was being released against his wishes. He stated that he made the decision to keep this information preserved in a sealed status and he was not even consulted in regard to the matter.[789]

It might not have occurred to the new generation at Justice or in the federal courthouse in Foley Square to consult him. On his elevation to the Court of Appeals, Judge Kaufman had to relinquish, to a district judge, his guardianship over the sealed envelope containing Exhibit 8. His opinions and feelings about Exhibit 8 — about the Rosenberg-Sobell case, in fact — had become irrelevant. If a Sobell appeal ever reached his court, he would be expected to recuse himself.

Exhibit 8 quickly found its way into the mainstream media, which solicited opinions from scientists on the accuracy and importance of what Greenglass testified he had turned over to Harry Gold and Julius Rosenberg, and on his ability to have drawn the atom bomb sketches in Exhibit 8 without assistance.

In the main, those scientists who found the sketches and testimony to have been accurate and important, were skeptical of Greenglass' ability to have produced them without the help of experts; those scientists who found the sketches and testimony inaccurate or, in some cases, useless, believed that Greenglass might have created them unaided.[790]

Two and a half years after Exhibit 8 was released, Sobell was freed from prison. On January 14, 1969, after serving eighteen years of his thirty year sentence, Sobell became a parolee until 1980, when he became an entirely free citizen again.

Judge Kaufman's suspicion that President Johnson might use his powers to arrange with federal parole officials for Sobell's release had been justified. Sobell's release came during the last week of Lyndon Johnson's presidency. Lyndon Johnson had first signaled his interest in the Rosenberg-Sobell case in March 1953, when he began making inquiries on behalf of a constituent about the intervention of Pope Pius XII for clemency for the Rosenbergs. As President, Johnson received a considerable amount of mail and petitions on Sobell's behalf, much of it from the clergy and from prominent scientists and lawyers.

President Johnson was certainly aware that he was arranging for the release of a man whose heart was undoubtedly with the anti-Vietnam War picket lines at the Johnson White House, and with the exodus of war-avoiding young men on their way to Canada, and with the great peace demonstrations and other actions that had deprived Johnson of a chance to run for a second term. Perhaps he arranged for Sobell's freedom because he wanted his conscience to applaud him.

Justice seeks out Prosecutor Irving Saypol and Assistant Prosecutor Roy Cohn.

Chapter 14 | Officials blinded by the light, briefly

An American spiritual-political springtime...

Contemplate the year 1975, in which the people of the United States are twenty-two years older and wiser than they were in the year that an American president gave his approval, on two consecutive days, to putting library books and two young dissenters to the torch. This was the same president who, to the angry disappointment of political extremists, prevented the spread of the Korean War by bringing that war to an end, and by his appointment of Earl Warren as Chief Justice of the Supreme Court, thus accelerating a movement that began to sweep away obstacles to equality of education for all Americans. Torcher and peacemaker, both in one man.

A uniquely American spiritual-political springtime was slowly emerging from a fear-driven political landscape, weighted down and bloodied as it was by new unofficial wars in place of old, still affected by the ferocity of the American Century visionaries, but showing awareness that the Constitution was, in the minds of most Americans, the national scripture that kept order and stability and that in its grandest moments asserted the most humble were the equal of the most arrogant.

There were hints of the coming of this new time in 1954, when Senator Joseph McCarthy lost his weak franchise on patriotism, and in 1957, 1959, and 1960, when Congress passed increasingly stronger civil rights bills that made voting a universal American right not subject to entrance fees or tests of color or docility. In 1965, national immigration quota systems were abolished. In 1971, the voting age was lowered to 18, and the Supreme Court upheld the right of the media to disclose secret government documents — the Pentagon Papers — that described deceptions on the public by government officials in the conduct of the war in Vietnam. In 1975, former U.S. Attorney General John Mitchell and two of President Richard Nixon's advisors were found guilty of obstruction of justice, and illegal actions by the CIA were made public by a government panel.

Portents, some of vindication of the defendants, some of vindication of the prosecutors and the judge, were on their way. Behind the release of Morton Sobell, in 1969, lay a growing public awareness that the conduct and outcome of the Rosenberg-Sobell trial, regardless of the defendants' guilt or innocence, had been profoundly improper. In 1971, E.I. Doctorow's *The Book of Daniel*, a novel sympathetic to the Rosenbergs, was widely reviewed and read, and a drama, *Inquest*, by Donald Freed was getting enthusiastic reviews. In 1973, *The Implosion Conspiracy*, by Louis Nizer, a prominent attorney, which vindicated the officials and the judge, became a best seller. Free of any references, or citations, or an index that would facilitate researching Nizer's views and claims, the book created a salacious portrait of the Rosenbergs as sexual animals in prison, "pawing each other with wild abandon."[791] Nizer gave no sources for this "information," nor for any other events he described, nor even for the portions of the trial record he cited in his book. He made the startling claim that 112 federal judges had reviewed the defendants' appeals, and that all had found the appeals without merit. Nizer admitted, however, that he had resorted to "creative" addition to arrive at that number. The nine Supreme Court justices who had eventually voted 9 times against review were counted as 81 judges; the three judges of the U.S. Court of Appeals voted unfavorably against the defendants six times; Judge Kaufman and one other judge denied appeals three times, bringing the total to 112. But the actual number of judges was 9+3+2, or 14,[792] of which nine never reviewed the case. Nizer was sued by the Rosenbergs' sons for libel and for invasion of privacy; their suit led to an out-of-court settlement. Although a best-seller in its time, Nizer's book has not been treated by scholars or other serious students as a reliable source of information on the Rosenberg-Sobell case.

In 1974-1975, the Freedom of Information Act (FOIA) was passed as a response to a growing awareness by the American public that accountability by government agencies was essential to democracy. Over the dug-in-heels of nervous officials, there followed years of litigation to compel their obedience to the Act, to force them to let the sun shine on their in- and out-trays and their locked files. When the officials were finally compelled by court orders to comply or face contempt charges, they heavy-handedly blacked out substantial portions of the documents, leaving a great many of them barely readable. A committee formed twenty years after the execution of the Rosenbergs — the National Committee to Reopen the Rosenberg Case — estimates that the Justice Department and other government agencies have withheld 80% of the documents relevant to the Rosenberg-Sobell case.

But thousands of documents did see the light of day, and revealed the deceptions, suborned perjuries, *ex parte* meetings between the prosecutors and the judge, admissions of lack of evidence and of other official misconduct that had led to long years of imprisonment for Sobell and to Sing Sing's electrocution chamber for the Rosenbergs.

The FBI declares jail-informant heard Julius Rosenberg's confession...

In 1975, among the first documents Justice officials made available to the media were some they said clearly pointed to the guilt of Julius Rosenberg. The documents were FBI memoranda relating to Jerome Eugene Tartakow, an inmate-informant at the Federal House of Detention in New York in 1951, when Julius Rosenberg, awaiting trial, had been there. Tartakow's criminal record included convictions for pimping, desertion from the navy, car thefts, and armed robberies.[793] In 1955, he was tried, but not convicted, on a charge of kidnapping and sexually molesting an 11 year old girl.[794]

The FBI documents selected for compliance with the FOIA had Tartakow informing the FBI, before the trial, that Julius Rosenberg had confessed to him the crimes he would not confess to the FBI. The earliest FBI memorandum we know of that alludes to Tartakow is dated December 12, 1950, three months before the trial. According to Ann Mari Buitrago, an attorney who had knowledge of Tartakow's relationship with the FBI

> For his services, Tartakow constantly demanded recompense. Dozens of FBI reports document his demands for money, for special parole, for early parole, and for getting charges against him dropped as well as his threats to quit informing if his demands were not met.[795]

According to the *Washington Star* of November 13, 1975

> It is not clear from the documents — made public, ironically, in response to a lawsuit by the sons of Julius and Ethel Rosenberg in an effort to prove the innocence of their parents — whether Tartakow was deliberately planted in the prison by the FBI to gather information from Rosenberg, or whether he happened to be in prison and volunteered material to the Bureau.[796]

The *Washington Star* quoted a released FBI document

> While certain of the information furnished by Tartakow has been corroborated to some extent, the majority of it has not.[797]

The reason Justice officials gave for releasing, in 1975, what they described as the information they had received from Tartakow almost a quarter of a century earlier, was that in the earlier years they had still been "studying the possibility of prosecuting other suspected members of the alleged Soviet spy system" (the reader will recall that Justice officials had told the media, in those years, that they had more than 20,000 indictments in the works), but in the end they had decided to forego the prosecutions because "witnesses to testify from first-hand knowledge could not be found."[798]

None of the "confessions" by Julius Rosenberg to Tartakow were aired at the trial, ostensibly because Tartakow had told the FBI that he would refuse to testify, and none of the events he described were ever shown to have actually occurred.

That Tartakow played chess in prison with Rosenberg, while the latter was awaiting trial is true. It is also true that Tartakow was adept at ingratiating himself with others, including FBI agents as well as prison inmates and their attorneys. He was able to persuade Julius Rosenberg's lawyer that he could be trusted, on one occasion, to chauffeur the Rosenbergs' sons to Sing Sing to see their parents, being in a position to do so because the FBI had arranged for his early parole. Robert Lamphere, the FBI agent who was deeply involved in the Rosenberg-Sobell case, labeled Tartakow a "con man,"[799] but nevertheless described some of Tartakow's claims as valuable clues to espionage cases, although they were apparently not so valuable that they led to a single arrest or indictment.

What Justice officials would have wanted of Tartakow, in addition to the "information" they were unable to corroborate, were observations by Tartakow of signs that Julius Rosenberg's intransigence was weakening; that he was moody and anxious, that his conversations were laced with phrases and innuendos that revealed fright, indecision, anguish for himself and his wife and sons, and expressions of hostility to the Communist Party for abandoning him and his family.

Aside from lack of corroboration there was another problem with Tartakow's claims.

In their book, *We Are Your Sons*, Michael and Robert Meeropol, the Rosenbergs' sons, wrote that they learned from a psychiatrist and a social worker who visited the Rosenbergs at Sing Sing, that both their parents assumed that their conversations with other prisoners and with each other were "bugged."[800] Julius Rosenberg was an electrical engineer whose belief that his conversations in prison were being recorded would have been reinforced by his knowledge of its feasibility. Whether these conversations were actually recorded by prison officials is irrelevant; what is relevant is that the Rosenbergs believed that hidden microphones were present in the cells and elsewhere in the detention building, making it exceedingly unlikely that they would pass along to anyone the kind of information Tartakow claimed to have received from Julius Rosenberg.

ACLU acknowledges Rosenberg-era ACLU officials reported to FBI...

The accumulating criticisms of the ACLU, from its members and disappointed admirers, caused its leaders, in the 1970s, to acquire approximately 10,000 documents from the FBI, from which it was learned that J. Edgar Hoover and other Justice officials had played a direct role in shaping the ACLU's policy statements in the Rosenberg-Sobell case.

Among the revelations was that Morris Ernst, the chief counsel for the ACLU 1930-1954, had been passing information on ACLU activities to the FBI since 1942, and had been an attorney for J. Edgar Hoover, with whom he was on a first-name basis,[801] and that Irving Ferman, the Washington D.C. ACLU Office Director 1952-1959, also reported on ACLU activities to the FBI.

According to a memorandum from Aryeh Neier, the ACLU Executive Director, to the ACLU Board of Directors on September 6, 1977, among the ACLU affiliates Ferman had reported on to the FBI were those in Colorado,[802] California, Oregon, Massachusetts, Illinois, and Washington.[803]

Among other matters, Ferman reported to the FBI on October 3, 1956, of the "bombardment" of the ACLU, by its members, to adopt a less-prosecution-oriented policy toward Sobell's efforts for a new trial and/or a reduced sentence.[804] An FBI memorandum by Louis Nichols, dated November 21, 1956, reported that "Ferman told me in confidence that he protested vigorously" an ACLU staff counsel report favorable to an appeal by Sobell.[805]

Ferman was given an opportunity, by the 1970s ACLU, to comment on his passing of information to the FBI. Ferman alluded to a threat by the FBI to embroil the ACLU in litigation if the organization supported Sobell's appeals.

> However, I would be greatly remiss, and silence would be unconscionable, if I did not stress what Nichols [Louis B. Nichols, Assistant Director of the FBI] did to assist the ACLU during those most trying days so that its relatively small staff (as compared to today) could be affirmatively involved in protecting civil liberties, rather than being absorbed in defending itself. Only those who functioned in those days could understand the meaning of this observation.[806]

Other documents disclosed that Herbert Monte Levy, who was ACLU staff counsel from 1949 to 1955, had been "receptive to FBI suggestions about ACLU policies and programs."[807]

Levy was given an opportunity to reply to revelations of his relations with the FBI, and he began his response with a eulogy to the Director of the FBI.

> Firstly, it should be noted that the documentation should be considered in the context of the years to which it relates — years when McCarthyism was running rampant, years when J. Edgar Hoover was one of the relatively few government officials issuing a clear call to the defense of civil liberties.[808]

Levy denied his relations with the FBI were not known to the top leaders of the ACLU. He said it was Morris Ernst, the General Counsel to the ACLU, who had first introduced him to a high-ranking official of the FBI.[809] Further, that Levy and/or the ACLU executive director "would report on our meetings with the FBI to, either to the Board of Directors or to the appropriate ACLU committee..."[810]

Levy acknowledged that much became known about the FBI's "covert activities" in the 1970s, but in the 1950s

> the appearance we went by then was of the Director of the FBI who was sincerely and passionately devoted to the cause of civil liberties, even training FBI agents in the law of civil liberties.[811]

Another ACLU official, Patrick Murphy Malin, ACLU Executive Director from 1950 to 1962, sought "political information from the FBI on persons active in several affiliates,"[812] and, according to an FBI memo, "He is very much concerned over the inroads which the Rosenberg propaganda has made," and "is having problems with his 23 affiliates," particularly those "in Detroit, Los Angeles, Denver, and Seattle," and "he asked that we keep in mind alerting him if anything came up."[813]

On September 26, 1977, ACLU Executive Director Aryeh Neier wrote to Aaron Katz, head of a committee to reopen the Rosenberg-Sobell case,

> I think I should point out that the ACLU has been dealing recently with some of the legacies of the Rosenberg case. We initiated the effort to obtain the FBI files on the case...and, a few months ago, called on Congress to examine Judge Kaufman's *ex parte* contacts about the case with prosecutors and the FBI.[814]

Neier went on to write that "from time to time," he had repudiated a 1953 ACLU statement on the case.

> Aside from anything else, the death penalty made the Rosenberg case a civil liberties case. The question I will discuss with my colleagues is whether there is any other step we should take.

There was irony in the ACLU's officials' informant relationship with the Department of Justice. In its early days, the ACLU had condemned the use by Justice officials of informants in unions and professional associations, and had issued a pamphlet, titled, *The Nation-wide Spy System Centering in the Department of Justice*.[815] In the 1950s, the ACLU leaders had only to look into their mirrors for proof that the ACLU's early pamphlet was as relevant as ever.

The fact is, while millions of ordinary Americans were risking their reputations, employment and peace of mind by signing pleas for clemency for the Rosenbergs, ACLU leaders took the risk-free road of approving the verdicts, the death sentences and the illegal conduct of the prosecutors and the judge. It is likely the ACLU leaders were as frightened of the denouncers as were Justice officials and the judiciary. There's no shame in being frightened, but there is shame in betraying a trust.

So far as we know, the ACLU has never commissioned a post-execution study of the Rosenberg-Sobell case or, if it has, has chosen not to make its findings public. It would be a great act of public service for the ACLU to make a thorough study of the case at this time and to acknowledge that the defendants were tried for a crime they had not committed. Watch-dog civil liberties organizations, because of the trust they ask from the public, must own up to their own errors, just as they ask the government to do.

The State of New York v. Justice Irving Saypol...

In the mid-1970s, an event occurred that should have provoked another look by the media at the Rosenberg-Sobell case. The U.S. Attorney who had been the chief prosecutor in the case, and who immediately after the trial became a New York State judge, was indicted for perjury and bribery.

In 1974, the degree of corruption in the New York City judicial structure and the state's appointed prosecutors had become so flagrant, that Governor Hugh Carey felt compelled to appoint a special prosecutor, Maurice Nadjari, to investigate and bring indictments against them.

After two years of investigation, on May 13, 1976, Nadjari obtained indictments from a special grand jury against Supreme Court Justice Irving Saypol and Surrogate Judge S. Samuel DiFalco, two of nine judges he found to have engaged in corrupt practices.[816] Specifically, Nadjari charged Justice Saypol with arranging with Judge DiFalco to illegally permit Saypol's son to obtain $20,000 in commissions on the sale of an estate the son had appraised. The city's policy forbade persons who appraised estates to profit from their sales. In exchange, Justice Saypol agreed to name lawyers of Judge DiFalco's choice to lucrative court assignments.

The indictments charged Justice Saypol with one count of bribery and three counts of perjury, all of them felonies that could result in seven year prison sentences, and charged Judge DiFalco with one count of conspiracy and official misconduct. DiFalco had been Secretary of Tammany Hall, in the years prior to his nomination for the Surrogate judgeship.[817]

On May 17, 1976, the *New York Times*, in an editorial, wrote, "The seriousness of the accusations would suggest that they step down from the bench entirely, at this time."[818]

The two judges declined to do so, possibly because Tammany Hall had already started turning the wheels for their evasion of trial. On June 4, 1976, the New York State Court of Appeals issued a split decision, 4-3, removing jurisdiction of the Saypol/DiFalco cases from Prosecutor Nadjari and giving them to Tammany Hall's District Attorney for Manhattan. The divided court ruled that, when the governor had appointed Nadjari to uncover criminal activity in the courts, the governor meant for him to investigate criminal activity only in the criminal courts, not in the civil courts over which Saypol and DiFalco presided. Consequently, Prosecutor Nadjari had lacked jurisdiction to inquire into criminal activity by Saypol and DiFalco,[819] and the evidence he had gathered would not be recognized.

One of the judges on the appeals court was Sol Wachtler, later its chief judge, and still later, in 1993, indicted, tried and sentenced to fifteen months in prison for attempted extortion from a former mistress. Wachtler voted with the majority, to remove criminal activity by judges in the civil courts from the special prosecutor's jurisdiction.

On November 4, 1978, the appellate court unanimously dismissed the charges against Judge DiFalco. The Manhattan District Attorney declined to seek new indictments against Justice Saypol and Judge DiFalco.[820]

That ended the matter in the Tammany Hall way, with a wink and a nod and a prayer in the shadows. The unpleasant matter would never come up again.

Ten years later, Saypol's chief assistant at the trial, Roy Cohn, was disbarred for stealing funds from clients, suborning perjury, aiding and abetting racketeering, and other ethical violations.[821]

Judge Kaufman: a change of heart...?

Kaufman had spent forty years of his life battling the Rosenberg-Sobell case. He had intervened against legal appeals for Sobell, against the publication of books on the case, and against the staging of dramas inspired by the case in theaters and on television.

Rod Townley, author of a November 10, 1977, *Juris Doctor* article on Judge Kaufman, put a number of questions to former federal Judge Simon Rifkind, Kaufman's friend and defender and head of an ABA Committee seeking to clear Kaufman of charges lodged against him by more than a hundred lawyers and law professors. Townley asked Rifkind to comment on Judge Kaufman's denial of Rosenberg-Sobell motions without a hearing. Rifkind replied, "Nothing unusual about that, in my opinion."[822] Asked about Kaufman's disregard of the rules against *ex parte* meetings. Rifkind said, "I don't care what the rule says!"[823]

Another member of the ABA Committee, Judge Donald Fretz, a California Superior Court judge, took a historical view of Judge Kaufman's *ex parte* practice.

> I have to admit, [his critics have] got a point. In my court we wouldn't think of talking to the prosecutor and asking for this and that. But apparently in the fifties this went on all the time.[824]

Both replies were, in effect, acknowledgments of Kaufman's wrongdoing.

In the 1970s, Kaufman may have sought to create a more politically balanced persona for himself by ruling in favor of pro-First Amendment litigants, as he did in 1971, when he dissented from an appellate decision upholding the right of the government to prevent publication of what became known as the *Pentagon Papers*. The Supreme Court subsequently agreed with his dissent.

As the years went by, a truth may have become apparent to Judge Kaufman. A campaign over many years by powerful political groups to get him a seat on the Supreme Court would not succeed. Nineteen Supreme Court justices had been appointed by five Republican and two Democratic Presidents since the execution of the Rosenbergs, but he had not been among them.

Kaufman must have also been aware there was strong opposition to his being appointed to the Supreme Court within the Court itself. He undoubtedly knew that Justice Frankfurter, in a letter to Judge Learned Hand five years after the Rosenbergs' execution, made it clear that he would do everything in his power to keep Kaufman from obtaining a seat on the Supreme Court. Frankfurter wrote, "I despise a Judge who feels God told him to impose a death sentence...I am mean enough to try to stay here [at the Supreme Court] long enough so that K will be too old to succeed me."[825]

With time, the extreme political duress under which Kaufman had presided over the Rosenberg-Sobell case began to recede, giving way to a somewhat more civil atmosphere. Relieved of duress, a more moderate, even liberal, persona appeared. He wrote the first judicial order compelling schools to desegregate in the North; reversed a decision to deport John Lennon on the grounds that the deportation order singled out Lennon for political reasons; the Supreme Court agreed with his dissent from a Court of Appeals decision to bar publication of the Pentagon Papers; he wrote a decision overturning an order that the Communist Party disclose the names of contributors to its presidential candidate.

On May 1, 1990, Kaufman wrote an article for the *New York Times*, in which he urged a course by appellate judges that contrasted sharply with the course he had taken in the Rosenberg-Sobell case. In the article, titled "Speedy Justice — At What Cost," Kaufman urged Congressional action to overcome limitations imposed on appeals from death sentences by the Supreme Court. He wrote

> A majority of the Supreme Court and Congress appear
> preoccupied with the problems of delay caused by piece-
> meal and repetitious litigation rather than with the need
> to safeguard essential liberties.[826]

Without direct reference to the Rosenberg-Sobell case, he criticized decisions in capital case appeals that used technical errors or failures by defense counsel as reasons to deny relief to appellants.

While there are times when counsel for the defense makes a tactical choice to waive objections or claims, an inmate should not be precluded from relying on arguments omitted from the original proceeding because of counsel's error.

Perhaps a truth had come to him: he would have been happier now, in his later years, if during the mid-20th Century inquisitions, he had chosen to be a stiff-necked Jew and a mule-stubborn American.

Judge Kaufman died on February 1, 1992. Virtually every obituary called attention to him as the judge who had sentenced the Rosenbergs to death.

A verdict on the verdict by Judge Kaufman's peers...

At its 1993 annual meeting, the American Bar Association staged a mock-trial of the Rosenbergs. The presiding judge was Marvin E. Aspen, a Federal District judge since 1979. The role of prosecutors were taken by Thomas Sullivan, a former United States Attorney in the Northern District of Illinois, and Andrea Zopp, a former Assistant United States Attorney in Chicago. The defense was undertaken by Gary Naftalis, a former Assistant United States Attorney for the Southern District of New York, and Harry M. Reasoner, a former law clerk to a judge on the U.S. Court of Appeals. Actors portrayed the defendants and witnesses.

Two jury panels were chosen from an actual New York City jury pool, each of six lay persons. At the trial's end, one jury quickly came in with a Not Guilty verdict; the other jury deliberated for almost four hours, and came up with the same verdict.[827]

The "secret evidence": the Venona/FBI messages ...

Possibly to counteract the Not Guilty verdicts at the 1993 ABA meeting, in 1995, the CIA released the "secret evidence" that had been rumored to have been in the prosecution's possession. The "secret evidence" came from the Venona/FBI Project, the mission of which was to decode and translate encrypted cable messages that had passed between Soviet embassy officials in the United States and officials in the Soviet Union during World War II. Many cover names appeared in the messages, some for people in the public eye, some for Soviet officials abroad, and some for spies. The FBI's contribution to the project was to supply the decoders with possible true names for cover names.

Approximately 3000 such messages were decoded, the great bulk of which related to trade, lend-lease and other legitimate transactions between the two governments.

At the time the FBI placed David Greenglass' and Julius Rosenberg's files on Justice official's desks in Spring 1950, the FBI had some twenty decoded messages indicating direct or indirect contact in 1944-1945 between Julius Rosenberg and a Soviet espionage controller in the United States. In several of these, the real or first names of persons appeared, in others they were referenced by cover names. The messages were essentially evaluative, describing the age, backgrounds, education, political outlooks, marital status and employment of actual or potential spies. None of the messages described specific targets or acts of espionage. None of the messages were decoded in their entirety; on average, about 50% of each message was decoded and translated.

None of the messages were introduced at the trial, nor were any Venona/FBI decoded messages ever introduced at subsequent espionage trials.

Why the Venona/FBI messages never made it to the courtroom...

The absence of the relevant Venona/FBI messages from the Rosenberg-Sobell trial has been explained by some officials and writers as an unwillingness by the government to reveal to the Soviets their espionage code had been broken. But at some point before the trial in 1951, possibly as early as 1945, Venona/FBI Project officials knew the Soviets had discovered that their espionage communication code had been penetrated. According to the official Venona/FBI historians

> The Soviets apparently had monitored Arlington Hall's "Russian Section" [the site of the Venona/FBI project] since at least 1945, when William Weisband [an Egyptian-born linguist who was fluent in Russian] joined the unit.[828]

In 1950, Weisband fell under suspicion of being a Soviet agent, which, if the suspicion was justified, meant that the Venona/FBI operation was known to the Soviets in 1945. Those suspicions were never validated.

Another source of Soviet information about the Venona/FBI operation was British intelligence officer and Soviet agent "Kim" Philby, who told the Soviet KGB in 1944 that British cryptologists had turned their attention to Soviet ciphers.[829] Philby would have also told them that British and American intelligence agencies were cooperating in breaking the Soviet code. In 1949, Philby was actually at the Venona/FBI operation at Arlington Hall, Virginia, having been assigned by the British intelligence agency as liaison with American intelligence agencies.[830] But Robert Lamphere, the FBI liaison officer in the Venona/FBI Project, believed that the Soviets knew their code had been broken "even prior to the time Philby arrived in the United States in October 1949."[831]

What our officials did know was that, in 1945, the Soviets had substituted a new code for the broken one.[832] This became obvious to the Venona cryptologists when they discovered they could not decode Soviet cables originating in 1946 and afterward. This was five years before the Rosenberg-Sobell trial. In short, introducing Venona/FBI messages at the Rosenberg-Sobell trial would not have told the Soviet Union anything it did not already know.

An explanation for why the messages never made it to court appeared in 1956 in an FBI interdepartmental memorandum

> ...the defense probably would be granted authority by the court to have private cryptographers hired by the defense examine the messages as well as the work sheets of the Government cryptographers. Also, in view of the fragmentary nature of the majority of these messages, the defense would make a request to have its cryptographers examine those messages which [hidden word] has been unsuccessful in breaking and which are not in evidence on the premise that such messages, if decoded, could exonerate their clients.[833]

Joseph Albright and Marcia Kunstel, the authors of *Bombshell*, who accepted the authenticity of the messages, regarded the problem as

> a patch of uncertainty about the ancestry of the Venona decryption that would complicate any attempt by the U.S. Justice Department to establish a chain of evidence to permit the introduction of a decoded Soviet cable in any future spy trial.[834]

In short, the absence of the messages from the trial was due to the possibility that they might contain exonerative information, and might not withstand authentication tests. Documents introduced as evidence at trials in the United States must satisfy the "chain of evidence" rule, under which both the prosecution and the defense have the right to discover the origin and itinerary of every document placed into evidence by the other side. If a document is a copy or paraphrase or decryption or translation of an original document, each side has the right to compare the text of the document entered as evidence with the text of the original. If the text of the entered document is identical to the text of the original document, the entered document is authentic. If the texts are not identical, the document lacks authenticity, although it may still, under certain circumstances, be admissible as evidence.

If Justice officials had entered one or more Venona/FBI messages as evidence at the Rosenberg-Sobell trial, the defense attorneys, using experts in decryption and linguistics, would have had the right to compare the texts in the released messages with the texts in the original Russian messages.

The CIA, which was given custodianship of the Venona/FBI messages when the Project was terminated in the 1980s, rejected a request by an attorney for the Rosenbergs' sons to be permitted to compare the decoded messages relating to their parents with the original Russian messages. As this is written, the right to make the comparison is still withheld.

The Venona/FBI messages as "secret evidence"...

There are very credible indications the Venona/FBI messages were used after the arrests of the defendants by Justice officials as a means of persuading the public, from which the jurors would be drawn, that the defendants committed atomic espionage. The messages were shown in full or in summary form, to media officials and editors, columnists and commentators, and selected scientists, as "secret evidence" of the defendants' guilt. The manner in which this was done was described in 1999 in *Venona, Decoding Soviet Espionage in America*, the authors of which accepted the Venona decodings as authentic. They wrote

> While the Venona Project and the decrypted messages themselves remained secret, the substance of the messages with the names of scores of Americans who had assisted Soviet espionage circulated among American military and civilian security officials. From the security officials the information went to senior executive-branch political appointees and members of Congress. They, in turn, passed it on to journalists and commentators, who conveyed the alarming news to the public.[835]

The use of the Venona/FBI messages as "secret evidence" also became known to the authors and others through Harold Urey, the Nobel physicist who had been listed as a witness by the prosecution. In June 1953, Urey wrote to Joseph Brainin, the chairman of the Committee, seeking clemency for the defendants that several reputable scientists had informed him that they had been shown "secret evidence" of the defendants' guilt.[836]

It is not known whether the "secret evidence," shown to — but not left with — opinion-makers, before and after the trial, was identical to the Venona/FBI messages released to the public in 1995. What is certain is that the accusations disseminated in the shadows by bearers of "secret evidence" was given the imprimatur of authenticity by Justice officials and the prosecutors.

The authenticity of the Venona/FBI messages...

Now that we know that Julius Rosenberg, Morton Sobell, and David Greenglass did pass classified information to the Soviet Union during World War II, the matter of the authenticity of the Venona/FBI messages might be considered moot. But since the messages were probably released in 1995 to rebut the ongoing criticisms of the conduct of the trial, the matter of their authenticity continues to be relevant, and especially so in respect to the accusations in the oral indictment involving the atom bomb and the charge of treason.

The only reference to the atomic bomb in the formal indictment is an allusion to "sketches of experiments conducted at the Los Alamos Project."[837] In the oral indictment in the courtroom, the defendants were charged directly with conspiring to commit espionage relating to the atom bomb. There may be an intended reference to the atom bomb in one of the decoded messages — Message 1340 — which mentions that David Greenglass was assigned to a "plant," not otherwise described, in Santa Fe, NM. It is the sole message in which one may reasonably argue there is an indirect reference to the atomic bomb. Was that message authentic?

Testing the authenticity of the Venona/FBI messages...

The refusal by the CIA to permit the customary tests of authenticity of documents led the authors to search for a way around the ban on making direct comparisons of the released messages with the original Russian messages. Our object was to discover whether the possible reference to the atom bomb in Message 1340 led to action by the FBI or any other counter-espionage agency. In the course of our search, we made a discovery that has a bearing on the deceptive relocation of the time of the crime by Justice officials.

Venona/FBI Messages 1340, 1657 and 1053...

On September 21, 1944, the Soviet espionage center in New York sent Message 1340 to Moscow.[838] It reads

> Lately the development of new people [D% has been in progress]. LIBERAL (ii) recommended the wife of his wife's brother, Ruth GREENGLASS, with a safe flat in view. She is 21 years old, a TOWNSWOMAN [GOROZhANKA] [iii], a GYMNAST [FIZKUL'TURNITsA] [iv] since 1942. She lives on STANTON [STANTAUN] Street. LIBERAL and his wife recommend her as an intelligent and clever girl.
>
> [15 groups unrecoverable]
>
> [C% Ruth] learned that her husband [v] was called up by the army but he was not sent to the front. He is a mechanical engineer and is now working at the ENORMOUS [ENORMOZ] [vi] plant in SANTA FE, New Mexico.
>
> [45 groups unrecoverable]

The message was decoded and translated by Venona workers some time in 1948, according to a Venona report dated April 27, 1948.[839] Within the text of each message there are Roman numerals which, at the end of the text, identify real names or places or other data supplied largely by the FBI at some time after the decoding. In this message the cover names preceding Roman numerals are identified as: [ii] Julius Rosenberg; [iii] American citizen; [iv] probably a member of the Young Communist League; [v] David Greenglass; [vi] Atomic Energy Project. It is important to keep in mind that the Roman numeral identifications of real names were not in the text of the messages; they were made at a later time, with the FBI as their source. But the name 'Ruth Greenglass' is in the text decoded in 1948, as is her address.

There is an error in the description of David Greenglass as a "mechanical engineer," and in designating Santa Fe rather than Los Alamos as the site of the plant to which he was assigned. These may be errors made by the Russian encoders, the American decoders or translators, or in the information supplied to the Venona personnel by the FBI.

The inclusion of Ruth Greenglass' real name in the text of message 1340 might be attributed to human error, laziness or lack of encoding time, were it not for a greater improbability, the inclusion of her address. No other person in any of the released messages relating to espionage agents, whether by real name or cover name, is given an easily identifiable address. The inclusion of the address would certainly have alarmed the recipient in Moscow because a counterintelligence agent, without even penetrating the code, by reading the real name Ruth Greenglass and her real address, both clearly revealed in the text, would know exactly where to look for the spy and her husband, and it would be little trouble to discover her brother-in-law and his wife, although their real names did not appear in the text.

Stanton Street is a relatively short street in the slums of Manhattan's lower East Side, where I had gone to Hebrew School as a boy. If Message 1340 had been decoded and translated in 1948, as the Venona record shows, it would have enabled the FBI, within an hour, to have found Ruth Greenglass and, through her, her brother-in-law, Julius Rosenberg. A phone call to the Atomic Energy Commission would have resulted in the discovery that David Greenglass had been employed at Los Alamos in 1944-1945. A ring of atom-bomb spies would have been caught in 1948, two years before the arrests of the defendants began.

The record shows, however, that the earliest acknowledged FBI contact with Greenglass was in February 1950, and with Julius Rosenberg a week after Greenglass' arrest in June 1950. The FBI's first recorded contact with Ruth Greenglass was after her husband's arrest.

No action appears to have been taken on the information in Message 1340.

Another real name appears in the text of decoded/translated message 1657, that of Ethel (second name not given). This message was sent to Moscow on November 27, 1944.

> Information on LIBERAL's [ii] wife [iii]. Surname that of her husband, first name ETHEL, 29 years old. Married five years. Finished secondary school. A FELLOWCOUNTRYMAN [ZEMLYaK] [iv] since 1938. Sufficiently well developed politically. Knows about her husband's work and the role of METR [v] and NIL [vi]. In view of delicate health does not work. Is character- ized positively and as a devoted person.[840]

Robert Lamphere, in his memoir, puts the time at which this message was decoded as prior to June 4, 1948.[841] The message is also mentioned in a Venona special report dated August 13, 1948.[842]

If the two messages, both decoded/translated sometime in 1948, are com- pared, we learn from message 1340 that Liberal's sister-in-law is named Ruth Greenglass, that she lives on Stanton Street in New York City and that her hus- band is in the army, working at "Sante Fe;" and from Message 1657 that Liberal's wife's name is Ethel. If both messages were authentically decoded and translated, that is, based solely on what was in the original Russian messages, the FBI could have within an hour or two harvested two families of spies, the Greenglasses and the Rosenbergs.

Following the message, a number of identifications are made: [ii] Julius Rosenberg; [iii] Ethel Rosenberg, nee Greenglass; [iv] Member of the Communist Party; [v] Probably Joel Barr or Alfred Sarant (note: two suspected spies); [vi] unidentified.

No action appears to have been taken on Message 1657.

There is a third message in which a real name appears in the text, No. 1053, which mentions Max Elitcher, who testified at the trial that Julius Rosenberg and Morton Sobell repeatedly invited him to join them in espionage, an invitation he testified he repeatedly ignored. The message states that Liberal traveled to Washington, D.C. to recruit Elitcher into a spy ring.[843] Lamphere put the date of decoding of this message as "spring of 1948."[844]

This gives us a friend of Liberal's to lead us to Julius Rosenberg in 1948, if the other two messages were somehow not comprehended by the Venona staff or by FBI Agent Lamphere. But the chronology of events tells us that this third message that points directly to the Rosenbergs and the Greenglasses was also not acted on in 1948.

Two years later, on June 27, 1950, Lamphere sent a memorandum to Meredith Gardner, the senior decoder/translator in the Venona Project

> Since the referenced memorandum [of June 23, 1950] was prepared it has been determined that one JULIUS ROSENBERG is probably identical with the individual described as ANTENNA and LIBERAL in that memorandum. It is also believed now that DAVID GREENGLASS is identical with the individual described as KALIBR, and that RUTH GREENGLASS is identical with the individual known under the codename OSA.
>
> ***
>
> More complete details concerning these individuals will be furnished to you at a latter date.[845]

Lamphere's memorandum appears to be a deception intended to support a relocation of the time of discovery of the crime and the defendants.

Before analyzing the reasons for the relocation, let us assume that Justice officials did not act on the information in the three messages because they wanted to keep the defendants under surveillance in order to discover their accomplices and Soviet contacts. Seemingly, the surveillance, if there was one, was unproductive over the two-year span between the emergence of the messages in summer 1948, and the arrests of the defendants in summer 1950, because no surveillance-related testimony was given at the trial, no new acts of espionage were exposed, and no accomplices were discovered. Nor would a two-year surveillance operation account for Lamphere's 1950 memorandum to Gardner. Gardner knew the messages had been decoded and translated and, with input from Lamphere, finalized in 1948. Nor would a two year surveillance operation account for Lamphere's 1950 memorandum to Gardner. There would be no reason to conceal from Gardner that a surveillance was undertaken as a result of his staff's successful decoding and translation operation.

The most logical explanation for the 1948-1950 discrepancy is that Justice officials were not certain what should be done with the information they were given in 1948. The Cold War had not yet reached the intensity that it displayed at the end of 1949, when the United States learned that the Soviet Union had created its own atom bomb. A trial in 1948 or before the end of 1949 would have been conducted in an atmosphere in which prosecutorial claims of hostility by the Soviet Union might not have been be sufficiently credible. Justice officials had not forgotten the series of failures in the *Amerasia* case (1945), the Redin case (1946), and the first Hiss trial (1948-1949). And, not of least concern, prosecuting an all-Jewish cast of defendants at any time could produce unforeseen difficulties.

In the fall of 1949, the news that the Soviet Union had exploded its own atom bomb, and the immediate outcries in Congress and the media for an atomic first-strike against the Soviet Union, created an entirely new situation. These were signals to Justice officials they must move ahead with indictments that would conform to the prevailing Cold War agenda.

The FBI injects ethnicity into the Venona/FBI messages...

When the dedicated Venona code breakers and translators teased out coherent portions of the coded messages flowing between the Moscow espionage center and the spy controllers in the United States during World War II, they found hundreds of cover names, although not all of them were for spies. So assiduously did the Soviet espionage apparatus cling to masking real names by cover names that in the years 1942-1945, the years covered by the messages, real names were not used even for public figures and places: President Roosevelt was "Captain," Great Britain was "Ostrov," Winston Churchill was "Boar," the Comintern was the "Big House," Washington, D.C. was "Carthage," London was "Sidon," New York City was "Tir," and so on.

The FBI's role in the Venona Project was to provide the code breakers/translators with lists of real names of persons who might be the persons referenced by the cover names. Because of the FBI's politically and ethnically skewed files, almost 50% of the initial 50 real names the FBI provided to the Venona operation to match the cover names in the first 99 decoded messages, were Jewish. About 7% were non-Jewish foreign born. The rest were native-born.[846] As a result, genuinely real names were not found for more than 90% of the cover names.

The official Venona historians gave no indication that the unmatched cover names might find their matches anywhere else than in the skewed "suspect population" files. In their view, the unidentified cover names belonged to clever American Communist spies who had succeeded in covering their tracks with the help of Communists in government. The CIA/Venona historians outrightly attacked Presidents Roosevelt and Truman who, they declared, had lagged behind the Republican Party in searching for and exposing Communists.[847] They also castigated the Supreme Court for upholding Constitutional protections for persons labeled 'Communists'

> The Supreme Court's decision in *Yates v. U.S.,* handed
> down in June 1957, all but voided the Smith Act as a tool
> for prosecuting [Communist] Party leaders.[848]

In the account of the Venona/FBI operation written by the CIA-appointed Venona historians, and in the memoirs of Robert Lamphere, no acknowledgment is made of the singularity of the preponderance of Jewish names — 17 times greater than their percentage of the population — proffered by the FBI as suspected spies. Perhaps they saw nothing singular in the proffer because it conformed to their own mindsets on ethnicity and loyalty.

The officials of the Department of Justice, from the Attorney General down, likewise saw no skew in imputing disloyalty to Jews in far greater numbers than among any other sections of the population. In September 1950, in a letter to the Immigration and Naturalization Service (INS), James M. McInerney, Assistant Attorney General, forwarded the names of 34 suspects "connected with the Soviet espionage group" who might seek passports. Of the 34 names, 18 (53%) were identifiably Jewish.[849] The letter did not request that the "suspects" be detained.

One year later, on October 9, 1951, McInerney sent the INS another letter in which the previous list was pared down to 12 individuals, six of them definitely Jewish. The "suspects" were not being sought for crimes, nor were indictments pending against them. The letter contained the comment

> In addition, only notification of intended departure is requested, and no steps should be taken to detain any of the individuals...[850]

David Greenglass's confession to perjury on CBS' *60 Minutes* television
program, broadcast December 5, 2001. (Page 372)

Interviewer:
>...you did not have a memory at the
>time of Ethel typing up the notes?

Greenglass:
>I had no memory of that happening.
>None whatsoever.

Interviewer:
>And did (federal prosecutor Roy)
>Cohn encourage you to testify that
>you saw Ethel typing up the notes?

Greenglass:
>Of course he did.

Chapter 15 | Motivations, confessions, mortality, icons emerging

Was Julius Rosenberg motivated to forestall a future genocide...?

In the years immediately following release of the Venona/FBI messages, support for their findings was tendered by a number of books, articles and interviews involving former officials of the Soviet Union's espionage apparatus.

The most relevant of these is Alexander Feklisov's *The Man Behind the Rosenbergs*, which was published in France in 1999, and in the United States in 2001.[851]

Feklisov described himself as Julius Rosenberg's case officer.[852] He wrote that Julius Rosenberg had provided him with information on military technology, including "minor" information on the atom bomb through David Greenglass.[853]

Feklisov wrote that he had had approximately 50 meetings with Julius Rosenberg, but none with Ethel Rosenberg, and that Rosenberg had been solely motivated by his belief that the Soviet Union was modeling itself on socialist-egalitarian principles, and believed that a strengthened Soviet Union would stand in the way of the future emergence of another Holocaust-driven state. Feklisov, who said he still believed in Communism, wrote about himself and Julius Rosenberg in 2001,

> I fully understand how our commitment to Communist values, hatred of exploiters and sympathy for the oppressed, the sincere enthusiasm in working at the creation of an era of equality and social justice may appear ridiculous today. Nevertheless, like millions of men and women all over the world, we believed in those ideals from the depths of our soul and we were ready to sacrifice our lives for them. Was Julius in the dark about the purges, the political trials and the repression of the Stalin era? He never discussed the subject with me and appeared convinced that the revolution could not avoid violence...
>
> ***
>
> Our ideological agreements were also strengthened by the thought that the human race was fighting an enemy attempting to erase thousands of years of civilization...
>
> ***
>
> ...The issue that most troubled him was the extermination of the Jews...[854]

Next to last (?) confession…

On December 5, 2001, fifty years after giving his testimony at the Rosenberg-Sobell trial, David Greenglass confessed, on a CBS *60 Minutes* television program, to having perjuriously testified against his sister and brother-in-law at the instruction of the prosecutors, in 1951.[855] Earlier in 2001, in Sam Roberts' *The Brother*, Greenglass similarly confessed to perjury. He committed the perjuries, he said, because "nobody ever told me that's what they were going" to do, that is, execute the Rosenbergs. He went on,

> That's neither here nor there. As long as they had something over my head about my wife and my family, then they could probably get me to do anything that would preserve them. That's the facts. There's no getting away from that. And most men would do that. Not just me.[856]

Asked about the notes he had testified Ethel Rosenberg typed up, Greenglass said at his television interview

> Greenglass: To this day I can't even remember that the typing took place…I don't even think it was done while we were there.

> Interviewer: But what you do remember is that you did not have a memory at the time of Ethel typing up the notes?

> Greenglass: I had no memory of that happening. None whatsoever.

The interviewer asked why Greenglass had given his false testimony. Greenglass replied that he was told to do so by Saypol's chief assistant, Roy Cohn.

> Interviewer: And did Cohn encourage you to testify that you saw Ethel typing up the notes?

> Greenglass: Of course he did.[857]

Greenglass was asked whether, if he met the Rosenbergs' sons, he would express regret for the role he had played in their parents' deaths. Greenglass gave a one-word answer: "No."

The interviewer asked Greenglass whether he could explain why the Rosenbergs chose to die rather than break their silence. Greenglass replied: "One word — stupid."

The interviewer asked, "And you're sitting here today — a man with a clear conscience?" Greenglass replied, "Absolutely. I sleep very well."

Greenglass' statements to the FBI, the author of *The Brother* wrote, went beyond naming the Rosenbergs, citing a memorandum from Hoover stating that Greenglass had "provided information about individuals and alleged espionage activities" which, if made public could not "adequately insulate David Greenglass from civil suits."[858] Meaning that Greenglass had not only perjured himself in respect to the Rosenbergs, but also in respect to others, or else there would not be fear of civil suits against him by persons who might prove that he had falsely implicated them in espionage. Hoover's ultimate concern would not have been that Greenglass might be sued, but that any lawsuit against Greenglass for libel would inevitably put the FBI, and Hoover himself, in a bad light.

Why did Greenglass confess to having perjured himself? He gives few clues to what led him to do so. Perhaps it was to deny responsibility for his sister's and brother-in-law's executions, and to justify what he had done by saying that any other man in his position would have done the same. Or, he may have been "getting back" at Saypol and Cohn, whom he had outlived, for their treatment of him, and especially for the fright he must have undergone when his status as a co-conspirator had been changed to co-defendant after the Rosenberg's arraignment.

There was also the matter of financial gain. Greenglass agreed to provide his statements to the author of *The Brother* "in return for a share of the proceeds" of the sale of the book.[859] We do not know whether he was paid by CBS for his televised confessions. As this is written, David Greenglass is still with us. Does he have one more confession to make?

Helen Sobell...

Helen Sobell, who had spent a major portion of her life seeking justice for her husband and the Rosenbergs, may have been unaware of David Greenglass' confessions, which he made five months before she died. She had been suffering from Alzheimer's disease for ten years. The authors had visited her ten years earlier, shortly after the first symptoms of Alzheimer's had appeared. Ten years prior to that, she had earned a doctorate in computer education and, about that time, she and Morton Sobell were divorced.

Icons emerging...?

The Rosenberg-Sobell case has inspired investigative journalism, legal and scholarly books, films, television shows, plays, art exhibits and musical compositions in which the Rosenberg couple have been either central to their themes, or in which they had been recognizably present. A transition may be underway, in which the Rosenbergs may acquire iconic identities in the public's imagination.

The most recent examples of this were memorable scenes in the film *Angels in America*, in which Roy Cohn, played by Al Pacino, is depicted in his hospital bed dying of AIDS, still infused with belligerent brightness and anger, disdaining to use patriotism as a cover for the relentless trail he left of books in flames, human electrocutions, reputations and careers crushed, clients defrauded and deceived. He finds himself immobilized by AIDS, the 20th Century's most relentless mass disease. He is in the grip of an hallucination in which Ethel Rosenberg, played by Meryl Streep, is in his hospital room, many years older than the young woman he last saw in the courtroom in which he helped prosecute her.

She is listening calmly to his defense of his right to have lived. She is unable to forgive him, and yet, witnessing his agony, sings a tender lullaby to him and, after his death, helps a Cohn friend recite the Hebrew prayer for the dead. Neither remorse, nor regret, nor blame, nor praise, nor innocence, nor guilt are relevant to the scene. The audience recognizes Ethel Rosenberg. She and her husband were that young couple who chose to defy government officials in the early 1950s, even at the cost of their lives. Roy Cohn is remembered because, not yet twenty-four years old in 1951, he told David Greenglass to choose whether his sister or his wife would face electrocution.

Iconization is a process by which large numbers of people find unusual qualities in individuals called to their attention by history, qualities that transcend what once may have been important questions about their actions. This process may be underway for the Rosenbergs. Time has leeched away details of the Rosenbergs' history that, in an earlier time, may have been headline news, and has left us only with a couple and their friend, whose passion led them to accept death before what they regarded as the dishonor of falsely confessing to treason. The details are grist for history, the passioned defiance is grist for imagination and self-questioning.

Iconization by the public is like the tide. Public officials cannot stop it.

Quote from Supreme Court Justice David Davis (appointed by Abraham Lincoln) telling us, very plainly, that when the President wants to suspend the Constitution, the problem is not with the Constitution but with the President. (Page 385)

The Constitution of the United States is a law for rulers and people, equally in war and peace, and covers with the shield of its protection all classes of men, at all times and under all circumstances.

No doctrine involving more pernicious consequences was ever invented by the wit of man than that any of its provisions can be suspended during any of the great exigencies of government.

Such a doctrine leads directly to anarchy or despotism, but the theory of necessity on which it is based is false, for the government, within the Constitution, has all the powers granted to it which are necessary to preserve its existence, as has been happily proved by the result of the great effort to throw off its just authority.

Chapter 16 | An ending and a beginning

Hundreds of millions of voices throughout the world had been raised to stay the Rosenbergs' executions. A Pope who had spent his life denouncing Communism and Communists added his voice to save the Jewish couple he knew were Communists. The Pope's coreligionist, a Knight of the Vatican, who headed the United States Department of Justice, locked his Pope's plea in a drawer so that it would not come to his President's attention. He was followed by another Attorney General who ensnared the Chief Justice of the Supreme Court in an illegal *ex parte* hearing and extracted from him an illegal commitment to have the Supreme Court dismiss an order for a stay of execution he had not read and that had not yet been written.

On a Jewish Sabbath eve, June 19, 1953, a young American Jewish couple declined to make counterfeit confessions to having committed treason against the United States. The husband, out of misplaced idealism, had committed a crime for which his indictment made no claim that he had harmed the United States. That crime was inflated to "treason" by reckless and opportunistic officials, prosecutors and the judge to satisfy a political agenda. To have confessed to the uncommitted crime, for which Justice officials cynically demanded the names of accomplices who would likewise face the threat of execution for an uncommitted crime, was beyond the Rosenberg's capacity to satisfy. They would be sending family members and friends to their deaths, making orphans of their children and burdening their futures with an unearned shame.

Julius and Ethel's agony had fallen on them at a time when the details of the tragedies of the Holocaust were becoming known. The Rosenbergs could not see themselves doing what small numbers of European Jews had done: saving themselves from the crematoria by finding other Jews to take their place. If they thought of their refusal to confess to the uncommitted crime as martyrdom, it was not to Communism, but to a venerable American maxim: death before dishonor, death before a shattered conscience.

A reparation of honesty...

As long as official and media accounts continue to maintain that the crime of the Rosenberg-Sobell defendants was treason, we will be extending the life of a politically-inspired falsehood. We will, also, be encouraging another generation of prosecutors to treat the Constitution as an ignorable standard because it does not license the practice of deceptions and perjuries in order to gain convictions.

To have tried and punished the defendants for what they did would have led to an unexceptional trial. To have tried and punished them for a crime they did *not* commit did exceptional harm to American justice.

A reparation of honesty is owed to the nation, for the monumental and dishonorable misuse of law, the courts and the presidency in the Rosenberg-Sobell case.

Honesty is also owed because of the peril our officials have added to a long imperiled people. In the all-Jewish cast of defendants, and in the unprecedented peacetime death sentences, Justice officials, the presiding judge and the president created a recklessly false corroboration for the *Protocols of the Elders of Zion*, a gift to international anti-Semitic organizations beyond their wildest dreams. A gift "made in America."

A reparation of honesty is also due the children and grandchildren, and all the descendants of the Rosenbergs and Sobell, and to those of the Greenglasses as well. The Greenglasses could not withstand the threats to their lives, and were unconscionably exploited by Justice officials to testify perjuriously in the perverse political and abased atmosphere of mid-20th Century America.

Some other mid-20th Century Americans are still unjustly imprisoned, some have died, some were murdered in prison. We write of men and women who were convicted for their beliefs, not their actions. Or were guilty of one crime but prosecuted for another, in which they were found guilty and imprisoned or executed. Among the cases that continue to confront the judicial system and the public with misconduct by prosecutors and judges are those that involved Alger Hiss, Leonard Peltier, Mumia Abu-Jamal, Jonathan Pollard, and a number of cases involving American and foreign Muslims.

Their children and grandchildren, and those who follow, are burdened by unjust histories. The greatest burden of all is to the nation as a whole. It is *our* reputation for fair justice, honesty and humanity that remains scarred to this day, and into the future, unless we redress the wrongs done in our name.

The nation has a history of offering redress in cases that have resisted closure because the doubts of guilt were based on stubborn facts.

> In 1915, Leo Frank was convicted in Georgia at a trial rife with anti-Semitism, for raping and murdering a young Christian girl, for which he was sentenced to death. We described his exoneration by the State of Georgia.

> Tom Mooney, a labor leader, was tried for murder in 1916, found guilty, sentenced to death, unofficially pardoned and freed in 1938, and officially pardoned in 1961.

> Nicola Sacco and Bartolomeo Vanzetti, two anarchists, were tried, in 1921 for murder and were executed in 1927; fifty years later Massachusetts Governor Michael

Dukakis issued a proclamation that read, in part, "We are not here to say whether these men are guilty or innocent. We are here to say that the high standards of justice, which we in Massachusetts take such pride, failed Sacco and Vanzetti."[860]

In the Scottsboro case, 9 young black men were tried for rape of 2 women in Alabama, in 1931, all were sentenced to death. All charges were eventually dropped for five of them, three were paroled in 1950, one escaped.

A good recent example of the righting of prosecutorial deceptions is the 2009 Department of Justice request that the case against convicted Senator Ted Stevens of Alaska be dismissed because of prosecutorial misconduct.

The Soviet Union and Czechoslovakia made reparations of honesty within a decade of the Moscow-Prague miscarriages of justice in 1952-1953.

The time is long overdue for us to clean our own house.

The skewed "suspect population" lists are still in service and expanding...

The misleading and tragedy-laden FBI suspect population lists for finding spies and saboteurs are now bigger, although no better, than they were sixty years ago. In May 2009, the *New York Times* ran a headline that read: TERROR LIST WRONGLY INCLUDES 24,000, WHILE SOME ACTUAL SUSPECTS ESCAPED IT.[861] The full FBI list to which the *Times* referred comprised 1.1 million names, including those of Senator Edward M. Kennedy and Representative John Lewis, both of them vigorous civil rights advocates. The *Times* also wrote that "Muslim activists and others have been listed for political reasons," and quotes an ACLU official as saying that "all sorts of problems that have larded" up the FBI lists, and that "the whole thing just really needs to be torn down" and replaced.

The real problem is that the FBI has been and is now a secret "thought police" operation, with a focus chiefly on Americans and foreigners who are critical of the *status quo* or of government policies they consider unConstitutional and contrary to democratic and egalitarian goals. About a quarter of a century ago, the FBI began filling its file cabinets with the names of Muslims, both American and foreign. Muslims now occupy the FBI's attention in the same way that Jews, blacks, and civil rights advocates did in the 1950s. It is not incompetence that has "larded" up the FBI's lists, but a reliance on "suspect populations" in which beliefs, ancestry and blood are taken as indicia of hostility to the United States, as well as "proofs" of criminal conduct. There follow arrests based on profiling rather than on scrupulous police attention to what, who, where and when.

With the addition of the Muslim suspect population to the lists, the percentage of the nation regarded by law enforcement agencies as potentially disloyal from birth — indigenous Americans, African-Americans, Hispanics, Jews and Muslims — rose to 28%. But the actual size of the combined suspect populations is much greater. Judging from the current "anti-terrorist" surveillance programs that cover more than a hundred million Americans, our total "suspect population" now includes the majority of the nation.

"Suspect population" lists are hidden shields for the guilty in all crimes, from speeding to spying. The American spies-for-pay for the Soviet Union never made the FBI's suspect population lists because they lacked the prejudicial qualifications of ancestry and beliefs. If any of the FBI directors of the past ninety years had had a taste for the hard work that honest policemen do, they would have known that spies-for-pay for our designated enemies would not likely be found in street demonstrations on behalf of the nations they served, nor would they call attention to themselves by picketing the White House, nor would they ever utter a word of criticism of the FBI.

A new direction must be given to the FBI, to protect the nation from more miscarriages of justice originating with genealogical and philosophic lists of presumed potential enemies of the United States. Lists of candidate-suspects that number in the millions are toxic absurdities with a potential for spawning monumental tragedies. The billions of taxpayer dollars spent on compiling and updating these files serve only to finance the most backward, regressive and anti-democratic bureaucracies in government. The rationale that the FBI multi-million skewed lists do lead to a spy on rare occasions would be more credible if the sheer number and origins of the lists did not shield a dozen or more professional expert spies-for-pay for every amateur ideology-driven spy discovered. The amateur spy and the many professional spies would both have been found by good police work that was not burdened by the mythology that genes and pride in the First Amendment are markers for treason.

The Constitution: America's scripture or a contraband doctrine…?

The movement for a new trial and clemency in the Rosenberg-Sobell case was made possible by the nation's Constitution, which requires that trials be transparent so that prosecutorial and judicial misconduct and deceptions in the courtroom are discoverable.

As this is written — in November of 2009 — public trials and transparency in national security trials are no longer the norm. The system of justice in place in the 1950s was bifurcated in the 1970s, leaving the nation with two judicial systems, one based on the Constitution in civil cases and "ordinary" crimes, such as murder, rape, theft, fraud and so on, while a second judicial system, created solely by the Executive and Congress, not provided for in the Constitution or by an amendment to the Constitution, has jurisdiction over "national security" and other cases the Executive describes as relating to security.

In the new, non-Constitutional system of justice, tangible evidence of guilt plays a decidedly inferior role in the process, while ancestry, "beliefs" or "sentiments," and assumed motivations are treated as evidence of criminal allegiance and actions. Lay jurors, the triers of fact in the Constitutional court system, are entirely absent in the alternative system, in which trials are military in character, with military personnel who are dependent on the Executive for promotions, assignments, and life-styles, acting as judges and jurors.

The new justice system is Executive-oriented. Prosecutors who fail to issue indictments in compliance with the Executive's agenda are summarily dismissed, as witness the firing of eight U.S. Attorneys in 2005.[862] The following year, a federal judge in the unConstitutional counterfeit judiciary resigned, apparently because he would not continue to be a party to the illegal and unConstitutional uses to which the new judiciary was being put.[863]

In the first months of the new administration, with President Barack Obama in the White House, and Eric H. Holder as Attorney General, the Executive argued in court for retaining the debased court system that began with President Jimmy Carter's administration and should have ended when President Barack Obama took office. There is presently no end in sight to the grief that will continue to be generated by sham courts that are governed, not by the Constitution, but by transient tenants of the White House.

The "old" procedures — arrests for probable cause, lawful interrogations, access to lawyers and speedy trials — have been "legally" abandoned for the new suspect populations. More than 1000 Muslims were secretly arrested immediately after 9/11; access to lawyers was denied them for very long periods of time, in some cases for years; torture as a means of interrogation had the White House tenant's and Congress' blessing. The public does not know, to this day, how many were actually tried and how many remain "detained" in prisons of which we are unaware.

Our new president has declared torture during interrogation to be illegal and immoral, but he enables its return in the future by declining to have those who authorized and practiced torture indicted for their criminal conduct. Indeed, those he protects from accountability were the professional descendants of those who committed the same crimes against "suspects" among the indigenous American populations, and the slaves and the descendants of slaves in the 18th, 19th and 20th Centuries. The permissive memoranda by lawyers in the federal government, who found "legal" rationales for brutality, sadism, and genocide against these early populations, were the precedents for current opinions "legalizing" illegalities, cruelties, and sadism against members of 21st Century suspect populations. Had the earlier lawyers and interrogators been tried for their illegal actions, there might have been no such practices in our own time. If those who most recently endorsed and practiced illegal sadistic interrogations are not held accountable under the law, the option of torture will remain a shameful staple of "justice" far into the future. How then will we be held different from totalitarian sadistic governments elsewhere in the world? By what right will we call ourselves Americans?

Spare the rod, spoil the nation: a new strategy for governing...?

The debasement of our system of justice was not limited to the creation of a counterfeit court system, but spread to the Constitutional court system as well. The "repugnant philosophy" left no part of government untouched, and altered the outlook of the Department of Justice and of law enforcement agencies of states and municipalities in respect to the population as a whole. The new outlook can be summed up in a phrase: *Spare the rod, spoil the nation!*

Over the past half century, spanning ten presidents and many hundred of governors, the rod has fallen more heavily on Americans than ever before in the nation's history. As a result, the United States, arguably the most democratic nation on earth, is now the largest incarcerator of human beings on the planet. The United States, with less than 5% of the world's population, incarcerates more than 23% of the world's prisoners.

In 1950, when our population was 150,000,000, our total federal and state prison population was 166,123; in 2003, with a population of almost 300,000,000, the prison population was 1,409,280, or 8 times higher than it had been in 1950. The United States now imprisons 750 per 100,000 Americans; for Russia, the number is 628. The two nations lead the world in incarcerations, just as they do in their atom bomb arsenals.[864] A prediction attributed to the Department of Justice is that if the growth of our rate of incarceration remains unchanged, the time is not far off when one out of every 20 adult Americans will spend time in prison during his/her lifetime.[865]

Because our law enforcement agencies are firmly wedded to their suspect population outlooks, one of every nine African-American men between the ages of 20 and 34 is incarcerated; the comparable figure for white men in that age group is one in thirty. Among women between the ages of 35 to 39, one of every 100 African-American women is imprisoned, compared to one of every 355 white women.[866]

Of the world's estimated 21,000 prisoners awaiting execution in 2006, approximately 16% were on America's death rows. That is more than three times greater than our percentage of the world's population.[867] That may be because elsewhere in the world fewer heads of state are permitted to resort to executions to deal with critics, agitators, skeptics, non-confessors, and psychopathic or demented murderers. One hundred nations now prohibit their political leaders from taking the lives of citizens for any reason whatsoever. Among them are Great Britain, France, Spain, Germany, Italy, Belgium, Denmark, Poland, Finland, Greece, Sweden, Canada, Mexico, Venezuela, Cambodia, and Rwanda. In the United States, the District of Columbia, and 13 states have abolished the death penalty: Alaska, Hawaii, Iowa, Maine, Massachusetts, Michigan, Minnesota, New Jersey, North Dakota, Rhode Island, Vermont, West Virginia, and Wisconsin.

In spite of the fact that nearly 40% of the states have abolished the death penalty, executions in the United States have gone up at an accelerated rate over the past thirty years. From 1977 to 1991, a period of fifteen years, we executed 157 persons; over the next fourteen years and five months we executed 872,[868] a sixfold increase.

Had something happened to the American character that raised the rate of incarceration and executions of Americans to a ferocious first place among nations?[869] Or had something happened to America's leaders that made them more punishing?

Increased incarceration rates are worldwide, although none as sharply as that of the United States. This is likely due in great part to the growing hostility by the world's populations to the men and women, elected or self-selected, who govern them. Their hostility is reciprocated by their leaders, who respond by legislating new crimes, and new laws, and enforcing old ones more rigorously. By these steps, they believe they can compel the great majority of the dissatisfied human race to swallow disasters, poverty and disappointment in silence.

It falls to law enforcement agencies — police, sheriffs, prosecuting attorneys and judges —, to exhibit to the population the ever-growing stern mindset of national political leaders. Inevitably, arbitrariness, arrogance and essential indifference to law characterize the behavior of law enforcement personnel, and especially the behavior of prosecutors.

An example: in February 2003, the Supreme Court of Missouri considered an appeal by a death row inmate to have his murder conviction reopened on the basis of new evidence. Frank A. Yung, a Missouri assistant state attorney, opposed the appeal and was asked by one of the judges

> Are you suggesting that even if we find Mr. Amrine is actually innocent, he should be executed?

Mr. Yung replied
> That's correct, your honor.[870]

Mr. Yung's reply would have been unthinkable to other prosecutors sixty years ago. So would secret trials. So would torture to obtain confessions. So would America as the prison capital of the world.

The gap...

On a world scale, the ultimate source of the growing hostility between rulers and the ruled is the steadily widening gap between the appetites of 1%-of-population blocs and the modest aspirations of most human beings for the wherewithal to feed families, raise and educate children and to live long enough to experience nostalgia for times past.

Sociologists, criminologists and other scholars have found an unmistakable relationship between a government's incarceration rates and its priorities. As long ago as 1998, our government became last among all nations in the percent of the value of Gross Domestic Production allotted to services to the populations, and first in the rate of incarceration of its citizens.[871]

The long way home...

How have we come such a long way from the Constitutional system of sixty years ago? Almost every deceitful stratagem against due process prohibited by the Constitution in the 20th Century has become standard operating procedure in the first years of the 21st Century. The violations of the Constitution recognized six decades earlier are violations no longer. They have been written into law by Congress and by Presidential Orders.

The counterfeit court laws and Executive Orders pose an unprecedented danger to the American public, even apart from denial of Constitutional protections to defendants. They have a chilling effect on freedom of discussion, debate and advocacy, and undermine the power of public opinion to resist and redress the tragedies that follow the adoption of extremist "repugnant philosophies" by Justice officials and sections of the judiciary.

The most recent debasement of the Constitution and the laws has been justified by what our past president labeled the "war on terrorism." A long-deceased distant cousin of that president, Supreme Court Justice David Davis, appointed to the Court by Abraham Lincoln at a time of great stress and uncertainty, found such a rationale pernicious. A civilian who had opposed the Union side in the Civil War and who had been sentenced to death by hanging, appealed his conviction and sentence. The government's response was that, in time of crises, such as war, the President's will, not the Constitution, was the law of the land.

Writing for the Court, Justice Davis said

> The statement of this proposition shows its importance, for, if true, republican government is a failure, and there is an end of liberty regulated by law.[872]

Making a specific reference to the Civil War, Davis wrote

> The Constitution of the United States is a law for rulers and people, equally in war and peace, and covers

with the shield of its protection all classes of men, at all times and under all circumstances. No doctrine involving more pernicious consequences was ever invented by the wit of man than that any of its provisions can be suspended during any of the great exigencies of government. Such a doctrine leads directly to anarchy or despotism, but the theory of necessity on which it is based is false, for the government, within the Constitution, has all the powers granted to it which are necessary to preserve its existence, as has been happily proved by the result of the great effort to throw off its just authority.[873]

Justice Davis was telling us, very plainly, that when the Executive believes that the Constitution is inadequate to protect the nation, the problem is not with the Constitution but with the Executive.

Illusions of Final Solutions...

The Rosenberg-Sobell case was an infinitesimally small stitch in the ever-expanding wild tapestry of human history, a tapestry seemingly without deliberate design in any direction. The stitchers are us, a species whose present characteristics emerged only some 5000 generations ago. Our long ago ancestors lived by values that were true for virtually all of them, because the life of each individual was a microcosm of the life of everyone. We are not like that any longer. The disparities among us in meeting biologic, physiologic and emotional needs are enormous. The lives of the poor or laboring vast majority are not microcosms of the lives of the small minority of humans who will never face the mutilations of poverty, the physical suffering of the hungry or of those with untreated diseases or the inconsolability of those from whom everything has been taken.

History tells us that social conflicts have no everlasting solutions. The American Revolution did not free all Americans to tend to their flocks and reap the golden grain of their fields; the Civil War did not free all Americans from the cruelties of unrewarded labor; the New Deal did not put bread on every table; the victories over Nazi Germany and Imperial Japan did not beget peace in America or anywhere else in the world.

The Russian people once hailed Communism as the "final solution" to a wretched way of life, and they are finding now that capitalism can give them greater freedom and greater wretchedness. The German "final solution" made every German an accomplice in the enslavement and murder of millions of men, women and children.

Only a perpetually nervous and delusional 1% of our population believe in "final solutions." They believe that if they create new laws enforcing docility, build more prisons, more solitary confinement centers, more detention camps, more rendition routes, more "alternative" interrogation chambers, more gallows, more electrocution chairs, more needle-execution kits, the disappearance of critical and rebellious humans will follow as surely as night follows day.

If the non-delusional majority seeks a modest sort of Eden for the future, it will not be inspired by "finality" but by modest visions. It will compel the recognition of a child's right to live a natural life by constraining empire builders for whom a child's life counts only as something to fill a uniform and a military coffin. It will put bread on the tables of the many rather than bread on the already overflowing tables of bread in the homes of the few. It will bring healing to all and not only to those who can pay for it. It will sensibly restore the Constitution to its place as America's guiding scripture. And it will end the cascade of counterfeit laws by which the Constitution is trumped by a 1% agenda.

If we have the courage to create the next temporary solution to our problems, we will begin by finally acknowledging that two centuries of unchecked growth in the power of gargantuan corporations and banks has been accompanied by a disastrous decline in democratic government and in the expansion of dead-end solutions to the problems of the overwhelming majority of Americans.

The power of a million voters is as nothing against the power of a few lobbyists in the pay of the financial, manufacturing, defense and political overlords. The wishes of voters are as nothing compared to the megacorporation bribes taken by the overwhelming number of elected members of Congress.

It will take the miracle of struggle to restore our Founders' dreams. The middle and working classes need an assurance that their jobs and professions will be given the same protection accorded to property, and their occupations, homes, farms, cars and little leisure boats will be protected against termination, seizures and foreclosures. If a well-regulated business sector is permitted, the mid-size business firms will be protected against unscrupulous competition and hostile takeovers; the storekeeper and merchant and family farmer will be protected from marauding speculators. The 99% will be shielded from the 1%.

Such an America will not be utopia, but a respite from more than 200 years of recurrent assaults on the lives of the majority of Americans. It will be a very modest Eden. The serpent will still be there, caged, a reminder to us not to heed the lure and siren calls of an unaccountable, irresponsible and life-indifferent parasitical monstrosity that must never again be trusted with our fate or that of our children.

Our almost-Eden will have its tensions, its unpredictable fluctuations, and there will be days when its streets will be on fire. And then, on to the next temporary miracle of improvement. This seems to be humankind's way.

Tough love...

A small but moving stitch in the tapestry of America was written by a former hero of the 1% — George F. Kennan — who told us, after the Rosenbergs were sentenced to death, why we must protect and proclaim the Americanism of the multitudes with all our strength, why we must revere America with tough love.

> ...America is something in our minds and our habits of outlook which causes us to believe in certain things and to behave in certain ways, and by which, in its totality, we hold ourselves distinguished from others. If that goes there will be no America to defend.[874]

Heaven and earth...

Emily looks down at us and then at Joseph Brainin. They are sitting at the right hand of God.

Emily says to Joe, "Joe, do that thing you do."

Joe looks at his watch and looks down at us. "Friends and descendants," he says, "The clock is ticking for you..."

Paris rally for clemency for the Rosenbergs, late spring 1953

Appendix | The clemency movement abroad

The Committee was concerned that our government might regard appeals for clemency from abroad as interference in the internal affairs of the United States. This had been the pre-war position of the State Department, which had opposed criticism of Mussolini's and Hitler's destructive attacks on democracy and minorities until the Axis powers attacked Pearl Harbor. Since the end of World War II, however, our government had been expressly critical of the judicial system of the Soviet Union and its satellites, and had been especially condemnatory of the arrest and trial of Cardinal Josef Mindset, of Hungary, and his imprisonment, in 1949, for life on his conviction of treason.

Most Committee members did not believe we could use our government's criticism of the Soviet political trials to justify criticism from abroad of our conduct of the Rosenberg-Sobell trial. Politically-motivated executions and harsh sentences were routine in the Soviet Union, but not at all routine in the United States. The Soviet public was prohibited from protesting judicial assaults on life and liberty in their country, but the U.S. public was free to question the fairness of trials and to organize public support for persons we believed had been victims of a miscarriage of justice.

We understood some support for clemency would undoubtedly come from politically-motivated sources. Even support from anti-Communist sources would be denigrated by government officials and the media — if the media carried news of such support, which was not at all certain. Our concern was justified. The State Department initially labeled all clemency appeals from abroad as "Communist-inspired" and, when the sources of clemency appeals were undeniably anti-Communist, State officials declared that those sources, including conservative government and religious leaders, had become "Communist dupes." In respect to the Pope's intervention, several of our government officials protested that the Vatican was inappropriately interfering in a purely American affair, leading *L'Osservatore Romano* to observe

> It is again displeasing that in the intervention of the Holy Father, some should pretend to see an intrusion of a "foreign citizen." The Holy Father is a sovereign and in this case appeared the more majestic in that, divested of any national particularity, he became a herald of a principle which transcends particularistic regions and touches the highest summit of the Christian and human spirit.[875]

What is most apparent in the petitions and statements of clemency supporters abroad was that they came overwhelmingly from admirers of the United States.
Those for whom we had always been a beacon were now praying that the new
extremist-crafted American slogans — *Better Dead than Red* and *The Constitution
is not a Suicide Pact* — were fleeting American idiosyncrasies, as Prohibition
had been.

There were also specific disappointments with post-World War II America
by friendly admirers abroad. One disappointment was our welcome to "ex-Nazis"
as newly-found friends, who only a few years earlier our officials had described to
the world as murderous and inhuman. The people of occupied Europe and Africa
could speak volumes about the treatment they had suffered at the hands of the
Germans, an experience that had no parallel in America's history.

Reading the pleas for clemency by pro-American government and religious leaders, eminent writers, scientists, military men, artists, heroes of the
Resistance forces that fought the Nazis in every country of Europe, one will find,
not hostility to the United States, but affection and admiration and — at times
— puzzlement.

Their statements, as relayed to us by our embassies abroad, make it clear
that a grant of clemency would not have made our friends feel they had wrung
a concession from us, but a sign that we were still what our admirers always
thought we were.

The largest clemency movements were led by non-Communists and anti-
Communists, partly as a result of their early appearance at a time when the
Communist Parties were indifferent or opposed to efforts for clemency. The
early clemency movements began in the winter of 1951, and spring of 1952. The
Communist-led clemency efforts abroad were begun in the fall and winter of
1952. The late efforts by Communist leaders reflected a truth: the rank and file
of the Communists were voting with their feet and were supporting the non-
Communist and anti-Communist clemency movements.

In the early months of the European clemency movement, the American
missions' reports to the State Department described clemency, in their words, as a
"Commie" campaign of hatred against the United States. They could not do otherwise; they were victims of the same fears haunting all our government officials since
the end of World War II. Department of Justice and State officials, already belea-
guered by Congressional and media accusations of being "soft" on Communism,
did not dare to *not* brand all clemency movements, anywhere in the world,
as Communist.

As the months passed, however, our missions' reports to State began to
call attention to certain realities. One such reality was that the arguments for
clemency were being supported by many in the media and public life who had
read the trial record. Another reality was that our embassies and consulates were

denied copies of the trial record by the State Department because Justice officials regarded the trial record as an apocryphal book. They referred to portions of the record at times, but they were uncomfortable with journalists and political figures who wanted to read it themselves in its entirety. It was the trial record many European lawyers, journalists, and political leaders quoted to our representatives, only to be answered with evasive expositions on our laws and judicial system and, specifically in respect to the Rosenberg-Sobell case, a kind of dragnet rhetoric that impugned doubters and critics as naive dupes of Communists.

Clemency movement in France...

In a cable to State from Paris, C. Douglas Dillon, our ambassador to France, wrote that "the great majority of French people of all political leanings feel that the death sentence is completely unjustified..."[876] This may have been seen by the State Department as a sign of French ingratitude, since France was one of the beneficiaries of the United States-financed Marshall Plan for rebuilding national economies that had been destroyed by the German occupation. But the United States had, at the same time, undertaken the Turnabout in which those who had destroyed those economies were now being heralded as American allies.

Germany's seizure and devastating occupation of France was very much alive in French memory. Half a million French lives had been lost, many of them casualties incurred by participants in the French Resistance. The French were clear on who had murdered, raped, pillaged, burned and humiliated them, and had done so three times over the seventy years preceding the Turnabout. The wounds to the French were not old news.

The American Turnabout, with its message to the French that they had expended their lives and limbs in the wrong war, against the wrong enemy, and must now begin to think of being bled, lamed and buried again in what some American political leaders were saying would be the right war, was astonishing and abhorrent to them.

There were also other undercurrents that attracted wide support to the clemency movement in France and other European countries. That all the defendants were Jews was inescapably thought-provoking. The spectacle at Foley Square touched a nerve in the French public, which was still sensitive to the Dreyfus affair, in which a small number of senior French Army officials and their supporters in government had tarnished the nation's reputation with a gross anti-Semitic forgery. The spectacle affected the people of almost all European countries that had been occupied by the Germans because a number of former political leaders had collaborated in the round-up of Jews to be sent to the German death camps.

On December 4, 1952, the embassy in Paris had telegraphed State

> ...non-Communist press (LE MONDE, Nov. 25) front
> page feature by Andre Fontaine entitled "time of

suspicion" pooh-poohed Rosenbergs were spies and suggested they were scapegoats for American anti-Semitism. "Is it mere chance," he wrote, "that the accused are Jews? In Prague as in Washington racism has not lost all demagogic attraction...A malady of suspicion that has overcome East is now contaminating little by little democracy that holds itself to be the beacon of freedom."[877]

The telegram cited two other non-Communist newspapers, *Figaro* and the conservative pro-Gaullist *Parisian Libere*, as also being critical of the conduct of the United States in the Rosenberg-Sobell case.

On that same day another telegram was dispatched to State from the embassy.

Truth is that facts of Rosenberg espionage case have never been satisfactorily presented to French public and even our friends often are at a loss know what to believe. Therefore, Emb strongly recommends that suitable means be found provide Fr press, preferably through Fr correspondents in US, with convincing review of history and evidence Rosenberg case at earliest opportunity.[878]

On December 11, 1952, a dispatch from State to Paris and London assured the embassies that "DEPT gathering all additional documentary material possible on Rosenberg case and will send soonest for use UR [State abbreviation for 'your'] discretion."[879] It was also airpouching "85 pages of verbatim testimony of principal witness David Greenglass," and sending six articles on the case that had appeared in the *New York Post*, as well as "full text of statement by American Civil Liberties Union" and other materials.

On the following day, December 12, State and Justice officials met to review the situation. A State official told the meeting

the press in several European countries was giving incredible publicity to the Rosenberg case...what disturbed us was the fact that even some of the liberal, though non-Communist, papers were handling the case and the manner in which it was being handled indicated either a definite bias of [or?] a woeful ignorance of the real facts in the case. I said that I would like to have the assistance of the Justice Department...[880]

A Justice official told the meeting that Justice too had been "receiving protests from organizations throughout the world attacking the conduct of the Rosenberg case," and

> the Justice Department was convinced that there was one organization which was behind all these protests. They are confident that the National Committee to Secure Justice for the Rosenbergs is a Communist inspired, if not dominated, organization and they are making every effort to have this Committee placed on the Attorney General's list of subversive organizations.[881]

The officials at the meeting agreed the Europeans should be told that David Greenglass' testimony was supported by "other testimony" given at the trial[882] (the witnesses giving the "other testimony" were not identified); that Judge Kaufman had no option but to mete out the death penalties because the alternative — 30 years imprisonment — would have been inadequate punishment; the nature of the Rosenbergs' offense made it impossible for the prosecutors to provide tangible evidence of their guilt; it is common to give government witnesses lesser sentences than to defendants; David Greenglass had sufficiently "skilled hands" and "practical knowledge" to create accurate sketches of the atom bomb "even many years later;" there was no deceptive intent in listing eminent scientists as witnesses to testify against the defendants, although not calling them to do so, because the defense could have called them as its own witnesses; Judge Kaufman had instructed the jury not to be biased against the defendants; during the pre-testimonial stage of the trial, the defense could have removed any jurors they thought were anti-Semitic (this was a *non sequitur* reply, since the French press did not claim that there was anti-Semitism among the jurors, but that there was an anti-Semitic influence in the Justice Department, and in other American government circles as well).

The United States Information Service, America's voice in Europe, also attempted to respond to the critics but, according to a dispatch from Paris to State, its efforts "seriously complicate efforts to present truth" by its factual errors.[883] Among these errors was a statement that "Sobell had been sentenced to death;" that the defendants had been convicted for "transmitting US atomic secrets to the Soviet Union;" and the prosecution "produced more than 100 witnesses" although the actual number was 23.

These various responses to the critics did not have the desired impact on the press or lawyers, scientists, clergy or the general public in France or elsewhere. Ambassador Dillon assigned Ben Bradlee, then a press attaché to the embassy, who in later years became famous as editor of the *Washington Post* when it ran its expose of the Watergate scandal during the Nixon years, to prepare a factual and definitive analysis of the case that could be used by American missions throughout the world. Bradlee described the situation:

> We were starved for information about the case. But we didn't know anything about the case...At the end we must have sent a dozen cables to the State Department saying 'give us information about this case' so we can combat what was becoming, especially in France, very, very difficult.[884]

Since at least two major non-Communist newspapers, *Le Monde* and *Les Temps_Modernes*, were citing the trial transcript as their basis for doubting the guilt of the Rosenbergs,[885] Bradlee felt obliged to read the trial record, a chore that required him to return to the United States, since Justice officials would not make the trial record available to the embassy. But even travel to the United States for that purpose was frustrated for a while because, Bradlee was told, funds were not available for that purpose.[886]

After funds were found, Bradlee returned to the United States to read the trial record. He "stayed only a few days in New York" where he wrote the analysis for the Ambassador.[887] Since Bradlee spent only a few days at his task, it is likely that he read only those portions of the trial record selected for him by Justice officials.

Bradlee's analysis ran to 18 legal-size pages, the first page of which gave a chronological-legal history of the case; seven pages were given over to the prosecution's case; one page described the Rosenbergs' and Sobell's defense; one page described the prosecution's rebuttal to the defense; four pages were taken to emphasize adherence by the prosecution to the proper formalities in the conduct of the case; one page, titled *The Verdict*, did not mention the verdict at all but dealt, instead, with the witnesses; two pages dealt with the sentences, proving their conformity to the law; and the final pages dealt with questions being raised by the press abroad, giving answers that conformed to those cited earlier.[888, 889]

The "analysis" did not mention that the Supreme Court had refused to review the trial record.

Bradlee was young and naïve, in 1952. He could no more see the papered-over perjuries and deceptions in the Rosenberg case than he could have imagined that twenty years later he would approve two reporters' monumental expose of a President who, like the prosecutors and judge in the Rosenberg-Sobell case, had entangled the government in an historic deception.

Ambassador Dillon sent the Bradlee analysis to editors, journalists and important political figures in France, and to 17 American embassies in Europe and Asia.[890]

Within a week of making the Bradlee document available to the French media and political figures, the embassy reported to State that its "efforts to counteract Communist propaganda about Rosenbergs have produced results."[891] Paris' largest circulation newspapers were running stories and editorials based on the "Analysis," and were emphasizing

> careful study shows Rosenbergs fairly convicted and guilty as charged, and all have attacked 'outrageous' Communist distortion of facts.

But the assignment to Bradlee, to prove the fairness of the trial, did not address the underlying issues that were stirring European opinion. The crime had been committed on behalf of an ally at a time when the bulk of the German army was being engaged by that ally, an engagement that had aided the French Resistance movement even before the Americans and the British opened a Second Front in 1944. What the French and other Europeans could not understand was the label of treason attached to the defendants, nor could they fathom — having passed through half a decade of daily executions by the Germans — the executions facing the defendants for having aided the ally.

For that reason, the embassy's relief was short-lived. Actually, its first reports to Washington had been highly selective. It was soon reporting that *Le Monde*, for example, "generally stuck to the line that conviction made possible by climate of hysteria in U.S.," and had to acknowledge that the Bradlee analysis did nothing to reduce French editorial, political or religious support for clemency.[892]

On the day following the above dispatch, the embassy reported to State that the implacably anti-Communist Socialist Party was releasing a resolution on the Rosenberg-Sobell case, which read

> The Directing Committee of the Socialist Party without taking a position on basic issue involved, in view of the reasonable doubt which exists regarding the guilt of Rosenberg couple, urgently requests President Truman to remit the death sentence in order to avoid the irreparable.[893]

On January 9, 1953, the embassy reported to State that the pro-government newspaper, *Figaro*, had run a front page plea for clemency on the grounds that the Communists were deliberately conducting the campaign to make it appear that a grant of clemency would be a victory for them. The editorial ended its plea

> Don't play their game. Don't give them these martyrs. It would be a wonderful victory over Communism if hangings of Prague were answered by clemency of Washington.[894]

The Socialist Party newspaper, *Socialist Populaire*, in an editorial stating that after being "submerged" by United States documents, "it is possible that the Rosenbergs were part of Soviet Spy Ring, but they were convicted on testimony of only one witness," which was not permitted under French law. The editorial "dismisses corroborating witnesses by name and calls for executive clemency."[895] That the Bradlee analysis being circulated by the American embassy among French officials, lawyers and editors was no match for the trial record was exemplified by a letter to President Eisenhower from Paul Villard, a leading French attorney who had been decorated by the United States for his bravery in combat in World War II.

> ...I have read the complete transcript of record of the Rosenberg case, which was lent to me for two days; all I knew about the case before was the news published in my daily newspaper, the European Edition of the *New York Herald Tribune*... As a general rule, I do not like the idea to make a personal interference with the justice of another country, especially a friendly country as the United States of America. But after reading the official report of the case, I could not refuse to give my name and my help to the Comité Français pour la Défense des Rosenberg... I had the honor to fight with the American Army...and I keep the Bronze Star Medal, with Oak Leaf Cluster, which was awarded to me for combat duty, as a precious symbol of this everlasting brotherhood in arms. It is in this spirit that I pray the Lord and hope the cruel sentence passed upon the Rosenbergs will not be executed and that finally their innocence will be recognized."[896]

On January 12, 1953, the American consulate in Marseille, in the south of France, described protests against the Rosenbergs' death sentences, including delegations to the consulate with petitions for clemency, one of which was "led by a young priest." It cited an editorial on the Rosenbergs in *La France* that read, in part

> The execution of these two spies would greatly serve the politics of Moscow...That is why we think that a measure of grace would be well-received by the civilized world, which deems it sufficient that the guilty ones be put where they can do no harm.[897]

In Lyon, the consulate reported, in mid-January, that a meeting of forty "Lyonnais intellectuals" had been held, at which a protest against the death sentences was signed "by all those present. The text of this note is scarcely worth repeating..."[898] The consulate complained that Lyon's leading newspaper, *Le Progrs*, had run an editorial on January 10, the headline of which read: *The execution of the Rosenbergs would be a moral defeat for the free world.*[899]

Similar news of clemency activity came from Bordeaux and elsewhere.[900]

On February 22, the *New York Times* reported that the Rosenberg-Sobell case had become "TOP ISSUE IN FRANCE."

> Petitions have been circulated among persons in almost every field of intellectual and manual activity. Mass meetings of protest, such as the one that filled the Velodrome d'Hiver (the equivalent of Madison Square Garden), have been staged from time to time.[901]

Describing the clemency campaign as Communist-inspired, the story went on to say that public opinion "is, on the whole, hostile to executing the Rosenbergs."

> Almost without exception there is a feeling that the sentence has been too harsh and smacks of procedures adopted in Communist countries.

In mid-February, after Eisenhower's denial of clemency, the embassy in Paris cited an editorial in the non-Communist *Franc-Tireur.*

> One had right to hope that Eisenhower, master of party which elected him, would not fear reprisals from public which applauded him. However, with sang-froid which is intended to appear political, he has rejected pardon, without even differentiating between Julius and Ethel, without finding slightest extenuating circumstances.[902]

On February 14, the embassy reported that most of the French newspapers "had long expressed hope that death sentence would be commuted and now, with almost complete unanimity, they deplore rejection of clemency plea." *Le Monde's* reporter in the United States referred to the great difference in sentences given the Rosenbergs and David Greenglass.[903]

The pro-government *Figaro* asked

> But would not cause of freedom been better defended by more generosity? Certainly, democracies have right to defend themselves. But their nobility consists of using only their own arms, and rejecting those of totalitarianism.[904]

The *Franc-Tireur* headline for an editorial read: *Freedom has no need for a hangman*. The rightist *Aurore* wrote, "President of the United States was pitiless at moment when pity would have cost justice nearly nothing."[905]

The news in February that Pope Pius XII had intervened for clemency and that his plea had been suppressed by Justice officials since December 1952, and that Judge Kaufman had set a new execution date for the week of March 9, resulted in an upsurge of pro-clemency communications to the embassy, which reported, on February 18, that it had "received well over thousand protests since President's declaration against clemency in addition few thousand previously." The report noted that the number of protests "considerably exceeds that any former Communist campaign..."[906]

Among the prominent new clemency supporters in France was François Mauriac, an anti-Communist Catholic writer who had won the previous year's Nobel Prize for literature. Others who were in or close to the government who spoke out for clemency were Andre Mornet, Chief Government Attorney for France; Gilbert de Chambrun, a descendant of Lafayette (who had fought in the American Revolution and had persuaded Louis XVI's government to send an expeditionary force of 6000 soldiers to support American troops against the British); and several generals who had been active in the French Resistance.[907]

Mornet, who had presided at the trial of Marshall Henri-Phillipe Petain at which Petain was charged with collaborating with the Nazis when he governed occupied France (Petain was sentenced to death, but the sentence was commuted to life imprisonment), wrote

> I have a very painful impression, a lingering doubt, about the testimony in the Rosenberg case. The inequality of the treatment of the defendants in this case disturbs me greatly because it seems that a brother confessed and sent his sister to the death house in order to escape with a light sentence.[908]

General Le Corguille wrote

> It is with very great sadness that we are shown once again that a great friendly nation for which we have always had a loyal understanding and high esteem, finds itself today, by a mistake of its government, enmeshed in a great miscarriage of justice of the most inhuman kind.[909]

In April, the embassy reported that the discovery of a David Greenglass memorandum to his attorney, in which he acknowledged that at the behest of the FBI he had attested to events of which he had no knowledge, "has put case back in spotlight."[910] The dispatch went on to say that news of the memorandum "is prominently played by most papers." In addition, "Commie press also reported that two newspapermen from the *National Guardian*" had found the console table, which Greenglass testified Rosenberg said was given to him by the Russians.[911]

The embassy report, signed by Dillon himself, said that it was urgent to obtain "all possible material to counter-act latest propaganda" and suggested that Assistant U.S. Attorney James Kilsheimer

> may be able to provide answers. At present, only Commies are vouching for authenticity of Greenglass statement.[912]

A return dispatch from State informed Dillon

> Kilsheimer nor interested officers Justice Dept have knowledge any statement by Greenglass such as one cited *Combat* as QTE new evidence QTE. Kilsheimer requests copy statement or April 18 edition *Combat* be sent him immediately so he can make official denial of authenticity document which he confident is fraudulent.[913]

The embassy immediately sent a photostat "of alleged Greenglass statement" to Kilsheimer, as well as copies of the stories in *Combat* and the Communist *Humanité*, with a request that "if official denial to be made would appreciate copy plus any background soonest."[914]

Four days later, on April 28, State replied to Paris

> Will forward soonest obtainable declaration which Kilsheimer obtaining from Greenglass regarding spurious document published *Combat*.[915]

On May 4, Merritt N. Cootes, a State Department official, distributed to State and Justice Department officials a memorandum of a conversation he had had with Kilsheimer regarding the Greenglass memorandum

> I called Mr. Kilsheimer and called his attention to today's article in the *New York Times* on the Rosenberg case. He said that as I would gather from this article, complications had arisen in the FBI investigation of the alleged Greenglass document.[916]

Cootes wrote that Kilsheimer removed himself from the inquiry by suggesting that Cootes ask the Justice Department's Criminal Investigation Division for a statement.

The "complications" mentioned in Cootes' memorandum arose from *a New York Times* story of the same day which quoted O. John Rogge, Greenglass' attorney, as authenticating the Greenglass memorandum.[917]

As though Rogge's authentication of his client's memorandum was not to be believed, State sent an airgram to a select number of embassies on May 6, 1953, informing them

> As soon as the FBI investigation of the source and authenticity of the document has been completed the mission will be notified.[918]

The airgram stated that the fact that the Greenglass document "was used for propaganda purposes casts doubt on its authenticity and raises the question of whether" the Rosenbergs' attorney was "spinning the case out to obtain a maximum anti-American propaganda effect."[919]

Nine days later, on May 15, Dillon, bowing to the reality that State and Justice officials would continue to pretend that they could not determine whether the Greenglass document was genuine, and that the world press would interpret that stance as confirming its authenticity, told State outright that it was in American interests to grant clemency to the Rosenbergs.

> This mission has concerned itself particularly with Rosenberg case and has undertaken all possible measures designed to inform and persuade French opinion on scrupulous fairness of trial...
>
> At the same time, fact of matter is that even those who accept guilt of Rosenbergs are overwhelmingly of opinion that death sentence unjustifiable punishment for offenses as revealed by trial, particularly when compared with prison terms meted out to British scientists Allan Nunn May and Klaus Fuchs.
>
> In addition to this...latest doubts aroused as to reliability Greenglass testimony by publication statement — allegedly in Greenglass handwriting — whose authenticity not (repeat not) yet denied...[920]

The statement was sent to State under a procedure that limited its reading to a few officials.[921]

An "Eyes Only" telegram was sent by Acting Secretary of State General Walter Bedell Smith to Dillon, which read

> UR views on Rosenberg case appreciated and carefully studied. Since case has gone twice to Supreme Court

which has not yet handed down decision on latest appeal
and since appeal for clemency to President has been
rejected, I do not feel there is any further recommendation at this time, which I can make to the President. I
have however forwarded to him your TEL and this reply
in order that he may be informed of UR views.[922]

Dillon persisted in his warnings to State. As an indication of how widespread sentiment for clemency was in France, and how ineffectual the recommended responses by State had become, the reports he received from the consul
at Strasbourg must have surprised even him. Strasbourg was the city closest to
the Saar, whose largely German inhabitants, in a plebiscite in 1935, had voted by
an overwhelming majority for union with Nazi Germany. After World War II, the
Saar was occupied by the French.

In a dispatch on May 28, 1953, the consulate at Strasbourg reported that
the Saar's "most widely read paper," the *Saarbruecker Zeitung*, which had "always
been extremely reserved in any criticism of the United States,"[923] was supporting
clemency for the Rosenbergs; that it considered a recent ultimatum made to the
Rosenbergs by the Attorney General to confess or die as an act of "extortion;"
and had expressed the hope that "the American judicial process has not also been
infected by the 'McCarthy bacillus.'"[924]

On June 5, 1953, the pro-American *Le Monde* ran an editorial titled
"Bargaining With Death," which began

"The Rosenbergs will have chosen their own fate." These
words summarize the meaning of the deal offered the
Rosenbergs by the Justice Department[.[If they refuse
to talk, the[y] will be executed on June 18 at 11:00 p.m[.]
If they confess, their lives will be spared but what a
confession, since their guilt has never been concretely
established...

The mere reading of the documents of the trial, as we
have often said, has instilled doubt in many minds.[925]

The editors of *Le Monde* chose, in the same editorial, to call attention to the
near-silence by the American press on the case, and suggested

fear of being accused of pro-Communist sympathy by
some McCarthy has become stronger than the fear of
Communism itself...[926]

On June 9, Dillon wrote State once again that he and his principal advisors
"would be very pleased if it should be possible to commute death sentence."[927]

A Dillon "Eyes Only" cable to State, on May 19, in which he had first recommended clemency, had been "leaked" within government circles, causing a certain amount of anxiety and consternation among top officials and Congressional leaders. The best explanation for Dillon's stance was that he was a hard realist, but that explanation did not sit well with extremists. Senator Alexander Wiley of Wisconsin, on reading Dillon's cable, said he could not believe that Dillon had written it.[928]

A few words are in order here on Ambassador Dillon. He was immune to being denounced as a Communist or Communist dupe for his position on clemency, for two reasons: 1) The White House did not want Dillon's stand on clemency to become public; 2) the Dillon family was immensely wealthy and powerful.

On June 10, Dillon sent another "Eyes Only" cable to State, saying that he had had "a long conversation last night with Madame Bidault." She was the wife of Georges Bidault, the French foreign minister and founder of the Christian-Democrat party. Speaking for her husband, she told Dillon

> that mercy was a Christian, democratic idea completely foreign to Soviet Communist doctrine. The exercise of mercy in this case would further highlight difference between Western liberal and free traditions and the Soviet Communist way of life.[929]

On June 12, Dillon was notified by the Strasbourg consulate that its walls had been defaced with slogans reading "U.S. Go Home" and "Free the Rosenbergs." Several delegations had called at the consulate, among them representatives of students at the Faculty of Medicine[930] and the Protestant theology school.

On that same day the consul at Lyon notified Dillon

> the Consulate is in receipt of a resolution signed by many of the members of the Catholic Faculty in Lyon and specifically approved by Cardinal Gerlier, Archbishop of Lyon and Primate of the Gauls, deploring the carrying [out] of the sentence of the Rosenbergs on humanitarian grounds but without attempting to judge as to their guilt or innocence. A leading editorial in to-day's *Echo Liberte*, a strongly rightist and catholic daily of Lyon, expresses the same views...[931]

Also on that same day, Dillon reported to State that a very substantial number of petitions had recently been brought to the embassy, and that their signers "include distinguished scientists from College de France, well known lawyers friendly to the United States and similar groups and individuals."[932]

He also reported that over the past two weeks there had been an increase "in non-Communist appeals for clemency," including an appeal for support for clemency to Francis Cardinal Spellman in the United States from a committee headed by François Mauriac, the Catholic writer who had won the 1952 Nobel Prize in literature. Dillon also related that the press had printed the text of a clemency message from Cardinal Feltin, Archbishop of Paris.

New editorials for clemency had also appeared in the Catholic *La Croix, Paris-Presse, Le Monde, Figaro.* The latter described the published letters of the Rosenbergs "as 'an extraordinary document.'"[933]

On June 15, Dillon reported a further increase in the number of appeals for clemency, and that the anti-Communist *Socialist Populaire* carried a "detailed analysis of text of latest finding" by Judge Kaufman, which rejected the latest appeal, and stated

> that political motivations rather than objective judicial process must have lain at basis of his refusal to reopen case. Parallel is drawn with Dreyfus case.[934]

Dillon added

> Numerous lawyers, who are basing themselves on such details of case as are available from rather extensive press accounts, are joining move to ask executive clemency, especially in light alleged new (repeat new) evidence, lest 'the irrevocable' take place and reopening of case at later time be rendered impossible.

Dillon also related that the minister of the American church in Paris "has asked me to forward Rosenberg appeal, adopted unanimously by General Assembly of Reformed Church of France," and that he had received a clemency appeal from the Bishop of Orleans, and that "French scientists in increasing numbers are also delivering petitions to Embassy science attaches."[935]

On June 16, Edouard Herriot, President of the French National Assembly (the equivalent of the U.S. House of Representatives), sent a plea for clemency directly to the White House. Herriot was widely respected by the French, because at the age of 68, he had risked his life and freedom by protesting against the German-approved Vichy regime during the occupation. He was arrested and deported to Germany, where he was imprisoned for three years.[936]

That same day Dillon reported to State that the embassy was receiving clemency petitions at the rate of 500 per day, "with petitioners lined up outside doors at some point yesterday."[937] Three leading Frenchmen, former Premiers Edgar Faure and Jean Paul-Boncour, and Nobel prize-winner Leon Jouhaux, had sent an appeal to the President, saying

> [J]ustice among men is fragile and fallible; it finds real
> grandeur only in generosity and clemency.[938]

Faure had been premier in 1952, had participated in the Resistance movement during German occupation, and was a De Gaullist nationalist; Paul-Boncour was an independent who had voted to continue the war against Germany from Algiers after the Germans occupied France; and Leon Jouhaux, an anti-Communist labor leader who had been sent to a concentration camp by the Germans, had received the Nobel Peace Prize in 1951.

The anti-Communist *Aurore* accepted the guilt of the Rosenbergs as a fact but editorialized

> It's no longer question of justice, but of pure humanity.
> Washington fears that commutation of Rosenberg sentence will appear to be victory for Communist petitions.
> This fear is baseless. If President gives Rosenbergs right
> to live, it will be honest men of all countries, opinions
> and religions who will approve.[939]

The non-Communist *Franc-Tireur* wrote much the same

> It is no longer question of procedure, innocence, or
> guilt. It is question of humanity...He [Eisenhower] will
> not only save lives of two human beings, but he will well
> serve prestige of United States.[940]

Foreign Minister Bidault, with whose wife Dillon had had the conversation described earlier, now asked Dillon to call on him. Bidault told Dillon that the President of France, Vincent Auriol, had sent him a letter for transmittal to President Eisenhower. The letter expressed

> Auriol's serious concern over the Rosenberg case and
> his hope that the President could see his way clear to
> commute the sentence...He [Bidault] then said that he
> personally agreed with the sentiments in the letter.[941]

Auriol, like so many other popular political figures in France, had been imprisoned, in his case for three years, for his opposition to the German-approved Vichy government during the German occupation.

On June 16, Secretary of State John Foster Dulles received a memorandum from a Special Assistant, informing him "that not only the Communists but also the non-Communists are concerned about the case."[942] It pointed out that members of the French government were warning that "the execution of the Rosenbergs would stir up considerable anti-American feeling in Western Europe..." It pointed out further

> Since January 15, 94,495 letters concerning the
> Rosenberg Case have been received in the Department
> from abroad. Over ninety per cent were from Europe
> and almost all recommended clemency.[943]

On June 18, Dillon reported to State that a meeting of 7,000 Parisians had sent the following telegram to President Eisenhower

> In this hour of choice, when entire world turns toward
> you, people of Paris, united as never before since lib-
> eration, beg you not (repeat not) to make an irreparable
> gesture. For honor United States, for honor of humanity,
> pardon Rosenbergs.[944]

Dillon reported that the embassy had received more than 2,000 petitions that day, "25% more than previous high of Tuesday. Grand total petitions received now approximately 12,000." The total number of signatures on the petitions was not given.

At Notre Dame Cathedral in Paris, a special hour of prayer was held by the Christian Committee for Revision of the Rosenberg Trial, with the approval of Maurice Cardinal Feltin, the Archbishop of Paris.[945]

Early on June 19, Dillon sent another "Eyes Only" cable to State, declaring that in view of the widespread feeling in France for clemency

> I feel that it is most important to take the strongest pos-
> sible action to counteract anti-American feeling that
> will ensue if Rosenbergs are finally executed.[946]

Dillon suggested that the President make a "strong and relatively detailed statement" explaining our legal system and somehow counteracting the feeling

> that penalty is too heavy because it is the first execution
> of spies in peace time...I feel it is most important that
> French get impression that President has given serious
> consideration to case in recent days, particularly to the
> pleas of those who are friendly to us.

In view of Dillon's unsuccessful appeals, from January to June, for fact-based statements from Justice to counteract the clemency movement in France and elsewhere, his suggestions on this day may have been inspired more by frustration and pique than by hope. It is likely that he already knew that none of what he asked for — the detailed explanations of the facts in the case, the President's acknowledgment of the feelings of "those who are friendly to us" — would be forthcoming.

Six months after the executions, the consulate in Strasbourg sent State a report on an exchange of letters that had been printed in a Saar newspaper, dealing with the future of the Rosenbergs' sons.[947, 948] One of the letters was written by Adolph Franke, a former official in the Nazi government in the Saar. Franke's letter argued that in the United States only Jews and Communists had favored clemency.

> I shall not base my stand on the fact that our Lord and Saviour himself drove the buyers and sellers from the Temple...How Jesus could threaten "Woe unto you, scribes and pharisees! Ye children of snakes and vipers!"
>
> ***
>
> ...in America it was only a little group, chiefly Communists and a certain number of Jews (who thereby performed no service to Jewry), who protested against this execution...They [the Rosenbergs] even made their children into enemies of human society...for the children are bound to believe that their parents — practically angels — were guiltless when executed.[949]

It is doubtful that the consulate sent the report to State to demonstrate how effective it had been in counteracting clemency support in the Saar. It was more likely sent as a cautionary signal that our executions of the Rosenbergs had relit the passions of the fanatical zealots of the Holocaust.

Clemency movement elsewhere in Europe

The clemency campaign in other European countries was especially strong among those whose populations, like the French, had been subjected to occupation and cruel executions by the Germans, and who had created, at great risk to their lives and families, stubborn and effective resistance movements supported by virtually every segment of society. The occupied European nations had used the inability of Germany, engaged in a life-and-death struggle with Soviet armies, to commit sufficient military forces to destroy their resistance movements. Even after their liberation, when the old disparities between the poor and the rich gave rise to conflicting agendas for the future, the ideals of freedom and amity expressed during the Resistance still retained a tangible hold on the thinking and sentiments of the men and women who had risked their lives to make the Nazi-led New World Order disorderly and unworkable. It was galling and provocative to them that two Americans had been condemned to death for aiding their wartime indispensable ally.

In Belgium, support for clemency for the Rosenbergs crossed all class and political lines.[950, 951, 952, 953, 954, 955, 956] Paul Henri-Spaak, a former prime minister who championed the establishment of NATO as a barrier to Stalin's aspirations in Europe, told the U.S. ambassador that the Rosenbergs' death sentences represented "the worst aspects of anti-Communist hysteria."[957]

Belgian's Queen Elizabeth wrote to President Eisenhower

> I do not want to interfere in your country but let me put my voice into the prayer on behalf of humanity to beg you dear President to save the life of the Rosenbergs.[958, 959]

Similar appeals for clemency crossed class and political lines in Denmark,[960, 961, 962, 963] and Norway. In some areas of Norway, the Germans had burned entire villages to the ground and had deported the men, women and children to concentration camps.[964] The Germans had also warned the general population that 100 hostages would be taken and put to death for every German killed.[965] Consequently, the Rosenbergs' death sentences evoked bitter memories of the executions in the not so distant past.

Early in January 1953, contrary to a report by our embassy that there was little interest in the case in Norway,[966] the sentiment for clemency was strong enough for the anti-Communist *Arbeiderbladet*, which was close to the government, to print an appeal for clemency.

> The decision is at present in the hands of President Truman. One of his last acts as head of the State should be to grant clemency. We are awaiting with hope the last word of the President."[967]

One goal of the Resistance, in occupied Holland, had been to protect the Jewish population, which may have been a factor in the widespread support by the Dutch for clemency. Nevertheless, in December 1952, our embassy at The Hague attributed the clemency campaign entirely to the Communist Party, but explained that "the campaign for signatures has been more of a success than any of the Party's protest drives in the past. The number of signatures on the protests is from five to ten times larger than in similar campaigns."[968, 969, 970, 971] Favorable news stories on the campaign were appearing in the anti-Communist and the Catholic press, and large public clemency meetings were being held for overflow audiences.[972] In June 1953, the embassy reported that the liberal *Het*

Vaterland "while attacking Communist appeals for clemency, itself makes plea for Rosenberg reprieve."[973] The dispatch to State conceded that the *Het Vaterland* editorial

> represents accurate statement what is undoubt-
> edly widely held Dutch view that death sentences in
> Rosenberg case should be commuted life imprisonment.

The dispatch also acknowledged that in "private conversations high government officials, members States General, many editors have told Embassy officers" of a

> growing view United States showing signs excessive
> indulgence emotionalism contrasted with more sober
> and rational approach to politics by conservatives in
> Netherlands, Britain, elsewhere.[974]

The report concluded that "commutation of sentence to life imprisonment on humanitarian grounds would receive overwhelming favorable response in Netherlands."[975]

Widespread support for clemency also emerged in Sweden,[976, 977, 978, 979, 980, 981] one of the few countries not overrun by the Germans, although its government felt compelled to permit one of Hitler's mountain divisions to be transported across northern Sweden for an attack on the Soviet Union's Arctic region.

Likewise in Finland, where anti-Soviet and anti-Communist feelings ran high due to the invasion of Finland by the Soviet Union in 1940. Finland had been an informal ally of Germany by allowing German troops to use Finland as a base for troop movements against the Soviets.

On March 6, 1953, the U.S. embassy at Helsinki reported receiving approximately twenty petitions for clemency, some of which the embassy believed were identifiably Communist. But

> From that point onward there has been the greatest
> diversity of language and of formality in presentation,
> ranging from fairly well written typed communications
> of a persuasive and argumentative character to bluff
> scrawls signed in pencil by thirty or forty laborers on
> sewer projects in Turku.[982]

The people of the British Commonwealth had suffered nearly a million dead and maimed, and a quarter million missing, at the hands of the Germans and the Japanese. In London itself, 80,000 men, women and children had been killed or wounded by German bombs, and a million Londoners had fled the city and its devastated environs. The American Turnabout was puzzling and threatening to the British public, however much their leaders attempted to explain and justify it. In the 1945 elections, Winston Churchill, one of the architects of the victory over the Germans, was ousted by the British electorate in part because he was sending out signals that the war against Germany might have to be followed by war against the Soviet Union. It was not that there was love for the Soviet Union; it was that there was an urgent need for peace so that the survivors and their children could get on with their lives.

The Communist Party in Great Britain was very small, and every other political party was strongly anti-Communist. Terse acknowledgments that clemency appeals were being received at the American embassy in London began in the fall of 1952, and continued to receive begrudging acknowledgment thereafter.[983, 984] Requests to State for legal documents with which to refute "Communist propaganda" for clemency were answered with evasions.[985, 986]

A pro-clemency member of Parliament, Sidney Silverman, wrote

> ...To exact the supreme penalty from these two unfortunates in these circumstances is to make the Rosenbergs personally responsible for all the errors of all the statesmen of the world which, since the end of the war, have so tragically lost the peace for which we all hoped...[987]

While it continued to report to State on increasing support for clemency by British lawyers, scientists and the clergy, among them C.E. Raven, chaplain to Queen Elizabeth,[988, 989, 990, 991, 992, 993, 994, 995] our embassy suggested to State that it might be advisable to launch a diversionary anti-Communist propaganda campaign centered on the theme that "CP membership means individual has sold soul to foreign power."

In Ireland, there was a small clemency movement, mainly sparked by the Irish Workers' League, a Communist organization.[996] Most of the clemency actions seemed to have come from trade union organizations,[997] and women's groups, although sentiment for clemency was also expressed in the non-Communist press. After the executions, the embassy in Dublin reported that the *Irish Times*, while not questioning the guilt of the Rosenbergs, was critical of President Eisenhower's refusal of clemency.

...the cause of anti-Americanism has been favoured deplorably by an action which, reported in all its grim details, must seem to simple and non-political people everywhere to conflict strangely with the noble pronouncements of humanitarian principles with which official utterances from the United States are spiced so generously.[998]

In West and East Germany, the clemency movement had to address a defeated, angry and demoralized people who had staked their lives on the belief that their poverty after World War I had been engineered by the Jews and Communists, and on the premise that their blood and intellect required them to cleanse the world of Jews. Driven by fevered visions, the Germans enthusiastically lit the racial and political cleansing ovens and engulfed the world in war. For eleven years, their visions brought them ecstatic victories, which were followed by two unbelievable years of bitter defeats, after which the visionaries were branded criminals, the gateways to the new world order were clogged with prisoners, and the streets were filled with starving, homeless, and bewildered Germans.

In the seven years since the Aryan dream ended, the Germans had cleared away most of the rubble in the streets, and had begun to restart their factories and stores and began to teach their young again. At first, there seemed a dearth of heroes for the children to admire and emulate, except in whispers. The victorious enemies had heroes: Eisenhower, De Gaulle, Zhukov, Tito, Resistance fighters, Tommies, GI Joes.

And then, miracle of miracles, small rays of light from west and east began to pierce the German darkness. The Americans and Russians had begun a Turnabout, welcoming some of the unsung German heroes to their lands. Thousands of them, actually. This had to be food for thought. Perhaps the victors were beginning to see the light. Perhaps the new world order was not in ruins, but only a dream deferred.

This was the mindset, we believe, not of all Germans, but of many Germans, and especially those Germans who had deftly avoided tribunals like those at Nuremburg, the Germans with whom the victors had made a purposeful peace. These were the Germans our ambassadors and consuls cited in their dispatches as the voices against clemency.

As we read the language of the anti-clemency Germans, we hear echoes of the language used against the Jews in general during the Nazi years, including libels of treason. But the language of our consular officials is also revealing: while they labeled virtually all pro-clemency sentiments in Germany as Communist-inspired, they at no time expressed the thought that here, in the home of the Holocaust, the German anti-clemency sentiments might be inspired by anti-Semitism.

There was, nevertheless, a clemency movement in Germany, although not among the people with whom our consular officials lunched. A good part of the clemency movement may have been inspired by Communists in East and West Germany, but because of the rigidly uniform attribution of Communist inspiration for virtually all clemency communications in dispatches to State, it is impossible to know to what extent there was a German clemency movement independent of the Communists.

In January 1953, the U.S. High Commissioner in Bonn (the capital of West Germany) notified State that two non-Communist Hamburg newspapers were supporting clemency. The *Hamburger Anzeiger*, in an editorial written by the chief editor, argued

> an act of mercy for the Rosenbergs would indicate that in the United States there was 'freedom of fear through superior strength.' The *Hamburger Echo* carried an article by a member of the Bundestag, the legislative branch of the West German area, in which he "declared that he was not convinced that the case against the Rosenbergs was sufficient to warrant such a harsh conviction and referred to it as a possible repetition of the 'Sacco-Vanzetti tragedy.'"[999]

The following month the U.S. High Commissioner sent State three excerpts from 3000 German communications related to clemency.

The first excerpt read

> I have lived in the Russian Zone for six years. If people like these (the Rosenbergs) lived there they would already be dead. What are you waiting for?

The second excerpt read

> Kill them at once.

The third read

> Exchange the traitors to the motherland for German prisoners of war and then send the two to Russia. That will be punishment enough.[1000]

On February 18, the *New York Times* carried a news story, under the heading ROSENBERGS USED IN 'HATE U.S.' DRIVE, which declared

In East Germany and probably throughout the
Communist world, the coming execution of Julius and
Ethel Rosenberg is being used on an unusually large
scale to incite hatred of the United States and western
democracies.

* * *

Today's issue of *Neue Zeit*, organ of the Christian
Democratic Union in East Germany, charged that
Department of Justice officials had conspired to sup-
press the Pope's message to then President Harry S.
Truman so as to prevent any pressure being placed on
the President by the Roman Catholic population of the
United States.[1001]

A February dispatch, to State from the American consul in Frankfurt (East
Germany), declared

Non-communists who have expressed their views concerning the case have been almost unanimous in considering the Rosenbergs as guilty not only of high treason
but of a most serious crime against the whole of humanity, and seem to feel that their death sentence was fully
deserved.[1002]

That same month, a Berlin dispatch to State included a copy of a letter con-
cerning the Rosenbergs from Bishop Otto Dibelius, Chairman of the Evangelical
Church in Germany to Samuel Calvert, President of the National Council of
Churches of Christ in the United States. The letter read, in part

I have been asked by various serious Christian groups
of the German Democratic Republic [East Germany]
to use my influence that the death sentence for the
two Rosenbergs is not carried out. It is not necessary
to point out that I do not pretend to have a judgment
on such a case living in Germany...However I think that
the National Council through you should know there
are Christians in the Evangelical Church in Germany,
who seriously have raised their voices against the death
sentences.[1003]

A West German newspaper that had earlier advocated clemency, the *Neue
Presse*, reversed itself after President Eisenhower denied clemency in February,
writing that it "respected the judgment of a man who viewed his high and difficult office as an order from God, namely Eisenhower."[1004]

The Italian public was confused and alarmed by the American Turnabout. The Italians held the Germans responsible for 400,000 deaths, 153,000 of them civilian, of which 67,000 were inflicted on them after September 1943, when the Germans stationed in Italy became their *de facto* enemies. It seemed incongruous to the Italians that two Americans who had been found guilty of passing information to the nation that had borne the brunt of eradicating Germany's deadly power had been sentenced to death.

The fiction that, in December 1952, the Pope had simply "reported" to McGranery that he had received communications favoring clemency contained one element of truth — that there was clemency sentiment in Italy. In October 1952, that sentiment, although mislabeled as to its origin, was acknowledged in a terse one-sentence report from our embassy in Rome, which read

> Emb beginning receive Commie protests Rosenberg execution.[1005]

Our embassy officials in Italy initially derided the clemency campaign and its supporting petitions, as being written in the "characteristically cramped scrawls of persons who have had little education."[1006, 1007] Not until February 1953, *after* the Pope's intervention became public, did our embassy and consulates in Italy report that there was significant support for clemency in Italy by persons and groups that were plainly anti-Communist, such as one by Giuseppe Saragat, the head of the Social Democratic Party, who was one of Italy's national heroes, and who later became President of the Italian Republic.[1008] The anti-Communist pro-government newspaper, *Mattino*, described President Eisenhower's February rejection of clemency "as shock for those who had hoped he would start his civilian office with a clemency gesture."[1009] On February 13, the embassy reported that the Vatican newspaper, *L'Osservatore Romano*, had announced that Pope Pius XII, "As he has compassionately done in several other similar cases, also in this case he has not failed to intervene..."[1010]

The *New York Times* noted that the clemency campaign had "found the ground particularly favorable in Italy and succeeded in arousing a great part of public opinion in their [the Rosenbergs'] favor," and that "even many anti-Communists feel that the evidence failed to prove beyond a shadow of a doubt that the Rosenbergs were guilty."[1011] In June, our embassy reported that a pro-clemency appeal had been unanimously adopted by the Rome City Council; that the pro-government newspaper, *Momento*, had editorialized, "There is nothing else to do now but send plea for mercy to President Eisenhower,"[1012] and "The Vatican radio, in a special broadcast in several languages, spoke of the sympathetic attitude of many Roman Catholics throughout the world toward appeals for clemency for the condemned couple."[1013]

Immediately following the executions the editor of the conservative newspaper *Stampa* wrote

> ...worst of all and repugnant to our conscience is fact that up to last Rosenbergs were played with as cat does with a mouse: your lives will be saved if you confess your guilt and denounce your accomplices. That is ugly.[1014]

The very small country of Luxembourg, bounded by France, Belgium and Germany, with a population, in 1953, of well under half a million persons, had a very small clemency movement. Its relevance here arises from the fact that over 90 percent of the population was Roman Catholic, and that when it was occupied by the Germans, in 1940, no one was willing to collaborate with the occupiers, and the Germans had to govern Luxembourg themselves.

On June 13, the *Wort*, a Christian Social newspaper, wrote

> If we follow the Catholics of France and other countries in recommending the review of the Rosenbergs' trial to the American courts, then we do this, because we are against any mistake in justice, any lack of procedure, any appearance of an unsatisfactory investigation and defense possibilities, especially as in this case two human lives are at stake and the future of two children...[1015]

In Switzerland, the oldest democracy in central Europe, the American legation reported, on January 15, 1953, that it "does find certain articles on the Rosenberg case carried in responsible papers a bit disturbing."[1016] It quotes a columnist *in La Sentinelle*, a non-Communist newspaper.

> I find it ground for the utmost anxiety that the United States should have reached the stage, in their struggle against Communism, of borrowing some of the Soviets' most abject methods.

Another non-Communist newspaper. *Journal De Genève*, printed a front page editorial which conceded that the Rosenbergs might be guilty, but expressed great uneasiness because the case stems from the atmosphere created about the Rosenberg case by politicians who have made a career out of anti-communist purges.[1017]

On June 16, the consul in Geneva reported to State that it had issued a statement to the Associated Press, stating that clemency

> petitioners are lending themselves, wittingly or unwit-tingly, to a Communist campaign which has as its objective only deceptive propaganda with no thought of the issues involved. The Rosenbergs have received a full and fair trial and have been afforded every legal process under American laws.[1018]

One day before the executions, the anti-Communist *Neue Zuercher Zeitung* observed that "a merciful action will seldom be regretted by those who have enough strength to reach such decision."[1019]

There were no known clemency movements in Poland and Hungary, where anti-Semitism was kept alive by Communist governments. In 1946, 15,000 Polish Jews, who fled eastward in 1940-1941, returned to Poland to find their previous homes, but were driven away. In Kielce, the returning Jews were attacked, leaving 41 dead and 60 wounded.[1020] The Jews fled again, this time westward. Toward the end of the Rosenbergs' lives, the Polish Red Cross was authorized by the Polish government, to offer the Rosenbergs asylum in Poland. The State Department dismissed the offer as impertinent.

Jews, returning to their homes in Hungary, met the same fate as those in Poland.[1021] In late 1950, a veritable epidemic of "little pogroms" took place in major Hungarian cities; earlier in the year the Hungarian Communist government had successfully encouraged the firing of Jews from all places of employment.[1022] Nevertheless, there did appear some isolated instances of non-political expressions favoring clemency. On June 9, the legation in Budapest informed State

> Usually reliable Hungarian contact reports that many lib-eral but non-Communist Hungarians are unhappy over Rosenberg case. This is not due influence Communist propaganda but to feeling that their execution would not quite fit in with concept Anglo-Saxon justice.[1023]

Clemency movement in Canada...

Our embassy and consulates in Canada adopted a more aggressive stance against the clemency movement than our missions did anywhere else in the world. For one thing, they attributed the clemency campaign largely to Jews and Communists. It is also evident from editorials and columnists in Canadian newspapers that our embassy and consulates led them to believe that the Supreme Court had reviewed the trial record and had upheld the verdicts and sentences. In addition to labeling clemency a Jewish/Communist movement, our Canadian embassy and consulate representatives threatened economic and other reprisals against radio stations and newspapers that sold time or space to clemency supporters, and turned the names of Canadian clemency supporters over to the Canadian police and to the FBI.

In the late fall of 1952, we heard from a Canadian committee that had been formed with the same objectives as ours — a new trial and/or clemency — that asked to be provided with information, and wrote that it anticipated that local committees would be formed in Montreal, Ottawa and other cities. The Canadians were already creating their own informational materials and had begun a letter-writing campaign that drew instant attention from C. Frederick Mullen, the Director of Public Information of the U.S. Department of Justice.

On November 10, 1952, Mullen recommended that the names of Canadian clemency supporters be sent to the FBI by the American embassy and consulates in Canada, and that their names also be sent to all "ports of entry, for I would judge that these people are probably communists and therefore excludable."[1024]

A month later, on December 13, our consul in Montreal notified State that the "patronage of the particular theater" a consulate employee attended, outside of which clemency supporters distributed handbills, "is 50% from the Anglo-Saxon ethnic groups and 50% from the Jewish group." The employee "described the persons handing out the cards as 'well-dressed young Jewish women.'"[1025] The employee did not reveal how the clemency supporters' ethnicity was determined.

On January 2, the consulate in Toronto was picketed by 75 persons carrying placards for clemency; the consulate reported to State that "a good many of the women were members of the United Jewish Peoples Order," which it described as "a Communist organization."[1026]

On January 4, a public clemency meeting, attended by 2,300 people, was held in Toronto, at which an American writer, Alfred E. Kahn, was a featured speaker. An embassy officer who had been at the meeting reported

> I could identify no one but a midget woman of about 40 who has been described to me as an important local Communist.[1027]

On January 9, the embassy notified all the consular offices that there were now clemency activities in "Ottawa, Montreal, Toronto, Regina, Winnipeg and

Vancouver," and that there had been "mass meetings in the larger cities, picket-ing, distribution of pamphlets, and the presentation of signed petitions."[1028]

On January 14, the embassy reported on clemency activities and petitions in Ottawa, and reported that it had been picketed by 300 persons.[1029]

A recording had been played at a public meeting, entitled *They Shall Not Die*, produced by the Labor Theater of San Francisco, that "developed more or less in soap-opera style on the theme that the Rosenbergs were accused, tried, and now were to be executed all unjustly." The report observed, "It is notable that in the course of the meeting no speaker introduced anti-Semitism."

Finally, the report said that, although "Canadian officials have privately expressed their unhappiness at these activities in Canada,"

> the highly influential secretary of the Privy Council, Jack Pickersgill, took the position that from an overall political point of view, and especially from the point of view of countering any charges of anti-Semitic preju-dice in the U.S., perhaps it might be well to commute the sentence.[1030]

On that same day, the consulate in Winnipeg reported that it had obtained information from an informant on the proceedings at a public meeting called by the Winnipeg Committee for clemency held at the Hebrew Sick Benefit Hall, which was attended by persons associated with a number of "Communist" groups, including the United Jewish People's Order.[1031]

On January 15, the consulate in Montreal reported that a letter in the non-Communist *Gazette* from a Rev. R. A. Cameron had mentioned an admission from the FBI that a prosecution witness had given perjured testimony at the trial. The Consul asked the embassy to provide it with information so that it could "swat down promptly what I presume to be just one more lie."[1032]

The consulate in Windsor sent State examples of informational materi-als distributed during a clemency demonstration. Among them was a leaflet that asked why the United States was engaged in freeing Nazi war criminals who had been sentenced to death, while seeking to carry out the death sentences of the Rosenbergs.[1033] The leaflet listed eleven convicted Nazi war criminals, four of whom had been sentenced to death, the others to long prison terms. The four whose death sentences had been commuted were Field Marshal Albert Kisselring (convicted for the massacre of 335 Italian hostages in 1944), General Eberhard von Mackensen (convicted for the same crime as Kisselring), General Kurt Gallenkamp (convicted for executing Allied paratroopers), and Franz Kirenschmalz (convicted for extermination of Jews at Auschwitz). All four were freed by 1952. Six of the remaining seven who had been sentenced to long prison terms were freed in 1951 or 1952. The seventh, Ilse Koch, was sentenced to life imprisonment for murderous atrocities at Buchenwald; she hanged herself in her prison cell in 1967.

On January 26, the Toronto consulate sent State a transcript of a half-hour radio broadcast on station CKEY, sponsored by the Canadian Committee to Secure Clemency for Julius and Ethel Rosenberg, at the end of which listeners were urged to join Albert Einstein, Harold Urey, and 1500 American ministers in petitioning for clemency for the Rosenbergs.[1034]

The cover message from the Toronto consulate, preceding the transcript, declared that the broadcast was "pernicious" and was paid for by an individual "reported to be an undercover member of the higher circles of the Communist Party of this city," and was also an officer of a "Communist-controlled" union. The consulate reported that copies of *They Shall Not Die* could be obtained by calling a telephone number that was listed in the name of "the head of the Jewish element of the local Communist Party."[1035] The message stated

> The first indication that such a broadcast would be given appeared in the form of an advertisement in the Conservative *Globe and Mail* on the morning of January 19, and the Consulate General thereupon took steps to bring pressure to bear for a cancellation of the broadcast. This was done with the concurrence of the Embassy in Ottawa, which stipulated that the Consulate General was not to expose itself as the source of intervention to have the broadcast stopped.[1036]

Since Canadian authorities declined to order the radio station to cancel the broadcast, the consulate arranged for "a scathing article on the broadcast" to appear in the *Toronto Telegram*.

Unless radio station CKEY can be reined in, the message went on, it could be used "even more extensively for anti-American attacks," but the consulate recognized that action by an American official to limit the radio station's rights

> must be discreet in order to avoid a basis for adverse general publicity regarding attempts on our part to meddle in Canadian internal affairs and rights of free speech.[1037]

The message raised the possibility that the radio station owner could be "convinced that his failure to have his station change its attitude would adversely affect his own material interests in a very tangible way." There was the possibility, the message went on, "of influencing American advertisers or their Canadian subsidiaries in regard to their use of CKEY," although there might be the stumbling block that advertisers might not want to abandon the marketing reach of the radio station and other media sources also controlled by the station's owner.[1038]

On February 17, the Toronto consulate announced that it had succeeded in curbing CKEY's sale of time to "Communists or fellow travelers."[1039]

In a dispatch on January 29, the consul in Hamilton reported that the consulate had been picketed by persons who

> were obviously Semitic in appearance and most of them had a foreign look. They were roughly dressed in working clothes and had obviously come from work to the picket line.[1040]

The consul also took credit for providing a broadcaster with material that included the misinformation that the Supreme Court had reviewed the case, "which made the broadcast possible."[1041]

On February 20, State sent the embassy in Ottawa a "Memorandum of Conversation" between an official of the Canadian embassy in Washington and a State Department official regarding Canadian opinion on the pending execution of the Rosenbergs which was at odds with the American embassy and consul reports.

The Canadian official said that he had requested the conversation to

> let the State Department know of the feeling which exists on the question of the Rosenberg executions in Canada.
>
> ...there was widespread concern over this matter in Canada which extends to circles which have nothing to do with Communist propaganda and which are not subject to fellow-traveller influences.[1042]

On May 28, the consul in Montreal reported a number of clemency activities, including picketers in front of the consulate, who were "completely dispersed" by the police who also confiscated their placards."[1043] An informant told the consulate that two women clemency advocates were "long-time communists," although there was "no record" that one of them "was suspected of subversive activity," nor was there any record of the other woman in the files, although "several male members" of her family "are listed as members of the Labor-Progressive Party, the United Jewish Peoples' Organization or other subversive organizations."[1044]

On June 10, the consulate in Montreal sent an employee of the consulate to a "Save-the-Rosenbergs" public meeting, "in the hope of identifying any American citizen residents of this area who might take part in the meeting."[1045]

The consulate employee reported that Emily Alman introduced the speakers.

> There were many Jewish-looking people; young couples; the old and the young. I saw no one I recognized, and remained inconspicuous at the back of the hall; many of us had to stand during the entire meeting.[1046]

The employee, who acknowledged in her report that she had arrived after the meeting had gotten under way, was mistaken in respect to Emily: Emily never arrived at the meeting, having become ill at Newark Airport, and was hospitalized; she had had a miscarriage.

On June 12, the consulate in Toronto reported that a public meeting for clemency had been held the previous evening at which Helen Sobell, the wife of Morton Sobell, and Stephen Love had spoken. The local press estimated that 1,000 persons attended the meeting, although the police said only half as many were there and that "80% of those in attendance were said to be members of the United Jewish People's Order, a communist front organization."[1047]

On June 19, the consulate in Toronto reported that there had been "round the clock picketing" since June 16, with the number of picketers varying "between a high of over 400 to a low of a dozen in the early hours of the morning. A high proportion of the picketers have been Jewish," and that during the evening hours "a number of passing motorists have booed the picketers and some have shouted 'go back to Russia.'"[1048]

On June 22, the consulate reported that when it had become apparent that the Rosenbergs would be executed, the number of pickets had increased to "600 and 700, about half of whom were women, and predominantly Jewish."[1049]

Clemency in the other Americas...

In the nations south of us, their situations, in the 1940s-1950s, had many elements in common: extreme poverty, rigid caste systems that discriminated against indigenous populations, often with genocidal effects. With some exceptions, most south-of-the border governments at that time were sympathetic to the interests of American-owned corporations.

The people of those nations were gifted with extraordinary writers and artists who were regarded as voices for the mute, whose partisanship was guileless, visceral and spiritual. This was even true for the small number who were Communists, almost all of whom abandoned their political partisanship when faced with the choice of compassion or dogma. Among the voices for the mute were poet Pablo Neruda and novelist Gabriel Garcia Marquez, both Nobelists, and artists David Siqueiros and Diego Rivera, who brought their people's sufferings to the world's attention. Many of these writers and artists, through contact with American tourists, students and anthropologists and archeologists who supported clemency, were persuaded to lend their names to the clemency movement. They were, of course, instantly labeled Communists and Communist-dupes by our embassies and consuls.

Our nearest southern neighbor, Mexico, had been embroiled in the Rosenberg-Sobell case since August 1950, when FBI agents apparently bribed several Mexican policemen to kidnap Morton Sobell, his wife and two children from Mexico and bring them across the border to Laredo, Texas, where a waiting U.S. immigration official accepted Sobell as a "deportee" from Mexico.[1050]

An embassy report, dated June 16, 1953, contained a translation "of the only editorial which has thus far appeared in the conservative press of Mexico City appealing for clemency in the Rosenberg atomic spy case."[1051] The editorial also expressed doubt of the guilt of the Rosenbergs and correctly noted that the Supreme Court had never reviewed the trial.

The editorial from the conservative *Excelsior* read, in part

> The case of Julius and Ethel Rosenberg — accused and apparently convicted — though they have not confessed to the crime, — of having sold to the Soviet Government the vital secret of the atomic bomb — continues to agitate the entire world. Petitions for clemency are pouring into the White House at Washington signed by North American citizens, political figures, prelates, writers, scientists and artists of many other nations...
>
> ***
>
> It is hoped, therefore, that President Eisenhower...will permit himself to be softened by the tears of the small children of the alleged "atomic spies." Those two little ones, actually, are the real victims, that is, the innocent victims of the crime which their parents probably did not commit.[1052]

In Cuba, a highly unpopular dictator, Fulgenicio Batista, had suspended the Constitution in an effort to prevent his overthrow. By that time criticism of him from almost every quarter — conservative to Communist — was so great that he could only partially enforce efforts to illegalize his opposition.

On February 19, 1953, our embassy in Havana reported the

Communist campaign to win clemency for Julius and Ethel Rosenberg has received considerable help, at least in Cuba, from the publication of pictures showing the two Rosenberg children at Sing Sing, holding valentines, dolls, or in other poses which cannot help stirring emotion in favor of their cause...These agencies [United States news services] no doubt find the pictures of definite 'sob story' news appeal, but may fail to realize their propaganda value for the Communists.[1053]

The embassy dutifully reported that most of the clemency communications it received had originated with the Communist Party.[1054]

In Nicaragua, governed by the dictatorial "shoot and loot" Somoza family that had been in power since the 1930s, a post-execution letter from the embassy at Managua to C. D. Jackson, publisher of *Life* and a close aide to President Eisenhower, explained why the Ambassador could not respond directly to Jackson, who had inquired what the reactions to the clemency campaign had been.

Ambassador Whelan, who had to go to Leon to attend a State funeral (General Somoza's mother-in-law) asked me to write you at once regarding the reaction in Nicaragua to the Rosenberg case.

There was almost none. Newspapers carried the usual A.P. and U.P. wire stories, but they were not overplayed. There have been no editorials on any phase of the trial or the execution of the judgment.

The few Communists in the country do not dare meet or stage demonstrations because of President Somoza's strong anti-red policies.[1055]

Argentina was governed by Juan Peron at the time, but, under the pressure of the old ruling cliques and the army, he was beginning to turn on his liberal and labor supporters of the past, perhaps because without his wife Eva, who had died in July 1952, he could no longer endure the hardships of the journey he had begun with her in 1945.

On January 29, 1953, an embassy dispatch quoted from an English-language newspaper, *Buenos Aires Herald*, which declared that "the trial and sentence has not been questioned," and "Since there was no recommendation for mercy there should have been no further impediment to the carrying out of the sentence."[1056]

On February 4, the embassy transmitted two pro-clemency letters, which were not translated, to State, with a handwritten note saying, "Protests in the Rosenberg case are not being dignified by a reply."[1057]

On April 7, the embassy reported to State that it had received petitions for clemency with "several thousand signatures."[1058]

On June 16, the disinterest in the case implied by embassy reports to States was shown to have been wishful thinking. On that day, the embassy notified State, "Recent Buenos Aires editorials Rosenberg case advocate commutation or stay to give them 'benefit of doubt,' alleging key prosecution witness compromised as confessed criminal...Embassy mail sharply increased with 1000 letters received last four days protesting or urging clemency."[1059]

Our embassy in Brazil informed State, on January 15, 1953, that the Communist Party was behind a clemency campaign for the Rosenbergs. "This propaganda has been energetically combated in the responsible press, with extensive use of USIE material."[1060] Since the numbers of signers of clemency petitions were in the thousands, the embassy explained that a "large portion of the signatures in all cases probably reflects the Brazilian antipathy to capital punishment rather than support of the communist campaign or belief in the couple's innocence." Our consuls in Brazil turned clemency signatures over to the Brazilian police.

The last available dispatch from Brazil is from the consul at Porto Alegre. It is dated June 16, and reads

> I have the honor to report that the Consulate has been requested by the President of the City Council of Porto Alegre to transmit to President Dwight D. Eisenhower a resolution passed by the City Council asking that the President pardon the Rosenbergs.[1061]

Uruguay was one of the few South American countries in which, under the prodding of a moderately democratic government, the economic situation was improving for the general population.

On February 23, 1953, the embassy at Montevideo reported that although it had received a small number of appeals for clemency for the Rosenbergs this display of sympathy for the condemned pair does not reflect any general sentiment voiced in the local press, most of newspapers expressing instead the view that the Rosenbergs have been afforded a fair trial and all reasonable consideration.[1062]

By June, to the surprise of the embassy, the clemency movement had grown to the point that *El Pais*, a newspaper which "is customarily very pro-American," had published an article on the Rosenberg case which "is a great boon to the Communist inspirers of the save-Rosenbergs, damn-the-United-States-as-fascists" campaign. The article in *El Pais* read, in part

> In Europe, high dignitaries of the Catholic Church, many French writers, the League for the Rights of Man and lawyers have gone on record against the death sentence. But in the United States, perhaps because of 'McCarthyism,' which has placed even the independents on the defensive, only a few voices are heard outside the defense organized by the Rosenberg committee.[1063]

Paraguay, at the time of the clemency campaign, had been governed for the preceding six years by six presidents, none of them distinguished by competence or honesty.

We have a single dispatch from the embassy at Asuncion, dated June 23, 1953, which quotes two post-execution editorials in the local newspapers.

The first, in *La Tribuna*, was described as "a strong denunciation of capital punishment, 'the wretched triumph of death, imposed by men on men.'" The dispatch stated that a "confidential source" identified the writer of the editorial as "a Communist," a description that the embassy believed to be true, because the editorial also said

> We do not defend the position, guilty or innocent, of the Rosenbergs...the 'justice' of death fell with all the force of law on the pair. Today Julius and Ethel Rosenberg are a sad remembrance for humanity.[1064]

The second editorial, which appeared in *La Union*, the newspaper of the conservative Colorado Party, was more satisfactory to the embassy.

> In contrast to the Tribuna editorial, the "Comentarios" writer expressed the belief that real justice was accomplished...

Guatemala was another nation in turmoil, this time as the victim of a destabilization program initiated by the CIA, in 1951, that included the recruitment
of civilian and military forces to oust Jacobo Arbenz, the legally elected
president. The immediate beneficiary of the destabilization program was the
United Fruit Company, which had vigorously opposed a land reform program
undertaken by Arbenz. At the time of the clemency campaign the destabilization
program was in full swing, although Arbenz' ouster would not take place until
the following year.

In December 1952, our embassy reported to State that "A significant number
of the fifty eight Deputies in the Guatemalan Congress went on record in support
of a Communist cause recently by signing a petition to President Truman for the
lives of Julius and Ethel Rosenberg."[1065] The embassy listed the names and
political affiliations of fifteen of the signers, but identified only four of them as
Communists.

On February 20, 1953, the embassy reported that both *Nuestro Diario*,
which supported the government, and the Communist newspaper, *Octubre*,
had "carried numerous articles pointing out the 'injustice' of the sentences," and
reporting protests against them by local groups.[1066]

On June 18, the embassy reported that 19 more members of Congress had
sent a petition for clemency to President Eisenhower, and

> the normally pro-American newspaper *La Hora* on June
> 13 carried a front-page editorial suggesting that it would
> be impolitic for the United States to carry out the sen-
> tence against the Rosenbergs.[1067]

From Costa Rica, governed at the time by a democratically elected government, our embassy at San Jose sent State translations of an article and an editorial
that had appeared in two non-Communist newspapers.

The editorial appearing in *La Prensa Libre,* on June 17, stated

> The fields of Korea have become a cemetery for the cream
> of the liberating armies...It is clear that the Rosenbergs
> will die in the electric chair, which should in justice
> receive those who are responsible for this 'treason'.[1068]

The article appeared in *La Nacion,* on June 18, after Supreme Court Justice
William O. Douglas granted the Rosenbergs a stay on the grounds that they may
have been tried under the wrong law. It continued,

He [Justice Douglas] has given them the benefit of the
doubt, in line with a principle of legal justice.

Clemency movements elsewhere in the world...

In Africa, the British and French governments were faced with popular
movements that would eventually compel them to yield sovereignty over Africa
to the Africans.

We have only two American consular dispatches, from what was then the
Union of South Africa, that relate to clemency for the Rosenbergs, both of them
immediately after the executions. The first is from our consulate at Cape Town,
dated June 22, 1953, which deals with a delegation that had been sent from a public meeting to the consulate to protest the executions. The consul wrote

> Not wishing to dignify the proceedings with a personal
> appearance, I requested Vice Consul Morris to receive
> the deputation on my behalf with instructions to inform
> the leader of the party that I was "unavoidably detained
> elsewhere," and that he was receiving the group as my
> personal representative. I also instructed Morris not to
> formally accept the resolution or to convey the impres-
> sion that the Consulate General would take any action
> toward transmitting the protest to Washington...[1069]

The second dispatch, also dated June 22, is from the consul at Port Elizabeth,
and stated

> The sentiments of the American community so far as it is
> possible to ascertain is unanimous that the Rosenbergs
> were guilty of treason and that the sentences should
> have been carried out long ere now.[1070]

Algeria, in northwest Africa, which had been under Vichy rule during
World War II, had a growing independence movement that the French government hoped to divert by incorporating Algiers into France, although this did not
end the agitation for independence. At the time of the clemency campaign, agitation was still going on and, in 1954, independence was achieved.

The American consul reported on June 25, 1953, that from June 5 to June
23, it had received 482 communications for clemency, for which the Communists
were "obviously responsible,"

> but a few apparently originated with non-communists.
> Among the latter group the most prominent persons
> was Leon-Etienne Duval, Bishop of Constantine.[1071]

In Tangiers, an "international zone" in North Africa, the American consul, in a dispatch dated June 25, 1953, cited at length an editorial in *Espana*, a Spanish daily, which opposed clemency as a Communist tactic against the free world. The consul noted, however, that *Espana* "has been one of the very few, if not the only newspaper in this area to consistently present the American viewpoint on the Rosenberg case in a favorable light."[1072]

In Tunisia, a French protectorate, a strong nationalist movement was engaged in guerrilla warfare that succeeded in winning independence in 1956.

A dispatch to State from Tunis dated June 22, 1953, states, "Rosenberg case coverage by local French press exceeds lineage any American issue recent years... General sentiment critical death penalty not on basis legal merits but emotional and dramatic aspects..."[1073]

Tripolitania (Libya) had been the scene of fierce battles between British and German troops in World War II. In 1951, its three provinces became the independent kingdom of Libya.

On January 21, 1953, the American legation passed on to State a letter it had received from the President of the Jewish community of Tripolitania on December 31, 1952, which read, in part

> Will God illuminate and protect all deeds of your Government, and in particular this act of human clemency which all the Jewish Community of Tripolitania invokes heartedly.[1074]

Egypt, at that time under a constitutional monarchy, was undergoing the stress of a strong movement for independence from Great Britain. The monarchy was toppled in 1952, and an independent Republic was proclaimed on June 18, 1953.

Early in 1953, the government had shut down six "Communist line" newspapers, several of which had urged their readers to support clemency for the Rosenbergs. Whether any or all of these newspapers were "Communist line," or whether that description was levied against all opposition newspapers, we do not know.

A dispatch from the embassy at Cairo, dated February 6, 1953, stated that the embassy had received "134 signatures on petitions and coupons, indicating the failure of the Communist sponsors to interest Egyptians in the subject."[1075] The embassy also reported receiving a petition bearing 101 signatures from "students at the Faculty of Law, Ibrahim University," which it did not attribute to Communist influence.

Iraq, in southeastern Asia, was being erratically governed by competing interests, among them British commercial interests, an underage heir to the Iraqi throne whose powers were exercised by a regent, groups of conservative and liberal politicians who had weak constituencies, and who were also pitted against one another along generational lines. It was not until 1946 that political parties were permitted, but the first elected government was quickly overthrown by the military. In 1952, after another popular uprising, civilian, but not democratic, rule was returned.

On July 15, 1953, our embassy in Baghdad reported that the only press comment on the Rosenberg case was contained in an editorial in the Muslim *Al-Sijl*. The embassy cited the newspaper as warning the Arabs against hostile moves by Israel, and quoted it as saying, "Jews pretend to be loyal nationals, at the time they are actually fifth columnists."

The paper then went on to argue that "the Jews were able to steal the atom bomb secrets and passed them to the Soviets as payment for the latter's recognition of Israel."

> Several Iraqi officials commented to members of the Embassy that the President's refusal to intervene in the case was evidence that the administration is not automatically a captive of pro-Jewish lobbies, and related this to assurances of impartiality with respect to the Palestine problem.[1076]

Israel was governed at the time by successive coalitions of labor, liberal, conservative and religious parties under David Ben-Gurion, Israel's first President. It was a contentious time, with great numbers of Jews streaming into Israel from Europe, Asia, Africa, and, in smaller numbers, from the United States.

The matter of clemency was related to a fundamental survival issue: without aid from the United States and private aid from American Jews, the vast numbers of Jews flowing into Israel would face homelessness and starvation. Thus, any action among Israelis that appeared to be critical of the United States was

regarded by some in Israel as a form of treason. Among the most forceful proponents of this point of view were the leaders of major Jewish organizations in the
United States, all of whom had gone on record as vigorously opposed to clemency
for the Rosenbergs.

On November 19, 1952, the *New York Times* reported that 20 Israeli rabbis
had sent an appeal for clemency to President Truman. The appeal did not question the fairness of the trial, but acknowledged an awareness of the Rosenbergs'
insistence on their innocence and the possibility of a miscarriage of justice, and
pointed out that incarceration in lieu of execution would provide the Rosenbergs
with the possibility that

> some day they would be able to prove their innocence.
> In such case your conscience and the conscience of the
> United States would be clean [.] No innocent life shall
> have been taken guiltlessly.[1077]

The appeal contrasted the "millions of guiltless Jews who lost their lives at
the hands of the Nazis...and the clemency that was extended to the perpetrators."
The appeal concluded

> God alone knows the whole truth. May this, your clem-
> ency, be a fitting crown to your great career.

On December 9, 1952, the American ambassador in Tel Aviv informed
State that Rabbi Itzhak Herzog, Chief Rabbi of Israel, had asked him to convey
his appeal for clemency for the Rosenbergs to President Truman, saying that he
had been approached by a relative of the Rosenbergs to do so, and that he had
been told

> the action for which they have been condemned to
> death was committed by them during the war at a time
> when Soviet Russia was still an ally of the United States.
> This, while no excuse, is to some extent an extenuating
> circumstance. I have also been told that this couple have
> two children of tender age, who if the sentence is carried
> out, would become orphans and whose innocent lives
> would be ruined forever.[1078]

On January 8, 1953, the embassy reported that *Haboler*, a Zionist publication
"had a long feature article which contrasted Rosenberg case with recent Prague
trial and implied that clemency would further dramatize difference."[1079] Further,
that a "December 6 article in *Jerusalem Post* by its US correspondent...asserts
guilt proven, but describes sentence 'as cruel and unusual punishment contrary
to Eighth Amendment,' and designed to bring pressure on them (Rosenbergs)
to talk.'" On January 7, an editorial in the *Jerusalem Post* "entitled 'The Quality

of Mercy' rejects Communist line, but appeals for commutation of sentence on humanitarian grounds."

On June 18, the embassy reported that *Davar*, the organ of the labor federation, wrote, on June 14, that "majority Israelis hope for last minute 'act of mercy,' not because they believe in innocence accused, nor to support Communists for whom affair 'only serves as another point in their hypocritical propaganda,' nor primarily because of Jewish factor, 'although it does enter into calculations here,' but because they believe in democracy, 'which is strong enough and, in face of the many gallows of totalitarianism, under obligation to refrain from executing a sentence against which there is no redress.'"[1080]

The report cited the *Jerusalem Post* of June 17, as saying that the "case is now overwhelming for President's exercise of clemency, which would be an act of mercy tempered with justice, since conviction based on indorsement [sic] from 'self-confessed traitor' who recently 'reputed to have revoked his evidence;' punishment unusually severe for peacetime; Rosenbergs have 'passed through valley of death' several times during last two years; Supreme Court decision [relating to Justice Douglas' stay of execution] June 15 divided." The report ended by citing comment in *Jerusalem Post,* that if the President decides not to grant clemency, his decision would lead to "the suspicion that the tendency to panic has gone so far in the United States that justice with mercy is no longer possible."

On June 23, following the executions, the embassy reported that none of the anti-Communist newspapers editorialized that justice had been served by the executions. *Hatzofe*, a religious newspaper, quoted the Rosenbergs' attorney as saying that "American democracy died with the Rosenbergs." *Maariv*, an independent newspaper expressed an apprehension, also voiced by a left-wing newspaper, *Al Hamishmar*, that "choice of Jews as scapegoats in United States witch hunt causing apprehension in Israel towards fate United States Jewry." The newspapers associated with the Histadrut, Israel's largest labor federation, were "sharply critical of Communist attempts make political capital out of Rosenberg case but expressed opinion death sentence should have been commuted as blow against totalitarianism."[1081]

On August 7, 1953, Warren Olney III, U.S. Assistant Attorney General replied to a request from Israel's Assistant Attorney General Benjamin Pepper for more information on legal aspects of the case. Olney outlined the legal history of the case, from the conviction of the defendants to the execution of the Rosenbergs, but declined to send Pepper copies of the defense and prosecution briefs, "as the Department of Justice does not have these documents available for distribution."[1082]

On July 14, the American consul in Jerusalem reported, "The Arab refugees in Palestine were well pleased with the execution of the Rosenbergs, according to Dr. Thomas Lambie, chief representative in Palestine of the Independent Board for Presbyterian Foreign Missions."

> It appears that, for some time, the refugees had taken a deeper interest in the whole case than had been generally realized — much more so than the resident population. True, there was one editorial in *Ad Difaa* following the execution itself, asserting that the Rosenbergs' action was typically Jewish in its betrayal of the nation to which they were supposed to owe allegiance and in its contribution to the Communist cause (which to the Palestinian is something almost exclusively a Jewish movement). [1083]

The consul's report went on to say that among the Arab refugees there was, at first, "doubt as to whether America could call on sufficient courage and integrity to withstand the pressure of organized Jewish opinion...and so when the original death sentence was maintained and defended and then finally executed, the refugees were overjoyed."

Dr. Lambie, the report added, "felt that the net effect of the execution was to create a warm glow for America..."

News of the clemency movement from our embassies and consulates and news sources in India, China, Indochina, Vietnam and New Zealand were similar to those we have already cited from other countries. From New Zealand came a plea for clemency from the Very Rev. C. W. Chandler, Dean of Waikato, in Hamilton, who wrote that he was "of the opinion that the evidence is of a very slender character." [1084]

In Australia, the *New York Times* reported, on June 19,

> Leaders of the Anglican, Jewish, Presbyterian, Methodist and Congregational Churches and of the Church of Christ in Sydney, Australia, joined in signing a cable to the President asking him to exercise "your prerogative of clemency." [1085]

On June 4, 1953, the Department of Justice sent our consul in Perth the names of Australians who had written to the White House in support of clemency, to be passed on by the consul to the Australian police.

Notes on references and Index

1. The letters 'AN' preceding reference file numbers refer to the Authors' Numbers given to documents, which can be found in the Emily and David Alman Collection at the Boston University, Howard Gotlieb Archival Research Center.

2. References to the 'Committee' (capitalized) refer to the 'National Committee to Secure Justice in the Rosenberg/Sobell Case.'

3. Abbreviations:

ACLU	American Civil Liberties Union
ADL	Anti-Defamation League
AEC	Atomic Energy Commission
AJC	American Jewish Committee
AP	Associated Press
CR	Congressional Record
DA	David Alman
EA	Emily Alman
DG	David Greenglass
DOJ	Department of Justice
ER	Ethel Rosenberg
FBI	Federal Bureau of Investigation
HUAC	House Un-American Activities Committee
ISA	Internal Security Act of 1950
JCAE	Joint Committee on Atomic Energy
JR	Julius Rosenberg
MS	Morton Sobell
NCRAC	National Community Relations Advisory Council
NPACT	National Public Affairs Center for Television
OJR	Law firm headed by O. John Rogge
OSRD	Office of Scientific Research and Development
RG	Ruth Greenglass
RSC	Rosenberg/Sobell Committee materials

4. The "Trial Record" refers to the 1715-page verbatim trial record of the Rosenberg/Sobell case published and distributed by the Committee. The numbers in parentheses following the page numbers in the Committee's Trial Record are those of the original court Trial Record.

Endnotes

1. 12/01/52: Affidavit of FBI Agent Harrington: AN.691-15-16 (AN 2674x)
2. 12/01/52: Affidavit of FBI Agent Roettling:AN 2674-148-9
3. Undated: NPACT:AN 510-4 to 514-4-5
4. 12/05/01: *60 Minutes*/CBS/*The Traitor*
5. Transcript Federal Grand Jury, Southern District New York, 08/03/50, p. 9142
6. Appellant's petition to Supreme Court, October Term 1952, for Writ of Certiorari, *Julius Rosenberg and Ethel Rosenberg v. U.S*, pp. 32-3:AN 2680
7. ibid, pp. 33-6
8. ibid, p. 33
9. ibid, p. 34
10. ibid, pp. 31-2
11. ibid, pp. 33-4
12. 09/14/08: *NY Times*
13. 12/26/51: *NY Times*
14. Kennan, George F., "Where Do You Stand on Communism?" *NY Times Magazine*, cited in *Dennis v. U.S.*, Justice Felix Frankfurter concurring, 341 U.S.554-556
15. 05/13/76: *NY Times*
16. von Hoffman, Nicholas, *Citizen Cohn*, Doubleday, NY, 1988, pp. 454-61
17. Trial record, p. 181(227)
18. ibid, p. 1550 (2338)
19. CCNY president's punitive powers against anti-fascist protests were not as great as President Herbert Hoover's. Several years before the expulsion incident at CCNY, Major General Smedley Butler, ex-commandant of the U.S. Marines, and twice rewarded with the Congressional Medal of Honor, was threatened with a court martial and forced to retire by Hoover for denouncing Mussolini, the dictator of Italy, as a "mad dog."
20. Feklisov, A.; Kostin, S., *The Man Behind the Rosenbergs*, Enigma Books, NY, 2001
21. Feklisov, pp. 119-20
22. Radosh, Ronald; Milton, Joyce, *The Rosenberg File*, Holt, Rinehart, Winston, NY, 1983, pp. 54-6
23. Roberts, Sam, *The Brother,* Random House, NY, 2001, p. 68-9
24. 01/03/44:War Dept:AN 125
25. 10/02/44:War Dept:AN 334
26. 07/27/50:FBI:AN 152a
27. 07/20/50:FBI:AN 369; AN 327a
28. Trial record, pp. 1176-7 (1746-9)
29. 12/15/41:Hoover/Naval Intelligence: AN 2673
30. Sobell, Morton, *On Doing Time*, Charles Scribner's Sons, 1974, p. 58

31.   ibid, p. 33

32.   ibid, p. 37

33.   09/18/08: *NY Times*

34.   Sobell, p. 61

35.   09/23/53:Sobell affidavit: AN 1554

36.   Wexley, John, *The Judgment of Julius and Ethel Rosenberg*, Cameron & Kahn, NY, 1955, see photostats p. 650

37.   ibid, see photostat p. 651

38.   Prosecution Exhibit 21

39.   Prosecution Exhibit 22 (a) (b)

40.   Prosecution Exhibit 23 (a) (b)

41.   Prosecution Exhibit 24 (a) (b)

42.   Schneir, Walter and Miriam, *Invitation to an Inquest*, Penguin Books, Baltimore, 1973, p. 340

43.   Neville, John F., *The Press, the Rosenbergs and the Cold War*, Praeger, Westport, CT, 1995, p. 25

44.   Had the prosecution found any evidence, either tangible or through interviews with David Greenglass' fellow soldiers, that he was attempting to recruit them to the Communist Party or for espionage, his attempt would have certainly been made known at the trial. In 1946, the Justice Department indicted Carl Marzani, a journalist and former OSS employee of, among other acts, "teaching the principles of communism to men in said Military Forces...to the end that the Communist Party might get control thereof and thus bring about a revolt against the Capitalist System." (Carl Marzani, *The Education of a Reluctant Radical: From Pentagon to Penitentiary,* Topical Books, 1995, pp. 208-9). Marzani was only one of a number of individuals indicted for trying to "get control" of the United States Army, Navy and Air Force on behalf of the Communist Party. Marzani, who had helped pick the targets for the World War II bombing raids on Tokyo, was convicted and sentenced from one to three years. His jail mate was ex-Congressman J. Parnell Thomas, one time Chairman of the House Un-American Activities Committee, who had been convicted of defrauding the United States, for which he was sentenced to six-to-eighteen months in prison.

45.   Schneir, pp. 392-6;Affidavit/Bernard Greenglass:AN 691-24; Trial record, pp. 1088-9 (1615-7)

46.   Trial Record, pp. 664-5 (949-50)

47.   ibid, pp. 663-7 (948-53)

48.   ibid, p. 676 (967-8)

49.   ibid, pp. 564-5 (801-4)

50.   Schneir, 391-6

51.   Trial record, pp. 459-60 (645-6)

52.   06/19/50:OJR/file:AN 143a

53. 02/03/53:DOJ/White House:AN 1293, p. 3

54. Ashman, C.R. *The Finest Judges Money Can Buy*, Nash Publishing, 1973, pp. 270-7

55. 05/13/76 *NY Times*: AN 2635a

56. Hoffman, p. 272

57. Zion, Sidney, *The Autobiography of Roy Cohn*, Lyle Stuart, Secaucus, NJ, 1988, pp. 65-7

58. Gentry, Curt, *J. Edgar Hoover*, Norton, NY, 1991, p. 422

59. 03/16/51:FBI Memo/Whearty; Zion, p. 77

60. Sachar, Howard, M, *A History of the Jews in America*, Vintage (Random), NY, 1992, p. 328

61. ibid, pp. 301-8

62. http://en.wikipedia.org/wiki/Leo_Frank

63. Slater, Elinor and Robert, *Great Moments in Jewish History*, Jonathan David, 1998, p. 24

64. ibid

65. Francis, David R., *Russia from the American Embassy*, NY, 1921, p. 214

66. "Zionism versus Bolshevism: A struggle for the soul of the Jewish people" *Illustrated Sunday Herald (London)*, February 8, 1920, cited at http://www.fpp.co.uk/bookchapters/WSC/WSCwrote1920.html

67. http://ddickerson.igc.org/The_Protocols_of_the_Learned_Elders_of_Zion.pdf

68. Ackerman, Kenneth, D., *Young J. Edgar*, Carrol & Graf, NY, 2007, p. 342

69. Donner, Frank, *The Age of Surveillance*, Knopf, NY, 1980, p. 121n

70. Gribetz, Judah; Greenstein, Edward L.; Stein, Regina, S., *The Timetables of Jewish History*, Simon & Schuster, NY, 1993, p. 383

71. Sachar, p. 297

72. Hoover, J. Edgar, *Masters of Deceit*, Henry Holt, NY, 1958

73. ibid, p. 255

74. ibid, p. 270

75. Heale, M.J., *American AntiCommunism*, Johns Hopkins Univ. Press, Baltimore, 1990, p. 188

76. Hoover, p. 5

77. Subcommittee to investigate the administration of Internal Security Act and other internal security laws to the Senate Committee on the Judiciary, "*Protocols of the Elders of Zion*", 1964, p. 2

78. Sullivan, William, *The Bureau: My Thirty Years in Hoover's FBI*, W.W. Norton, 1979, p. 273

79. Donner, p. 121n

80. ibid

81. Loftus, John and Aarons, Mark, *The Secret War Against the Jews*, St. Martins Press, NY, 1994, p. 187

82. Gribetz,, p. 377; see previously cited Gribetz, p. 383

83.   Morse, Arthur, D., *While Six Million Died*, Hart Publishing, NY, pp. 65-7
84.   ibid, p. 82
85.   *U.S. v. Remington* 191 F 2d 246,252
86.   Schneir, p. 314
87.   09/19/50:DOJ/Saypol:AN 121e
88.   Hoffman, p. 369-70
89.   08/08/53, *Saturday Evening Post*, cited in Wexley, pp. 249-50
90.   Hiss, Alger, *In the Court of Public Opinion*, Alfred A. Knopf, NY, 1957, p. 214
91.   ibid, pp. 289-98
92.   Luce, Henry, *Ideas of Henry Luce*, Atheneum, NY, 1969, p. 113
93.   http://www.cnn.com/SPECIALS/cold.war/episodes/06/1st.draft/pravda.html,
       p. 2; retrieved 08/18/08
94.   Senator Pat McCarran, Nevada: 1950 CR 14186
95.   09/11/45:War Dept:AN 39
96.   Cook, Blanche Wiesen, *The Declassified Eisenhower*, Doubleday, NY, 1981, p.
       345-6
97.   02/12/46:War Dept:AN 1374
98.   McCullough, David, *Truman*, Simon & Schuster (Touchstone), NY, 1992, p. 517
99.   Whitfield, Stephen J., *The Culture of the Cold War, 2nd ed.*, Johns Hopkins Univ.
       Press, 1996, p. 38
100.   08/1/50 *NY Times*, p. 1
101.   McCullough, p. 761
102.   Oshinsky, David M., *A Conspiracy So Immense*, Free Press, NY, 1983, p. 106
103.   Reuben, William A., *The Atom Spy Hoax*, Action Books, NY, 1955, p. 149
104.   Carmichael, Virginia, *Framing History*, U. Minnesota Press, 1993, p. 36, citing
       George Kennan in internal State Department document, 1948, quoted in Harold
       Pinter, "Language and Lies," *Index on Censorship 17*, No. 6 (June-July 1988), p. 2
105.   Carroll, James, *House of War*, Houghton Mifflin, Boston, 2006, pp. 215-6, citing
       Snead, David L., *The Gaither Committee*, Ohio State University Press, Columbus,
       1999, p. 63
106.   Kennan, George F., "Where Do You Stand on Communism?" *NY Times Magazine*,
       05/27/51 p. 7, cited in *Dennis v. U.S.*, Justice Felix Frankfurter concurring, 341 U.S.
       554-556
107.   Hixson, Walter L., *George F. Kennan*, Columbia Univ. Press, 1991, pp. 165-6
108.   06/29/50, Pegler, Westbrook, *NY Jnl-American*, p. 3
109.   Oshinsky, p. 104
110.   Manchester, William, *The Glory and the Dream*, Little, Brown, Boston, 1974, p. 402
111.   Warren, Earl, *The Memoirs of Earl Warren*, Doubleday, Madison Books ed. 2001,
       p. 6
112.   U.S. Code Annotated, Title 50 Internal Security Subch I Sec 781 (1), p. 442
113.   ibid Subch I Sec 781 (15), p. 444

114. ibid Subch II Sec 811 (12), p. 470

115. ibid Subch II Sec 811 (14), p. 470

116. ibid Subch I Sec 781 (9), p. 444

117. ibid Subch I Sec 794 (a), p. 466

118. 1950 CR 14440

119. 1950 CR 14258

120. 1950 CR 15188

121. Kanfer, S., *A Journal of the Plague Years*, Atheneum, 1973, p. 39

122. 1950 CR 15536

123. 1950 CR 15288

124. 12/27/55 *NY Times*: AN 218

125. Fariello, Griffin, *Red Scare*, Norton, NY, 1995, pp. 40-1

126. ibid, p. 203

127. Hunt, Linda, *Secret Agent*, St. Martin's Press, NY, 1991, pp. 6-40

128. For details of wartime trading with Nazi Germany by a score of United States major corporations, see Higham, Charles, *Trading with the Enemy*, Dell, NY, 1983

129. Hunt, p. 25

130. 10/01/45/War Dept/German scientists/AN 3005

131. Hunt, pp. 1-2

132. Simpson, Christopher, *Blowback*, Weidenfield & Nicolson, NY, 1988, pp. 222-5

133. ibid, pp. 27-8

134. 1950 CR S17103-4

135. 1950 CR S17104-5

136. 1950 CR S17105-6

137. Ryan, Alan A.,Jr., *Quiet Neighbors*, Harcourt Brace Jovanovitch, NY, 1984, pp. 29-30

138. Hunt, p. 44

139. ibid, p. 218

140. ibid, pp. 44-5

141. For additional accounts of the numbers and functions of Nazis in America and of Nazis subsidized by our government to remain in Germany for special tasks, and the retreat from deNazification, see Craig Roberts' *The Medusa File*, Consolidated Press International, Tulsa, OK, 1997

142. 07/97 *Dateline:World Jewry*, World Jewish Congress, NY, p. 1 AN 1436

143. Hunt, p. 56

144. Mason, R.A., Taylor, John W.R., *Aircraft, Strategy and Operations of the Soviet Airforce*, Janes, London, 1986, pp. 28-9

145. Holloway, David, *Stalin & the Bomb*, Yale, New Haven, 1994, p. 110

146. Katz, Lyber, "Stalin's AntiSemitism Documented," in *Jewish Currents*, July-August 1997, Vol. 51, No. 7, p. 20 et seq AN 1435

147. Hunt, p. 255

148. Roberts, Craig, *The Medusa File*, Consolidated Press International, Tulsa, OK, 1997, pp. 67-71

149. *U.S. v. Stanley* 483 U.S. 669, 673 (1987), citing *Chappell v. Wallace* 462 U.S. 296, 300 (1983)

150. *U.S. v. Stanley* 483 U.S. 669, 687-688 (1987)

151. Shirer, William L., *The Rise and Fall of the Third Reich*, Touchstone (Simon & Schuster), 1990, pp. 1095n-6n

152. 07/06/50:DOJ/file:AN 361

153. 08/02/50:DOJ/Hoover:AN 389

154. Gentry, pp. 338-9

155. Klehr, Harvey & Radosh, Ronald, *The Amerasia Spy Case*, UNC Press, 1996, p. 119

156. Gentry, p. 346

157. ibid, p. 344

158. ibid, p. 346-7

159. Reuben, pp. 113-8

160. 07/19/50:JEH/DoJ:AN 151g

161. Gentry, pp. 424-5

162. Zion, p. 72

163. 02/8/51:JCAE:AN 3201, p. 14

164. Exhibit 8, atom bomb sketch: AN 1486

165. Schneir, p. 465

166. Schneir, pp. 350-4

167. 08/08/50:FBI Lab/FBI:AN 315

168. Romerstein, Herbert; Breindel, Eric, *The Venona Secrets*, Regnery, Washington, DC, 2000, p. 227

169. Moss, Norman, *Klaus Fuchs*, St. Martin's Press, NY, 1987 p. 3

170. Lowenthal, Max, *The Federal Bureau of Investigation*, Harcourt Brace Jovanovich, NY, 1950, p. 438

171. Lamphere, Robert J., *The FBI-KGB War*, Random House (Berkeley Books ed.) 1987, p. 143

172. 07/02/46:WarDept/Hoover:AN 267

173. Lamphere, p. 147

174. 07/18/50:AEC/from FBI:AN 263

175. Hoover, J. Edgar, "The Crime of the Century", in *20 Reader's Digest Books*, Reader's Digest Association, Pleasantville, NY, 1953, p. 73

176. ibid, pp. 75-6

177. ibid, p. 78

178. ibid, p. 66

179. ibid, p. 82

180. Sullivan, p. 183

181. ibid, p. 82

182. ibid, p. 83

183. Trial Record, p. 800 (1152-3)

184. Wexley, p. 50

185. Williams, Robert Chadwell, *Klaus Fuchs, Atom Spy*, Harvard Univ. Press, Cambridge, 1987, p. 200

186. 07/11/50:DOJ:AN 122, p. 2

187. Wexley, pp. 44-6

188. ibid, p. 47

189. Schneir, Chapters 10, 13, 27, 29

190. 09/24/65: Gold, Harry, 84-page letter to attorney: AN 2513-9; ('Gold letter')

191. ibid: AN 2513-2

192. 06/19/50:DOJ/File:AN 376

193. Schneir, p. 83

194. ibid, pp. 363-4

195. Hoover (*Crime...Century*), p. 84

196. 06/02/50:FBI/Gold statement:AN 142a

197. Undated FBI memorandum: AN 106-67

198. Trial record, pp. 564-5 (800-2)

199. Joint Committee on Atomic Espionage (JCAE), *Soviet Atomic Espionage*, U.S. Govt Printing Office, 1951, p. 6

200. 05/10/45:War Dept/William L. Laurence, pp. 4, 14-5, 17: AN 2-4

201. JCAE, p. 4

202. undated:DOJ:AN 245

203. date deleted:FBI re DG: AN 843

204. undated:DOJ/DG:AN 293, p. 122

205. Smyth, H.D., *A General Account of the Development of Methods of Using Atomic Energy for Military Purposes Under the Auspices of the U.S. Government 1940-1945*, U.S. War Dept., Washington, DC, 1945, p. 20

206. Trial record p. 611 (871-3)

207. ibid, p. 451-3 (632-5)

208. 11/07/57:DOJ-Benjamin F. Pollack:AN 775, p. 111

209. 09/19/50:DoJ/AN 121e

210. Roberts, S., pp. 417, 483; 12/05/01: *60 Minutes*/CBS: *The Traitor*

211. 08/23/50 memo: OJR associate: AN 691, p. 19-21

212. ibid, p. 21-2

213. Trial record, p. 1624 (2469)

214. Higham, Charles, *Trading With The Enemy*, Barnes & Noble, NY, 1983, pp. 74-5

215. 06/28/50:DOJ/file:AN 138

216. Horne, Gerald, *Black and Red*, SUNY, Albany, 1986, p. 178

217. 02/06/51:AEC/Beckerly: AN 134

218. 02/08/51:JCAE:AN 3201

219. ibid, p. 2
220. ibid, p. 3
221. ibid, p. 5
222. ibid, p. 25
223. ibid, pp. 2-3
224. ibid, pp. 11-2
225. ibid, pp. 14-5
226. ibid, p. 6
227. ibid, p. 18
228. ibid
229. ibid, p. 8
230. ibid, p. 14
231. ibid, pp. 26-7
232. ibid. pp. 27-8
233. Trial record, p. 62 (44-5)
234. ibid, pp. 64-6 (47-51)
235. *In Fact,* begun in 1940 by George Seldes, investigated and analyzed media handling of current events
236. Trial record, pp. 68,71 (52-4, 59-61)
237. ibid, p. 59 (38-9)
238. ibid
239. ibid, p. 61 (42-3)
240. ibid, p. 74 (63-5)
241. ibid, p. 75 (64-6)
242. 02/06/53:DOJ:AN 1472
243. Trial record, pp. 51-2 (25-7)
244. ibid, p. 156 (184-5)
245. ibid, p. 180 (225-6)
246. ibid, p. 181 (226-8)
247. 06/?/50:David Greenglass/OJR:AN 222
248. Trial record, pp. 590-1 (841)
249. ibid, p. 498 (701-2)
250. Schneir, p. 465
251. Trial record, pp. 499-500 (703-6)
252. ibid, p. 501 (706-7)
253. ibid, p. 502 (709)
254. ibid, p. 508 (719)
255. ibid, p. 610 (870)
256. ibid, p. 611 (870-2)
257. ibid, pp. 611-3 (874-5)
258. ibid, pp. 609-13 (866-75)

259. ibid, p. 611 (871-2)

260. ibid, p. 916 (1337-8)

261. ibid, p. 403 (557-8)

262. 09/12/61:DOD/Schneir:AN 531

263. 08/22/66: *Morton Sobell v. U.S.*/amended petition to U.S. District Court:AN 1521, p. 36-7

264. ibid, p. 34

265. Trial record, p. 443 (621)

266. ibid, p. 510 (722)

267. ibid, p. 704 (1010-1)

268. ibid, p. 1523 (2291)

269. Transcript Federal Grand Jury, Southern District New York, Ruth Greenglass, 08/03/50, p. 9142

270. Radosh, pp. 163-4

271. 02/08/51:JCAE:AN 3201, p. 14

272. Radosh, p. 165

273. Roberts, S., p. 483

274. 12/05/01:*60 Minutes*/CBS: *The Traitor*

275. 03/15/51 *NY Times*, p. 1, cited in Neville, p. 41-2

276. Wexley, p. 489

277. Trial record, pp. 756-7 (1087-8)

278. Transcript of Record for Supreme Court, *Rosenberg v. U.S*: Affidavit of Ass't U.S. Attorney J.M. Foley: AN 2674-142-5, pp. 1-4

279. Decision, U.S. Ct. of Appeals, *U.S. v. Rosenbergs et al* 200 F.2d 666,670 (2nd Cir. 1952): AN 2679, p. 320

280. Trial record, pp. 706-7 (1013-4)

281. ibid, p. 521 (738-9)

282. ibid, p. 1054 (1563-4)

283. ibid, p. 1211 (1802)

284. 07/17/50:FBI/Rosenberg inventory:AN 369; AN 327a

285. Circa 03/14/53: Macy affidavit:AN 691-25-26

286. 03/30/53:FBI/DOJ:AN 2729

287. 04/20/53:DOJ:AN 2726

288. 07/17/50:FBI/Rosenberg inventory:AN 369; AN 327a

289. Lamphere, p. 193

290. 05/4/53:FBI:AN 2731

291. Roberts, S., p. 417

292. ibid, p. 482

293. 06/02/50:FBI/Gold statement:AN 142a

294. Trial record, pp. 821-4 (1186-90)

295. ibid, pp. 824-5 (1191-3)

296. ibid, p. 455-7 (639-42)

297. ibid, p. 828 (1196a-7)

298. 06/?/50:David Greenglass/OJR:AN 222

299. Wexley, pp. 386-91;407-10

300. see Schneir, Chapters 27-29

301. Transcript Federal Grand Jury, Southern District New York, Harry Gold, 08/02/50, p. 9099

302. 12/23/51:FBI/Gold/Greenglass:AN 418

303. Trial record, p. 826 (1195)

304. ibid, p. 827 (1196)

305. 06/02/50:FBI/Gold:AN142a, p. 3

306. Trial record, p. 826 (1193)

307. Wexley, p. 386

308. ibid, p. 411

309. Gold letter, p. 45

310. Trial Record, pp. 821-2

311. 08/01/50:DOJ/Gold:AN 108-16-17

312. Trial record, p. 815 (1177-8)

313. ibid, p. 828 (1196a-7)

314. Gold letter, p. 42

315. ibid, p. 57

316. ibid

317. Wexley, p. 407

318. Schneir, pp. 386-7

319. Gold letter, p. 34

320. undated:DOJ/AEC:AN 106-68

321. Trial record, 824 (1191)

322. ibid, p. 456 (641)

323. Williams, p. 191

324. Wexley, p. 400-1

325. Schneir, pp. 391-6

326. ibid, p. 394

327. 08/26/66:FBI/DOJ:AN 1263

328. Swearingen, M. Wesley, *FBI Secrets*, South End Press, Boston, 1995, pp. 116-7:AN 3000

329. Trial record, pp. 527-8 (747-9)

330. ibid, pp. 1277-8 (1900-1)

331. ibid, pp. 1424-5 (2124-7)

332. ibid, pp. 1425-6 (2125-7)

333. ibid, pp. 1427-8 (2127-30)

334. ibid, pp. 1428-9 (2130)

335. ibid, p. 1429 (2131)
336. 12/01/52:Affidavit of FBI agent Roettling:AN 2674-148-9
337. Trial record, pp. 1429-30 (2131-2)
338. ibid, p. 1431 (2132-3)
339. 08/23/50 memo from Rogge associate on Pilat's conferences with Saypol AN 691, 19-21
340. Pilat,Oliver, *The Atom Spies*, G.P. Putnam's Sons, NY, 1952, p. v
341. ibid, p. 287
342. 12/01/52:Affidavit FBI Agent Harrington:AN 691-15-16 (AN 2674x)
343. Trial record, pp. 1613-4 (2449)
344. ibid, pp. 1064-7 (1578-83)
345. ibid, pp. 1067-8 (1583-4)
346. ibid, pp. 1069-70 (1585-7)
347. ibid, pp. 1075-6 (1596)
348. ibid, p. 1076 (1596-7)
349. ibid, p. 1079 (1600-1)
350. ibid, p. 1079-80 (1602)
351. ibid, p. 1080 (1602-3)
352. ibid, pp.1082-3 (1606)
353. ibid, pp. 1164-5 (1730-1)
354. ibid, p. 1174 (1744-5)
355. ibid, p. 1175 (1745)
356. ibid, pp. 1176-8 (1747-9)
357. ibid, pp. 1178-9 (1749-51)
358. ibid, p. 1185 (1760-1)
359. ibid, p. 1186-8 (1763-6)
360. ibid, pp. 1187-90 (1766-8)
361. ibid, p. 1190 (1769)
362. ibid, p. 1201 (1786-6a)
363. ibid, p. 1220 (1814)
364. *Grunewald v. United States*, 353 U.S. 391, 1957
365. Trial record p. 1454 (2170)
366. ibid, p. 1475 (2207)
367. ibid, pp. 1494-5 (2241)
368. ibid, p. 1507 (2264)
369. ibid, p. 1508 (2266)
370. Zion, p. 68-9
371. Trial record p. 1511 (2270)
372. ibid, p. 1511 (2271)
373. ibid, p. 1515 (2277-8)
374. ibid, pp. 181-2 (227-9)

375.   ibid, p. 1535 (2311-2)

376.   ibid, p. 1535 (2312)

377.   ibid, p. 1550 (2337)

378.   ibid, p. 1550 (2338)

379.   ibid. p. 1553 (2344)

380.   ibid, p. 1558 (2352)

381.   ibid, pp. 1566-7 (2366-7)

382.   ibid. p. 1573 (2379-81)

383.   ibid, pp. 1574-5 (2380-1)

384.   ibid, pp. 1575-6 (2383-4)

385.   ibid, p. 1578 (2387)

386.   ibid, p. 1580 (2390)

387.   ibid, p. 1584 (2399)

388.   ibid, pp. 1602-3 (2429-32)

389.   ibid, p. 1606 (2436-7)

390.   ibid, pp. 1606-7 (2437-8)

391.   ibid, p. 1613 (2449)

392.   ibid, p. 1615 (2452)

393.   ibid, p. 1614 (2451)

394.   ibid, pp. 106-7 (109-11)

395.   02/06/53:DOJ:AN 1472

396.   undated:NPACT:AN 512-4

397.   undated:NPACT:AN 514-3

398.   undated:NPACT:AN 514-2

399.   ibid

400.   Radosh, p. 272

401.   undated:NPACT:AN 510-2

402.   undated:NPACT:AN 511-5

403.   NPACT: AN 511-6-7-8

404.   undated:NPACT:AN 510-9-10

405.   undated:NPACT:AN 510a-4

406.   undated:NPACT:AN 510a-7

407.   ibid

408.   undated:NPACT:AN 513-3

409.   ibid

410.   Reuben, p. 295

411.   The date page and other pages are missing from our copy of the minutes, but the
       minutes make it clear that the meeting took place some time after the trial and
       before the executions. We have pages 43 (746) to 50 (753); Senator Hickenlooper's
       statement appears on pages 48 (751) to 49 (752). AN 3200

412. Stember, Charles Herbert, et al, *Jews in the Mind of America*, Basic Books, NY, 1966, pp. 78-9, Table 19

413. Morse, Arthur. D., *While Six Million Died*, Hart Publishing, NY, 1967, p. 137

414. Reuben, p. 295

415. FBI, *A Report to the American People on the Work of the FBI 1993-1998*, Chapter 2, p. 8

416. FBI press release 02/20/01

417. FBI, *A Report*, Chapter 2, p. 8

418. ibid

419. Richelson, Jeffrey T, *A Century of Spies*, Oxford Press, NY, 1995, pp. 278n, 279-82

420. Earley, Pete, *Confessions of a Spy*, G.P. Putnam's Sons, NY, 1997, p. 329

421. ibid, p. 329; see also Norman P. Hamilton, *Accused: The Spy Left Out in the Cold*, Horizon, 1989

422. Richelson, pp. 396-8

423. FBI, *A Report*, Chapter 2, p. 9

424. Barker, Rodney, *Dancing with the Devil*, Simon & Schuster, NY, 1996

425. FBI, *A Report*, Chapter 2, p. 7

426. ibid; see also 221 F. 3d 542 (4th Circuit 2000)

427. Earley, p. 329

428. 02/20/01:FBI Press release

429. 02/18/96: FBI-CIA joint press release

430. Hewlett, Richard G.; Anderson, Oscar E., Jr., *The New World 1939-1946*, Vol. 1, U.S. Atomic Energy Commission, 1962; Atomic Shield 1947-1952, Vol, 2, 1969

431. ibid, Vol. 2, p. 482

432. Kahn, David, *Hitler's Spies*, MacMillan, NY, 1978

433. Rhodes, Richard, *The Making of the Atomic Bomb*, Simon & Schuster, (QPB) NY, 1986, p. 605

434. Groves, pp. 207-23

435. McCullough, p. 288

436. Breuer, William, *Nazi Spies in America*, St. Martin's Paperbacks, NY, 1989, pp. 212, 265-6

437. http://www.fbi.gov/intelligence/di_timeline.htm, retrieved 04/10/09

438. 06/21/43:Message 961:AN 2741B

439. Feklisov, pp. 55-6

440. ibid

441. Williams, p. 189

442. ibid, p. 192

443. *NPACT Show # 1*, Robert Lamphere, August 21, 1973, Public Broadcasting System, pp. 1-4, 2-8

444. Groves, pp. 47-8

445. Higham, p. 163

446. ibid, p. 175
447. ibid, p. 176
448. ibid, p. 177
449. Simpson, Christopher, *The Splendid Blond Beast*, Common Courage Press, Monroe, ME, 1995, p. 62
450. Higham, p. 161
451. ibid
452. Simpson, p. 96
453. Higham, p. 161
454. ibid, p. 33
455. ibid, p. 37
456. ibid, pp. 61-2
457. Harington, John, cited in *Bartlett's Familiar Quotations*, Little, Brown & Co., Boston, 1992, 16th ed., p. 160
458. 10/31/50:AEC:AN 291-5-7
459. ibid
460. ibid
461. ibid
462. ibid
463. ibid
464. ibid
465. ibid
466. *Time*, 07/21/47
467. Wexley, p. 88n
468. http://www.jonathanpollard.org/sentences.htm
469. 12/26/51 *NY Times*
470. 10/19/51 et seq:Contributions ledger:AN 615
471. Dean, William; Axel, Larry E., *The Size of God: The Theology of Bernard Loomer in Context*, Mercer U. Press, 1987
472. 07/21/52:Cronbach/Alman:AN 223
473. 08/3-5/55:HUAC:AN 791, pp. 2127-30
474. 08/03-05/55:HUAC:AN 791, pp. 2127-30
475. 05/10/55: *NY Times*:AN 1423
476. 04/17/52:FBI:AN 2633h, p. 6
477. 08/25/56:HUAC:Trial By Treason:AN 1406, pp. 25-6
478. Trial record, p. 51 (25)
479. ibid, p. 411 (570)
480. Wexley, p. 558
481. 06/19/50:OJR/file:AN 143a
482. Wexley, p. 606
483. ibid, pp. 604-5

484. ibid, p. 605
485. ibid
486. ibid
487. 12/26/51:*NY Times*
488. 03/20/52:FBI:AN 1415
489. 04/02/52:ADL:AN 1414
490. 05/18/52:NCRAC:AN 1461
491. 06/05/52:AJC:AN 1460
492. ibid, p. 3
493. ibid, p. 6
494. ibid, p. 4
495. 06/23/52:Kaufman/Fineberg:AN 1412
496. 05/02/52:ACLU memorandum:AN 2278
497. ibid, p. 1
498. ibid, p. 2
499. ibid, pp. 2-3
500. Circa 1953:*Petition to SC for rehearing*:AN 2681, pp. 5-6
501. Trial record, p. 1535 (2313)
502. ibid, p. 1550 (2338)
503. 12/04/52:ACLU:AN 2277, p. 2
504. ibid
505. ibid
506. 03/27/52:DA-EA:AN 667
507. 03/29/52:DA-EA:AN 644
508. 03/30/52:DA-EA:AN 668
509. 03/31/52:DA-EA:AN 649
510. 03/31/52:DA-EA:AN 646
511. 04/03/51:DA-EA:AN 669
512. 04/09/52:DA-EA:AN 653
513. 04/10/52:DA-EA:AN 647
514. 04/13/52:DA-EA:AN 655
515. 08/25/56:HUAC:AN 1406, pp. 15-21
516. 03/15/54:NY FBI/Hoover:AN 2633k
517. 04/22/53:FBI:AN 2633h, p. 7
518. ibid, p. 8
519. 02/17/53:FBI:AN 2633g
520. 03/30/54:FBI:AN 2633L, p. 2
521. ibid, p. 1
522. 04/22/53:FBI:2633h, pp. 4-5
523. 12/?/52:*NY World Telegram*:AN 970
524. Rosenberg, pp. 162-3

525. 04/26/53:RSC:AN 801

526. 07/53:RSC:AN 803-14

527. 03/20/45:War Dept::AN 337

528. 02/28/92: *NY Times*

529. Manchester, pp. 3-18

530. www.en.wikipedia.org/wiki/Eddie_slovik

531. Warren, p. 6

532. Meeropol, Michael, ed., *The Rosenberg Letters,* Garland Publ., NY, 1994, p. 518

533. 01/28/53:NY Post:AN 2725

534. Patterson, William, L., ed., *We Charge Genocide*, International Publishers, NY, 1970, pp. 58-122

535. 02/20/53:DOJ(Foley/Olney):AN 1287

536. Meeropol, Robert and Michael, *We Are Your Sons*, Houghton Mifflin, Boston, 1975, pp. 183-4

537. 01/05/53: *Washington D.C. Herald-Tribune*:AN 924

538. 01/05/53:*NY Times*:AN 3001

539. 01/13/53:*NY Times*:AN 3002

540. 08/25/56:HUAC:AN 1406, pp. 36-7

541. Circa 1953:RSC:AN 2552, NY 4,7,11,14,17,20, OH 11,22, Penn 30, Wash 6, Wisc 4, Texas 1

542. 01/09/53:Application for Clemency:AN 2678, p. 22

543. ibid, p. 23

544. ibid, p. 24

545. 08/25/56:HUAC:AN 1406, p. 35

546. 08/25/56:HUAC:1406, p. 34

547. 01/09/53:Daily Worker:AN 928

548. 01/20/53:ibid:AN 927a

549. ibid; HUAC AN 1406, pp. 67, 78, 82

550. 01/05/53:Poling:AN 1459, p. 1

551. ibid, p. 2

552. *NY Times*, 02/14/53

553. 02/13/53:*NY World Telegram*:AN 1334

554. 02/14/53:*Washington Post*:AN 1336

555. 02/13/53: Rome/State:AN 1078

556. *NY Times*, 02/15/53

557. 02/14/53:Stitt/J.Dulles:AN 1227

558. 02/16/53, *NY Times*

559. 03/11/53:*Daily Worker*:AN 809

560. 02/16/53:Vatican:AN 2672, pp. 3-8

561. Meeropol (*We Are...*), p. 172

562. 02/20/53:Epstein/Cronbach:AN 425

563. 02/09/53:Shoshone/White House:AN 1043

564. 02/13/53:New Hampshire/White House:AN 1044

565. 02/12/53:New York/White House:AN 1046

566. 02/12/53:Pennsylvania/White House:AN 1045

567. 02/23/53:*Daily Worker*:AN 937

568. Neville, p. 103

569. ibid

570. Shirer, pp. 1095n-6n

571. Oshinsky, p. 279

572. 02/14/53:*NY Times*:AN 931

573. 04/21/53:White House memo:AN 1014

574. 02/27/53:DOJ:AN 1289

575. 03/03/53:LBJ/State:AN 1106

576. ibid, p. 2

577. ibid, p. 3

578. 04/16/54:State Dept:AN 783

579. ibid

580. Heale, p. 188

581. 03/24/53:ibid:AN 942

582. 02/20/53:ibid:AN 936

583. 03/30/53:*NY Times*:AN 943

584. 06/19/50:OJR:AN 143a

585. 05/01/53:E. McCarthy/Committee:AN 222, p. 2

586. 05/04/53:*NY Times*:AN 939

587. ibid

588. 05/04/53:*NY Post*:AN 981

589. 05/04/53:OJR:AN 2734

590. ibid, p. 3

591. ibid, p. 4

592. 05/06/53:OJR:AN 2735

593. Radosh, p. 370

594. ibid, p. 369

595. Trial record, p. 1054 (1564)

596. undated:Aaron Schneider, interviewed by Emily Alman:AN 1319, p. 3-4

597. 04/06/53:*Daily Worker*:AN 945

598. Neville, pp. 114-24

599. 03/30/53:AJC:AN 1410

600. Gentry, Curt, *Frame-up*, W.W. Norton, 1967, p. 422

601. *NY Times*, 06/19/53, p. 1

602. ibid, p. 8

603. McCullough, pp. 489-90

604.   American Institute of Public Opinion, cited in petition to Supreme Court, October Term 1952, for Writ of Certiorari, *Julius Rosenberg and Ethel Rosenberg v. U.S.*, p. 12:AN 2676

605.   ibid, p. 13

606.   ibid, p. 14

607.   *Delaney v. U.S.* 199F 2d 107

608.   ibid, pp. 112-3

609.   ibid, p. 114

610.   Supreme Ct., Oct. Term 1952, *Julius Rosenberg and Ethel Rosenberg v. U.S.*, Brief for U.S. p. 14-5:AN 2691

611.   ibid, pp. 16-7

612.   12/01/52:U.S. Dist. Ct. C134-245:AN 2704, p. 6

613.   12/31/52:opinion, *U.S. v. Rosenberg et al.*, U.S. Ct. of Appeals, Docket Nos. 22570-22571:AN 2679, p. 318

614.   Ibid

615.   undated:NPACT:AN 514-3

616.   undated:NPACT:AN 511-5

617.   Circa 03/14/53:Macy affidavit:AN 691-25-26

618.   06/08/53:Opinion, Judge Kaufman re petition for hearing:AN 2677, p. 3

619.   ibid, p. 4

620.   ibid, pp. 3-4

621.   ibid, p. 5

622.   12/01/52:Affidavit FBI Agent Harrington:AN 2674x

623.   12/31/52:opinion, *U.S. v. Rosenberg et al.*, U.S. Ct. of Appeals, Docket Nos. 22570-22571:AN 2679, p. 323

624.   Supreme Ct., October Term 1952, No. 687, *Julius Rosenberg and Ethel Rosenberg v. U.S.* Reply Brief, pp. 5-6:AN 2692

625.   06/?/50:David Greenglass/OJR:AN 222

626.   Trial record, p. 1623 (2468)

627.   Sharp, Malcolm P., "Was Justice Done?" *Monthly Review Press*, NY, 1956, p. 156

628.   06/08/53: Kaufman decision; AN 2677, p. 10

629.   Trial record p. 609 (868-9)

630.   ibid, p. 610 (869-70)

631.   ibid, p. 611 (871-2)

632.   Roberts, S., pp. 281-5

633.   Appellant's petition to Supreme Court, October Term 1952, for Writ of Certiorari, *Julius Rosenberg and Ethel Rosenberg v. U.S.*, pp. 67-8:AN 2680

634.   Supreme Ct., Oct. Term 1952, *Julius Rosenberg and Ethel Rosenberg v. U.S.*, Brief for U.S. p. 9:AN 2691

635.   ibid

636. 02/31/52:opinion, *U.S. v. Rosenberg et al.*, U.S. Ct. of Appeals, Docket Nos. 22570-
      22571:AN 2679, p. 322

637. Brief in opposition to defendants appeal to U.S. Circuit Court of Appeals: AN 2691
      pp. 17-9

638. Decision, U.S. Ct. of Appeals, *U.S. v. Rosenbergs et al*: AN 2679, p. 320

639. ibid, p. 321

640. *Cramer v. U.S.*, 325 U.S. 1 (1945) 24

641. 11/05/52:DOJ:AN 626

642. 12/31/52:opinion, *U.S. v. Rosenberg et al.*, U.S. Ct. of Appeals, Docket Nos. 22570-
      22571:AN 2679, p. 324

643. Schneir, p. 177-8

644. Supreme Ct., October term 1952, Petition for cert, *Morton Sobell*, No. 112, pp. 2-19
      AN 2685

645. Supreme Ct., October term 1952, Brief in opposition, *Morton Sobell*, No. 719, pp.
      8-9: AN 2701

646. Supreme Ct., October term 1953, Brief in opposition, *Morton Sobell,* No. 497, pp.
      13-8: AN 2693

647. Supreme Ct., October term 1952, Petition for cert, *Morton Sobell*, No. 112, pp. 45-7
      AN 2685

648. ibid, p. 35

649. ibid, p. 34, citing 195 F.2d at p. 602

650. undated:Aaron Schneider interviewed by Emily Alman:AN 1319, pp. 5-12

651. 05/15/53:Paris/State:AN 742, pp. 1-2

652. 06/09/53:Paris:State:AN 740

653. Loftus, John; Aarons, Mark, *The Secret War Against the Jews*, St. Martin's Press, NY,
      1994, p. 90, citing R. Harris Smith, OSS, p. 215

654. ibid, p. 39

655. 02/02/53:DOJ/FBI:AN 847a

656. 01/22/53:CIA:AN 847, p. 2 (9)

657. ibid

658. 02/27/53:FBI/DOJ:AN 1288

659. Meeropol (*Letters*), pp. 676-87

660. ibid, p. 677

661. ibid, p. 686

662. ibid, p. 687

663. 06/05/53:DOJ:AN 1477

664. Neville, p. 125, citing the *National Guardian* of 06/15/53

665. Gentry, p. 419

666. Cook, p. 105

667. Loomer, Bernard M., "A Mercy Call at the White House", *The Progressive*,
      September 1953, pp. 1-2:AN 2522

668. Supreme Ct., October term 1952, Petition for Rehearing, *Julius/Ethel Rosenberg v. U.S.* No. 111, pp. 13-4:AN 2681

669. Edelman, Irwin, *Suppressed Facts in the Rosenberg Case*, self-published, Los Angeles, CA, 1953:AN 2575

670. 05/10/55:*NY Times*:AN 1423

671. Swearingen, pp. 116-7

672. 06/12/53:Urey/Eisenhower:AN 691-26

673. 06/12/53:Affidavit of Fyke Farmer, p. 5:AN 2686b

674. Trial record, p. 1454 (2170)

675. ibid, pp. 1612-3 (2447-9)

676. 06/15/53:*NY Times*:AN 955

677. 06/15/53:*Washington Post*:AN 956

678. 06/16/53:*NY Times*:AN 959

679. ibid

680. ibid

681. Meeropol (*Letters...*) 06/16/53, pp. 705-9

682. Sharlitt, Joseph H., *Fatal Error*, Charles Scribner's & Sons, NY, 1989, p. 65

683. 06/16/53:DOJ:AN 2533ad

684. ibid

685. 06/17/53:*Washington Post*:AN 963

686. Loomer, AN 2522, pp. 1-2

687. ibid, p. 2

688. 06/17/53:Douglas' stay of execution:AN 858

689. 06/17/53:Atomic Energy Act:AN 1559

690. 06/17/53:Douglas:AN 1562

691. Sharlitt, p. 83

692. ibid, p. 85

693. 06/17/53:*Daily Home News* (New Brunswick, N.J.):AN 1397

694. ibid

695. 06/18/53:*NY Times*:AN 2608

696. Warren, pp. 304-6

697. 06/19/53: *NY Times*

698. Sharlitt, p. 117

699. Kinoy, Arthur, *Rights on Trial*, Bernel Books, Lexington, MA, 1983, 1984 p. 115

700. ibid, p. 120

701. ibid, p. 122

702. ibid, p. 123

703. 06/19/53:Black, 346 U.S. 297-8

704. 06/19/53:Frankfurter, 346, U.S. 309

705. 06/19/53:Douglas, 346 U.S. 312-3

706. Sharlitt, p. 131n

707.   ibid, p. 72, citing *Philip Elman, an Oral History*, Columbia University, Vol. 4, p. 226

708.   Brownell, Herbert, *Advising Ike*, Univ. Press of Kansas, 1993, p. 244

709.   04/26/45:Frankfurter memorandum:AN 173, p. 2

710.   ibid, p. 3

711.   05/28/45:Frankfurter:AN 166

712.   Trial record, pp. 890-1 (1298-1300)

713.   06/20/53:*NY Times*

714.   Meeropol (*Letters...*) pp. 697-9

715.   06/19/53:The White House:AN 190

716.   Meeropol (*Letters...*) pp. 702-3

717.   Gentry, p. 427

718.   ibid

719.   07/19/50:FBI/DOJ:AN 151g

720.   Gentry, pp. 420-1

721.   Gentry, pp. 427-8

722.   undated:Aaron Schneider, interviewed by Emily Alman:AN 1319, p. 14

723.   *NY Times*, 06/21/53

724.   06/22/53:*NY Daily News*:AN 1424

725.   06/22/53:*NY Daily Mirror*:AN 799

726.   06/21/53:Cronbach:AN 440

727.   03/17/54:*NY Times*

728.   "The Rosenberg Case": *Columbia Law Review*, Vol. 54, No. 2, February 1954 p. 223
       AN 2526

729.   ibid, p. 227

730.   ibid, p. 244

731.   ibid, p. 260

732.   05/11/54:FBI:AN 847-22

733.   ibid

734.   Groves, p. 63

735.   Meeropol, Robert and Michael, *We Are Your Sons*, Houghton Mifflin, Boston,
       1975, pp. 220-47

736.   05/03/54:DOJ/NY Court:AN 995

737.   Circa 1956:FBI/re authors: AN 1343

738.   10/23/56:FBI/re surveillance Almans:AN 463

739.   02/19/57:FBI/re recruiting pharmacist to report on Almans:AN 457

740.   06/23/57:FBI/re request Hoover permit interview with Almans:AN 458

741.   07/18/57:FBI/re Hoover denial request interview Almans:AN 458a

742.   Reuben, William A., *The Atom Spy Hoax*, Action Books, NY, 1955

743.   Wexley, John, *The Judgment of Julius and Ethel Rosenberg*, Cameron & Kahn, NY,
       1955

744.   08/04/55 HUAC hearings: AN 782, pp. 296 et seq; 340 et seq.

745. 12/22/55:Emplymt denial DG/RG:AN 1279
746. 04/22/53:FBI:AN 2633h. pp. 6-8
747. 08/21/53:FBI:AN 2633b
748. 09/10/53:FBI:AN 2633c
749. Lamphere, pp. 2-7
750. 03/30/54:FBI:AN 2633L, p. 1
751. ibid, p. 2
752. ibid, pp. 3-4
753. 04/8/54:FBI:AN 2633m, pp. 1-2
754. 04/16/54:FBI:AN 2633n
755. 04/21/54:FBI:AN 2633o
756. 12/10/54:FBI:AN 2633i
757. 01/19/54:FBI:AN 2633j
758. 04/27/54:FBI:AN 2633p
759. 05/05/54:FBI:AN 2633q
760. 07/15/54:FBI:AN 2633s
761. 08/27/54:FBI:AN 2633u
762. ibid, p. 3-4
763. ibid, p. 6
764. 08/29/54:Sobell/Dreyfus:AN 2633v
765. 09/01/54:FBI:AN 2633w, p. 7
766. ibid, p. 5
767. 10/13/54:FBI:AN 2633x
768. 11/11/54:Helen Sobell/JEH:AN 2633y, p. 1
769. 11/24/54:FBI:AN 2633ab
770. 03/15/55:FBI:AN 2633ac
771. Sobell, p. 437
772. 11/07/57:DOJ:AN 775, p. 111
773. 11/12/57:FBI:AN 470a
774. 01/13/59:AEC:AN 474
775. 02/04/59:Bishop/President:AN 538a
776. 03/06/59:DOJ;AN 468
777. 03/24/59:DOJ:AN 1249
778. ibid, p. 2
779. 03/27/59:AEC/White House:AN 538b
780. 01/27/60:DOJ/AEC:AN 475
781. 12/21/62:FBI:AN 519i
782. 02/06/53:opinion, *U.S. v. Morton Sobell*, U.S. Ct. of Appeals, No. 151:AN 2703, p. 1138
783. 03/24/65:FBI:AN 519a
784. 10/16/65:FBI:AN 519b

785. ibid, p. 2

786. 05/02/69:FBI:AN 519c

787. Swearingen, pp. 116-7

788. 04/14/66:DOJ:AN 519k

789. ibid

790. 08/22/66:*Morton Sobell v. U.S.*/amended petition to U.S. District Court:AN 1521, p. 36

791. Nizer, Louis, *The Implosion Conspiracy*, Doubleday, NY, 1973, pp. 395-6

792. ibid, pp. 493-5

793. Schneir, p. 475

794. 08/04-11/79:*New Republic*, Letter from Schneirs, p. 26:AN 1239

795. Buitrago, Ann Mari, "The Fraud of the Century", *Our Right to Know,* Fund for Open Information and Accountability, Inc., NY, 1983, pp. 15-6:AN 847B

796. 11/13/75:*Washington Star*:AN 203

797. ibid

798. ibid

799. Lamphere, p. 214

800. Meeropol (*Sons*), p. 392

801. 09/06/77:FBI re ACLU:AN 2709, pp. 2-3

802. ibid, p. 3

803. ibid, p. 4

804. 10/03/56:ACLU:AN 2711

805. 11/21/56:FBI:AN 2718

806. Circa 1977:ACLU:AN 2717, p. 2

807. 09/06/77:ACLU:AN 2709, p. 4

808. 08/03/77:ACLU:AN 2720, p. 1

809. ibid, pp. 5-6

810. ibid, p. 6

811. ibid

812. 09/06/77:ACLU:AN 2709A, p. 5

813. 08/20/56:FBI:AN 2714

814. 09/26/77:ACLU:AN 2721

815. Gentry, p. 136-7

816. 05/13/76:*NY Times*:AN 2635a

817. 05/23/76:*NY Times*:AN 2635b

818. 05/17/76:*NY Times*:AN 2635c

819. 06/04/76:*NY Times*:AN 2635d

820. 06/21/76:*NY Times*:AN 2635e

821. 06/24/86:*NY Times*

822. Townley, Rod, "A Specter is Haunting Irving Kaufman", in *Juris Doctor*, Vol. 7, No. 10, November 1977, p. 24 AN 1242

823. ibid

824. ibid, p. 23

825. Radosh (*Rosenberg File*), pp. 411-2, citing *The Brandeis/Frankfurter Connection*, by Bruce Allen Murphy, Oxford Univ. Press, NY, 1982, p. 331

826. 05/01/90:*NY Times*:AN 641

827. 08/11/93:*New York Law Journal*: AN 798

828. Benson, Robert Louis; Warner, Michael, *Venona – Soviet Espionage and the American Response 1939-1957*, National Security Agency, Washington, DC, 1996, p. xxvii

829. ibid, p. xiv

830. Haynes, John Earl and Klehr, Harvey, *Venona: Decoding Soviet Espionage in America*, Yale Un. Press, New Haven, 1999, p. 51

831. Lamphere, p. 81

832. Richelson, Jeffrey T., *A Century of Spies*, Oxford U. Press, 1995, p. 226, fn

833. 02/01/56:FBI:A.H.Belmont/L.V. Boardman: http://foia.fbi.gov/filelink.html?file=/venona/venona.pdf; retrieved 12/16/07, p. 8:AN 3010-8(70)

834. Albright, Joseph; Kunstel, Marcia, *Bombshell*, Times Books, NY, 1997, pp. 207-8

835. Haynes/Klehr, p. 14

836. 06/30/53:Urey/Brainin::AN 1419

837. Trial Record, pp. 5-6 (d1-d3)

838. 09/21/44:Message 1340:AN 2744

839. 04/27/48:Venona report:AN 2757

840. 11/27/44:Message 1657:AN 2748

841. Lamphere, p. 98-9

842. 08/13/48:Venona report:AN 2757B

843. 07/26/44:Message 1053:AN 2740

844. Lamphere, pp. 93-4

845. 06/27/50:Lamphere/Gardner:AN 2590

846. Benson, Warner, pp. 199-450

847. ibid, pp. xviii, xx, xxiv

848. ibid, p. xxix

849. 09/28/50:DOJ/INS:AN 387a

850. 10/9/51:DOJ/INS:AN 399

851. Feklisov, A., Kostin, S., *The Man Behind the Rosenbergs*, Enigma Books, NY, 2001

852. ibid, pp. 129-36

853. ibid, p. 278

854. ibid, pp. 119-20

855. 12/05/01:*60 Minutes*/CBS/*The Traitor*

856. Roberts, S., pp. 496-7

857. 12/05/01:*60 Minutes*/CBS/*The Traitor*

858. Roberts, S., p. 465

859.   ibid, p. 472

860.   Watson, Bruce, *Sacco and Vanzetti*, Viking, 2007, p. 365

861.   05/07/09:*NY Times*

862.   03/07/07:*NY Times*

863.   12/21/05:*Washington Post*

864.   Pew Center on the States, Associated Press, 02/28/08

865.   http://inhisserviceweb.com/prison_statistics.htm; retrieved 02/14/08

866.   see Pew Center, above

867.   http://www.deathwatchinternational.org/the_facts.php; retrieved 01/21/10

868.   http://www.clarkprosecutor.org/html/death/dpusa.htm; retrieved 03/14/08

869.   http://albany.edu/sourcebook; see Table 6.28

870.   *NY Times*, 02/24/03

871.   Downes, David; Hanson, Kirstine, "Welfare and Punishment", *Crime and Society Foundation*: www.crimeandsociety.org.uk\

872.   Ex parte Milligan, 71 U.S. 125

873.   ibid, pp. 121-2

874.   Kennan (*NY Times Magazine* 05/27/51)

875.   02/13/53:Vatican:AN 2672, p.7

876.   05/15/53:Paris/State:AN 742, pp. 1-2

877.   12/04/52:Paris/State:AN 1224

878.   12/02/52:Paris/State:AN 1223

879.   12/11/52:State/Paris:AN 708

880.   12/12/52:State:AN 735

881.   ibid, p. 3

882.   ibid, p. 1

883.   12/23/52:Paris/State:AN 1230

884.   Neville, p. 80

885.   ibid, p. 81

886.   ibid, p. 82

887.   ibid, p. 88

888.   01/7/53:Paris/State:AN 710 (Bradlee analysis)

889.   01/7/53:Paris/State:AN 710A (last page of Bradlee analysis)

890.   12/20/52:Paris/17 U.S. embassies:AN 1229

891.   01/07/53:Paris/State:AN 1222

892.   ibid

893.   01/08/53:Paris/State:AN 576

894.   01/09/53:Paris/State:AN 1228

895.   ibid, pp. 1-2

896.   Rosenberg, pp. 158-9

897.   01/12/53:Marseille-State:AN 1295

898.   01/14/53:Lyon/State:AN 574

899. ibid, p. 2
900. 01/22/53:Bordeaux-State:AN 572
901. 02/22/53:*NY Times*:AN 800
902. 02/13/53:Paris/State:AN 593
903. 02/14/53:Paris/State:AN 594
904. ibid, pp. 1-2
905. ibid, p. 2
906. 02/18/53:Paris/State:AN 571
907. 03/25/53:*Daily Worker*:AN 1313
908. ibid
909. ibid
910. 04/20/53:Paris/State:AN 1220
911. ibid, p. 2
912. ibid
913. 04/20/53:State/Paris:AN 1133
914. 04/24/53:Paris/State:AN 1484
915. 04/28/53:State/Paris:AN 1131
916. 05/04/53:State/Paris:AN 739
917. 05/04/53:*NY Times*:AN 939
918. 05/06/53:State/select embassies:AN 737
919. ibid, p. 2
920. 05/15/53:Paris/State:AN 742, pp. 1-2
921. ibid, p. 2
922. 05/19/53:State:AN 743, p. 4
923. 05/28/53:Strasbourg/State:AN 570
924. ibid, p. 3
925. 06/05/53:Paris/State:AN 1225, pp. 1-2
926. ibid, p. 2
927. 06/09/53:Paris:State:AN 740
928. 06/09/53:State:AN 741
929. 06/10/53:Paris/State:AN 752
930. 06/12/53:Strasbourg/State:AN 567
931. 06/12/53:Lyon/State:AN 568
932. 06/12/53:Paris/State:AN 569
933. ibid
934. 06/15/53:Paris/State:AN 566
935. ibid
936. 06/16/53:Paris/State:AN 914
937. 06/16/53:Paris/State:AN 561
938. ibid
939. ibid

940. ibid
941. 06/16/53:Paris/State:AN 765
942. 06/16/53:State:AN 779
943. ibid, p. 2
944. 06/18/53:Paris/State:AN 557
945. 06/19/53:*NY Times*:AN 1385
946. 06/19/53:Paris/State:AN 751
947. 12/29/53:Strasbourg/State:AN 555
948. ibid, p. 4
949. ibid, pp. 5-6
950. 01/09/53:Brussels/State:AN 1184
951. 01/11/53:Brussels/State:AN 753
952. ibid
953. 01/27/53:Brussels/State:AN 749
954. 01/27/53:Brussels/State:AN 754, p. 2
955. ibid
956. 01/16/53:Antwerp/State:AN 716
957. 06/08/53:Brussels/State: AN 748
958. 06/15/53:Queen/President:AN 917
959. 06/18/53:State/Brussels:AN 1177
960. 12/01/52:Copenhagen/State:AN 1196
961. 05/18/53:Copenhagen/State:AN 1195
962. 06/16/53:Copenhagen/State:AN 1198
963. ibid, p. 2
964. Shirer, p. 993
965. ibid, pp. 956-7
966. 01/08/53:Oslo/State:AN 1186
967. 01/13/53:attributed by Ce Soir to *Arbeiderbladet* on document not otherwise identifiable:AN 881
968. 12/23/52:The Hague/State:AN 1166
969. 01/06/53:Amsterdam/State:AN 1172
970. 02/17/53:The Hague/State:AN 1167
971. 03/20/53:The Hague/State:AN 1164
972. 06/13/53:Dutch Clemency Com./Committee: AN 887
973. 06/15/53:The Hague/State:AN 1169
974. ibid
975. 06/17/53:The Hague/State:AN 1170
976. 03/11/53:Stockholm/State:AN 1192
977. 03/17/53:Stockholm/State:AN 1194
978. 04/22/53:Takman/Committee:AN 882
979. 06/23/53:Stockholm/State:AN 1193

980.   ibid
981.   06/25/43:Goteborg/State:AN 619
982.   03/06/53:Helsinki/State:AN 1191
983.   10/31/52:London/State:AN 1206
984.   11/21/52:London/State:AN 1114
985.   11/28/52:State/London:AN 1115
986.   11/28/52:London/State:AN 1205
987.   Rosenberg, p. 159
988.   ibid
989.   12/09/52:London/State:AN 1210
990.   01/06/53:London/State:AN 1203
991.   02/16/53:London/State:AN 1202
992.   06/08/53:London/State:AN 1201
993.   06/08/53:London/State:AN 1209
994.   06/11/53:Manchester Clemency Committee:AN 886
995.   07/09/53:London/State:AN 1208
996.   06/17/53:Dublin/State:AN 1200
997.   01/02/53:Union Council/State:AN 1211
998.   06/25/53:Dublin/State:AN 1199
999.   01/28/53:Hamburg (West Ger)/State:AN 1100
1000. 02/04/53:Bonn/State:AN 1092
1001. 02/18/53:*NY Times*:AN 812
1002. 02/18/53:Frankfort (East Ger)/State:AN 1089
1003. 02/12/53:Berlin (3-zones)/State:AN 1099
1004. 07/01/53:Bonn/State:AN 1085
1005. 10/21/52:Rome/State:AN 1081
1006. 12/24/52:Milan/State:AN 1083
1007. 01/19/53:Rome/State:AN 1079
1008. 01/12/53:Rome/State:AN 1080
1009. 02/19/53:Rome/State:AN 1077
1010. 02/13/53:Rome/State:AN 1078
1011. 02/22/53:*NY Times*:AN 800
1012. 06/16/53:Rome/State:AN 1076
1013. 06/19/53:*NY Times*:AN 1385
1014. 06/22/53:Rome/State:AN 1074
1015. 06/16/53:Luxembourg/State:AN 1174
1016. 01/15/53:Bern/State:AN 730
1017. ibid, p. 3
1018. 06/16/53:Geneva/State:AN 731
1019. 06/19/53:Bern/State:AN 732
1020. Sachar, p. 556

1021. ibid, p. 556

1022. Gribetz, p. 512

1023. 06/09/53:Budapest/State:AN 1215

1024. 11/10/52:DOJ/State/INS:AN 627

1025. 12/13/52:Montreal/State:AN 622

1026. 01/02/53:Toronto/State:AN 1140

1027. 01/04/53:Toronto/State:AN 756, p. 3

1028. 01/09/53:Ottawa/All consular offices:AN 582

1029. 01/14/53:Ottowa/State:AN 579

1030. ibid, p. 3

1031. 01/14/53:Winnipeg/State:AN 758

1032. 01/15/53:Montreal/State:AN 1123

1033. 01/19/53:Windsor/State:AN 709

1034. 01/26/53:Toronto/State:AN 760 (also 01/26/53:Toronto/State:AN 1121)

1035. ibid

1036. ibid, p. 2

1037. ibid, pp. 2-3

1038. ibid, p. 4

1039. 01/17/53:Toronto/State:AN 761, pp. 1-2

1040. 01/29/53:Hamilton/State:AN 759

1041. ibid, p. 2

1042. 02/20/53:State/Ottawa:AN 762

1043. 05/28/53:Montreal/State:AN 578, pp. 1-3

1044. 05/28/53:Montreal/State:AN 764

1045. 06/10/53:Montreal/State:AN 620

1046. ibid, p. 2

1047. 06/12/53:Toronto/State:AN 774

1048. 06/19/53:Toronto/State:AN 773

1049. 06/22/53:Toronto/State:AN 772

1050. Wexley, pp. 658-9; AN 658

1051. 06/16/53:Mexico,D.F./State:AN 1148

1052. ibid, p. 2

1053. 02/19/53:Havana/State:AN 1048

1054. 06/18/53:Havana/State:AN 1050

1055. 06/29/53:Managua/State:AN 915

1056. 01/29/53:Buenos Aires/State:AN 1063

1057. 02/4/53:Buenos Aires/State:AN 1065

1058. 04/7/53:Buenos Aires/State:AN 1067

1059. 06/16/53:Buenos Aires/State:AN 1064

1060. 01/15/53:Rio de Janeiro/State:AN 1060

1061. 06/16/53:Porto Alegre/State:AN 1058

1062. 02/23/53:Montevideo/State:AN 1054

1063. 06/17/53:Montevideo/State:AN 1056

1064. 06/23/53:Asuncion/State:AN 1053

1065. 12/20/52:Guatemala/State:AN 1146

1066. 02/20/53:Guatemala/State:AN 1147

1067. 06/18/53:Guatemala/State:AN 721

1068. 06/18/53:San Jose/State:AN 1151

1069. 06/22/53:Cape Town/State:AN 613

1070. 06/22/53:Port Elizabeth/State: AN 612, pp. 1-2

1071. 06/25/53:Algiers/State:AN 1155

1072. 06/25/53:Tangier/State:AN 719

1073. 06/22/53:Tunis/State: AN 1153

1074. 12/31/52:Tripoli/State:AN 919

1075. 02/06/53:Cairo/State:AN 595

1076. 07/15/53:Baghdad/State:AN 596

1077. 11/19/52:Rabbinic appeal/President:AN 1454

1078. 12/09/52:Tel Aviv/State:AN 611

1079. 01/08/53:Tel Aviv/State:AN 610

1080. 06/18/53:Tel Aviv/State:AN 609

1081. 06/23/53:Tel Aviv/State:AN 607

1082. 08/07/53:DOJ/Israeli DOJ:AN 326

1083. 07/14/53:Jerusalem/State:AN 605

1084. Rosenberg, p. 164

1085. 06/19/53:*NY Times*:AN 1385

Index

A

CPSIA information can be obtained at www.ICGtesting.com
Printed in the USA
LVOW04s2117150415

434712LV00031B/1022/P